The Struggle for Sea Power

Also by Sam Willis

*In the Hour of Victory: The Royal Navy at War in the
Age of Nelson*

* * *

THE HEARTS OF OAK TRILOGY
Fighting Temeraire: Legend of Trafalgar
The Admiral Benbow: The Life and Times of a Naval Legend
The Glorious First of June: Fleet Battle in the Reign of Terror

* * *

THE FIGHTING SHIPS SERIES
Fighting Ships: From the Ancient World to 1750
Fighting Ships: 1750–1850
Fighting Ships: 1850–1950

* * *

Shipwreck: A History of Disasters at Sea
*Fighting at Sea in the Eighteenth Century: The Art of Sailing
Warfare*

The Struggle for
Sea Power

A Naval History of
American Independence

SAM WILLIS

ATLANTIC BOOKS
London

First published in hardback in Great Britain in 2015 by Atlantic Books, an imprint of Atlantic Books Ltd.

10 9 8 7 6 5 4 3 2 1

A CIP catalogue record for this book is available from the British Library.

Hardback ISBN: 978 1 84887 8 464
E-book ISBN: 978 1 78239 7 403
Paperback ISBN: 978 1 84887 8 471

Printed in Great Britain by TJ International Ltd, Padstow, Cornwall

Map artwork by Jamie Whyte

Endpaper image: Detail from *Attack of the rebels upon Fort Penobscot ...*, 1785 (*Map image courtesy of the Norman B. Leventhal Map Center at the Boston Public Library/Richard H. Brown collection*)

Frontispiece image: Detail from *Campagne du Vice-Amiral* [*sic*] *Cte. d'Estaing en Amêrique ...* by Pierre Ozanne (*Courtesy of the Library of Congress*)

Atlantic Books
An Imprint of Atlantic Books Ltd
Ormond House
26–27 Boswell Street
London
WC1N 3JZ

www.atlantic-books.co.uk

For Tors

'With an undiscribable pleasure I have seen near a score of years roll over our Heads, with an affection heightned and improved by time.'

* Abigail Adams to John Adams, 12 December 1782

'To produce a mighty book, you must choose a mighty theme.'
Herman Melville

CONTENTS

PART 3　World War, 1778–1780

PART 4　American Independence, 1781

ILLUSTRATIONS

Colour section

1. *View of the Narrows between Long Island & Staaten Island* ... by Archibald Robertson, 1776 (*Spencer Collection, The New York Public Library*)
2. *Forcing the Boom on the Hudson River* by Dominic Serres the Elder, 1779 (*Melford Hall, The Firebrace Collection/ National Trust*)
3. *The British landing at Kip's Bay, New York Island* by Robert Cleverley, 1777 (*National Maritime Museum, Greenwich, London*)
4. *The landing of the British forces in the Jerseys* ... by Thomas Davies, 1776 (*The Miriam and Ira D. Wallach Division of Art, Prints and Photographs: Print Collection, The New York Public Library*)
5. *New England Armed Vessels in Valcure Bay, Lake Champlain...* by Charles Randle, 1776 (*Library and Archives Canada, Acc. No. 1996-82-2*)
6. Sketch of Fort Ticonderoga, 1777 (*Courtesy of The Fort Ticonderoga Museum*)
7. Sketch by Hector McNeill from *Naval Documents of The American Revolution, vol. 9* (United States Government Printing Office, Washington, 1986)
8. *Washington Crossing the Delaware River* by Emanuel Gottlieb Leutze, 1851 (oil on canvas, copy of an original painted in 1848) (*Metropolitan Museum of Art, New York, USA/Bridgeman Images*)

Black & white illustrations

CHARTS

AMERICA BEFORE THE WAR

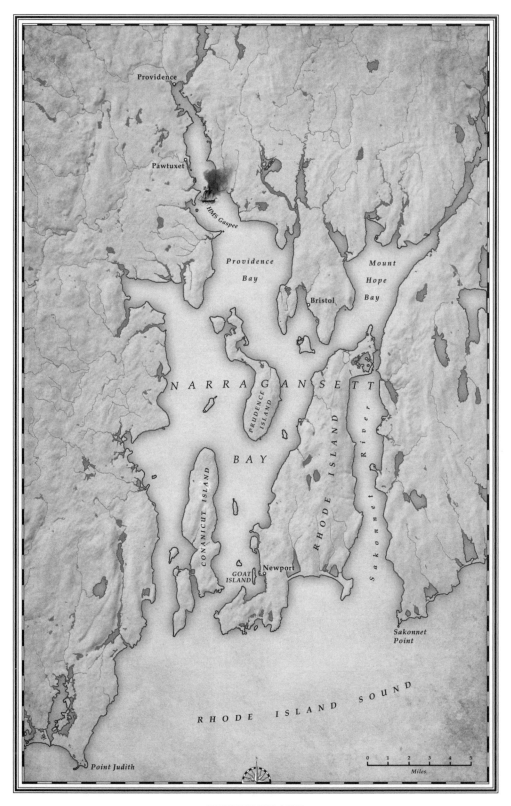

RHODE ISLAND

Lexington 5 miles
Concord 11 miles

Somerville
Powderhouse

Mystic River

Sinking of
the *Diana*

Chelsea Creek

HOGG
ISLAND

Bunker
Hill

NOODLE'S ISLAND

Charles
Town

Cambridge

Charles River

Cambridge

Marshes

Long Wharf

BIRD
ISLAND

APPLE
ISLAND

*Back
Bay*

*THE
NECK*

BOSTON

GOVERNOR'S
ISLAND

DEER
ISLAND

Dorchester
Heights

Castle William

CASTLE
ISLAND

Boston Harbour

SPECTACLE
ISLAND

THOMPSON'S
ISLAND

LONG ISLAND

Lighthouse on
*LITTLE BREWSTER
ISLAND*

Alderton
Point

MOON
ISLAND

*Hull
Bay*

Quincy Bay

Hingham Bay

Nahant Bay

N A H A N T

Nahant
Point

*Broad
Sound*

*Massachusetts
Bay*

Weymouth Fore River

Back River

Weymouth

Monatiquot River

0   1   2   3
Miles

BOSTON

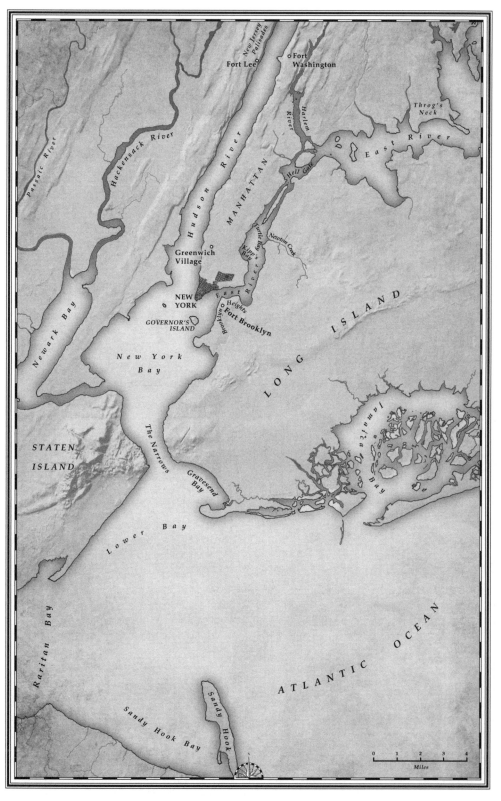

NEW YORK TO QUEBEC, PART I: NEW YORK AND THE LOWER HUDSON

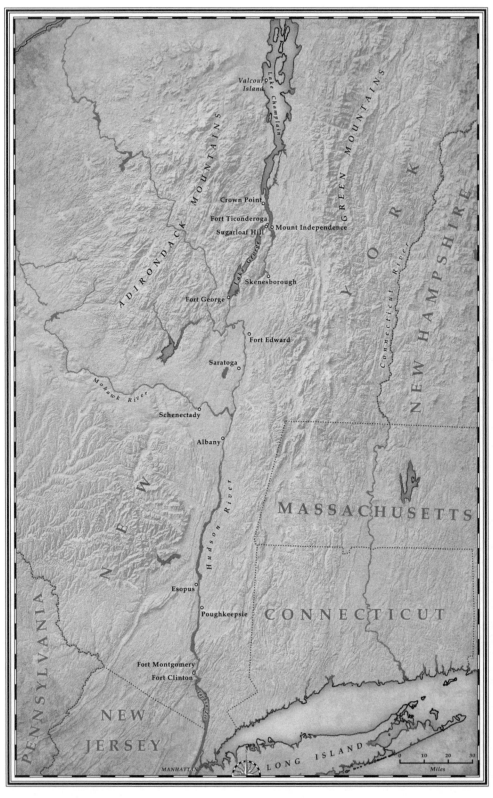

NEW YORK TO QUEBEC, PART 2: HUDSON HIGHLANDS AND LAKE CHAMPLAIN

NEW YORK TO QUEBEC, PART 3: ST JEAN TO QUEBEC

Quebec

Chaudière River

Saint Lawrence River

Trois-Rivières

Lac-Saint-Pierre

Sorel

Saint François River

Richelieu Rapids

Richelieu

Richelieu River

Fort Chambly

Montréal

St Jean

ÎLE DE MONTRÉAL

ÎLE DE JÉSUS

Lake Champlain

PROVINCE OF QUEBEC

NEW YORK

NEW HAMPSHIRE

MAINE

Miles
0   10   20   30

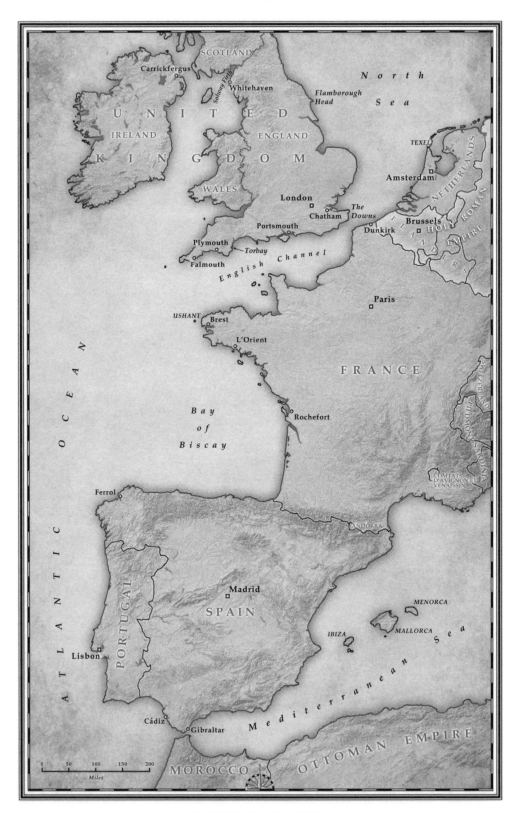

NORTHERN EUROPE

THE CARIBBEAN

ST KITTS
NEVIS
ANTIGUA
English
Harbour
MONTSERRAT
GUADELOUPE
DOMINICA
MARTINIQUE
Pigeon
Island
Cul de Sac
ST LUCIA
ST VINCENT
St George's
Harbour
GRENADA
BARBADOS
TOBAGO

Gulf
of
Mexico

Vera Cruz
Campeche

NEW
GUATEMALA
SPAIN
HONDURAS

Havana

CUBA

Black River
Settlement

JAMAICA

SAINT
DOMINGUE
SANTO
DOMINGO

Caribbean Sea

C a r i b b e a n   S e a

Orinoco   River

NEW
GRENADA

GUYANE
GUYANA
Cayenne

BRAZIL
(Portugal)

PACIFIC   OCEAN

French Possessions
British possessions
Spanish possessions

0   100   200   300   400
Miles

THE RED SEA AND INDIA

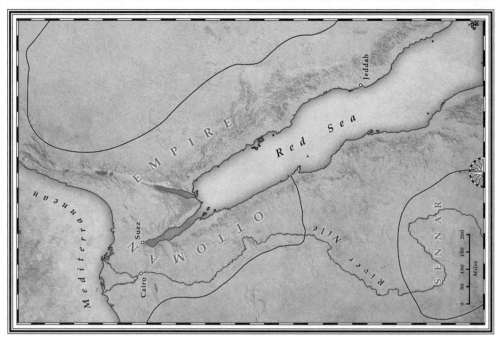

THE GULF COAST

THE CHESAPEAKE BAY

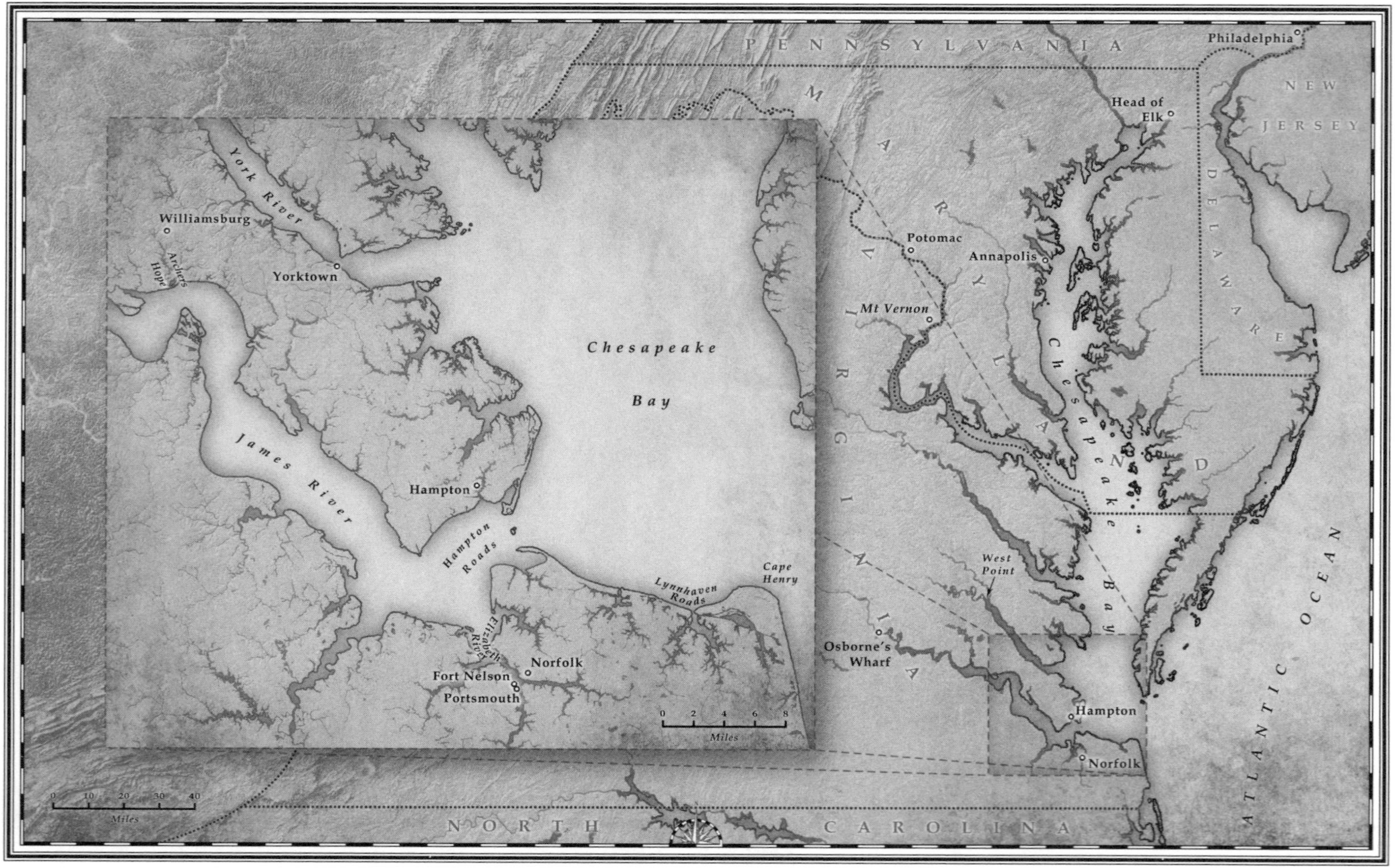

NEW JERSEY

PENNSYLVANIA

DELAWARE

MARYLAND

VIRGINIA

NORTH CAROLINA

ATLANTIC OCEAN

Chesapeake Bay

Philadelphia

Head of Elk

Annapolis

Potomac

Mt Vernon

West Point

Osborne's Wharf

Hampton

Norfolk

Chesapeake Bay

Cape Henry

Lynnhaven Roads

Norfolk

Elizabeth River

Fort Nelson

Portsmouth

Hampton Roads

Hampton

York River

Yorktown

Williamsburg

Archers Hope

James River

Miles
0 2 4 6 8

Miles
0 10 20 30 40

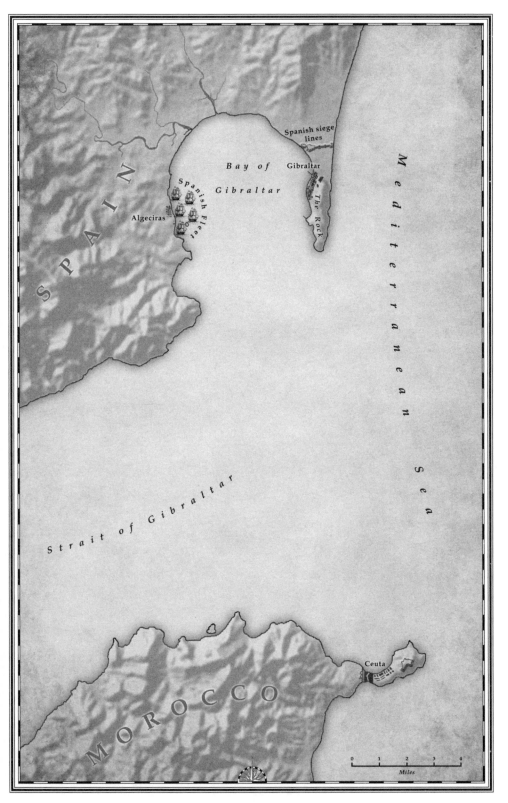

GIBRALTAR

FOREWORD

This book has been a joy to write. It has taken more than five years and I have travelled far and wide in my research. I have visited countless new places and met countless new faces. The faces made the places enjoyable. As a maritime historian, I believe it is essential not only to visit the locations where history unfolded, but also to get out on the water and experience them. I can now say that, in the process of researching this book, I have sailed, rowed and sometimes even swum up and down the Delaware and Hudson rivers, where I trembled at the currents where the rivers meet the sea; around Long Island Sound and the Chesapeake Bay, where I marvelled at the blue-shelled crabs and sniffed nervously for sand-banks; up and down the James and York rivers in Virginia; and to and from New York, Boston and Newport, Rhode Island, where I was bewildered by the density of the summer fog. I have explored by sea numerous coastal villages in both Massachusetts and Connecticut, and I have even been lucky enough to portage a replica eighteenth-century bateau from Lake Champlain to Lake George and then sail it down that most beautiful stretch of sparkling crystal water, the first time that this has been done for 200 years. I have marvelled at the challenge of waging naval war in the heat, trade winds and relentless ocean currents off Antigua, Barbados, St Lucia and Martinique. I have been foxed by the fog off Brest, by the swells off La Corunna, and by the currents in the Bay of Gibraltar. I have both been becalmed and nearly sunk in the English Channel. I have studied books, enjoyed letters, pored over maps and hefted artefacts in dozens of libraries, archives and museums from London to New York, from Paris to Antigua.

The helpers have a special place in my heart. First I must thank the Society for Nautical Research whose generosity funded a crucial part of my research in America. I must also thank the American National Maritime Historical Society and Burchie Green, who welcomed me with such open arms. I have relied heavily on a rowdy crew of scholars who are all so generous with their knowledge and time. Michael Duffy, Roger Knight, Jonathan Dull, John Hattendorf, Nicholas Rodger, Andrew Lambert, Richard Harding, John Tilley, Olivier Chaline, Michael Crawford, Alan Jamieson, Robert Bellamy, David Manthey, Steven Park, Carl Borick, Jim Johnson, Gareth Cole and Arthur Lefkowitz all offered invaluable historical help. Others helped with their company during my research or by opening doors for me. I am indebted to Carol Bundy, Edward and Jane Handler, Simon and Laura Tucker, and Jonathon Band. Andrew Bond has been a constant presence in the last decade of my writing and Nicholas Blake an invaluable sounding board as a naval historian and wordsmith. Thank you all.

SW
Trafalgar Place, November 2014

'Is it possible that a people without arms, ammunition, money, or navy, should dare to brave a nation, dreaded and respected by all the powers on earth?'
Extract from a letter published in the *New York Gazetteer*, 29 December 1774

'In any operation, and under all circumstances, a decisive naval superiority is to be considered as a fundamental principle, and the basis upon which every hope of success must ultimately depend.'
George Washington to Count Rochambeau, 15 July 1780

PREFACE

Once I heard an American boatman, with his boat trapped hard against rocks by a raging current, and with the boat's stern-line hard as iron, scream for more slack as she began to grate and grind against sharp granite. You could see that he felt every blow as if he were receiving the wound himself. The boat was being subjected to gross moral indignity as much as to actual physical injury. With her hull exposed and her motions awkward, the tableau felt unnatural, it felt wrong. The boat-man's eyes bulged, his chest swelled and he bellowed an order.

Now, in this situation, a British seaman would shout 'Ease!' or 'Slack!', referring directly to the stern rope that was bar-tight, the tether that was holding the boat back from the safety of the open water. But Americans have another word, and theirs refers to the boat rather than to the lines by which she is held. As this particular situation worsened from accident to crisis, with the boat shuddering with every blow, the boatman set his shoulders back and roared at me – for it was I who held that stern-line – 'Liberty!'

The problem was not that the stern-line was too tight, but that his precious boat, which encapsulated his livelihood, was trapped, pinned, restrained, imprisoned. The problem was not with the line but with the *person* who was holding the line, the *person* who was denying that ship her liberty. The problem was with me.

I was immediately enchanted by the way that the word 'liberty' survives in American but not in British maritime lan-guage. In a split second I began to write this paragraph in my head; in another, to the soundtrack of more splintering wood and American thundering, I began to write this book about how thirteen British colonies in America won their independence – in their eyes, their liberty – from Britain between 1775 and 1783.

Five years later I have completed it, and it is time for me to say sorry. So I'm sorry, Fred. I'm sorry that I wasn't paying attention and that your precious boat was damaged. On the banks of that river we had our own mini maritime revolution, and when I finally started to pay attention and eased off that line, your beautiful boat won her liberty.

INTRODUCTION

How do you begin a naval history of the greatest war of the age of sail? Consider the scale of the problem. From first gasp to final whimper, the American War of Independence lasted a decade and was the longest war in American history until Vietnam two centuries later. It involved no fewer than *twenty-two* separate navies and was fought in five different oceans, as well as on land-locked lakes, majestic rivers, barely navigable streams and ankle-deep swamps. It involved more fleet battles than any other naval war, one of which was the most strategically significant naval battle in all of British, American or French history. Those battles were fought by some of the largest fleets of sailing warships ever to set sail, and some of them by the strangest and most eclectic fleets in history, including one that was taken to pieces, dragged twelve miles overland, and then rebuilt and launched on a lake.

The war bursts with tales of heroism and cowardice, loyalty and treachery, political blood-letting, military ingenuity, medical innovation and stunning incompetence. It encompassed tidal waves, three of the worst Atlantic storms on record, the gravest invasion threat faced by Britain since the Spanish Armada in 1588, shipwrecks, smuggling, riots, mutinies, convict labour, treasure ships, slavery, financial collapse. There were nervous breakdowns, epic feats of survival and endurance, as well as love stories, epidemics, miserable evacuations and narrow escapes. There were unstoppable invasions, unprecedented shipbuilding programmes, one of the longest sieges in history and one of the most outrageous examples of military treason in history, horrifying and systematic cruelty, a 'floating' town, spies, the world's first military submarine and a native Indian tribe descended from shipwrecked slaves.

Starring in this spectacular were historical figures of the highest distinction, from George Washington and George III of England to Louis XVI of France, Charles III of Spain and Catherine the Great of Russia. While naval officers of great fame such as John Paul Jones, Abraham Whipple, John Manley, George Rodney, Samuel Hood, Horatio Nelson, the comte de Grasse and the bailli de Suffren navigated the oceans, Titans of political and diplomatic history, including John Adams, Benjamin Franklin, George Germain, the Earl of Sandwich, Lord North, the comte de Vergennes and the conde de Floridablanca, navigated the labyrinthine corridors of power. Countless unsung heroes, meanwhile, made their mark on history in a myriad ways, and all of this happened in a conflict that dramatically shaped the modern world.

So how *do* you begin? The answer, you might be surprised to hear, lies with a woman precariously balancing a model of a fully rigged sailing warship on her head.

In the summer of 1778 a new and bizarre fashion swept Paris as ladies began to wear their hair in a style known as *à la Belle Poule*. The Paris salons and society balls were transformed as dozens of ships sailed by on elaborately coiffured heaving swells of curled and powdered hair. What on earth was going on?

A perfect historical puzzle, it encapsulates everything I love about history. Sufficiently bizarre to seem ever so human, it also hints at far deeper historical themes and questions than the tastes of Parisian women and the techniques of Parisian hairdressers in the last quarter of the eighteenth century. Sailing warships, after all, were the tools of war and empire. They were used to protect trade, fight battles, transport troops and blockade enemy fleets. They represented staggering investment on a scale that, if mismanaged, could bankrupt nations. Those ships were engineering achievements of the very highest calibre that have been compared with the construction of

A contemporary cartoon of a fashionable French lady wearing her hair 'à la *Belle Poule*'.

medieval cathedrals, and the dockyards that maintained them were the largest industrial sites that then existed.

Sailing warships were thus the very opposite of fashionable whimsy. Clearly, something quite remarkable must have happened, perhaps thousands of miles from Paris, to have had such an influence on urban society as to affect fashion in such a profound and remarkable way. This is what I discovered.

On 17 June 1778 a British frigate, HMS *Arethusa*, in company with a smaller armed naval ship, was patrolling off Cornwall when she came across a French frigate, the *Belle Poule*. The two frigates hove to within firing distance of each other, and the British ordered the French to return with them to the bosom of the main British fleet for inspection.

The French had long been covertly assisting the Americans with their rebellion, but Britain and France were not yet at war. In Paris, however, the moment for the declaration had finally arrived and a message had already been sent to Brest, ordering the *Belle Poule*'s captain to engineer a confrontation that could provide a pretext for war. He therefore refused to follow the British and opened fire. The ferocity of the subsequent engagement surprised the *Arethusa*, and though neither ship was taken, the British ship was severely damaged and her captain forced to break off the action.

The French crowed over their success. Anticipation of this exact moment had been rising for three full years and had reached fever pitch. Horrified by their humiliation in the previous Anglo-French conflict, the Seven Years' War (1754–63), the French had rebuilt their navy. The American rebellion had given them the excuse they needed to join a conflict that could return French diplomatic prestige to its accustomed level, and the *Belle Poule* action was interpreted as evidence that the dream could come true. At the same time it was the most visible evidence possible to the Americans, whose rebellion was then wilting after a year of unexpected bloom, that the French really were coming to their assistance and that they would bring with them the one thing that the Americans lacked and yet desperately needed if they were ever going to win this war: a navy that could contest control of the seas with the British.

These themes had already been popularized in Parisian society, chiefly through the efforts of one man, Benjamin Franklin. The canny Franklin had spent a year and a half in France acting as a commissioner from the American Continental Congress. His role, and that of his two colleagues Arthur Lee and Silas Deane, was to nurture friendship between the two nations and secure both political and military aid. He was a revelation. He knew his way round the minefields of French eccentricities, having visited before the war as a scientist promoting his convincing theories about electricity and lightning. The French loved him, and Franklin's major triumph was to make the American cause not just politically and diplomatically appealing but *fashionable*.

Thus, in the summer of 1778, both French society and the French government were primed for something dramatic and the *Belle Poule* action provided the spark. France officially declared war and French ladies began to appear with their coiffure *à la Belle Poule*. Viewed in a crowded room, the ships would constantly appear and disappear, rise and fall, pitch and roll in an extraordinary and involuntary theatrical display. What at first sight seems entirely absurd was, in fact, a rather clever piece of performance art, way before its time, that thrived on the contrasts that it exposed and delighted in. It brought all things maritime and naval – which is to say all things tough, hard, frightening, dangerous, wet, outdoors and masculine – deep into the perfumed, feminine warmth and cosy chatter of a high-class indoor party. Unsurprisingly, the French absolutely loved it.

My discovery of that extraordinary image was the principal inspiration for this book, for it was soon clear that 'The Great Hair Mystery' was just one piece of a far greater jigsaw. My subsequent research slowly uncovered what I believe to be the most intriguing naval story in history.

* * *

It is no longer necessary to entirely bemoan a lack of maritime or naval perspective in our histories of American independence. There are now excellent histories available on numerous aspects of the maritime war, such as the various roles of the Royal Navy, the French navy, the Spanish navy, the American navy, the maritime economy, privateers, fishermen, shipping, logistics and leadership. These focused studies are supported by an ongoing project of astonishing scale to publish significant documents pertaining to the war at sea. Under the aegis of the US Naval History and Heritage Command, the *Naval Documents of the American Revolution* series has been running since the mid-1960s and has become an important historical document in its own right. It now stands at twelve volumes, each well over 1,000 pages long, with forewords from several generations of American presidents: from Kennedy through Johnson, Nixon, Ford, Carter, Reagan, Clinton and Bush to Obama.

Nevertheless, no attempt has yet been made to unite or combine these many themes into a comprehensive narrative naval history of the war. As a result, the role of sea power tends to retain a limited profile in our most general histories of the war. Indeed, it is most commonly restricted to a single example, the battle of the Chesapeake in 1781, when the defeat of a British fleet by the French led to the isolation and sub-sequent surrender of an entire British army at Yorktown in Virginia. Cornwallis's capitulation led directly to the fall of the bellicose North government in Britain and its replacement by one committed to ending the war. Thus is the link between sea power and American independence made manifest.

This argument has been well made by many historians and I make no attempt to challenge it here, at least not directly. What I have tried to do, however, is to extend this idea of the influence of sea power to the *entire* war, rather than to one isolated and very short-lived battle in a single location, whose influence is more debatable and far more complex than many suspect. What I have set out to do, essentially, is to provide the reader with a proper maritime and naval context within which to place the more widely known battle of the Chesapeake. By doing so, I hope to demonstrate that sea power did indeed influence the American war, but not in the way that one might suspect.

Within this broad approach, I have been careful to follow certain rules or themes. The first is that I do not restrict my 'naval' history to formal and established navies. It is often not appreciated that sea power can exist without navies – that is, without the formal funding stream, infrastructure, bureau-cracy, professional manpower, permanence and warships that the term 'navy' suggests: an idea that is particularly true of this war. Twelve of the thirteen rebellious colonies formed their own 'navies' without any formal administrative or logistical infrastructure, and even before these were created on paper, some of the colonies already wielded significant sea power. The same can be said of the Continental Navy, which represented the rebellious colonies acting together. Ships fighting on behalf of the Continental Congress exercised sea power long before the Continental Navy actually came into existence.

I have also been careful to include the role of privateers, because the relationship between navies, state formation and privateers is far too complex to be separated. A privateer, after all, cannot be a privateer until he has received a licence to conduct private warfare that has been issued by a state: you cannot have non-state maritime violence if a state does not exist first. Thus the rise of American privateers is an essential, if surprising, part of the story of American independence.

My second rule is to make no distinction between navies operating on rivers and freshwater lakes and those operating on oceans. The contributions made by the former to this war are of equal significance to those by the latter. Naval historians tend to make a false distinction between 'inland navies' and those that disputed 'command of the sea', but contemporaries saw no difference. They simply talked of 'command of the water',[1] an excellent phrase that has sadly gone out of use. If you are struggling to see a lake in the same terms as an ocean, I urge you to stand on the shores of Lake Michigan in a storm. You will not want to go out in a boat. Shallow it may be, but that shallowness and the relatively short fetch of the shores make for particularly brutal conditions on the water. And what about rivers? Rivers were to an eighteenth-century army as railways were to armies of the nineteenth century, but these were no passive, gently bubbling streams but evil and treacherous tongues of brown water whose currents could create whirlpools big enough to suck down a fully manned cutter. Figures do not survive, but it is safe to assume that during this war hundreds, perhaps thousands of sailors drowned in rivers, or otherwise died fighting on, in or near them. Most of the riverine warfare I describe in this book, moreover, happened on the lower reaches, where powerful ocean-bound currents met relentless land-bound tides. Operating vessels in such conditions was the ultimate test of seamanship. The slightest misjudgement could endanger the lives of everyone aboard, and with them the success of an entire military operation. Historians have tended to ignore men who fought in these liminal areas between land and sea, but I have the utmost respect for them. Indeed, one should remember that, for all his lack of 'naval' experience and understanding, Washington was the son of riverine Virginia and, of necessity, an experienced river boatman.

My third rule is not to restrict my narrative to the fates of Britain and America. Readers already familiar with the war will know of the major roles played by the French and Spanish fleets but may be less familiar with the roles played by those belonging to the Dutch, the Russians, the Danes, the Swedes, the native American Indians and by the East India Company's navy, the Bombay Marine.

My fourth aim is to try to bring together what is conventionally kept apart by emphasizing the links between these apparently separate navies and the seemingly separate theatres in which they operated. This is a major departure from previous approaches.[2] Trade ran from Britain and America to Newfoundland, Africa, South America, the Caribbean, the Mediterranean, the Baltic, the Indian Ocean and beyond, and where trade went, navies followed. The transient presence of foreign-bound trade convoys in home waters always carried significant historical significance, especially if they were captured. Each theatre, moreover, was affected by what was happening elsewhere in the world. If, for example, a major naval threat was posed to Britain in the English Channel, then one, or perhaps all, of the British forces in American, Caribbean, Mediterranean and Indian waters would be weakened to strengthen the Channel Fleet.

Such connections had a profound impact on the outcome of the war. The situation at Gibraltar, that lump of rock at the entrance to the Mediterranean, repeatedly set the war in America on a different course, while the situation in the

Caribbean constantly affected everything on both sides of the Atlantic. One contemporary put it simply: the war in America 'has and ever must be determined in the West Indies'.[3] There are even direct links between the construction of a canal system in northern France and American independence.[4] The way that these theatres interacted is both a fascinating intellectual puzzle and the key to understanding how the war developed. Exploring these unexpected links has been one of the most enjoyable aspects of writing this book, and the strength of them is most eloquently described by a single, captivating fact: a warship in the Pennsylvania State Navy was named *Hyder Ali*, after the warlord then fighting against the British 5,000 miles away in India.[5] If you need any more convincing, consider this: everyone knows that the first shot of this war was fired between soldiers on Lexington Common in 1775, but did you know that the last was fired between warships at the battle of Cuddalore in the Bay of Bengal on 20 June 1783?

The fifth rule is that I have tried to emphasize the various different ways that sea power affected the war and the nations in question. The obvious military narratives concern fleet battles, invasion and blockade, but such a traditional view misses a great deal. There are numerous strands to this narrative – the effect of sea power on strategy, internal politics, diplomacy, economics (and of course hairdressing) – but consider for now the arrival of the British fleet off New York in 1776, because it makes a significant point that transcends all of these themes. Before it fired a single shot or unloaded a single soldier, its mere presence dramatically altered the situation in New York. It terrified the rebels, gave hope to the loyalists, triggered a massive civilian evacuation causing untold misery to thousands, and affected the economy. Time and again the presence, or even just the anticipated presence, of a naval fleet had such an effect, and the war was particularly sensitive to it. In 1778 and 1780 just the *rumour* that the French were sending a major fleet to America dramatically changed the war. To understand the impact of sea power on the war, therefore, one must first realize that military commanders and civilians reacted not only to the reality of enemy sea power – measured in soldiers landed or cannon-balls fired – but also to its promise, and sometimes even to its ghost: the effects of sea power often lingered long after the fleets themselves had vanished.

This may be a naval history, but it is a history more of people than of ships, and I have also been careful to emphasize how navies affected people's lives in a far more personal way. The American Revolution meant that the sea, in some way, touched many more people than it had before the war. Throughout this war, an unknown number of people, but measured easily in the thousands, took to the sea in military operations or civilian evacuations and thereby experienced the world in a new way. A charming feature of the period resulting from this is that so many diaries are filled with awe at the majesty of nature. Here are narwhals, flying fish and icebergs, even islands covered in so many birds that, if startled, they would darken the sky.[6] Those same diaries are also filled with shock at the unique life of the sailor – the smell, the cramped conditions, the hot, the cold, the damp, the noise, seasickness. All of these goggle-eyed innocents were baptized in sea power by the war. For them the scale and potential of the world expanded during this period, their horizons broadened. This war was nothing less than a vital moment in the history of the human race reconnecting with itself, and with our world, by sea.

An interesting offshoot of this approach is that I have taken care to emphasize the reverse image – the intriguing paradox of sailors operating and fighting ashore – and this soon became a dominant theme. Almost every major military operation had a significant maritime component, for it was impossible to move any meaningful distance around colonial America without quickly finding oneself confronted by a river, estuary or lake which was impassable without significant maritime resources and skills. One of the most important parts of Washington's army – and, on several occasions, *the* most important part – was a regiment of mariners from Marblehead, Massachusetts. On more than one occasion land-battles were contested entirely by sailors on both sides firing naval guns from land-batteries. The presence and, perhaps even more so, the *absence* of sailors at critical moments in crucial theatres sent this war hurtling off in unexpected directions.

Another significant approach I have adopted has been to explore the little or completely unknown maritime aspects of otherwise well-known campaigns. Consider the famous battles of Lexington and Concord. Known most widely for the skirmishing on Lexington Common and in the woods on the way back to Boston, there were key naval aspects to the operation at both its beginning and end that directly affected its outcome. Then, the way that the battle was interpreted in Britain, which turned on the key question of who fired first, was directly influenced by a trans-Atlantic maritime race for intelligence. Consider also Benedict Arnold's 'march' through the Maine wilderness to Quebec in 1775, one of the best-known military campaigns of the period. This was actually an amphibious operation from start to finish. Arnold's troops first sailed from Newburyport in Massachusetts to the Kennebec River in Maine in a fleet of eleven ships and then headed into the wilderness with a fleet of 220 bateaux, which brought them down to the banks of the St Lawrence, but on the wrong side of the river to Quebec. Even the final act of the 'march', therefore, was a voyage. And what of Washington crossing the Delaware in 1777, sparking a hugely significant revival of American fortunes? Now that maritime operation *is* famous, one of the most famous maritime operations of the war, but did you know that Washington actually crossed the Delaware *four* times? Its popular title is actually misleading: 'Washington's Crossings' would be far more accurate. Finally, at least for now, what of the most famous naval event of the war, the battle of the Chesapeake and Cornwallis's surrender at Yorktown? Intriguingly, Cornwallis was not as isolated in Yorktown as we might think, helplessly stranded and waiting for naval rescue; in fact he had nearly 1,000 sailors embedded with his army and a fleet of sixty-eight ships to hand. Sixty-eight!

Above all, however, I have tried to emphasize just how difficult it was to wage naval war of any type in this period and the different ways that difficulty could be experienced. Naval warfare, for example, raised unique problems simply because of the slowness of communication. It would usually take at least a month for a message to travel across the Atlantic and, of course, twice as long to receive a reply. Key decision-makers, therefore, were working not with real-time information but with historical documents; in a curious link across the centuries, military commanders had to analyse information as historians.

The idea of a naval 'strategy' as we might conceive it was also rudimentary. The word did not even exist. That is not to say that planning or strategic thought was not attempted, but that war planners had only a loose understanding of exactly how one theatre of war would affect another, while capability was so limited and unpredictable that, when combined with the slowness of communication, any real planning was far more likely to fail than succeed. Sea power was hardly a surgical instrument of war, and this was not an era of men leaning over huge chart tables moving little model ships around: so many here to meet this threat; so many there to put pressure on that government; so many here to defend trade or blockade the enemy. Indeed, if there is one prominent theme to emerge from the operations described in this book, it is that, with only a handful of exceptions, *none* of them worked out as planned. The weather also played an immense part. Naval warfare in the age of sail was always influenced by the weather, but its impact seems to have been particularly severe in this war.

At the level of tactics, naval operations were confounded by limitations in signalling and by the fact that there was no shared inter-service doctrine. In essence, this meant that a fleet under one commander in one part of the world would operate with different signals, tactics and doctrine from another fleet, though from the same nation, elsewhere in the world. It is, in fact, more helpful to think of a navy not as one navy but as numerous different navies that worked in different ways. This did not make for reliable performance. Fleets working in international alliances suffered particularly severely from this type of problem. It was almost impossible to get different fleets within a single navy to co-operate with each other, let alone different fleets from different navies.

From the point of view of the economist and administrator, navies were enormously expensive to run and very difficult to maintain at any level of strength. Men had to be found to man the ships, and those men then had to be fed, clothed and kept healthy. In some theatres, such as the Caribbean, this was a herculean task and one at which everyone failed, but then, as we shall also see, every naval administration failed at this task even in the comfort of home waters. The occasional examples of success in this war within a war, when fleets were well manned and healthy, become fascinating exceptions.

All navies faced similar problems, but both old and new navies also had their own unique challenges. While the British, for example, were struggling with the problem of getting 5,000 sailors into a fleet without infecting one another with typhus, and the French with how to source sufficient nails to secure sheets of copper to their ships' hulls, the Americans grappled with problems specific to fledgling navies. What rules and regulations should the men abide by at sea? How were prizes to be distributed and administered? Even the most basic questions took up time and mental effort. Who was going to design the uniform? And what was it going to look like?

This struggle *with* sea power is one of the most important themes of this book. Yes, it describes the struggle *for* sea power that was fought between various nations, but it also explains how the difficulty of wielding sea power shaped the modern world. True, the battle of the Chesapeake turned the tide towards America and her allies at a crucial moment and can therefore be seen as an example of how sea power affected the war; but, in many respects, it is the exception that has been used to prove the rule. Time and again, it is held aloft as an example of how the magic wand of sea power could be waved to bring nations and empires to their knees, but nothing could actually be further from the truth. The war by then had become a maze without any exits, not because of the potency of sea power, but because of the difficulty of wielding it.

And yet with every dead end met, with every failure and disappointment suffered, the expectation of the success that could be achieved with navies remained curiously unaffected. It was almost as if the enormous investment expended on sea power gave it the right, like a spoiled child, to get away with anything, preventing any significant critical analysis by those who had borne it. In every country, in spite of staggering naval expenditure, it remained the case that politicians who made policy had no detailed knowledge of naval affairs and few expert advisers, and lacked any appreciation of how chance and the weather could ruin everything as easily as bad planning. The concept of a 'chain' of events is therefore almost completely unhelpful in this war. Far from being tightly joined by iron links, events were flimsily connected like a house of cards. There was, correspondingly, a constant sense of apprehension and drama from 1774 right up until the Peace of Paris in 1783, and throughout this long period, there was a total absence of any realistic expectation attached to sea power. The *promise* of sea power remained far more powerful than the reality, so that, in a curious way, this is a story about blind faith – it is a story of faith in the god of sea power.

This difficulty of wielding sea power lies at the heart of the most fascinating question of the age – one of two questions that are central to this book: how did a loose collection of colonies, without any standing army or navy, win its independence from the most powerful country in the world, a country which wielded such sea power that it could block out the sun with its sails and hide the surface of the sea with its ships? Washington himself believed that, in the future, the story of American independence would actually be considered a fiction:

For it will not be believed that such a force as Great Britain has employed for eight years in this Country could be baffled in their plan for Subjugating it by numbers infinitely less, composed of Men oftentimes half starved; always in Rags, without pay, and experiencing, at times, every species of distress which human nature is capable of undergoing.[7]

The numbers are compelling. At the start of the war, Great Britain, with the largest navy in the world, had committed nearly half of its commissioned ships to America and had successfully transported nearly 50,000 highly trained troops 3,000 miles across the Atlantic. It was an astonishing achievement. There, they faced an army that was no more than 20,000 strong, consisted in large part of hastily trained militia, had few experienced leaders, and was supported at sea by nothing more than a handful of ships without any supportive infrastructure. How on earth did the British lose?

The second question is intimately linked to the first: how and why did the war end with the Americans winning their independence, in spite of the fact that, by then, Britain was in a position of exceptional strength at sea – far stronger, even, than she had been at the start of the war?

On the surface, both questions appear to pose propositions as incongruous as the idea of a fashionable woman, anxious above all else over the way she looks, appearing in public with a ship balanced on her head. But as we have already seen, this was an extraordinary period of history in which the inconceivable was conceived and the impossible was an article of faith.

This inclination towards disbelief and a consequent acceptance that the independence of America was somehow preordained should not therefore lead us away from historical investigation but towards it, and in this book I will show how a naval and maritime perspective unlocks these mysteries and many more. Not only does a study of sea power in this period help us understand the events that led to American independence, but also it helps us understand sea power itself and the way that it has influenced history, for, ultimately, this was a war at sea that encourages us to think about what a war at sea actually is.

PART 1

AMERICAN REVOLUTION
1773–1775

1

BRITISH PYRE

It was surprisingly difficult to destroy a warship in the age of sail. The first problem is that warships were immensely difficult to sink. There are several reasons for this. The first is that, as the water in the hull rose, it became relatively easier for a tired crew to pump the water up onto the weather deck and then out over the side. The second reason is linked to the first: as the hull filled with water, the rate of influx decreased because of the pressure of water that had built up inside the hull; it would soon reach a state of equilibrium in which the water coming in would be balanced by the water being pumped out. This bought time, often far more than sailors expected, and we now suspect that many stricken ships were actually abandoned by their crews far too soon.[1] Given sufficient time and material, moreover, wooden ships could easily be repaired from the same material from which they were built. They were, in that respect, essentially organic: you could take a piece from here to mend it there; you could mend a rudder with a spar; a spar with a rudder; a piece of hatch coaming with a hull plank.

This all meant that the only way to destroy a wooden ship utterly was to burn it and that ship-burning carried with it a powerful symbolic element. Decisive, determined and greatly feared, to burn a ship was to kill a ship. Ship-burning was also symbolic because neither the activity nor the remains could be easily concealed. The spectacle created by a burning sailing ship is similar to that created by a burning church, because both create a vast pyramid of fire: the masts and sails of the ship conduct the fire in the same way as the steeple of a church, and the ship's hull feeds the fire in the same way as the church's nave. Gun-ports act like windows and allow the fire to breathe. Depending on the size of the hull, the masts of a warship could be anywhere between 50 and 220 feet above sea level, and the flames would burn higher still, 20 or even 30 feet above the top of the mast. The thick black smoke of burning timber and tar would then drift with the breeze for miles. Given the right landscape and atmospheric conditions, such a fire could be seen for 30 miles in any direction. But perhaps most importantly of all, a ship burned in a shallow river would not disappear. Ships' timbers are too large and too damp to be destroyed completely, and the waters are too shallow to cloak the evidence. Either the entire ribcage of the hull's beams or a few significant chunky timbers would survive as an enduring reminder of the violence that once destroyed her, as well as the method chosen for that destruction. To burn a ship was therefore to create an enduring spectacle that linked the present with the past across a bridge of maritime violence. It was a statement as much as an action and a symbol as much as a tactic. It was intensely and consciously provocative.

Burning a ship, however, raised a surprising number of problems. First, the fire would be difficult to start. It is an established fact of seafaring that all wooden ships leak, a factor of the way they are built and the stresses they are put under in their working lives. Wooden hulls torque and twist, constantly opening and closing the seams between the planks. The hull of any wooden ship is always damp, and in the bowels of the hull – the bilge – it is always wet. If a fire is to destroy a ship, it must be carefully set in the correct location and with appropriate material.

Secondly, an alert crew, especially a British naval crew, could quickly put out the fire. Consider this: the newest British chain-pumps in the 1770s, operated by only four men, could spill a ton of water onto deck in 43.5 seconds,[2] and there was an endless supply of it – it came from the sea. The crew were certainly motivated to use their pumps: there were never enough boats to take the entire crew to safety. If a ship took fire, some men would burn and others would drown. All crews of British warships were, unsurprisingly, acutely aware of the dangers of fire.[3]

To successfully set fire to a warship, therefore, first required the crew to be neutralized. This could be achieved in one of two ways: either by a bold approach from a heavily armed ship or by some element of surprise. The method chosen on the sand-banks of Narragansett Bay in Rhode Island, on 9 June 1772, was surprise by stealth, followed by deception.

*   *   *

The attackers' target was the British schooner HMS *Gaspee*, a ship that had been patrolling the waters of Narragansett Bay since early 1772, enforcing British customs laws. On 9 June she chased the *Hannah*, a packet-boat bound for Providence from Newport. The *Hannah*'s captain refused to heave to and led the *Gaspee* a merry dance before the latter struck the sand on Namquit Point off Pawtuxet. The possibility that the *Gaspee* was lured to her fate cannot be discounted.[4] The *Hannah* fled the scene.

The *Gaspee* could have been left alone to refloat with the tide and continue her business of irritating the local Rhode Island merchants and inhabitants, but as she lay so vulnerable and so close to shore, the opportunity was too good to miss. Her attackers came in boats from the nearby towns of Providence and Bristol. They had no cannon and they were facing the well-trained crew of a British warship led by a captain notorious for his unforgiving violence. Everything depended on surprise. Time was also limited because the tide was coming in and the *Gaspee* was sure to refloat.[5] Her attackers pushed off, wet feet braced in front of them. Stroke. Stroke. Stroke.

Their main concern was noise because the moon was invisible that night, and the attackers had blackened their faces and hands.[6] Oared craft make a surprising amount of noise. If you are ever strolling up the Cambridge Backs, ambling along the Isis in Oxford or striding along the banks of the Thames in Connecticut, and you are lucky enough to see a crew of eight cutting through the river, shut your eyes as the shell surges past.

It appears to glide, but the oars splash, the rowlocks clunk, the hulls make the water ripple, creating a distinctive whooshing noise, while the crew grunt, pant, growl and curse. The more men there are, the more noise the crew collectively, and unavoidably, make. A twenty-man crew forcing the blunt hull of a mid-eighteenth-century cutter through the water would be an orchestra of maritime effort. One technique that might reduce the noise, but by no means eliminate it, was to muffle the oars by putting some cloth, canvas or leather around the part of the oar that rested in the rowlock.

These men, more than sixty in total in eight boats and perhaps as many as two hundred in seventeen boats, depending on whose testimony you believe,[7] kept impressively quiet and got very close before they were seen. A British lookout challenged the boats three times and three times the challenges were ignored.

Stealth now made way for deception. Within sixty yards of the ship, one of the boats' leaders, a man named Abraham Whipple, stood up and claimed, inaccurately, that he was the local sheriff. He was, in fact, a merchant, and brother-in-law of Chief Justice Stephen Hopkins.[8] It was a bid to buy time to get the boats closer, and it worked.

* * *

Consider now the position of the *Gaspee*. The majority of any warship's armament, regardless of her size, was on either side. To bring her guns to bear, therefore, a ship had to present her broadsides to the enemy. If she could not move, she became immensely vulnerable at bow or stern. The way to attack a large, stationary ship at night with a flotilla of small boats was therefore to pull, as quickly as possible, for the ship's bow or stern, and to keep as far as possible from the broadside guns and their gun-ports. Of the two, the bow was always preferable for an attack from low-lying boats. With anchor cables hanging from the side or piercing the sea at a shallow angle, and with the rigging of the bowsprit reaching out across the sea, the climbing was good there, while at the stern there was often a large glass window, which made climbing tricky and increased the likelihood of being spotted.

The goal was then to get on board as quickly as possible before the sleeping crew could be sufficiently roused to defend their ship from a position of strength. The British ship being attacked was actually an American-built schooner, no more than forty-nine feet long. The Americans would have known such craft well: they would have known that her crew numbered no more than thirty, and they would have known the rough layout of the ship below decks. The success of the plan rested on the assumption that the crew could be surprised with many of them still down below. Defending the decks of a ship from an attack launched from below deck was relatively easy. The companionway ladders were steep, narrow and few. Only one or two sailors could ever get up at a time, and if any became injured or were killed, they would then block the passage of those behind.

The attackers thus pulled for the *Gaspee*'s bow as quickly as possible. One British sailor estimated that only three minutes passed between the strangers being sighted and their climbing on deck.

Most of the *Gaspee*'s crew were asleep and undressed. The lamps were extinguished and the arms chest was locked. It is easy to argue that their lack of preparation was a failure of command, but it is also helpful to see it as a measure of the confidence that the British captain felt at that time and in that location. This was, after all, a *British* warship from the Royal Navy – the very navy that had recently dominated the oceans in the Seven Years' War (1754–63) and which had helped Britain carve out the largest maritime empire that the world had ever seen. Rhode Island was one of no fewer than twenty British colonies in North America.* The captain of the

---

* The twenty consisted of the thirteen colonies that eventually rebelled: Massachusetts, New Hampshire, Rhode Island, Connecticut, New York, New Jersey, Pennsylvania, Delaware, Maryland, Virginia, North Carolina, South Carolina and Georgia; and the seven that did not: East Florida, West Florida, Quebec, Nova Scotia, St John, Newfoundland and Rupert's Land.

Gaspee clearly felt as secure as if he had run aground off the coast of Devon or Cornwall. There is an important level of expectation here, a theme that runs throughout this book. The British expected their sea power, exercised and conceived here on a local scale, to be sufficient to cow the citizens of Rhode Island. But they were wrong.

The schooner's commander, Lieutenant William Dudingston, stood near the forward shrouds and ordered the mysterious boats to stand clear. A commanding position it may have been, but he presented an easy target for Joseph Bucklin, who crouched in the bow of one of the boats and eyed along his musket. As soon as his target was steady, he pulled the trigger and shot Dudingston in the arm, the musket-ball unfortunately ricocheting into his balls, or – in the roundabout way of a polite eighteenth-century witness – 'five inches below his navel'.[9] He immediately collapsed, pouring blood from his groin. No doubt he screamed. The attackers, meanwhile, forced themselves aboard like a wave smashing its way through the scuppers and over the bulwarks. The few crewmen who stood to meet them were clubbed to the ground with wooden handspikes. Dudingston was surrounded 'and told to beg my life'.[10] He swiftly surrendered his ship. The crew were secured and the Americans set about the task of burning their prize.

*   *   *

The way to burn a ship was this. First, you had to open the gun-ports to ensure a good through-draft. This was often a problem. As the fire spread, the ropes that held the gun-ports open, hinged from above, would quickly burn, thus closing the gun-port lids and denying the fire the oxygen it needed to spread.*

Secondly, you had to pile some kind of kindling in the centre of the ship. Dried heather, reeds or birch, two or three

---

* This is why gun-ports on fireships were always hinged at the bottom, so that the fire could not suffocate itself with its own success.

feet long and tied in bundles, were ideal. The kindling could then be covered with a layer of material known as quick-match – strands of cotton dipped in saltpetre and gunpowder. Pitch, tar, olive oil, camphor and sulphur were also excellent accelerants. The fire had to be set sufficiently distant from the ship's magazine to allow time for the fire-setters to row themselves to safety. Five minutes was enough if a boat was to hand with a strong crew.

The fire then had to be lit. Sometimes this was done with more quick-match, but a 'port-fire' – essentially an eighteenth-century version of a fire-lighter – might also be used. Compositions of saltpetre, powder and sulphur packed into paper cases, these would burn for about twelve minutes, long enough to ignite substantial sections of timber.[11] If everything went to plan, the fire would spread evenly, the flames would lick out of the hatches and catch the masts, yards and sails, and the ship would become a fierce pyre. Guns might go off, paint would sizzle and pop, masts would creak and groan as the rigging gave way. The burning detritus would hiss as it fell into the sea. The fire would grow, live and breathe as the ship would break, moan and die. This is exactly what happened to the *Gaspee*.

2

AMERICAN ORIGINS

Revolutions are rather like oil slicks. Once they have begun, they can leach in any direction for any distance, and it becomes impossible to find a beginning or an end. No part of the oil is first and no part is last; it simply exists. All one can do is sample the oil for what it can tell us. In a similar way, any event chosen as the 'beginning' of a revolution is always going to be inadequate in one way or another. The best one can do as an historian is to choose an event that directly suggests or indirectly reflects as many significant issues as possible, and that is why the burning of the *Gaspee* is particularly important. I make no claim that it was the start of the American Revolution, nor do I claim that it was the start of American maritime hostility in the 1770s: the first claim would be unhelpful, the second manifestly false. The *Gaspee* does help, however, by encouraging us to think about the outbreak of the American Revolution in several important ways.

The first is to emphasize the maritime nature of many of the confrontations between colonial rebels and British armed forces in the early 1770s. So often the start of the war is measured from clashes between armed rebels and British redcoats at Lexington and Concord on 19 April 1775, when Massachusetts militia fought off British soldiers determined to seize stockpiles of military supplies. Others look to the Boston Massacre of 5 March 1770 as an important precursor to Lexington and Concord, when Bostonian civilians were killed and injured by British redcoats attempting to calm a demonstration against the Townshend Acts, new legislation that imposed an array of taxes on the colonies and tightened up customs enforcement.

Both of these are, of course, important events in the timescale of revolution, but it is also important to realize that the years between them were alive with other examples of rebellion and, particularly, with maritime-focused examples of rebellion.

Long before the destruction of the *Gaspee*, we know that the fort on Goat Island in Newport Harbour, Rhode Island, fired at the customs schooner *St John* on 9 July 1764; that, in 1768, local residents seized and scuttled the revenue sloop *Liberty* in Newport Harbour; that, in November 1771, a Philadelphia mob damaged a customs schooner and imprisoned her crew.[1] We also know that Massachusetts' fishermen rose up in their opposition to British policies and that there had been several riots over the impressment of American colonists into the Royal Navy, with Boston as the epicentre. This had a long history. On one occasion in 1747 a group of Royal Naval officers were actually kidnapped in Boston and held until a group of impressed Americans were released. By the end of the 1760s the British were unable to press American sailors ashore – indeed, it has been argued that countering the British impressment of American sailors on American soil was the first significant victory of the American Revolution.[2]

The importance of the maritime nature of these early flares of rebellion is that they could so easily spread down the liquid highway of the eastern seaboard. Every one of the British American colonies had a significant coastline, and although some groups of settlers had penetrated as far as 200 miles inland, the focus of every colony was at, or near, the sea. The sea was both a focus of rebellion and the means by which the rumour and reality of rebellion spread.

The *Gaspee* incident, however, was more than a maritime event, it was a *naval* event, and that too is highly significant because it raises the important questions of why she was attacked and of who attacked her – questions that help us understand both the *Gaspee* incident and, more broadly, the complex motivation for rebellion that ultimately led to revolution.

In 1772 no one knew that there was going to be a war within

three years. The key point to realize here is that the *Gaspee* incident was a brief crisis in naval power that happened during a period of peace. Naval power is too often and too easily associated with naval war, but that is to ignore the important activities of navies in peace, particularly the activities of the Royal Navy. A key part of its day-to-day work in American waters in the 1770s was the suppression of smuggling. Wars created debt that was reduced by increased taxation; increased taxation led to increased smuggling; and decreased navies led to an increase in the population of seafarers with nothing to do. The result was that there was usually an explosion of smuggling in times of peace.

Peacetime naval power therefore became far more personal and far more intrusive to the coastal population of the nation in question. In times of war the great ships usually fought their battles clear of the home horizon, on many occasions thousands of miles clear of that horizon. One of the paradoxes of naval power in wartime is that the majority of the people it benefited knew so little about it. For the domestic population, naval power in time of war was something obscure, something that existed through rumour, something that was experienced through terse description in newspapers, occasional artwork, and storytelling in pubs and coffee houses. In peacetime, however, naval power came home.

Tension between the Royal Navy and coastal populations was particularly acute in 1770s America. Britain and the American colonies had increasingly begun to confront each other over issues relating to taxation. The British empire was deeply in debt after the Seven Years' War (1754–63), a debt which now cost the government £5 million per year in interest alone at a time when the government collected only £8 million in revenue.[3] The British government believed that the American colonies should contribute to paying that debt off on the basis that they had clearly benefited from the results of the Seven Years' War. There was a real sense of unfairness underlying this in Britain. Some estimates claimed that British taxpayers were actually paying as much as ten times more in taxes than their colonial counterparts,[4] but the Americans also saw an imposition of tax as unfair: they had no representation in Parliament, so why should they be taxed?

Smuggling therefore became a way of flexing colonial muscle against the hated tax, but it was also an attractive proposal in 1770s America because it was so likely to succeed. Anyone who has sailed up the east coast of America will know of its mind-boggling length and variety, from towering cliffs to low-lying bluffs, with forests that run down to the sea, marshlands, lagoons, mudflats and mile upon mile of windswept beaches. A colonial customs service existed, but it was too weak to make a significant number of seizures.

To assist, the customs service began to deputize British naval officers. In this crucial period before the outbreak of war, therefore, British naval officers in North America actually carried two commissions: one from the Admiralty and one from the Treasury. In effect the British declared a modified, maritime form of martial law, typically the preserve of locations where there had been a breakdown of civilian authority or where an occupying force ruled over a conquered foe. British naval officers were encouraged in their role by being allowed to keep a substantial percentage of any illegal goods that they seized.[5] This was all unpleasant and provocative, and a frank admission that the British government was unable to perform one of the basic duties of any civil government – to collect revenue.

The link between tax and customs, the Royal Navy and American resentment over their tax burden was thus made explicit, and it was worsened by the method of policing. With such a weak force, even when boosted by naval officers, the British resorted to a tried and tested method of enforcing discipline: they acted occasionally and in few locations but with great vigour. In the same way that pirates might be hanged to discourage piracy, so smugglers were now severely punished to dissuade smuggling. In several cases, British naval officers were excessively violent, intrusive and demanding, and perhaps none more so than Lieutenant William Dudingston of the *Gaspee*.[6]

The problem in 1770s America created by the relationships between war and peace, and the navy and taxation, was well summed up by Benjamin Franklin, who, in his *Rules by Which a Great Empire May be Reduced to a Small One* of 1773 – the year after the *Gaspee* incident – wrote a passage which deserves to be quoted in full for its passion and insight:

> Convert the brave, honest officers of your navy into pimping tide-waiters and colony officers of the customs. Let those who in time of war fought gallantly in defence of their country-men, in peace be taught to prey upon it. Let them learn to be corrupted by great and real smugglers; but (to show their diligence) scour with armed boats every bay, harbour, river, creek, cove, or nook throughout the coast of your colonies; stop and detain every coaster, every wood-boat, every fisher-man; tumble their cargoes and even their ballast inside out and upside down and, if a penn'orth of pins is found unen-tered, let the whole be seized and confiscated. Thus shall the trade of your colonists suffer more from their friends in time of peace than it did from their enemies in war.[7]

* * *

The *Gaspee* was attacked because the local population was exasperated with Dudingston. He had developed a reputation as a violent, uncaring man who took pleasure in terrorizing the locals. The newspapers called him 'cowardly and insolent' and 'a disgrace to his profession'.[8] According to the *Providence Gazette*, he was 'haughty, insolent and intolerable' and had been 'personally ill-treating every master and merchant of the vessels he boarded, stealing sheep, hogs, poultry, &c. from farmers round the bay, and cutting their fruit and other trees for firewood'.[9] For these Rhode Islanders, their isolated rebel-lion was no theoretical cause, no matter for political philoso-phers in ivory towers; it was very real, very personal, and they were very, very angry. And, as always with anger, it was par-ticularly potent because it concerned concepts of reasonable or fair behaviour.

If the broader question concerned the fairness of being taxed, the specific question in this case was how a British naval officer, as a direct representative of the monarch carrying the King's Commission, should behave. Those rebels, as British subjects, believed that Dudingston had behaved improperly, that he had shamed the reputation both of the navy and of Britain herself. A crucial factor in their motivation was that, not only had they had enough of Dudingston, but they were fed up with the failure of the British system to keep him in check – a motivation that was shared in numerous other maritime-oriented attacks on British officials.[10]

One of the leaders of the attack was a man named John Brown, a wealthy merchant and the future founder of Brown University. Brown had tried to solve the problem of Dudingston through official channels three months earlier but with no success; it only led to the most acrimonious correspondence between the governor, Joseph Wanton, and Admiral John Montagu.[11] This, therefore, was not the Rhode Islanders' first response to Dudingston's behaviour, but their last.

The lesson of the *Gaspee* attack was that official channels of grievance and policing seemed broken. So often the American Revolution is presented as a caricature of Americans fighting for liberty from British tyranny with the implication of over-regulation that comes with such an interpretation, but in fact the colonists needed more control from a governing body that understood their particular problems and interests. The paradox of the *Gaspee* and of other similar demonstrations of dissent is that the rebels were creating disorder because they wanted to *contain* disorder.

A key indicator of this is the relative lack of violence used in the *Gaspee* attack. It was a bold and vigorous attempt against the ship, certainly, but the only man who was wounded was the vessel's commander, and there is plenty of evidence that he was shot in the balls by accident. The rest of the crew had no more injury than bruising from handspikes, and the attackers gave their word that the crew would not be harmed.[12] The destruction of a ship may seem bad, but consider how much worse it could have been: in the early years of the French Revolution the figures of hated authority were butchered like dogs.

Even with their blood up the actions of other American rebels in this period were similarly characterized by restraint and control. The Boston Tea Party is the best-known example. Then, gangs of enraged merchants and smugglers, who were all set to lose out from new legislation, threw tea worth £10,000 into Boston Harbour. The important point for this story was how the demonstration was staged: it was highly organized, exceptionally efficient, entirely non-violent, deliberately theatrical and carefully symbolic. Even as they threw the tea into the harbour, they replaced a broken lock to demonstrate that their 'quarrel' was not against property or order, and one man who stole a small amount of tea was made to run the gauntlet and his coat nailed to the whipping post.[13] Similar non-violent events occurred at the same time up and down the eastern seaboard – a strong display of unity throughout the disparate colonies in both the motivation and style of rebellion.[14]

Such acts, of which the *Gaspee* was an important part, were designed to demonstrate American responsibility as much as they were the scale of American anger. At this stage the question of independence simply did not exist: the Americans wanted to be treated justly and fairly as British citizens; they still felt closer to Britain than they did to one another.

*   *   *

A careful understanding of the British response to the *Gaspee* attack also highlights many problems with the wider British response to rebellion that ultimately led to revolution.

The basic point was that the British government misunderstood the motivation for rebellion. For all the American moderation in their rebellion and the reasonableness of their requests, the American rebels were continually portrayed in Britain as mindless thugs, pirates, smugglers, law-breakers, anarchists – as an infestation of radicals that needed to be exterminated. There was no room for negotiation in London, and so the rebels' actions condemned them even when those very actions had been deliberately chosen to convey a message of moderation. The highest-ranking British military officers, General Thomas Gage and his naval counterpart Admiral John Montagu, must share responsibility for this misinterpretation, but if one reads their correspondence, the role that Montagu played stands out.

Montagu had arrived in 1771, when the rebellion was yet to reach crisis point, and his fear of rebellion served to realize his worst nightmares. He saw rebels in shadows and anarchy in well-meant demonstration; he turned his back when he should have opened his eyes and ears; he encouraged an iron fist when a kid glove was required. His letters back to the Admiralty were entirely devoid of any understanding and full of condemnation of American treachery and insurgency.[15] The role of Montagu and other Royal Naval officers in propagating this belief is an unmistakable part of the British failure in America. It is a reminder that, when policing and administering distant colonies, especially in times of crisis, the subtle mind of an experienced diplomat was required, when in fact that role too often fell to the highest-ranking naval officer on station, regardless of his abilities in that field.

To make matters worse, sea power was a particularly sensitive tentacle of empire and perhaps the most effective way to send a message directly to London. After all, this was not just the navy: it was the *Royal* Navy. The navy itself was big and impressive, but the *idea* of the navy was even bigger and even more impressive. The link between the monarch and his navy had existed from the time of Henry VIII, but in the 1770s it had grown particularly close thanks to the careful nurturing of that relationship by the Earl of Sandwich, the First Lord of the Admiralty. To attack the Royal Navy was directly to provoke the king.

The point about the *Gaspee* attack, therefore, was not just that British authority had eroded, but that it had eroded to the point that the Americans had burned a ship of the Royal Navy. That message got through loud and clear. In fact it worked so well that the Americans were about to discover just how very sensitive the British were about their navy.

*　　*　　*

No blame was attached to Dudingston, who was sent to a French spa to recover from his wounds while the British politicians stamped and cursed. Unable to see the burning of a British warship as anything other than piracy or treason, they decided to impose British authority, symbolically as well as in effect, by declaring that those responsible would be dragged 3,000 miles across the Atlantic to be tried in Britain. To identify those responsible, a Royal Commission was set up in Newport, the capital of the Rhode Island colony, and given extraordinary powers of investigation.[16] An enormous sum of £500 was promised to anyone who could identify any of the rebels, and £1,000 to anyone who would betray the leaders and the man who shot Dudingston.[17] This was the first time that British politicians in London had acted to punish any of the numerous examples of violence that had taken place against British maritime authority in North America.[18]

The constitutional principle behind the inquiry – that the British were going to extradite the offenders – was widely despised in America.[19] Appointed to a commission that was openly ridiculed, the Commissioners, who were all prominent men with personal interests in New England, ensured that it remained toothless and did everything in their power to irritate Montagu. When the Commissioners summoned him from Boston, he at first refused, but when he did arrive flying his admiral's broad pennant, the fort on Goat Island summarily ignored his presence. Montagu was incensed.[20] Realizing what was afoot, he understood that, in spite of the best intentions, nothing would ever come of the inquiry. He was quite right. The inquiry did not obtain sufficient evidence to apprehend a single suspect.[21]

Meanwhile, false stories circulated concerning the summary powers of the Commission of Inquiry and Montagu's intent to lay waste to Rhode Island.[22] Eleven of the thirty-eight newspapers in colonial America had reported the *Gaspee* incident within weeks of it happening, and it became the subject of one of the most influential and bestselling pamphlets of the revolution. In Boston a little-known minister named John Allen used the *Gaspee* affair as a basis to launch an attack on greedy monarchs, corrupt judges and conspiracies – all key concerns in the subsequent ideological hype over independence. His sermon *An Oration upon the Beauties of Liberty, or the Essential Rights of the Americans* was reprinted seven times in four colonial cities and became one of the most popular pre-independence pamphlets of colonial British America. It was also the most widely read sermon and the most popular public address in the years before independence.[23]

The story of the *Gaspee* affair thus became a cause célèbre, a flame in its own right to heat American blood. The burning pyre that had lit up the Rhode Island night now persisted through print, guiding Americans towards rebellion. Boston patriot Samuel Adams, who could see as clearly as anyone the significance of the burning of a British warship at that time and in that location, wrote six months after the attack, 'Such an Event as this will assuredly go down to future Ages in the page of History',[24] but he never could have imagined the scale, depth and complexity of the story that page would tell.

* * *

The stringency of the measures taken against the *Gaspee* attackers was exactly mirrored in British policy towards America in the subsequent years, culminating in what became known in Britain as the 'Coercive Acts' but in America as the 'Intolerable Acts'. The most significant legislation, the Boston Port Act of 31 March 1774, closed the port of Boston until the East India Company had been repaid for its tea lost in the Boston Tea Party, brought the Massachusetts government under direct control of the British government, and made the extradition of Americans to Britain for trial explicitly legal.

This policy of aggressive coercion was the brainchild of the Lord Chief Justice, the Earl of Mansfield, who spoke in rousing terms quoting none other than Gustavus Adolphus, the famed Swedish warrior king: 'My lads, you see these men. If you do not kill them, they will kill us.'[25] Everyone in Parliament loved this rhetoric and newspapers soon joined in. Boston was a 'nest of locusts',[26] and 'a canker worm in the heart of America, a rotten limb which (if suffered to remain) will inevitably destroy the whole body of that extensive country'.[27]

The only measured far-sighted thinkers were the Duke of Grafton, the previous prime minister and now Lord Privy Seal, and Lord Dartmouth, Secretary of State for the Colonies. Dartmouth's pacific tendencies were restricted by loyalty to his stepbrother, the prime minister Lord North, which meant that Grafton was the only man to make any detailed concilia-tory proposal. His suggestion, for peace commissioners to be sent to America to settle grievances on the spot, was roundly ignored and eventually led to his resignation in 1775.[28]

The policy of aggressive coercion was also assumed with the poor condition of the British economy in mind: matters were so bad that, as the embers of rebellion flared, the British actually reduced their naval budget.[29] There wasn't enough money for an overpowering campaign, but there was enough for a stinging slap in a single location – Massachusetts. Boston, therefore, was blockaded by sea from 1 June 1774. Any ship caught running the blockade was to be seized, along with her cargo. The only exceptions were ships carrying supplies, food or fuel for British troops and Boston's civilian population.[30]

The British, however, simply did not have the naval power to back up their strategy. British ships were too few and of the wrong type. The mighty ships of the line that constituted the heart of the British battlefleet and which had won the previous war were useless in sheltered, shallow inlets like Narragansett Bay and Boston Harbour. Even frigates were too large. To blockade Boston and police the entire coast of North America,

Montagu had at his disposal no more than one significant ship of force, three or four small frigates, and a dozen sloops and schooners.

In an attempt to enforce the Boston Port Act, he stationed eight of his precious ships in Boston Harbour, which might seem like sufficient force to blockade a single harbour but was woefully inadequate. The term 'Boston Harbour' is misleading. It suggests an enclosed space, perhaps accessed through a narrows, but in practice Boston Harbour was actually defined as stretching from Nahant Point in the north at the very end of modern Nahant Island, all the way to Point Alderton in the south, the modern town of Pemberton.[31] The entrance alone to this 'harbour' is almost eight miles wide and at its farthest point is some eight miles from land. That area of sea itself was a navigational nightmare, strewn with at least forty small islands and smaller sand-banks that littered the approaches to Boston.[32]

The tiny squadron was further cursed by manning and supply problems and the poor condition of its ships. Boston may have been the centre of British naval power in this period, but there was no dockyard there; in fact there were no major British naval docking facilities *anywhere* on the coast of North America. The nearest limited facilities were in Halifax, Nova Scotia.[33] The constant sea-time thus wore out both ships and crews, and this in turn led to impressment, which further infuriated the Americans.[34]

Even though the British naval force was inadequate, this was a key moment in the changing relationship between the Americans and the Royal Navy. These ships were now part of a hostile fleet, and Montagu was a hostile flag officer rather than a friendly station commander.[35] At the end of June he was replaced by Vice-Admiral Samuel Graves, who had no more success than Montagu in keeping Boston closed. His ships repeatedly ran aground on hidden mudflats, and he cursed at how small boats passed freely in the shadows of the British warships, 'creep[ing] up and down to and from Boston, in and out of the harbour in the night'.[36] Meanwhile, the naval focus on Boston meant that the rest of the New England coast was left wide open to smugglers. From the summer of 1774, Rhode Island, Connecticut, the Delaware River and Philadelphia had no naval presence at all, and by now the customs service was impotent.[37]

Landed in an extraordinarily difficult position, it certainly did not help that Graves, like Montagu, was easily provoked and suspicious, was unable to get on with his counterpart in command of the British troops in Boston, General Thomas Gage, and was unwilling to take any initiative to tackle the problems that he faced. A close friend of Lord North condemned Graves as 'a corrupt admiral without any shadow of capacity'.[38] It is likely that Graves's appointment was the result of his friendship with the First Lord of the Admiralty, the Earl of Sandwich, who should shoulder some of the blame for his failure.[39] This issue of competence in command of the North American station was to become a recurring theme.

This early period of rebellion is therefore characterized by a curious and contradictory effect of British political and military power: it occurred and then endured in American consciousness because of British military and political strength, but also because of British military and political weakness. By taking advantage of transient weakness in specific locations, the Americans revelled in their defiance of a British naval power that had crushed other countries, but the failure of the British then to do anything about those acts of rebellion lessened American respect for British military power, particularly for her naval power, and encouraged the colonies to come together.

A direct response to the Intolerable Acts was the formation of the first Continental Congress of September 1774, held in Philadelphia. Though never conceived as a permanent body, this was still a major step towards state formation for the rebellious colonies.[40] Representatives of twelve colonies* met to consider their response to the Intolerable Acts and determined

* Georgia did not send a representative, hoping for British help against Indians on their frontier.

on a boycott of trade designed to take advantage of their significant position in the Atlantic trade system – a tactic they had previously used to help force the repeal of hated legislation.[41] Indeed, the Americans believed themselves to be in a position of strength. One contemporary commented: 'America, impressed with the exalting sentiments of patriotism and of liberty, conceived it to be within their power, by future combinations, at any time to convulse, if not to bankrupt the nation, from which they sprung.'[42] The Americans had no army and no navy, but they certainly were not going to lie down in the face of this new British aggression.

3

EUROPEAN GUNPOWDER

Here are some interesting facts about gunpowder. On home service a British First Rate man of war – that is to say, a three-decked ship of 100 guns – would stock somewhere around 525 barrels of powder. Each barrel was of uniform size and contained 100 pounds of powder. There were 2,240 pounds in a British (long) ton, so we can work out that a single First Rate man of war carried more than 23 tons of gunpowder on home service. Even a small sloop, of the type that patrolled the coasts of America in the 1770s, carried 126 barrels of powder, a little over 5½ tons. On foreign service, where there was less opportunity to renew the stock, the figure was even higher for all ships.[1] For the single period for which we have decent figures, the Napoleonic Wars, we know that the Royal Navy consumed some 80,000 barrels of powder every year. The implication is clear: if a state was going to wage a war in the eighteenth century, it had to be able to source a great deal of gunpowder for a long period of time.

It also had to be able to source good-quality powder. Old powder was less potent than new powder; powder that was manufactured with good-quality ingredients was more potent than powder that was not; powder that was well mixed to the proportions appropriate for the chosen ingredients was more potent than powder that was not. Those ingredients, in name at least, were always the same: saltpetre, charcoal and sulphur. In practice the quality of the charcoal depended on the type of wood that was burned, the best being alder, dogwood or hazel, and also on the technique of the burning. Similarly, the quality of the saltpetre and sulphur depended on the source and the extraction and purification techniques. Each raw ingredient was ground and weighed before being mixed, milled, sieved, dried and then re-formed into large or fine grains depending on its intended use. Finally it was glazed with graphite to make it more durable.[2] If the manufacturing process was incorrectly carried out at any of these crucial stages, the quality of the gunpowder would suffer.

The biggest problem that the Americans faced at the start of their revolution was access to these materials. Saltpetre could be manufactured or dug out of the ground domestically, but the manufacturing process took considerable time and saltpetre found naturally in the ground was always insufficient in quantity.* The best-quality saltpetre in the largest quantities came from India. Other good sources were found in Russia, Germany and Spain. Sulphur was also very difficult to access, and the single best source of good-quality sulphur available in commercial quantities was Sicily. Even if these ingredients were found in America, the colonial powder-making industry was far too immature to produce the amount of powder necessary to ignite a revolution.[3]

This all meant that, if the Americans were going to rebel, they would need to import vast quantities of gunpowder by sea. Other military stores were important, of course, not least lead for shot, flints for flintlocks and the firearms themselves, but the principal problem was powder. With no powder there would be no revolution. At this critical stage, therefore, the ability of the colonies to rebel became in large part a question of sea power, focused on their ability to smuggle gunpowder by sea past British warships or to transport British powder, seized in maritime raids on forts and ships, safely up rivers into the interior. All of this began to happen while the British were trying to impose the Coercive Acts on Massachusetts.

* * *

* It was usually found in the floors of barns, where animal and plant waste eventually produced saltpetre in the damp conditions.

A group of European maritime powers were more than willing to trade in military stores with the Americans. The British had become so dominant in the aftermath of the Seven Years' War (1754–63) that France and Spain, their traditional enemies, were happy to see the balance of European power shift away from Britain back towards them, and neutral countries such as the Netherlands and Russia were more than happy to profit from a British civil war – a contentment shared by merchants everywhere. This was a period characterized more by entrepreneurial sharks exploiting pre-existing maritime trade contacts than by political ideologists inciting others to rebellion.[4]

What made matters worse for the British – and a significant enabling factor for the American rebels – was that several European countries had a presence in the Caribbean which, because of the direction in which the north-easterly trade winds blew, was directly en route between Europe and North America. Each of these countries, moreover, had a large and established mercantile marine with time-honoured trading routes and long-standing American trading partners. Crucially, each also had a significant navy to bolster any stance they took in relation to the British–American conflict. In 1770 the combined French and Spanish navies were 14 per cent larger than the British, and by 1775 that figure had risen to 25 per cent. The Dutch navy, very roughly a third of the size of the French and half that of the Spanish, was also a significant force.[5]

The British, faced with a rebellion 3,000 miles away and a crippled economy, were desperate to avoid provocation of any of these countries. The threat of French, Dutch, Russian and Spanish sea power, imposed by their navies doing nothing more than sitting in their dockyards, hung like a cloud over British policy towards America. By their mere existence, these distant navies all influenced this embryonic stage of rebellion.

*   *   *

The initial British effort to prevent the importation of gunpowder to America was unfocused and hamstrung by logistical and diplomatic weakness.

Ships bound for America from British waters were policed in home ports, but it was not until 22 December 1775 – *eighteen* months after the passage of the Coercive Acts – that Parliament passed the Capture Act, which declared the American colonies in a state of open rebellion, authorized the seizure of all American ships and prohibited trade with America.[6] Until then the British were legally restricted to searching only those suspicious ships that were within two leagues* of British territory, and they could do nothing at all about American ships in foreign ports or indeed about foreign ships on the high seas.

Pressure was put on the Dutch, via the Prince of Orange himself, to stop their trading with America, but what, in practice, could be achieved politically or militarily when confronted with the merchants of Amsterdam who, in the words of one contemporary, 'would sell arms and ammunition to besiege Amsterdam itself'?[7] The Spanish made no attempt whatsoever to limit trade in arms with the Americans and were particularly active in smuggling munitions up the Mississippi.[8]

Under the guidance of the foreign minister, Charles Gravier, comte de Vergennes, a dedicated, prudent and idealistic politician utterly committed to resurrecting French political and military power, the French were both brazen and sly in their help of the Americans. One ruse was to load American ships with gunpowder in a French port but to issue the ship with false French papers and even to man the ship with French officers who would conduct any negotiations with British naval officers.[9] They also set up a company, cunningly called 'Roderigue Hortalez et Compagnie' to disguise its French origins, through which they shipped to America some 30,000 muskets and 2,000 barrels of powder.[10] In abject terror of provoking a naval arms race, British politicians actually instructed the navy not

---

* A measure of distance equal to three miles.

to intercept French ships carrying munitions and supplies to America in European waters.[11]

In the Caribbean, powder simply poured into, and then out of, French Martinique, Spanish Cuba and the Dutch Antilles. There were simply too few British ships here to be in any way effective – four slow cruisers to cover the entirety of the Leeward Islands station – and the merchants worked together to defy the Royal Navy. There is good reason to think that many of these players were British merchants.[12] The British envoy to the Dutch island of St Eustatius, a key location in the powder trade, threw his hands in the air: 'All our boasted empire of the sea is of no consequence,' he raged, 'we may seize the shells but our neighbours will get the oysters.'[13] This was military power undermined by mercantile power; this was sea power weakened by a lack of political alliances with foreign nations.

With such a gaping net in Europe and the Caribbean, an increased responsibility fell on British ships in American waters to stop the smugglers, but it had been clear for some time that the North American squadron was too small even to blockade Boston Harbour, let alone the entire coast. In 1774 the British had twenty-six ships to blockade the east coast of America *and* to support the British policy of the coercion of New England. Hugh Palliser, a leading British naval officer and strategic thinker, thought that they needed twenty-two to blockade Boston alone.[14] Vice-Admiral Graves in Boston simply stood no chance, even though he had received some limited reinforcements in the winter of 1774.[15] In a telling letter to the Admiralty in April 1775, he wrote that 'smuggling is carried to such a height, and so systematically followed, that without the utmost vigilance and care, there is no detecting them [the smugglers] to condemnation'.[16] On the rare occasions when smugglers were actually seized by Graves's ships, no contraband arms or ammunition was ever secured, and on 19 March 1775 he admitted to the Admiralty: 'I am extremely mortified that notwithstanding the King's Ships and Vessels have been very active all this Winter, no seizures of any

Consequence have been made.'[17] The British squadron in the Chesapeake was equally impotent.[18]

The result of these combined failures was that over 90 per cent of all the American powder used during the first two-and-a-half years of the struggle for independence was imported to America by sea.[19]

* * *

The other source of gunpowder – of far less significance in terms of quantity than imported powder, but of far more significance in terms of direct American–British confrontation with the antagonism it both revealed and provoked – was the powder that already existed in the colonies. Although usually considered in terms of land-based operations, the struggle for this powder had significant maritime themes.

Powder was stored throughout the colonies in specially designated buildings, tended by men who knew the fickleness of their charge. A fine example of a powder house from the period survives in Somerville, Massachusetts. In 1774 this was already seventy years old and had been converted from its original use, a windmill. A perfect powder house, it stood high on a hill, a good six miles from Boston, where any accidental explosion would cause no harm to the city itself. It was also sturdily built of brick and sufficiently large to house all of the powder of the Province of Massachusetts as well as the powder designated to individual towns within that province: gunpowder storage and distribution was not simply a question of logistics but of bureaucracy and law.

This was one of the largest caches of powder in the colonies, and when, in August 1774, Thomas Gage heard detailed reports that it was being systematically emptied of powder belonging to the towns surrounding Boston, he launched a lightning amphibious raid to secure what was left. Two hundred and sixty men rowed from Boston in thirteen long-boats and pulled for the Mystic River. They followed the ever-narrowing river deep inland before disembarking and racing across open country to the powder house. With dawn breaking at their backs, they carried the remaining barrels to the longboats and then cruised down the river and then across the bay to Castle William, the island fortress some distance offshore at the mouth of Boston Harbour.

The boats provided the troops with the mobility and speed they needed to achieve the surprise that was essential to its success. Given sufficient warning, the remaining powder would have vanished in the night and the troops would have found nothing but a building echoing with missed opportunity. Gage's safeguarding of the Massachusetts powder was a bold move made by a man who refused to be left behind by swiftly changing events. He secured the powder that was rightfully his and he denied it to his enemy. Unfortunately, however, his actions made many of the existing problems much worse.

As news of the operation spread, the Americans were both outraged and alarmed by the idea of armed British troops marching around the countryside. The American concern – and this was characteristic of so many of these flare-ups between British forces and the colonists from 1772 onwards – was enflamed by wild and inaccurate rumour. In this case there were claims that six Americans had died and even that Gage's operation was only the first move in a co-ordinated British offensive. Some even claimed that the British warships were bombarding Boston.

None of this was true, but it was exactly what so many of the committed rebels actually wanted to hear and it served to persuade the uncertain of the righteousness of the rebel cause. Civilian mobs gathered in larger numbers than had even been seen in New England. One Boston customs commissioner, Benjamin Hallowell, was unfortunate enough to be discovered in a sumptuous carriage. 'How do you like us now, you Tory son of a bitch?' howled one of the mob.* Hallowell leapt from his carriage, forced his liveried servant from his horse and galloped for Boston.[20]

---

* 'Tory' is a term used to describe an American loyal to the British crown.

By securing the Massachusetts powder, Gage had opened the floodgates to a torrent of rage that had been building in the Massachusetts countryside, and the Americans responded to Gage's raid in kind, launching several focused and daring amphibious raids to secure powder from British coastal forts in Portsmouth in New Hampshire, Newport and Providence in Rhode Island, and New London in Connecticut. Only a narrow escape saved an entire British ship loaded with ordnance from falling into rebel hands off Rhode Island.[21] All of these American successes were made possible by inadequate British sea power that should have linked these isolated coastal fortresses together with a chain of patrolling warships.[22] Things did not all go well for the Americans and there were a few other successful British operations, but we know that, by an impressive concerted effort throughout the colonies, in this period the rebels secured somewhere in the region of 80,000 pounds of gunpowder from stores in British hands.[23]

Against this background Gage wrote to London with news that 'the whole country was in arms and in motion',[24] and he made it quite clear that the situation on the ground had changed alarmingly. The question was no longer one of tea or tax but of guns, powder and bullets – the currency of war. In a terrible mistake that the British would repeat throughout the war, Gage's crucial dispatch was not sent to London via a fast naval ship but by a slow merchantman that took no less than seven weeks to reach Whitehall.[25]

News of this type convinced Lord North that the policy of coercion had failed, and in September 1774 he unexpectedly chose to dissolve the government six months before its scheduled ending, to create a new one that would be free from the burden of past colonial strategy and would not have to interrupt its policy on America for an election.[26] North won with a large majority and it was this government that was in place for the majority of the subsequent war. Their language immediately hardened with Lord Dartmouth taking the lead. He declared that Massachusetts Bay was in a state of rebellion and that conflict could not be avoided.[27] George III oversaw everything with grim approval. 'The dye is now cast, the colonies must either submit or triumph.'[28]

In this atmosphere of unravelling control, Graves surrounded Boston with ships. Nothing is more indicative of the changing situation than the fact that, in April, Graves surveyed the channels between Charlestown and Boston and ordered the largest ship in his squadron, the *Somerset*, to anchor between the two towns.[29] The smuggling of powder was, by now, far from Graves's mind; he was now worried that the rebels would actually launch an amphibious invasion of Boston.

Gage soon received orders to take decisive action by targeting rebel leaders and disarming the population. He also received another injection of reinforcements, while Graves was informed that six sloops were being built in the Royal Dockyards, all for him.[30] This was part of a limited naval mobilization in 1775 that was still wholly inadequate for the challenge that faced Graves.[31]

As so often in this period, rumour of Gage's new orders reached American shores long before the orders actually reached Gage, and the orders themselves soon found their way into rebel hands. Both sides had a full twelve days to skitter nervously amid full knowledge of the storm that was coming.

*   *   *

The basic story of the subsequent British campaign that began with fighting in the New England villages of Lexington and Concord and ended with the British forces desperately fighting their way back to Boston is well known, but the role of sea power in that campaign is not as well known as it should be.

It all began on the evening of 18 April 1775. The movement of the fleet's boats told its own story as they were gathered together from all over Boston into a great bobbing raft under the stern of the Third Rate *Boyne*. As so often with British military operations, the earliest hard information was to be had at the seafront, straight from the mouths of British sailors who were sent ashore on errands, the secrets spilling from their mouths like the coin from their pockets.[32]

Soon the Americans had detailed intelligence that confirmed the harbour-front rumours and named the target. The detail was so specific that some historians suspect none other than Gage's wife as the spy who betrayed the British plan. By mid-afternoon the Americans knew that the British were heading for Concord, a hard day's march from Boston – a hothouse of rebel activity where the Provincial Congress met and the location of a cache of rebel powder. It just so happened that Gage had heard rumours that the rebel leaders Samuel Adams and John Hancock were there.

Through a network of runners and spies the information quickly came to the ears of Paul Revere, a silversmith who acted as a messenger and co-ordinator for rebel activities and interests. He and another man, a tanner by the name of Richard Dawes, then set off, primarily to warn Adams and Hancock. Dawes went by land, across the defended neck which joined Boston to the mainland, but Revere first set off by sea. Shortly after 10.15 p.m. he headed to the shore opposite Charlestown, found his boat and set off with two others. 'It was then young flood, the ship was winding, and the moon was rising', he later wrote of a moment that stuck in his mind because, blocking his way, was the 64-gun *Somerset*. Revere could not hide himself in river traffic because there was none: the ferries had been seized and all 'boats, mud-scows and canoes' banned from taking to the water. His only hope, therefore, was that the British sentries would be slack or the darkness would hide his crossing. He was lucky. His little boat bobbed silently past the massive hulk of the creaking *Somerset*, the event immortalized in Henry Wadsworth Longfellow's poem 'Paul Revere's Ride': 'A phantom ship, with each mast and spar, / Across the moon like a prison bar.' Revere was across.

The British troops, meanwhile, were preparing for their own crossing of the harbour. They chose not to get to the mainland via the neck but, as everyone had already worked out, by the flotilla of boats that had been so obviously mobilized that afternoon. Shortly before Revere crossed Boston to his hidden boat, British troops marched to a scarcely populated stretch of coast known as Back Bay, divided by a narrow stretch of ink-black water from the Cambridge marshes, a landing point chosen for its isolation.

With the tide running swiftly against them, naval crews struggled with their cargo of soldiers. To keep together in the darkness, the boats were connected to each other at bow and stern in chains of three or four. There were too few boats to take the men over in one crossing, and it was a full two hours before they were all across. They disembarked and stood shivering in the Cambridge marshes, wet to their waistbands as they waited for the navy to return with their supplies. Time passed. Revere, meanwhile, had made his crossing undetected and swiftly because his route had taken him inland at an angle, with the tide.[33]

The subsequent events twisted and turned in countless ways. The British eventually marched inland. They were cold, wet and late. Revere was captured on his way to Lexington but subsequently released. In spite of several warnings, the men of Lexington were unprepared for a British attack. Hancock and Adams narrowly escaped. An unidentified shot began a full-scale engagement on Lexington Common, while another engagement was fought at Concord. Eight times American militias held their ground against British troops, and twice the British lines were broken. The British then retreated in the face of highly effective skirmishing tactics that devastated the British ranks. They were chased all the way back to Charlestown, where they were finally left alone by the Americans. The Royal Navy took the shattered remains of the expeditionary force back to the relative safety of Boston. The wounded went first, but there were so many of them that it took the navy three hours to ferry them all to Boston.[34]

General William Heath, commander of the rebel militia, saw too much strength in the British position as they closed on Boston and called off the chase. Graves, no doubt to talk up his own role in halting the American advance, believed that it was the fear of his ships alone that had prevented the British troops from being routed and had secured the safety of Boston.[35] The *Somerset* was still anchored in the channel between Boston and Charlestown where, in the words of Graves, it kept the inhabitants of Charlestown 'in awe'.[36] To that mighty presence Graves now added a ring of boats right around Boston. Every ship was kept clear for action and any spare boats were hauled alongside the larger ships and armed.[37]

British naval power certainly played a role in this campaign, therefore, and had things been done differently, there might well have been a markedly different outcome. If the navy had been more subtle and more efficient with its preparations, British troops might have had more success in their attempts to surprise the inhabitants of Lexington and Concord. Adams and Hancock might have been captured. Bloodshed might have been avoided. From the American perspective, an absence of British ships in the channel between Charlestown and Boston might have led to a direct assault on Boston.

On the evening of 19 April the countryside around Boston reeled from the fighting, and the rumour mill began its manic grinding. Stories of half-seen events of shocking violence were told alongside blatant falsehoods and established facts. Had a British soldier really been discovered lying on the roadside with no ears? Had he even been scalped to mimic the Indian way of warfare? Had British soldiers fighting their way back to Boston really burst in on a family and massacred them all? What really happened in that orchard, where the vile rumour of atrocity grew like so much mistletoe on the bows of the apple trees? And, of course, there is the question at the heart of the story that was so well hijacked by both sides that we still do not really know the answer: who fired the first shots on Lexington Common? As one contemporary wrote: 'At all corners People inquisitive for News – Tales of all Kinds invented, believed, denied, discredited.'[38]

Truth and fiction blended together on numerous levels. The Americans understood the events in a different way from the

British; farmers in a different way from soldiers; soldiers who had been there in a different way from soldiers who had not; men in a different way from women; children in a different way from adults. But in the coming months, what actually happened would become less relevant than what people *thought* had happened. Thus began a race for public opinion that was ultimately of far greater significance to the war than the men, women and children who actually died during the Lexington campaign; and it was, of course, a maritime race, because the dispatches of both sides had to be taken to England by sea.

*   *   *

The British seem to have acted first by drawing up their own version of events and sending it home. News of the British account reached the members of the Massachusetts Provincial Congress, who immediately wrote a letter to Benjamin Franklin in London, explaining how 'Our enemies, we are told, have dispatched to G[reat] Britain a fallacious Account of the Tragedy they have begun'.* They included in their letter their own account, which they instructed Franklin to print and disperse 'thro' every Town in England' and also to give copies directly to the Lord Mayor, Aldermen, and Common Council of the city of London – men and organizations known to be sympathetic to the American cause.[39]

With a greater awareness of the significance of this news than either Graves or Gage, or at least with a greater awareness that time was crucial to its interpretation, the Massachusetts Provincial Congress then quickly commissioned John Derby, a highly experienced Atlantic sailor from Salem who owned a very fast ship, the *Quero*, to take the American dispatches to England. He was not allowed the time to load a cargo and was ordered to keep his mission secret from any other soul until he had cleared the Grand Banks. His was the first maritime

* Franklin was actually on his way back to Philadelphia, so the letter was received by Arthur Lee.

mission authorized by a governmental authority in American history.[40]

The British made no such preparations, and their dispatches were sent on the first available ship, a cumbersome merchant-man called the *Sukey*. She was a hippo to *Quero*'s marlin; a wallowing 200 tons, the *Quero* a slip at 60.[41] The American dispatch reached Southampton on 27 May, a full fortnight before the *Sukey* arrived – a fortnight in which a stunning amount of damage was done to the British cause. The key point, of course, was who fired first. The Americans were desperate to paint the British as the aggressors – here again is the idea of non-violent rebellion that had so coloured the *Gaspee* affair.

Derby arrived in London on the evening of 28 May and passed his bundle of evidence into the hands of the Lord Mayor of London, John Wilkes. The stock market immediately dropped a point and a half.[42] It was well known that Gage's dispatch had already been sent but had not arrived, and Lord Dartmouth, representing a ministry in 'total confusion and consternation',[43] did his best to calm the situation by publishing in the *London Gazette* a caution directed to all who had read, or were going to read, the American account. Writing from the 'Secretary of State's Office, Whitehall' to add some extra authority to his letter, he declared:

> A report having been spread, and an account having been printed and published, of a skirmish between some of the people in the Province of Massachusetts Bay and a detach-ment of His Majesty's troops, it is proper to inform the publick that no advices have as yet been received in the American Department of any such event. There is reason to believe that there are dispatches from General Gage on board the *Sukey* ... which, though she sailed four days before the vessel that brought the printed accounts, is not arrived.[44]

But Graves's version of events, which stressed the role of the Americans in starting the fight and warned of false reports, came far too late – later, in fact, than other American ships from Virginia and New York which further confirmed the version brought by Derby.[45] Tearing his hair out, Dartmouth wrote back to Gage, admonishing both him and Graves and urging them, in the strongest terms, to send such dispatches in the future by 'one of the light vessels of the fleet'.[46]

The battle at Lexington and Concord thus became a disaster for the British on a far greater scale than the military event itself. A stunning turn of events, by no means was this the only time that the spread of news by sea was going to affect the war, nor was it the only time that the first account of a significant event to arrive in Britain was American.* Before news arrived, sympathy for the American cause was almost non-existent in Parliament, though elsewhere it did exist, and this news made it spread.[47] 'The Bostonians are now the favourites of all the people of good hearts and weak heads in the kingdom,' wrote Lord North, 'their saint-like account of the skirmish at Concord, has been read with avidity … [and] believed.'[48]

The impact of Derby's news was given more momentum by a sorry shipload of 170 soldiers wounded at Lexington, who came ashore at Plymouth along with a cargo of women widowed and children orphaned in the battle. One witness wrote:

A few of the men came on shore, when never hardly were seen such objects! Some without legs, and others without arms; and their clothes hanging on them like a loose morning gown, so much were they fallen away by sickness and want of proper nourishment … the vessel itself, though very large, was almost intolerable, from the stench arising from the sick and wounded.[49]

---

* The first account of Bunker Hill to reach British shores was also American (Hinkhouse, *Preliminaries*, 183–4). So too was the surrender of Cornwallis at Yorktown.

For the few who witnessed this hideous cargo and the many thousands who heard versions of it through the virus of rumour that spread the news so swiftly, the invisible glory of distant war had become visibly gory. The public could now see the results of war first hand, and they didn't like it.

There was surely more strife to come, however, as a trident of hardened and distinguished British major-generals – William Howe, Henry Clinton and John Burgoyne – was already on its way to replace the naïve Gage. Upon their arrival, military orders would supersede civil law, forts and redoubts would be strengthened, rebel military stores would be seized, and all suspected of treason arrested. The generals were full of vim and muscle, piss and vinegar. Burgoyne was nicknamed 'General Elbow Room' because it was said that he had declared: 'Well, let *us* get in and we'll soon find elbow-room.'[50] What the generals did not know, however, was that an American militia force of 20,000 men had already surrounded Boston and that, elsewhere, the Americans had already made the bold, far-sighted and courageous decision to attack where the British were not looking. While Burgoyne was priming his elbows to put down a rebellion that the British believed was isolated in Massachusetts,[51] the Americans did something entirely unexpected: they invaded Canada.

4

CANADIAN INVASION

The Canadian campaign of 1775–6 is particularly important for what it tells us about early American sea power.
The birth of American sea power is too often and too easily
confused with the birth of the American navy, but they are
entirely separate events and need to be treated as such. It is too
often overlooked that sea power can exist without navies,[1] and
the Americans were about to demonstrate exactly that.

The lakes that linked North America with Canada were
already a well-established theatre of maritime war, having
played a key role in the Seven Years' War (1754–63). The northerly route inland from the eastern seaboard of America is barred
by mountains that run from the banks of the St Lawrence all
the way to Georgia. There are two significant routes through.
The first is the Mohawk Valley, which runs west from the
Hudson and through the Appalachian Mountains. The second
is via the Hudson River to Lake Champlain, which offers a
pass through the Adirondack and Green Mountains. Once a
few tricky rapids have been by-passed, that route directly links
New York with Quebec by water.

The strategic key to that route was Fort Ticonderoga,
built on a promontory at a dramatic narrowing of Lake
Champlain.

The British had spent a fortune strengthening the area after
the French abandoned it in 1759, but it had since decayed. In
1775 the tiny garrison in the fort was formed of invalids more
than soldiers, and they were burdened, in military terms, by a
significant settlement of women and children. Worse still, the
garrison was living in blissful ignorance of the events in the

south, whiling away the spring days in the stunning Vermont wilderness.

Descending on them in May 1775 from that very wilderness, then known as the New Hampshire Grants, was a feral band of men called the 'Green Mountain Boys', led by a happy-go-lucky rogue called Ethan Allen. By all accounts Allen was an absolute scoundrel. He had wanted to attack Ticonderoga for nearly six months and had finally been commissioned to do so by a group of Connecticut businessmen. Another man, meanwhile, cut from altogether different cloth, was also descending on Ticonderoga. This was Benedict Arnold, a successful merchant with a bearing of natural authority, and he was there with the blessing of the Massachusetts Committee of Safety.* Near Ticonderoga Allen and Arnold blundered into each other, joined forces and made their way to a safe location on the other side of the lake, where they could spy on the fort and plan their next move. But here was the problem: although the fort was in touching distance, they didn't have any boats to get there.

Allen sent a handful of men to Crown Point, a British fort a little to the north, in a bold move to hire some boats from the British garrison. He also sent men to the nearby civilian settlement of Skenesborough. The main force, meanwhile, waited in the fragrant darkness of a grove of spruce trees at Hand's Cove opposite Ticonderoga, where they found a single bateau. And the night ticked away. With every passing hour they risked discovery. No news or boats appeared from Crown Point, and in Skenesborough the thirsty party had been severely side-tracked by a cellar full of 'choice liquors'.[2] Allen's subsequent comment that 'it was with the utmost difficulty that I procured boats to cross the lake' is full of frustration:[3] this was nearly the death knell of the entire operation.

---

* Committees of Safety were formed in 1774 to monitor the British government. By 1775, with the British royal officals expelled, they were undertaking governance roles of their own.

Fearing discovery, Allen crammed as many men as he could into the single bateau at Hand's Cove and ferried them across the lake. By the time the boat returned for another load, a second bateau had been found, and they made the crossing together. Allen managed to get just eighty-three men across before dawn, though mercifully unseen.[4]

Those few men – farmers and backwoodsmen – were nevertheless enough to take the fort from its unsuspecting defenders. The entire operation was utter chaos. Allen rushed around like a madman trying to find the officer in charge, shouting 'come out you damned British rat!',[5] and when one of the senior officers eventually appeared, he did so without his trousers on.

And so Ticonderoga fell, a fort that is now famous for two extremes of siege history: a fierce and proud defence in 1758 by an outnumbered French and Canadian force against an overwhelming British attacking force; and the laughable capitulation in 1775, by a rabble to a rabble. As with so many instances at this early stage of the revolution, the forces that changed history were slight.

The Americans also captured Crown Point and then Arnold set about changing the path of history. He realized that if the whole venture was not to be in vain, he would have to capture more British forts that guarded the lake at other key points, and then, to hold those positions as well as Crown Point and Ticonderoga, he would have to secure maritime control of the lake itself by seizing it from the British. The British lakeside forts did not exist in their own splendid isolation but were linked to each other and to other powerbases and sources of military strength by the strands of sea power. The British exercised and projected that power with a flotilla of bateaux dominated by a 70-ton armed sloop, HMS *George*, stationed to the north of Champlain. To secure the *George* and at least some of the bateaux was therefore to secure the lake: the Americans would have to take to the water, and Allen – a landlubber through and through – now deferred to Arnold, a maritime man.

But how would they do it? The *George* was 100 miles further north, at Fort St Jean on the Richelieu River, which linked the northernmost reaches of Lake Champlain to the province of Quebec. Not only would Arnold have to get there in force, but by doing so he would be invading a foreign country. The only vessels he had to transport his men were those they had used for the original crossing and a few more small craft captured at Ticonderoga. Arnold's solution to this problem is a fine example of how one can come to wield extensive sea power from very humble resources.

Arnold sent a detachment of men in a handful of boats to Skenesborough, where there was a wealthy man, a loyalist and the founder of the settlement, named Philip Skene. Like many wealthy men who live near water then and now, Skene had bought himself a large boat, a fine schooner that he had named after himself. That schooner was Arnold's stepping-stone to the *George* and its capture was as crucial to the success of the entire operation as was the initial assault on Ticonderoga.

The *Skene* was taken without a struggle and Arnold began to fit her out for a man-of-war with the limited resources he had at his disposal. He renamed her *Liberty*. Designed for sailing on the lakes, she had a shallow draft and a handy ketch rig with a square yard on the foremast for running downwind. Arnold also armed two large bateaux with bow guns and fitted them with thick hawsers to their bows so that they could be towed by the *Liberty*. With his little flotilla complete, Arnold raised anchor and set sail for the north. Allen followed in four bateaux.

Achieving total surprise, Arnold captured the *George* without any loss on either side. He renamed her *Enterprise*.[6] He now had a powerful sloop, a schooner and six armed bateaux. More importantly, the British now had no ships at all on the Champlain–Hudson waterway; for the foreseeable future it was in American hands and secure.

On his return to Ticonderoga, Arnold consolidated his achievements. New captains were appointed to the *Liberty* and *Enterprise*, experienced sailors were appointed alongside landsmen to sail the ships, and a small band of soldiers was transformed into marines. He hired a surgeon and a surgeon's mate, and organized the distribution of blankets, uniforms and pay. He set his men to making spare sails and cutting planks to make more bateaux. He then scoured the surrounding country for all the oars he could find, to deny them to the British as much as to provide the Americans with spares. He eventually secured 927 feet of oars.[7] Arnold thus made a neat little navy out of nothing but hope, and it immediately paid a dividend when a boat carrying the British post from Quebec to New York was intercepted, allowing Arnold to write a detailed report to Congress detailing the number and location of British troops in Canada.[8]

This was crucial information for future American strategy as it revealed just how precarious the British position was, the Canadian garrisons having been stripped to help with the defence of Boston.[9] It was clear that the door was open for an invasion. Within only three weeks of the fall of Ticonderoga the Second Continental Congress authorized a plan to invade Canada. This was, in itself, a crucial step towards independence because, by authorizing the invasion of a foreign country, the Second Continental Congress was acting like the representative governing body of a nation state.[10]

* * *

The invasion would be two-pronged. Arnold, now a commissioned colonel in the Continental Army, planned to lead a group of men on a surprise attack via the wilderness of Maine. The energetic and resourceful Philip Schuyler, meanwhile, who had been placed in command of the small fleet at Ticonderoga, planned to invade via Champlain, take Montreal and then rendezvous with Arnold at Quebec.

If Arnold arrived at Quebec before Schuyler, his presence would draw British defenders away from Montreal, thus making Schuyler's task easier. If, on the other hand, the British defenders were entirely focused on the defence of Montreal, Arnold might even find Quebec undefended. If,

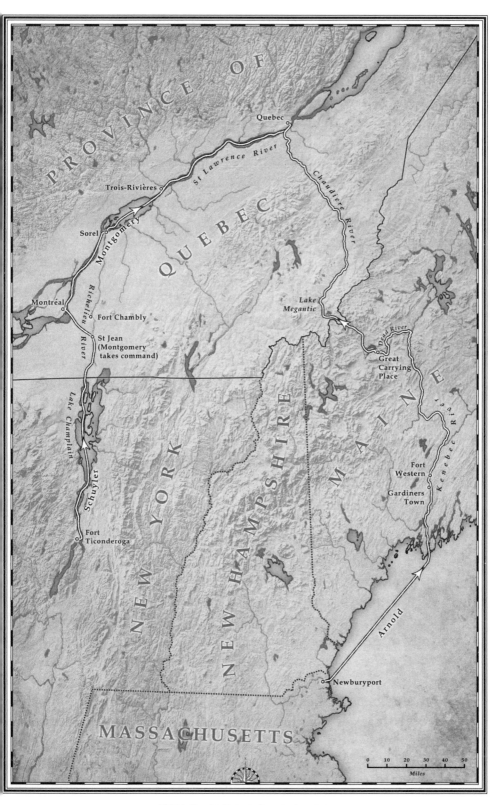

THE INVASION OF CANADA

however, a long siege was necessary, the timing of the strike was perfect. Planned for the autumn, the strike would fall with the St Lawrence on the point of freezing, which would in turn prevent any relief from getting through to the British garrison until the spring.

First, however, both Schuyler and Arnold had to get to Canada. Both movements were significant maritime operations. Schuyler planned to take his force from Ticonderoga up Lake Champlain, into the Richelieu River, on to Montreal, and then down the St Lawrence to Quebec. Arnold, meanwhile, would take his force by sea from Newburyport in Massachusetts to the mouth of the Kennebec River. From there he would travel 350 miles to Quebec by water with the exception of a twelve-mile hike between two major rivers known as the 'Great Carrying Place'. His route would take him up the Kennebec River to the Dead River, down into Lake Mégantic, and then down the Chaudière River to Quebec. This extraordinary escapade has become known as 'Arnold's March', which is entirely misleading; it wasn't a march at all, but an amphibious invasion.

Schuyler burst into Ticonderoga, a tornado of effort. When he arrived on 18 July, there were sufficient boats to transport 200 men; by 23 August he was able to transport 1,300 men equipped with provisions for twenty days. Delighted at his achievement, he still knew his weakness: for all the men he had raised and boats he had built, the Americans had only six nine-pounder cannon and only one gun carriage.[11] Schuyler was also unwell and was forced to hand over command to Richard Montgomery. In contrast, the British by now had a fully armed schooner to defend the Richelieu, the 16-gun *Royal Savage*, and numerous armed boats. Nonetheless the Americans headed north to attack the fort and shipyard at St Jean, the focus of the British military presence after the fall of Ticonderoga. The fort fell after a brief siege, the turning point of which was the destruction of the *Royal Savage*. It was a major victory for the Americans, not only because they had destroyed the only remaining British naval presence on the river but also because they subsequently seized the British shipyard, along with its valuable shipbuilding and naval stores. An inventory made after the capture lists six anchors and anchor cables, spare sails, compasses, pitch, oil, tallow and rigging blocks.[12]

Nearby Fort Chambly was also taken with another magnificent stock of military supplies including 'naval stores for three vessels'.[13] Montreal then fell after a lengthier and more carefully planned siege, and with it even more stores fell into American hands, this time a cache of ordnance.[14] Before the surrender the city was carefully evacuated of British troops and 'as many Canadian Tories as were inclined to go',[15] who crammed themselves onto the limited British shipping – the first of many such maritime evacuations caused by this war.* It did not end well. Initially trapped by poor weather, a brig, three armed vessels and eight transports subsequently fell into American hands at Sorel, sixty miles downriver from Montreal.[16] The defenders, however, had held on long enough to buy the garrison at Quebec a few more crucial days before they were attacked.

*   *   *

From Newburyport in Massachusetts Arnold took 1,050 men to the Kennebec River in Maine in a fleet of eleven schooners, by some margin the largest fleet of sizeable American ships yet assembled for a military operation. It was an obvious opportunity for the British to strike. The fleet was unarmed and unescorted, the ships slow and cumbersome, described by one soldier as nothing more than 'dirty coasters and fish boats'.[17] The passage, moreover, was nearly 100 miles and took five days.[18] Through indifferent seamanship one transport ran aground soon after leaving, and her troops had to be transferred to other ships, worsening the overcrowding. Many of the soldiers were incapacitated by seasickness in the filthy weather that cursed the voyage. One 'became very seasick and *such* a seasickness, making me feel so lifeless, so indifferent whether

---

* Others were the evacuations of Boston in 1776, Philadelphia in 1778, Newport and Gibraltar in 1779, Charleston and Savannah in 1782, and New York in 1783.

I lived or died!'[19] A single British cruiser could have taken the entire fleet and Arnold's operation would have been stillborn, but with Graves's gaze firmly on Boston and such limited naval resources to hand, the British only found out about Arnold's operation twenty-seven days after the fleet had sailed.*

Upriver in Gardinerstown, meanwhile, the shipwright Reuben Colburn had received an order to build 200 four-oared bateaux. The choice of boat type was sensible because bateaux were simple to build and maintain, but there was not enough money to build them properly. The boats were commissioned at £2 each, but we know that, in 1774, a civilian bateau cost £3 17s.[20] Not only were the bateaux underfunded but the promised monies never arrived, perhaps something that Colburn suspected would happen.[21]

The next problem was the time available: he had just two weeks. Those 200 bateaux required 1,000 knees to be cut and shaped for frames; 16,000 feet of white pine boards; 10,000 nails to fasten them together; 800 oars, allowing four per boat; and 800 setting-poles.[†] It was a mammoth task, and the fact that it was completed within fourteen days has been seen by many historians as an achievement to celebrate. In reality, however, the necessary speed of their construction had a direct bearing on the quality of their finish. First, the shipwrights were forced to use unseasoned timber to meet such an order. Any wooden-boat builder will tell you that, depending on the species, green wood can be anywhere between 70 or even 100 per cent heavier than seasoned wood. Arnold's boats, therefore, were exceptionally heavy; we think that each weighed around 400 pounds,[22] roughly the same weight as a small piano. This was a crucial consideration because the boats would have to

---

* NDAR II: 132, 331. On the way to the Kennebec Arnold's ships passed the ruins of the English colony founded in 1607 by Sir John Popham, a sister colony to the successful one at Jamestown. Those early settlers had hated the severity of the Maine winter so much that they built a ship from the surrounding forests – the first ever ship built in North America – to take them home.

† A setting-pole is used to propel a craft through the water, pushing against rocks or the riverbed.

be carried as well as rowed. The second problem was that there were nowhere near enough nails to meet the order. The solution was not, as it could have been, to build fewer and stronger boats, but to use fewer nails per boat. It is particularly ironic that, among the artefacts that are still routinely discovered along the trail of Arnold's march, there are often nails. In fact, from the artefacts alone one would assume that his men actually travelled with pockets full of nails.*

Another aspect of the construction that may have fatally weakened the bateaux was the method by which the oars were mounted. The most efficient way to mount an oar is between two thole-pins, set upright in the gunwales. To equip every bateau in this way, however, Arnold would have needed a total of 1,760 pins, assuming four oars per bateau. No doubt this taxed the already overloaded shipwrights. The quick and easy solution in this situation would be to abandon thole-pins and simply cut a hole in the top streak of the boat, a solution to the thole-pin problem but one that would have significantly weakened the boats.

And then, of course, there was the voyage. Historians have tended to gloss over the specific boatmanship problems of handling fleets of bateaux, but they are of course crucial to our understanding of Arnold's mission.

Arnold finally left with 220 bateaux, each roughly four feet wide. Although they were dispatched upriver in three separate groups, the size of the groups was still large enough to cause problems. Each company consisted of between thirty-six and sixty-four boats. Consider first the problems of securing these bateaux to the shore. Ideally each bateau would be tethered to the shore at right angles and given enough room to swing with the current or wind without knocking into her neighbours. In reality that was impossible, but so too was it impossible to pack the boats perfectly at right angles to each other against a meandering shoreline.

---

* Those artefacts, including axe-heads, cutlery and belt buckles, can be seen at Reuben Colburn's house, now preserved as a State Historic Site.

If the boats were given four feet of room on each side, the 220 boats would have taken up well over a quarter of a mile of riverbank. If tethered end to end, they would have stretched over a mile. Even the smallest of the flotillas, perhaps consisting of forty boats or so, would have taken up at least 320 feet if moored at right angles to the riverbank. Such a relatively short distance of clear riverbank would have been very difficult to find. It is likely, therefore, that the craft were moored as close together as the shoreline would allow, and – almost always overgrown – this would have necessitated the ships being tethered directly alongside each other, where they would chafe, rub and bang, generally working themselves loose.

Bateaux are also relatively cumbersome craft, particularly in strong currents. Waves, sometimes several feet high, are a continual curse on large rivers, and they buck anything from their back with the ease of an unbroken stallion. Large rivers that run through forests, moreover, regularly carry logs at several knots that act like battering-rams, while hidden dangers from branches and tree-roots, set at vicious angles like stakes to stop a cavalry charge, constantly lurk underwater.

To work such a craft in such conditions required boatmanship of the highest order and of a very particular type. Because of the cumbersome nature of oars and setting-poles, just one sailor working out of synch would cause absolute havoc in a small boat. Even the greenest of novices would soon realize that rowing at the edges of a straight but fast-flowing river is sensible because there is less stream, but knowing where to steer when faced with unforeseen obstacles requires much deeper knowledge of boatmanship in general and also of the particular river. It is something that can be acquired only through considerable experience.

It is also important to remember that Arnold was voyaging *up* the Kennebec. He was able to harness the tide as far as Fort Western at Augusta,* but thereafter every inch was hard

---

* Fort Western was built in the Seven Years' War (1754–63) and is now beautifully restored. It is the oldest log fort in the United States.

won. Rowing or poling upstream is dispiriting and exhausting. When faced with rapids, there were three main options. In shallow water, though nothing greater than waist-deep, the crew could get out and wade alongside the boat, thus reducing the vessel's draft and maintaining control. In deeper water the boats could be 'lined' – essentially pulled upstream by ropes running ashore. The last resort was to land all the boats, empty them, and carry them through the woods, but Arnold had no carriages and there were no roads. In this scenario, his men would have to put those enormously heavy boats on their shoulders and blunder through the undergrowth.

The subsequent catastrophes that beset Arnold's expedition were the result of poor planning, poor boatmanship and bad luck.

* * *

Between Kennebec and the Dead River they struggled against swift-flowing streams. It was a major problem for his men, many of whom, it was now clear, were inexperienced boatmen. Arnold soon wrote to George Washington, offering this as an excuse for his delay: 'we have had a very fatiguing time, the Men in general not understanding Batteaus.'[23] It is likely that many of them had lied about their experience to get on the expedition.

Many of the bateaux simply fell apart, and some were destroyed or lost downriver in accidents. At one stage the waters of the Dead River, so named for its usual passivity and almost total absence of current, rose eight feet in as many hours, possibly the result of the tail of a hurricane that had passed up the east coast from the Caribbean. All the bateaux leaked despite constant attempts to caulk them, and some shipped great quantities of water, easily enough to ruin or entirely wash away the crucial casks of provisions. Many of the casks themselves seem to have been entirely inadequate for such a maritime journey and were not even made to be waterproof.

Arnold's men had to carry the boats further than they had

ever imagined would be necessary, and it is certain that carrying them split the seams further, made the boats even more
leaky and crippled the men.[24] Their shoulders were rubbed
to the bone. 'I would heartily wish the infamous construc-
tors who, to satisfy there [sic] avaricious temper, and fill there
purses with the spoils of their country, may be obliged to
trust to the mercy of others more treacherous than themselves,
that they might judge the fear and undergo the just reward
of their villainy,'[25] spat one soldier, and another commented:
'Could we have then come within reach of the villains who
constructed these crazy things, they would have fully experienced the effects of our vengeance ... Avarice or a desire to
destroy us, perhaps both, must have been their motive.'[26]

Some of the companies got lost. The raised water meant that
the edges of lakes and rivers merged, transforming a simple
navigational challenge into a nightmare for the inexperienced.
The rations ran out and the men ate their dogs, cartridge boxes
and soap to survive, a diet augmented with tree sap.

Only seven of the original 220 bateaux and less than half
of Arnold's men made it to Canada, and they were utterly
ruined, both physically and psychologically, by their ordeal.
They suffered from a range of debilitating symptoms and illnesses, including gout, rheumatism, dysentery, angina, distemper, diarrhoea, constipation, pneumonia, swollen limbs and
'infestation', though Arnold himself was relatively unscathed,
having travelled most of the way in a fast, manoeuvrable, light-
weight native birch-bark canoe paddled by Indians, which he
later swapped for a pirogue – another type of light canoe that
can easily be taken onto land.

To make matters worse, the British in Quebec, who had
long since known that Arnold was coming as rumour dripped
out of the forest,[27] had removed every object that could float
from the shore of the St Lawrence opposite Quebec where it
was expected that Arnold would emerge. When he and his
men finally limped and crawled out of the wilderness on 8
November, Arnold was thus presented with the same problem
he and Allen had experienced at Ticonderoga that summer:

how to get at his target across a large stretch of water. Guy Carleton, the governor of Quebec, had taken most of Quebec's soldiers with him to meet the Americans near Montreal, and so Quebec was garrisoned by a tiny force and could have fallen with only the gentlest of pushes, but Arnold's force was crippled and now stranded.

It took Arnold five days to find enough craft on the Chaudière, some forty canoes,[28] to take his surviving men across the mile-wide St Lawrence, though each of the craft would have to make three trips there and back – that is to say, six actual crossings – and they would have to do so without being spotted by the Royal Navy vessels, the sloop *Hunter* and the frigate *Lizard*, which were now patrolling that stretch of water with their boats manned and their men armed.[29]

Between 11 p.m. and 4 a.m. in the early morning of 14 November Arnold transported just over half of his men across the water. At one stage they had to lie flat on their paddles to avoid being seen by a sentry boat. One of their canoes broke apart mid-stream.[30] These dangers negotiated, the weather then turned and the operation had to be abandoned for the night. The rest of the force, leaving a rearguard of sixty, followed over the next couple of nights but were spotted by an armed British boat right at the very end of the operation.[31] Impressively, the exhausted Americans fought off the subsequent attack by well-equipped British sailors. Some 675 men now stood outside the walls of Quebec, where they 'Paraded & Marched up within ½ a Mile of the walls and gave them Cheers'.[32]

Although they had failed to prevent the Americans from crossing the St Lawrence, the presence of those British ships did prevent Arnold from leading his men in a mad dash to take Quebec. It was a crucial deflection. The horrors of his voyage through the wilderness, combined with the task with which he was now faced, caused him to pause for thought, and he came to the conclusion that his men were too few and too weak to try anything on their own. Arnold thus decided to postpone his attack until the arrival of the Americans making their way to Quebec from Montreal. This decision thus rendered Arnold's entire expedition pointless: he and his men could have just come with the American fleet up Lake Champlain. The story survived, however, and it became inspirational. It was, in the words of one resident in Quebec, 'an undertaking above the common race of men', and Dr James Warren, then speaker of the Massachusetts General Court, wrote to Samuel Adams comparing Arnold's march 'to Hannibal's or Xenophon's'.[33]

In Montreal, meanwhile, the American army, now under the command of Brigadier General Richard Montgomery after Schuyler, being unwell, had returned to Ticonderoga, missed a clear opportunity to capture or kill Guy Carleton, governor of Quebec and a gifted and experienced soldier. To capture Carleton may very well have been to capture Quebec. Carleton, disguised as a farmer, slipped out of Montreal at night in a boat paddled by the oarsmen's hands for silence, and they managed to slip through the American river blockade a few miles downstream.[34] Safely back in Quebec, Carleton then roused the few British troops and made crucial preparations for the city's defence. In doing so, he took sailors from ships to defend the walls and ordered the ships to unbend their sails to prevent any faint-hearted from escaping.[35] The subsequent campaign was thus the earliest of the war's numerous major land campaigns in which British sailors fought ashore.

Montgomery rendezvoused with Arnold under the walls of Quebec and they attacked on New Year's Eve. Montgomery led the attack and was killed, Arnold was wounded, and Quebec held. Not all was yet lost, however. The Americans were still at the walls of Quebec and the British inside were nervously looking to the ice-bound horizon for relief from ships that might never come. The only news they received had come from Howe, who, writing from Boston in early October, had warned that the season was far too advanced for naval relief.[36]

*   *   *

As soon as news had arrived in London of the American attack on Canada, however, a scheme had been adopted to relieve Quebec. A driving force in the scheme was George

Germain, an experienced politician who had taken over from Lord Dartmouth as Secretary of State for the American Department in early November. He would go on to direct the British war effort for most of the war.[37] The contributions of Hugh Palliser, then a Lord of the Admiralty, were particularly valuable to Germain because Palliser had taken part in the 1759 capture of Quebec and had subsequently been governor and commander-in-chief of Newfoundland.[38] If anyone understood the logistical and seamanship challenges of sending a naval relief into the St Lawrence, which would be frozen until the beginning of May at the very earliest, it was Palliser. Sandwich also buzzed with energy.[39] The relief, led by Captain Charles Douglas in the *Isis*, set sail from the Nore on 22 February 1776, the departure delayed by ice. Every day that the ships were delayed caused Sandwich untold grief: 'For God's sake get the *Isis* down to Blackstakes the next spring tide ... your being ready to leave the land early in February is of the utmost importance to the publick service, I think the fate of Quebec depends on it.'[40]

Douglas had made something of a name for himself in the late 1760s by conducting a series of experiments off the coast of Lapland to investigate deep-sea temperatures. When he wasn't inventing thermometers to measure temperature at depths of 260 fathoms – so deep it took over thirteen minutes to pull the thermometer back up again – he investigated local rumours of the Kraken, giant sea-worms and a huge mythical Dutch whirlpool. His official record of the time he spent off Lapland makes fascinating reading.[41] He had witnessed the 1759 capture of Quebec as a commander, and therefore knew the St Lawrence first-hand, and had served as a flag officer in the Russian navy, based in St Petersburg in the frequently frozen Baltic, in 1764–5. He had also served on the frozen coasts of Newfoundland in the 1760s.[42] Douglas was not just another sea officer, therefore, but – like Palliser, the brains behind the operation – one carefully chosen to fit the challenge posed.

And what a challenge it was. Entire books have been written about the difficulties of sailing ships through pack ice,[43] but suffice it to say here that you have to be able to cope with the numerous optical illusions that are caused by ice and which have grave effects on navigation; you have to be able to identify the *type* of ice you are sailing through – floes, blocks or pancakes, made of salt or fresh water; you have to be able to identify the age of the ice, which affects its intrinsic strength; you have to be able to predict if the ice will compact or expand, freeze or melt, all of which it can do with little notice; you have to understand that, when working in ice, your ship will always move in the direction of least resistance, not in the direction chosen by the helmsman; you have to maintain momentum at all times, especially when working in convoy. In short, the challenge of getting anywhere near Quebec was immense, a battle in its own right.

The British fleet split into two, the *Isis* leading a frigate and a sloop, with the transports and another sloop following. The going was excruciatingly slow and the ships had to force their way through 100 miles of dangerous floating ice even to get to the St Lawrence. Unsurprisingly, they fixed fenders on the sides to protect the hull. Once there, they discovered that twenty more miles of heavily packed ice protected the estuary. Douglas refused to accept that he was beaten and simply rammed his ship into a wall of ice, 'ten or twelve feet thick', to see what happened. Luckily for Douglas and his crew, and also for the British in Quebec, the ice, rather than the bow of his ship, disintegrated. 'Encouraged by this experiment,' wrote Douglas,

> We thought it an enterprise, worthy of an English ship of the line, in our King and Country's sacred cause, and an effort due to the gallant defenders of Quebec, to make the attempt of pressing her, by force of sail, thro the thick, broad and closely connected fields of ice, as formidable as the gulph of St Laurence ever exhibited, to which we saw no bounds, towards the western part of our horizon.[44]

By nightfall they had made their way twenty-four miles into the ice, 'describing our path all the way with bits of the sheathing of the ship's bottom, and sometimes pieces of the cutwater'.

Occasionally they stuck fast, and as they were unaware of what they would find at Quebec, the troops were unloaded and exercised on the ice. Time and again they would set every stitch of canvas on the ship, heave against grapnels set in the ice, and shift the ship's ballast to try and break her free; and occasionally it worked, only to find themselves beset again almost immediately and forced to repeat the entire exhausting process.[45] Nine days later, and after 'unspeakable toil' for fifty or sixty leagues, Douglas arrived in Quebec, the *Isis* being one of the earliest ships ever to have done so. It was 6 May. And it was a stunning achievement. Understandably, Douglas was immensely pleased with himself.[46]

The American strategy was dramatically and directly altered by the arrival of Douglas's convoy. They immediately retreated from Quebec to Sorel and then, after several weeks of sustained British reinforcements arriving amid the constant crash of salutes, they skulked all the way back to Trois-Rivières and abandoned their invasion. This was the last time that the Americans attempted to make Canada their fourteenth colony, though the idea was mooted several times more during the war: in 1778, 1780 and 1781.[47]

The arrival of the British ships not only saved Canada but also provided an important psychological fillip to the local Canadians and Indians. When the main victualling fleet appeared in late spring, the presence of over eighty sail in the very heart of Canada had a profound impact. The impression gained of awesome maritime strength was long-lasting, and Canada remained a potentially hostile threat to the Americans throughout the war.

In the north, therefore, the ideological boundaries of the revolution seemed to have been reached. Too often the shape of the modern United States and Canada is associated with Wolfe fighting the French at Quebec in 1759. It should, instead, be associated with the British naval patrol that spotted Arnold crossing the St Lawrence in November 1775 and with Captain Charles Douglas fighting the ice in the mouth of the St Lawrence in the new year of 1776.

5

COLONIAL SEA POWER

Back in Boston the rebels began to flex their muscles at sea as soon as the changed situation post-Lexington became apparent. For all their impressive numbers, the American soldiers encamped upon the hills overlooking the city remained toothless, even though, on 14 June, the Second Continental Congress had used those men to form a new 'Continental Army'. In those initial months after Lexington they lacked everything that an army needed: powder, leadership, a logistical infrastructure, medicine, transport and, worst of all, guns. The British also had a significant weakness, however. With the surrounding countryside cut off by the presence of the rebel army, *everything* that was required to sustain the garrison, the navy and the civilian population in Boston now had to come from the sea. The rebels therefore knew that they could severely damage the British position by targeting British shipping and the British maritime infrastructure in the immediate vicinity of Boston: the lighthouse that would guide the trans-Atlantic supply ships and packet-ships safely in; the island caches of livestock, powder, shipbuilding supplies and hay; the store schooner, where the British kept so much of their maritime stores; even one of the small British warships themselves anchored in the shallows of Boston Harbour. If that maritime fingerhold could be broken, then the British could be driven from America.

While the American soldiers pitched camp on the hills around Boston, therefore, a parallel bustle was raised – in and around the jetties and wharfs of Boston Harbour, up the wooded creeks and muddy inlets of Massachusetts Bay, and on the banks of the Charles, Mystic, Danvers, Weymouth Fore,

Weymouth Back, Monatiquot, North, Indian Head, Saugus and Neponset rivers – in a hell for leather race for anything that could float. Its significance struck both Gage and Graves at roughly the same time. Gage told Graves to seize 'all the Boats you can lay your hands on everywhere', and Graves later recalled how 'all scows, sloops, schooners & boats of every Kind' had to be secured, and at all costs. The Americans, meanwhile, were doing exactly the same thing and became increasingly aggressive. Off Dartmouth, a little to the south of Boston, two British tenders manned by British soldiers sent to steal sheep were taken by rebels and the men imprisoned. Inevitably this led to more armed confrontation.[1]

The boats successfully secured by the British were kept under guard just to the south of the long wharf, and those by the Americans were spirited inland to hidden caches, in 'swampy Land & Woods'. Some were piled onto wagons and then hauled from Charlestown to Cambridge, which nestled up the Charles River, an easily defendable location where the fledgling American army was encamped.[2] Shipbuilders throughout New England, meanwhile, were ordered to build craft, and oars were gathered and stockpiled.

Soon enough, all along the coast and up the rivers, bundles of twigs that hid the distinctive shape of boats' hulls were cast aside, screens of foliage were swept back and the Americans took to their craft, sometimes in great shoals, to harass the British in every way they could.

* * *

The Americans' favourite craft was the whaleboat. Double-ended, which made landing and relaunching so easy, they were rowed by ten to sixteen men – a sizeable force in its own right that took on significant proportions if whaleboats were used together in fleets. They were like Viking raiders, launching lightning raids on strategic targets. This included attacks on local fishermen who were supplying the British garrison: rather cleverly the rebels thus imposed their own kind of blockade on the British who were blockading Boston.

There were notable successes against the lighthouses on Little Brewster Island at the mouth of Boston Harbour and on Thatcher Island off Cape Ann. Both were excellent raids conducted in the utmost secrecy. One British officer ruefully observed how 'the Flames were generally the first Notice of their Intentions',[3] such a telling comment for its implied naivety as much as for what it says about the boldness of the Americans. It is astonishing that the British were surprised that the Americans would attack Boston's lighthouses when they were the key to the entire maritime infrastructure that was sustaining the beleaguered British forces in Boston, and the removal of coastal navigation markers is an ancient tactic of maritime war.

The scale and tempo of the whaleboat attacks were such that British anxiety became infectious.[4] Exhausted lookouts jumped at shadows and nervous officers wrote to Graves, whose growing desperation is palpable in his letters to the Admiralty. There was soon real concern that the rebels might have the temerity to attack one of the larger warships in Boston Harbour, perhaps even the largest of them all, the 70-gun *Boyne*. British naval officers were diverted from other missions to meet the threat.[5] James Warren sensed the change in the wind. He wrote to his friend, the astute lawyer John Adams, declaring the British 'more afraid of our whaleboats than we are of their men-of-war'.[6]

*   *   *

The Americans held all the initiative, constantly testing the strength of British sea power to discover and expose its limits. A major breakthrough was perhaps inevitable and it came in early June. A large band of rebels had launched a whaleboat attack on Noddles Island and Hog Island, which were used by the British as stores for livestock, maritime supplies and hay.[8] The admiral's nephew, Lieutenant Thomas Graves, slipped anchor on his armed schooner, the *Diana*, and took her as close to land as possible to fire on the rebels.

The admiral had given his nephew the most specific instructions that he was only to stay until the tide changed and the younger Graves dutifully turned his ship back to Boston, but the change of tide brought with it a change in the weather too. The cooling breeze that had so surely brought the *Diana* across the harbour died, and with it the confidence of her captain and crew. She began to drift as the ebb gathered pace. News flashed around the harbour, from rebel to rebel, like the sun reflected in a network of mirrors. By early evening, in the words of Samuel Graves, 'the whole Country was alarmed'.[8] A team of British boats was launched to take the *Diana* in harness like a coach and four while militia poured down to the coast.

Some 2,000 armed rebels, led by General Israel Putnam, lined the shore and busied themselves around two large field pieces they had dragged into position. The *Diana*, meanwhile, now being towed by British boats, was making painfully slow progress within touching distance of the rebels, who took leisurely pot-shots at the sweating, groaning men sitting in their open boats, skin prickling for the hot sting of lead.

Two oarsmen died and several were wounded, and the *Diana*'s progress slowed enough for the tide to win the race. Two feet of water became one foot, and then six inches, and then, with a sickening thud, she stuck fast in the clinging mud of Boston Harbour. The water relentlessly drained towards the sea around her. At three o'clock in the morning she heeled onto one side and an hour later a path to the schooner from the shore was dry. The *Diana*'s crew abandoned ship and climbed into the *Britannia* sloop which had come to her aid. By four o'clock the estuary was completely dry and the rebels marched through the mud to take away her cannon, empty her sail locker, steal what clothing and money was aboard, and then burn her as she lay helpless.

Just like the *Gaspee*, the *Diana* burned like a giant warning fire, but this time she burned within clear sight of Boston, under the very noses of the British armed forces, with thousands of witnesses lining the beaches, watching from rooftops, hanging out of windows. This was no great strategic victory such as the capture of Ticonderoga, but it was a hostile act in the lion's den itself that displayed both American courage and resourcefulness and convinced many of the direction that the revolution was taking. If, as was so clear, the revolution was succeeding in spite of the Royal Navy, then its providence seemed manifest. It also raised the interesting question of what could be achieved if such daring could be prosecuted on a much larger scale, and in that thought lay the seed of another idea – one that would lead to the creation of the American navy.

* * *

The man with the idea was George Washington: by profession a surveyor and farmer from Virginia, by limited experience a frontier soldier, by political demand the new commander-in-chief of the Continental Army.*

In 1775 Washington knew more about farming than anything else. Like many thousands of Americans, however, he had fought with the British in the Seven Years' War (1754–63). That military training had taught him the basics: the difference between a well-fortified and a poorly fortified position; the dangers of raw sewage in camp; the importance of discipline, good food and water; the value of well-maintained arms. For all that experience, Washington had never commanded more than a regiment, and after the Seven Years' War he had left the service for Mount Vernon, an estate that commanded thousands of acres of prime slave-farmed Virginian tobacco land.

Washington's personal experience of sea power was non-existent and his first-hand experience of the sea nearly so. The only voyage he appears to have been on occurred in 1751 when he was nineteen. Then, he had sailed to Barbados with his brother, who was ill with tuberculosis and sought the popular

---

* The fighting so far, though by no means exclusive to New England, had focused on New England, and it was there that the British remained in force. It was politically important, therefore, that command of the Continental Army, and thus the man wielding the resources of all the colonies, should not be a New Englander. From the outset, the man chosen to lead the Continental Army was chosen for his origin as much as for his experience; he was to be both a leader and a unifier.

tropical air. Surviving documents from that voyage are very revealing. As soon as his ship tasted the Atlantic swells, Washington took up a notebook, ruled some lines and began to make a rudimentary log-book. It is the action of a young man deeply enthused by this new environment and stimulated by the challenge of recording the things he saw in their correct way, for George did not write as a landlubber on a sea voyage but learned to imitate the phrases and abbreviations of the mariner. He particularly enjoyed the demanding challenge of identifying strange ships on the horizon from their silhouette. Was it a trader or a warship? If so, what type and how large? What nationality? Often overlooked, this was one of the most important skills of an officer in any navy.[9] This, clearly, was the work of a man with maritime potential.

Washington may have lacked experience in sea power, but it is too easy to overlook his knowledge of waterways and skill at boatmanship. He may well have been a 'farmer' – a traditional seaman's insult – but he was a farmer in Virginia, and in the 1770s all farmers in Virginia had a keen nose for matters maritime. Virginia was a colony that constantly looked to the sea. The most significant aspect of the Virginian economy was the exportation of tobacco, and vast fleets, well over 100 ships strong, made an annual migration to Virginia to move the tobacco crop from its magnificent natural harbour at Hampton Roads back to Europe.

With Hampton Roads as its primary maritime focus, Virginia also has 112 miles of coastline so deeply scarred by rivers and inlets that it creates a tidal shoreline nearly thirty times larger than its coastline, some 3,315 miles. There is, in fact, so much water in Virginia that it was impossible to travel in the colony without frequent use of boats. In Washington's youth forty-three ferries operated on the James River and its tributaries alone, twenty more on the York River, twenty more on the Rappahannock, fifteen on the Potomac and two on the Nottoway.[10] He was brought up beside rivers, the Rappahannock as a child and the Potomac as a man. So while he had no experience of sea power, he did have experience of boats on rivers which would certainly come in handy.*

When offered command of the Continental Army in June 1775, Washington accepted but with a rather loud, important and honest caveat: 'Tho I am truly sensible of the high honor done me in this appointment, yet I feel great distress from a consciousness that my abilities and military experience may not be equal to the extensive and important trust.'[11] Nonetheless, Washington was picked because he was a natural leader, a thoughtful and careful speaker, and the very embodiment of authority.

Washington began to work with sea power as soon as he arrived at Cambridge in early July 1775 and immediately organized whaleboats to patrol the waterways as part of a package of precautions taken to prevent surprise British attacks.[12] For the first eight weeks or so of his command, however, he was a powerful voice in a group of men who spoke against those who urged the Americans to take to the sea in a far more ambitious way: in ocean-going armed ships. For these anti-navy men, to challenge the Royal Navy at sea was crazy and their opposition 'loud and vehement'; this was a child 'taking a wild bull by the horns'.[13] They baulked at the seemingly endless political, logistical and financial implications of sending large armed ships to sea. Samuel Chase, a delegate from Maryland, simply declared it the 'maddest idea in the world'.[14] The idea of a navy was even questioned by those colonies with significant natural harbours and waterways, particularly those colonies around the Chesapeake and Delaware.[15]

This disagreement over a possible American navy was symptomatic of numerous disagreements between the colonies at this stage in the war. In fact the question of whether or not there should even be a war was still very much open, and a petition for peace in May 1775 – the Olive Branch Petition

---

* On a December night in 1753 Washington had attempted to cross the ice-choked Monongahela on a raft he and a companion had built. He fell in trying to fend off the ice floes. This river experience and knowledge is relevant to his subsequent escape from Brooklyn and the crossing of the Delaware in 1776.

– had, among other things, stalled the creation of a colonial navy.[16] This was no coincidence. The construction of a navy was behaviour intimately associated with an independent nation state. The idea of a colony raising armed ships to fight the Royal Navy was simply unprecedented – and clearly illegal. Raising an army, on the other hand, as they already had done, was not, because raising militias was an ancient colonial right and the army outside Boston was, in reality, a collection of long-established militias: engaging with the British certainly was illegal, but existing was not.[17] This was a period of hazy lines and boundaries that were kept deliberately hazy by both sides as they jockeyed for position. The overt adoption of a navy would have irrevocably hardened those lines. It would have been provocative to any state, but particularly so for the British simply because of the size and reputation of her navy. In many ways her navy defined Great Britain. In these circumstances the Americans who had drafted the petition realized that the overt establishment of a navy would have been nothing less than a tacit declaration of independence, and any chance of reconciliation, or even of delaying the war to allow them time to strengthen their hand, would have been impossible.

It was essential, therefore, that the politicians should come to terms with the revolution before they could come to terms with the navy, which is why the subsequent Congressional resolutions to establish a navy shadow perfectly the gradual hardening of the official stance towards Britain, for the two went very much hand in hand. Indeed, naval developments in America in this period were fundamental in resolving the great question of independence versus reconciliation.[18]

*　*　*

A cabal of men with significant maritime experience and knowledge drove that process. Some could see the strategic value of taking to the sea, while others, among them shipbuilders and merchants, had a vested interest in that dream.* Washington was the first who had to be convinced of the value of the sea by the pro-navy men because, while the politicians of the Continental Congress bickered and jockeyed, playing a different game, Washington could act, even without Congressional approval. Upon his arrival at Cambridge he was faced with a shocking shortage of military stores, in particular gunpowder, of which there was enough for only nine shots per man. An added weakness was a total lack of heavy artillery, which Washington believed could be solved by dragging to Boston the British cannon that had been captured at Ticonderoga. He sent a mission to the north to deal with the cannon while, relatively safe from attack in Cambridge as a consequence of British timidity, he concentrated on the problem of powder and military stores. Thus Washington turned his mind to the sea.

There was certainly no problem with shipbuilding resources, skill or supplies. North America was already a maritime state with a maritime economy. Shipbuilding was the colonies' single largest industry, producing some 35,000 tons of ships per year and no less than a fifth of the entire British merchant fleet.[19] The rebels certainly had the manpower: the Massachusetts coast was swarming with seamen thrown out of employment by the interruption of their trade that had been caused by the British blockade of Boston, and many of their fishing schooners were lying idle.[20] In need of a quick and cheap solution, at the end of the summer of 1775 Washington decided to arm at Continental expense a handful of merchant ships and send them out to act against British supply ships. He began with just one but ended with seven, all leased to 'The United Colonies' and all with orders to seize 'such Vessels as may be found on the High Seas or elsewhere, bound inward and outward to or from Boston, in the Service of the ministerial Army ...'.[21]

The first to be commissioned and leased to Congress, thus

---

* These pro-navy men included John Adams, Stephen Hopkins, Silas Deane, John Langdon, John Glover, Christopher Gadsden, Richard Henry Lee and Joseph Hewes.

becoming the first 'American' naval vessel, was the 78-ton schooner *Hannah*. She is a vessel that remains one of the most dominant figureheads of the early American navy and one that has fascinated generations of history lovers, but the most interesting thing about her is that, even after dedicated investigation by numerous scholars, we know far less about her than many people suspect. In fact we know almost nothing about her at all.

We know that she was commissioned on 2 September 1775 under the command of a Nicholas Broughton, and that she sailed on her first voyage three days later,[22] but we have very little idea of what she looked like. No wreck survives to measure, preserve and discuss. Unlike other vessels in Washington's fleet, there are no bills or accounts for her fitting out, and certainly no descriptions, portraits or sketches. In fact the only plans that survive for any schooner from the period immediately before the revolution are in the National Maritime Museum in Greenwich, England, and there are just four. Only two actually date from the war years, and each is significantly different from the other.[23] The best we can do is compare her to a surviving portrait of a ship [*see fig. 14*], the *Baltick*, built in an adjacent town on the same Merrimac River within two years of the *Hannah*.[24] There is not even any contemporary evidence that the rebel schooner which engaged HMS *Nautilus* on 10 October 1775, long thought to have been the *Hannah's* finest hour, was actually her. Perhaps it was, but not one contemporary source actually says so. One historian has described the constancy with which her name fails to appear in official documents as 'disturbing'.[25]

This lack of information about the *Hannah* may seem surprising, but when viewed in the context of the time and the location, it is not, and that makes it interesting; in fact it is an important reminder that she was just one of several small ex-fishing vessels being fitted out at the time in Massachusetts. In the aftermath of Lexington there were glimpses of colonial sea power up and down the coast, fuelled by a changing perception of the British as well as by a changing perception of the Americans themselves: they suddenly saw themselves as empowered and it was catching. They now acted to deny the British their demands for colonial supplies of livestock, food and fuel and to protect their own maritime trade from British harassment.[26]

This was a period of intense excitement and maritime bustle throughout New England, caused by several institutions and numerous private individuals all acting independently – a distinctive characteristic of the rebellion as a whole at this time. Thus, while the shipyard at Beverly in Massachusetts was busy fitting out the *Hannah*, numerous American shipyards were also filled with the sound and smells of caulkers hammering and tarring seams; with the calls of men striving for unison to sway heavy masts and yards aloft; with the unmistakable thunk of heavy iron munitions being loaded on deck. Together, they created an atmosphere crackling with promise and excitement. After months of stalemate, finally the Americans were taking the fight to the British at sea. Yes, Washington had commissioned some schooners on behalf of the army, but at roughly the same time a mini-flotilla consisting of a schooner and two sloops was seized from the British in Machias, Maine by Jeremiah O'Brien, an action in which a British midshipman was fatally wounded and which still features highly in American naval lore.[27] The colony of Rhode Island, meanwhile, had taken the leap that Congress was unwilling to take and had committed to creating its own navy; Georgia commissioned a sloop to seize a British ordnance transport; and Massachusetts had been on the brink of making the same decision since early June. Urged to action by a resolution of the Continental Congress of 18 July 1775 that each colony should provide for the protection of its own harbours and navigation,[28] twelve of the thirteen colonies who rebelled created navies.* It was an important naval development, but the resolution was still couched in terms of defence, the operations

---

* The only colony that rebelled but did not create a navy was Delaware, though for many years it was believed that New Jersey also did not create a navy. Scheina, 'Matter of Definition'.

were to be focused on local waters, and the ships were to be administered by each individual colony. These moves were all carefully judged because they were not, yet, the actions of an independent state.

* * *

These colonies armed fishing vessels, built their own fighting ships, and organized flotillas of whaleboats, galleys, fireships and floating batteries. The navies' roles were as varied as the craft they consisted of. Some chose to attack British trade and harass British warships; others existed just to protect people, livestock or stockpiles of materiel; for some the defence of a single significant waterway or landing spot was their only purpose.

Pennsylvania was the first to build specially designed ships: galleys armed with a single cannon in the bow. Their role was to defend Philadelphia, the seat of the Second Continental Congress, by protecting the Delaware and its mighty estuary. Pennsylvania also built eight 'chains' of fire-rafts – each chain consisting of six rafts, and each raft 25–35 feet long and equipped with a vicious prong of barbed iron sticking out from its bows to ensnare its target. With such a significant waterway in their midst, and one that was patrolled by British warships, the role of the Pennsylvania Navy was more than just defensive, and their galleys and guard-boats were particularly active in preventing Tories from shipping supplies downriver to British forces.[29]

The Virginians, better endowed with shipbuilding and naval industry than any other state, including a ropewalk at Warwick on the James River, built the largest of all the states' navies. The force consisted primarily of galleys, armed with one and sometimes two heavy cannon, for the defence of the Potomac River and the main hub of their colony, Charlestown.[30] The Virginians, along with the North Carolinians, were particularly concerned about an important navigation, via Ocracoke Inlet, which gave access from the Atlantic to Pamlico and Albemarle Sounds, and from there deep inland via numerous rivers. The two colonies' navies worked together in its defence. Well defended from this moment on, Ocracoke became a major supply channel for the rebel armies.[31] Making the most of their local knowledge, these navies specialized in shallow-drafted vessels that could nip in and out of the sand-bars of Virginia and the Carolinas.

The Connecticut navy was created principally to protect New London, one of the largest and most important seaports in New England and by far the best deep-water harbour on Long Island Sound. Well protected, it went on to become a major base for American warships and privateers of all types. The Connecticut navy is particularly noteworthy for having a dedicated spy-ship 'to run and course from place to place, to discover the enemy, and carry intelligence'.[32] It was also responsible for the most provocatively titled ship in any of the state navies: the *Oliver Cromwell*.

Georgia and South Carolina worked together to bottle up the British force in the key port of Savannah and were responsible for one of the most entertaining episodes of the entire war. On 27 June the governor of Savannah, James Wright, wrote a desperate plea to Samuel Graves in Boston because rebel boats had blockaded Savannah: 'And thus you see, Sir … that they have it in their power to plunder any thing, that arrives here, and do just what they please.'[33] He then begged for the assistance of 'a sloop of war of some force' to disperse the rebel craft. The letter fell into rebel hands and, rather brilliantly, was simply replaced with one of their own composition which painted a rosy picture of events in Savannah. One can almost sense the joy in writing this letter: 'It gives me the highest pleasure to acquaint you, that I now have not any occasion for any vessel of war, and I am clearly of opinion that his Majesty's service will be better promoted by the absence than the presence of vessels of war in this port.'[34]

Each navy had its own carefully protected identity, often expressed visually through flags, though this is becoming far less clear-cut than was once thought. For many years the most famous state navy ensign was that which was believed to belong to the South Carolina State Navy: a vivid red and blue stripe with a snake slithering over the motto 'Don't tread on me'. The latest research, however, makes it clear that there is no direct evidence at all linking this flag with South Carolina in this period. There is also evidence that the flag most commonly associated with the Massachusetts State Navy – a white flag with a green pine tree over the inscription 'Appeal to Heaven' – was also used by most of the state navies.[35]

This was a time of inspiration, energy and naïve excitement. The Maryland commissioners insisted that the men enlisted in their navy were visions of perfection, with 'able bodies and perfect in all their Limbs and Sight of Sound Health without Ruptures or other visible Infirmities, above five Feet four Inches and above sixteen and under fifty years of age: and if above forty they must be of robust Constitution'.[36] It would not be long before they, and all the other colonies, came to realize just how difficult it would be to man their ships with anyone at all, let alone with such models of maritime excellence.[37] Nonetheless, the summer and autumn of 1775 are characterized by increased military power and a growing sense of identity for each colony – a change that reflects what was happening politically in Philadelphia.

There, the Second Continental Congress was hardening its stance towards Britain, though it was still not overtly seeking independence, and it was also reassuring representatives of the individual colonies that they would continue to retain their own freedom and independence from each other. The early history of the state navies therefore reflects the attitude of Congress both towards Britain and towards its own states, and it is actually against this background – one of increased separateness among the colonies, rather than of increased unity – that one should consider the next stage in the development of American sea power, the creation of the Continental Navy.

* * *

By October 1775 a significant change had occurred among the American politicians in Philadelphia. A proposal from the

Rhode Island General Assembly to form a Continental Navy to threaten British supply lines and protect American trade had been put to Congress in August but had been shelved – it had just seemed too radical. Ideas of reconciliation were still cherished by many and the creation of a Continental Navy was as good as any declaration of independence.[38] By October, however, significant momentum had gathered behind those who believed that separation was essential, and one manifestation of that political change was Congress's commitment to create an American navy. The creation of that navy was both a manifestation of that political realignment and a reason for its growing support over the coming months: by creating a navy many came to believe in both the possibility and the advantages of independence. Even in these early months, the rumours of a navy, even the *idea* of a navy, generated support for the rebel cause.

The process began on 13 October 1775 with approval of a resolution that

> a swift sailing vessel, to carry ten carriage guns, and a proportional number of swivels, with eighty men, be fitted out with all despatch, for a cruise of three months, and that the commander be instructed to cruise eastward, for intercepting such transports as may be laden with warlike stores and other supplies for our enemies, and for such other purposes as the Congress shall direct.[39]

Soon after another vessel was commissioned for the same purpose, and these initial orders rather opened the floodgates. Those two ships, originally to be of 10 guns, became one of 10 and one of 14, and then two more were recommended, much larger, at 20 guns and then 36 guns. By mid-November four ships were being converted in Philadelphia. Then came a significant step-up. In December it was resolved that, rather than convert any large existing ships from traders into warships, they would actually build from scratch thirteen frigates and they would so so at the ludicrously exact cost of $866,666.66: five of 32 guns, five of 28 guns and three of 24 guns.[40] They would be built in seven of the thirteen colonies to make best use of the available workforce and presumably to ensure that as many colonies were involved as possible: four in Pennsylvania, two each in Massachusetts, New York and Rhode Island, and one each in Connecticut, New Hampshire and Maryland. Soon after work had begun on those frigates, the programme was expanded yet again with another significant step-up. Now three 74-gunners – ships large enough to be classified as 'ships of the line' – were to be built, as well as five more large frigates.[41]

This was now a truly massive commitment that would have major repercussions on the course of the war and the shape of the nation that was fighting it. To design, build, victual, man and operate these ships would require a significant centralized infrastructure. Just as the creation of the American navy was both a manifestation and a cause of political realignment in the relationship between Congress, the colonies and Britain, so was it also a manifestation and cause of increased centralization of American government. The creation of the navy is an integral piece of the picture that led to the rise of America as a fiscal-military nation state – to the printing, raising and borrowing of money and the creation of a bureaucracy to oversee the spending of the money it generated.[42] This is why the birth of the American navy reflects the birth of America itself.

* * *

Before the Americans could build a navy at sea, they first had to build a navy on paper. Congress eventually established a three-man committee tasked with preparing an estimate of the expenses. This mini committee, consisting of Silas Deane of Connecticut, John Langdon of New Hampshire and Christopher Gadsden of South Carolina, was the first American governmental supervisory body of the navy.[43] It soon expanded to seven members and was tasked with more responsibility.*

---

* The additional men were John Adams of Massachusetts, Richard Henry Lee of Virginia, and Stephen Hopkins and Joseph Hewes of North Carolina.

This Marine Committee laid out the basic structure of the navy: it created a system of wages; designed a uniform; conceived a set of rules and regulations; established a prize-share system; outlined expectations of conduct and boundaries of authority; drew up a list of crimes and punishments;* and addressed the questions of divine services, courts martial and terms of enlistment. At this stage the Marine Committee was also responsible for operations.[44]

It all started off with high levels of expectation and plenty of enjoyment. The committee met every evening on the second floor of a tavern in Philadelphia. John Adams remembered the meetings as 'the pleasantest part of my Labours for the four years I spent in Congress' and was detailed in his appreciation of the 'wit, humour, anecdotes, science and learning' that characterized the meetings and their convivial aftermath.[45] At exactly this time he wrote to James Warren: 'We begin to feel a little of a Seafaring Inclination here'[46] – a line of thrilling immediacy that encapsulates the hope and energy of the time, when those pro-navy men had finally received the Congressional approval and encouragement that they had long sought.

This peak of naval vitality is significant if one is going to appreciate fully the torpor that, long before the end of the war, poisoned the American naval administration. Now back-slapping in a smoky room above a tavern, hunched with inspiration over blank pieces of parchment, reassured by a relatively stable currency to fund their dreams, these men would eventually find themselves utterly worn down by the never-ending problems they encountered. This is because building any navy in any location at any period in history was always an immense struggle. It took endless time even for those with the requisite experience and skill honed through failure. Running a navy successfully also required political dexterity, financial ingenuity, administrative efficiency, logistical robustness and excellent

---

* In general these followed the Royal Navy pattern but were less severe. Fowler, 'Esek Hopkins', 8.

leadership. Yet none of the men on the Marine Committee had any experience of naval administration, and there was not a single dry dock anywhere in North America – not one.[47]

If one considers that these challenges – often too much for a navally inclined nation to overcome even in peacetime – were increased under the intense pressure of war and were further multiplied by the fledgling nature of the American state itself, then failure, if not inevitable, was highly likely. At the very least the operational capability of the American navy, if it ever made it to sea, would be significantly compromised – something that was immediately apparent when it became clear that the Americans were barely able to arm their ships at all. The British had discouraged ordnance manufacture in the colonies. The first American naval guns, therefore, were a hodge-podge of discovered, stolen and imported pieces intermingled with a tiny handful of cannon newly cast from recycled door-knockers and church bells.[48]

The question we must ask, therefore, is how much of an impact such a small and fragile navy would have on the shape or direction of the war. To find the answer we must look beyond the obvious or traditional tools of naval warfare. At this stage of the war, the flag that these ships flew was of far more significance than the guns that they mounted. The first ensign of the Continental Navy – the Grand Union flag – was made up of thirteen red and white stripes with the British Union flag in the upper left corner next to the flagstaff [*see fig. 12*]. It is likely that its attraction lay in the fact that it could easily be made by sewing six white strips of cloth horizontally across the field of the easily accessible red ensign, or 'meteor' flag, of England.[49]

The first known naval use of the Grand Union was 3 December 1775, when it was hoisted by Senior Lieutenant John Paul Jones over the new commander-in-chief Esek Hopkins's flagship, the *Alfred*, newly purchased for the Continental Navy and then lying in the Delaware River.[50] Thousands cheered it and wished the *Alfred* Godspeed – a reminder of the value that this nascent American sea power had in forging a sense of unity among the existing supporters of the rebellion and in drawing the uncommitted to its flag.

That flag was first saluted by a foreign country nearly a year later, on 16 November 1776, by Fort Orange on the Dutch Island of St Eustatius. Significantly, British forces in nearby St Kitts witnessed the salute. They were furious and ordered the Dutch to 'formally disavow the salute to the rebels, punish the culprit and recall and dismiss the Governor of St. Eustatius ... His Majesty will not delay one instant to take such measures as he think due to the interest and dignity of his crown.'[51]

The naval use of this flag is important because it was a Band-Aid for the festering wounds that were the reality of American politics in the winter of 1775 and the new year of 1776. The country was deeply divided between rebels and loyalists, and both factions were themselves divided regarding the most appropriate way forward. The Second Continental Congress was taking significant steps towards centralization of power, but it did not have consent of the governed – *de jure* authority. In fact the rebellious colonies shared only three things: one was George Washington, another was the Continental Army that he commanded, and the third was this new Continental Navy. Washington and his army were both stuck in Boston. The navy, however, could go wherever it wanted and it could take its flag with it. It could, in essence, export the revolution, and show the world that the rebellious colonies were acting as a sovereign state with major pretensions at being a world power. In doing so it would present a simple, strong face to the revolution that hid its complex, weak nature. It is impossible to overstate how important this was at exactly this stage. It was quite clear to everyone that the revolution would not survive without a great deal of help, but to secure that help – essentially to attract foreign investors willing to buy into the revolution – it would have to take its own first wobbly steps. The creation of the Continental Navy must be seen in this light: it was nothing less than a declaration of independence.

*   *   *

The final ingredient of colonial sea power that emerged in this period – one that also reflected the growing centralization of power in America and served to advertise abroad the rebellious colonies as a nation state – was privateering. A privateer was a privately owned ship whose captain held a 'letter of marque and reprisal' that gave him the legal right to seize vessels and their cargoes belonging to a particular nation, in this case Britain. This was of significance in America in late 1775 because, by authorizing non-state violence, these letters of marque implied the existence of a nation state. The authorization of privateering, moreover, was a crucial part of all European state behaviour in this period. All the significant European maritime powers – Britain, France, Spain, Portugal, Holland, Denmark, Sweden, Russia – issued letters of marque in wartime. As with the creation of the Continental Navy, this is another example of the Americans inching towards independence simply by behaving on an international stage as if they were independent. The need to do this was well summarized by Richard Henry Lee in April 1776:

No state in Europe will either Treat or Trade with us for so long as we consider ourselves subjects of G[reat] B[ritain]. Honour, dignity, and the customs of states forbid them until we rank as an independent people.[52]

Every letter of marque, therefore, was in its own way a declaration of independence, and many of them pre-dated the formal declaration of 4 July 1776. The first suggestion of issuing such letters came from a particularly radical member of the Massachusetts Assembly, Elbridge Gerry,[53] in October 1775, but it was not until March 1776 that the relationship between Britain and America had sufficiently fractured for Congress to feel able to issue them. This link between state formation and privateering is why John Adams referred to a bill that passed through the Massachusetts House of Representatives recommending the institutionalization of privateering as one of the most important documents in the history of the revolution.[54]

It is no coincidence that, in this period, the Americans, hitherto bound by the British Navigation Acts and thus restricted to trading with British ships, also opened their ports to foreign trade. This – an outright rejection of the British mercantile system – was yet another act that would be felt around the world; for it was both deliberately provocative of British maritime and naval power and also the first step in forming foreign alliances that the Americans and British knew would be crucial to their cause – and they would not be able to ask for foreign help without offering some form of trading privilege in return.[55] These developments demonstrate clearly that winning independence in war was just one part of the journey to independence; behaving independently before the break was also crucial. Yet again, it is John Adams who saw the path for what it was. 'Have you not seen the Privateering Resolves?' he wrote to James Warren. 'Are not these Independence enough for my beloved Constituents? Have you seen the Resolves for opening our Ports to all Nations? Are these Independence enough? What more would you have?'[56]

The rise of privateering created its own problems for the Americans, however. First among these was the competition for naval resources between the various navies, State and Continental, on the one hand, and the privateers on the other. The owners of privateers were commercially beholden to make privateering an attractive opportunity to mariners. Such forces did not run the Continental Navy. Congress offered a regular wage that a privateer owner did not, but for the promise of that wage and also to help pay for the Continental war machine, a sailor aboard a Continental warship received a smaller portion of any prize than his compatriot aboard a privateer. A crew sailing under the flag of the Continental Navy or a state navy would share no more than a third of the value of their prize, unless that prize was an enemy warship, in which case the portion rose to a half. A privateer owner and crew shared the full value of their prize, whatever the prize, and they were more than happy to sell any black sailors they might capture as slaves or to keep them to boost their own crew.[57] The risk was certainly worth running. One privateer owner explained the maths: 'It is well worth risquing largely for one arrival will pay for two, three or four losses. Therefore its best to keep doing something constantly.'[58]

Ship-owners were also cunning in making their ship financially attractive in other ways. Debt-ridden sailors were an easy target and could be lured into service by pre-selling the shares of a cruise for a given figure. The investor, often the ship-owner himself, would then keep any prize money received over and above the figure paid.[59] Prize courts were set up in Baltimore and Philadelphia to process the claims quickly and efficiently, in no more than a matter of weeks, so the privateer sailors could plainly see a commitment to realizing their dreams of rapid wealth. The system was transparent and visibly worked, in direct contrast to that surrounding the Continental Navy in this period. Put simply, you were more likely to get paid if you were serving on a privateer, and when you were paid, it was likely to be more than if you were on a navy vessel. This tension between the private interest and the collective interest would create problems for American sea power throughout the war.

By the spring of 1776 the Americans were sufficiently committed to privateering that it had become streamlined, with pre-printed and even pre-authorized privateering commissions, and it was not long before the number of privateers in each colony exceeded the number of craft in its navy.

* * *

If considered together, the combined potential of whaleboats, state navies, the Continental Navy and privateers was now significant. The British had a serious problem on their hands. The question remains, then: what did these various strands of American sea power actually achieve in this early period?

It would be more than possible to write an entire chapter on the frustrations and failures of early American sea power. There were manning problems, arming problems, logistical problems, tactical problems, shipbuilding and seamanship problems, political interference, personal enmity, insubordination, unwarranted aggression, fraud, bribery, mutiny, litigation, lightning strikes, ship fever, rotten victuals, drunkenness and greed. It is not a period or topic that reflects well on the Americans. John Adams said that officers scrambled for rank and pay 'like apes for nuts' and worried one another 'like Mastiffs'; Washington noted that the crews caused him inexpressible 'plague, trouble and vexation' and that 'licentiousness & every kind of disorder triumphantly reign' in the navy.[60] It is a wonder they achieved anything at all until one considers their targets.

At this early stage, most British supply vessels destined for American waters sailed unprotected.* Neither were they armed nor did they sail with an armed escort. They were sourced, loaded and crewed in British waters 3,000 miles away, where there was no conception of the danger posed by the rise of American sea power. Upon their arrival they were then too far removed in both distance and time for administrators to react sufficiently quickly to the changing situation. The problems were exacerbated by confusion at the level of the British government that supervised the sending of stores and supplies to America. In 1775–6 the operation was supervised by three different agencies of the British government: the Treasury, responsible for army provisions; the Ordnance Board, responsible for artillery, arms, munitions and engineers' stores; and the Navy Board, responsible for army clothing, camp equipment, naval stores and presents for the native Indians. These three agencies worked without supervision or co-ordination and often in direct competition with each other for scarce resources. Administrative confusion in London was the inevitable result.[61] Although the Americans were beginning to bristle at sea, most British supply ships continued to sail

---

* The most valuable ships carrying arms and army camp equipment were given escorts, though after 3,000 miles of trans-Atlantic voyage they often found themselves separated when they finally arrived in America. This is exactly what happened to the *Nancy* (see pp. 98–100).

unarmed and without escort, arriving off the eastern seaboard in blissful ignorance of the threat they faced. This all caused utter consternation for the British in America.[62]

British merchant ships in British waters were also unprotected. Hitherto the public focus of the war in Britain had been beyond the distant horizon. It seemed to be a war of principle and ideology, not of bullets, blood, bandages, death and property theft. British merchant ships pootled around the British coast undefended and unescorted, sailors whistling and smoking pipes as the sun set and rose on their never-changing routine. They were at peace with their traditional enemies, France, Spain and Holland. There was no threat, only profit. Life was idyllic.

The situation in the Caribbean was different because of its proximity to America. Here the war at sea felt far more vivid. French, Dutch and Spanish ships carried supplies to their islands, and American merchant ships hovered around the coasts ready to smuggle those supplies to America. British merchant ships, meanwhile, carried on their trade along well-known routes at predictable times of year. Anyone with an ounce of maritime and local knowledge would be able to target them. There were insufficient British ships stationed in the Caribbean to protect them. They were vulnerable and they knew it.

* * *

For all this British weakness, the primary story of American naval operations in this period is one of disappointment. The *Hannah*, the first ship hired by Washington, the great maritime hope of the rebel army, failed to meet the expectations heaped upon her. Seven of her first eight captures were American vessels that had to be returned to their American owners with damages paid for goods pilfered by the crew.[63] None of the thirteen frigates, which were supposed to be at sea by the spring of 1776, were ready until 1777, and four never got to sea at all. There was, however, the occasional startling success that was sufficient to maintain momentum behind the great expectations of American sea power that so coloured this period.

The most spectacular success of the Continental Navy was the capture, in November 1775, of the unprotected British brig *Nancy* almost within sight of the British in Boston. We can only imagine the effect on Captain John Manley and the crew of the *Lee* when they opened *Nancy*'s hold and climbed down into her musty depths. They would have smelt the unmistakable aroma of dormant arms and ammunition, of latent energy, in enormous quantities. There were 2,000 muskets and cartridge boxes, 3,000 twelve-pound cannon-balls, 4,000 six-pound balls and 150 carcass shells, an incendiary projectile cunningly engineered to set fire to anything in its path. There was a mortar, a short and wide artillery piece for bombardment. There were also ropes, lanterns, saddles, harnesses, kettles, frying-pans, nails and countless other essentials for waging war. There were even seven dismantled ammunition wagons that the Americans used to steal their prize away to the rebel army camp at Cambridge.[64] There was so much aboard her that it took two months to fully unload the cargo. Thousands cheered the haul, paraded through Cambridge. A capture that mattered both materially and symbolically, Washington called it 'an instance of divine favour',[65] while Howe raged that Washington now had 'all the requisites' for burning Boston or the British ships that guarded it.[66]

Other successes were noteworthy. By December 1775 American whaleboats had secured control of the entire north shore of Massachusetts Bay, a key strategic advantage in their fight to drive the British out.[67] Four major troop transports were captured off Boston* and nine victualling ships.[68] The first notable fight between British and American naval ships was the engagement off Rhode Island between HMS *Glasgow* and the *Andrew Doria* in April 1776, in which the *Glasgow* was

---

* The first of only two major seizures of British troops at sea in the war, the other being the convoy capture in 1780 by a combined Franco-Spanish squadron of six companies of the 91st Regiment en route to the West Indies.

forced to flee 'yelping from the mouths of her cannon like a broken-legged dog'.[69] The first British warship to be captured – and therefore the first enemy ship captured by a United States naval vessel – was HMS *Hawk*, captured on 4 April 1776 by Abraham Whipple in the *Columbus*.[70]

In March that year American sea power really began to stretch its legs, and Esek Hopkins, with John Paul Jones in his crew, led a small squadron on a successful raid on Nassau in the Bahamas and captured seventy cannon and fifteen mortars. It was the first engagement of what later became the US Marine Corps.[71] By the end of 1776, to the utter horror of British merchants, politicians and the public, American privateers were regularly conducting operations in the Caribbean and in European waters. One of the earliest captures in European waters, and possibly the first, was made by the privateer *Rover* of Salem, which seized four British merchant ships off Cape St Vincent in the summer.[72]

Captures close to home particularly stung, but far more numerous and economically significant raids occurred in the Caribbean. William Bingham, an emissary of the Continental Congress stationed on Martinique, orchestrated American privateering in the Caribbean. They cut out merchant ships and fishing vessels, raided towns and captured slaves. In one attack on Barbados they took goods valued at £2,000.[73] In Bingham's first six months on the island, 250 British ships carrying cargoes worth more than $10 million were waylaid in the West Indies.[74] He took a skim from every capture and returned to America in 1780 one of the richest men in the nation; he became a founder member of the first bank in America, which was therefore financed by the profits of American sea power.*

These captures transformed the perception of the war in Britain. Everyone knew that the Caribbean was the source of the vast majority of Britain's wealth, and the British were

* Bingham died in Bath, England, in 1804. There is an impressive memorial to him in Bath Abbey.

particularly sensitive about naval warfare of any type conducted off British shores. American privateers thus directly
enfranchised the British population in the conduct of the war,
expanding the scale of the political problem. Quite simply,
American privateering changed both the nature and the
development of the war.

* * *

In yet one more and perhaps surprising way, American sea
power was instrumental in the march towards independence. We have seen how the establishment of a navy and the
issuing of letters of marque were, in their own way, declara-
tions of independence, but the role of American sea power
is also spliced into the actual history of the Declaration of
Independence itself.

Just as, after Lexington and Concord, the Americans used
their existing maritime infrastructure to rush their version
of the news of the battle around the colonies and across the
Atlantic, so did they when the colonies signed their Declaration
of Independence in July 1776, a document which hardened
the stance of the rebels and which outlined ideas whose spread
would be crucial to the ultimate success of the revolution. The
problem with the Declaration of Independence, however, was
that it would carry only a fraction of its desired impact if none
of the rebels' potential allies – both at home and abroad –
knew about it. It had to be broadcast to as wide an audience as
possible and as quickly as possible, and American ships played
a little known but major role in that dissemination – a role
that is clearly demonstrated by a fascinating discovery, made
in an English archive, in July 2009.

It is unknown exactly how many copies of the Declaration
of Independence were made in its first run (the Dunlap
broadside) – it has been suggested that there were around 200 –
but we do know that, until 2009, only twenty-five copies were
known to exist. Then, a researcher discovered a copy in the
collections of the British National Archives in Kew, London.
It was found in a section of British naval letters sent back to

London in the summer of 1776.[75] It is likely that the broadside was captured at the same time as an American merchantman or warship: for it to end up in the Admiralty archive, that copy of the Declaration must have been captured at sea.

There was an established postal route north from Philadelphia to New York and Boston, but the route south was far more problematic and, if speed was a concern, involved sea travel. We know that the Dunlap broadside took just three days to get to Baltimore, four to New York, seven to Rhode Island, eleven to Massachusetts, and two weeks to Virginia, and twelve days after that, on 2 August, it reached South Carolina.[76] We know that it was deliberately sent abroad. The *Andrew Doria*, a Continental Navy vessel, took a copy of the Declaration to the crucial Dutch island of St Eustatius, through which the rebels were importing vast quantities of military supplies, where it was presented to the island's governor. The Committee of Secret Correspondence, meanwhile, sent a copy on board a fast brigantine to Bordeaux and then on to Silas Deane in France. News also went very quickly north by ship, up the Hudson and Lake George and then into Lake Champlain, reaching Ticonderoga on 16 July. The text first appeared in a London newspaper in the second week of August 1776, and from there news travelled to Scotland, Ireland, Holland, Germany and Scandinavia. By 24 August it reached Dublin, by the 27th Madrid, by the 30th Holland, by the 31st Vienna, by 2 September Denmark, and by the 4th Florence. Only two months after Congress had passed its resolution, word of independence reached Warsaw.[77] This successful dissemination of the Declaration of Independence was one of *the* major success stories of American sea power in 1776.

For all these successes, however, there were countless failures and frustrations, and when, in December 1775, the Royal Navy captured its first American naval ship, the *Washington*, the thin veneer of American sea power was exposed.[78] She was surveyed and found to be so utterly awful that she was deemed unsuitable for British operations on the high seas, or in the words of the British carpenter who surveyed her, 'totally unserviceable ... unfit for war ... not fit for sea'.[79] This was a strong judgement indeed considering the British were then as desperate for shipping as they had ever been. Other American captains occasionally let the disguise slip. William Coit joked that his guns dated back to the Pilgrim era and that firing more than one at a time 'would split her open from her gunwale to her keel'.[80]

Nonetheless American ships achieved just enough to annoy the British and force them to deploy increasing numbers of naval craft in America, the Caribbean and home waters, thus stretching their already thin naval resources almost to breaking point.[81] Sandwich realized the problem and urged full mobilization, but in vain. In fact British politicians had put so much faith in the success of the Coercive Acts of 1774 that they had actually reduced the numbers of both shipwrights and sailors in the navy.[82] The British had thus scuppered their own ship, the result of an understandable failure to foresee the exact strategic problem that was posed by American sea power in 1776.* The British may have been surprised by the military competence displayed by the American rebels at Lexington and Concord, but they were entirely thrown off course by the Americans taking to the sea. One contemporary neatly summed it all up:

> Naval captures, being unexpected, were matter of triumph to the Americans, and of surprize to the British. The latter scarcely believed that the former would oppose them by land with a regular army, but never suspected that a people, so unfurnished as they were with many things necessary for arming vessels, would presume to attempt any thing on water.[83]

---

* For years the blame was attributed to a failure to keep the navy adequately maintained in the peace that followed the Seven Years' War (1754–63), but the record of peacetime naval upkeep between 1763 and 1775 was only slightly worse than the norm. Baugh, 'Why did Britain?', 145. For a criticism, see Wilkinson, *British Navy*, 4n.

Howe realized the dangers of this and wrote to Dartmouth in December, warning that a naval threat 'will hurt us more effectually than anything they can do by land'.[84] The moment the Americans took to the sea, even in their limited way, the traditional British strategy of putting down rebellions with a show of force led by an army was undermined. Naval officers were desperate for orders, but the entire naval hierarchy and, above them the politicians, were paralysed.[85] The unchallenged birth of American sea power demonstrates so clearly that the British had misunderstood the nature of the beast they were trying to kill. Graves lamented that 'whilst the Americans were preparing for, nay making war, we were only passing and making Acts of Parliament'.[86]

The question posed now was: just how much damage could the Americans inflict on the British before they realized their mistake and rectified it?

6

BRITISH EVACUATION

In the summer of 1775 the British army was under siege in Boston and the situation there was mirrored, if in a diluted sense, elsewhere in the colonies. Up and down the eastern seaboard British troops and loyal Tories were forced into enclosures and, if there were none to hand, into British warships. Isolated and threatened, in several significant locations British authority in North America persisted through its warships alone.

Governor Josiah Martin of North Carolina fled to the *Peggy* in the Cape Fear River, Governor James Wright of Georgia to the *Scarborough* in the Savannah River, and Governor Sir William Tryon of New York to the *Duchess of Gordon* in the North River. Significantly, he took with him the officials of the Parliamentary Post, another British institution that collapsed in this period.[1] The situation in Virginia was particularly noteworthy. John Murray, Earl of Dunmore and governor of Virginia, had been chased out of the capitol, Norfolk, and had sought refuge with his family on HMS *Fowey*, which had also become the new home of the Williamsburg powder magazine. As soon as Dunmore left terra firma, royal government in Virginia collapsed. He was, in his own words, 'reduced to the deplorable and disgraceful state of being a tame spectator of Rebellion'.[2] Riled, he realized that his ships could be turned to some use – that they could become a focal point of British strength to attract local loyalists and, far more provocatively, the thousands of disaffected slaves in the south. Dunmore was sitting on a bomb in more ways than one.

On 7 November 1775, aboard the *William* in Norfolk

Harbour, Dunmore issued a proclamation, offering emancipation to any slaves willing and able to bear arms who could get themselves to his fleet. There was a flood of escapes, all of them necessarily maritime-based. Two weeks after the proclamation a group of slaves came down the James River in a thirty-foot vessel but were captured. Soon after, seven broke out of a local jail and 'went off in a pettinger', a type of dugout. In an interesting example of British sailors affecting the revolution through the message that they carried rather than through their cannon or boarding axes, British tenders cruised up and down the river all summer, in the words of one Virginian, 'using every art to seduce the negroes'.[3]

Dunmore's use of British sea power had a paradoxical effect on the revolution in the south. On the one hand it generated some support for the British and increased the number of men who could bear arms or sail their ships, but on the other it alienated many potential friends whose livelihoods were tied up in the local slave-run economy. Thomas Jefferson said that the proclamation raised the country 'into a perfect phrensy'.[4] The problem was simply one of numbers. In 1776 the population of America was 2.5 million and a fifth of those were slaves. The proportion varied from state to state, but in Virginia, Dunmore's state, 40 per cent of the population were slaves. This was not just an issue of the British encouraging the slaves to escape; by arming them and turning them against their owners, Dunmore was exploiting one of the deepest fears of the south. The slave-owners' reaction was vicious. A fifteen-year-old girl was caught on her way to Dunmore and received eighty lashes followed by hot embers poured on her bleeding back. Others who were caught were mutilated or sent to the lead-mines, ultimately a slow ticket to the grave. Few were actually executed.[5]

Nonetheless, 800 or so slaves reached Dunmore's fleet, around 200 within the first few weeks alone, and their success inspired many others – perhaps 4,000 in total – to run to the British throughout the war. Three slaves who reached Dunmore's fleet via HMS *Roebuck* came from Washington's own plantation. Some British captains also interpreted Dunmore's decree to allow them to free any slave working as a mariner on a captured American vessel.[6]

Some of the slaves were skilled watermen and pilots, and proved of great value to the British. This was no coincidence. Most of the slaves who escaped to the British fleet were the ones who could escape; they were maritime workers from Hampton, Norfolk and Portsmouth, and they were following a well-established pattern of slaves in northern America using the sea as an escape route.[7] This was a key moment in the revolution. Hitherto the Royal Navy had been seen primarily as a tool of oppression, but for these Virginia slaves it symbolized the chance (though certainly not the guarantee) of freedom. It symbolized the hope of a new life.

*   *   *

Back in Boston the pot had been simmering since a titanic struggle for Bunker Hill, overlooking the harbour, had left the British in control but with Howe mourning the loss of 40 per cent of his attackers, dead or injured. The sides now peered at each other divided only by a barricade on Boston' s neck, 'almost near enough to converse', said Washington.[8]

Elsewhere the relationship between the British and Americans worsened, principally as a result of the actions of Samuel Graves. Seemingly liberated by the carnage suffered at the hands of the Americans on Bunker Hill, in the summer and autumn of 1775 Graves authorized several naval bombardment raids of American coastal towns as a means of subduing the insurrection. Only one was carried out, on Falmouth (later Portland, Maine), but it had the opposite effect to that which was, naively, intended: American maritime activity increased and resentment of the British grew. The 'British Barbarians' were condemned for their 'malicious Purpose ... to execute, their unrelenting Vengeance by every Means in their Power'.[9]

Everything then changed dramatically in Boston on the morning of 4 March 1776 when the British were astounded to see the Americans hauling heavy artillery into position on

Dorchester Heights, which overlooked the city. Henry Knox, sent to Ticonderoga by Washington to haul back the artillery seized by Arnold a year earlier, had succeeded in his herculean mission of hauling 120,000 pounds of guns 300 miles through snow and ice. Howe's immediate response was to assault the heights in a re-run of Bunker Hill, but with the assistance of some timely bad weather, sense prevailed.[10] The British would evacuate.

In the subsequent fortnight every sailor, soldier and willing Tory was transferred onto a British ship. It was a massive logistical exercise. The ultimate destination was irrelevant, and we are certain that most of the evacuees and soldiers had no idea where they were headed. What mattered was simply this: the entire city of Boston was going to sea. It is possible, but by no means certain, that Howe agreed an unofficial truce with Washington to ease the embarkation process. Washington's whaleboats remained tied up in muddy creeks, his armed schooners bided their time, hoping to track the convoy when it finally made it to sea, and Knox's guns stayed silent. The biggest irony of all was that, when this crux finally arrived, the Americans never needed the powder they had been so desperate to attain.

When news of the evacuation finally arrived in London, the behaviour of the British troops was applauded, not least by Lord North, who claimed that the British had embarked 'with all possible coolness and regularity ... perfectly at their ease'.[11] Howe himself had been careful to describe how they had left 'without the least molestation by the rebels',[12] and Molyneux Shuldham, the new naval commander who had taken over from Graves in March, celebrated the fact that the troops were embarked without the loss of a man.[13]

The political challenge was to make this seem like an act of choice, but on the ground in Boston the reality had been quite clear. 'Never [were] troops in so disgraceful a situation ...', wrote one American, 'I pity General Howe from my soul.'[14] Washington agreed: 'By all accounts, there never existed a more miserable set of beings, than these wretched creatures now are.'[15]

Central to the problem was Howe's desire to provide passage for loyal Tories. The British, even in evacuation, had to be seen to protect those who favoured British rule. It was a valuable political point and it set an important precedent for several other large-scale evacuations as the war progressed. The result, however, was that the operation became a total mess. It was far from dignified, as one witness wrote: 'It was not like the breaking up of a camp, where every man knows his duty. It was like departing your country, with your wives, your servants, your household furniture, all your encumbrances.'[16] In the stampede to get men and baggage on board, the ladders to the wharves were repeatedly broken, 'no care taken of them'.[17] They were taunted: 'The Tories with their brats and wives / Have fled to save their wretched lives.'[18]

Everything that could not be loaded aboard was smashed and thrown into the harbour, which became thick with sodden timber and detritus, a tide of broken furniture like the aftermath of a tsunami. Piles of goods and belongings were abandoned, along with 220 horses.[19] The Americans sat and watched as the pressure of civil war forced the British to destroy their own belongings and abandon their own homes. The Americans later claimed that some Britons with medical knowledge – the words they actually used were 'Doctors of the diabolical Ministerial Butchers' – deliberately mixed arsenic with medicines and left it behind.[20]

Space at Boston's wharves was limited, so whenever a ship was full, with white faces and shining eyes peering out of portholes, it drifted away from its jetty with the tide and made its way to Nantasket Roads, which, ironically – having been settled soon after the Plymouth Colony in 1620 – was one of the oldest areas of British control in America. There, 'men, women, and children, parents, masters, mistresses, were obliged to pig together on the floor', wrote the wealthy, disgusted Benjamin Hallowell.[21] This was a grim time – the ships rolling sickeningly at anchor with no canvas to steady them, the cramped passengers with no idea of their destination. Those ships that had arrived first at Nantasket endured this for more than a fortnight. At least one man threw himself overboard and drowned.[22] Washington thought this was only to be expected, if not a little overdue: 'One or two have done what a great many ought to have done long ago – committed suicide.'[23]

When, on 25 March, the fleet was finally ready to sail, it carried 11,000 people including 8,906 troops, 1,100 loyalists and 553 children. One witness claimed the fleet was over 170 strong and appeared 'like a forest'.[24] It stretched nine miles out to sea and it took ten days before the final British sail dipped into the eastern horizon, even though it was still enormously short of the tonnage that they actually required. Forced onto reduced rations by the unplanned overcrowding, the British headed for their naval base at Halifax, Nova Scotia, which was entirely unprepared for such an enormous influx of humanity.[25]

The Americans beamed as Howe left. 'Surely it is the Lord's doings and it is marvellous in our eyes', wrote Abigail Adams.[26] James Thatcher, a surgeon in Washington's army, described 'the unspeakable satisfaction' of watching them leave 'wafting from our shores the dreadful scourge of war'.[27]

* * *

What a moment. The British had been driven from their New England stronghold, and the only other significant body of British civilians, troops and ships in America was now to be found in Dunmore's hideous floating town off Virginia.

The pillars of hope raised by Dunmore's recruitment of hundreds of slaves had now come crashing down. His naval surgeons had been faced with a serious problem. Most of the slaves were not inoculated against smallpox because the idea of inoculation had been fiercely resisted in Virginia. Dunmore's surgeons tried to inoculate as many as possible, but hundreds – two-thirds in total – swiftly died; their bodies thrown overboard 'tumbled into the deep, to regale the sharks'.[28] Dunmore himself said that 'there was not a ship in the fleet that did not throw one, two or three or more dead overboard every night'.[29] Diseased, bloated bodies bobbed to the shore, a worrying advertisement to would-be escapees of the true cost of fleeing to the apparent safety of British ships.

The Americans loathed Dunmore both for freeing the slaves and for his violent ways. And by now he had become the first fully fledged villain of the revolution. 'For more than a twelve-month past, [he has] perpetrated crimes that would even have disgraced the noted pirate BLACKBEARD', wrote the *Virginia Gazette*.[30] 'If Britain had searched through the world for a person the best fitted to ruin their cause ... they could not have found a more complete agent than Lord Dunmore', wrote another.[31]

In London the British had cooked up an idea to support Dunmore's attempts to raise loyalist support and recruit slaves. The navy would appear in strength off Charleston, South Carolina, the key port in the south. It is ironic that the men who had pushed this loyalist-focused policy were the same southern governors who had met such sustained ferocity from the rebels ashore that they had been forced to move their entire administration and families on board British warships for their own safety. One gets a vivid sense that, attempting to wield authority from the sea, these men had entirely lost touch with the momentum and characteristics of the revolution on land. It was a problem that would dog the British throughout the war: distant warships were excellent for imposing block-ades and blasting seven shades of hell out of enemy ships, but they were no place to test the wind of popular sentiment on terra firma.

This conceptual misjudgement was then matched by opera-tional incompetence, and the subsequent raid on Charleston in June 1776 became the naval equivalent of Bunker Hill. A direct assault on a well-fortified American position on Sullivan's Island in Charleston harbour led to horrific casualties in the British force. Three British frigates grounded, one of which had to be burned by the British. Every man on the British flag-ship's quarterdeck was either killed or wounded, and the naval commanding officer, Commodore Sir Peter Parker, had his trousers shot off.[32] The Americans loved the story and quickly composed a song: 'I've the wind in my tail, / And am hoisting my sail, / To leave Sullivan's Island behind me.' Another began, rather brilliantly, 'If honour in the breech is lodged ...'.[33]

In one key respect, however, Charleston was far worse than Bunker Hill because – unlike Bunker Hill – it was, ultimately, a failure. The rebel fort that defended the harbour entrance, Fort Moultrie, withstood the fire of an entire squadron of British warships. The surgeon of Parker's flagship *Bristol* wrote in astonishment: 'This will not be believed when it is first reported in England. I can scarcely believe what I myself saw on that day ... One would have imagined no battery could have resisted [the Royal Navy's] incessant fire.'[34] Another contemporary boggled at the conviction of the Americans, an echo of the British response to the American defence of Bunker Hill: 'We were told the Yankees would not stand two fires, but we never saw better fellows ... All the common men of the fleet spoke loudly in praise of the garrison.'[35]

At Charleston the British couldn't even retreat with dignity. One British transport packed with Scottish soldiers ran aground; the soldiers were taken captive and the ship burned to the mud. This was the first major British naval operation of the war and it had been an unmitigated disaster. They limped away, though they used the time to bombard Wilmington in North Carolina and recruit hundreds more slaves. One of the men who sought refuge in the British fleet, having escaped his owner's flour mill on the Cape Fear River, was none other than Thomas Peters, who later became a significant leader of black loyalists in exile.[36]

*   *   *

Taken together, the Americans had achieved an enormous amount in 1775 and in the first half of 1776, while the British had tried to quell what they believed to be an isolated rebellion. They had won battles at Lexington and Concord, shocked the British at Bunker Hill, taken control of Lakes George and Champlain, invaded Canada, taken to the sea in armed ships, forced the British to evacuate Boston and defeated the

Royal Navy at Charleston. It was easy to get carried away by this unexpected success. On 28 March 1776 the Massachusetts General Court thanked Washington and wished him luck in his retirement.[37] What the Americans did not know, however, was that the British had already decided to evacuate Boston – Knox and his cannon had merely forced their hand – and the reason that they had decided to evacuate Boston was chilling. A city on an island approached via awkward navigation and surrounded by high hills was an inadequate bridgehead for a major amphibious invasion, which needed a wide and clear anchorage, gently sloping beaches to land men, guns and horses, and easy access inland. This mattered now perhaps more than it ever had, because in the spring of 1776 the British were planning the largest amphibious invasion in their history.

PART 2

CIVIL WAR
1776–1777

7

BRITISH ATTACK

The men placed in charge of the attack were General William Howe and his brother, Admiral Richard Howe. William had already experienced the war, having been sent to Boston to assume command just prior to Bunker Hill, an experience that had chastened him severely. Richard was a naval officer of immense experience and creativity, but from the perspective of the politicians who would be managing him, he was awkward, conceited and happy to bear a grudge. He had a particular distaste for Germain to whom he had not spoken since 1758.[1]

The Howes planned to subdue the rebellion by combining the psychological impact of a massive armada with repeated offers of conciliation. Richard Howe had insisted that they be appointed peace commissioners as well as military leaders as a condition of his accepting command. Their strategy was perfectly encapsulated in the names of the troop transports sent with them from Britain: *Good Intent, Friendship, Amity's Admonition, Father's Good Will* – a classic example of political intent expressed through the maritime sphere. The Howes had personal ties with America, not least because their elder brother, Brigadier-General George Howe, had been killed in the Seven Years' War (1754–63) and was a hero in America, particularly in Massachusetts, which had voted £250 for a monument to his memory to be erected in Westminster Abbey.[2] Their desire to broker a peace is understandable, but they would have done well to read and consider the maritime signals being sent in their direction from the colonies. Names of ships in the service of the state navies included *Oliver Cromwell, Tyrannicide, The*

Rising Empire, Independence, Republic and *Freedom*. By the summer of 1776 the Howes' idea of conciliation was a year out of date, everything having changed after Bunker Hill, particularly since Graves's destruction of the port of Falmouth.

The two ideologies that these ships' names reflected were now incompatible but there was confusion in London. Sandwich offered no clear direction in this period; Germain was against the idea of conciliation in any format; and North had been unhelpful and uncertain about the idea of using the Howes as peace commissioners. But the Howes' standing – as senior and experienced military figures with knowledge of and personal ties to America, as Members of Parliament and leading aristocrats with close ties to the king – was sufficient to see their demands accepted.[3]

The issue of the Howes' role as peace commissioners, moreover, was only one subject of debate. Another had been the question of what type of military force to send to America. North had been very much in favour of a large naval force to bring the rebellion to its knees by effective blockade – essentially having another stab at the Coercive Acts but with an appropriately sized naval force – but Germain and others had favoured the use of the army. It is clear that the decision was influenced by naval considerations. It was felt that the naval option would be too slow and too costly, and – most important of all – that a full-scale naval mobilization would encourage the French and the Spanish to war.[4] This disagreement and uncertainty over the appropriate course of action – negotiated peace versus coercion, army versus navy – was notably different from the general consensus that had led to the imposition of the Coercive Acts. The actual arrival of civil war had divided British opinion in both Parliament and throughout the country, and that division was to have a significant impact on the war's future.[5]

*   *   *

The strike would fall on New York. There was adequate anchoring ground in Raritan Bay and plenty of beach space on Staten

Island and Long Island to land and protect an army. Crucially, to hold New York was also to secure access to the Hudson and thus to that key maritime route which ran from New York to Canada via Lakes George and Champlain. This route could therefore be used to sever New England, always considered by the British to be the beating heart of the rebellion, from the rest of the rebellious colonies. It was believed that the enemy army, if not destroyed in the first attack on New York, could be trapped in New England and dealt with by the British at their leisure. To take New York was therefore to crack the shell of the rebellion.

It was one of the largest and most complex military operations ever undertaken by Britain and the largest force ever sent across the Atlantic. A total of 32,000 troops were escorted by seventy-three warships – half of the entire Royal Navy in 1776 – together with another vast fleet of transports and supply ships embarking from various points in Canada, Germany, Ireland and England – so many that nearly the entire British merchant fleet was sucked into service.[6] The scale of what was being attempted shocked the French who were observing keenly. A leading French diplomat in London wrote to Paris:

> When we recall that the original purpose behind this enormous expense was to impose a small tax on America, we seem to see an Alchemist of a new kind throwing into his crucible everything that is made of gold and precious metals in order to turn it into lead: this ruinous and mad war is the reverse of the Philosopher's stone for England.[7]

Husbands said goodbye to wives and fathers to children. Many were to experience British sea power for the first time, some were to cross the Atlantic for the first time, and many more were to experience the *sea* for the first time. This was always the case in major eighteenth-century wars, but it was particularly so in this war because a significant number of soldiers sent to America in British ships were German mercenaries bred for combat on the plains and in the mountains of northern Europe. In fact, nearly a third of all troops sent to

America during the war – around 29,000 – were German mercenaries of one sort or another, collectively known as 'Hessians' because the majority came from Hesse-Kassel.[8]

One Hessian soldier was heartbroken by the thought of travelling so far. 'Dearest Wife, never have I suffered more than upon my departure this morning. My heart was broken; and could I have gone back who knows what I might have done ... Guard most preciously the dear ones. I love them most fondly.'[9] Those whose journeys paused in Plymouth were frankly astonished by the scale of the British naval infrastructure there: 'the admirable and costly docks, the harbour fortifications, the citadel, the ordnance and supply depots – where much abundance prevails – and the hospitals for seamen and soldiers; all of which reflected the greatness and wealth of England.'[10] On the subsequent voyage the Hessians seem to have suffered horrifically from seasickness, being 'not as good sailors as those from the other European nations',[11] and they filled their diaries with wide-eyed panic at Atlantic storms and revulsion at life at sea: 'the pox above-board, the plague between decks, hell in the forecastle, the devil at the helm', wrote one.[12] Finally, and to their intense relief, they reached America. 'Land! Land!' wrote a soldier of their elite infantry regiment, the Jägers, 'Only a person who has rediscovered land after a strange sea voyage can imagine the joy we felt.'[13] The hardened British sailors who transported them would have wallowed in this Hessian misery.

Commodore William Hotham was given command of the armada, nearly 100 strong, and the burden almost killed him. He wrote: 'You may well think that the last fourteen weeks of my life have been made up of trouble, vexations, and anxiety; indeed to such a degree that I hope I shall never again experience the like.' Subsequently, he attributed the success of such a large undertaking to luck – more 'than one can expect should fall to the share of most men'. It is unclear if he was being modest or just honest, but probably a little bit of both. It is far more certain that Admiral Howe was absolutely delighted with him.[14]

The first stage in this 'ruinous and mad war' was the occupation of Staten Island by General Howe and Admiral Shuldham. For the waiting Americans, the tension was unbearable. They barely slept, 'ready to turn out at a minute's notice'.[15] Lookouts strained their eyes waiting for the leviathan of British sea power to emerge from the deep and heave itself above the eastern horizon. When it did, even though this was only the vanguard of the main British force, the Americans were awestruck. Private Daniel McCurtin wrote: 'when, in about ten minutes, the whole bay was full of shipping ... I declare that I thought all London was afloat.'[16] The British knew that the Americans were stunned: 'The rebels (as we perceived by the Glasses) flocked out of their lurking Holes to see a Picture, by no means agreeable to them.'[17]

The arrival of Admiral Richard Howe with the rest of the force a fortnight later was not without mishap, his flagship striking the ground several times before anchoring, but there was absolutely no sense of threat from the Americans, only the deafening cheers of the British troops and sailors. There was something of a carnival atmosphere, not unlike a huge summer fete. Howe's captain, Henry Duncan, thought it 'a most delightful spot'.[18] The ships were anchored close to shore where curious Americans could observe them in some detail. So close to shore, such a large fleet created an optical illusion because one had no choice but to see the ships themselves rather than the gaps between them: one tended to see nothing but the space that they occupied rather than the space that they did not. A mass of timber reached high into the sky and deep in perspective towards the horizon. Now only ever visible in two-dimensional, meaningless shapes on contemporary charts and plans, the sheer volume of three-dimensional space that a fleet of this size would occupy is difficult to conceive, and in that ignorance we share an experience with the majority of colonial Americans. It is so easy to think of this period as the 'age of sail', with the implication of familiarity that goes with it, but large fleets were utterly alien to most observers. Indeed, only those civilians who lived in close proximity to

large naval bases would ever have seen such a gathering of warships and transports so close to shore. The scene was captured
by a British engineer, Archibald Robertson [*see fig. 1*].

*   *   *

Often the impact of British sea power ashore is considered
only in terms of the soldiers that the ships carried in their
damp bellies, but the mere presence of the British fleet off
Staten Island immediately altered the nature of the war for
those living in the city and transformed the lives of thousands
of New Yorkers. Anyone who lived in New York knew how
vulnerable they were to attack from the sea. Manhattan was
almost surrounded by water, with the East River on one side
and the Hudson on the other; in fact native Indians knew
it as Manahata, meaning 'the place encircled by many swift
tides and joyous sparkling waters'. British warships anchored
offshore would be able to target almost any part of the city.
The American general in charge of the defence, Nathanael
Greene, knew this well. In his words you can almost feel him
shiver. 'What to do with the city, I own, puzzles me', he wrote.
'It is so encircled with deep, navigable water that whoever
commands the sea must command the town.'[19]

Even when Shuldham's small vanguard of forty ships was
spotted on 29 June, New York erupted into chaos. Alarm guns
were fired and bells were rung, triggering a mass exodus –
'the sick, the aged, women and children, half naked, were
seen going they know not where.'[20] They certainly ended up
leaving New York. By the time the British finally attacked, the
population of New York had been reduced to 5,000. A matter
of weeks before it was 27,000.[21] 'My God, may I never experience the like feeling again', wrote Henry Knox to his brother
before disguising his fear by shouting at his wife Lucy, telling
her off for not having left before.[22]

The presence of the Royal Navy also triggered violence by
awakening dormant pro-British supporters. New York was
a hotbed of Tories who were well aware that a strike would
shortly fall on New York and who were waiting for the

moment that British masts were visible to act. As soon as they crossed the horizon, the tension erupted. In marked contrast to the runaway slaves who had fled to Dunmore and Clinton, many of those willing to join, or at least help, the British at New York were influential and wealthy, and immediately sent supplies and intelligence to the British fleet. There were even well-founded claims that, as soon as British warships anchored in the harbour, the governor, William Tryon, would distribute pardons to defectors. A group of Tories planned to use the arrival of the fleet as the moment to spike rebel guns in return for pardons and bonuses. The presence of the navy even sparked dastardly plots to kidnap and poison Washington – plots in which the Royal Navy played a key part.[23]

The rebel response to this loyalist muscle-flexing was sudden and savage, the response coloured and determined by the presence, rather than the action, of the British fleet. American boats patrolled the coast around Manhattan and Long Island to prevent Tories from getting across to the British ships. Tories suspected of spying, aiding the British or somehow threatening the Americans were caught and tortured. Washington had one suspected traitor hanged in public as a warning and 20,000 people witnessed it – almost all of New York.[24]

The presence of the British fleet brought with it a sense of apocalypse. 'The time is now near at hand which must probably determine whether Americans are to be free men or slaves ... the fate of unborn millions will now depend, under God, on the courage ... of this army', wrote Washington.[25] The natural fear caused by the proximity of British warships was then exacerbated by a raid up the Hudson, in which a small British squadron of three ships was taken straight through defences sunk in the river and then straight past their shore batteries – a moment full of significance and drama captured by Dominic Serres the Elder in a stunning image that is based on eyewitness sketches [see fig. 2].

The squadron then bombarded the city, and for the first time British cannon-balls flew through New York and Greenwich

Village, where three entered 'Captain Clarke's House' and one lodged itself in the headboard of Miss Clarke's bed.[26] The 'shrieks and cries' of the women and children were, according to Washington, 'truly distressing and I fear will have an unhappy effect on the ears and minds of our young and inexperienced soldiery'.[27] Much to Washington's irritation, many of the American soldiers just stood and gawped, and only half of the artillerists even manned their guns, being utterly transfixed by this new and shocking spectacle of British sea power. Washington condemned the 'weak curiosity' that 'makes a man look mean and contemptible',[28] a judgement that seems a little unfair. It was a sight that would have stopped people in their tracks, eyes on stalks, mouths chattering: British sea power had a physical effect on those who witnessed it. We also know that the British did receive some casualties: one of the ships' captains, Hyde Parker, reported a total of nine killed and eighteen wounded aboard the three ships.[29]

The British knew that they had filled the Americans with 'astonishment',[30] and Howe greatly appreciated the role that captains Hyde Parker and James Wallace, the ranking officers, had played in expanding the aura that already surrounded British sea power with their raid. He immediately recommended them both for knighthoods.[31]

All the while, further reinforcements and refugees joined the British fleet at New York, but the build-up in strength was not as flawless as the evident size of the fleet, the psychological impact of its presence and the successful raid up the Hudson would suggest. Seasick and weak soldiers arrived on over-packed transports from England, and barely more than half of the 950 horses survived the voyage; Clinton and Parker's force returned, damaged and disgraced from Charleston; and the shattered and disease-ridden remnants of Dunmore's floating town, whose collapse in strength had forced him to conduct a 'predatory war' simply to survive, skulked in from Virginia.[32]

If one adjusts the lens through which the force at New York is viewed, these three new additions were a hideous trinity of British sea power, a powerful corrective to the display of strength already achieved. Such was the paradoxical nature of British sea power in this period and in this location: awesome and feeble, inspiring and lacklustre, dominant and self-destructive. The Howes made final offerings of peace, but in the shadow of their strong and weak armada, they were rejected. Too much water had already passed under the bridge. In a last-ditch meeting between Admiral Howe and an American delegation sent by Congress, Benjamin Franklin, with a 'sneering laugh', made it clear that it was too late for conciliation. He argued that, because 'Forces had been sent out and Towns destroyed',* the Americans 'could not expect happiness now under the <u>Domination </u>of Great Britain'. For his part, Howe was unable to offer anything in return if the rebels 'would not give up the system of Independency'.[33] And so it came to an attack.

*   *   *

The problem that now faced the British was this: how, exactly, would they get 35,000 troops, their heavy guns, their horses, and their baggage, tents and countless tons of apparel ashore, to a location from which they could threaten New York? It is worth pausing to consider the logistical challenge in some detail because, in the shadow of the failed Charleston expedition, it leads us to a better understanding of the grand capability of British amphibious sea power in the 1770s, if the plan was well considered. Indeed, by the 1770s the British had developed sophisticated doctrine and practices for joint operations that would influence the war from its beginning to its end.[34]

The landing was planned for Long Island, a short hop across the bay from Staten Island, where most of the troops were camped. The advantage of seizing Long Island lay in the high

---

* Franklin is probably referring to the naval bombardment of Falmouth in the aftermath of Bunker Hill in October 1775, authorized by Samuel Graves, and the destruction of Norfolk in January 1776 by Dunmore.

ground on its north-western shore overlooking Manhattan, together with the low-lying, gently sloping, sandy beaches on its southern shore, which so lent themselves to an amphibious landing.

The British had one crucial factor in their favour: this was not an amphibious operation from ships to shore, but one conducted from shore to shore. The troops, therefore, were able to organize themselves into their divisions on the Staten Island beach from where they could easily embark. This was always an enormous advantage as it allowed the horses, which hate being at sea, crucial time to recover ashore.[35] Forming up in this way at sea was also time-consuming and dangerous.

Cavalrymen were all required to be strong swimmers and horses swim naturally and well, but they cannot cope with distances of much more than a mile. The distance between Staten Island and Gravesend Bay, the chosen landing spot, was at least one mile and might be as many as three, depending on the embarkation points and route. It is likely, therefore, that the horses were taken in boats across to Gravesend Bay, possibly in craft specially designed with stalls. The troops were certainly loaded into specially designed landing craft known as 'flatboats'; flat-bottomed, they were easy and safe to beach and disembark. The sailors manned the oars and the soldiers sat in rows along the inside facing each other. The boats had a removable tiller and rudder and were cleverly constructed in a way that allowed them to be easily stacked on the decks of transports.

The next challenge was to get the army ashore in the right order and formation. An army that is not in battle formation is useless. The soldiers do not know where to go and the officers do not know who to command or where to look for their own orders. It was essential that the troops were landed in a way that allowed them to perceive themselves as an army in the midst of an operation, rather than as an army simply moving from A to B. The solution was to travel in battle formation. The loaded flatboats would rendezvous offshore and form up. Each boat would be distinguished by a number painted on its bow and by a flag denoting the division it carried. Then, with warships ahead, astern and abeam, orchestrated by a special signalling system that allowed the ships and the flatboats to work in harmony, the fleet would head for shore, in utter silence and with no firing from the flatboats.[36]

Sometimes a separate naval squadron would bombard the enemy defences to provide as much time and space as possible for the troops to land. The boats would be run ashore and a grapnel thrown over the side to act as a kedge, while sailors leapt into the surf to hold the bows steady. The soldiers clambered over the side, into the surf, and then waded ashore. The first to land would be the specialized light infantry – grenadiers or Hessian Jägers. Highly mobile, experienced and aggressive, they would secure the landing site and enable the main body of infantry to land in waves.

The flatboats would then return to their source of men to reload and then make the journey all over again. There were usually several journeys: the flatboats that the British had were excellent but there were never enough.

Heavy guns were also transported in specially designed landing craft with a bow that could be lowered, to allow the guns to be run straight onto the beach on their carriages – an eighteenth-century equivalent of the more familiar landing craft of the Second World War.[37] The soldiers all carried two or three days' worth of rations, depending on the scale of the operation envisaged and the distance that they would travel from shore. They were also provided with a canteen full of a mixture of rum and water, sixty rounds of ammunition and two flints. Then, while the army fought its way ahead, the navy would tirelessly secure its lines of supply: by no means was their job done once the soldiers had been landed.[38]

* * *

The American army, which had been transported efficiently from Boston to New York by sea[39] – a little-known achievement of American Sea power in this period – had then made certain that 'every kind of watercraft … that could be kept afloat'[40] was secured for their own use and denied to the British, but they did nothing to prevent the actual landing when it came on 22 August. The British had absolute command of the local waters, and the Americans a poor intelligence network. Washington therefore had no idea exactly where the British would strike. He admitted that the potential of British sea power had left him 'in a state of constant perplexity',[41] and as a direct result the American forces were divided when the strike finally fell as a full-blooded, single and focused assault on Long Island.

With HMS *Rainbow* anchored at an angle where she could cover the landing site and protect the seventy-five flatboats, eleven bateaux and two galleys waiting quietly in formation under the command of William Hotham, at 8.30 a.m. the signal was raised for the boats to go ashore at Gravesend Bay. The operation was mightily impressive both in its execution and in its impact:

> in ten minutes or thereabout 4,000 men were on the beach, formed, and moved forward ... by 12 o'clock or very soon after, all the troops were on shore, to the number of 15,000, and by three o'clock we had an account of the army being got as far as Flat Bush, six or seven miles from where they landed.[42]

The Hessians formed part of the preliminary invasion force, and so too did the runaway slaves who had joined Clinton's and Dunmore's regiments of black loyalists. Not only were the British invading, but also they were doing so in exactly the way that was certain to enrage the Americans by using foreign mercenaries and by turning their own slaves against them. The experienced British sailors and soldiers were well aware of the mixed nature of the invasion force and celebrated the achievement of their invasion 'effected without the loss of a man, except two or three Hessians, who were killed through their own faults'.[43]

* * *

The subsequent battle for Long Island was more of a rout than a pitched battle, though the Americans retained spirit and pride throughout and always kept an eye out for anti-British propaganda. The British drove the Americans from the field but nothing would drive away the stories of Americans being skewered to trees by Hessian bayonets, being decapitated by Highland broadswords, or being harnessed to British gun-carriages to pull them through the mud for want of horses.[44] The British perspective was a little rosier: 'it was impossible for troops to behave better than every corps of ours did; the Hessians behaved exceedingly well.'[45]

The victory at Long Island was not what it could have been, however. The Royal Navy had failed to get into the East River and thus outflank the retreating American army, and once the main battle of Long Island had been fought and won, the British army had failed to press home its advantage. Even while this was happening, the trapped American army was growing because Washington made the mistake of sending reinforcements into a hopeless position. The result was that the American army teetered on the Brooklyn shore with the mile-wide and fast-flowing East River behind it, while the British dug in on Long Island. American defeat was a certainty if the armies remained like this. Washington understood what had to be done, and for the first time in the New York campaign, he acted decisively and with great clarity. To avoid capture, perhaps even to ensure the survival of the revolution, he would have to evacuate his army across the East River before the British army attacked his lines or the Royal Navy blocked his escape.

*　*　*

Such a maritime evacuation of an army and its equip-ment is one of the most difficult of all military operations and Washington oversaw the operation personally, scarcely dismounting for forty-eight hours. The evacuation began under cover of darkness and in enforced silence. Wagon-wheels were muffled; no one was even allowed to cough. The troops were ordered to move to the shore, while every available boat 'from Hellgate on the [Long Island] Sound to Spuyten Duyvil Creek [on the Hudson]' was taken to the Brooklyn shore by the many men in Washington's army who could row and sail. We know next to nothing about the type of craft used, but it is likely they would have included flat-bottomed vessels for loading cannon and horses.[46] This maritime operation was led by John Glover's regiment of mariners from Marblehead, assisted by Israel Hutchinson's regiment of fishermen from Salem, Lynn and Danvers. Both Glover and Hutchinson were experienced mariners and were well liked. Everything about the 'soldiers' in their ranks spoke of the sea. They wore blue jackets, white caps and tarred trousers – the uniform of fishermen from the Grand Banks, where the harshness of life at sea had forged them into units who knew how to overcome hardship and also the value of discipline and teamwork.[47]

The American position was so precarious that, even for these sailors, pretence was maintained – these boats, it was claimed, were to be used to ferry the injured to Manhattan and to ship over reinforcements to fight the British. Fires in the American camps, meanwhile, were kept burning to deceive the British lookouts. When dawn came, however, the operation was still incomplete, even though some boats had made the crossing as many as twelve times, each time with water lapping over the gunwales from overloading. Panic set in. At one stage too many men boarded a boat that threatened to capsize, and Washington himself picked up a huge stone and threatened to 'sink [the boat] to hell' unless they all got out, which they did.[48] With dawn, however, came a fog as dense as cotton wool that cloaked the last few boats as they rowed in across to the safety of Manhattan.

A similar but little-known operation evacuated the American troops on Governor's Island.[49] In total, 9,500 American soldiers and their stores, horses and all but five of their cannon were evacuated in a single night and not a life was lost. The battle for Long Island had been a disaster for the Americans, but the evacuation was a triumph that must rightly take its place among other contemporary examples of maritime evacuations in close proximity to the enemy.* It confirmed in the minds of his soldiers, and the politicians who watched on from Philadelphia, that Washington was, indeed, the right man for the job and that the American army, if it put its mind to it, could achieve impressive operational feats. Thus from defeat on Long Island the Americans drew strength.

It was certainly a failure by the Royal Navy. They had tried to prevent an American maritime escape by sailing up the East River, but they had been baffled by contrary winds and foul weather. Indeed, five different ships on five separate occasions had tried and failed to get into the East River to surround the American army.[50] It was certainly an opportunity to crush the rebels that went begging. Even to get into the East River in good numbers, a small lookout boat, stationed in the East River, could have passed word to the army that the Americans were escaping. It seems that the British never considered that the Americans would be capable of moving so many men over such a long distance in such a short time. The army had underestimated the tenacity and fighting spirit of the rebels at Bunker Hill and the navy had repeated the mistake at Charleston. Here – and not for the last time – the navy underestimated their logistical capability and maritime skill.

*   *   *

Nearly three weeks went by before the British were ready for the next assault, a period remarkable for a single event which passed by with barely a raised eyebrow. On 6 September the *Turtle*, a craft built by David Bushnell of Connecticut which was able to travel underwater, made its maiden hostile voyage. The *Turtle* is now considered an important precursor of military submarines, but we know very little indeed about it. There are no contemporary illustrations at all – the famous image of the *Turtle* is an exercise in nineteenth-century imagination.[51] This proto-submarine was towed from Manhattan towards the

* For example, Toulon 1793, Puerto Rico 1797, and Corunna and Walcheren 1809.

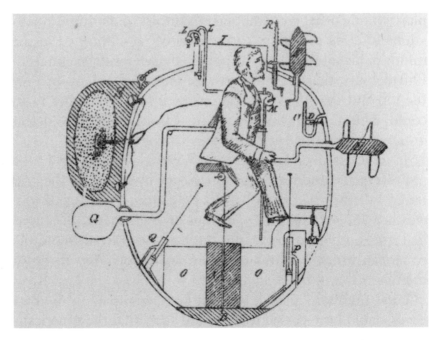

This famous image of the *Turtle* was drawn in 1875 by an American naval lieutenant,
Francis Barber.

anchorage of Admiral Howe's flagship the *Eagle*, where it was
cast adrift. Her operator, Ezra Lee, spent two hours working
across the tide towards the *Eagle*. We know that the *Turtle* was
operated by a system of pedals and cranks to turn the propeller
and pump water from the ballast tank, a process flawed by its
complexity.[52] We also know that Lee's compass was broken.
Working across the rapid tides of the harbour while constantly
having to check location and direction would have rapidly
driven Lee to the point of collapse. Unable to attach the explosive device, crammed with 150 pounds of gunpowder,* to the
Eagle's hull, Lee 'thought the best generalship was to retreat
as fast as I could'. The device later exploded in the East River
'throwing up large bodies of water to an immense height'.[53]
The failed attack on the *Eagle* is the best known of the *Turtle*'s

* An enormous amount. A typical cannon at the time required just four pounds
of powder to be fired. Considering the rarity of powder in the colonies, this suggests
significant investment and belief in Bushnell's invention.

activities, but she also went on to attack, unsuccessfully, the frigates *Phoenix*, *Roebuck* and *Tartar*, which were anchored downstream of Fort Washington prior to running the river defences on 9 October.[54]

Such diversions aside, the British spent these weeks consolidating their control of Long Island and planning for the next assault. This was launched directly into Manhattan at Kip's Bay on 15 September, under cover of a ferocious shore bombardment by five British warships which had anchored unnoticed, in close formation, at night, within fifty yards of a hostile shore – a seriously impressive feat of seamanship. The subsequent bombardment was an impressive feat of gunnery. One sailor claimed that, on one ship alone, they expended 'five thousand three hundred and seventy-six pounds of powder'.[*] The fire of the British ships at Kip's Bay was shocking even to those hardened by war. Ambrose Searle, General Howe's private secretary, exclaimed, 'So terrible and so incessant a roar of guns few even in the army and navy had ever heard before.'[55] A soldier in the American lines later described how 'all of a sudden there came such a peal of thunder from the British shipping that I thought my head would go with the sound'. He then 'made a frog's leap for the ditch and lay as still as I possibly could, and began to consider which part of my carcass would go first'.[56]

Not only did the bombardment hammer the American defences but also it created a giant wall of smoke, behind which came the flatboats, ghosting out of Newtown Creek and down from Turtle Bay. A British witness declared that the 'water covered with boats full of armed men pressing eagerly towards the shore, was certainly one of the grandest and most sublime scenes ever exhibited'.[57] Others noted how it was 'highly dramatic', a 'most striking spectacle' and 'a most magnificent

---

[*] The maths behind this suggests that it is not actually possible. It works out at an average of one round per gun every two minutes, assuming both broadsides were firing. It is unlikely that this could have been achieved either by the crew or without the guns exploding. Many thanks to Dr Gareth Cole for help with this. NDAR VI: 844–6; Laughton, *James Journal*, 31.

sight'.[58] The landing on Long Island was no doubt impressive, but the key difference here was that Manhattan itself was being attacked rather than an isolated stretch of Long Island beach, which meant that many more Americans, both civilians and soldiers, witnessed the event. We know that, as the British landed, the surrounding hills 'were cover'd with spectators'.[59] It is not surprising that Robert Cleveley, a young clerk on the 64-gun *Asia*, which was involved in the action, chose to preserve it in a famous painting, which for years was mistakenly identified as the landing on Long Island [*see fig. 3*]. Historians who were too quick to think of the Long Island landing as the key set piece of this operation are now coming to appreciate just how much Kip's Bay meant both to the British forces who took part and to the many Americans who witnessed it.

The British sailors were rightly proud of their success. As they advanced through the smoke, the German troops sang hymns and the British shouted profanities.[60] Once ashore, the British cut westwards across Manhattan, but waiting for more troops to come ashore and unwilling to extend their lines too far from the sea, they failed to make the connection from shore to shore, thus allowing all the American soldiers to the south of Kip's Bay, at the tip of Manhattan Island, to escape northwards. The British had captured New York but let the American army escape – again.

Soon after the British took control of New York several fires were started deliberately in various locations in Manhattan. Before long nearly a quarter of the entire city was in flames. The flames were clearly visible from the British ships, and Duncan, Howe's captain, took charge, summoning all lieutenants and ordering boats from every ship to assist. 'A great number' of British sailors were soon ashore tackling the blaze, but it had already taken too many large buildings and the wind spread and fanned the flames.[61] In exasperation the British savagely attacked an American found with a burning torch cutting the handles of fire-buckets. A Highlander cut off his torch-bearing hand and the sailors hung him upside down by his heels. Others were caught trying to escape with 'faggots dipp'd in brimstone'. To one British soldier this was nothing but an 'excess of villainy' and clear evidence of the different characters of the two nations.[62]

The Americans were not the only ones capable of wanton destruction. An eyewitness recorded how British soldiers plundered the King's College library, one of only eight key academic centres in the colonies. 'This was done with impunity', wrote one witness, 'and the books publicly hawked about the town for sale by private soldiers, their trulls, and doxeys. I saw an Annual Register neatly bound and lettered, sold for a dram ... I saw in a public house on Long Island nearly 40 books ... under pawn from one dram to three drams each.'[63]

Looted, badly damaged but nonetheless intact, New York became the largest loyalist stronghold in the colonies. Operations continued for a short while. Another landing was made at Throggs Neck, which required some impressive seamanship to navigate through the rocks and whirlpools of Hell Gate, and operations were also conducted further up the Hudson.* When Forts Lee and Washington, guarding opposite banks of the Hudson, were taken, the *Turtle* was discovered and burned.[64] Washington personally witnessed the capture of Fort Washington and openly wept when it fell, with a loss of 146 cannon and more than 2,800 captured men, who could not be saved because the Americans had no boats of any sort on the Hudson to evacuate the men to New Jersey. Two-thirds of those men died in the next eighteen months in British prison ships anchored in Brooklyn's Wallabout Bay.[65]

The rest of Washington's men retreated inland to New Jersey, committed to avoiding any more pitched encounters or occupying any location at all from where the British could use their sea power to advantage: it is no coincidence that, after the disastrous New York campaign, Washington never let his army get anywhere near a significant body of water that the Royal

---

* On 4 December Duncan took forty-three transports through Hell Gate in a single day, an impressive achievement that was rightly praised by Admiral Howe. Laughton, 'Duncan Journals', 137; NDAR VI: 1245–6.

Navy could control. There was also an inherent weakness in that maritime strength, however. The British had executed their landings with skill, but, unwilling to stretch their supply lines too far from the sea and fearful of losing large numbers of troops so far from a source of replenishment, they had been unable to destroy the American army as they had so fervently hoped. As long as the army existed, the rebels had hope. Albeit bedraggled and on the run, Washington still refused to enter into negotiation with the British and no leading rebels defected.* The spirit of revolution thus held.

*   *   *

Although the capture of New York facilitated the British strategy of cutting off New England, it immediately became clear that New York was a poor harbour for a naval force. Sailing into and, more importantly, out of New York in a square-rigged ship was extraordinarily demanding because of the narrowness of the river at New York, the turn at Staten Island, the narrowness of the opening at Sandy Hook, and the sand-bars which jut southwards from Long Island. Only very specific wind and tide conditions made it possible to enter or leave New York with confidence, and in the winter any attempt could be jeopardized by the harbour freezing. Howe's eyes therefore settled on Narragansett Bay in Rhode Island, and in particular the colony's capital with its fine harbour, Newport. With easy access to numerous deep-water anchorages, Rhode Island also had the advantage of being closer to the Gulf Stream than New York, which meant that its waters were much less likely to freeze. It was also the home of an annoying American naval squadron under the command of Esek Hopkins. The British therefore adopted a joint plan. The navy would take control of Newport Harbour and town while the army, under Cornwallis, would drive Washington out of New Jersey.

The Howes sent Clinton and Parker to Newport with 7,000 men in fifty-one transports escorted by fifteen warships. The

---

* Though 5,000 civilian loyalists did. Gruber, 'Lord Howe', 240.

fleet sailing out of Lower New York Bay into the Atlantic Ocean seemed uncommonly beautiful to Frederick Mackenzie, an infantry lieutenant on one of the transports. He wrote on 4 December:

> This Evening, just as it grew dark, our ship being among the headmost in the fleet, we had an opportunity of viewing a most beautiful seapiece from our cabin windows. The fleet was going down the sound before the wind, those ships which sailed the worst having all their sails set, the others such as were necessary to keep them in their respective stations. The sun having set from under some very thick clouds, a streak of reddish colour between those clouds and the horizon, shewed the fleet astern of us, and just discernable. The perspective was very fine: in the farthest distance we could perceive some of the sternmost ships, with their mast heads and top gallant sails, reaching about half way up the red streak: according as the ships were situated nearer to us, less of them appeared; in some only their topsails, in others nothing more than their Courses. But the principal object in the piece was the *Brune* Frigate; this ship had nothing more than her three topsails set, and she was exactly at that point of distance in which no part of her could be seen but her lower masts and rigging, her hull being below the horizon, and her sails above the red streak. What was seen of her had a singular appearance. The stillness of the sea added much to the beauty of the piece, which would have afforded an uncommonly fine subject for a painter.[66]

At Newport the British made another impressive amphibious assault, overseen by Commodores Hotham and Parker, who had been instrumental in the success at New York. This time the invasion was carried out from ships at anchor, a demonstration that the British could invade as easily from ships as they could from shore to shore. There was no resistance.[67] Hopkins and his fleet fled upriver towards Providence. Disappearing inland, their topsails were spotted by lookouts on the leading British ships.[68] This was a significant coup for the British.

The American frigates *Warren* (32 guns) and *Providence* (28) and the armed ship *Columbus* (20) were all now neutralized, extinguishing in the work of a moment months of effort and thousands of dollars.* Hopkins was subsequently relieved of his command.[69]

With the capture of Newport the British secured a fine harbour and also a key commercial centre, which had risen in prominence throughout 1775 as Boston had declined under British army occupation.

*   *   *

Cornwallis, meanwhile, launched himself into New Jersey with an impeccably planned crossing of the Hudson, organized and defended by the Royal Navy, followed by a tricky climb up the mighty New Jersey Palisades [*see fig. 4*]. The British made it to the top, thanks alone to the fact that the Americans had failed to guard the easily defensible summit. The British soldiers then waited for the sailors, who were world leaders in the art of heavy haulage over testing terrain, to bring them their guns. Those sailors pulled eight field guns – four three-pounders, two six-pounders, two howitzers – and all of their ammunition boxes up 300 feet of sheer cliff. It was not the last time that British sailors changed the war by carrying guns across awkward terrain.[70]

And then the chase began. The British constantly expected to catch the Americans, but they refused to stand and fight, and their progress across New Jersey was relentless. At night the British would camp in expectation of battle in the morning, only to find the field deserted again. This was not a mad dash but an inexorable, steady movement, like the tide going out. At Brunswick, Cornwallis narrowly missed Washington crossing the Raritan River – a real opportunity wasted – and he then paused for six days, waiting for William Howe to appear with fresh reinforcements. During those six days, Washington

---

* One of Hopkins's ships, the *Alfred*, captained by a certain John Paul Jones, was at sea and escaped inland incarceration.

made it safely to the Delaware River, where he found the ferry crossings choked with civilians and sick and wounded soldiers fleeing for their lives. One girl thought of the scene as the Day of Judgement.[71]

With such a significant body of water at his back, this could have been a disaster, but the Americans had learned a lesson from the fall of Fort Washington which had been caused by a lack of boats in the Hudson. On or about 1 December 1776 Washington had written ahead to Colonel Richard Humpton, a former British officer, to gather all the boats in the vicinity of Trenton.[72]

The Delaware River lies between Pennsylvania and New Jersey, and Congress's home was in Philadelphia, also on the Delaware. The Pennsylvania Navy, therefore, was one of the most impressive of all the colonies' navies because part of its role was to protect Congress. Its strength lay in the thirteen galleys that patrolled the rivers and estuaries to the north and south of Philadelphia, craft that were useless in any kind of open sea but effective in rivers. With a keel of around fifty feet and a beam of around thirteen feet, they were relatively small if compared with other colonies' galleys, but they were ideally adapted to their location. They were rowed by twenty double-banked oars but were also equipped with two removable masts rigged with lateen sails. Designed to be highly manoeuvrable, they could overcome the frequent natural river obstructions and obstacles that littered the Delaware. They also had a very shallow draft and were double-ended, so they could be landed and relaunched easily and safely. Heavily armed with a single, heavy cannon in the bow and numerous swivel guns amidships and aft, the crews were also armed to the teeth with pikes, cutlasses and muskets. Philadelphia shipwrights were renowned for their skill and these galleys were fine craft. Shortly after they were built, Maryland, New Jersey and Connecticut had sent representatives to observe them.[73]

Nine of the thirteen galleys were dispatched to meet Washington at Trenton, along with all the river craft they could find forty miles in either direction.[74] Every boat that they did not take they destroyed, an operation so effective that, when Tory Joseph Galloway later scoured the surrounding country for watercraft, all he could find was one scow, four bateaux and two boats on a millpond.[75]

Washington then crossed the Delaware from east to west, from danger to safety, in yet another amphibious operation of staggering scale, performed under the greatest of pressure, mostly at night. They lit huge bonfires on either shore to light the way. Dancing shadows that played on the screaming horses and bellowing men 'made it rather the appearance of Hell than any earthly scene'.[76] Another described it as a 'grand but dreadful sight'.[77] A group of lightning-fast Jägers rampaging ahead of the British army reached the river on the night of 8 December. The transportation of the American army across the Delaware had taken every available boat three full days of constant crossing, and the Jägers witnessed the last American boats leaving the shore when only 300 paces away.[78]

While the British slowly advanced towards the river, the American army occupied the western bank and the Pennsylvania galleys conducted regular patrols from Bordentown, five miles or so south of Trenton, right down to the northern limits of Philadelphia. They reported on enemy movements and guarded against Tories and spies crossing the river to get to the British. Their crews also destroyed bridges that crossed the New Jersey creeks and bombarded any riverside towns seen to harbour enemy troops. Conditions on the galleys were ghastly. On 17 December the galley *Effingham* had no more than three blankets and three rugs for twenty-eight men. Manning the vessels was also difficult, and there is some suggestion – though with more than a whiff of propaganda about it – that captured Tories were impressed as oarsmen. Nonetheless, it was clear that the Pennsylvania Navy posed a serious challenge to the advancing British.[79]

Just as the British had controlled the waters around New York, so did the Americans now control the upper Delaware. The British arrived at Trenton, where they could, in theory, have used the '48,000 feet of boards'[80] available there to build river-barges to boost the number of pontoon boats on wagons that were following the British army. The British certainly had the equipment and experience to hand to build a bridge of pontoon boats across the river,* but any such British crossing would have been performed under the guns of Knox's artillery on the opposite shore and those of the fearsome Pennsylvania galleys. The Pennsylvania Navy thus altered the war simply by existing, the first significant occasion that the war was affected by an American 'fleet in being'.[81]

To undertake such a crossing under fire was unthinkable and, even if it had been achieved, would have divided the British army and cut it off from its source of supplies, which stretched all the way back to New York. With the British and Americans thus glowering at each other across the Delaware, General Howe, quite rightly, ordered his army to stand down for the winter, to consolidate the significant ground that he had won in New Jersey. This was good fertile land densely populated with Tories, and it had been deliberately taken to provide a garden for the British army. Howe and Cornwallis headed to New York, and the latter 3,000 miles further, all the way home to his beautiful, beloved and ailing wife. This, it seemed, was a job well done. The British now controlled Staten Island, Long Island, Manhattan, New Jersey, Rhode Island Sound and Narragansett Bay. Far to the north, meanwhile, the British had also begun what then seemed another inexorable conquest.

---

* As they did to cross the Hudson during the Burgoyne campaign in 1777 and also the Arthur Kill, which separates Staten Island from New Jersey, in 1780. For more details, see Lefkowitz, *Long Retreat*, figs. 14 and 15.

8

FRESHWATER FLEETS

In Canada the British troops had been enormously successful, chasing the Americans all the way back to Lake Champlain. Just as in the New York campaign, however, there had been several occasions when the British might have prosecuted their attack with more vigour and forced the Americans into decisive battle.[1] It would not have taken much to capture or destroy them utterly. In tattered clothes starving men were ravaged by smallpox. They died where they fell at the side of trails, on riverbanks, in makeshift tents. The sick were laid on the bare boards of leaky boats, 'drenched in the filthy water of that peculiarly stagnant muddy lake, exposed to the burning sun'.[2] An American army surgeon 'wept till I had no more power to weep' at the sight of America's revolution putrefying in its extremities as if it were suffering from frostbite.[3] Its popular heart was in New England and its political head was in Philadelphia. Insufficient blood could be pumped to Canada.

The Americans headed to Ticonderoga to recover while the British rested in Montreal. They were suffering from a similar, if diluted, problem. To reach Montreal the British soldiers had spent at least three full months in transit at sea, in cramped, unhealthy conditions, where they had been unable to exercise and to drill. British ships had successfully deposited them on the other side of the world, but in doing so had gravely weakened them. If British military might was a musket-ball fired from British shores, at Montreal it could be caught in bare hands as it fell from the sky to the feet of the enemy. This was a recurring problem for the British throughout the war.

Their sea power gave them the reach that they required, but its potency decreased with both distance and time. Nothing could happen in Canada until the troops regained their health and consolidated their position.

All newcomers goggled at the density of the Canadian forests, the extraordinary height of the trees, the endless water-colour skies, but this was just another life-changing experience that their journey had provided. For most the trans-Atlantic journey itself had been life-changing as they had passed through countless different maritime landscapes and tasted the life of the mariner for the first time. They had seen islands of ice 'some three times higher than our main top mast head and formed in the most romantic shapes, appearing like large castles, when the sun shone on them, all on fire'; islands of rock covered in thousands of birds, where 'had we fired a gun … the air would be darkened two or three leagues round'; and fights between 'swordfish' (probably narwhals) and whales whose battles appealed greatly to the martial-minded soldiers on a voyage to war. In the fog-bound creepy waters of the northern banks – a 'kingdom of cod fish' – anything seemed possible and the experienced sailors teased the green soldiers with crazy stories, one of which involved a large fish which could escape capture by 'turn[ing] itself inside out like a pocket'.[4] This sailors' gaze had its particular benefits when viewing the land. One sailor noted that Quebec looked stunning from the sea, a real contrast to how miserable it actually was inside the walls.[5]

The arrival of the fleet at Montreal was another opportunity for the colonials to be wowed with the might of British sea power, just as they had been at New York, though this, perhaps, was even more impressive because Montreal was so far inland and the river so narrow. Even for the British who had spent three months in the fleet, it was a sight 'well worth seeing'.[6] It was, however, impossible for any vessel to go further towards Champlain than Montreal because of the fabled Richelieu Rapids – twelve miles of boiling water on the Richelieu River between Chambly and St

Jean that disgorged from the lake down seventy-five verti-cal feet. The challenge for the British was now somehow to project their sea power beyond these rapids because Quebec would only be secure if Lake Champlain was made secure.

The British were semi-prepared. On his retreat from Montreal in 1775, Guy Carleton had begged for shipwrights and seamen to build a fleet on the lake to 'drive out the rebels',[7] and he had been answered with fourteen prefabri-cated gunboats and ten flat-bottomed boats, which had been transported to Quebec disassembled, in the holds of trans-ports.[8] With them came twenty shipwrights from Glasgow and ten house carpenters from Portsmouth. This is clear evi-dence of the pressure that the British dockyards were already under to provide shipping for the massive New York and Canadian campaigns, and for trade protection elsewhere in the American colonies, the Caribbean and the Channel. They sent house carpenters to Canada because there were simply no British shipwrights spare anywhere in Britain.[9] The few gunboats they brought with them were nothing like enough, however. They would have offered a useful boost to British sea power on the lake as conceived at the start of 1775, but Arnold's early raid and Montgomery's later successful drive to Quebec had entirely destroyed British sea power on Champlain and had provided the Americans with a mini-navy of reasonably powerful ships – an irony that was not lost on the British soldiers.[10]

The British, therefore, not only had to establish a navy on Lake Champlain by getting past the Richelieu Rapids, but they also had to seize control of it from the Americans, and that could not be done by bateaux and flatboats alone. At the very least they needed to get three large ships into the lake, as well as enough boats to carry the army.

The first job was to cut a road through the forest, which was achieved with gangs of Canadians, raised under the aus-pices of an ancient French law designed for large-scale projects of public labour, some of whom, it is claimed, were forced to work in chains.* Even after the road was cut, the effort was still immense. Three schooners – the *Lady Maria*, the *Carlton* and the *Loyal Convert* – and a gondola were selected to be carried overland. Their yards were uncrossed, the masts unstepped and their planking cut down. They were then put on rollers made from huge stripped tree-trunks and dragged past the rapids using cables fixed to windlasses every twenty yards.[11] At first the schooners were found to be too heavy for the soft road and the roller-logs sank. The operation had to be abandoned and then recommenced once the schooners had been further cut down. With the roller-skating ships came a quilted convoy of bateaux, flatboats and longboats, and an endless chain of men struggling with guns, shipbuilding stores and provisions. Among their number were teams of ship carpenters, taken from the British transports and warships at Quebec.[12]

The men knew that they were part of something special. One wrote home with a dash of understated pride: 'What will seem most surprising to you is, that we are now hauling three large armed Vessels over Land, for twelve Miles, to the Lakes.'[13]

These ships would bring British strength on Champlain to a potency similar to the Americans', but parity had never been the traditional British way of warfare at sea. They had won the previous war through examples of military ingenuity, yes, but also through dominance by numbers and might, and Carleton was prepared to leave nothing to chance. His eyes therefore settled on the skeleton of an unfinished 180-ton warship in Quebec, far larger than anything that was being dragged through the woods. This was HMS *Inflexible*, a three-masted sloop, and Carleton saw in her the promise of glory, if only she could be moved.

---

* The accusation of slavery has echoes elsewhere in 1776. There were claims that Pennsylvania Tories were forced to man the oars of rebel galleys on the Delaware and that captured rebel soldiers were harnessed like oxen to British gun-carriages after the battle of Long Island. Bird, *Navies in the Mountains*, 189; Baxter, *British Invasion*, 120.

He turned to the ingenious Lieutenant John Schank, a clever soul renowned for inventing a pulley system that allowed him to raise or lower his cot without actually getting out of it, an achievement for which he was affectionately known as 'old purchase'.[14] Schank labelled the *Inflexible*'s timbers, organized teams to knock them down, floated them upriver to a fleet of thirty waiting boats, and then transported them to Montreal. From there they were carried through the woods to St Jean which, in a matter of weeks, had been reborn, following its American destruction, as a fully functioning British royal dockyard.

There, the three smaller ships and the *Inflexible* were reassembled at immense speed. Lieutenant James Hadden recalled how

> [the *Inflexible*'s] keel was laid the second time on the morning of Sept 2nd 1776, and by sunset on that day, not only was she as far advanced in her new locations as she had been at Quebec, but a considerable quantity of fresh timber was also got out and formed into futtocks, top timbers, beams, planks, &c.; as it was no uncommon thing for trees, growing at dawn of day, to form parts of the ship before night.[15]

Rebuilding the *Inflexible* at all was an impressive achievement, but there is some suggestion that Schank actually lengthened her keel by nine feet to ensure that she drew less water – a spontaneous redesign which would have made the job of rebuilding her all the more complicated and all the more impressive as a result.[16]

Meanwhile another craft – a quite extraordinary craft – was built from scratch. Aptly named the *Thunderer*, she was designed as a massive floating gun-platform. With a flat bottom and a square bow, she was technically a 'radeau', though some ninety feet long, thirty feet wide and armed with fourteen eighteen-pounders and four eight-inch howitzers, she was far larger and far more heavily armed than any radeau anyone had ever seen before.[17]

The Germans gawked at this demonstration of naval power and efficiency.[18] Such a high-pressured operation did not go off without incident, however. On one occasion a tree was felled far too close to the camp and, falling in an unexpected direction, landed on a tent, crushing and killing instantly its three occupants. A telling accident, it suggests how much time pressure these men were under: you only take the closest tree if you are worried about the time or effort wasted in felling a more distant one. Thereafter an order was issued that no trees should be felled within 100 yards of the camp. Carleton retained absolute focus throughout the operation, oozing discipline that one soldier considered a 'rigid strictness ... very unpleasing'.[19] He had left the backdoor to Canada open once already, and this time he was going to close it – and keep it firmly shut.

For fear that the Americans were planning a surprise attack, native Indians, recruited as allies, launched a spying mission to the other end of the lake in their bark canoes. They made use of a technique whereby they could paddle in absolute silence, an exceptionally difficult skill to master.[20] The Americans, however, were totally focused on their own shipbuilding. A lightning attack in bateaux by the British would undoubtedly have destroyed the American shipbuilding programme and finally scattered their sick men, but that was not the only British intent. Yes, they wanted to secure the lake, but they wanted to do so in a way that demonstrated British naval might. In Charles Douglas's words they wanted to achieve 'absolute dominion over Lake Champlain'.[21] It is important to realize that Carleton's strategy revolved around the symbolism of naval majesty as much as it did around the reality of naval control – an echo of the Howes' strategy at New York. Viewed in hindsight, it seems as if the British, both in New York and on Champlain, had been blinded by their own naval capability.

The British shipbuilding was completed in ninety days: an epic feat of naval construction in an unfamiliar environment, all achieved by house carpenters working under the instruction of ships' carpenters, supervised by a tiny team of sixteen Glaswegian shipwrights, one of whom cut himself so badly with an adze on just the third day that he was unable to work.[22] This astonishing achievement has no historical parallel. In July the British had no ships on this land-locked lake, but by the beginning of October they had a ship-rigged sloop, two schooners, a gondola, an enormous radeau – quite probably the largest radeau ever built – twenty gunboats, twenty-four unarmed longboats, twenty-four armed longboats, and 450 bateaux to carry troops and provisions.[23]

The launch of the *Inflexible* was a particularly special occasion. Her keel had been laid on 5 September and she had been launched just twenty-four days later. Five days after that her rigging had been completed. On 10 October she was ready to sail, a masterpiece of management by John Schank, who had constructed a novel 'sled-like machine' on which she slid into the river.[24] Yet again there was a feeling in the British forces of something special having been achieved. 'It certainly was a noble sight to see such a vessel on a fresh water lake in the very heart of the Continent of America & so great a distance from the sea', wrote one soldier.[25] Douglas wrote of his 'unspeakable joy' at seeing the *Inflexible* afloat only twenty-eight days after her keel was laid. He thought that the builders' 'prodigies of labour … almost exceed belief'.[26] The construction was not without mishap. While rigging her, the young Edward Pellew, then a midshipman but a future naval captain of immense fame, was thrown into the lake along with all the rigging. Pellew soon surfaced to everyone's relief and shimmied up the rigging again. This, Pellew's first great escape, was a story that Schank later told his grandchildren: 'He was like a squirrel.'[27]

Manning and arming the fleet was certainly a problem, but the British muddled through by using the resources they had at their disposal at Quebec and Montreal. The soldiers were trained by the sailors to work on this unfamiliar element until they could move their motley fleet together into line ahead or abreast according to signal. When done correctly, this 'had a pretty effect'.[28] They were also trained in the tricky business of embarking and landing with safety and in the even trickier business of attacking and boarding other boats 'should the Rebels be foolish enough to attempt opposition on either Element'.[29] If you do not think this required much training, try standing up in a small boat and then imagine being surrounded by armed men, who are all trying to stand up without getting in the way of the oars or everyone else's swords and muskets. It would require all of your attention to stay on your feet, unharmed by your colleagues, let alone to attack or repel an enemy.

Carleton, a soldier wholly out of his element, made no attempt at command, which he gave to Captain Thomas Pringle, an interesting choice because it was *not* Captain Charles Douglas, the highest-ranking naval officer in the fleet and the man who had overseen its construction. Pringle was undoubtedly competent and went on to have an impressive career, reaching flag rank, but in the autumn of 1776 he was only a captain and a green one at that – he took command before his promotion to captain had even been confirmed. His second-in-command was a lieutenant, James Dacres. And yet this was a major British naval fleet and a key part of the British strategy to subdue the colonies. It was the only means by which Canada could be protected and the only means by which an invasion route to New England could be opened from the north. Guy Carleton was a high-ranking and experienced soldier but he had no maritime experience at all and there was no British naval flag officer of equivalent rank to oversee operations on the lake, to offer naval and maritime advice to Carleton, or to stand up to him in discussion and debate. At New York General William Howe had Admiral Richard Howe as a sounding board, a check and a balance, and the relationship had worked both ways, but here in the wilds of Canada there was nothing like this shared command. In the long term this weakness would have serious consequences.

For now, however, the fleet was raring to go and there is no evidence that it was plagued by any self-doubt. Momentum was clearly with the British both in Canada and elsewhere.

The Howes had consolidated their position in New York, Cornwallis was preparing to chase the Americans out of New Jersey, and Clinton was waiting to strike against Newport. The British strategy of securing Canada and isolating the rebellion in New England was nearly complete. First, however, they had to drive the Americans out of Lake Champlain.

*   *   *

The Americans, meanwhile, had been performing their own version of a shipbuilding miracle at the far southern end of Champlain, at Skenesborough. The largest settlement on the lake, Skenesborough had all the major attributes required to become an ad-hoc shipbuilding centre. Surrounded by good timber and iron ore, it was equipped with two sawmills, a forge and a good launching site, though significant work still had to be done to realize its potential. Just as the British had expended significant effort in turning St Jean into a shipbuilding centre, so did the Americans sweat in and around Skenesborough before they could even begin ship construction. There were also logistical challenges to be met further south to link the Hudson with Lakes George and Champlain more effectively, not least the construction of an adequate road northwards from Fort Edward on the Hudson and clearing an important creek.[30]

In the following four months the Americans built eight 53-foot gondolas,* four 72-foot galleys,† and finished constructing a cutter, the *Lee*. They had harvested oak, spruce and pine from the local forests; recruited sailors, wheelwrights, colliers, sawyers, shingle-makers, miners, rope-makers and iron-workers from New Hampshire, Massachusetts, Connecticut, Rhode Island and even Virginia; lured with the promise of exceptionally high wages shipwrights from Pennsylvania,

---

* Quick and cheap to build they were flat-bottomed and ugly, designed for maximum capacity with minimum draft. Propelled by long sweeps with a single mast amidships.

† The galleys were larger than the gondolas and carried more, lighter ordnance. Round-bottomed, they were rigged with two lateen masts.

Maine, Massachusetts and Connecticut; sourced 500 blocks, miles of rigging and anchors from Albany, Poughkeepsie, Esopus and Schenectady on the Hudson; found guns and ammunition; battled malaria and smallpox; succumbed to indiscipline, corruption and theft; and endured endless logistical and supply problems. Hour-glasses, spy-glasses, speaking trumpets, cutlery, bowls, pistols, cutlasses, fishing nets, 800 pounds of chalk to whiten the ship's rails to allow sailing at night, and of course tons of food and drink all had to come to Skenesborough from elsewhere in the colonies. The means by which they conjured this manpower and these goods to Champlain is a subject worthy of a book of its own.[31]

The American achievement was therefore different from the British, who had been far more prepared for their challenge and could draw men, material and supplies from nearby Montreal, Quebec and the massive British fleet itself. Their achievement was certainly no less impressive and, like the British feat, was brought about by some exceptional men.

Ever since he had been forced to hand over command of the invasion of Canada to Montgomery, Schuyler had remained behind in Ticonderoga overseeing the establishment of supply lines and the flow of craftsmen up to the lake. He had raged against the 'laziness of the scoundrels' and the 'rascality' he had found there,[32] and it is certain that the American army in Canada only avoided self-destruction because of his efforts at Ticonderoga. Montgomery praised his 'diligence and foresight'.[33]

When Major-General John Sullivan assumed command of the Canadian Department,* Schuyler had been careful to impress upon him the value of American naval power on Champlain. Among numerous pearls of wisdom, he wrote: 'By keeping a naval superiority on the lake we shall be able to prevent the enemy from penetrating into the inhabited part of

---

* After the death of Montgomery at the battle of Quebec, command passed in turn to Brigadier-General David Wooster, who was incompetent and was recalled, and thereafter to Major-General John Thomas, who died of smallpox.

these colonies.'[34] Schuyler, in short, had seen what was coming and had done everything he could to prepare for it. Command over American forces at Ticonderoga and on Lake Champlain had, by then, passed into the hands of Horatio Gates, another man of great energy and insight, and the fine work continued. This could easily not have been the case. When Gates assumed command, he was, by his own admission, 'intirely uninform'd as to marine affairs',[35] and naval history is littered with examples of men, inexperienced in the maritime world, who have crumbled in the face of its unexpected eccentricities and unique burdens. One of Gates's most important decisions was to place Benedict Arnold, a maritime man who also knew the geography, in charge of the shipbuilding effort in Skenesborough. He was also well served by Colonel Jeduthan Baldwin, chief engineer at Ticonderoga, who was responsible for rigging and arming the fleet and who lived and breathed his task as the days melted into each other. 'I have my hands & mind constantly employed night & Day except when I am a Sleep & then sometimes I dream',[36] Baldwin wrote in his diary. One can almost see the cloud of anxiety and the mountain of work that cast their shadows over him. Another man utterly absorbed by the task was Captain Richard Varick, Schuyler's secretary. The quantity of correspondence Varick processed in this period is astonishing.[37]

By July 1775 the supply lines to the south were fully open, and there were more than 200 skilled shipwrights in Skenesborough and twenty-five blacksmiths.[38] Valued so highly, they were paid more than any enlisted man or officer in the Continental Navy with the exception of the commander-in-chief, Esek Hopkins.[39] The boats were quickly made, each gondola in no more than a few weeks, but they were also well made, and thanks to the wonders of maritime archaeology and the crystal-clear freshwater of Lake Champlain, which preserves timber as if it were a scientific sample pickled in formaldehyde, you can see one of them today: the gondola *Philadelphia*, on display in the National Museum of American History in Washington DC.

The *Philadelphia* was discovered in 1935 upright, her mast still stepped, and was raised and excavated in a pioneering excavation. It is from a minute examination of the boat itself that we can say with confidence that she was well made. The joints are well crafted, the planks well cut, the fastenings secure. We now excavate ships in a very different way from how we did it in 1935, but even then the salvors were careful enough to save much of the material that survived in and around the boat, including buttons that had come from British uniforms, specifically from soldiers of the 26th Regiment of Foot, whose stores had been captured in Montreal during the American invasion of Canada in 1775.

No doubt the *Philadelphia*'s crew was buoyed by such physical examples of their recent success, for these were cherished treasures that inspired confidence and kindled hope, but they must also have been anxious. At the other end of the lake the British were building a far larger fleet, spearheaded by a three-masted ship and supported by the largest radeau any of them would ever have seen or even believed possible – something out of a nightmare. In fact, if one ignores entirely the other twenty-three armed boats and ships in the British fleet, the firepower of the *Inflexible* and the *Thunderer* alone outgunned the entire American fleet.[40] The Americans knew about this discrepancy. To make matters worse, they were badly under-manned, most of the men had no naval experience at all, and far fewer than they had hoped had an adequate grasp of maritime skills. As soon as the boats were on the water, it became clear that many of those who claimed maritime experience had done so for the extra money and had been creative with the truth.[41]

If it ever came to battle, the Americans would stand no chance and they knew it. Arnold was given specific instructions to avoid an engagement if the British appeared in greater force. 'It is a defensive War we are carrying on', wrote Gates, 'therefore no wanton risque, or unnecessary Display of the Power of the Fleet, is at any Time to influence your Conduct.'[42] Stubborn and proud, Arnold ignored his orders.

Schuyler had devised the idea of building a fleet as a means to delay the British by forcing them into building their own. A calculated challenge to British military and particularly naval ego as well as a problem posed to British military strategy, it had worked very well indeed. Here is another example of a 'fleet in being' affecting the war. Carleton could have saved significant time by building a naval force that was adequate to transport his far superior army down the lake to face any threat posed by the sickly and weak Americans. What he chose to do, however, when faced with an American ship-building programme, was to outbuild the Americans so that he could dominate them utterly with a display of force that would have a psychological as well as a military impact. He could have driven the Americans out with an efficient military strike designed around the intended result; he chose to drive them out with a naval regatta, flags flying, trumpets blaring, a demonstration of imperial might and reach rather than a demonstration of military efficiency. And that decision changed the war.

On 24 September Arnold anchored his little fleet in the lee of Valcour Island, his position well recorded by eyewitnesses [*see fig. 5*]. The British came down the lake in all their pomp, rubbing their hands over the effect that the sight of their fleet would undoubtedly have on the Americans. And they were right. 'The moment a three-masted ship made her appearance, being a phenomenon they never so much as dreamt of,' wrote one witness, '[they] ran into immediate and utter confusion.' This was a British victory 'in working as much as fighting', and they were rightly proud of it.[43]

As expected, the subsequent battle was hopelessly one-sided. The mighty *Thunderer* was unable to force her massive, ugly, blunt hull into the wind and so could not take part in any of the fighting, but she wasn't even needed. All but four of the American force were either captured or destroyed by just a fraction of the British fleet.[44] The young midshipman Edward Pellew made a name for himself, taking command of the *Carleton* when the lieutenant in command of her was injured.* He was mentioned in dispatches and promised a promotion as soon as he reached New York.[45]

In the aftermath of the battle, Carleton decided to halt the British advance because the season was already turning. The British showed their sails at Ticonderoga on 28 October but left just four days later with snow already on the ground.[46] Carleton returned north like a boxer retreating to his corner, leaving Arnold, bloodied but swaying in his. Charles Douglas characteristically became overexcited by the victory and saw in it 'the certain Re-establishment of our Nation's Affairs, + the utter Ruin of the Rebel cause in Canada – I hope soon in all America',[47] but the reality was quite different. The American retention of Ticonderoga was a significant strategic development that could not be so easily overlooked, and, perhaps more importantly, American sailors and troops who had escaped death or capture at Valcour were now free to make an impact elsewhere in the war. Washington certainly needed the men. Chased by Cornwallis out of New Jersey to the far side of the Delaware, he was now ready to strike back, to try something that might shake up the British and perhaps rekindle the fire that warmed American dreams of independence. Washington sent messages north; Arnold sent men south. The focus of the war shifted from north to south. But would the momentum of the war change with it?

* Again, notice how low-ranking the British naval officers are in this fleet. See NMM: BGR/9 for a lieutenant doing a captain's job at Valcour.

9

AMERICAN RIPOSTE

On the west bank of the Delaware things were looking grim for Washington. His army had shrunk by 90 per cent, the soldiers' annual enlistments having ended as November had arrived. The Continental Congress had abandoned Philadelphia for Baltimore and granted Washington the power to direct the war unilaterally. Between 1774 and 1776 the revolution had grown from an idea to a physical reality with military backbone, but unless something was done now, it would become a will-o'-the-wisp again. Washington admitted to his brother that 'the game [was] pretty near up',[1] and he later recalled 'trembling for the fate of America'.[2] At the same time, however, he was a beacon of bristling energy and health in the midst of his shattered army, and he plotted his next move, something that would rouse the spirits of his men. He envisaged an 'important stroke', a 'lucky blow'. He would seize the initiative; set the beat of a new campaign; demonstrate that the revolutionary cause, embodied by his army, was still alive.

The potential to do so clearly existed. British troops on the New Jersey side of the river had been reduced in number for the winter and divided to guard a lengthy frontier. They had no rivercraft. The key to the American chances therefore lay in the bateaux and armed galleys in the Delaware. Given favourable weather and water conditions, they could cross the snaking Delaware at numerous points and at any time they chose. The British had lost the initiative the moment that they forced the Americans back beyond a maritime border that they did not control.

THE PENNSYLVANIA CAMPAIGN

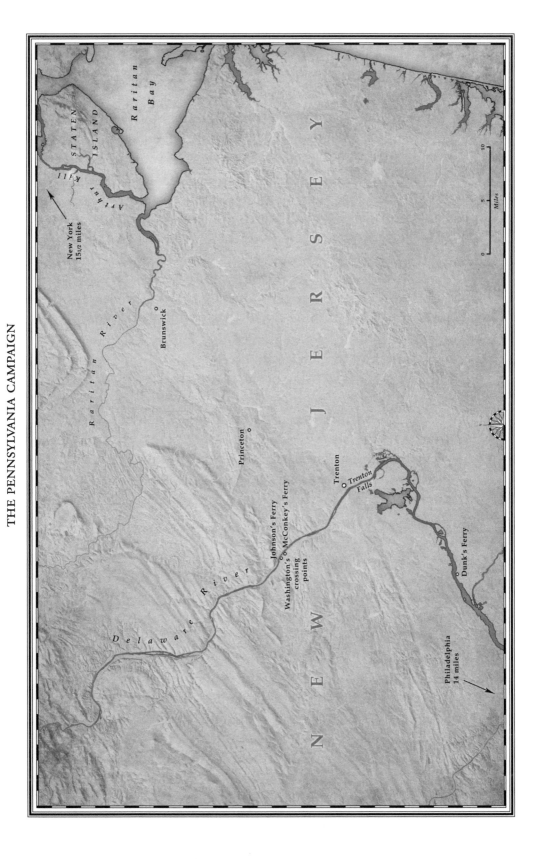

*   *   *

The campaign that followed is one of the most widely known of all military campaigns. In brief, Washington took 2,400 men and their equipment across the Delaware and defeated a weaker Hessian force at Trenton. Eight days later the Americans fought off a vigorous British counter-attack, led by Cornwallis, who had marched 6,000 reinforcements from New York. In the aftermath of that battle, Washington disappeared into the night before attacking the British rearguard at Princeton. Those victories dramatically swung the New Jersey campaign back in favour of the Americans, who eventually drove the British out of New Jersey with the exception of a small bridgehead maintained around Perth Amboy, a little to the south-west of New York.[3]

Washington's crossing of the Delaware is widely recognized as the most decisive single day in the creation of the United States and was immortalized in Emanuel Leutze's iconic 1851 painting *Washington Crossing the Delaware* [*see fig. 6*], an image of maritime struggle which occupies a favoured place in the heart of the American nation. In many ways it is an American parallel to J. M. W. Turner's *The Fighting Temeraire*, which so intrigues the British.[4]

Viewed in real life at the Metropolitan Museum of Art in New York, Leutze's painting is vast, as full of clear and open sky as it is of men struggling to force their boats along their ice-bound path. Washington stands tall, one leg raised on an oarsman's bench. His long, curved cavalry sabre – a ridiculous weapon to wear in the narrow confines of a boat – hangs prominently below the luxurious lining of his cloak. In his right hand, which rests on his knee, he grasps a telescope. He is surrounded by a motley collection of men. At the bow and wielding a boat hook is a frontiersman in a fur hat and buckskin jacket; behind him, fending away a floe with his oar, is a Scottish migrant in his bonnet; to his right, pulling hard on an oar, is a black crewman in a short sailor's jacket; behind Washington is Lieutenant James Monroe, a future president of the United States, in his uniform struggling with the flag; below the flag is a feminine-looking sailor, perhaps a woman in a man's clothing; behind her, cowering near the gunwale, is a man who might be a merchant; and towards the stern are two men who might be farmers, one severely wounded, both wrapped in cloaks with broad-brimmed hats.

So many people on a such a small craft would have put the gunwales under, but by focusing on this single event, Leutze illustrates the revolution as a united struggle for freedom enacted by men and women from a variety of backgrounds, and he captures themes such as endurance, racial and sexual equality, leadership and faith.* For those seeking a deeper understanding of the American counter-attack, however, particularly its maritime dimensions, the painting is more than a little unhelpful.

The first point to make is that the crossing was not a single event. In fact, after his initial retreat across the Delaware to escape Cornwallis, Washington subsequently crossed the Delaware not once but three times: once on the night of 25 December, then back across after the battle of Trenton on the 26th, and then back again into New Jersey on the 29th prior to the battle of Princeton. On each occasion the entire American army, complete with horses and artillery, was loaded onto boats and ferries, transported across a swollen river packed with ice, and then disembarked.

Each operation was a feat of maritime skill in its own right and each was made possible by the presence of sailors in Washington's army, the same men who had helped Washington's army escape from the British army at Brooklyn. The action was led by the Marblehead sailor John Glover, who had personally advised Washington on the maritime logistics of a night crossing. It is nice to know that he did so with the deadpan, dry confidence of a working sailor dealing with a landlubber baulking at a maritime challenge. When the details

---

* Painted at a time when Leutze's own country, Germany, was in the grip of revolution, it was designed to inspire and encourage his country's revolutionaries.

were explained to Glover, he simply said 'not to be troubled about that, as his boys could manage it'.[5] It is understood that Glover's assent led directly to Washington going ahead with the operation.[6]

To assist the Marbleheaders, numerous skilled maritime hands from Philadelphia and the Pennsylvania Navy had joined Washington's force the moment they had reached the Delaware. These men, in the words of one witness, were 'a hardy set of youths belonging to the water service and amply equal to any boating duty'.[7] They carried Washington's army across the Delaware 'ferrying over the last reserved hopes and fortunes of our country, through the booming ice-crags of that stormy Christmas night',[8] and also fought alongside the soldiers at both Trenton and Princeton. 'There, sirs, went fishermen of Marblehead', recalled Henry Knox, 'alike at home upon land or water.'[9]

The first of those crossings – the one that Leutze purportedly depicted in his painting – was achieved in the dead of night and in a snowstorm. Witnesses complained of the snow and sleet driving into their faces from a fierce north-easterly gale. John Greenwood, a fifer in a Massachusetts regiment, simply said that 'it blew a perfect hurricane'.[10] Although the Americans used every boat that they could get their hands on, the majority of the boats were the local 'Durham' boats. High-sided, double-ended, large and roomy, these boats were designed to carry pig iron to and from the Durham ironworks upriver. It is likely that the American soldiers and sailors stood in them to cross the river.

The other main source of local transport was the large ferries that regularly crossed the Delaware at the narrow points that Washington chose as the focus for his counter-attack. Indeed, he chose those points precisely because they were relatively narrow and relatively safe and were well-established ferry crossings. A 'ferry' in this instance was a large flat-bottomed barge, perhaps even secured to stout cables running across the river. Designed to transport large and heavy coaches, they were ideal transport for Washington's horses and artillery. We know that Washington used at least thirteen ferries of this type in his various crossings.[11]

Perhaps Washington himself travelled across in a smaller vessel such as that depicted by Leutze, but, even so, his safety would have been entrusted to a crack crew of experienced Pennsylvania or New England mariners. The American cause may have been precarious as they crossed, but Washington's boat would have been expertly and safely navigated. He was too precious a commodity to be allowed to stand on one leg in a tiny boat during a storm at night.

The waters in Leutze's painting are also too calm for the wind-whipped swollen river that was scarred by sleet and heavy rainfall as if the Delaware itself had fallen to smallpox. The presence of large ice floes was very real, though they would not have appeared as the mini-icebergs of Leutze's painting. Rather, they would have been flat, broken pieces of pancake ice. They were not a trifling nuisance but caused immense problems. At Dunk's Ferry the ice formed into a solid mass jutting out from the east bank, strong enough to hold the weight of a man but not that of a horse or a field gun. There, the attempt to cross was abandoned. Still further downstream, where the tumbling rapids of the river at Trenton Falls met the tidal waters of the Delaware estuary, the floating ice backed up into an ice jam that made any crossing impossible.*

Finally there is the flag in Leutze's painting to consider. Certainly it is likely that flags were transported with the army, though the one in use at that time was not the 1777 'Betsy Ross' version of the Stars and Stripes depicted in the painting, with its stars in a circle, but the Grand Union flag, with thirteen red and white stripes and a British Union flag in the top left quarter next to the flagstaff – the same ensign flown by the Continental Navy. If, as is certainly possible, Washington was taken across in a galley provided by the Pennsylvania Navy, their ensign, had they been bothered to fly it at night,

---

* Even today ice floating down the Delaware can create an ice jam at this location in a matter of hours, lying five feet deep across the entire width of the river.

would have been a green pine tree on a white background with 'Appeal to Heaven' embroidered above.[12]

*   *   *

The first crossing was a mighty struggle. Knox, who knew a thing or two about hard work having dragged the British guns captured at Ticonderoga in 1775 all the way back to Boston, declared the labour 'almost incredible' and only achieved 'with almost infinite difficulty'.[13] One witness claimed that Knox's 'stentorian lungs', which projected his voice through the sleet and wind like cannon-fire, were essential to the entire operation's success.[14] Washington oversaw everything on the bank of the river, wrapped in his cloak. One officer was deeply impressed. 'I have never seen Washington so determined as he is now', he wrote,[15] and one is immediately transported back to the shores of Brooklyn, where Washington oversaw that evacuation with such intense focus. The formidable maritime challenge immediately derailed Washington's plans for a pre-dawn raid and the first contact did not occur until 8.00 a.m. So audacious was his move, however, that surprise was complete. The Hessians in Trenton were routed.

Impressive enough; consider now the challenge of the second crossing. Glover's mariners and the men from the Pennsylvania Navy, already exhausted, now had to ferry back across the river an army crippled by battle weariness and enemy bullets, and burdened with 896 prisoners and captured supplies. They achieved it by noon. The journey was made all the more treacherous by the fact that many of the American soldiers had plundered the Hessians' rum supply; it is no coincidence that more men fell in on the way back across the Delaware than on the way over. One American soldier guarding the Hessians remembered how they stood knee-deep in icy water 'so ... that their underjaws quivered like an aspen leaf'. Another complained of the rain, sleet and ice, which made this return journey so tough.[16]

On 29 December the third actual crossing of the river, but the second time that Washington crossed from west to east, was by far the largest logistical feat.* Eight separate crossing points were used and Knox, assisted by John Glover, shipped forty cannon and their associated carriages and ammunition boxes – that is well over 800 tons of artillery – across to the eastern shore, along with all their associated horses. This was a highly significant quantity of artillery because, in the context of eighteenth-century warfare, it represented an enormously high proportion of guns to men.† This in turn mattered because of the poor weather: muskets did not work if priming pans got wet, but cannon could be used in rain or snow.[17]

This crossing was also threatened by significant river ice, perhaps even worse than that which they had encountered on Christmas Eve. We know that the Delaware had actually frozen right across on the night of the 28th. Regardless of what happened next, the logistical feat itself would have left a deep impression on the American soldiers. This was the action of a serious, professional army. It is interesting that few accounts survive for this final crossing. By now, it seems, Washington's men were so fed up with going backwards and forwards over the Delaware that the novelty of the labour had worn off; but as one soldier remembered, 'owing to the impossibility of being in a worse condition than their present one, the men always liked to be kept moving in the expectation of better-ing themselves.'[18] Yet again they tasted success, this time at Princeton on 3 January, where they repulsed a vigorous attack from Cornwallis before counter-attacking brilliantly.

*   *   *

The impact of these crossings shook the New Jersey ground. Nathanael Greene, one of Washington's four principal gener-als, estimated that the Americans captured or killed up to 3,000 enemy soldiers in only two weeks.[19] In a stroke, the

---

* If one considers the retreat from Cornwallis on 7 December as the first cross-ing, this was in fact the fourth; the second and the third being the famous attack and retreat of 25 and 26 December.

† The expected proportion of guns to men in traditional European armies was around two or three per 1,000 men. Callahan, 'Henry Knox', 246.

apparently unstoppable momentum of British land forces had been halted. Washington's clarity of thought and leadership rescued his reputation, which had begun to show significant cracks after his dithering and tactical naivety in New York. The American cause itself, ideologically strong though physically weak before Trenton, was given a major boost and the British began to see the war in a new light.

Reports of the action caused consternation in London. At first George III's court denied it had even happened and Lord North tried to suppress the news.[20] The subsequent British withdrawal from New Jersey, intended as a market garden for the British army in New York, meant that no solution to the army's supply problem could be quickly found in America. General William Howe sent a hang-dog letter to the Treasury, explaining that 'all supplies must continue to be sent from hence [Britain] & no certain dependence had of obtaining them in America'.[21] The impact of crossing the Delaware was therefore felt thousands of miles away in the mid-Atlantic, where it kept unwanted pressure on British maritime supply lines and created further opportunities for American naval vessels and privateers. It also placed an added strategic burden on the Royal Navy on the eastern seaboard of America because the British army was clearly vulnerable if stretched too far from the sea, as it had been in New Jersey.

And all the while the French looked on, bathing themselves in the warm light of British defeat.

*   *   *

The Americans next showed their maritime strength and resourcefulness at Philadelphia. Washington's army had spent the winter of 1776-7 at Morristown, a little to the north and west of New York, while the British planned a major new offensive. They chose not to attack the American army in or near their camp for fear that Washington would lure them into the interior, stretching their supply lines. Instead they chose to rely on what they knew best, on what gave them a marked advantage over their enemy: they chose to rely on sea power.

One could argue that General Howe was blinded by the promise of British sea power as Carleton had been in 1775 during the construction of his unnecessarily large fleet on Lake Champlain. British strategic planning was, in some respects, a victim of British naval success. Howe's decision was influenced by British sea power as a type of security blanket. He wanted a guarantee of success and the navy provided him with one. Howe knew that his brother's ships gave him the opportunity to strike at will with immense strength and surprise. In direct contrast to the unpredictability of army campaigns, as clearly demonstrated by Lexington, Bunker Hill and Trenton, a naval campaign seemed to come with the promise of easy and quick victory. But what should the target be?

Above all, the British now needed to recapture the initiative and what better way to do that than to seize Philadelphia, the political powerbase of the revolution and the largest and most dynamic metropolis in the colonies? [22] Rumours of hordes of loyalists in Pennsylvania just waiting for the opportunity to join the British abounded. Dunmore had raised hundreds of slaves, and in New York hundreds of loyalists had significantly aided the British invasion. There was no reason to doubt the rumours of Pennsylvania Tories queuing up to help. These men would solve the Howes' constant worries over troop and sailor numbers. Thus the British focus fell on Philadelphia. William Howe told Germain of the plan, who, so far distant in London, had little choice but to agree.[23]

* * *

A naval attack on Philadelphia, however, posed a number of problems. Less than 100 miles by land from New York, it is more than double that by sea, and the journey requires a ship to sail on nearly every point of the compass. The ship must head south-west towards Staten Island, south-east into the lower bay, east out past Sandy Hook, south down the Atlantic coast, westwards towards the Delaware, north-west up the estuary, north and then finally north-east to Philadelphia. This mattered because most square-rigged sailing ships, and certainly all heavy and cumbersome troop transports, were unable to make significant headway, and at times any headway at all, in a windward direction. If the weather gods were not in your favour, such a convoluted voyage could be set back months by delays, just waiting for the right wind. Once there, the narrow and shallow Delaware would be far more difficult to attack than the broad and deep-flowing Hudson had been. Following the abject failure of the Hudson River defences, moreover, the Americans had learned valuable lessons, and this time they had the formidable galleys of the Pennsylvania Navy to lead the defence.

All of this created a great deal of uncertainty in the timing of the British operations in Philadelphia, but time was now the one thing that mattered most to the British. As General Howe prepared to strike south with the help of his brother's ships, Burgoyne in the north prepared to lead another invasion, in Carleton's footsteps, down Lake Champlain. The original idea was that Howe would sail north from New York and meet Burgoyne on the Hudson, severing New England. Howe's commitment to a naval attack on Philadelphia thus potentially threatened Burgoyne's success, though Germain had sanctioned Howe's plan, albeit with the rather significant addendum that he expected the Philadelphia campaign to be completed in time for Howe to help Burgoyne.[24]

This was a major misconception in the logistical requirements of the Philadelphia campaign. It would be impossible to achieve both goals in a single campaigning season as Germain expected, and the naval men knew it. By July the majority of General Howe's senior officers had advised him against a move on Philadelphia, but he was unwilling to listen or to change his plan. We now think that this reflected misplaced confidence in Burgoyne and an underestimation of American military capability, rather than the wilful sacrifice of a fellow fighter. Deep in the heart of Howe's planning was a belief that Burgoyne would not actually need his help, a belief shared by Burgoyne himself.[25] It is also certain, however, that numerous flawed assumptions were worsened by an almost total lack of communication between the two men.

*   *   *

The Philadelphia campaign began with the Americans in an ignorant panic. Washington had heard rumours that General Howe was stripping timber from houses in Brunswick, New Jersey, presumably to build soldiers' cots and horses' stables on transports, and it was plain to anyone that there was a 'great stir' among the British shipping at New York.[26] Washington, however, had no idea of Howe's intention. He found it 'impossible to decide with certainty' where they were headed,[27] and was unable 'to form any satisfactory judgment of the real motions and intentions of the enemy'.[28] This was exactly the value of British sea power that Howe was seeking to exploit. Washington gained some comfort from intelligence that the British were recruiting Delaware pilots, but nonetheless, even when the British left Sandy Hook, Washington was left 'in a state of constant perplexity and the most anxious conjecture'. In the same letter to Congress he described 'the amazing advantage the Enemy derive from their ships and the Command of the water'.[29] The day before the British left, Washington still claimed the British intentions were 'puzzling and embarrassing beyond measure' and still believed that a campaign up the Hudson was likely.[30] The Massachusetts Board of War, meanwhile, feared for Boston.[31]

The British voyage started badly and got worse. It took them five full days to get over the bar and into the Atlantic. On 23 July 13,000 troops on 225 ships with 652 women and children on board set sail from New York – another massive movement of bodies by sea.[32] The destination remained secret: the American bewilderment was curiously matched on the British fleet. Some thought they were heading for Virginia.

Almost immediately the ships were beset by calms and south-westerly winds. Most of the horses died in the stifling heat.[33] When they finally arrived at the mouth of the Delaware, General Howe abandoned his plan for a direct maritime assault, his decision influenced by three things: he had received intelligence of impressive river defences; he was wary of the Pennsylvania Navy; and he had received intelligence that Washington was already in position to pounce on a British landing.[34] His unarmed transports needed an isolated and safe location where the men could land unopposed, as they had done so well at New York and Newport the previous year. In hindsight, all of Howe's reasoning can be criticized: the defences were far upstream from where he needed to land; the Pennsylvania galleys were weaker than the navy's convoy escorts; and the intelligence he had received about Washington's location was false.

Awash with these misconceptions, Howe headed even further south, for the mouth of Chesapeake, 120 miles away. This was Philadelphia's backdoor, though it required *another* 160-mile journey up the Chesapeake from its mouth to Head of Elk, an anchorage a short march from Philadelphia. There, the argument went, the troops could be landed 'without any molestation', the horses given time to recover, and the transports anchored 'in perfect security'.[35] Andrew Snape Hamond, the ranking officer of the British squadron at the mouth of the Delaware, was furious, as he believed that all of these requirements could be met in the Delaware as long as they did not venture too far upriver. The decision to commit the fleet to 280 more miles at sea went down very badly indeed in the fleet.[36] When Washington finally guessed Howe's intentions, he considered it a 'very strange' route.[37]* As the weeks went by in London with no news of Howe's progress, a wag published an advertisement in the *St James Chronicle* asking if anyone had seen him. Unsuccessful attempts to find him had

---

* Of the many 'what ifs' that surround the American War, one of the least discussed, but perhaps the most interesting, must surely be the result of a British landing somewhere safe on the Delaware estuary, perhaps at Marcus Hook, fifteen miles or so to the south of Philadelphia. Washington's army would have posed no more of an obstacle than it later did at Brandywine, and the British campaign would have been shortened by several crucial weeks, perhaps even months.

apparently been made in Knightsbridge, on the Serpentine, and in the lost and found office in Holborn.[38]

The journey from Delaware Bay to Head of Elk could, at best, have taken two days; it took two weeks. The rebels lit fires all along the banks of the Chesapeake to signal their approach, and letters detailing the enemy's location flew ahead.[39] Howe's men finally landed at Head of Elk thirty-four days after they had left New York, cloaked in stuffy summer misery – though, once again, rightly proud of their achievement.[40] The higher reaches of the Chesapeake were such a navigational nightmare that they were certain that the Americans would be impressed by the British fleet even being there, let alone by the fact that they had navigated there without a single vessel running aground.[41] The brilliant Andrew Snape Hamond conducted the operation.[42] Some things, however, were disastrous. Most of the horses had died from sunstroke and 'putrid & bilious Fevers'.[43] The sailors had stuffed themselves with the delicious blue Chesapeake crabs, but it had done little to raise their moods and they still chewed over the fact that Howe had chosen a ridiculous route. 'It is a barbarous business and in a barbarous country', wrote one. 'The novelty is worn off and I see no advantages to be reaped from it.'[44]

As had happened at New York, the visibility of British masts in the offing transformed the situation in Philadelphia and it suddenly became a very dangerous place to live if you were a loyalist.[45] Washington attempted to counter the significant psychological burden of the British fleet's presence by marching his 12,000 troops through the city in a carefully stage-managed display of American fortitude and hope, with every soldier turned out as smartly as he could be and with a green sprig (a symbol of victory) in his hat or hair.[46] It did nothing to stem the rising tide of panic, and as the British approached, Philadelphia was evacuated in a similar crazy stampede to that which had happened in New York, with 'wagons rattling, horses galloping, women running, children crying, delegates flying'.[47] Congress fled for safety to Lancaster and then to York, Pennsylvania.[48] Slaves fled their masters, though, with the Delaware blocked up by the Pennsylvania Navy, this was not the same scale of maritime evacuation as had been seen in Virginia.[49] As soon as the British were within spitting distance, the mood dramatically changed and loyalist gangs started roaming the streets performing citizens' arrests.[50] In the British fleet there was a misplaced but intense feeling of anticipation created by the overwhelming strength of British sea power, just as there had been at New York. 'In all probability a day or two will decide the fate of America', wrote one British soldier.[51]

The British took Philadelphia on 26 September after fighting two major battles, at Brandywine and Germantown, but they did not take the Delaware River, a failure that proved immensely significant.[52] With New Jersey in American hands no British force in Philadelphia would be secure until maritime access could be guaranteed up the Delaware. Until then, Howe's army – some 18,000 strong, together with twice as many loyal citizens, refugees and camp followers – was, effectively, trapped.

*   *   *

The day after the British arrival, British artillery forced the American frigate *Delaware* to run aground and surrender in full view of the city,[53] but British ships were unable to make any significant headway against the American defences further downriver.

It is important to realize that the Delaware was, and still is, very unlike the Hudson, which flows slowly and in few, deep, channels. The Delaware, in contrast, was notorious for its shifting sand-bars and numerous channels. These natural obstacles were carefully and cleverly integrated into the American defences, which had benefited from French engineering expertise. Washington himself had taken a personal interest,[54] and this use of French military knowledge and experience was both a major step forward for the American military machine and a significant change in the nature of French aid.

The core of the American river defences consisted of *chevaux*

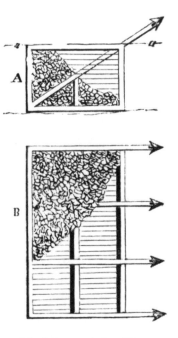

A profile (A) and plan view (B) of *chevaux de frise*. The iron-tipped spikes were about thirty feet long and their construction at Philadelphia supervised by Captain Thomas-Antoine de Mauduit du Plessis, a French engineer.

de frise. Huge timber chests made out of tree-trunks 65 feet long and 2 feet in diameter stacked twelve high to a height of almost 25 feet, they were lined with thick pine planking, filled with stone ballast and chained to each other in staggered lines. One was placed at Billingsport twelve miles below the city and another between Fort Mercer on the New Jersey side and Fort Mifflin, which guarded the Pennsylvania side of the river at the confluence of the Delaware and Schuylkill rivers. Iron-tipped timber stakes projected from the chests at 45 degrees. All navigational markers were removed and a secret channel through the *chevaux* was revealed only to ten pilots, all sworn to secrecy.[55] Those men were also sworn to 'use [their] utmost skill and endeavours' to prevent being captured by the British.[56] The sheer scale of these obstacles was dramatically brought to life in the 1930s when the US Army Corps of Engineers dredged some of their remains out of the Delaware.[57] A section of one of the iron-tipped spikes, 11 feet 2 inches long, was found in the seabed off Fort Mifflin as recently as 2007 and is now preserved in Philadelphia's Independence Seaport Museum.*

Highly mobile rafts, galleys and fireships from the Pennsylvania Navy and Continental Navy, which co-operated well, linked these sunken defences with fortifications ashore.[58] Shoals in the river and swamps on the landward side protected both Forts Mercer and Mifflin. The defences were well chosen, well designed, well located and well manned, and their combined role was well integrated with the army's movements, at Washington's explicit command. 'Let us join our Force and operations both by land and Water in such a manner as will most effectually Work the Ruin of the Common Enemy, without confining ourselves to any particular Department', he wrote.[59] Commodore John Hazlewood commanded the fleet with commitment and skill. The Philadelphia defences, in short, were everything that the Hudson defences had not been in 1776, when the British had so casually and repeatedly swanned up and down the Hudson to inflict terror and rain death on the heads of American soldiers and citizens.

The British were constantly interrupted and harassed in their attempts to clear the river. It took them thirteen days just to get past the first defences.[60] The British captain in charge of the operation, Andrew Snape Hamond, resorted to bribing the American galleys to leave him alone in exchange for the 'King's pardon'.[61] His offer was not taken up. The second major line of defences could not be cleared until Fort Mifflin, guarding them from Mud Island, was reduced. But that, in General Howe's words dripping with understatement and irritation, was a 'tedious operation'.[62] The Americans put up a mighty defence of Fort Mercer at the battle of Red Bank on 22 October, which further demonstrated their mettle and the quality of their river defences. Hazlewood had the pleasure of writing to Washington the following lines: 'early this

* One other is known to exist and is now located at the Camden County Historical Society in New Jersey.

PHILADELPHIA

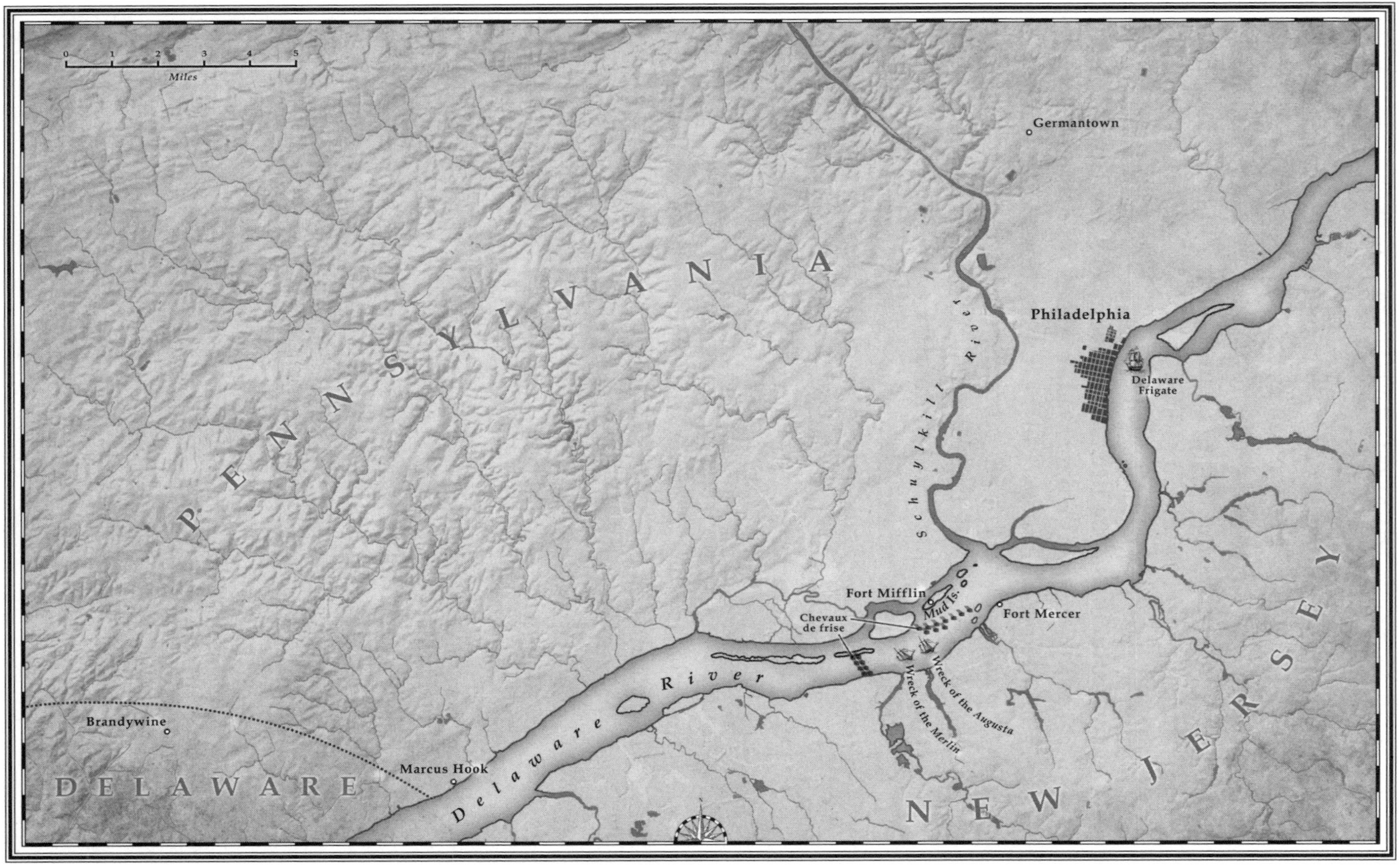

morning we carried all our Galleys to Action, & after a long & heavy firing we drove the enemys Ships down the river.'[63] To cap the American achievement of frustrating the British, the 64-gun British ship *Augusta* had exploded in the thick of the action, providing the Americans with yet another example of British naval bungling which was well used by pamphleteers and cartoonists. The British claimed it was a horrific accident caused by a stray flaming wad, but it is also certain that the guns of Fort Mifflin were firing heated shot and that there was a hailstorm of fire coming from the galleys and floating batteries. Most of the sailors escaped, but forty sick seamen and the chaplain burned to death in the sickbay.[64]

The explosion was heard for miles around. The pamphleteer Thomas Paine, then a volunteer aide to Nathanael Greene, witnessed it on the road between Germantown and Whitemarsh. He wrote: 'We were stunned with a Report as loud as a Peal from a hundred Cannon at once, and turning round I saw a thick smoke rising like a Pillar and spreading from the Top like a Tree.'[65] In Philadelphia the explosion 'felt like an earthquake'.[66]

A moment clearly laden with significance, John Adams believed the defence of the Delaware, encapsulated by the destruction of the *Augusta*, to be the turning point of the war, and his over-optimism was shared.[67] The Pennsylvania Navy was given a vote of thanks from Congress for its part in the action.[68] Even today it remains a powerful symbol of the grit of American rebellion. The *Augusta's* wreck was raised in 1869 and timbers from her hull were used by the Daughters of the American Revolution to clad and furnish the New Jersey Room in their Continental Hall in Washington.[69] Nor was the *Augusta* the only casualty of that day: skewered by one of the *chevaux de frise*, the *Merlin* was abandoned and burned to prevent her from falling into enemy hands.[70] The Americans hungrily fell on the corpses from both vessels, stealing their rings and pulling their gold teeth. There was an enormous amount to loot. Guns, clothing and naval stores were spirited away inland.[71]

Thus Philadelphia fell to the British, but American bite ensured that the river remained in American control, sucked British naval resources into Pennsylvania, and left the British army and loyalists in the city isolated. Of even greater significance, however, was that, far to the north, Burgoyne had also become isolated. The Philadelphia campaign had been delayed, but there was no doubt that the Royal Navy, already regrouping and reinforcing after Red Bank, would eventually triumph in the Delaware and that Howe would be safe. But there was no such confidence regarding Burgoyne.

10

BRITISH SURRENDER

During the winter of 1776 neither the British nor the Americans, once again at either end of Lake Champlain, had been idle. The British took their fleet back to St Jean, where the vessels' masts and rigging were removed. It was so cold that the ice which formed so quickly around their hulls had to be broken every morning to save the British ships from being crushed.[1] The momentum behind British shipbuilding, begun under Carleton in the summer of 1776, was maintained into 1777, though the frenzy of effort that had led to the creation of Carleton's fleet now became more focused.

The challenge now was to build a *really* powerful ship. Yes, the British had built the three-masted sloop *Inflexible* in 1775, which had been far larger than any American ship on the lake, but the story of her success was really one of logistics: of cutting a road through the woods, of dragging the timber and materiel up the Richelieu Rapids, and of building the ship in under thirty days. The British now wanted a still more impressive symbol of their sea power, both in terms of its reality on Lake Champlain, and in terms of the potential of British sea power. A sloop, after all, was only a sloop – an unrated warship – even if its construction had represented a singular feat of logistics and engineering.

The British, therefore, spent the winter of 1776 building a *proper* warship – a 26-gun Sixth Rate frigate nearly twice the size of *Inflexible*. She would be the biggest ship yet built on Lake Champlain, and the biggest ship built on any of the American lakes, ever. She was to be named the *Royal George*, yet another example of significant imagery and symbolism used in the maritime landscape of this war. Not only would she control the lake, but she would also embody British royal authority, might and naval power in the northern colonies.

* * *

The Americans, in direct contrast, had abandoned any attempt to contest naval control of Lake Champlain. All they had left of their navy was a handful of boats, a single sloop, and very few sailors. The gondola *New York*, which had been under-manned with only forty-five men at Valcour, now had a crew of eleven.[2] Nonetheless, the Americans worked extraordinarily hard to defend the route southwards down Champlain at the Ticonderoga narrowing.

The fort's defences were improved and they also fortified the hill directly opposite Ticonderoga, which they christened Mount Independence. Under the guidance of the resource-ful farmer-turned-engineer Colonel Jeduthan Baldwin,[3] they built a boom and a floating bridge 700 feet across the lake, from Mount Independence to Fort Ticonderoga. This, it was hoped, would block the passage of any British ship.

The bridge was anchored to twenty-two massive caissons – timber-lined chests the size of large cars full of stones, similar to those which anchored the Delaware's *chevaux de frise*; these were manhandled into position on the ice before the ice was cut away beneath them, plunging them to the bottom of the lake.* One of the few mentions of the building operations appears in Baldwin's journal on 10 March 1776, just nine days after the work began. It simply, and chillingly, reads: 'the ice began to fail'.[4]

The spaces between the sunken piers were then filled with 'separate floats, each about fifty feet long and twelve wide, strongly fastened together with iron chains and rivets'.[5] A boom and 'double iron' chain was laid alongside the pontoon

---

* The remains of these caissons, together with some of the thousands of artefacts that were thrown or dropped into the lake, are on display at the excellent Lake Champlain Maritime Museum.

bridge. An impressive achievement of maritime engineering, it is visible in several contemporary illustrations,[6] [*see fig. 7*]. Various diary entries record pride in its achievement. 'It does honor to human mind and power,' wrote one, 'it may be compared to the work of Colossus in the fables of the heathen.'[7] Only time, however, would tell if the Americans had expended unimaginable effort wrapping a steel garrotte around the neck of the lake or simply decorating it with a necklace of shells.

They waited for the British, a lull in the storm. They had no blankets, 'nothing but the Heavens to Cover them', but took their pleasure where they could. On one spring evening the soldiers at Ticonderoga sat down to eat a plate of fried fish and roasted pigeon. A certain Lieutenant Childs would not have enjoyed the pigeon because he had shot his left hand off while hunting them.[8]

*   *   *

The man who led the British attack down Champlain in 1777 was Lieutenant-General John Burgoyne. The king and George Germain, who already disliked Carleton, had taken badly the news of Carleton's failure to press his attack after Valcour.[9] Burgoyne, equipped with driving ambition and close to both the king and Germain, made certain that he was on hand to argue his case.[10] He won command of the northern army while Carleton was ordered to resume command at Quebec. The change in command was perceived as more than a little unfair among the British troops, and it was ill judged. Burgoyne, like Carleton, was a soldier rather than a sailor, and yet Carleton had demonstrated so clearly that any operation down the lake was a massively complex naval problem, in terms of both logistics and strategy, and one that required a high-ranking and experienced naval commander to oversee. Burgoyne was a light cavalryman.[11]

The fleet that he came to command was deeply impressive. Behind the new and mighty *Royal George* came the ships built the previous year: the sloop *Inflexible*; the radeau-on-steroids *Thunderer*; various schooners and cutters; and three American prizes seized at Valcour – the *Washington* galley, the cutter *Lee* and the gondola *New Jersey*. There were also forty-four armed gunboats, twenty-three longboats and 260 bateaux. There was so much firepower here that the *Loyal Convert, Washington* and *Lee* were stripped of their guns to make more space for stores, provisions and artillery, and several gunboats that had been sent from England in pieces were left unassembled. The need for seamen was so great that every sailor was sucked inland from the fleet of transports in Quebec, which were abandoned at their moorings, unmanned.[12]

Not only was Burgoyne's fleet bigger than Carleton's had been, but also the men were now experienced in living on these boats and fighting from them. One soldier proudly described his tented area at the stern of his gunboat: 'about 6 feet by 5 ... sufficient to contain a small *Table* & your *Baggage* &c and cou'd be kept constantly covered when not *Rowing* against the *Wind*.' The men had also learned how to create a tent when at anchor, by making two basic A-frames with four oars, joined down the centre by a fifth, over which they draped their sail.[13] These men were adapting to their unique maritime environment. On 13 June, just before they left St Jean and headed south, the 'Standard of England' was hoisted aboard the *Thunderer*, a banner under which to rally and a psychological boost for these British forces in Canada about to re-enter American waters.[14]

Under the command of Skeffington Lutwidge,* the fleet moved systematically down the lake, between seventeen and twenty miles per day. They travelled successively in brigades, the second taking the encampment of the first and so on, always leaving at daybreak. When, finally, the entire army joined together, the effect was astonishing: 'the most complete and splendid regatta you can possibly conceive. A sight so novel and pleasing could not fail of fixing the admiration and attention of every one present.'[15]

---

* Lutwidge had been the captain of HMS *Carcass* for the Arctic voyage of 1773 in which Horatio Nelson had served as a midshipman.

An army of Indians led the fleet in large birch canoes, with twenty or thirty soldiers in each, followed by the main British army in bateaux supported by the gunboats. The *Royal George* and *Inflexible* sailed in the centre of the fleet, towing two huge booms, which could be used to divide the lake to protect British shipping and territory from American raids such as that launched by Arnold in 1775. Generals Burgoyne, Phillips and Riedesel followed in pinnaces, surrounded by a British brigade and a German brigade. The camp-followers, officially numbered at 225 women and 500 children, but closer to 2,000 according to subsequent claims, came behind them.[16] This was an entire city afloat, not just an army, a massive naval invasion that dwarfed the previous year's already impressive effort. One British soldier wryly noted: 'Upon the appearance of so formidable a fleet, you may imagine they were not a little dismayed at Ticonderoga.'[17] The British knew the psychological impact that such a display of force, logistics, ingenuity and perseverance would have. And they were right.

*   *   *

In the middle of the Atlantic, meanwhile, two particularly intrepid ladies, both wives of officers, were making their separate ways to America, and they both left diaries which are among the most engaging primary sources that survived the war. It was by no means unusual for women to travel with the army, but it certainly was unusual for such high-ranking women to travel on campaign. Their diaries provide some of the clearest evidence that the war forced all sorts of people to sea for all sorts of different reasons, and the maritime experience that they enjoyed (or loathed) changed their lives.

The first we shall meet is Frederika Riedesel, wife of the Hessian general Friedrich Riedesel. Frederika had been unable to travel to America with her husband because she was pregnant with her third child. When that child, a third daughter, was born in March 1776, she began to make preparations for her journey. In April 1777, while her husband was preparing to reinvade Champlain from St Jean, she set out for Canada from Spithead aboard a ship owned by a rich, one-legged merchant.* Frederika and her three children were almost instantly, and terribly, seasick, but after three full days of unremitting nausea and dizziness they were dancing on deck to fife and drums. Later, when the weather turned rough again, Frederika was better prepared and swiftly discovered the sailors' cure for seasickness: keep busy. She wrote at the time: 'I had no time to be sick, as my servants were sicker than all the rest, and I had to take care of my three children alone. I believe there is no better preventative against seasickness than to keep busy.' Her servants also seem to have been particularly unlucky: one slammed her fingers in a door when the ship took a big roll and another hurt her chin. In contrast with many of the surviving accounts of soldiers crammed into stinking transports, Frederika had a charming crossing. She ate magnificently, 'five or six dishes daily, all excellently cooked', and her only real concern was the welfare of her children, with whom she shared a bed, during storms; she was terrified that she would crush one of them. She knitted manically to pass the time: by the end of their 2,760-mile voyage, she had finished a night-cap for her husband, two purses, seven caps 'and a number of other small articles'. The rest of her journey down through the lakes was considerably more alarming, not least when she and her daughters inadvertently camped on an island known to the locals as the charming-sounding Île à Sonnettes, which actually translates as 'Rattlesnake Island'. Well-meaning British sailors from her naval escort built a huge fire and spent all night making as much noise as possible to frighten off the snakes. She was doubly shocked the next morning when 'we found on every side the skins and slime of these nasty creatures, and accordingly, made haste to finish our breakfast'.[18]

Lady Harriet Acland, wife of Major John Acland, meanwhile, had also crossed the Atlantic, and with her mother. She also kept a wonderfully detailed journal of her voyage on the

---

* His other leg was bitten off by a shark while bathing in the West Indies. M. L. Brown, *Baroness von Riedesel*, 25.

transport ship *Kent*, though there is some suspicion that at least some of the journal was kept by an as yet unidentified man. Not only is the Acland journal a detailed diary but it is a detailed maritime log, full of observations of weather conditions, miles travelled each day, latitude readings, records of communication with other ships, and even observations on the impact of war rumours on the crews of the fleet. On 10 April she noted with some mirth how Captain Winchester turned out 'with great alertness' to attack what he thought was a whale, which turned out to be a bundle of hay. The bundle of hay, at least, is physical evidence that they were sailing the same waters through which a horse transport bound for America or Canada must recently have passed. She also managed to see 'penguins' in the middle of the North Atlantic, an impressive indeed. It is more likely that she saw great auks, now extinct. One of her most striking memories was a stunning aurora borealis: 'None of the Company had ever seen any thing at all equal to it in England, the edges of the streaks of light were of a beautiful purple, & sometimes green, & the outline excessively noble, in the shape of large rocks.' Once arrived, and like so many soldiers who had already travelled to Quebec in the war, she and her companions were stunned by the beauty of the Canadian landscape, and even claimed that it felt as if 'we were walking on magic ground'.[19]

* * *

The British fleet, meanwhile, had made its way down Lake Champlain and had arrived to find the few surviving American ships at anchor beyond their famous bridge and boom, where they remained, out of range, while patrol boats continually criss-crossed between Ticonderoga and Mount Independence.[20] Command of the American defences on Champlain had by now shifted into the hands of Arthur St Clair, promoted for his service with Washington at Trenton.* The Americans were con-

---

* Note that he was promoted above Arnold, which became a major source of grievance and a factor in Arnold's subsequent treason.

fident. The boom and bridge, they felt, were well constructed. They watched as the British probed the boom and returned to out of the range of gunshot.[21] The Americans exhaled.

The defenders had food; they had gunpowder and shot; they had water. What they did not have, however, was an appreciation of the ingenuity and skill of British sailors and engineers. The problem with the American defences was that they were dominated by a high ridge, 760 feet above water-level at the summit, known as Sugar-Loaf Hill, so named because it looked like a sugar-loaf when approached from the south. A gun emplacement on the hill would endanger the American positions at Mount Independence and Ticonderoga, and of course the American ships at anchor in the bay. The Americans had noted this strategic weakness but had dismissed it; indeed, the officer who officially raised the possibility that the Sugar-Loaf could be scaled and armed 'was ridiculed for advancing such an extravagant idea'.[22] They simply did not think that the British would be able to get to the top. But they could, and they did. 'Where a goat can go a man can go, and where a man can go he can drag a gun', reasoned Burgoyne.[23] Using the same logistical and haulage skills which had allowed them to hoist guns to the very top of the towering New Jersey Palisades prior to the New Jersey campaign in 1776 – a skill at which British sailors excelled – the British established a gun emplacement on Sugar-Loaf Hill on 5 July 'by hoisting cannon from tree, to tree, till they reached the summit'.[24]

On the same day 'a large ship',[25] presumably the *Royal George*, approached the American bridge and boom. That boom, which had taken such effort to build and which had appeared to be well constructed, was painfully, achingly and shockingly broken by the British at just their second attempt. One witness claimed that it took about as long to break the boom as it did to describe its breaking.[26]

The Americans fled in a desperate scramble down the lake in 200 bateaux and five armed galleys that were full of soldiers, armaments, supplies, invalids and camp-followers. This was yet another entire army afloat, yet another waterborne retreat within close proximity of the enemy and executed at night. The British raced after them, once again displaying matchless seamanship in their large ships, 'notwithstanding the communication is so narrow in some places that the Ships Yards almost touched the Precipices which over hung them'.[27] Everything was frantic. At Skenesborough Jeduthan Baldwin, the farmer-engineer who had helped build the failed boom and bridge, lost all his baggage, papers, 6,491 dollars of public money and spare clothes, and then had to march 110 miles through the woods till he was 'very dirty and uncomfortable'.[28]

The British missed the Americans at Skenesborough by only two hours, though there were still a few stragglers to gloat over. They took great pleasure in seeing the American officers 'scampering for their baggage'[29] and succeeded in capturing two American ships, the *Trumbull* lugger and *Liberty* schooner. None of the other vessels could be saved from fires that had been started by the Americans. American sea power on Lake Champlain thus ceased to exist. The fires of the burning ships lit the night, illuminating the path that they, and the revolution itself, had to take. They took to the woods.[30]

St Clair and his men knew they had disappointed their superiors and feared for their future. One soldier wrote: 'No event could be more unexpected nor more severely felt throughout our army and country. This disaster has given to our cause a dark and gloomy aspect.'[31] The word 'unexpected' leaps out here and is a powerful reminder of the utterly misplaced confidence that the Americans had felt in their defences at Ticonderoga. This was American maritime and naval naivety at its very peak and a strong contrast with the French-inspired genius of the Delaware defences. Here, the British felt, was proof that the Americans had 'no men of military science' in their ranks.[32]

Washington was apoplectic. He described it as 'an event of chagrin and surprise not apprehended, nor within the compass of my reasoning'.[33] So much time, effort and expense had been wasted. The career of the talented Philip Schuyler was ruined.[34] Horatio Gates replaced him in command of the army's Northern Department. Would he be able to stop the seemingly unstoppable British?

*   *   *

As things stood in the first week of July 1777, the British had advanced to Skenesborough at the very bottom of Lake Champlain, having left 900 men to defend Ticonderoga and Crown Point. The Americans, meanwhile, had vanished into the woods heading for Fort Edward at the top of the Hudson. The British also planned to head to Fort Edward, but unlike the Americans, they had a choice of routes available to them. They could either follow the Americans through the woods into the unknown, or they could head back up Lake Champlain to Ticonderoga where its western shore came within about a mile and a quarter of Lake George along a well-used portage route. The British had even prefabricated special carriages to assist in the expected portage.[35] With no American ships to challenge the British, the voyage back up Lake Champlain could be made swiftly and safely, and the next voyage down Lake George would also be guaranteed to be swift and safe. Once regrouped at the foot of Lake George, Burgoyne would then only face a short march along well-used roads to Fort Edward on the Hudson, his railway to the south.

The British had slaved for months to build a force that could dominate the lakes and had bled to achieve that dominance at Valcour Island. Now that absolute control had been achieved, however, it was not utilized. Burgoyne, a soldier, chose to take his main force not by water – an element entirely alien to him – but into the woods, along a sixteen-mile road that crossed a creek forty times and passed through endless bogs and thickets. A tiny portion of the British force, meanwhile, would travel to Fort Edward via Lake George. Around a hundred bateaux would be dragged into the woods with Burgoyne's army.[36]

It was a poor decision, made by a man who did not understand the role of sea power in this inland campaign and who later defended his decision in terms of morale. To go backwards, he claimed, was to retreat.[37] It is important to note that his decision was made in total isolation from the navy. As had been the case with Carleton's fleet, the highest-ranking naval officer on Champlain under Burgoyne was a captain, Skeffington Lutwidge. Significantly junior in rank to Burgoyne, he also lacked any first-hand knowledge of the theatre. The presence of a naval flag officer at this key moment in the war might well have changed everything.

Lutwidge remained with his fleet and Burgoyne took the men into the woods. Although Burgoyne still faced numerous maritime problems in reaching and travelling down the Hudson, the highest-ranking naval officer in his army was now the twenty-year-old midshipman Edward Pellew, who was placed in command of a small body of sailors embedded in Burgoyne's 5,000-strong army.

Schuyler, at Fort Edward, instantly sent his soldiers, many of whom were experienced woodsmen, back into their element with instructions to fell trees, destroy bridges and break dams. Life for the British in the woods immediately became a misery. Those few men sent by boat to Fort Edward via Lake George, meanwhile, were having a thoroughly splendid time. The return voyage to Ticonderoga and portage to Lake George had gone swiftly and easily, and in total absence of the enemy, their diaries are full of observations of nature – a nest of rattlesnakes here, a good fishing spot there – all interspersed with 'many pleasing & romantic prospects'.[38]

The Americans in the woods began to scent blood. Militiamen flooded to join Gates while Burgoyne was held up. Burgoyne had taken only a matter of weeks to travel by water all the way from Canada, down Lake Champlain to Skenesborough, but now on land it took him a full month to travel a handful of miles to a position just south of Fort Edward, and in that crucial window the Americans built an army large enough to fight him.[39]

Meanwhile every step that Burgoyne took stretched his supply lines further. They already ran nearly 400 miles back to Montreal, and then, on 13 September, having waited to stockpile supplies, he deliberately severed those lines by cross-ing the Hudson on a bridge of boats made by British sailors under Edward Pellew's command. Once across, the bridge was broken up to help float the army's supplies downriver. Burgoyne was fully aware of the implications and had written: 'from the hour I pass the Hudson's River and proceed towards Albany, all safety of communication ceases'.[40] Never a man for turning back, his only option once across the Hudson was to break through the American lines.

* * *

Hope of relief from the south was not entirely lost, however. General Howe was in Philadelphia but he had left behind in New York Henry Clinton, who, now fortified with 2,000 extra troops, had sailed up the Hudson under the naval command of the competent and reliable William Hotham.[41] It was the most daring incident in Clinton's entire career, another fine example of British sea power penetrating deep into enemy ter-ritory. Often overlooked, this was no easy task. The Hudson at this point is narrow and surrounded by high mountains that baffle the wind. At West Point it is particularly bad because of Bear Mountain to the west and Anthony's Nose to the east. The river current races to New York, but it is also tidal, and powerfully so, the tide often forcing the river inland at three knots. Working a single large ship, let alone a fleet of large ships, this far against the current, or with the tide, required immense seamanship skill.

Fort Montgomery and Fort Clinton, on the western bank of the Hudson guarding a narrowing where the river forms an S-shaped curve, were captured in a surprise attack on 6 October.* The attack on Fort Clinton was prosecuted by Henry Clinton and the fort was defended by James Clinton and George Clinton, and hence it became known as the Battle

---

* Unlike Fort Clinton, many of the original features of Fort Montgomery still survive; it is well worth a visit. The United States Military Academy at West Point is located at the site of Fort Clinton.

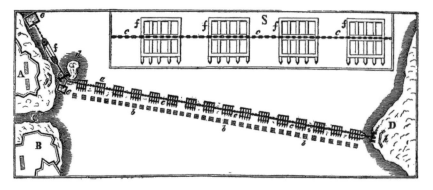

A contemporary illustration of the 1777 Hudson River chain broken by the British and subsequently dismantled.

A: Fort Montgomery. B: Fort Clinton. C: Poplopin's Kill. D: Anthony's Nose.

a: Floats to Chain. *b b b*: Booms in front of Chain. *c c c*: Chain.

d: Rock at which the Chain was secured with large Iron Roller. *e e*: Cribs and Anchors.

f: Blocks and Purchase for tightening Chain. *g h*: Ground Batteries for defence of Chain.

S: Section showing Floats and Chain. *c c c*: Chain. *f f f f*: Floats.

of the Clintons.[42] Another great chain and boom, made of logs fifty feet long with pointed ends,[43] guarded the Hudson at Fort Montgomery. This boom was taken by the British but, in direct contrast to the one at Ticonderoga, it was so strong that the British chose to capture the forts that guarded its western end rather than risk their hulls forcing it. The Americans were forced to burn their two frigates on the Hudson: the *Congress* near Constitution Island, the *Montgomery* immediately to the west of Anthony's Nose.[44] The resourceful British later raised the cannon from their wrecks.[45]

Clinton and Hotham rampaged as far as Esopus, fifty miles from Albany, where they were stopped by well-positioned American cannon, and waited for Burgoyne to break through. But Burgoyne was struggling. Behind his back, the Americans, under the intrepid John Brown, had raided the British supply depot on Lake George where they captured 200 bateaux, over 300 British soldiers including twelve officers, and a huge stockpile of weapons and baggage. They released 188 American prisoners who, according to Brown, 'came out of their Holes and Cells with Wonder and Amazement'.[46] Brown then took his attack into Champlain in a small schooner and numerous captured gunboats, and he briefly reignited the flame of American sea power on the lake before British gunnery forced him to retreat back to Skenesborough. Burgoyne, therefore, was surrounded.

The only glimpse of hope was that the Hudson still lay between the American and British armies, though that did not exactly guarantee security. In one instance a bold American soldier swam across the Hudson and stole a British officer's horse grazing in a field opposite. He then did it again and got one for his captain.[47] Edward Pellew, whose heroism was witnessed by Burgoyne, foiled another daring raid on the British army's supply barge.[48] The temperature rose. Battle was coming.

* * *

When it came at Saratoga, the American attack was noted for the courage displayed by John Glover's Marblehead mariners, who had now come north after their victorious Trenton campaign. They fought like wild animals. One witness noted that 'even the stolid Hessians expressed their amazement when they saw these brave Marbleheaders dash through the fire of grape and canister over the dead bodies of their comrades, through the embrasures, over the cannon, with the same agility with which they formerly climbed to the maintop, or traversed the backstays, bayoneting the cannoneers at their posts'.[49]

The battle fell in a rush towards the Americans, and a few days later, when the British generals discussed their options and first formally considered surrender, Edward Pellew – remember he was no more than a twenty-year-old *midshipman* – was asked to sit in on the council of war as the highest-ranking naval 'officer' present. Burgoyne's campaign is so often held up as an example of what could happen if a British army operated too far from the navy in terms of supply lines and firepower support, but it should equally be held up as an example of what could happen if a British army undertook significant maritime operations without integrated naval leadership. In such operations the army needed to be close to the navy in terms of both distance and command. It certainly didn't help that General Howe was in Philadelphia and not in New York from where he could head up the Hudson, but without a significant naval presence with Burgoyne there is every reason to think that his branch of the campaign would have failed anyway.

Pellew rather boldly asked if he and his sailors could make a run for it and escape the noose because 'he had never heard, he said, of sailors capitulating',[50] but his request was denied. The British army, including Pellew's sailors, surrendered on 17 October. The Americans granted surprisingly generous surrender terms to the British, allowing the soldiers to be shipped home on the promise that they would not fight again, a privilege usually reserved for officers. It has been argued that this was the result of Clinton's ominous presence with a naval force just forty-five miles south of Albany.[51]

Glover and his mariners, so experienced and now so trusted, were put in charge of the prisoners, who were marched back to Boston and from there sent to Newport. It was at first intended to send them back to Britain but, suspecting bad faith, Congress suspended the embarkation and they remained in America as prisoners until the war's end.[52] British sick and wounded were allowed to be transferred out of the woods to the lakes and then back to St Jean, where many of them were loaded aboard the radeau *Thunderer*. Her roomy hold, first designed to hold ammunition and weaponry to kill and maim Americans, was now crammed with dead and dying British soldiers, at least 150 sick. To make the irony complete, off Windmill Point on Lake Champlain, she sank, drowning those helpless men who were unable to move their limbs already shattered by American artillery.[53]

As an officer, Pellew was paroled and sent home with two major pieces of news: he had to tell the prime minister that an entire British army, 6,222 strong, had surrendered, leaving the British war effort in America hanging on a spider silk; and he had to tell his parents that his seventeen-year-old brother John, who had served in the doomed army as a private soldier, had died in the fighting. One wonders which was the harder news to break.

11

AMERICAN SEA POWER

The British surrender at Saratoga is traditionally seen as the defining moment in the French decision to intervene in the war, but to be understood properly, that intervention needs to be seen within a broader context: one that includes an understanding of French naval preparation but also one that takes into consideration the contribution made by American sea power during 1777, in terms of both success and failure.

Arnold's fleet at Valcour and the Pennsylvania Navy at Trenton had both been instrumental in halting major British advances in the winter of 1776. The Pennsylvania and Continental navies were then key players in the defence of the Delaware in 1777. The British finally broke down those defences in late November after a naval assault of staggering ferocity against the Delaware forts.[1] 'When the firing had in some measure subsided', wrote one American soldier huddled in Fort Mifflin, 'I found ... the fort was as completely ploughed as a field ... If ever destruction was complete,' he wrote, 'it was here.'[2] The captured American frigate *Delaware* took a significant part in the attack and facilitated the crossing of British troops to the New Jersey forts whose capture, by troops under the command of Cornwallis, completed the victory.[3]

The first British sloops and small vessels reached Philadelphia on 23 November, and four days later more than sixty British ships were riding off the city.[4] The Delaware was thus opened, but fifty-nine days after the army had entered the city. Utterly isolated until then, the British soldiers had begun to starve along with the civilian population. The poor suffered particularly badly during those weeks.[5] The stout defence of the

Delaware had demonstrated that the opportunity to blow the Americans down easily had passed and that the British army, if isolated in this way, was shockingly vulnerable.

Elsewhere the Americans had achieved some potent successes exploiting the decision made in 1775 by British politicians to avoid full naval mobilization. The result of that decision was that the British army had been transported to New York and then to Philadelphia in great force, but elsewhere, in the words of Augustus Keppel, 'Things had an extreme disagreeable appearance.'[6] Sandwich had urged North to re-arm, but even after Bunker Hill, the latter had insisted on budgetary stringency. He had, in fact, forced Sandwich to make significant savings in naval expenditure, which were achieved by reducing the dockyard workforce. Orders for ships of the line virtually ceased until late 1777.[7]

American whaleboat raids were a constant pain in and around Long Island Sound. At Sag Harbor, Long Island, on 23 May 1777, the Americans led an amphibious attack against a slumbering British force, burned twelve British ships and took ninety prisoners without losing a single man.[8] Boston, meanwhile, had become a lair of American privateers crowing over their successes. One British naval captain, taken into Boston as a prisoner, was astonished:

> Boston harbour swarms with privateers and their prizes; this is a great place of rendezvous with them. The privateersmen come on shore here full of money and enjoy themselves much after the same manner the English seamen at Portsmouth and Plymouth did in the late war; and by the best information I can get there are no less than fifteen foreign vessels lately arrived in the harbour with cargoes of various articles.[9]

These privateers were particularly active on the Grand Banks, where, according to Admiral John Montagu, Governor and commander-in-chief of the British naval forces in Newfoundland, writing from St John's in Newfoundland, they 'committed great depredations among the fishermen'.

Montagu was quite clear that he was fighting a losing battle, that his squadron was outnumbered and that, until he was reinforced, the fishery would come to a standstill.[10]

Under the guidance of William Bingham, American privateers continued to cause havoc in the Caribbean. Bingham by now had developed a cunning system whereby he commissioned ships manned almost exclusively by Frenchmen but with a requisite single American aboard, allowing them to be classed as American privateers. If they met a merchantman, they took her, but if they were stopped and inspected by a British cruiser, 'the Men all speak French and show French papers'.[11] The Caribbean continued to be the single most important location for American privateers, the economic impact of captures there far outstripping those anywhere else.[12] By February 1777 American privateers had contributed to the collapse of four major West Indian merchant companies.[13] It was in this theatre that the young Horatio Nelson, serving as a lieutenant on HMS *Lowestoffe*, really cut his teeth in warfare at sea.

The Caribbean had been a major weakness for the British since the start of the war. The key difference in this period was that the tempo and reach of American privateer attacks elsewhere increased dramatically with their own, unique, impact on the war. In June three American privateers working together captured no fewer than fourteen British merchantmen in the Firth of Clyde, eleven of them taken in five days. In England and Scotland, Lambert Wickes, a merchant from Maryland now holding a commission in the Continental Navy, and the Irish-born Philadelphian Gustavus Conyngham, another ex-merchant, became bogey figures for this American success. On one cruise alone Wickes captured eighteen British merchant ships in the Irish Sea, almost within sight of English shores, and Conyngham captured sixty ships in less than eighteen months. The British losses led to Germain writing a sarcastic letter to Admiral Howe in which he congratulated him for allowing swarms of enemy privateers to get into European waters.[14]

The Americans did their best to take advantage of European ports through deception, ruses and collusion, and the French and Spanish trod a fine line between assisting American privateers by offering them shelter and supplies and heading off British diplomatic outrage.[15] The comte de Vergennes insisted on enforcing the neutrality of France only when Lord Stormont, the British ambassador, presented him with evidence so conclusive that no other option was possible.[16] By no means were the French happy with this, however: the Americans were trampling all over their carefully laid plans, and they were not to be forced into war with Britain before they were ready. The Americans were also pushing the boundaries of Spanish assistance. Conyngham openly used Spanish ports as a base from where he could prowl Biscay and as far south as the Canaries, an excellent route for the interception of Caribbean-bound trade.[17]

By taking more effective measures to protect their trade, the British had stopped the very easy pickings that had characterized 1775–6.[18] Nonetheless, as many as 300 British merchantmen were taken in 1777.[19] Such figures, however, can divert one's attention from the real issue. The vast British maritime economy was particularly sensitive in the Caribbean, but even there – and certainly everywhere else – it was able to absorb these losses, and there is no evidence that the American privateering effort did anything to shorten the conflict.[20] It is far more useful to see the American successes of 1777 in terms of their political and diplomatic impact on the war rather than in material terms measured against the British economy. These privateering successes were part of the broader narrative of American successes in 1776 and 1777. Together, they demonstrated on an international stage that the Americans were committed to their revolution and that the British were vulnerable, and they heightened tension between Britain and her traditional European enemies. In short, they created the opportunity for foreign intervention.

*   *   *

At the same time, however, American sea power had also demonstrated, and with stunning clarity, that an intervention was absolutely essential if the revolution was going to succeed, for overshadowing these successes was a mountain of failures that signalled just how badly the Americans were struggling.

Those failures were encapsulated by the fate of the thirteen American frigates that had been commissioned amid such excitement and expectation in 1775. Ever since then the Marine Committee had been struggling desperately with the unprecedented challenge of building, arming, rigging, manning and then using men-of-war in an appropriate fashion. A key problem was that the same body of men responsible for the administration – the Marine Committee – was also responsible for the young navy's operations. An attempt was made in April 1776 to ease the burden by setting up two separate regional Navy Boards to concentrate on building, manning, outfitting and supervising expenditure. For the first time this extended the management of American naval affairs to include men who were not members of Congress. The Americans thus took their first step in the creation of a separate bureaucracy for naval affairs, a key development in any national navy.[21]

Perhaps the most daunting challenge of all for this young navy was to live up to the dreams of the public it represented. 'Expectations run high', wrote James Warren, now an elected member of the Massachusetts Provincial Congress, to John Adams with gritted teeth, having acknowledged a bewildering array of problems, not least that the authority of the Navy Board was 'contemptible' and that 'all ideas of Oeconomy seem to be lost'.[22] A key weakness, now acutely felt, was that no American leader had any experience of the British Admiralty or Navy Board or, indeed, the respective institutions of any other navy. The man with the closest experience was Christopher Gadsden, who had served in the Royal Navy as a purser. Allied to this problem was the sheer burden of work that now fell on Congress, which was serving as both legislature and executive, its work executed via a variety of inefficient committees. There was, in fact, no settled American government until the

Articles of Confederation were finally ratified in March 1781; everything until then was ad hoc, unreliable, cumbersome. The Continental Congress had been designed as a forum where representatives of the colonies could air their views on matters of mutual concern, not for supervising the conduct of a war. Congress was plagued by inter-state feuds, duplication of responsibilities and irregular attendance. It was occasionally impossible to find sufficient members for the Marine Committee even to meet.[23]

The first American frigate to be launched, on 10 July 1776, was the 26-gun *Randolph*. Her maiden voyage was a total disaster. Her fore and main masts were rotten and crashed overboard. Sickness then struck and many of her crew died. Nineteen British prisoners of war who had been signed on to her crew to boost numbers mutinied and were narrowly defeated. She staggered into Charleston on 11 March. Her captain, Nicholas Biddle, was an experienced mariner, one of the few American naval officers who had served in the Royal Navy. Biddle simply said that it was 'one of the most disagreeable passages that I have experienced'.[24] Since then, the *Delaware* had been captured at Philadelphia; the *Washington* and *Effingham* had been hidden twenty-five miles upstream on the Delaware at Bordentown before being scuttled to deny them to the British; the *Congress* and *Montgomery* had been destroyed on the Hudson to prevent them from falling into Clinton's hands; the *Trumbull* drew too much water to get out of the Connecticut River where she had been built; the *Virginia*, built at Fells Point in Maryland, was trapped in the Chesapeake by a British blockade; and the *Warren* and *Providence* were blockaded in Narragansett Bay by the British in Newport and, in their inactivity, the crews of Esek Hopkins's squadron had been torn apart by squabbling.[25] Only three of the frigates – the *Raleigh*, built in Portsmouth, New Hampshire and the *Hancock* and *Boston*, built in Newburyport, Massachusetts – made it to sea with any chance of success, and those of the 32-gun *Raleigh* were particularly slim: when she was launched, her builder confessed, 'am Sorry to say, [I] can form no Idea where the Guns are to com[e] from.'[26] Richard Hart, a Portsmouth merchant, subsequently wrote to Abraham Whipple, now a captain in the Continental Navy, and signed off with a wry comment: 'We have a fine ship, at her moorings. Wish we had the Cannon &c.'[27] She eventually sailed with only a handful of guns for Brest, where it was hoped she would find some more. She enjoyed some limited success on the way, including a scrap with a small British sloop, HMS *Druid*.[28]

The *Hancock* and *Boston*, based in Boston, had the best opportunity of any of the American frigates. The British had taken nearly every available naval ship with them on their Philadelphia campaign, leaving the New England coast almost unprotected.[29] In May the *Hancock* and *Boston* set sail with a fleet of privateers and briefly seized control of New England waters. One British officer writing from Newport commented on how it had become 'absolutely necessary to avoid a separation, as he [Captain John Manley of the *Hancock*] had a force infinitely superior to us; which was the cause of our losing a vast number of valuable prizes'.[30]

The Americans, however, were never able to realize the full potential of their force. Soon after they reached the Grand Banks, the privateers immediately abandoned the frigates, reasoning that such a concentration of American ships was likely to attract the attention of any nearby British warship. And they were right. It was not long before rumours reached Boston that the British, horrified at the loss of naval control, had sent eight frigates after them.[31] The privateer captains had no interest at all in risking their vessels in battle with the British. Thus the opportunity to work together, by forcing the British merchantmen to scatter and then catching them in a well-coordinated net of American armed ships, vanished.

The second problem was that Manley and Hector McNeill, captain of the *Boston*, loathed each other. 'McNeill and Manly it is said like the Jews and Samaritans will have no Connections of Intercourse', wrote Warren before they left. He was understandably anxious about what might happen.[32]

The American frigates plodded on alone, and after a narrow escape from a far more powerful British warship, the 64-gun *Somerset*, they fell in with some prey that they could handle themselves: the 28-gun British frigate *Fox*. The *Fox* fled but was chased, and was chased well in a display of competent seamanship and tactical nous by Manley in the *Hancock*. The *Boston* soon joined the fight, and when she could no longer steer, the *Fox* surrendered.[33] McNeill made some atmospheric sketches of the battle from the decks of the *Boston* [*see fig. 8*].[34]

The victory papered over some serious cracks in American sea power. It had been far from easy. Some of the *Hancock's* crew had shown 'strong signs of fear and dismay', and Manley had been forced to urge them on like a dervish:

> [Manley] ran continually from one end of the ship to the other, in his waistcoat, his shirt sleeves tucked up to his shoulders, flourishing and swinging a great cutlass around his head, and with the most horrid imprecations, swearing he would cut down the first man who should attempt to leave his quarters.[35]

If the *Boston* had not been there as well, it is more than likely that the *Hancock*, rather than the *Fox*, would have struck.

The American victory was also short-lived. They captured a merchantman on the way back to Boston but were then caught by a British squadron under the command of the excellent George Collier. The *Fox* was recaptured along with the *Hancock*.[36] McNeill in the *Boston* escaped back to the Maine coast, but it became clear that he had abandoned Manley. 'Capt. McNeill's reputation on his first Appointment was Extreemly good', wrote Warren. 'It seems to be now reversed.'[37] McNeill was later court-martialled for abandoning Manley, found guilty and dismissed from the service, and the whole sorry tale was laid to rest in July when the *Hancock* was defeated in battle and captured by the British. By the summer of 1777 it had become painfully clear that, in the words of the

Reverend William Gordon in a letter to Adams, 'Maritime affairs have been most horribly managed.'[38]

* * *

The successes and failures of American sea power in 1777 are therefore important if we are to understand the extraordinary diplomatic changes that happened next. The Americans' operations had advertised commitment and ambition, but at the same time had betrayed weakness and incompetence.* The French had begun by offering them arms and powder, but they now clearly needed money, men, engineering knowledge, shipbuilding supplies, large cannon, and access to European and Caribbean ports. Without this they would be unable to conduct their own war at sea, to protect their own shipping or to give their failing economy a crucial boost.[39]

American ships had also facilitated any possible French intervention by transporting key diplomats – Silas Deane, Ben Franklin, John Adams – as well as intelligence to and from France.[40] Franklin's arrival in the *Reprisal* was by far the most significant: this was the first Continental warship to be seen in European waters. She made quite an impression, arriving in Nantes in November 1776 with two prizes in tow.[41]

During this period the French had grown ever closer to their final, decisive commitment to intervene and had travelled far down that road long before the British surrender at Saratoga in October. Then the French foreign minister Vergennes had commented on the possibility of gaining revenge over Britain for the humiliation suffered by France in the previous war: 'the opportunity would be seductive and it would be a sublime effort of virtue to refuse it', he had written.[42] Their motivation, however, was far more mixed than this suggests and far more important for the future of France.

Their aim, rather, was a readjustment of the balance of power that would recover for France the diplomatic prestige

---

* So too had the poor performance of Washington's army at New York in 1776 and then Brandywine and Germantown in 1777.

lost in the Seven Years' War (1754–63). Before that war, France had been a powerhouse of European style, political and military power. The French now wanted to hold once again the dominant hand in European politics, to place herself '*en position d'arbitre*'.[43] In the 1770s Vergennes was particularly concerned about the growing influence of Russia in the balance of European power,* and Britain was an ally of Russia. A weakened Britain therefore meant a weakened Russia, and there was an explicit assumption in France that Britain would be gravely damaged if it no longer had a monopoly on American trade. At the same time it was envisaged that France, rather than Britain, would become the dominant trading partner with the United States and that Britain might even then be encouraged to work with France against expansion by the eastern powers.[44]

Any premature pressure on the French naval infrastructure would threaten this grand vision of the future. The ships had to be ready, the crews mustered and trained, and the dockyards prepared for a lengthy campaign with stockpiles of timber, rigging supplies, munitions and food. If they were not adequately prepared, the Royal Navy would crush them utterly, and once war was declared this would not just be a question of American independence but of the survival of the French maritime empire: it should not be underestimated just how much the French risked by allying themselves with the Americans and how correspondingly cautious they were about the exact moment of commitment. The fate of a relatively small British army blundering around in the Hudson Highlands was hardly a priority concern.

Even as Burgoyne and Gates clashed in battle at Saratoga, the French dockyards were a hive of activity. In May 1776 the French could boast twenty-five ships of the line; by 1 January 1777 it was thirty-seven; a year later they had fifty.[45] All the while the relative naval strength of Britain and France

---

* In 1772 Austria, Russia and Prussia, working together rather than against each other as they had done for generations, dismembered Poland, taking a fifth of her population and a quarter of her territory. Dull, 'Tragedy', 81.

converged because the British had failed to mobilize their navy in 1776 and the Royal Navy was suffering from a natural cycle of decay which meant that ships built at the height of the previous war, the Seven Years' War (1754–63), were now being broken up faster than new ships were being built to replace them. Finally, and far too late, the British ordered a full-scale naval mobilization in January 1778, but they were now at least fifteen months behind the French. The British also began to build ships at an unprecedented rate in this period, far faster than the French; fifty-five frigates were built in 1778 and 1779 alone, and in those years eighteen ships of the line were also ordered – ships that would take at least three years to build, and ships that would, once launched, tip the balance of naval power significantly back towards the British. In 1777, therefore, the French knew that, for the first time since 1690, they could achieve near-parity with the British. That parity would come in 1778, but they were then likely to lose it again in 1779 when the enlarged British fleet could be fully manned by impressing sailors returning from overseas trade. The window of opportunity to strike a blow on their own, therefore, was just a year.[46]

Under the careful guidance of Vergennes the French would not rush their commitment. They knew they had an advantage and they were not prepared to jump the gun; in fact they used every possible delaying tactic available to them, just to perfect the state of their naval forces and to give them more time to try to woo the Spanish into joining the fight.[47] The result was that this was the one and only time between 1688 and 1815 that the French embarked on a naval war with two full years to build and repair ships and stock up the yards.[48] Even when the chance to take an open stance by officially assisting a squadron of American privateers appeared in 1777, the French refused to help and expelled the American squadron, all because their naval preparations had yet to be finished.[49]

While Vergennes waited to launch his naval Armageddon, the help offered to America subtly increased. As 1777 slipped into 1778, more French ships arrived in America with significant and now varied cargoes, not least the *Flamand*, which carried 500 barrels of sulphur for making gunpowder and none other than Baron von Steuben, the former staff officer of Frederick the Great. Arrivals like these were joyously broadcast in the local newspapers and the Americans could sense a change in the wind.[50] It was clear that the rebellion, which had grown into a full-scale civil war, would soon change again, this time into an international conflict. It was about to change from a naval war dominated by cruisers, whaleboats and bateaux to one that was dominated by ships of the line. The timing of that intervention had less to do with Burgoyne surrendering at Saratoga than with the readiness of the French navy.

By the time Burgoyne surrendered at Saratoga the French were waiting only for the king's approval to enter the war.[51] But was that good news or bad for America? The answer was not as clear as you may suspect.

PART 3

WORLD WAR
1778–1780

1778

12

BOURBON ALLIANCE

From the relatively austere shores of both Britain and America it was easy to ridicule the French in the 1770s. Consider their clothes. The French certainly looked odd to anyone who wasn't a Frenchman or in thrall to French fashion. When the French upper classes were viewed from an outsider's perspective, their appearance alone was enough to cause some serious sniggering. Hairstyles, as we have heard, were ridiculous. Even men's hair, which was relatively tame compared to women's, was covered with pomade or powder, and their costume littered with fascinating absurdities. The men, for example, would carry a cocked hat, but never wear one; their coats were cut away to such an extent that they only met at chest level and severely restricted any movement. 'I have no more use of my arms than an Egyptian mummy' was a satirical comment in a play.[1] Those coats were elaborately decorated with buttons or badges of enormous size and variety. Some were embroidered or enamelled with topographical, political or even theatrical scenes or ornamented with paintings under glass, insects, minerals, objects of natural history, comic riddles, the portraits of the twelve Caesars, the latest kings of France, Ovid's *Metamorphoses* ... the list goes on and on.

'It is difficult to imagine', wrote one Frenchman, 'the idea Americans entertained about the French before the war. They considered them ... as a kind of light, brittle, queer-shapen mechanisms, only busy frizzling their hair and painting their faces, without faith or morals.'[2] Before he saw his first real live Frenchman, one American believed them to be 'pale, ugly specimens who lived exclusively on frogs and snails'.[3] A

'With porter roast beef & plumb pudding well cram'd, Jack English declares that Monsr
may be D—d. The soup meagre Frenchman such language don't suit. So he grins
indignation & calls him a brute.'

splendid cartoon of 1778, 'Politeness', encapsulates the differ-
ences between the austere, manly English and the bewigged,
snuff-sniffing, dandyish, effeminate Frenchman.[4] The excitement about a potential alliance with France, therefore, was
tinged with some serious misgivings, the result of these and
numerous other 'ancient prejudices'[5] – or, in the words of
Abraham Whipple, 'natural enmity'.[6] The resulting violent
cultural clash, in the form of a military alliance between a
young liberal Protestant republic and an ancient despotic
Catholic monarchy, is one of the most fascinating moments in
the entire eighteenth century.

The famous marquis de Lafayette is often taken as a shining
example of brotherly love between the rebels and the French
fighting for nothing more than elusive liberty, but in reality he
was the exception and French motivation was complex. The
French were universally distrusted in America; in fact the first
French officers to arrive there were met with abhorrence. John

Adams is a classic example of the most common American perspective: he distrusted all Frenchmen on sight and on principle.[7] One American was simply astounded when he met his first group of French troops, simply because they appeared so normal: 'A fine body of men, and appear to be well officered', he wrote, a little disappointed. 'Neither the officers nor men are the effeminate beings we were heretofore taught to believe them. They are as large and likely men as can be produced by any nation.'[8]

The British had far more first-hand experience of the French than the Americans and were consequently less hung up on caricature and prejudice. Nonetheless, they utterly loathed them. The Earl of Chesterfield, writing in the previous Seven Years' War, had described them as 'Our great and natural enemy', and another army officer in the same war wrote how the British soldiers had 'an implacable hatred against the French, who are the enemies of all mankind'.[9]

A major source of British hatred was fear, caused by the fact that the French had a massive navy. As an island nation the security of Britain was only vulnerable to a country that could wield sea power and the closest and most dangerous threat always came from France. In the 1770s that British fear was based on a realistic perception of French naval capability. An efficient system of spies regularly informed the Admiralty of developments in French naval dockyards.[10] The French had rebuilt their fleet and reformed their naval infrastructure and administration since the end of the Seven Years' War (1754–63), and the British knew all about it. The general consensus was that, by 1778, 'the French Navy was never in so good order, nor the magazines of every kind so completed, nor the Sea Officers so disposed for action, to recover (as they acknowledged themselves) their lost honour'.[11] An interesting by-product of this healthy wariness of French naval strength was that, once France entered the war, the opposition to naval impressment that had characterized the war so far completely vanished. Such opposition was now considered nothing less than unpatriotic.[12] It was all very well campaigning for rights and liberty when the British and Americans were fighting a civil war, but when the French were involved ... well, that was another matter entirely.

King Louis XVI's first naval minister was Anne-Robert-Jacques Turgot, a brilliant man, so good that, within weeks, he was plucked away from the navy to take charge of the royal finances themselves. His replacement, however, was equally impressive. Antoine-Raymond-Gaulbert-Gabriel de Sartine, head of the Paris police and chief administrator of the city of Paris, became one of the ablest naval administrators his country had ever seen. Tactful, prudent, courageous, innovative and meticulous, his mind was exactly what the French navy required.[13] Sartine did more than anyone else to turn the French navy into a force that could rival, and even defeat, the British. His was a crucial naval mind to balance the political wile of Vergennes.

Louis XVI had overseen all the changes. Though weak and easily manipulated, he had a natural interest in maritime affairs that had been encouraged since boyhood. Carefully schooled in naval matters by one of the most talented marine artists of the age, Nicolas-Marie Ozanne, he had spent many happy hours playing with toy sailing ships on the pond at Versailles. The king's avid interest in all things naval translated into personal patronage of talented men in the naval administration. Louis firmly believed that a strong navy was exactly what France required to secure its future and regain its rightful position in the balance of European power.

The changing diplomatic situation in Europe in the 1770s was uniquely advantageous for this new focus on the French navy. An alliance between France and Austria – the Peace of Teschen of 1777 – had calmed long-standing tension between the two countries, and the French could also rely on the 1761 'family compact' which tied Spain as an ally in case of a European hostile threat. In 1778, therefore, France was able to turn its back on its land borders with the Low Countries, Rhineland and Italy, and look to the sea.[14]

The chances of success against the British now even seemed,

in numerical terms, promising. By no means were numbers of ships everything to sea power in this period, though the French had also invested significantly in everything else that went with them. All three of the major French naval dockyards had recently been remodelled,[15] and they were now bursting with stores. The ships' magazines were packed with the most potent gunpowder on the planet. Under Louis XVI French gunpowder-manufacturing had been utterly transformed under the hand of the gifted chemist, administrator and work-aholic Antoine Lavoisier. In 1777 he was at the very peak of his powers and was hurtling towards his 1778 discovery – one of the most important of modern chemical discoveries – of how combustion works, and particularly the role played by oxygen. It is no coincidence that his discovery was central to the chem-istry of explosions, and Lavoisier soon became the most influ-ential man in the French scientific world. By 1777 the French were manufacturing two million pounds of powder per year.[16] The sailors were ready to use this powder: from 1767 provision was made for systematic naval gunnery drill once a week.[17]

The young officers would have been well educated and would have benefited from a relatively new initiative, the Marine Academy, which was founded in 1752 and designed to encourage scientific thinking within the navy. They would have studied mathematics, geometry, hydrography, drawing and shipbuilding, and were also given their practical skills by experienced boatswains who taught them ship-handling, gunnery, stowage and rigging. When ashore, they spent three afternoons a week visiting the dockyards' workshops and building slips;[18] when at sea the most senior midshipmen were required to keep their own logs, with their own daily reckon-ing, which was regularly shown to the captain. Most were sent on missions to various countries, including Great Britain, to study different aspects of building, administering, maintain-ing and operating navies. Most benefited from the new French 'squadrons of evolution' – training exercises conducted under the command of the comte de Guichen in 1775 and the comte du Chassault in 1776.[19] Both commanders used highly original ideas developed in the 1760s by French theorists who led the world in thinking on naval tactics.[20] These cruises taught the officers to judge speed and position in a fleet by eye; to keep station at night by following the wake of the ship ahead as it glowed in the moonlight; to anticipate the manoeuvres of their fellow captains; to squeeze the very best performance from their ships in a variety of conditions.

The crews were raised by a system of naval conscription, designed to ensure that large numbers of men would have knowledge and experience of the maritime environment. To maintain their health, schools of naval medicine had been established at the main naval dockyards of Brest, Rochefort and Toulon.

These developments now made the French a particularly dangerous enemy. In practice, however, so much could still go wrong because of the many problems inherent in wielding such sea power. Operations could misfire because of basic navigational errors; thousands of sailors would die if the ships were not kept clean; the chaos of fleet battle in deep oceans endangered almost all attempts at command and control; manning systems and dockyard efficiency could collapse under the pressure of war. The Americans, with no naval history behind them and no naval administrators or career naval officers to advise them, did not realize this, and they heaped expectation upon the French navy. They may have loathed the 'Frenchman' but they loved his ships. The French – purely because of their navy – were seen as the saviours of the revolution. Thus the alliance, made in February 1778,* was associated in America with a fascinating and paradoxical mixture of distrust and exceptionally high levels of expectation. 'Wine, meats, and liquors abounded, and happiness and contentment were impressed

---

* On 6 February France signed a treaty of 'amity and commerce' with America and a separate defensive alliance. The treaties were more than the Americans could have hoped for: it was agreed that neither could negotiate peace without each other's consent and, best of all, the French promised to fight until the Americans had achieved independence.

on every countenance', wrote the Hessian General Johann de Kalb.[21]

The key question of 1778, therefore, was how would the French navy live up to those American expectations? It started very well indeed.

*   *   *

As in all British wars, the first naval action was highly significant and the public waited with baited breath for news that could herald so much. They knew it was coming: French naval officers were spreading rumours that the two countries were at war weeks before the actual declaration.[22] The 'first shot' of any war was always burdened with the weight of international politics. Britain and France both had defensive treaties with other European countries, which required assistance to be given, in the shape of arms and money, to their partner country if attacked. Britain held a defensive treaty with the Netherlands, and France with Austria. The key question surrounding this first naval engagement, therefore, was who fired the first shot. In reality, of course, the answer to that question was always unclear. Either it actually was unclear who had in fact fired the first shot, or the subsequent reports twisted the truth. The British had already come off very badly from just such an engagement, at Lexington in April 1775, when both sides had been desperate to paint the other as the aggressor – a fight within a fight that was plainly won by the Americans, who had rushed their version of events across the Atlantic first. How would the opposing sides now fare at sea?

On 17 June 1778 a small French squadron was sent out from Brest to ascertain the strength and location of British forces in the Channel. Two frigates, the *Pallas* and *Belle Poule*, were spotted, chased and brought to heel. According to custom, the British captains then demanded that their French counterparts travel with them to see the British commanding officer, Admiral Augustus Keppel, on his flagship. The *Pallas's* captain agreed; the *Belle Poule's* refused, simply saying: 'that cannot be, Sir'.[23] The British frigate *Arethusa* fired a warning shot across her bows, whereupon the French unleashed their entire broadside into the hull of the British ship. There followed a terrific battle in which both ships found it very difficult to manoeuvre in the fluky winds. The British frigate, 200 tons smaller than the French, lost her mainmast just ten feet above the deck and was even less able to manoeuvre than her adversary. Drifting with the tide towards the French coast, the ships slugged at each other like prizefighters unable to land the knockout blow, the canvas at their feet spattered with blood and littered with teeth. Eventually it became clear that the *Arethusa* was unable to continue the fight and the *Belle Poule* escaped. News of the action, meanwhile, had reached Keppel, who immediately detained the *Pallas*. Keppel also mopped up two smaller ships from the French squadron.[24]

With such visible and dramatic evidence of the first clash between the two nations, journalists and politicians on both sides of the Channel feverishly set to work, spinning the story to make even more telling blows. A report appeared in the *London Gazette* on 27 June, which emphasized that the British had fired a shot across the French bows for not complying with their desire to escort them to Admiral Keppel. The French, apparently with no warning, then fired a full broadside into the *Arethusa*, which was within very close range. From the British perspective, it was also, and rightly, feted as a battle fought on the very lap of the Frenchman, against the odds, and it generated a very well-known song, simply titled 'The Arethusa', which emphasized these salient points:

> On deck five hundred men did dance
> The stoutest they could find in France
> We with two hundred did advance
> On board the *Arethusa* ...

> The fight was off the Frenchman's land
> We forc'd them back upon the strand,
> Of the gallant *Arethusa*
> And now we've driven the foe ashore
> Never to fight with Britons More ...

In France, however, the battle found an even more enthusiastic audience, one willing to embrace the battle in a way that few could have foreseen. The key point was that the French had sent an insignificant force of two frigates and two smaller ships to sea, which had, apparently, blundered into the entire British Channel Fleet and been driven back to find safety under the protective rocks of their own coastline. In doing so they had fought with great success, disabling their British opponent.*

No one in his or her right mind would believe that the captain of the *Belle Poule* had deliberately chosen to place his ship in the path of such a force, still less to start a fight within sight of it. In France, therefore, the battle was described as an affront to the French king, as an affront to his flag, to his seas, to his pride, to his nation, to his subjects. Louis explained his decision to declare war on Britain in exactly these terms in a letter to naval minister Sartine that was subsequently published. A similar letter, also with direct reference to the *Belle Poule* action, was sent to the French West Indies.[25] Frenchmen now had reason of their own to feel aggrieved, to feel bullied; they could legitimately paint the American cause as *their* cause, as a fight for liberty against the dastardly British, seen through the lens of the *Belle Poule* action as an insatiable imperial monster unfairly dominating the seas.

The real story, however, is more complicated. The timing was perfect. The French navy was now fully mobilized and the French were now prepared to show their hand and fight. It was essential, however, that the British were painted as the aggressors. Keppel found evidence on board the captured ships that the battle was the result of a carefully planned trap by the French. The ships' captains had explicit orders to provoke the British into 'what they may pretend to construe into an insult or act of hostility'.[26] The French, therefore, carefully manipulated the theatre of naval war to generate new enthusiasm

---

* Perhaps a part of the French fascination with this battle was the fact that the *Arethusa* was actually a French frigate, which had been captured in the previous war.

and reinforce existing support, both within France and on an international stage, for their alliance with America.

A well-organized publicity coup maybe, but no one was prepared for the extraordinary fame that this battle would subsequently achieve. Since the arrival of Benjamin Franklin it had become fashionable to be interested in America, and chic women now took on the challenge of celebrating the *Belle Poule* action, of linking themselves with the resurrected French navy and with the American cause, by creating that hairstyle – *à la Belle Poule* – which began, and inspired, this book.

In France war against Britain was on every tongue. Lieutenant Clocheterie, commander of the *Belle Poule*, was personally decorated by the king, and there was every hope that the French navy was once more, as it had been a century before under the great Louis XIV, equal to the British. The *Belle Poule* action seemed to suggest so; the French hoped so; and the Americans expected so.

For exactly this reason, the impact of the alliance in Britain was also severe and became the key element in a significant change of perception by the British of the Americans. The war had changed from a civil war to a more easily understood foreign war, with a resulting hardening of stance towards the rebels who suddenly now seemed more foreign, hostile and dangerous than they ever had before. 'America willingly became the dagger of France, and lent herself to be the instrument of the assassination of her parent', wrote Lord Lyttelton.[27] 'Are rebels and traitors our brethren, and fellow-subjects?' asked a letter in one British newspaper, 'are they not now aliens, and enemies? And what hope have we they will be our friends again, who are joined with Frenchmen, and Papists?'[28] This change of gear is more commonly associated with the battle of Lexington or the Declaration of Independence, but in reality it was the alliance with France, and particularly the entry of the French navy into the war, which changed everything.[29] Renouncing their allegiance to the king was *nothing* compared with the Americans jumping into bed with the French to embrace their sea power.

13

FRENCH FIREPOWER

The French entry into the war had an immediate impact on the *type* of sea power that was exercised and contested. Hitherto, relatively small warships had conducted the sea war in America. Admiral Howe's flagship *Eagle*, from which he had commanded the attacks on New York and Philadelphia, was a two-decked 64-gun Third Rate. It was chosen for its shallow draft and for its compromise between firepower and manoeuvrability. When Howe arrived in America, it was far more powerful than anything that the Americans could summon. Most of the other large ships in America were 50- and 44-gunners, obsolete classes of ship that had been reintroduced in the mid-1770s specifically in response to the challenge of war in America. Back in British waters, however, a 64-gun ship of the line was barely adequate even to be called a 'ship of the line', with the implicit assumption that it was powerful enough to hold its own in a line of battle. In the previous war the backbone of the line of battle had become 74-gunners – long, sleek, formidable ships.

With the French entry into the war, everything suddenly changed because the French had very large ships and the British were afraid of invasion.[1] They were right to be afraid: with so many troops in America, in February 1778 the entirety of England and Wales was garrisoned with only 14,471 troops.[2] French sea power and fear of invasion went hand in hand. In recent memory people could recall the several invasion scares of the Seven Years' War of the 1750s and the War of the Austrian Succession in the 1740s, and folk memory recalled the Nine Years' War in the 1690s, when Louis XIV had raised vast fleets in an attempt to seize control of the Channel as a crucial precursor to invading and replacing the Protestant William of Orange with the Catholic James Stuart.

To face the new French naval threat in 1778 the British now needed a different type of navy from the one they had in America; they needed a navy that consisted of the largest moving objects in the world – three-decked First Rate ships of 90 guns or more – to provide focus points in battle for long chains of 74-gunners.

The ship that encapsulated these hopes, this strength, this investment, and the newest First Rate in the navy, was HMS *Victory*, named for the *annus mirabilis* of 1759, when Britain had repeatedly beaten the French at sea. *Victory*'s subsequent famous history has in some respects played against her. She is now known worldwide as the only surviving ship from the Revolutionary and Napoleonic Wars and as Nelson's flagship at Trafalgar. But she is, in fact, the only surviving ship of the line from the War of American Independence – a far more impressive feat.

The *Victory* is enormous. If you have not seen her, one of the quickest ways to get a sense of just how massive she is is to consider her anchor cables. They have a circumference of 24 inches, roughly the same as a mature birch-tree. The cable itself, at least 600 feet long, weighed something like 4.5 tons, far more when wet. When she was fitted out for service in the Channel Fleet in early April 1778, sixty-five men were needed simply to get her anchor cables aboard.[3] Those cables were used to raise a two-ton anchor using two capstans, each of which was fitted with twelve capstan bars, and six men pushed each bar. No fewer than 144 men were therefore required to raise just one of HMS *Victory*'s anchors.

A comparison with Howe's flagship HMS *Eagle* is useful here to get a sense of the difference in sea power between 1776 and 1778. The *Victory*'s full complement was 850 men, 350 more than the *Eagle*. The heaviest guns of the *Eagle* were 24-pounders, whereas the *Victory* was designed for

42-pounders on her lowest deck.* The result was that the weight of broadside of *Victory's* lowest deck was larger than all of the guns on the *Eagle's* broadside added together. On 1 May 1778 *Victory's* powder stores were stocked with 42,000 pounds of gunpowder – that is the explosive capacity of 25.2 tons of TNT.[4]

Victory was destined to be the flagship of the Channel Fleet and, more than that, she was destined to be one of *seven* three-deckers in that fleet, one of the most powerful fleets of sailing warships ever assembled. The British pinned their hopes on *Victory* as the fleet's material and symbolic figurehead. She was widely considered then, and has been ever since, one of the finest examples of a three-decker ever to have been built, with beautiful lines that translated into surprisingly impressive speed and manoeuvrability for such a large vessel. Unusually, the king visited her as the final touches to her fitting-out were completed.[5] In this way and others, George brought a bristling energy to British preparations. Utterly outraged by the French joining the war, he had since threatened to abdicate rather than concede America's independence.[6]

This energy from the king flowed down through the Admiralty and Navy Boards and into the dockyards, both royal and private. In an attempt to reduce the damage of lost time, a greater number of shipbuilders than ever before were engaged to build ships in this period and resources committed in hitherto unknown amounts.[7] Expectations of British naval success, in both the navy and the public, soared. Significantly, however, one man was cowed rather than inspired by the challenge of fighting the French at sea. Unfortunately for the British it was Lord North, the prime minister. On receiving news of the French declaration he immediately asked to resign, claiming that capital punishment was preferable to his anguish of mind.[8] Conscious of North's political skill at this time of deep political division, the king refused. From that moment

---

* They were changed to 32-pounders by Keppel in the summer of 1778.

on, a man who was both weak and unwilling led the British war effort. It was not a good mixture.

*   *   *

The first opportunity to test each other's mettle arose in July 1778. *Victory*'s admiral was Augustus Keppel who, with the advent of war with France, had finally found an opportunity to serve in the war. Born into the Rockingham Whig aristocracy, Keppel was an opinionated opposition politician and had refused to fight in America – a significant loss to the British war effort. He had been one of the leading naval officers, if not *the* leading naval officer, of his generation. His naval career began at the age of ten and he was made captain at the age of nineteen – nearly two years in age earlier than Nelson. An experienced fighting sailor with knowledge of amphibious operations and well liked by his men, Keppel would have been a perfect choice to share command with Carleton and Burgoyne in the lakes, and it has been made clear how a naval mind could have significantly altered the campaigns of 1776 and 1777. There was no doubt, however, that in the summer of 1778 Keppel was a little rusty; he had, in fact, been ashore for fifteen years.

His second-in-command was Hugh Palliser. Slightly older than Keppel though still three years his junior because of Keppel's lightning promotion, Palliser was another competent officer. He sat on the Admiralty Board and was well respected and liked by his men. He was, however, a staunch Tory and thus ideologically opposed to Keppel. Nonetheless, both men were committed career naval officers, both men had fought the French over a life-long career, and both men now faced a threat that they understood and were committed to destroying: Keppel and Palliser sailed to war as naval brothers, not as rival politicians.

Their crews, however, were not so experienced and skilled. Remember that war in America had already been draining British resources of fighting sailors for four years. By the summer of 1778 the British were unable to man the ships of the

Channel Fleet until the merchant fleets from the Caribbean and Mediterranean had made their annual return voyage. Most of the crews, therefore, were pressed into service and had very little time to work together, to form the links of trust and respect – or, indeed, of mistrust and wariness – that allowed the best fleets to perform competently. Boatswains needed to know the quirks of their men just as sailing masters needed to know the quirks of their ships. The French may have had no more recent battle experience than the British, but they certainly had more experience of naval seamanship, acquired through training squadrons in the early 1770s. Furthermore, the man who had led one of those training squadrons, the comte d'Orvilliers, was now in command of the Brest fleet.[9]

D'Orvilliers's early military career had been in the army, but at the age of twenty he had joined the navy. In 1778 he was sixty-eight years old, a true veteran of French sea power who had served in both the War of the Austrian Succession (1740–8) and the Seven Years' War (1754–63). Of particular interest, d'Orvilliers had fought at the battle of Minorca in 1756. Then, the British admiral John Byng had been sent with a fleet to relieve British-held Minorca, a crucial key to British naval strength in the Mediterranean besieged by the French. The fleets met and the French fought a skilful defensive action, teasing Byng by regularly drifting away to leeward while retaining a dominant position between the British and Minorca. Not only was d'Orvilliers equipped with a well-trained fleet in 1778, therefore, but he also had personal experience of one of the finest defensive naval actions of the century.

D'Orvilliers's orders in the summer of 1778 have been criticized by generations of naval historians for being inadequately aggressive,[10] but they were also entirely realistic. Sent out on a month's cruise in the approaches to the Channel, he would protect French trade and American privateers while threatening both incoming and outgoing British trade. In so doing he would maintain an already impressive level of French seamanship in his skilled sailors while improving it in the unskilled. His presence alone would reinforce the pre-existing and strong belief in Britain that the Brest fleet was a very serious threat indeed, thereby hobbling British naval strategy and forcing it to remain Channel-focused. He had specific orders to avoid battle unless the odds – determined by a comparison of the number of ships in his and the British fleet – were very much in his favour.[11] This was sea power carefully applied and well understood, a reflection of the cunning Vergennes and sensible Sartine behind it.

Keppel, meanwhile, was cruising the western approaches, protecting British trade, when he received intelligence that the French were preparing to sail with a fleet that would outnumber his own. He headed back to St Helen's, the fleet anchorage in the lee of the Isle of Wight, where he received reinforcements that would make the fleets roughly equal in number – twenty-nine French to thirty British* – though the British would have a marked advantage in number of guns: 1,950 French to 2,280 British.[12] Keppel headed back out to sea, this time in the knowledge that d'Orvilliers was out there somewhere, probably to the west and north of the island of Ushant.

*　*　*

To understand what happened next, and to be able to place those events in a realistic framework of expectation, it is first necessary to stop and consider a number of crucial factors relating to fleet battle under sail.

The first and most important point to make is one that is most often overlooked: relatively small squadrons had achieved most of the overwhelming British fleet victories of the previous two wars.† This is not a coincidence. Fleet command in the

---

* When the fleets fought on 27 July, the French had lost two during the previous night's manoeuvre, thus giving the British a slight numerical advantage.

† Boscawen defeated de La Clue at the battle of Lagos in 1759 with eight ships of the line; George Anson defeated de la Jonquière with a squadron of fourteen ships of the line at the first battle of Finisterre in 1747; Edward Hawke defeated the marquis de l'Etanduère with fourteen ships of the line at the second battle of Finisterre in the same year. Only the battle of Quiberon Bay in 1759 stands out as a decisive action in which quite a large fleet was used in the attack, when Edward Hawke defeated Conflans with twenty-four ships of the line.

age of sail was extraordinarily difficult. Signalling systems were very limited throughout the eighteenth century and it was all too easy for signal flags to be missed in the gun-smoke that clouded the battle. Station-keeping was also very difficult. The warships were cumbersome, all manoeuvres took a great deal of time to execute, and most manoeuvres, in particular tacking, were unreliable. All warships, moreover, performed differently. Uniformity of performance was impossible. As a rule, things went wrong. The one consideration that reduced the negative impact of these awkward truths was the smallness of a squadron. A small squadron was more likely to be able to concentrate its fire on a given location; a small squadron was more likely to be able to see and then react to its commander's orders; a small squadron was more likely to be able to act together as a single unit, rather than as a confused jumble of ships.

The two fleets that now faced each other at Ushant in the summer of 1778 were enormous. Keppel had thirty-one ships of the line, and when he initially left Brest, d'Orvilliers had thirty-two. They were unwieldy. Keppel's fleet, when sailing in line ahead, was nine *miles* long. On one occasion when Keppel gave the order to anchor, the entire rear third of the fleet was so far behind the van that they were unable to come to anchor in the desired place until the next day.[13] Hitherto, such large fleets had never produced a decisive result in any eighteenth-century battle, and in every decisive battle won by a large sailing fleet in the years that followed the enemy was either trapped or willing to stand and fight until the battle was decided one way or another. This had nothing to do with tactical ideas but was the nature of sailing warfare. Ideas of concentrating ships on a part of the enemy line or of disrupting the enemy line were as old as the line of battle itself. The problem was making it happen against an enemy who did not want to stand and fight. Experienced naval minds knew this, and for that reason several leading British thinkers and decision-makers were relatively unconcerned about what d'Orvilliers might actually achieve.[14] Another key factor to consider is that, unlike the British, the French had no ships in reserve at Brest: the nearest were in

Toulon.[15] By no means, therefore, could they risk the type of confrontation that the British public so feared.

D'Orvilliers sailed in full knowledge that, in the haunting words of Sartine, 'the eyes of Europe' were on his fleet.[16] On 23 July the fleets made first contact and d'Orvilliers cleverly and skilfully won the weather gage from the British during the night. From that moment on, if Keppel had wanted to attack the French, he would have had to tack his fleet, probably several times, to get anywhere near them – and that assumed that the French would not try to escape to windward or, if they did, that the British had superior windward performance. Such manoeuvring, moreover, was very likely to create divisions in his fleet, if not outright chaos, which would either force Keppel to stand his attack down or present d'Orvilliers with a wonderful opportunity to counter-attack by dividing and overwhelming a section of the British.

Unsurprisingly, therefore, the fleets continued like this for four entire days while the British hoped for a change in the wind; eventually it shifted enough to allow the British to close the gap. Keppel fortified his crew with an allowance of grog while a squall brought the fleets close enough for a distant action to commence. The fleets passed on opposite tacks at a deathly slow pace. The angle of attack meant that the British rear, under Hugh Palliser, suffered particularly severely in the ships' rigging from excellent French gunnery. Keppel later claimed that the effect of their gunnery was 'beyond any degree I ever before saw',[17] testament to the quality of French gunpowder and the training of the French sailors. The tactic of firing high put immense pressure on the relatively untrained British crews. We know that Keppel's crew were forced to unbend a main topsail in the thick of the action, a tough and demanding job requiring precise teamwork on deck and aloft as well as perfect communication between the two teams.[18] To do this in the middle of battle with smoke obscuring their vision, the sound of cannon-fire deafening their ears and enemy shot snapping in the air around their heads and feet was an immense challenge. Faced with many similar challenges, Palliser's flagship and several others were unable to rejoin the British centre and van squadrons to launch another attack.[19]

The battle fizzled out. No ships were lost on either side, though the statistics of dead and injured were at least encouraging to the British. Relatively speaking, the British had more guns per ship than the French, and it appeared that those guns, when fired at the enemy hulls, were effective at smashing the timber and killing the men.* After the first pass, the French fleet formed neatly into line as the sun set. The next morning they were twenty miles distant and soon entirely out of sight, their job done. The French had not won a crushing victory, but they had not tried to win a crushing victory. Rather, as one officer said, they had 'beaten you as much as the kind of battle that had been fought, would permit them'.[20] D'Orvilliers had followed his orders to the letter. He had taken his fleet out, he had fought only once, and he had prevented his fleet from being defeated while delivering a stinging slap to the enemy.

We know that the French suffered from cohesion problems and communication problems in their own way and that one French flag officer, the duc de Chartres, shouldered some blame for preventing the French fleet from continuing the action. Still, they performed well enough and comparatively so much better than the British that, for once, British naval officers came away scratching their heads, deeply impressed with the quality of French seamanship they had witnessed. 'It is a general observation of the Officers of the fleet, that no ships could be fought better or better managed than the Enemies ships were, their line was formed very exact', wrote one sailor.[21] Another commented that 'The French behaved more like seamen, and more officer like than was imagined they would do, their ships were in very high order, well managed, well rigged and ... much more attentive to order than our own.'[22] Yet another, in a particularly telling description of the

---

* There were 133 dead and 373 wounded in the British fleet, compared to 161 dead and 513 wounded in the French. Clowes, *Royal Navy*, III, 422.

workings of the French fleet, explained how the French frigates, bustling around the main fleet, passing messages this way and that, providing support as and where it was needed,

> showed an alertness … not equalled by any of ours. When their signals were at any time thrown out to make sail, they were in an instant under a cloud of canvas; when they returned to their admiral, or were called to him, they run close up to his stern with all sail set, when in a moment all disappeared but the topsails. If a ship was but at a small distance, if called to the admiral, she immediately spread all her sail, even to stunsails, if they would draw.

'This appears to be not only seamanship,' he concluded, 'but the brilliancy of it.'[23] This was only one part of an all-round display, however. The effect of French gunnery had been so severe that, after Sandwich had inspected the fleet in Plymouth, he declared in Parliament he could not have believed the scale of the damage if he had not seen it himself, and the boatswains' damage reports are eye-opening.[24] Richard Kempenfelt, a British naval officer with a keen interest in signalling and tactics, was so frustrated by the evident gulf in performance that he was inspired to develop an entirely new signalling system for the Royal Navy.[25]

Regardless of the battle's result, this clear demonstration of competence, even of outright superiority, single-handedly changed the war. From that moment on the presence of any French fleet in European waters had to be taken very seriously indeed. The desire to win the war in America now had to be balanced with the necessity of keeping the French out at home, and the balance of naval power around the world had to be struck accordingly.

*   *   *

Some interpretations of the battle of Ushant see it as a potential turning point in the war on the basis that it was a failure, by the British, to utterly destroy the French Brest fleet. Such an argument, however, depends entirely on the assumption that such a victory was possible, when the potential of fleet battles to create such a clear-cut solution was clearly inadequate, particularly so when one admiral, who was both crafty and skilled, had orders to do everything he could to avoid it. The assumption that Keppel could somehow have 'annihilated' the French fleet and removed it permanently from the strategic equation is naïve. The best that could have been hoped for was for the French to become divided during the night, allowing the British to capture an isolated squadron of, say, six or seven French ships. But even then the French would still have had a fleet of twenty-three of the line in Brest, more than enough to continue to influence the shape of the war. The key advantage of the size of their fleet was that the French could measure its impact in the long term, and they knew it. 'The great disadvantage the French have hitherto had in every naval war, arose from the beginning it with too small a force – The loss of one or two squadrons undid us,' said the comte de Maurepas, a former naval minister and Louis XVI's unofficial chief minister, 'but that will not be the case now.'[26]

The impact of naval battles, however, always has to be measured both at sea and ashore, and in this instance the impact ashore was immensely influential, far more so than the guns fired and musket-balls exchanged on that day. The nature of the war had already ensured that political divisions ran deep and the entry of the French into the war did nothing to unite the British politicians. In fact, quite the opposite happened and divisions deepened.[27] Ushant was then used as ammunition to strike political blows against the incumbents, particularly the prime minister, Lord North, and the First Lord of the Admiralty, Lord Sandwich.

The problems began in the press. In the weeks after the battle the British flag officers had been getting on very much as they had before, but now repairing their ships and focusing on the likelihood of the French fleet leaving Brest again. What happened next is a classic example of the politics of the period aggravating problems rather than initiating them.[28]

An opposition newspaper suddenly piped up, blaming Palliser for Keppel's inability to relaunch an attack on the French. Palliser, whose squadron had tasted most of the action and had been crippled by French gunnery, was understandably furious. The journalist responsible must have rubbed his hands with glee when Palliser rose to the bait and demanded that Keppel publicly refute the allegations, and Keppel refused.

The navy had previous experience here. Something similar had happened in 1744 at the battle of Toulon, when Admiral Thomas Matthews had been unsupported in the face of the enemy by Richard Lestock. Those events, however, had been more clear-cut. Matthews and Lestock loathed each other; Keppel and Palliser did not. Neither Matthews nor Lestock was particularly well liked or respected, and neither had particularly impressive careers; both Keppel and Palliser were liked and respected, and both had impressive and lengthy careers. Although they were no doubt politically wary of each other, there is no evidence at all that they did not share a professional respect for each other, or that they had deliberately failed to help each other because of a personal or political feud.

Palliser, whose reputation was on the line, had no choice but to react when Keppel refused to refute the public accusations, and here again is an interesting crossroads. Perhaps Palliser could have forced a public apology from Keppel by publishing his own version of events and encouraging others to do the same, but he chose to take a far more extreme route, and here a peculiar circumstance intervened which forced the confrontation in an unpleasant and unwanted direction. Palliser demanded a court martial of Keppel, his senior officer. Sandwich, loyal to Palliser as a fellow member of the Admiralty Board and a supporter of his policies, granted his wish. A different scenario – perhaps *any* different scenario – would have had a different impact. By supporting Palliser over the senior commanding officer of his Channel Fleet, Sandwich essentially threw Keppel to the wolves, severing an important bond of professional trust. It was a serious mistake.

'Who's in fault? NOBODY a view off Ushant. The Anatomists will have it that it can
have no Heart, having no Body-but the Naturalists think if it has a Heart, it must surely lay
in its Breeches.'

And so the case went to court, to the utter outrage of most
naval officers. Politicians, naval officers and the public were
forced to split into camps, neatly known as the Montagus (for
those who supported Palliser and his benefactor Sandwich,
whose family name was Montagu) and the Capulets, a pun
on Keppelites. The press produced some fantastic cartoons,
including one which showed Keppel as nothing more than
a head wobbling on top of some spindly legs, thus allowing
the artist to claim that the indecisive action at Ushant was
'nobody's fault' – no *body's* fault – while firmly pointing the
finger at Keppel. At the same time the artist could comment
that such a peculiar-shaped being 'can have no Heart having
no Body – but the Naturalists think if it has a Heart, it must
lay in its Breeches'. In the background Ushant was depicted as
a confusion of smoke and sailcloth.

Palliser had simply wanted Keppel to acknowledge that the public criticism of his second-in-command was unjust, but now Keppel was being tried, and make no mistake, he was being tried for his life: in 1756 Byng had been tried for failing to do his utmost to engage the French at Minorca, had been found guilty and had been executed on his own quarterdeck. These charges, however – and as everyone knew – were ridiculous. Keppel had done well to force an engagement at all, doggedly chasing to windward over four days and waiting for an opportunity. When that opportunity had arisen, he had taken it in the only way that he could, and had succeeded in bringing the French to an engagement. That the French were unwilling to stand and fight was certainly not his fault, nor was there much that he could have done about it. Every naval man knew that.

Now there was another crossroads that further exploded this trial into the public consciousness. Uniquely, and by a special Act of Parliament, it was held on land, rather than on board ship, thus allowing large numbers of onlookers and reporters to witness the unfolding events. Naval court martial, usually professional, austere and private, thus became public political theatre. Public interest was unprecedented and journalists became heavily involved. This, also, was a significant change: hitherto the legitimacy of the war had been the main topic of discussion; after Ushant it was its conduct. Simultaneously, the Opposition sharpened its teeth.[29]

Keppel was acquitted to riotous celebrations in a result that was interpreted as a strike against the government and against Sandwich. Mobs took to the streets. The issue at stake had evolved from seamanship to politics to human justice. Palliser was burned in effigy and his house destroyed; Lord North was forced to protect himself and his house with armed guards; the homes of Sandwich, Lord Lisburne, Lord Bute, Lord Mulgrave and Germain were all attacked. The gates of the Admiralty were pulled down.[30] A pro-Palliser song lamented:

And is it thus, ye base and blind,
And fickle as the shifting wind,
Ye treat a warrior staunch and true,
Grown old in combating for you?
… Go learn of him whom ye adore,
Whose name now sets you in a roar,
Whom ye were more than half prepar'd
To pay with just the same reward,
To render praise where praise is due,
To keep his former deeds in view
Who fought and would have died for you.[31]

Palliser felt that he had no choice but to demand a court
martial of his own to clear his name, but his demand of a court
martial on Keppel, his superior officer, had done more than
enough to ruin his name in other, and perhaps more meaningful, ways. Palliser's trial went ahead, but it was not conducted
with anything like the razzmatazz that had been attached to
Keppel's. He was also acquitted. In fact it was found that he
had acted with honour and courage and that his conduct was
'in many instances highly exemplary and meritorious'.[32] He
was, however, chastised for failing to signal to Keppel that his
flagship was disabled – a slap on the wrist that carried far more
weight handed down in court than it otherwise would have
done. Naval men knew that ships became damaged, that it
was difficult to signal, that Palliser, had he not been damaged,
would have joined with Keppel. They also knew that, if Keppel
had been able to reunite his fleet, he would have tried once
more to attack the French.

The result of all this was that the British naval officer corps
was gravely and unnecessarily damaged. At a time when the
Royal Navy needed every knowledgeable officer it could get,
neither Keppel nor Palliser, though both were reprieved, ever
served afloat again, nor did some of their most experienced
senior officers. It was extraordinarily difficult to gain experience of fleet battle and the British were throwing theirs in
the bin. There was a very shallow pool from which to find

replacements. A pro-Keppel pamphleteer concluded one tirade with the thoughtful and excellent line that he would 'be *lov'd*, when he is *lack'd*'.[33] All this tension, of course, filtered down to the lower decks. *Victory* and *Formidable*, the respective flagships of Keppel and Palliser, were berthed separately for fear that their crews would fight it out.[34]

The Royal Navy thus did more damage to itself in the battle's aftermath than the French had inflicted in the actual battle. The expectation of British naval success in home waters, so dominant in the run-up to battle and so necessary because of the repeated failures in America, burst. An American prisoner in a British gaol in Portsmouth noted:

> we have seen a vast number of men come in from the ships, in boats, whom we suppose to be wounded ... This was England's pride – the fleet that was to sweep the seas, and accomplish such wonders. Alas! Many of them are disappointed of their expectations, for in their first engagement, they were worsted.[35]

Cornwallis's wife Jemima summed up the change: 'I am really so bilious as to think our army in America, Fleets everywhere, Possessions in the West Indies, &c., &c., &c., will be frittered away and destroyed in another Twelve months.'[36]

The British were now in uncharted waters. Traditionally, the navy gave them security, safety, confidence and hope, but all of this had been stripped away by Ushant. To make matters worse, Jemima was right to fear for British possessions beyond the Channel. In the summer of 1778 not only had the French sent d'Orvilliers into British home waters, but they had also sent another squadron, under the fiery comte d'Estaing, to America. The 1778 campaign was a double strike. Would the British be able to fight off the French in America or would they fail as Jemima and many others now so feared?

14

BRITISH SURVIVAL

The first French warship to arrive in American waters, the first concrete evidence of significant French military aid, was the frigate *Nymphe* commanded by le chevalier de Sainneville, which arrived in Boston on 5 May 1778. A mere lieutenant, he was treated almost regally. Trailed by a crowd of all ages, Sainneville dodged the many and repeated questions fired at him by the Bostonians, like a wily politician on campaign, commenting on French intentions 'but without saying anything'.[1]

All American hopes had been placed on a French alliance but no one knew exactly what it would bring. The Americans were both joyous and wary; this meeting sparked both the release of tension and the birth of new concerns. Would the French come and drive the British from the sea in a dramatic clash between battle fleets? Would they land an army and fight the British on American soil? This odd breed of man also, of course, fascinated them. Some refused to believe the evidence of their eyes that Sainneville and his crew appeared quite normal and spread rumours that several had been caught hunting frogs in the pond at the bottom of Boston Common.[2] The anticipation of French aid also had an interesting effect on the American economy because merchants rushed to take advantage of prices that would inevitably rise once the French and British both had large battle fleets in American waters. In turn, this halted the relentless depreciation of the American currency, which had been sliding downhill since 1776. Life in America was thus changed by French sea power before the French ships even arrived.

* * *

D'Estaing's fleet leaving the Mediterranean, 16 May 1778.

The first significant French force sent to America was d'Estaing's naval squadron. His mission had been long in the planning; he had, in fact, left his base at Toulon for America on 13 April 1778, more than two months before the *Belle Poule* action was even fought and war between Britain and France was openly declared.

He had kept his destination secret, only revealing it to his officers twenty leagues west of Cape St Vincent: the middle of the Atlantic was the only place safe from British spies. He also carried orders to begin hostilities against Britain when twenty leagues even further west, where he could act in the knowledge that no news would reach Britain for weeks, if not months.[3]

D'Estaing's primary responsibility was to cross the Atlantic to find and fight the British fleet, the first time in French naval history that a French squadron had been given such explicitly aggressive orders.[4] He had been well equipped to do so, with twelve ships of the line and five frigates, more than a match for Admiral Howe's higgledy-piggledy fleet of small ships scattered along the American coast. D'Estaing and his men, moreover, had been roundly encouraged to fight. Under a new law the French sailors would receive a significant prize, 600 *livres* per cannon for each enemy warship sunk or burned.[5] D'Estaing overflowed with energy. One of his officers said he had the 'enthusiasm and fire of a man twenty years of age'.[6] He was actually forty-eight and time would tell if the appearance of youth alone would be enough to command a highly complex naval operation against a skilled enemy on an unknown shore thousands of miles from home. For one thing was certain: d'Estaing did not overflow with experience.

In Britain worries about French sea power had reached fever pitch thanks to the talent of Lieutenant Clocheterie of the *Belle Poule* and Admiral d'Orvilliers, commander of the French fleet at Ushant. D'Estaing, however, bore no comparison. He had begun his career in the army and had since transferred to the navy where, owing to close connections with the king, his promotion had been swift. Many of his fellow naval officers, experienced naval men all, were outraged.[7] He was at heart a soldier with no knowledge of, or feel for, the sea. His courage was unquestioned, as was his experience of campaigning ashore, but he understood neither the whims and caprices of naval warfare nor the immense influence that a squadron could exert if used with great subtlety. To make this weakness worse, d'Estaing was often unwilling to seek counsel from those around him who had the knowledge that he lacked. The French performance at sea hitherto had created legitimate expectations of French sea power in and around the British coast. Considered use of both immense fleets and small squadrons had been allied with excellent execution and accurate firepower. By placing d'Estaing in command of the squadron sent to America, however, Vergennes had seriously undermined the tower of expectation that had been built in America, and the Americans had no idea at all that this was the case: when they saw d'Estaing's topsails breaking the horizon and ships flying the distinctive white French naval ensigns, their hearts leapt. The idea that competence and operational effectiveness could vary to astonishing degrees within a navy was unthinkable to them. It was one of the most important lessons that they would learn in the coming war.

The voyage was notable for its unusual length. D'Estaing

took thirty-three days to travel from Toulon to Gibraltar and then another fifty-two days to cross the Atlantic.[8] It is unclear why he took so long and the poor sailing qualities of the ships he was given must bear some responsibility, but the voyage was long enough for the network of merchants, naval ships and fishermen who populated the mid-Atlantic Ocean and were sympathetic to the British cause to send news westward faster than d'Estaing's fleet could travel. One British packet-ship wheezed into Philadelphia with the horrific news.[9] The news was received there particularly badly because, now staggering from the shock of having to wage a naval war with France as well as a land war with America, the Cabinet had decided to abandon Philadelphia, to free up troops for a campaign against French Caribbean colonies.[10] They were now in no position at all to defend themselves from a hostile fleet.

The British took care to burn every vestige of American sea power on the Delaware before they left.[11] The evacuation was yet another massive naval operation. Howe made the bold and impressive announcement that the Royal Navy would give any civilian who wanted it, together with his family and his property, transport to New York.[12] It soon became clear, however, that there were insufficient ships to honour this promise. It was a major political blunder. 'No man', wrote one royal official, 'can be expected to declare for us when he cannot be assured a fortnight's protection.'[13] The British relationship with the loyalists, upon whom they had heaped so much expectation for the conduct of the war, was thus damaged.

Those who had the muscle or influence crammed themselves aboard a cumbersome evacuation fleet to rival, in both size and misery, the one that had left Boston in 1775. Yet again, carts overloaded with household goods were dragged to the harbour and, yet again, British sailors maximizing space on their ships for bodies and food threw anything else into the sea.[14]

With all the space on Howe's ships taken up by loyal civilians, the least trustworthy Hessians, and a last-ditch and utterly toothless peace commission led by the Earl of Carlisle,* Henry Clinton, who had now taken over General William Howe's role as commander-in-chief of the British army in America, had no choice but to take his army to New York overland.[15] A sorry, vulnerable parade that stretched twelve miles across New Jersey, Washington seized the opportunity to attack it at Monmouth, a significant strike against Cornwallis that created fresh enthusiasm for the American cause. The Americans, meanwhile, had regained the key port of Philadelphia, which became one of the leading privateer ports for the rest of the war. Hundreds of slaves, mostly young men, fled with the British for New York. When the Americans retook Philadelphia, they found a black community that was largely composed of children, the elderly and women.[16]

All this upheaval, misery, strategic vulnerability and death had been caused by nothing more than the promise of French sea power – another striking example of how French warships affected both life in America and the shape of the American war before they even arrived.

*   *   *

Fortunately for the British, Admiral Howe, who had been given permission to return home, remained in American waters even while his replacement, James Gambier, settled into New York. Howe, who had been itching to get at the French, knew that his real talents lay in fleet warfare. He also knew that Gambier had no real talents.

Howe's formidable task was clear. He knew that naval reinforcements were arriving under John Byron, a naval officer of immense experience, who had been sent to America as soon as it became clear in London that d'Estaing had escaped and his location was known. This strategy of using small squadrons to react to French initiatives characterized British naval

---

* This was the last diplomatic attempt to end the war by negotiation. The fact that there were no more efforts made when several opportunities presented themselves was a major weakness in the British war effort. Dull, *Diplomatic History*, 123–4.

The French fleet entering the Delaware and chasing the frigate *Mermaid*, 8 July 1778.

strategy throughout the war. Sandwich, terrified of French invasion after their navy's competent display at Ushant, was responsible for it, prioritizing strength in home waters over strength abroad. Until Byron arrived, Howe would have to use his badly manned and small fleet of small ships to hold off a much larger French fleet, consisting of twelve large ships of the line designed and built for fleet battle.*

Howe's first priority was intelligence: if he knew exactly what the French were doing, then he could make the most effective use of his force. British cruisers were therefore sent south to find the French and to shadow them wherever they went. The French arrived at the Delaware on 8 July, terrifyingly close to the sailing of the vulnerable British evacuation fleet.

The French arrival was not without incident and one of their ships grounded on the sand-bar at the entrance to the Delaware. It raised the obvious point that, although the French warships were more powerful than those of the British, they were, necessarily, larger and drew more water.[17] For all its materiel weakness, therefore, Howe's fleet would be able to go to places where d'Estaing's could not.

* Howe's fleet consisted of six 64-gunners, two 50-gunners and some smaller ships. Clowes, *Royal Navy*, III, 399–401.

Having landed the Philadelphia evacuees in New York, Howe assumed a strong defensive position just inside the bend of Sandy Hook, New Jersey, with his ships positioned broadside to the main channel heading towards New York. The positioning of his ships was the result of careful study, deep knowledge of seamanship, and a willingness to share information with his subordinates:

> He sounded its several depths in person; he ascertained the different setting of the currents, and from the observations thus made, formed different plans with a view to the points of wind with which d'Estaing might resolve to cross the bar. These plans, with the grounds on which they rested, he daily communicated to the commodores and captains, soliciting their opinions, and desirous of profiting by their objections.[18]

With his ships anchored at bow and stern, Howe also had his sailors run extra lines, known as 'springs', to their own anchors, which meant that the broadsides of the British ships could easily be swung into new positions by manipulating the main anchor lines.[19] The naval defences were augmented with army positions, dug in on the Hook itself. With Howe's fleet positioned in this way, every French ship would be forced to sail past every British ship before entering the Narrows, and all this in a seaway renowned for its shallows and racing tides, and only at high tide on a day with a settled easterly or south-easterly wind. Any attack, therefore, would be both risky and predictable: the British would know how and when the French would come, and they would then have every chance of disabling the French ships as they headed to New York.

For several days the French lurked just to seaward of the Hook, 'in the form of an exact half-moon',[20] using the time to make contact with Washington, to water their ships and to sound the approaches to the Hook. In a week of the highest tension, these fleets of warships were only a mile or two apart,

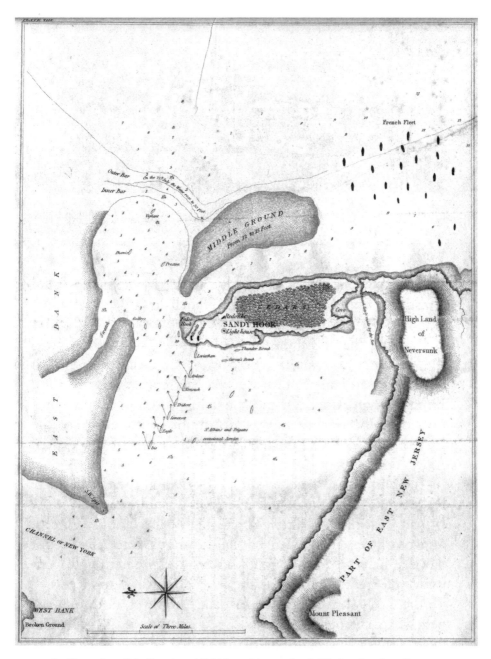

An illustration of the French and British positions at Sandy Hook, taken from Rear-Admiral Charles Ekins's *Naval Battles* (1824), one of the most detailed studies of naval tactics of the era and a pioneering English language study of naval tactics. Ekins joined the navy in March 1781, fought against the Dutch at the battle of the Dogger Bank in 1781 and relieved Gibraltar with Howe in 1782. He went on to enjoy a varied, long and successful career.

The French fleet anchored before New York, blockading the English fleet and intercepting the shipping trying to enter, 12 July 1778.

separated by the dunes of Sandy Hook – a memorable and arresting moment captured by the French artist Pierre Ozanne, who had sailed with d'Estaing.

Rumour that d'Estaing was off New York flashed across the Atlantic to France, where everyone held their breath in full of anticipation of success. In the words of John Bondfield, an American merchant in Bordeaux deeply committed to the war, there was 'no doubt of the entire of the [*sic*] English Forces would fall into the hands of the United Allied Forces'.[21]

The climax was reached on 22 July when there was thirty feet of water over the bar. The tension was intense and yet the British, just like the French, had high expectations. One of Howe's officers acknowledged that 'we ... expected the hottest day that had ever been fought between the two nations ... Yet, under Heaven, we had not the least doubt of our success.'[22] To the 'great surprise' of the British,[23] however, nothing happened. Concerned that his deep warships would get stuck on the notorious sand-bar that guarded the entrance to the Narrows and worried about the orientation of the channel running past the Hook, d'Estaing made no move at all.[24] One ship had already grounded at the mouth of the Delaware, and it was becoming rather clear that, without accurate, up-to-date hydrographical knowledge of the coast that they were attacking, French naval capability was severely restricted. It is remarkable that they had not anticipated this problem, and one strongly suspects that a seaman such as d'Orvilliers or a commander more willing to listen to his knowledgeable officers than d'Estaing would not have made such an error. The contrast with the way in which the British force was positioned and commanded by Howe could not have been starker.

Outfoxed for now, d'Estaing sailed, but the game was by no means up. He left New York with a very valuable piece of information – a key fact that would elude many other fleet commanders during the war and that would regularly affect its course: d'Estaing now knew where his enemy's fleet was, and therefore he knew where his enemy's fleet wasn't.

* * *

Howe was impotent for fear that d'Estaing was merely trying to lure him away before doubling back and striking again at New York. Until he had received concrete intelligence of d'Estaing's movements or Byron arrived with more ships, the British were immobilized by the presence of French sea power.

Nevertheless, Howe played his cards well in the given situation and found the loyalist population of New York more than willing to help. With the threat of the traditional enemy at hand, volunteers from the British transports in New York had flooded to his undermanned ships 'almost to a man',[25] and fishermen had offered to take their shallops to sea to look out for Byron and to bring him safely and as quickly as possible to New York.[26] Howe had acted decisively and with great skill, but in truth it had been a lucky escape for the British: if only d'Estaing had been able to make his crossing of the Atlantic in anything approaching a normal time frame, he would have found the British in a vulnerable, perhaps even hopeless state, in the process of evacuating Philadelphia.[27] Washington was keenly aware of how close they had come to such easy pickings. He was convinced that, had d'Estaing arrived sooner,

Clinton's army in Philadelphia would have shared the same fate as Burgoyne's at Saratoga.[28] There was, however, more than a single British army at stake here. If Howe's fleet had been intercepted or bottled up at Philadelphia, then New York itself would also have been defenceless. Little did he know it, but when d'Estaing was in mid-Atlantic, the war had been hanging on another spider silk.

Rear-Admiral John Byron, meanwhile, had been rushing as fast as he could to join Howe but was finding the going heavy. At least one of his ships had been rigged with weak masts that split and snapped, killing and wounding several of his crew – the poor state of his rigging a direct result of the pressure that had already been applied to British naval infrastructure and stores by the war in America.[29] Byron was also renowned for encountering storms and had been named for it by his crew. 'Foul Weather Jack' now lived up to his reputation. On 30 June he encountered a ferocious storm, perhaps the result of an unusual northwards course, which thrashed his ships until they were bedraggled shadows of the force they were supposed to be. In a matter of hours his 'reinforcement' squadron had become one that could barely cling to life, let alone offer a threat. The ships were shattered and scattered. One went home, two made it to St John's in Newfoundland, another sailed to Lisbon for repairs. The rest limped into New York, their rigs ruined and their crews in a desperate condition, ravaged both by the storm and also by an epidemic.[30] When Byron arrived, therefore, his ships had little practical impact on the balance of sea power in America. Howe would still have to make do with his rag-tag fleet.

Howe moved as soon as he heard from his ever-efficient network of frigates that d'Estaing was heading for Newport, Rhode Island, the key deep-water harbour captured by the British in 1776 and now held by a force of some 5,000 soldiers. It was a sensible move by the French. By now d'Estaing's fleet had been at sea for three-and-a-half months, and the only fresh provisions they had been able to acquire were those rowed out to the fleet when at anchor off Sandy Hook. They now desperately needed water and the crews were beginning to suffer from scurvy. The operational capability of the squadron was beginning to diminish rapidly.

If the French were going to make a significant and long-term difference to the balance of power in American waters, they needed a base where they could recover and from which to operate. Newport was ideal. It was, moreover, a target was well within their grasp. The British force at Newport was geographically isolated because the town lies on the western shore of Aquidneck Island and is vulnerable to being cut off from the mainland. A well-timed and well-organized attack with the French navy working closely with the American army could therefore lead to a swift victory that would change the shape of the war.

This plan, however, depended entirely on two things: the first was that the French and the Americans could actually work together; the second was that Howe would not interfere.

* * *

Washington dispatched Major-General Sullivan, who had led the American withdrawal from Quebec and since then fought at Long Island where he had been captured and subsequently released, from the American camp at White Plains outside New York to prepare a position against Newport, from where he could attack once the French navy had taken control of Narragansett Bay. To some this opportunity to work with French sea power seemed like a dream come true. 'You are the most happy man in the World', wrote Nathanael Greene, 'What a child of fortune.'[31]

D'Estaing's arrival, with 4,000 soldiers in twelve magnificent ships of the line, now cast a shadow over the British in Rhode Island, just as British ships had done in New York in 1776 and Philadelphia in 1777. The British knew that there was little they could do to prevent such a powerful squadron from forcing the main passage and blocking the entrances to Narragansett Bay. But in a bid to make that navigation as difficult as possible – and giving evidence of their desperation – the British sank thirteen of their valuable transports in key strategic locations in the outer harbour, eight of which have since been discovered by marine archaeologists.* They also burned and sank four frigates along the west coast of Aquidneck Island, two corvettes in the outer harbour near the transports, and three smaller armed vessels in the Sakonnet River. This self-inflicted destruction was the most substantial British naval loss of any campaign of the war, and all this destruction was caused by the presence alone of d'Estaing. He had yet to fire a gun.

With an American pilot on board every ship in his fleet, and with his flagship at the head of the line, d'Estaing forced the main passage into Narragansett Bay on 8 August. The squadron gave a 'rolling fire at the entire coast' as they passed.[32] The British batteries struck a few blows but were toothless; the progress of the French relentless. Ozanne caught the majestic arrival of the French fleet in a remarkable series of eyewitness sketches.

Safely in, d'Estaing positioned his ships at every entrance to the bay while Sullivan prepared to attack. At this stage, co-operation between the Americans and the French was impressive. D'Estaing disposed of his ships according to Sullivan's suggestions and even ordered his ships operating close to shore to follow Sullivan's orders.[33] But then, on the very day that Sullivan planned to advance at the head of a force swollen with thousands of volunteers inspired by the arrival of the French ships, Howe arrived with the British fleet. The French, blinded by a lack of frigates, had been caught unawares.[34] The Americans and French were about to discover how their new relationship would bear up under the strain of British sea power.

Howe's force was weaker than d'Estaing's, and significantly so: only eight were ships of the line, and only thirteen were

---

* It is likely that one of those ships is the *Lord Sandwich*. Originally built in Whitby, she was once none other than the *Endeavour*, Captain James Cook's ship on his first circumnavigation. Her presence in Rhode Island is important evidence of the pressure on British shipping caused by transport and supply problems. You can follow the ongoing search for *Endeavour* at www.rimap.org. See also Abass, 'Newport'; Abass, '*Endeavour* and *Resolution*'.

The French fleet entering Rhode Island. To the right in the distance they are shown under
fire from British Batteries on the present-day site of Fort Adams. Note the sunken British
transports to the left and one British ship on fire. Between the sunken ships and the French
fleet, batteries on Goat Island and Rose Island are firing. D'Estaing leads the fleet in his
flagship the 80-gun *Languedoc*.

larger than frigates.[35] He anchored off Point Judith and waited
to see what d'Estaing would do. The French fleet was in a
strong position and Howe's arrival would change nothing if
Howe subsequently did nothing. Sullivan would advance and
the British garrison in Newport would be captured. Simply by
adopting the position that he had, d'Estaing's fleet was being
effective. He did not have to do anything. Inactivity in the
face of an enemy was not d'Estaing's way, however, nor, in his
defence, was it part of his orders, which required him to be
proactive in finding and fighting the British fleet.

The relative advantages of the positions of the forces, moreover, was a matter of perception. Was it the British garrison at
Newport that was surrounded by enemies, with Sullivan on one
side and d'Estaing on the other? Or was it d'Estaing who was
surrounded, with Howe on one side and the British Newport
garrison on the other? D'Estaing certainly felt vulnerable. In
his words he was 'blockaded, locked up, and divided'.[36] A key
part of his concern was a mistaken belief that Byron would
shortly join Howe, thus removing the clear and extant superiority that he then had over the British fleet. If d'Estaing was
going to engage the British at sea, now was the time to do so.

Situation in the afternoon of 11 August 1778 when a hurricane disrupted the British and French manoeuvring for battle. Note the black squalls carefully depicted on the horizon.

On 10 August he made sail. Howe bolted south, buying time for Byron to arrive while contemplating a limited fleet action against d'Estaing's superior force.

The French had a brief opportunity to engage which they spurned.[37] With detailed knowledge of local conditions and outstanding skills in fleet command, Howe positioned himself so that he could take advantage of a predictable shift of wind – the regular easterlies that blow onshore in the summer evenings off the Rhode Island coast. If there was going to be a battle, Howe thus made certain that he would control it, a crucial advantage between two unevenly matched fleets. To make things easier, he moved from his flagship, the 64-gun *Eagle*, to the frigate *Apollo*, a rare example of an admiral in the age of sail choosing to command at a distance, rather than from his flagship, in the heat of the action.

Everything was set for the most interesting fleet battle in the age of sail that was never fought. A vicious storm, one so fierce and relentless that it lived long in Rhode Island folk memory, rose out of nowhere. Ships of both fleets were instantly 'all jumbled together', the sailors no longer able to test each other against the wrath of their enemy but utterly focused on fighting for their lives against the wrath of nature.[38]

In the storm's aftermath a number of British and French ships blundered into one another: the 50-gun British *Renown* into the 80-gun *Languedoc*; the 54-gun *Preston* into the 64-gun

D'Estaing's flagship the *Languedoc*, dismasted by a storm on the night of 12 August, is attacked by HMS *Renown* the following day.

Marseillais; and the 50-gun *Isis* into the 74-gun *César* – an action that one contemporary thrillingly labelled 'as brilliant as any on record in the history of the English navy'.[39] Feverish, maybe, it is at least certain that, in each of these actions, the British were massively overmatched by their French opponents, but still fought until they were forced to flee by the arrival of other French ships. Howe barely survived the storm. His ship, the *Apollo*, had been pushed to the very limit. Captain Hamond risked his life to get a cutter across to Howe's ship, where he found him 'sitting by the Rudder Head to which he was lashed and the ship in a deplorable situation, all the half ports washed out and the sea running through and through the cabin'. Hamond took command, ordered a jury-mast rigged to ease the motion of the ship, transferred the crew to his ship, the *Roebuck*, and towed the *Apollo* back to New York.[40]

When the French returned to Newport, the mood in their navy had significantly changed and the change was tangible ashore. The violence of the storm, the lurking presence of Howe and the temerity of the warships they had encountered after the battle seemed to have given d'Estaing pause for thought. 'The devil has gotten into the fleet', wrote Nathanael Greene to a friend.[41] It certainly had. Even with Howe safely back in New York, d'Estaing wanted nothing more to do with the plan to take Newport from the British and fell back on his orders which required him, if outnumbered, to find

The French fleet repaired at sea and re-formed, with the exception of the *César*, now making way, 17 August 1778.

safety in Boston. On 22 August the French left Newport and the Americans raged in their wake. From the perspective of Sullivan and his army, the French had 'abandoned' their allies 'in a most rascally manner ... inexplicable upon military principles'.[42] Their leaving was, unquestionably, a terrible blow to American morale, casting a 'universal gloom' on the army. Thousands of volunteers, who had joined Sullivan's army cradling hopes of victory born by the presence of French sea power, instantly left. Washington, however, saw d'Estaing's actions in a more nuanced light, appreciating the immense difficulties that d'Estaing had faced. The very fact that the French squadron still existed as a viable force after the storm was itself a deeply impressive achievement, and the French sailors' heroic efforts to repair the fleet at sea off the Delaware coast, where they had been blown by the storm, were carefully recorded by Ozanne.

One can sense from his sketch that he, as well as the sailors knotting and splicing the rigging, fishing the masts and yards, and bending the sails, knew that this was a crucial moment. Less easy to defend, however, is the fact that, inexplicably, the French fleet abandoned their anchors when they left Newport, cutting them free rather than taking the time to weigh and secure them.[43]

For a brief time the chase was on again because Howe, remarkably, had also managed to repair his ships under intense logistical and time pressure in New York. They sailed 'in full Cry after the French Fleet', but – partly because one ship, the *St Albans*, grounded near Cape Cod – they were unable to catch them up before 'Monsieur, to Our great mortification ... got into Boston'.[44] Perhaps wisely because of the awkwardness of Boston Harbour, Howe chose not to risk a lightning attack on the French in Boston.

With things in America thus carefully balanced but with the initiative now firmly in British hands, Howe handed over his command to Gambier and left for London to defend his conduct in the 1776 and 1777 campaigns in a public circus of recrimination that had been begun by Ushant and would continue for the rest of the war. The loss of Howe was another sorry blow to British naval power.

*   *   *

Washington lamented another grievous lost opportunity. He believed that the loss of the British army at Newport would have broken the British will to continue the war. In his words, he believed it would have landed 'the finishing blow to British pretensions of sovereignty in this country'.[45] Perhaps he was right; this could well have been Yorktown three years before the real thing.

As it was, nothing had been achieved apart from a serious souring of the American–French relationship and a startling reality check on the effectiveness of sea power. At the start of the campaign, d'Estaing had sent Sullivan kind words, pineapples and lemons; now Sullivan, never calm even at the best of times, sent him back letters dripping with bile in which he explicitly attacked d'Estaing's honour.[46] Even worse, American expectations of the efficacy of French sea power had been demonstrated to be false. The magic wand of sea power they had all so craved had simply failed to work. It had emitted a few sparks, but the all-empowering sorcery of sea power, which was supposed to make armies lie down with a single swish, remained elusive.

It was a sobering moment for everyone. The French were

finding the realities of prosecuting an aggressive naval strategy 3,000 miles from home extremely difficult. So many variables had to fall into place for it to work, and at every turn so far they had been thwarted: in turns by Mother Nature, by their own incompetence, and by a skilful enemy. The Americans were immensely disappointed. Abigail Adams summed it up: when the damaged French fleet limped into Boston having achieved nothing at New York or Newport, she wrote, 'I own I am mortified, because I never before saw the people so zealous, or so much engaged & Determined. I thought it portended success to our Aims.'[47] The French and the Americans were starting to realize that the struggle *for* sea power went hand in hand with a struggle *with* sea power. Abigail, shoulders back, chin high, wrote: 'in bold & difficult enterprises we should endeavour to subdue one obstacle at a time, nor suffer ourselves to be depressed by their greatness and their number.'[48] She had yet to realize, however, just how large and numerous those obstacles would be. Operational failure in the face of the Royal Navy was only the start of the Frenchman's troubles.

Rather brilliantly, d'Estaing had met Sullivan's rudeness with 'the painful but necessary law of profound silence',[49] but the manifest tension between the new allies erupted into violence in Boston. Classic prejudices of both nations were reinforced. The Frenchmen sneered at the appearance of the American soldiers on their 'bad nags', and the Americans at the French in their high-heeled shoes.[50] Indeed, the French behaviour at Newport became the subject of a humorous ballad that poked fun at d'Estaing:

> To stay, unless he rul'd the sea,
> He thought would not be right, sir,
> And Continental troops, said he,
> On islands should not fight, sir.[51]

This caricature of distaste for each other's cultures and harmless sniping actually hid something far more destructive. Yes, the Americans felt let down by what they perceived to be the French abandonment of Sullivan at Newport. But more importantly – especially for the folk of Boston – the French navy now represented competition for meagre resources at a time of nervousness and desperation.

The French fleet was given priority in the use of all ship-building resources and the Americans were expected to pay for the numerous repairs to the French fleet. In fact, the French navy dominated dockyard labour to such an extent that several American ships were left 'in a most destitute and forelorn situation'.[52] This all put immense pressure on the immature American Navy Board of the Eastern Department, based in Boston, which was unable to cope. In the words of John Langdon, they were forced to 'alter our minds'. He raged at 'the most extravagant expense, the exorbitancy of the demands ... the imposition of every kind we are obliged to submit to'.[53]

The French navy also affected the sensitive balance in Boston between the supply of and demand for food. The French fleet was the size of a large town and had appeared with no notice. To cope with such unpredictable demands required a logistical infrastructure matured over decades. The Americans had nothing of the sort, nor did they have the financial resources to compete with the French navy. With chests of specie and bills of exchange and thousands of hungry mouths to feed, the French had no scruples in outbidding Continental agents trying to feed the American armed forces.[54]

The arrival of the French fleet in Boston, therefore, meant that conditions for the American army and for American civilians in the city worsened. Several riots broke out, and it is no coincidence that one of the worst happened at a baker's shop, one of several set up along the seafront to provide bread for the fleet. A French officer tried to prevent an angry and hungry American mob from breaking into the shop and had been murdered. It was particularly unfortunate that the dead officer was the chevalier Saint-Sauveur, the first chamberlain of the French king's brother, the comte d'Artois. Desperate diplomatic attempts to ease the crisis followed, and in an impressive feat of spin-doctoring the British were officially blamed.[55] Wounds were healed over a large feast and an orgy of toast-making and mutual reassurance with a necessary bias towards the rebels. The Massachusetts House of Delegates agreed to erect a memorial in his honour.*

D'Estaing remained jumpy. When invited by the Americans to dinner, he insisted it was held at Colonel Josiah Quincy's house because it was in sight of the harbour: d'Estaing could not let his ships out of his sight.[56] Such dinners at least gave the American and French leadership a chance to study each other properly and, generally speaking, both sides were impressed. Abigail Adams managed to secure an invitation to the flagship where she saw 'entertainment fit for a princiss', which compared favourably with an earlier event, a sumptuous feast followed by 'Musick and dancing for the young folks'.[57] John Adams commented in a letter back that 'accounts from all hands agree' that there was 'happy harmony upon the whole between the inhabitants and the Fleet'. He also observed that 'the more this Nation is known, and the more their language is understood, the more narrow Prejudices will wear away'.[58] He may have been right, but this mixture of street-level violence and diplomatic curtseying is a distinctive feature of the alliance in this period, the one born from the other. The British, however, were not easily fooled. 'The French and the rebels are most cordially sick of each other, a most reciprocal enmity and contempt', wrote Gambier in New York.[59]

*   *   *

Towards the end of 1778 d'Estaing was ready to move again, his soldiers' clothing and equipment boosted by British army supplies that had been captured by American privateers. He had achieved nothing in the interim: the grand dreams of American sea power working in harness with the French had been proven entirely unrealistic. He had given the British

---

* In fact nothing happened for 139 years. Then, in 1917, when France and America were allies in another war, a memorial was finally erected in the King's Chapel Burying Ground in Boston. It is still there today.

a major scare at Newport and had forced them to destroy some of their own shipping, but he had not even captured or destroyed a single British warship, let alone worked with the American army to secure any territory.[60] Washington had forced Sullivan to apologize to the Frenchman, but winter had now arrived in New England and nothing more could be done. An opportunity to surprise and dominate the British still existed in the West Indies, however, and d'Estaing was never one to sit still for long.

On 4 November he ran from Boston with his powerful fleet for Martinique. On the very same day a British force under Commodore William Hotham left New York, also for the West Indies. This had nothing to do with d'Estaing's movement but was a much-delayed response to orders sent from London to shift the strategic focus of the war to the Caribbean. Both Britain and France could almost taste the easy victories waiting for them in the Caribbean, and they were both equally terrified of easy defeat. The arrival of French sea power in the war was the single cause of this major strategic realignment from North America to the Caribbean, a change that directly and immediately affected the likelihood of the British being able to retain their American colonies.

Hotham's force consisted of 5,000 troops in fifty-nine transports, protected by nothing more than a nominal naval escort, the most powerful ships being two 64-gunners. Even the inexperienced d'Estaing could have taken the entirety of Hotham's force with ease, had the two fleets met, and the entire British Caribbean would then have been in his lap. British luck held, however, and the fleets did not meet but sailed almost parallel with each other, in total ignorance, all the way to the West Indies – yet another extraordinary turning point in this extraordinary war.[61]

15

CARIBBEAN SEA

The Caribbean sugar islands were the principal source of British and French wealth, and their importance to the war cannot be overstated. George III summed it up:

> Our islands must be defended even at the risk of an invasion of this island, if we lose our sugar islands, it will be impossible to raise money to continue the war and then no peace can be obtained but such a one as He that gave one to Europe in 1763 never can subscribe to.[1]

The Americans also realized that a British defeat there 'will put our affairs on a favourable footing, and ... will effect the full completion of all our wishes, in securing the independence of America'.[2] The income from the Caribbean trade was important in itself, but the guarantee of its arrival gave Britain a far bigger borrowing capacity than its rivals. The British government essentially paid for the war by raising revenue against its sugar islands.

The islands lay like a great fleet of warships across the entrance to the Caribbean Sea, the Windward Islands to the south, the Leeward Islands to the north, and there was plenty to worry about. At the outbreak of war the British owned Jamaica, Antigua with its crucial naval base at English Harbour, St Kitts, Dominica, St Vincent, Barbados, Grenada and Tobago. The French were also heavily committed. They then owned Saint-Domingue (modern Haiti), Martinique, Guadeloupe, St Lucia and Cayenne on the South American coast.

All these islands were vulnerable to defeat in isolation. Distances in the Caribbean are far larger than many people suspect; it is well over 500 miles from the southern tip of the Lesser Antilles, which comprise both the Windward and Leeward Islands, to the northern tip, and from there it is well over 1,200 nautical miles to the westernmost tip of Cuba. To make matters worse, there were very few troops on the islands – around 1,000 British troops in the entire British Caribbean in 1778.[3] The islands' defence therefore relied almost entirely on sea power. It is no coincidence that more major fleet battles in this war were fought in the Caribbean than anywhere else.

With so much at stake, it was ironic that the demands of exercising sea power in the Caribbean were as steep as anywhere in the world. Any navy there would struggle against nature more than they would ever struggle against an enemy. Simply surviving in better condition than your enemy was to win a major naval victory.

Sea power in the Caribbean was governed by the predictable wind system. During the calm winter months the winds blew steadily, almost always from the east, and in the summer months storms and hurricanes rolled through with steady frequency. The currents caused by the meeting of the Atlantic and the Caribbean Sea in a stretch of water populated by numerous islands were also powerful and influential. With their large, blunt hulls, warships were poor at sailing to windward and vulnerable to currents of any sort. Local knowledge was a massive advantage.

The ships themselves fell apart rapidly in the Caribbean. Admiral James Young complained that 'the weather and climate destroys everything so fast it is with great difficulty we can keep them in repair'.[4] The shipworm – *Teredo navalis* – grew as large as a small snake in the warm water. The sun dried and frayed rope, and sudden squalls sprang masts and yards. Limited dockyard facilities – in Antigua, Barbados and Jamaica for Britain, and in Martinique for France – added a far greater significance to damage received in the Caribbean than to similar damage received in home waters. Even basic wear and tear could be problematic. There were no dry docks anywhere in the British or French Caribbean.[5] In a strange way, therefore, successful naval warfare in the Caribbean was actually all about minimizing any naval activity. This was always true but it was particularly true in 1778. Then the British problems were exacerbated by a shocking lack of stores and experience in the dockyard at Antigua. When war broke out, a ship's carpenter was working in the role usually occupied by a highly experienced master shipwright, and there were no masts at all 'fit for a frigate's main mast or larger'.[6]

The men always suffered in the Caribbean. Over one third of white immigrants died of disease within three years of arriving. The danger of sudden death was a constant topic of conversation among passengers on a voyage to the West Indies in 1775.[7] Ships on Caribbean service tended to be undermanned as a result, but the problem was particularly appalling in the overcrowded conditions of war. Writing to Germain in May 1778 about a proposed British Caribbean operation, General James Grant openly declared that 'more than half is not to be counted upon as fit for service after they have been a little time in the West Indies'. Grant, who had been at the Siege of Havana in 1762 in which 4,700 British troops had died – at least half of the regulars shipped out from Britain – and almost all from disease, added ruefully: 'I write from experience.'[8]

The particular problem was overcrowding of the larger warships because this could lead to outbreaks of typhus. Frigates and sloops were little troubled because they were light and airy, but two- and three-decked ships – the type that were now rapidly closing in on the Caribbean from America – could be death traps in a typhus outbreak. And yet again there was a problem that was particular to exactly this period: the naval hospital at Barbados had been closed since 1773.[9] Sailors started dying as soon as they started arriving for war. One young British sailor, arriving in 1778 on his first tour, recorded how

1. Drawn by a British engineer, Archibald Robertson, from a high point on Staten Island, this shows the moment on 12 July 1776 when the British build-up of naval power at New York was complete. Howe's fleet sails through the narrows and meets Shuldham's, already at anchor in Raritan Bay. Long Island is visible in the distance.

2. One of several versions of a painting by Dominic Serres the Elder of the British *Phoenix, Roebuck* and *Tartar*, accompanied by two smaller vessels, forcing the American river defences in the Hudson. The tips of the river defences can just be seen to the left of the ships. The narrowness of the river depicted here is misleading; the Hudson at this point is almost a mile wide.

3. The British fleet landing at Kip's Bay, 15 September 1776, drawn by Robert Cleveley, then a clerk on HMS *Asia*. Note the clear depictions of the flat boats – the characteristic British amphibious landing craft of the day.

4. The British landing and scaling the New Jersey palisades on 20 November 1776, an operation made possible by the skill and experience of British sailors in hauling heavy guns over difficult terrain.

5. A contemporary sketch of Arnold's eclectic fleet at Valcour Island on the morning of 11 October 1776, showing the schooner *Royal Savage* in the centre surrounded by a variety of craft. From the left we see another schooner, a galley, the gondola *Philadelphia* (now preserved in Washington) and another galley; from the right we see a galley, a sloop and several gondolas.

6. *Washington Crossing the Delaware* by Emanuel Leutze. A multi-layered allegory of the revolution painted seventy-five years after the event, it focuses on one of Washington's four crossings of the Delaware.

7. A sketch by a British soldier of the remains of the 'Great Bridge' built by the Americans between Fort Ticonderoga and Mount Independence in 1777. The bridge's pilings stretch across the lake. The vessel on the left is HMS *Inflexible*, built in just twenty-eight days at St Jean.

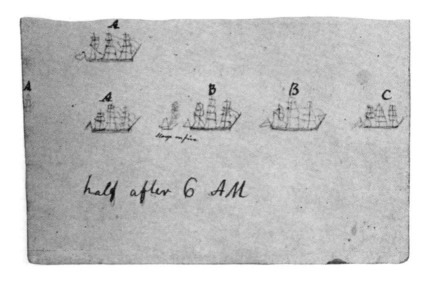

8. One of a series of brief sketches by Hector McNeill recording the relative positions of the ships in the duel between the *Boston* and the *Fox*.

9. & 10. Dominic Serres's two paintings of the Battle of St Lucia. The first (*above*) shows the engagement with the French fleet bearing down on the British at anchor and greatly exaggerates the closeness of the battle – the closest that the French ever engaged was at three-quarters of a mile. The second painting (*below*) shows the British fleet after the battle with the French leaving in the distance. Note that the British guns have been run out on their landward side, suggesting that they were fully expecting to be doubled or to have their line broken – a clear indication of their vulnerable mindset.

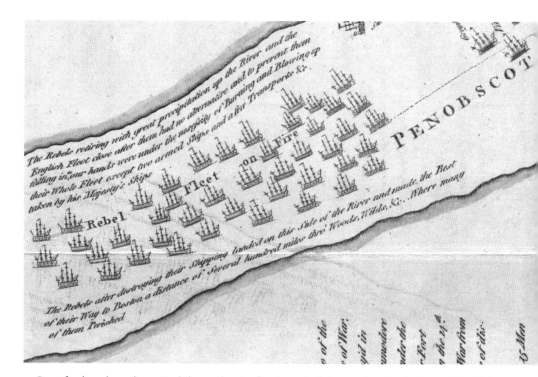

The Rebels retiring with great precipitation up the River, and the English Fleet close after them had no alternative and to prevent them falling in our hands were under the necessity of Burning and Blowing up their Whole Fleet except two armed Ships, and a few Transports &c. taken by his Majesty's Ships

Rebel Fleet on Fire

PENOBSCOT

The Rebels after destroying their Shipping landed on this Side of the River and made the Best of their Way to Boston a distance of several hundred miles thro' Woods, Wilds, &c...Where many of them Perished

11. Part of a chart drawn by an Englishman shortly after the end of the war, showing the destruction of the American fleet in the Penobscot River, August 1779.

12. A contemporary woodblock print of the Grand Union flag, the first ensign of the Continental Navy. It is notable for its similarity to the British East India Company flag.

13. One of many images that depict the destruction of the *Santo Domingo* at the Moonlight Battle, 1780. Rodney's flagship the *Sandwich* (90) dominates the foreground. The masts and spars of the *Santo Domingo* are shown cartwheeling into the sky behind her.

14. The *Baltick* of Salem, the best likeness we have of Washington's first armed ship, the *Hannah*.

15. Hunter House, on present-day Washington Street in Newport, the shore-based headquarters of the French fleet from August or September 1780 until August 1781. The house belonged to Colonel Joseph Wanton Jnr who abandoned it because of his loyalist sympathies. It is now open to the public.

16. One of several coins produced to commemorate Rodney's sack of St Eustatius and the 'punishment' of the Dutch in 1781.

we buried in six days about twenty seamen and seven marines, together with Lieutenant Thomas Philip Smith of the marines, and Mr. John Eglestone, master's mate. The 28th of this month the master, purser and surgeon was taken ill, and a few days after myself, gunner, surgeon's mate, and sixty more men were ill in severe fevers, during which time we had not men enough to work the ship, and Captain Bligh and one of the mates was at watch and watch.[10]

To make matters worse, at the outbreak of war there were inadequate food supplies in British naval warehouses even to sustain a small squadron. When Rear-Admiral Samuel Barrington arrived in the Caribbean to assume command, he discovered that, owing to contractor negligence, there were none of the naval stores that he expected to find. His men had to eat rice and yams instead of bread until the situation was remedied.[11] In the words of Barrington himself, it was the 'most wretched sickly fleet, without stores, and in a most shattered condition ... How we scrambled through I know not.'[12]

The British had not been ready for war in America; and they certainly weren't ready for war in the Caribbean.

*　*　*

The threat of naval war alone altered everything for those living in the Caribbean. Slaves on Jamaica outnumbered whites by twelve to one, and the plantation-owners felt vulnerable.[13] The slaves sensed that uncertainty and rose up, partly because they now had good reason to expect help from Britain's enemies, but more importantly because British naval ships, the most significant representation of British military authority in the Caribbean, were now absent chasing American privateers and watching the French: here the sudden absence of British sea power affected people's lives just as the sudden arrival of it had done in America.[14]

As the dark cloud of war hovered on the tropical horizon like a summer hurricane, costs of imported food, upon which the plantations relied because they had turned all of their land over to sugar, soared. In Barbados the price of flour increased fivefold in less than four years.[15] Profits plummeted. Slaves starved. All this happened before the battle fleets even arrived, and when they did arrive, the extant problems became worse. Sailors, in their thousands, now competed for already scarce supplies of food and water. Just one statistic is needed to reveal the horror of this impact of naval war in the Caribbean: one-fifth of Antigua's 38,000 slaves died between 1778 and 1781.[16] This is no coincidence: Antigua was a key British naval base and sailors were prioritized over slaves. Slaves had much to dread but naval war is often overlooked.

Unsurprisingly, therefore, almost everyone in the British Caribbean was against the war, though the majority of British subjects did stay loyal to the crown because they were utterly dependent on British imports and sea power for their sustenance and protection.[17]

*   *   *

In anticipation of this moment, the French had reinforced their islands of Martinique and Guadeloupe and had 8,000 troops at their disposal; before Hotham's arrival the British had fewer than 1,060 men fit for duty.[18] When Hotham did make it to the West Indies, moreover, the French had a chance to strike, which they spurned. D'Estaing had received intelligence that Hotham was near at hand but had wrongly guessed his destination to be Antigua, rather than Barbados. It was a desperately ill-informed decision. Antigua was an important dockyard but Barbados, being far to windward of all other islands, was the strategic key to the entire Caribbean. Again, one suspects that a man more fully immersed in the ways of naval warfare would not have made such an error, and d'Estaing's experienced naval officers knew it.[19] The French sailed to Antigua, and Hotham for Barbados. Yet another war-changing opportunity had been missed by the Frenchman: the British were still in the war but only by the skin of their teeth.

Waiting for Hotham in Barbados was the new commander-in-chief of the Leeward Islands station, Rear-Admiral Samuel Barrington. The celebrated Joshua Reynolds painted him just a year later and produced a magnificent study that oozes personality in a way that so few other portrait artists could achieve. Barrington stands proud, confidently gazing towards his future. He is satisfied as a leader, effortless in his confidence. He also appears resourceful and tough. By 1778 Barrington had been in the navy for thirty-eight years, and at the outbreak of war he had pestered Sandwich for command of the Leeward Islands. He was very keen.[20]

His orders were to attack French St Lucia, an island that the British had taken in the previous war and had returned with great reluctance at the peace. St Lucia was superb for its fine anchorages and its proximity to Martinique, the location of the main French naval base in the Caribbean. From St Lucia the British could keep an eye on the French without wearing out their ships by permanently cruising off the Martinique coast.

The French, however, had already seized the initiative under the command of the brilliant governor of Martinique, the marquis de Bouillé. They had captured the British ship that carried news of the outbreak of war and then captured two more, the frigates *Minerva* and *Active*, before the British knew anything about the declaration of war.[21] With more than ships in their sight, however, they quickly took Dominica, a key island that lay between the French possessions of Martinique and Guadeloupe. Dominica was also a valuable prize because it was the finest location in the entire chain in which to get both wood and water for a fleet at the same time. Its capture was therefore a serious coup for the French.[22] Lord Macartney, governor of Grenada, claimed that a single British ship of the line would have been enough to discourage the French or disrupt the invasion, an observation that appears exaggerated but was probably correct. The French had no significant warships to cover their landing, and de Bouillé only launched the invasion when he was certain that a single British frigate, which had been lurking around St Lucia, had gone.[23]

*　*　*

On 10 December Hotham finally arrived in Barbados and, now united with Barrington, headed for St Lucia. The British landing with 'ten regiments of the finest fellows that ever drew a trigger'[24] was unopposed in an operation overseen with exquisite precision by the brilliant Hotham, who had also superintended the landings at New York and Newport in 1776.[25] The achievement was remarkable for the awkwardness of the terrain: this was 'the most difficult country War was ever made in', wrote General Grant,[26] and another soldier noted that St Lucia was 'generally the Resort of noxious Animals'.[27] On one occasion Grant, in charge of the army, had to write a rather awkward letter to Barrington asking him to 'order every thing which has been carried ashore to be taken on board again, and brought round by water'.[28] This would have interrupted the important business of taking soundings and buoying the entrance to the bay and would have driven the sailors barmy.

There was no French naval presence to contest the landing but they were coming. Barrington had sent a handful of frigates ahead of the main invasion force to act as a net around St Lucia, to prevent news of the British invasion from reaching the French, but a vessel had escaped the trap and made it to Martinique.[29]

British sailors rowed 5,000 troops ashore at St Lucia and landed them amidst piles of stores, while the French battle squadron in Martinique spread its wings with shouts of confidence playing on the breeze. Expectations of French sea power delivering a victory were as high as ever, entirely and surprisingly undamaged by the previous six months' worth of disappointment in America. One Frenchman wrote: 'the capture of the [British] squadron, the transports and army was certain, the conquest of all the British islands was sure. The language at Martinique was "the fish are in the net, we go to draw it; the mouse is in the trap, it will shut of itself".' Another simply stated: 'You might read in every countenance, France is going to be victorious.'[30] But would d'Estaing let a fifth opportunity to strike a blow against a significant British force slip though his fingers?*

* * *

British scouts saw the French fleet at 5.00 p.m. on 14 December. Many of the troops were still on the beach and the rest occupied a tiny strong point overlooking the bay. The British transports were unprotected and the small force of small British warships was in no position to face a larger fleet of larger ships of the line. The frantic signalling from the British frigates was seen 'to our utmost astonishment' by British soldiers and sailors on the beach.[31] It was a moment of the highest drama. One witness said in rather rosy prose: 'Fancy our confusion and hurry when we counted from our masthead a French fleet of 13 sail of the line and twelve frigates standing in for us.'[32] The missing emotion here is fear.

Barrington's response to this appalling situation was exemplary. A sailor who visited his flagship shortly after the enemy had been sighted commented on his calmness; he later wrote: 'I was sent, a few minutes before the attack, on duty on board the *Prince of Wales*, and was astonished to see everything so clear for action, and particularly at the serenity of the Admiral's countenance, and presence of mind in giving orders.'[33] The British spent the entire night and all of the next morning preparing their position.

The transports were removed to a nearby inlet known as the Cul-de-Sac for its shape – a bulging bay with a narrow entrance, just like the bottom of a sack. The transports were warped into place in the body of the bay while the opening was closed shut by Barrington's warships anchored in a line. Barrington was particularly worried about losing valuable anchoring equipment, so difficult to replace so far from any major naval dockyard,

---

* The other four are: Howe evacuating Philadelphia, the French attack at Newport, Hotham leaving New York, and Hotham arriving in the West Indies.

and he ordered extra cables to be attached to the anchor cables and run back into the ships. A nautical equivalent of belt and braces, Barrington was not planning on losing his trousers.* Two frigates and a 20-gun post ship, too small ever to fight in a line of battle, had to take their place in that line and their crews prepare to meet the full broadsides of French ships of the line. The British ships were also severely undermanned as a result of illness, and many sailors had been sent ashore to drag guns into position and man the batteries. 'Fearful odds it was,' wrote one sailor, 'but [we] were resolved and hoped for the Almighty assistance in our trial.'[34]

There was too little daylight left for d'Estaing to have attacked on the night of 14 December, but Barrington's defensive preparations were not completed until 11.30 a.m. on the 15th.[35] With dawn coming a little before 6.30 a.m., there was plenty of time to have launched a morning attack before all the British ships were in position, but the French did no such thing. One British sailor wryly put it down to d'Estaing's 'politeness'.[36] Several hours later, with the British in a better but by no means ideal defensive position, the French attacked.

They had orders to heave to opposite the British line and to concentrate the fire of two French ships against every individual British ship. They were then to fight until the British ships struck. As many French ships as possible, meanwhile, would fight their way into the bay and attack the unarmed transports. Everything was set up for d'Estaing to achieve a very rare decisive naval victory.

The awful moment of waiting then came, a moment captured in a pair of magnificent oil paintings by Dominic Serres [see figs 9 & 10].† The British are anchored in a perfect line across the mouth of the Cul-de-Sac, the transports visible within the bay. From the west, meanwhile, the French can be seen filling the horizon and bearing down on the British position. What

---

* A life-long sailor, Barrington's approach is significantly different from d'Estaing's, who had carelessly abandoned his anchors when he left Newport.

† The two paintings have recently been reunited by the National Maritime Museum in Greenwich, London, and can now be seen together as always intended.

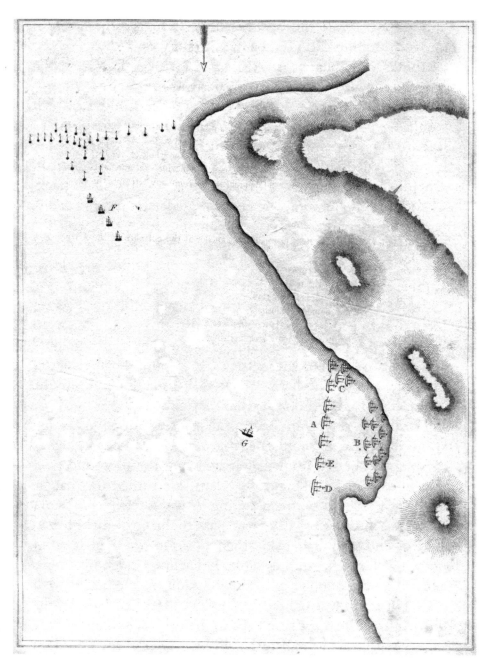

An illustration of Barrington's position at St Lucia from Ekins' *Naval Battles*. 'A' is
Barrington's fleet at anchor in the entrance to the Cul-de-Sac; 'B' is the fleet of transports;
'C' the frigates; 'D' is Admiral Barrington; 'E' is Commodore Hotham; 'F' is the French
fleet; 'G' is a French frigate reconnoitring.

you cannot see are the British sailors, staring at the horizon, hearts thumping clean out of their chests.

Things immediately started to go wrong, however. The French struggled even to get to the British line. The 'violent' current running between St Lucia and Martinique, which would have been known to any local sailor, set them far to leeward, and they were then baffled by fluky winds in the lee of St Lucia's great mountains. They appeared to British eyes 'disconcerted ... at a loss how to act'.[37] The first attack, when it eventually came, was a cannonade at a full mile's distance and therefore significantly different from that which is depicted by Serres. There were no British casualties at all and the ships were barely scratched. The second attack was closer, at three-quarters of a mile, but again, as one sailor wrote, 'the maneuvers of the Enemy ... betrayed great confusion'.[38] Again their gunfire had little effect on the British line and seems to have been particularly bad. Shot was seen to fly high and long, and one British sailor later retrieved a 42-pound ball a quarter of a mile inland. Another bewildered British sailor said simply: 'it was hard to determine at what they aimed'.[39]

Frustrated yet again by capricious sea power, d'Estaing swore that 'the profound grief that fills me will not influence my plans',[40] before immediately allowing the profound grief that filled him to influence his plans. He turned to what he knew best, a good bit of soldiering. It was a terrible decision. By now a number of days had passed since the British had landed, and they had made their position, on a high point known as La Vigie, impregnable. D'Estaing landed his troops and led a hare-brained full-frontal assault on the heights that ended in terrible slaughter. The French retreated back to the beach and several days later back to their ships, leaving – to the extreme distaste of the British soldiers – piles of their dead on the slopes of La Vigie which British soldiers and sailors later buried.[41]

Barrington, meanwhile, held his breath. His position was far stronger now than it had been when d'Estaing first attacked, but he knew he was still vulnerable, either to destruction by naval assault or to being blockaded into starvation. He was astonished, therefore, when d'Estaing sailed for Martinique.

The British had unquestionably escaped, thanks largely to the excellent relations between army and navy that had marked their operations. Of particular importance had been the permanent and effective umbilical link between army and fleet that had been set up and maintained by the fleet's boats and sailors, working like a line of ants to carry supplies and men to and from the fleet. Grant was careful to make Barrington aware of how grateful he was. He wrote a lovely letter in which he acknowledged how 'we give you a great deal of trouble and are infinitely obliged to you and the Fleet for the assistance you give us so cheerfully'.[42] It is interesting that he noted how jovial the sailors were because Barrington made a similar comment in a letter to his brother: 'Never had an Admiral a more glorious set of Officers under him; it is a pleasure to serve with such men, cheerful in the worst of times.'[43] And they certainly were the worst of times: his sailors had remained at battle stations fully for two weeks and had slept by their guns the entire time.[44]

Once the French garrison in St Lucia had stopped teasing the British about losing the battle of Ushant and had decided that trying to shoot holes through the British flag of truce was of limited entertainment, they eventually surrendered.[45] The British forces in St Lucia sat back and enjoyed the island's rum, available in such abundance that Grant worried 'it will flow in upon us, like a tide'.[46] It is likely that this was another curious side-effect of British sea power in the Caribbean: the sudden loss of the American rum market, policed by British privateers and the Royal Navy, had literally flooded the Caribbean with one of its major exports.[47]

* * *

Byron's fleet soon arrived from Newport to boost Barrington's numbers, but by then both fleets were utterly worn out, so short of men and stores that they were useless. Byron's ships had no sails 'other than what are on the yards' and not a single spare coil of rope, and his men were suffering particularly badly from scurvy and typhus. Nearly 1,500 of his men died of disease,* and they had run into a shocking series of storms. 'There surely never was so unlucky a fleet', wrote Grant.[48] Luck, however, was only one reason for Byron's condition. His orders to pursue d'Estaing wherever he went did not take into consideration important things like repair facilities and food supplies. His unexpected arrival in the West Indies put immense pressure on British naval resources, just as d'Estaing's had on American naval resources when he arrived unannounced in Boston in 1778. Byron's fleet immediately consumed 1,800 tons of naval stores which had been sent out the previous year for the Caribbean squadron.[49] These two examples are an important reminder that a flexible naval strategy only worked if there were sufficient resources in the likely operational locations, and the best British resources, as they always had been and always would be, were in home waters, not 3,000 miles away. In this respect neither the French in America nor the British in the Caribbean were actually able to cope with the sea power that they were attempting to wield.

With the main naval forces finally in the Caribbean, the situation, ironically, calmed down because neither side was either willing to take the initiative or capable of doing so. When they were in Boston, the French had taken the opportunity presented by such a lull in proceedings to enrage the Americans, and now they took the opportunity to enrage themselves. D'Estaing's string of missed opportunities and clear failures was starting to tell. 'Never will France have such opportunities again as we have had', lamented one bitter Frenchman; it was a campaign that was 'mortifying to the last degrees by the folly of our General, on every occasion, he having had the most favourable opportunities of signalizing himself'.[50] Like-minded French officers formed anti-d'Estaing cabals and his name became mud in Martinique. He was openly abused

---

* Part of the same epidemic, caused by overcrowded guardships, that ruined Charles Hardy's fleet in 1779 (see p. 292).

in the streets and rumours circulated that he was mentally unstable. It is unclear if they were true, but one thing is quite certain: d'Estaing's behaviour throughout the campaign of 1778 indicates a man out of his depth both with the strategic situation, as influenced by the practical restrictions of seaman-ship, and also with the specific seamanship challenges he faced fighting the British.[51] He would still have a shot at redemption, however.

The difficulties of wielding sea power had caused the French to fall out with their American allies and had fractured the relationship between the Commander and his own fleet. It had also caused them to lose St Lucia, a key Caribbean island. Even more worryingly, similar problems had begun to affect the war, and their empire, elsewhere: in fact, by 1778 their entire position in India was under threat.

16

INDIAN EMPIRE

It is tempting to view events in India during the maritime wars of the eighteenth century as somehow isolated from events elsewhere, but that would be a mistake. Yes, they were distant, but that distance created strategic problems that affected European navies and hence all waters in European naval control. It took between four and six months to travel by ship from Britain to India. The ancient canals running from Suez to Egypt, which had linked the Nile with the Red Sea, and thus the Mediterranean with the Indian Ocean, and thus Europe with India, had long since dried up. To reach India from Europe, therefore, one had to travel south past the Spanish lurking at Cádiz and the British at Gibraltar, then past various European-owned slaving stations on the west coast of Africa, before entering the vastness of the Atlantic, where the British also lurked on the rocky island of St Helena. Then one had to round the Cape of Good Hope, which was in the hands of the Dutch. The Cape was critical for its position mid-voyage, by which time all ships needed to resupply. Once round the Cape, the French lurked to the north and east in the islands of Mauritius and Réunion, then known respectively as Île de France and Île de Bourbon. The main European navies, therefore, could easily contest the route to India from Europe.

It is also important to realize that the American colonists viewed themselves as part of a broad British imperial jigsaw that transcended the Atlantic world. Yes, American connections with the Caribbean, Europe and Africa were particularly influential and vivid, but so too were the connections between America and Asia: remember, one of the key events which sparked off the revolution was the Boston Tea Party, an intense clash between the eastern and western hemispheres of British interest. Indeed, one of the most thought-provoking artefacts to survive from this period is a small, clear bottle in the collections of the Massachusetts Historical Society. Inside it are tea-leaves, harvested in Asia but then harvested again from the shoreline of Boston, near Dorchester Neck, the morning after the Boston Tea Party.

Tea, moreover, was only one part of this Asian equation: there was also a growing demand for luxury, exotic and military goods, and this demand was generated in America as much as it was in Europe.* The Americans felt a strong connection with India and with the Indians, who were also subject to British control. It is no coincidence that, later in the war, a Pennsylvania privateer was named *Hyder Ally* after the sultan of Mysore, Hyder Ali, the war-chief who rose up in an attempt to drive the British out of southern India at exactly the same time as the Americans rose up to drive them out of America. The relationship between Britain, India and America is particularly interesting in this period because, just as the British empire in America collapsed between 1775 and 1782, so did it start to grow in India, and the two are intimately connected. Those links were first felt long before the rebellion in America rose in spate. Indeed, an existing war with the Maratha empire in the mid-1770s was one of the key reasons that British politicians were unable and unwilling to give the growing crisis in America the full attention that it deserved.[1]

* * *

The naval set-up in India was unique. The East India Company was the key to British power in India because it was a willing ally of British imperialism. It raised its own troops and had its own mini-navy, the Bombay Marine. Even before the outbreak of war, it had five 20-gun cruisers and eight huge armed gallivats,

* The Indian trade was also the main source of saltpetre, the key ingredient in gunpowder.

powered by both oar and sail. It was a bit like a maritime police force. The ships were not designed to engage in warfare with ships from European navies but to protect Company shipping from local raiders and pirates, the ships of the Muscat Arabs, sheikhs in the Persian Gulf and the Maratha chiefs known as the Angrias. The Company also built and maintained its own large trading ships, which were usually armed.

To build and maintain ships, the Company needed a sound maritime infrastructure in India, and they had it in Bombay: a well-established dockyard including no fewer than three dry docks, two of which were capable of servicing ships as large as 74-gunners. Nearby were excellent facilities for graving several ships at once.* The local resources for cordage were excellent and there was a fine ropewalk. Timber resources were also plentiful. In particular, the forests of Malabar near Bombay were full of teak, one of the finest of all shipbuilding timbers for its resilience to tropical shipworm and rot and the fact that it did not swell in hot climates. There was even a peculiar local gum that was used to seal the seams of ships instead of pitch. The facilities were deeply impressive.[2]

Crucially, the East India Company was more than happy to share its facilities with the Royal Navy, but the French navy had nothing of the sort, either of its own or run by a French trading company that it could co-opt into helping project sea power so far from home. In fact the nearest French naval base was on the Île de France (Mauritius), 2,300 miles from the southernmost tip of India. Nonetheless, the French had serious imperial ambitions as well as significant possessions in India. They would soon find out that, in time of war, such imperialism without naval infrastructure was a pipe dream.

*   *   *

The initial exchanges between the British and French in India were horribly one-sided. The British already had an army at their fingertips, raised to fight an existing war with

---

* 'Graving' involves grounding a ship to work on her underwater hull at low tide.

the Marathas. They also had a tiny naval squadron under the command of Edward Vernon,* which was boosted with armed East India Company ships.[3] The French had managed to scratch together a squadron of similar force, under Admiral François l'Ollivier de Tronjoly, but they were burdened with the terrible 'what if' that hung over all their operations on the Indian coast: what would they do if a large number of their men were injured in battle? Where would they go to repair? How could crews depleted by battle sail damaged ships 2,000 miles back to safety? The idea was too appalling for words.

The British had one other significant advantage in 1778: in direct contrast to what had happened in the Caribbean that year, in India they knew that they were at war before the French knew, and the reason for this is particularly interesting.

A British entrepreneur, George Baldwin, had recently pioneered a route across the seventy-mile stretch of desert from Suez to the Nile, drawing on an earlier attempt to exploit this route by the adventurer James Bruce in 1768. British access to this area had become possible in the 1770s because of changing politics in Egypt, where the Mameluks had finally freed themselves from Turkish suzerainty. This created the opportunity to open new trade routes running from the Mediterranean to the Red Sea via Suez. The practicality of the system took some working out, not least the need for a detailed understanding, by British sailors, of the navigation of the 1,040 mile-long Red Sea. For generations this had been a Muslim lake, protected and cherished for its crucial role in the annual pilgrimage to Mecca, just inland from the Red Sea port of Jeddah.

In 1773 the Egyptian bey, Mehmed, summoned Baldwin to Cairo and encouraged the British to start using the Suez route, even offering to cut a canal to assist them. Although the canal never materialized, the British immediately increased their activity in the Red Sea and several voyages made by Royal Navy ships resulted in the creation of more detailed charts of

---

* Edward Vernon (died 1794) was nephew of the more famous admiral of the same name (1684–1787).

the Red Sea than had hitherto existed. This first exploitation and investigation of the Red Sea by British ships is almost completely unstudied by historians. A glut of fabulous material awaits an intrepid scholar.[4]

The result of this mixture of diplomacy and exploration was that, at the opening of the war, the British had an entirely new route for communications with India that was very fast, relatively safe and unavailable to the French. The war's outbreak then provided the publicity-hungry Baldwin with the perfect opportunity to prove both the worth of his system and how clever he was. It worked spectacularly. In his subsequent self-penned hagiography, it only took him seven pages before he congratulated himself:

> I had the satisfaction to convey the first advices of the war in 1778 to the East Indies, by means of which they were enabled, to the astonishment of all England, when the news arrived, to expel the French from India before succours could reach them, and add their possessions to our own.[5]

This is a rare example from this war of the British using sea power to great effect to transmit intelligence – something they had been woefully bad at hitherto.

The day after news of war was received in Madras via the British sloop HMS *Cormorant*, a decision was taken to attack the French and increase naval protection of British Bengal. The French settlement of Chandernagore, just up the Hughli River from Calcutta, was the first to be attacked and it fell as if made of paper. A major strike was then landed on the large trading post and root of French power in India, Pondicherry. Also chosen as a target for its vulnerability to British sea power, Pondicherry was the only place on the entire coast where a large amphibious landing could be made.[6]

The battle for Pondicherry saw a scuffle between the British and French squadrons with no ships taken on either side, but the French suffered many more casualties than the British and the British ships were badly damaged in their rigging.[7]

Tronjoly then fled the Indian coast altogether for the remote safety of Île de France, the squadron's disappearance witnessed with horror by the French troops in Pondicherry. His retreat was considered a shameful and criminal act, and there are clear parallels with d'Estaing's abandonment of Sullivan at Newport, but the lack of French naval infrastructure in India left him with no choice. Pondicherry fell after a siege in which British sailors played a major part both afloat and ashore,[8] and within five months so too did all the remaining French posts in India.

British ships thus dominated the Indian Ocean in 1778, but a storm was brewing and the British certainly felt insecure. Their presence in Bombay, Madras and Calcutta was as reliant on sea power as the army in America, and news of Burgoyne's defeat at Saratoga had certainly made some of the Bengal Council jittery.[9] This was not just the fear of defeat, but, specifically, the fear of being cut off from the safety and security provided by a navy, the umbilical cord linking such a distant settlement with home.

That fear, in turn, was partly informed by developments in Indian sea power. By driving the French out of India they had also provoked Hyder Ali, the sultan of Mysore, a man of immense influence who had promised to protect the French. Ali had his own cherished visions of sea power that are, generally, much neglected by Western historians. The Indians had an impressive tradition of building large ships, influenced by European shipbuilding styles and techniques that had been practised in Indian waters from the 1730s onwards.

In the 1750s Hyder had built a navy that consisted of thirty warships commanded by renegade European officers and a large number of troop transports. The majority of that navy had been captured or destroyed by the British during the Seven Years' War (1754–63), but Hyder's appetite for sea power remained.[10] In 1778, with war breaking out between the British and French and with internal conflict sparking tension between the British and Mysore, Hyder began to rebuild his fleet, employing Joze Azelars, a shipwright once in the service of the Dutch East India Company, to oversee its design and construction. The main bases of Mysore naval power were Mangalore and Bhatkal near Onore, which Hyder also strengthened by building a huge mole to protect the fleet.[11] We have one very rare description of this fleet, given by a travelling Englishman, in the midst of its construction at Onore:

> Here are two frigates building near the castle; one of thirty-two guns and the other of twenty-four guns. Being desirous to examine their construction, I went in company with two other English gentlemen near to them, without offering to go on board, lest it should give offence. The Governor, being there, overlooking the men at work, observed us walking away, very civilly invited us to go on board and examine them, adding that it would give him great pleasure if we would candidly give our opinions on them. We went on board both of them and were surprised to find the work so well performed, particularly as they were the first ships of great burthen that have been built in Hyder Ally's country. When finished they will be two complete frigates, being very strong and of a fine mould; they will have a prow and what they call 'grabs' and one of them is larger than a Bombay 'grab'.*

The final size of Hyder's fleet is uncertain. Sources survive which claim that his largest ships, perhaps eight in number, were armed with between twenty-eight and forty guns each,

---

* It is an interesting description for several reasons. The ships that Hyder built were not frigates as the Royal Navy knew them, and the fact that an Englishman has described them as frigates here must only be taken as a reflection of their impressive size and that they were armed on a single deck. The word 'grab' is an Anglicization of the Arabic *ghurāb*, referring to a highly manoeuvrable warship popular with corsairs. The hull of the *ghurāb* was distinctive for its low and projecting prow, described here, and it was rigged with the traditional triangular lateen sails of the dhow. They were built broadside to a river, in contrast to the European tradition of building ships stern to or bow to a river. Also, unlike the British tradition, these large Indian warships were launched using elephants, which would push them into the river at bow and stern, the ship inching its way down greased timbers. MacDougall, 'British Seapower', 304; Low, *Indian Navy*, I, 182.

and that this force was augmented by smaller, though still very powerful, vessels known as *pals*. Whatever its actual size, it is certain that the fleet was large enough to be significant for the balance of sea power in India. It could challenge the Bombay Marine, transport troops, raid British trade, blockade small towns, and make life more than uncomfortable for an isolated British warship. With so few European ships in Indian waters before the arrival of the main French and English fleets in 1780, such a small force could easily sway the balance of power at sea and influence broader strategy.

The route home via Suez, moreover, which had served so well in forewarning the British of war before the French, was far from secure. The initial successes of the British exploitation of this route served only to arouse the suspicion of the Turks, who believed that the increased British activity was merely a forerunner of a massive invasion of Egypt. They particularly feared for the sanctity of the Red Sea route as the key to the pilgrimage to Mecca and, in 1778, issued a decree forbidding all 'Frankish' ships from using Suez as a port. After the naval battle at Pondicherry Joseph Ellison, lieutenant of the sloop *Cormorant*, returned to Suez, where he met with a very rough reception. Seized by the Turks, he was only released when the *Cormorant*'s captain threatened to turn her guns on the town.[12] In spite of the success of British sea power at the end of 1778, therefore, India had suddenly become very distant, and British possessions very isolated.

Nonetheless, the British in India were now in a far better position than the French, and that development needs to be considered in the context of the other numerous and severe French disappointments of the 1778 campaign in both American and Caribbean waters. Only in European waters had the French showed any muscle and lived up to their self-generated new reputation. The clock, moreover, was ticking. The French navy was a house built on sand. France lacked the bureaucracy to fund a war via taxation, so they had resorted to borrowing vast sums of money, at enormously high interest rates, to fund their navy. A lengthy war was unsustainable for that reason alone, but there were others: the available pool of skilled sailors was limited, and French access to naval stores unreliable.[13] If they did nothing, they would soon find themselves outnumbered by the British in ships of the line and 50-gunners by almost 50 per cent.[14] If they were to stand any chance of realizing their ambitions for the war, it was quite clear to the French that they needed a game-changer – something that would dramatically alter the balance of power at sea. What they needed, unquestionably, was the Spanish navy.

1779

17

SPANISH PATIENCE

Long before war between Britain and Spain was officially declared, the spectre of Spanish involvement could be sensed throughout the British empire. It caused anxiety and bloodshed and directly affected the war.

In the new year of 1779 a naval expedition was sent to British settlements in Spanish Honduras to reassure British subjects of naval protection and to recruit native allies. Indian canoe flotillas had already been fully integrated with British naval operations on Lakes Champlain and George,[1] and the British intended to do the same in the western Caribbean if war with Spain erupted. With very limited resources available at the nearest British naval command in Jamaica, a young man of promise was needed for such a job, and Peter Parker, commander-in-chief at Jamaica, had just the man in his sights: Lieutenant Horatio Nelson. To fulfil this duty, Parker gave Nelson his first independent command, the brig HMS *Badger*, a captured American privateer.

Nelson was ordered to sail to the Mosquito Coast of Spanish Guatemala, making land at the Black River settlement. On his way he would avoid large French and American predators and hunt small prey. In that forgotten British corner of the world he would fly the British flag and collect the king of a reportedly friendly native tribe, the Sandy Bay Samboes, who were descended from shipwrecked slaves. He would then bring the king of the Samboes back with him to Jamaica for talks with Parker.

Nelson was only twenty-one and the war had landed this bizarre opportunity in his lap. One wonders how the *Badger's* crew took to him – this slim, freckly, light-haired boy with a Norfolk burr, the very picture of British innocence – because this really was a miserable posting. The *Badger* wasn't much of a ship. Brigs were notorious for being cramped and uncomfortable even in pleasant conditions, but the coast of Honduras in January was going to be about as tough as you could get – at least 80 degrees Fahrenheit with regular 70 per cent humidity. Everyone knew that such a climate led to fever. Then there was the coastal navigation to consider. One of the reasons that the Black River settlement was in its location was that it was difficult to approach from the sea, and hence was relatively secure from maritime attack. A British officer who visited the coast shortly after Nelson described the navigation around the area as 'dangerous beyond description'.[2] Then, of course, even if they made it ashore, the potentially hostile Spanish could be lurking around any or every corner.

The voyage, however, was uneventful. Nelson struggled to keep his ship and his crew together, but no more or less than anyone in a similar situation. He and his sailors fought a constant battle against the elements. The ship rotted beneath them. Nonetheless, Nelson and the *Badger* returned to Jamaica with King George of the Samboes, demonstrating competence by avoiding the numerous pitfalls of this first command. Unfortunately for Nelson, however, this very demonstration of competence would nearly kill him: he was now the highest-ranking British naval officer with detailed recent knowledge of the Honduras coast, and John Dalling, the governor of Jamaica, had set his heart on an elaborate and unrealistic scheme to seize vast quantities of land and treasure from the Spanish in Central America. Nelson could now help him realize those plans.

* * *

Another area of British concern was New Orleans, a Spanish enclave since the end of the Seven Years' War (1754–63), and the Mississippi River, which led north and provided navigable access deep into the American colonies. The Spaniards had long been ferrying key supplies to the rebels via this network. One of the most important but often overlooked items was money. The influx of Spanish specie via New Orleans became so extensive that, almost single-handedly, it had boosted the struggling Continental currency and become a commonplace means of exchange.[3] The Spaniards, moreover, had opened New Orleans to American privateers and warships and their prizes early in 1777, and used the port as a base to launch spying operations on nearby British Pensacola, once a Spanish colony.[4]

The British reciprocated with their own display of naval strength. They paraded off New Orleans and made increasingly frequent sorties up the Mississippi to protect British settlements and police the river. Those settlements were now horribly isolated. Rebel colonists, untrustworthy Spaniards and Choctaw Indians – who were allies of the Spanish – openly salivated at British vulnerability.[5] The British in turn sought help from the Chickasaw and Creek Indians, but the backbone of British strength lay in the sea power they could wield on the river. That 'strength', however, was very limited indeed and an American by the name of James Willing decided to strike.

A frustrated merchant with local knowledge, with a brother who had sat on the First Continental Congress, Willing proposed a raid down the Mississippi that was authorized by Congress.[6] On 11 January 1778 he sailed from Fort Pitt on the Ohio River in Pennsylvania with twenty-eight men in a sloop, the USS *Rattletrap*. As they headed south, various banditti joined his gang, and once they entered the Mississippi, some Spanish officers even came to his flag. Willing and his men systematically plundered every British settlement they came to and captured every British ship. They then sailed all the way to New Orleans, where the governor, Bernardo de Gálvez, gave Willing's men shelter in a public building and allowed them to dispose of their plunder at public auction. One Tory described this as 'aiding, assisting, abeting, entertaining, succoring &c. the rebels'.[7] Spanish and British warships closed in on New Orleans as the tension rose.

The relationship between Gálvez and Willing, however, and through them the relationship between the Spanish and the Americans, was less clear-cut and far more interesting than this apparently black and white picture suggests. Willing's raid is particularly important for what it tells us about the relationship between Britain and Spain in this period, because one of the British vessels that Willing captured was taken from a village well inside Spanish territory.[8] Unsurprisingly, the British were furious with the Spanish for 'allowing' it to happen in theoretically neutral waters, but perhaps more surprisingly, the Spanish were furious with the Americans for barging into the carefully stage-managed relationship that then existed between Britain and Spain.

The Spanish had long been committed to the war but, just like the French in 1778, were waiting until the time was exactly right to declare war, and they would not be pushed. An immensely delicate process, it was overseen by the talented conde de Floridablanca, the new Spanish minster of state who operated with precision under the guidance of the firm Spanish king Carlos III. Everything Floridablanca did was governed by patience and reason. He was a deeply impressive man and led the most efficient administration of any nation involved in this war. The governor of New Orleans, moreover, Bernardo de Gálvez, was equally level-headed and shrewd, and was certainly not going to let the Spanish masterplan be upset by the pesky Willing. Even when a British naval captain fired a shot into the city in the subsequent confrontation, Gálvez did not rise. In fact, he used the opportunity to publish a proclamation that laid down the strict rules of neutrality, and stated that Spain would continue to observe a 'perfect' neutrality.[9]

The situation escalated in the subsequent weeks as more British ships arrived, but Gálvez kept his calm and did so with both humour and style. It was a stately display of Spanish self-control in a city that was a boiling pot of tension, where loyalists and rebels 'hate[d] each other to an Excess'.[10] It was also a clear announcement that Gálvez was aware of the broader strategic issues and that he was willing to play the long game.

A major player in the war had arrived and the British needed to stand up and take notice.

*   *   *

The Spanish had a strong hand to play; they knew it, the French knew it and the Americans knew it. More than that, however, many Americans saw not only hope in the entry of Spain into the war but even a guarantee of victory. The wild expectation that had characterized the American assessment of French involvement in 1778 simply transferred itself to Spanish involvement in 1779. In January 1779 Washington wrote to a Congressional committee arguing that

> [it] is not only possible but probable the affairs in Europe may take a turn which will compel [Britain] to abandon America. The interpositions of Spain and the union of her maritime force to that of France would probably have this effect.[11]

He also admitted that the 'doubts' he had concerning the success of the revolution would 'all subside' if the Spanish 'would but join their fleets to France'.[12]

Everyone could see that the numbers made sense: if Spain, with fifty-eight ships of the line, allied with France, which had sixty-three, then they would have far more warships than the British, who had ninety. Somewhere, surely, they could make that difference count.

Before the Spanish could declare war, however, they needed several things to fall into place. The most important of these was for the French to agree to Spanish terms – it was, in effect, the price for their alliance, and the price was high. Above all the Spanish wanted Gibraltar back. The British had taken that rock and its anchorage at the mouth of the Mediterranean with barely a fight in 1704. Since then it had become a strategic key to the British maritime empire. The British presence there was like a splinter deep in the Spanish heel, and the British stubbornly refused to return it in the diplomatic dance that preceded Spanish intervention in the war. This was a key moment. D'Estaing's failure to achieve anything in America in 1778 had demonstrated the weakness of French sea power, and here the British had a clear diplomatic opportunity to keep Spain out of the war, which would have allowed them to squeeze the French at sea and dominate them utterly through blockade.

The Spanish also wanted Minorca back. A tiny island blessed with the finest harbour in the western Mediterranean, Minorca was only 100 miles from Barcelona, 200 from Valencia, a similar distance from the French naval base at Toulon and less than 200 miles from Sardinia. The perfect naval base from which to control the western Mediterranean, it also was in British hands.

The remaining demands were subsidiary, but they included clearing the British from East and West Florida. There was a clear link between these war aims and the Spanish crown: Florida, Gibraltar and Minorca had all been lost to Britain since the advent of the Bourbon dynasty in 1700. Further aims were the recovery of the coast of Honduras, a contested zone since the 1660s, and the island of Jamaica, captured from the Spanish in 1655. American independence was never a specific Spanish war aim but it was a significant part of their commitment because Spain agreed not to make peace with Britain without French consent, and France could not achieve peace until England recognized American independence. The Spanish would therefore ally with France and not with America, and Spain would never deal directly with American diplomats, but the American cause was still central to Spanish policy.[13]

The demands were enormously high, regardless of how they were to be achieved, but the Spanish had a clear idea of how to go about it and that plan was even written into the Treaty of Aranjuez to stop the French from wriggling out of it.[14] The plan was to invade England and to seize some territory, perhaps Plymouth or the Isle of Wight, and then to exchange it for Gibraltar. Such a move was specifically designed to force Britain's hand by creating a financial panic: this was sea power used carefully and precisely to influence politics. It was a new strategy, Bourbon invasion plans in previous wars having relied upon invasion to promote mass uprisings that would lead to a change of monarchy.[15] This new invasion plan depended entirely on the presence of the Spanish fleet, which, when added to the French, would in theory allow the allies to seize control of the Channel. Spain's diplomacy therefore relied upon the theoretical existence of its sea power, but its ability to act rested on the quality of that sea power, and this was the final piece of the puzzle that governed Spain's willingness to declare war.

The French were trapped. Their failure to defeat the British in a single campaign in America now left them at the mercy of the Spanish. In 1778 British mobilization had finally kicked in and the weakness of French sea power when compared with Britain's led to an almost total capitulation to these exorbitant Spanish demands.[16]

The Spanish had been making diplomatic promises since August 1778, but it was not until the spring of 1779 that the Spanish fleets were manned, armed and victualled. Spanish sea power was funded by Spanish treasure, mined from the New World, and in 1778 there were insufficient reserves of money to pay for a naval mobilization. The Spanish fleet could not be prepared, therefore, until the 1778 treasure ships arrived home. Expected in the summer of 1778, their failure to appear by the end of June had been deeply alarming, but they soon staggered in, the last arriving on 18 September from Vera Cruz, Lima and Havana. If the British had been able to intercept or even blockade any of these treasure fleets, the war would have taken an altogether different path. But they did not, and by April 1779 the money had been spent and the ships had been manned, supplied and loaded.[17]

The Spanish were finally ready to make their play, and on 12 April they signed their alliance with France in the exquisite Royal Palace of Aranjuez, a royal site since the fifteenth century that had been favoured by Philip II in the 1560s and enlarged by Philip V in the early 1700s and then by Charles III, his son. In 1779, therefore, Aranjuez was a sumptuous symbol of Spanish authority and tradition. The Americans were instantly fired up by the news. Washington wrote to Lafayette: 'The declaration of Spain in favour of France has given universal joy to every Whig while the poor Tory droops like a withering flower under a declining sun.'[18] The French were also delighted. D'Estaing, then at Cap François on the northern shore of Saint-Dominigue, immediately threw a party.[19]

The tangible threat of Spanish sea power also created a growing sense of inevitability and doom in Britain. Lord North, who had nearly suffered a breakdown when the French had allied with the Americans, again cracked. On 22 June 1779 he wept in the House of Commons.[20] As he had done when France entered the war, North again tried to resign and, yet again, the king denied his request. Perfectly miserable, North wrote to his brother: 'I am not my own master, I am tied to a stake and can't stir.'[21] All he could do was watch as the tide of Spanish sea power rose to his chin and drowned him.

It is useful to see these developments as a chain linked by expectations of sea power. At the start of the revolution the Americans had needed help in the form of sea power, and they had expected success to be delivered on a plate by the French navy. They had been disappointed. Now the French needed help in the form of sea power, and they looked to the Spanish navy. But would they and the Americans now be disappointed too? The Spanish had a massive navy, bases in the Caribbean and boundless ambition. If they joined the war, the combined Franco-Spanish fleet would utterly dominate the British. Surely this would tip the scales. How could it not?

18

BOURBON INVASION

It is helpful to think about the Franco-Spanish campaign to invade England in the summer of 1779 like this.

The challenge was immense, perhaps even too immense for it ever to succeed. Two fleets of differing nationalities in three locations had to meet at sea in or around the notorious Bay of Biscay. The timing was crucial because the operation had a finite end: the storms of the autumnal equinox would probably destroy an operation of any complexity within sight of the English shore. Almost everything, however, conspired to upset the timing of that meeting.

The fleets would come from Brest, Ferrol and Cádiz. The furthest points in that chain, Brest and Cádiz, are at least 1,000 miles away from each other by sea. The fact that the operation was planned for midsummer, when northerly winds hampered any voyage north from Cádiz, made that distance – significant in any case – even more of a challenge. Before they could leave the ships would have to be victualled and manned, a process that never worked according to strict deadlines, depending as it did on intricate relationships between a complex naval administration and a host of contractors. A moderate-sized warship would carry 1,000 tons of equipment and stores for a normal voyage, but the Cádiz fleet, burdened by the distance it would have to travel to and from the theatre of operations, would need at least five months' worth of supplies. Once purchased and prepared, how would the goods be transferred to the naval dockyards? Once there, how would they be stored? Once stored, how would they be loaded onto the fleet? Who would check the stores for quality? What should be done if the food or drink was found to be vile? The quantities in question were immense.

Even before the Spanish and French fleets met, therefore, the fleet commanders were forced to answer a question that would affect future operational capability. What was more important? Meeting on a designated date, and perhaps sacrificing readiness in terms of men and supplies to be there on time, or making certain that the ships were fully operational at the expense of the envisaged timetable? This question was based firmly on the realities of sea power in the 1770s; in no way was it the product of fevered pessimism.

To complicate matters still further, each of the three commanders would have to ask their own question, and their answers would be based on the conditions in their own dockyards. Each answer, therefore, would be determined by different conditions that were influenced both by the culture of the navy in question as well as by the unique logistical issues each dockyard faced. The problems in Ferrol, for example, would not be the same as the problems in Cádiz just because both dockyards were Spanish. Moreover, France and Spain may have shared a royal house but their navies were vastly different in terms of leadership, structure and administration. They worked in different ways and at different speeds. Their administrations also had different expectations. This was a massive problem in its own right, but to make matters worse the navies were at different stages in the war. The French were already strained from a year of operations. The Spanish, in contrast, had been preparing for war for two years or more.

The rendezvous was also going to be difficult and dangerous to achieve. When combined, the Bourbon fleet would outnumber the British Channel Fleet, but until that point each of the three Bourbon squadrons would be inferior to the British fleet. The British Channel Fleet, of at least thirty ships of the line and eight frigates, manned by 26,544 men and armed with 3,260 guns, was already united and alert. It was out of the question to assume that the immense preparations required for an allied Bourbon invasion of Britain would go undetected, and it was more than likely that the Channel Fleet would be waiting for them, patrolling to windward of the English Channel in the western approaches, from where it could swoop on its enemy. If the British had enough ships spare and enough advance warning, there was every reason to suspect that one, two or all three of the Bourbon dockyards in question would actually be blockaded by the British. It was certainly possible that each of the Bourbon squadrons would actually have to fight for its freedom before it could even attempt to rendezvous with the others.

Assuming that the rendezvous was somehow achieved and that there was still sufficient time to undertake an operation that season, the allied fleets would then have to train together. They would have to decide how the command structure between the two navies would work; they would have to agree on shared command and signalling systems, which would require careful translation; they would have to develop some kind of shared command culture within a few short weeks of exercises. As a rule, the larger a fleet, the more difficult it was to command. A fleet of thirty was considered extremely cumbersome, but this combined fleet would consist of around sixty ships.

The identity of the two navies is also important to consider here. Yes, the French and Spanish shared a royal house and were now allied with each other, but they also loathed each other. 'I foresee a fatal outcome', wrote one perceptive Frenchman. 'France and Spain, having neither affection nor esteem for each other, are going to ruin this business by mutual suspicion and recriminations.'[1]

Once the training had been satisfactorily completed, the allies would boldly head towards the Channel, take control of it by defeating the British, and then launch the invasion. To prevent this from happening, all the British had to do was to keep their fleet in one piece and operational. As long as the British fleet existed in some reasonable strength, the allies would be unable to risk unloading their men on the beaches. This, perhaps, was the biggest problem because, as had been so clearly demonstrated at the battle of Ushant, forcing one fleet to action when it didn't want to fight was the single most difficult thing to achieve in fleet warfare in the age of sail.

If, miraculously, all this was achieved, the final piece of the jigsaw was for the Bourbons to capture a significant portion of British territory, ideally Portsmouth. This, it was believed, would lead to an immediate run on the banks and the British government suing for peace. Time here was crucial: if this surrender did not happen quickly, the invading force would be vulnerable to blockade by British ships, cut off and forced to surrender.

There were, in short, so many ways that this operation could fail that it will come as no surprise to learn that it did. The French saw much of it coming. Vergennes had highlighted the 'innumerable chances [that] might ruin the enterprise'[2] but had been so anxious to secure the Spanish alliance that he had feared the dangers of pointing out logistical difficulty. The French ambassador to Madrid, the comte de Montmorin, explained the bind that they were in:

> I tread very warily when it is a matter of pointing out the difficulties in the way of any enterprise proposed by M de Florida Blanc; I fear that if I showed them as they really are I would ... give him occasion to reproach us ... for wanting to wage only a cold and lifeless war.[3]

Throughout the spring and early summer of 1779, therefore, the plans moved forward when they should have been forced to stand still.

This is what happened next.

* * *

The French and Spanish planned to meet in a large but specific area of sea just north of the Sisargas Islands, off the coast of Galicia, no later than 15 May. This did not happen. The French left Brest later than intended and even then they were not fully ready. They sailed with insufficient and poor-quality victuals, and insufficient surgeons and medical supplies, particularly those used to treat scurvy. Their ships were also undermanned, the shallow pool of available, skilled sailors having been savagely depleted by an epidemic during the winter. The despairing Vergennes described all those who had convinced him that the navy would be ready by 1 May as 'windbags'.[4]

The result of all this was that the gleaming, well-trained and eager French fleet of 1778 had entirely vanished. It now contained large numbers of inexperienced sailors, 'weaklings', convalescents and the outright sick who promptly infected everyone else. Still impressive in terms of its physical size, the fleet's muscle had withered. The excellent d'Orvilliers, at least, was still in command.

There were also problems with the Spanish fleet. The quality of the Spanish ships was irreproachable but that of their leading officers was suspect. The admiral of the Cádiz fleet, Don Luis de Córdova, was seventy-three and his immediate subordinates were easily criticized: Don Antonio Ulloa for his scholarly bearing; Don Caudron Cantin for his talent at intrigue and nothing else; and Don Miguel Gaston for his bullishness. The Ferrol fleet was commanded by Don Antonio d'Arce, who detested the French to a degree that affected his thinking and behaviour.[5]

The Spanish were also delayed. Unwilling to save time by initiating the operation before a formal declaration of war had been made,* they had also been delayed by Floridablanca's obsessive secrecy. He had made it a condition of the alliance that only a handful of people were allowed knowledge of the plans being made and, remarkably, none of them were experienced naval planners. When knowledgeable naval men were finally initiated, they had insufficient time to make the necessary preparations.[6] There was no time at all for a conference between the allied chiefs of staff to discuss things like signalling.[7]

---

* In direct contrast to the French in 1778, who had unleashed d'Estaing before war was made official.

Córdova did not even leave Cádiz until 22 June – that is, twenty days *after* the French had arrived at the rendezvous. They were then immediately caught in predictable northerly winds off the coast of Portugal, which further delayed their progress. By the time they arrived at the rendezvous the French had already been waiting for six weeks, enough time at sea to weaken even a healthy squadron. Their food was already starting to run out.

The combined fleet was seriously impressive in terms of size, at least. Sixty-six ships of the line strong, it was twice the size of the combined Franco-Spanish fleet at Trafalgar. They spent a single week practising manoeuvres. Effective communication was always critical in a fleet but particularly so in this one because the main force consisted of three divisions of ships, with every division consisting of ships from both countries.* The Spanish officers, however, did not understand the French signals when suddenly presented with them at the rendezvous point because the French instruction books that were supposed to have been sent never arrived. Even if they had arrived, the Spanish officers might very well have been bewildered to a point of incapacity or blinded by theory. We know from a surviving copy of the signal book they were using on the campaign that three-quarters of the book contained no fewer than seventy-six evolutions (fleet manoeuvres), all of which ignored the existence of an enemy.[8]

The British Channel Fleet was already at sea, now under the command of Charles Hardy, who had been chosen to replace Keppel on grounds of seniority and political neutrality, rather than experience or skill. At the instigation of the king, he was given the brilliant Richard Kempenfelt, a man with a wealth of experience, knowledge and respect throughout the service, who would serve as 'captain of the fleet' – a precursor to a modern admiral's chief of staff.

Hardy was cruising twenty miles or so south-west of the Scilly Isles when the allied fleet sneaked past and headed for

---

* Córdova led a 'reserve' of sixteen Spanish ships, a huge fleet in its own right.

Plymouth, where – inducing utter consternation – it was sighted from Maker's Point on the Rame Peninsula, at 1.00 p.m. on 16 August. First six, then eight more, and then all sixty-six of the allied ships appeared 'like a wood on the water'.[9] One British ship, the *Ardent*, was captured and another, the *Marlborough*, made her escape. As soon as he could make it to shore, her first lieutenant leapt on a horse and rode with a racing heart to Sandwich's house in London with the shocking news.

The Franco-Spanish fleet anchored and sent a cutter in to sound the approaches to Plymouth where, because of incompetent scouting, they thought Hardy was sheltering. Civilians in coastal areas moved inland while the militia was raised, the dockyard workers were armed, and tin-miners marched from Cornwall in their thousands. Orders were sent to British naval anchorages at the Downs and the Nore to block the eastern end of the Channel. Navigational aids were removed and all horses were removed from coastal areas – a decision that reflects British knowledge of the difficulty of transporting horses by sea. From his surviving correspondence you can almost see Vice-Admiral Molyneux Shuldham, the commander-in-chief at Plymouth, wringing his hands. 'At this important crisis and in my situation, I think I should fail in my duty if I suffered a day to pass without writing to you', he wrote to the Admiralty, with no more news to share. Naval officers were stationed in the tower of Maker Church in Cornwall to observe the enemy. The church tower stills stands today and is a haunting location to consider the threat pulsing ashore from the hostile fleet.[10] Meanwhile, the headline news, that the enemy were off Plymouth, filtered through to Hardy, who was still cruising off the Isles of Scilly. He immediately set sail, hoping to close the door on the allied fleet – to force them up the Channel, where they could be driven to their own destruction like the Spanish Armada* – but he was held back by rare easterly winds.

---

* In a curious twist of fate the man in charge of the British squadron in the Downs was named Francis Drake.

The allies, meanwhile, had achieved nothing. They had no idea where the British fleet was because they had not sent out any cruisers, nor, in a striking oversight, did they have any pilots with local knowledge of the south coast of England. They were forced to navigate 'by guess and by God', a mistake that has clear parallels with d'Estaing's ignorance of the American coast in the summer of 1778.[11]

The sickness that had tainted the French crews had, by now, turned into a full-blown and hideous epidemic, which the British knew about from a British sailor who had been captured, taken aboard a French 64-gunner and then released.[12] Thousands of sailors, both French and Spanish – though the latter seem to have suffered particularly badly – fell sick.[13] D'Orvilliers's only son died in the epidemic and the admiral himself had been weakened in his own way by a total absence of orders from Paris. Supplies of food were very low; some ships had no water at all.

On 29 August he finally gave up and headed for home. Hardy, reinforced with extra ships and winning his battle against the easterly winds, very briefly sighted his enemy. D'Orvilliers decided to offer battle but the poor condition of his fleet had reached the crucial tipping point at which it severely affected performance. The ships straggled and struggled to keep station; the Spanish ships were particularly bad. One French officer later said that they could 'overtake nothing and run away from nothing'.[14] They had no hope of getting anywhere near the British fleet. As a fighting force, the allied fleet was useless and now terribly vulnerable. Every day it grew weaker, and by the time it reached port at least 8,000 French and Spanish sailors and soldiers were either sick or dead – though ultimately the deaths were a low percentage of those disabled, a strong suggestion that the epidemic was not typhus.[15] The sickness in the Bourbon fleet allowed the British to dig up one of their favourite myths of failed enemy invasion: the sea, apparently, was so full of French and Spanish corpses that the inhabitants of Devon and Cornwall all stopped eating fish for a month.[16]

Hardy patrolled for a few days before returning to Spithead because his men were also starting to fall sick at a frightening rate – the result of a manning system that kept both pressed men and volunteers crammed together in unhealthy guard-ships before they were assigned to their naval ships.* The *Canada* and *Intrepid* were 'so sickly as to be almost useless'; the crew of the *Shrewsbury* were 'falling down with fever so fast as to deter me from sending any men on board her'; the *Monarch* was in a similar state; and the *Blenheim* was too badly manned to stay at sea for long. He was also running out of food and drink, though this is hardly surprising when one considers that the British Channel Fleet was consuming 150 tons of beer[†] per day.[17]

The summer campaign season thus closed and the British Isles were safe, for now. A contemporary article included the memorable quote: 'Never had perhaps so great a naval force been assembled on the seas. Never any by which less was done.'[18] As always, however, the impact of sea power must be measured in more ways than one. The allies had failed to invade, but by parading their fleet off Plymouth they had caused panic all over the south coast of Britain, which allowed the seed of fear that had been sown at the battle of Ushant to germinate. 'I think we have more reason to trust in Providence than in our Admirals', wrote Germain.[19] Shelburne and Richmond, leading politicians in the Opposition, described the crisis as the most awful the country had ever faced, comparable with the Armada.[20] Others looked back to that great Tudor confrontation in an attempt to come to terms with their situation. Among these was the evangelist John Wesley who, as a good Protestant, felt deeply threatened by the beast

---

* This was not remedied until 1781, when Charles Middleton introduced a system of 'slop ships' in home ports, where new recruits were stripped, washed and issued with clean clothes. Jamieson, 'Leeward Islands', 79.

[†] The equivalent of a quarter of a million pints. Each man was allowed a ration of a gallon of beer (around ten pints) per day, but there is plenty of evidence that in practice the men could drink as much as they liked.

of Catholicism. He wrote to Samuel Bradburn, a friend and fellow preacher:

> It is the judgment of many that, since the time of the Invincible Armada, Great Britain and Ireland were never in such danger from foreign enemies as they are at this day. Humanly speaking, we are not able to contend with them either by sea or land. They are watching over us as a leopard over his prey, just ready to spring upon us.[21]

The newspapers, far more interested in the threat of invasion than in the conduct of the war elsewhere, joined the party with enthusiasm. 'Fire your indignation at the thoughts of an invasion by the Monsieurs of France', urged one editorial.[22]

It was a disaster for the British both politically and militarily: politically, because it called into question the handling of the war; militarily, because it affected future operations. To prevent any such recurrence, Sandwich felt obliged to prioritize the Channel Fleet over others and to keep the ships at sea longer than he might otherwise have done, and in that decision lay the seed of defeat elsewhere. In a curious way, therefore, the allied invasion campaign was both an operational failure and, entirely inadvertently, a strategic success. Kempenfelt did his best to remedy the operational failure by innovating obsessively in addressing the problem of how a very large fleet could operate effectively against an even larger fleet. Never in the history of any navy, at any period before or since, have so many signal books and fighting instructions been issued by one man in the space of only twenty-seven months.[23] The strategic blunder of prioritizing home waters over foreign, however, had yet to make itself clear and the allies had no idea of the significance that their campaign would have. Before the fleet was even back in port, Vergennes wrote to Spain urging a new strategy. Thereafter Franco-Spanish fleets would assemble in the summer off the south coast of England, not to renew an invasion attempt but to keep British ships abroad outnumbered by threatening those at home. The Spaniards objected to the changed strategy, but Vergennes used Spain's financial weakness to force them into accepting.[24]

*   *   *

The Channel invasion, however, was not the only card that the French and Spanish had in play in 1779. The question now was, could they do any better elsewhere? Gibraltar was an isolated British rock that could easily be cut off from land and blockaded by sea. The British had no significant naval squadron at Gibraltar and there was an enormous Spanish naval base nearby at Cádiz. Surely, at least, the garrison there could be blockaded into submission. How could it not?

19

BRITISH RESOURCEFULNESS

Before the outbreak of war the Spanish had offered their neutrality to Britain in return for Gibraltar, an offer that the British had refused. Washington considered that decision 'more strongly tinctured with insanity' than any other yet made by Britain in the war,[1] but he had failed to consider the strategic problems faced by Britain through the lens of sea power. Gibraltar was nothing less than the key to the British maritime empire. It was used to monitor the Spanish navy in nearby Cádiz in times of peace and to blockade it in times of war; to protect British trade entering and leaving the Mediterranean; to police the Barbary corsairs who sailed from the north coast of Africa; as a wedge to hammer between the French naval bases of the Atlantic and the Mediterranean, to keep French sea power weak by keeping it divided; as a stepping stone for British operations heading into the western Mediterranean; and as a launching point for naval squadrons or trade convoys sailing from Europe to the West or East Indies. To lose Gibraltar was to endanger this entire system, the very system by which the British had become safe, rich and strong.

The Spanish began to build siege lines across the narrow isthmus that joined Gibraltar to Spain in the spring of 1779. The actual fighting, however, did not begin until September, when the wife of a British officer fired the first cannon at the Spanish lines, upon which 'every battery ... bellowed with rage, and vomited forth the most tremendous flames'.[2] By October 14,000 workmen were constructing defences around the Spanish camp and a Spanish fleet at Algeciras, just five-and-a-half miles across the bay from Gibraltar, was preparing to impose a maritime blockade.

In terms of ship type, the fleet was well chosen for the job in hand. A handful of powerful ships provided the backbone of the fleet and Vice-Admiral Antonio Barceló's flagship, a 74-gunner, dominated everything, riding at anchor 'most magnificently, exulting over a people shut up like poultry in a coup'.[3] The real action, however, would be conducted by a force of armed boats and specialist Mediterranean craft – xebecs and galleys – perfect for the challenge of exercising sea power in the Bay of Gibraltar.

The British naval force was tiny and toothless. Vice-Admiral Robert Duff flew his flag in the 64-gun *Panther*, which was supported by a single frigate, the *Enterprise*, and a small sloop, the *Childers*. A close observer would notice that the largest guns in the *Panther*'s armament were missing. As so often with British operations ashore in this war, sailors played a major part. Here, they built their very own battery from scratch, using the *Panther*'s guns.[4] Perhaps to hide their weakness, the crew of the *Panther* undertook regular exercises in both small arms and cannon fire – a show of muscle for Spanish benefit. The exercises also included regular seamanship drills such as raising and lowering topgallant yards, to keep the sailors practised and fit and – like the gunfire – to send a message of strength to the Spanish.[5]

In spite of this bluster, the clear imbalance of power in the bay was visible to the Gibraltarians in their eyrie, and it sparked yet another major civilian maritime evacuation.* Gibraltar was home to a British garrison, but it was also a major settlement, with particularly large numbers of Jewish and Genoese traders. Before the blockade began in earnest, refugees crammed into any boat they could find and made their way to the Moroccan or Portuguese coast, usually under the cover of night.[6]

---

* To go with the evacuation of Boston in 1775 and Philadelphia in 1777. There would be many more by the end of the war.

*   *   *

With more ships to hand the Spanish held the advantage in this balance of naval power, but it certainly was a balance: the Spanish did not dominate absolutely because they could not. The Bay of Gibraltar is vast, far too large to be physically cut off by a boom, and the British had made certain that the defences of the Rock were robust. The Rock, moreover, gave them an added advantage because of its height. British guns mounted high up could throw shot deep into the bay, and as the siege developed, designs were made for a 'depressing carriage' which could fire shot almost vertically downwards into the waters close to the British shore – an invention of great value and one of which the British were rightly proud.

In any contest between shore fortifications and warships, the stable shore fortifications always held the advantage. The crew of a warship had to manoeuvre their ship close to shore, always awkward because of coastal currents, shallow water and fluky winds. This was, and still is, a particular problem

Lieutenant George Frederick Koehler's 'Depressing Carriage', drawn by Koehler.

in the Bay of Gibraltar because of the dominant size of the Rock.

There was, therefore, something of an exclusion zone around the Rock into which the Spanish could only enter at great risk. Given advantageous wind and tidal conditions, this made it possible for ships of any size to break the Spanish blockade if they could only survive the likely chase on arrival or departure. Attempting it at night had a clear advantage.[7] As the siege dragged on, the rewards for such temerity became very high indeed, with huge prices paid for everyday goods, which only encouraged merchantmen to take the risks to get in.

The ability to run the blockade also allowed the British to launch lightning raids from Gibraltar against the regular merchant convoys that ran through the Straits. Gibraltar, after all, was located on what was then one of the busiest, if not *the* busiest, shipping lanes in the world. Yes, the British naval squadron was tiny, but it is important to remember that, rather like the ports on the American coast, Gibraltar was full of fishermen with fishing boats who were already well experienced in the dark arts of avoiding revenue cutters: it made little difference to them if they were escaping from a Spanish boat imposing a blockade or from one collecting tax. These vessels could hunt for vulnerable merchantmen as easily as they could go fishing.

With so many ships passing their door, moreover, they often had to do nothing at all but wait for damaged merchantmen, desperately seeking shelter of any sort, to fall into their lap. Any sailor who has spent more than a few days in or around the Straits will know that they are treacherous. The Atlantic rushes constantly into the Mediterranean, the prevailing winds come from the north and west, but powerful Levanter winds from the east can come and go with little notice. With dangerous shores to both north and south, the Bay of Gibraltar is the only safe haven. In this respect Gibraltar acted as a sort of giant maritime spider's web, and the British, who knew that their survival depended on such hapless prey, were always ready to pounce.

All this meant that although Gibraltar was dependent on maritime protection and supply for her survival, she was not as helpless as many suspected. The summer and autumn of 1779 is a perfect example. The last time that Gibraltar had received a major resupply was in April, yet the garrison had done remarkably well for itself since, capturing wine, brandy, wheat, cheese 'and other necessaries'. On one glorious occasion a windfall ship came in with 6,000 bushels of barley.[8] Demonstrations of self-sufficiency like this were good for both the stomach and the mind – a major morale boost to the garrison. It is significant that several first-hand accounts record the loss of one of the British privateers, the *Peace and Plenty*, which was chased ashore by a Spanish frigate and two galleys.[9] One can sense a loss of hope in those accounts; as long as the Gibraltarians had their mini-fleet of privateers, they knew that they could survive for a little longer.

The role of maritime protection and supply in relation to the garrison's morale is vividly highlighted by one particularly interesting event. One morning a sail was sighted making for Gibraltar. It was a cutter, rigged fore and aft, and clearly armed. The breeze blew from the north-west, cutting across the bay diagonally and blowing in a similar direction to the strongest of several currents in the Straits. In a large and showy display of sea power, far more than was actually required, the entire Spanish squadron weighed anchor, perhaps lured to sea by the friendly winds that would take them directly down upon their prey. Outgunned, the British waited to see what would happen.

The cutter, a British privateer, turned and apparently fled for the Barbary shore. The Spanish followed. Then, when the Spanish ships were well clear of their anchorage, when their sails were full of wind and when their giant, bluff hulls were just beginning to taste the pressure of the easterly current, the cutter's captain tacked, pointing her fine bow directly into the current and trimming her fore and aft sails as close as they could go to the north-westerly wind. She did not even need to be a fine sailing craft to outmanoeuvre the cumbersome

Spanish square-riggers, but she was handled with a fine touch. She first hung in the current, holding her own, before gradually edging forwards towards the Rock. Gradually she gained momentum until she finally sprang free of the current and made swift progress to the protection of the British anchorage. Two Spanish ships, including Barceló's flagship, realized what the British captain was up to, but they failed to counter his move and, for fear of being isolated near British guns, were forced to join the rest of the squadron, which had been caught cold and were now miles to leeward. They were, in fact, so far to leeward that they were unable even to return to Gibraltar until a Levanter blew.

It was an absolute triumph for the British. A single privateer captain had lured the entire Spanish squadron out of the bay. The blockade was lifted and it remained so for twelve days until the wind changed direction. Word raced through the Straits, up and down the coasts of Spain, North Africa and Portugal. During those twelve days, goods of every kind poured into Gibraltar. The privateer captain became a hero, his story a perfect allegory of what General George Eliott, the British commander of Gibraltar, wanted to inspire – a story of British pluck, courage and skill, a story of the few against the many.

The incident is also interesting because it raises a number of important questions about Spanish seamanship. It can be read in a number of ways. Perhaps the Spanish were competent seamen who had simply been duped by the privateer's temerity. Perhaps, however – surprising as this may seem – they were ignorant of the dangers that would befall their large square-rigged ships if they entered the current. Had they even considered the problem of returning to their anchorage against a wind and current that were both running directly offshore? There are many questions here and many possible answers, but none of them shine a positive light on Barceló and his men. It is also interesting that, at around this time, Captain George Montagu of HMS *Pearl* managed to capture a Spanish frigate off the Azores, even though only ten of Montagu's crew had ever served before in a man-of-war and the *Santa Monica* was significantly larger than the *Pearl*. The Spanish, it seemed, were raw indeed; an unkind historian might suggest that they didn't know what they were doing.

* * *

In the midst of all this Eliott shone like a beacon. A teetotal vegetarian widower, he was the perfect man for a siege. One of his major professional assets was his ability to see the broader strategic problem as well as the minutiae of siege tactics, and that vision saved the day on a number of occasions – once when he prevented Duff from throwing a major spanner in the works.

Hitherto, Gibraltar's precarious survival owed a great deal to the support of the sultan of Morocco, Mohammed I. He was a natural ally of the British because he was an enemy of the Spanish, who held the fortress of Ceuta, on the north coast of Africa more or less opposite Gibraltar. The sultan of Morocco wanted to expel the Spanish from Ceuta just as the Spanish wanted to expel the British from Gibraltar. Mohammed provided victuals duty-free to the Royal Navy and at reduced rates for the garrison. He also charged British ships reduced anchorage fees. He was a particularly valuable source of both corn and cattle, and provided safe passage for all of Eliott's official correspondence. This explains, for unwary historians, why Eliott's letters are all written in the flowery language of eastern courtesy and are signed from 'the slaves and servants' of the Arab leaders: the British could be surprisingly obsequious if it suited them.[10] Only a dash of this type of toadying by the British in America between 1773 and 1775 could have averted the entire war.[11]

Mohammed's friendliness did not exist without a price, however, and as tension increased on the Gibraltar peninsula, so did his price rise. Interestingly, the currency he valued most of all was the ability to exercise sea power in the Straits of Gibraltar. The sultan of Morocco therefore agreed to continue to help the British on the condition that they repaired and freshly fitted out four Moroccan frigates from British stores and with the expertise of British shipwrights at Gibraltar.[12] Three of these had been completed when Duff waded in, refusing to release any more naval stores for the sultan, but Eliott overruled him. More sensitive to the bigger picture, Eliott knew that, if the sultan took offence, the British would be denied crucial supplies in the future. Eliott described himself as a 'half-sea officer' and conducted all his business with one eye to the sea.[13] If the British had had more men like him in America in 1776–7, the war could have taken an entirely different course.

*   *   *

In 1779, therefore, the key balance was not between Spanish and British sea power but between Spanish incompetence at sea and British resourcefulness and diplomatic skill. The existing balance allowed Gibraltar to endure but it could not do so forever.

By November things had become desperate. Bakers sold their bread protected by armed guards and from behind locked doors. Civilians lived off thistles. They also began to burn precious fishing boats for firewood.[14] The civilians suffered far worse than the British soldiers or sailors, who were all prioritized with what little food and firewood was left; the price of naval protection was civilian misery.[15] By December Gibraltar was on the verge of collapse.

If Gibraltar was going to survive, core victuals required by the garrison – biscuit, oatmeal, peas and butter – had to come from Britain, and they had to come soon. But how would British politicians prioritize their plight? One thing was certain: by the winter of 1779 there were difficult decisions ahead because the façade of British sea power had already cracked. The situation in Gibraltar was bad, but it was just one more problem to add to a long list; a list that included the Channel and Western Approaches; the North Sea; the Irish Sea; various isolated British naval squadrons or garrisons in New York, the Chesapeake, the Mississippi, Mobile, Pensacola, Savannah,

Newfoundland and Canada; and the entire Caribbean from Barbados to Honduras. It was possible that a crisis would hit any of these locations. The question was, where? And could it be predicted and averted?

20

CARIBBEAN CRISIS

That crisis hit the Caribbean. In 1778 the British had lost the important wooding and watering island of Dominica but had captured the geographically significant island of St Lucia, from where they could watch the French at Martinique from a safe anchorage. British naval responsibilities, however, included far more than just watching the French at Martinique. The entire Caribbean was now awash with privateers and enemy cruisers: American, French and Spanish. The British economy and war effort, meanwhile, still relied almost entirely on the safe arrival of Caribbean trade. British commanders in the Caribbean were always, therefore, confronted with a difficult choice. Should they watch the enemy fleet and perhaps try and force battle if the opportunity arose? Or should they protect the crucial trade? In 1779 the man faced with this dilemma was John Byron, who had taken over command of the Leeward Islands station from Barrington. Byron's first challenge was to guarantee the security of a major British convoy gathering near St Kitts. Already postponed twice, its contents were needed desperately in London to boost the economy. Byron therefore abandoned his close observation of the French at Martinique and headed to St Kitts.[1]

D'Estaing, meanwhile, was itching to break out of Martinique. In the past few weeks he had received significant reinforcements which the British Channel Fleet had failed to prevent from leaving European waters and which Byron had failed to prevent from arriving in the Caribbean. The new British warships that had been ordered in 1778 were not yet ready and so reinforcements could not be sent. As a result the

British numerical superiority, which had been achieved in the Caribbean in late 1778, had been lost.[2] The French now maintained in the Caribbean in 1779 the same crucial numerical advantage that they had enjoyed in American waters in 1778. But could they make anything of it this time round?

Now ready, d'Estaing had been watching Byron as closely as Byron had been watching him: one of the ironies of using St Lucia as a naval base was that British movements were as clear to the French as French movements were to the British. The moment Byron's sails sank below the horizon, bound for the convoy rendezvous at St Kitts, d'Estaing acted, sending a small force to capture the nearby island of St Vincent, which was unprotected by any naval force and had only the barest defences on land. It fell on 17 June without so much as a whimper. D'Estaing, meanwhile, led a much larger force to Barbados – the windward-most island of the Windward Islands, the first stop for Caribbean-bound convoys and warships, and an island rich in sugar plantations and blessed with naval stores.

It was, in theory, a very good plan. Byron was nowhere to be seen and the jewel in the crown of the British Windward Islands was there for the taking. In practice, however, it was a terrible plan and betrays the same faults that had plagued d'Estaing's 1778 campaign. The operation failed because d'Estaing's ships were simply unable to make sufficient ground to windward. All sailing warships were large and cumbersome with bluff hulls that made them particularly susceptible to losing round easily to leeward, and their square rigs were poorly designed for sailing close to the wind. A nimble frigate, acting alone, had a good chance of making limited ground to windward, but a fleet of warships, further restricted by the challenge of keeping together, needed weather conditions to be as favourable as possible and the sailors to be at the top of their game to succeed. In this instance neither one nor the other was the case, and an experienced maritime eye would have immediately seen it. The Barbados operation therefore failed but, never willing to be beaten, d'Estaing set his sights on another British island: Grenada.

French warships at anchor at Saint George's Harbour, Grenada, showing the
disembarkation of French troops.

The wealthiest British island in the entire Caribbean after
Jamaica, Grenada was nevertheless almost entirely undefended; there were only eighty-four fit troops on the whole
island.[3] It was also to leeward of Martinique and therefore
easy to get to. The few soldiers on the island put up a brief
fight, allowing d'Estaing, the bull-headed soldier, another
chance to do what he did best – to lead his men in a
full-frontal assault shouting, '*Soldats en avant, suivez-moi!*' –
'Forward soldiers, follow me!'[4] The French secured the island
and took thirty richly laden merchantmen lying passively in
St George's harbour.[5]

Byron, meanwhile, had seen the St Kitts convoy safely on
its way and was heading back to St Lucia when he heard that
the French were attacking Grenada. He did not know that
the island had already fallen, nor did he know the size of the
French fleet. In fact he suspected, quite wrongly, that there
were fewer French ships than British.[6]

Not only was Byron's squadron outnumbered, it was also
in worse condition than the French. It had, in fact, been in a
shocking state when it first arrived in the Caribbean the previous year, and the Caribbean climate had only compounded the
problems. His men fell like flies to sickness and a large number
of his surgeons and their mates were ill.[7] Aware that they were
in the grip of an epidemic and that continued service in the
British fleet was akin to a death sentence, Byron's men deserted

like rats. He didn't even dare to sail to the naval dockyard at English Harbour in Antigua, usually a sanctuary for British ships in the Caribbean, because it had become renowned for desertion. There was little point taking the risk because the dockyard suffered from 'a total want of every kind of stores, but particularly of masts'.[8] The single most significant advantage that the British traditionally held over the French in the Caribbean – their access to quality repair facilities and naval stores at Antigua – had therefore been lost.

The result was that, in the summer of 1779, Byron commanded a fleet full of unhappy men on rotting ships with empty holds. To make matters worse, if it was at all possible, his squadron was now almost entirely out of water, having consumed what they had taken on their trip to St Kitts.[9] The very last thing that the British needed now was a battle.

Byron sailed in the hope that he could surprise the French, perhaps while they were still unloading their troops. The French, however, had already secured the island, and were now united, focused and ready to defend it. An efficient network of scouts warned them long in advance of the British arrival.[10] Naval battle in such a scenario was always tentative because the defending side would be unwilling to commit to a decisive encounter. To secure the island they simply needed to retain control of their anchorage, and we have seen at Ushant just how difficult it was in the age of sail to force an unwilling enemy to battle. Byron, who had never commanded a fleet in battle, was about to find out just how difficult it was.

His first problem was that his fleet was in very poor order because two sections of three ships had broken away from the main body. He was also burdened, and preoccupied, with a convoy of blundering transports full of troops. To allow the French to fall on a defenceless flotilla of transports would be catastrophic.

Byron signalled to attack the rear of the enemy fleet, which required those isolated sections of his fleet to pass within range of an overwhelming number of French ships. They fought

The battle of Grenada. The French fleet is shown in the foreground, the British in the background.

their way towards the enemy rear but were horribly damaged in doing so. A bold British captain, Robert Fanshawe of the *Monmouth*, wore out of line without orders, and attacked the van of the French fleet, to distract them from the crippled British ships in their rear – a move that was almost identical to the much more famous one made by Nelson at the battle of St Vincent in 1797.* Byron praised Fanshawe's move in his dispatch and the French were deeply impressed; it was reported that they toasted the gallantry of that 'little black ship' after the battle.[11]

Several British accounts recalled how the French fired at their rigging and then drifted away to leeward, thus preventing the British from engaging closely in their traditional manner, and Byron was careful to complain that the French ships sailed much faster than the British, allowing them to choose the range of engagement.† It is also clear that, once the full size of the French fleet became clear, Byron deliberately and quite sensibly kept to windward of the French to prevent them from doubling his line and attacking it from both sides at once. The

---

* An interesting parallel which is rarely mentioned. Nelson was in the Caribbean at this time. It is highly likely that he heard a detailed breakdown of Byron's battle and knew all about Fanshawe's manoeuvre.

† An important observation which counters the traditional view that the British ships sailed better than the French during this war, and which is intimately linked with the issue of coppering. T. White, *Naval Researches*, 27.

Admiralty later praised Byron's conduct: this was no situation to try anything rash.[12]

The battle drifted to a close with both fleets out of range and content to remain so. The French could easily have secured four isolated and dismasted British ships but did not. One of d'Estaing's subordinates, the fiery bailli de Suffren, blamed d'Estaing's want of seamanship skill for this failure. 'Had our admiral's seamanship equalled his courage,' wrote Suffren, 'we would not have allowed four dismasted ships to escape.'[13] Perhaps that is fair; but what is certain is that the prize of capturing four ships was not worth the risk of losing an entire sugar island newly prised from the British. Less likely but certainly possible, d'Estaing may very well have been making a remarkably restrained and impressive strategic decision.

Byron returned with most of his ships to St Kitts to repair in safety under the guns of British batteries.* The French threatened him at St Kitts twice but, to British astonishment, made no attack.[14]

*   *   *

French and British sea power were damaged in different ways by the battle. At least nine of Byron's fleet were badly damaged in the rig, many of them entirely dismasted, and the lack of available stores to get those ships quickly back to sea was the death knell of British sea power in the Caribbean for 1779. It was the worst British naval defeat for ninety years – since the battle of Beachy Head in 1690. The capture of St Lucia the previous year had put a deceptive glow on the shape of things in the Caribbean, but the loss of Grenada had revealed them for what they really were.[15] Byron, fed up with being expected to wage naval war with inadequate supplies, too few men and too few ships, resigned. Yet another leading British naval flag

* William Cornwallis, captain of the *Lion*, managed to raise some canvas on the stumps of his masts and claw his way to Jamaica, where he met the young Captain Nelson, thus sowing the seeds of a warm professional relationship that would last for the rest of Nelson's life. Cornwallis's account is in TNA: ADM 1/241, f.297.

The French fleet, shown in the foreground on the starboard tack, reconnoitring the British fleet at St Kitts, 22 July 1779. The British are shown beyond the French fleet, advancing along the coast on the port tack.

officer experienced in naval battle, to go with Keppel, Palliser, Howe and Barrington, was thus lost to the war.[*]

D'Estaing's fleet suffered many more casualties than the British,[†] a reflection of the thin construction of the French hulls. The French, however, were able to recover much more quickly than the British because they had a better supply of men available than the British did of masts. D'Estaing simply continued his campaign by taking 1,600 men from Saint-Domingue, 2,000 from Guadeloupe and patching the damaged hulls with whatever timber the shipwrights had to hand.[‡] In only a short time he had at his disposal a truly massive fleet, fifty-two ships strong, of which no fewer than twenty-two were ships of the line.

The British quaked in London, where the news was met with abject horror, and, in the Caribbean, where anxious eyes waited for the next strike to fall.[16] The British Caribbean fleet was immobilized and Jamaica, the engine of the entire British

---

[*] Though both Keppel and Howe returned at the war's end, after the fall of the North government.

[†] The French had a similar number of deaths (190 to the British 183) but far more killed and injured (759 to 346). Mahan, *Major Operations*, 81.

[‡] These new men included the first free black regiment to serve in the French military, the 'Volunteers of San Domingo'. Wilson, *Southern Strategy*, 137; Dull, *French Navy*, 161.

economy, was on d'Estaing's doorstep. A strike there would be an unparalleled and grievous wound against the British empire and it would probably force them out of the war. Nelson, who had been responsible for improving the island's defences, joked in a letter home that he might soon be learning to speak French.[17] Rumour of the danger they were under flew home in letters like this, and Barrington, furious, was now in London weaving tales of misery and woe, defending his actions by justifiably blaming those who had failed to provide him with an effective weapon with which to fight. 'Admiral Barrington is come home in very ill humour,' wrote James Cornwallis, brother of William, 'and represents our situation in the West Indies as truly lamentable, where we thought ourselves strongest ... we are every day in apprehension of some bad news. How different from the last war, when we were only accustomed to hear of victory.'[18] The British were on the verge of disaster.

21

FRENCH INCOMPETENCE

L uckily for the British, whose empire was sitting like a fat grape beneath d'Estaing's heel, the eighteenth-century sailor's fear of the weather saved them. With the hurricane season fast approaching, even though he might still have struck at the British in Jamaica, d'Estaing abandoned the Caribbean. When the British finally discovered that he had left, they panicked, thinking that he had chosen to attack a major British naval base, probably New York, Newport or Halifax. Vice-Admiral Marriot Arbuthnot, the new commander-in-chief of the North American Station,[1] was furious that d'Estaing had been 'unattended, unobserved and without interruption to pursue any enterprize he might be daring enough to begin',[2] and in a complete fuss the British abandoned Newport, leaving Narragansett Bay and Rhode Island Sound wide open. Here, the threat of French sea power alone caused the British to abandon a hard-won and valuable position. Of less immediate significance but still with an impact on the war, d'Estaing's presence in American waters also caused Clinton to postpone a new plan to attack Charleston.[3]

The British were right, at least, in thinking that d'Estaing was heading to America, but they were wrong in supposing that he would attack a major naval base – an interesting difference which reveals the wide gulf in thinking between Arbuthnot and d'Estaing, between British and French perceptions of naval strategy. The Frenchman, in fact, had decided to head for the southern states, which had been struggling to fend off a British offensive launched in the dying weeks of 1778 that had culminated in the capture of Savannah. The

British offensive had been planned with the Caribbean in mind. British Caribbean plantations were suffering because the Americans had cut off the imports of rice, meat and timber that kept the plantations going, and Savannah was the key to that trade.

The city fell rapidly to a force of Scottish soldiers in November 1778. The plucky Georgia State Navy, which had boasted one of the earliest examples of a ship armed by the rebels with the explicit intention of attacking a British military vessel,[4] was destroyed. The behaviour of the rampaging Scots – some of them on their first operation after two years as American prisoners, having been captured by American naval ships outside Boston in 1776 – was horrific. It was so bad that, after the war, the Georgia legislature passed a law prohibiting Scots from settling in the state unless they had fought for the Americans.[5] As so often in campaigns in America during this war, the initial British assault was impressive but the long-term strategy it reflected was ill considered. Savannah became yet another isolated strong point on the eastern seaboard that was reliant on naval support but whose presence stretched the available naval resources too far.

The British had nearly been trapped in Philadelphia, Newport and New York, and they had been saved in Jamaica by the coming hurricane season. Now d'Estaing was on the loose again, bending his orders so that he could respond to numerous pleas for American aid, sent from the Continental Congress and the governor of South Carolina.[6] This time he was heading for Savannah. What would he make of this next clear opportunity to capture or destroy an isolated British garrison?

*   *   *

D'Estaing's attack on Savannah in October 1779 was influenced by the difficulties of waging war at sea from start to finish. His ships were struck by a storm shortly after their arrival at the mouth of the Savannah River. Neither the storm's arrival nor the extreme damage caused by it would have surprised an experienced mariner with detailed local knowledge of the coast of Georgia. A captured English sailor had warned the French that, off the Savannah coast at that time of year, 'an English squadron had never dared to remain for eight hours even in the most beautiful weather', and they were subsequently astonished that the weather remained fine for the first few days. It soon turned, however.[7] The storm fell on the fleet with such suddenness that many of d'Estaing's captains were unable to raise their anchors. Their only choice now was to head out to sea 'to escape destruction'.[8]

The storm lasted a week, and when the French returned, they were in tatters. Seven ships had lost their rudders and had to be steered by a recently invented system of ropes and tackles. The French *Magnifique* was so leaky that her sailors had to take out her guns, until she was hardly *magnifique* at all. The entire fleet lacked rope for running rigging, without which the sails could not be set.[9] This all meant that, to repair his ships, d'Estaing had to stay far longer at Savannah than he had ever intended, and it is likely that this changed his plan from a lightning attack to a full-scale siege.[10]

Congress was delighted that d'Estaing was there and crowed. Yet again they saw success written all over the sails of French ships, as if the disappointments in New York and Newport, and the excruciating tension caused by the presence of the French fleet in Boston, had simply never happened: they were utterly blinded by the 'promise' of sea power. 'We did proclaim a general Day of Thanksgiving, to be held in these States, on the ninth Day of December next, not doubting but a complete victory over all the British forces in Georgia was "fixt as Fate"', declared Congress, who held the 'most sanguine expectations of success'.[11] The local press in South Carolina simply bubbled with excitement.[12]

As far as the Americans were concerned, French sea power was about to save the day.

*   *   *

The reports d'Estaing had received about the weakness of the British position in Savannah were not entirely accurate, or at the very least they needed significant qualification. The real situation was this. The city was very well stocked after the British raids of that summer into South Carolina. They had enough flour to last 6,000 men until January, and enough beef and pork until March. There were very few substantial fortifications of any type, but the city was defended on three sides by the Savannah River, a significant obstacle in itself but daunting indeed when patrolled by a number of British naval vessels. Other vessels had been sunk to block the main passage to the city. There was, moreover, no shortage of manpower to build fortifications to protect the city's one undefended side, because the British had seized hundreds of slaves on their raids inland. They also had an ace up their sleeve in the talented, energetic and highly motivated Captain James Moncrief, the chief engineer of the British southern army.[13] The most significant weakness in the British defences was that the trained military forces were split between the city itself and Beaufort, a town a little to the north of Savannah in Port Royal Sound. If d'Estaing could strike hard and fast, he could do so before the British had the opportunity to unite their troops. Savannah, in theory, was there for the taking.

In practice, however, the French landings were poorly organized, poorly led and poorly executed. The first was on an island at the mouth of the Savannah estuary, which had been abandoned by the British. D'Estaing was so impatient to be ashore and to get to grips with the British that he landed in his fast, lightly manned cutter well in advance of the rest of his troops. Completely isolated, he then fell asleep while his men struggled in the open boats against the rising wind and turning tide. Many were unable to land that night and were forced to spend an uncomfortable night in their open boats.[14] The next day the rest of the army landed, paraded around an empty island and then re-embarked.

The second landing, this time on the mainland, was also a disaster. Again, the organization was shoddy, and a far larger body of men – 1,500 this time – was forced to spend the night in their open boats. The next day the wind and sea rose. One of the boats, rowed by men 'who knew not the difficulties which confronted them',[15] turned over, drowning everyone aboard. One witness claimed that, in total, 100 men died this way.[16] The position was also poorly chosen and d'Estaing raged that 'a post of a hundred men would probably have repulsed us'.[17] The wind then rose to another storm, forcing the warships to slip anchor again, thus abandoning the French army on the beach without any tents and with only three days' rations.

The utter chaos of these landings stand in marked contrast to the skilful efficiency of the British landings at New York and Newport in 1776, at Head of Elk for the Philadelphia campaign in 1777 and at St Lucia in 1778. It seems that the French had dreams of sea power that they were simply unable to realize.

The French at least knew about the British military outpost at Beaufort and had recognized its significance. They had stationed frigates at the mouths of both the Savannah River and Port Royal Sound to prevent the two from uniting. What they did not do, however, was block the route to Savannah from Beaufort that wound its way through coastal marshes. An American army under General Benjamin Lincoln had already made its way towards the French army camp and several armed rebel galleys – ideal craft for guarding the shallow inland waterways – had joined the French fleet. But nothing was done to block this passage, probably for want of local knowledge: we know that the French had no local pilots.[18]

The British, on the other hand, who had been exploring the coast for nearly a year, knew it well, and they knew about a passage through the marshes known as Wall's Cut, passable only by boats and small ships and only at high tide.[19] They sneaked through, guided by Lieutenant Goldensborough of the *Vigilant*, on the very same day that a French frigate was negotiating the sand-bars at the entrance, some seven miles away. Utterly overjoyed at their achievement of defying such a mighty force, the British sailors 'could not be prevented from giving three cheers'.[20]

SAVANNAH

D'Estaing and Lincoln, who had climbed nearby Brewton's Hill to observe Savannah, saw the whole ghastly scene unfold, as the British boats stole upriver toward the city uncontested. Furious, d'Estaing blamed the Americans: 'General Lincoln, who could and should have prevented this misfortune, saw it and fell asleep in an armchair', he wrote in disgust.* It would be wonderful to know what Lincoln thought of the French in return but, oddly, there is no hint in any of his correspondence of what he thought of his allies. It is not inconceivable that he destroyed any incriminating letters. A balanced assessment criticizes poor co-ordination between the allies.[21]

The result of this maritime sleight of hand was that British manpower in Savannah was as strong as it could have been, and was far stronger than the French had ever suspected or were in any way prepared for. They had left Martinique, the only French naval base in the Caribbean capable of providing the necessary supplies for such a large fleet, at the end of June; it was now September.

The French spent weeks building batteries for a long siege, but every day the condition of their sailors, abandoned on their ships, worsened. One account claims that thirty-five sailors were dying of scurvy every day. They were also severely short of water, which was shared out 'in a cruel way even to the sick'. The bread, which by now had been stored for nearly two years, was inedible, and there was a general lack of clothing, shoes and linen for bandages. The few sailors who were not in their hammocks 'were weak, of a livid colour, with the marks of death painted on their faces'.[22] The comte de Noailles claimed that, if only ten ships of the line had engaged them, the entire fleet would have been taken,[23] a conservative estimate if one considers that most of the fleet's guns and nearly all of her sailors were ashore and the rest were like zombies.

What d'Estaing thought of this is unclear. One French officer

---

* Lincoln was very fat and suffered from sleep apnoea.

noted how he 'appeared to have entirely forgotten his vessels',[24] while Lincoln himself noted how d'Estaing 'appeared exceedingly anxious about his Fleet'[25] – startlingly divergent views. On balance it is likely that d'Estaing was painfully aware of the state of his fleet but was himself suffering from the burden of expectation that had been heaped upon the shoulders of French sea power by both the French and the Americans. With such hopes so far unrealized on the American coast, he knew that this was his last chance to make an impact and perhaps to make amends for his abandonment of Sullivan at Newport. Thus the French remained at Savannah, literally digging themselves an enormous hole.

More time was lost because the Americans had almost no artillery and the siege guns would have to come from the French ships. The French therefore had to drag their naval guns, with their small wooden wheels designed for smooth gun-decks, overland. They then struggled to master the numerous logistical challenges of mounting naval guns, which were mounted on low carriages, in land batteries, which required them to be mounted on high carriages. To enable the gunners to hit their targets, the naval guns therefore had to be positioned on a raised platform, which exposed the gunners to enemy marksmen. They then had to be protected by a firing pit. These took weeks to build and, once firing began, ultimately slowed the rate of French fire. None of this was aided by the fact that, at the very start of the siege, a ship's steward mistakenly sent a barrel of rum to the forward batteries, rather than a barrel of beer. From the moment that the order to open fire was given, the gunners were roaring drunk for two days straight.[26]

By this stage the French were so desperate for men that the warships were almost completely evacuated.[27] In direct contrast to almost all British combined operations in this period, the French soldiers blamed the subsequent poor bombardment on the fact that d'Estaing had entrusted some of the most important batteries to his sailors.[28] The fifteen British batteries in Savannah were also armed, almost exclusively, with naval guns and were manned entirely by sailors.[29] This stage of the battle of Savannah, therefore, was almost a naval battle, contested between sailors with naval guns, but fought on shore between trenches rather than afloat between warships.

The French attack had little effect on the British positions. Exasperated, d'Estaing fell back on his favourite tactic, the good old-fashioned frontal assault – yelling, sword-wielding, musket-blazing. His men had been unable to build effective batteries with naval guns, his sailors were dying, and every day he spent on shore was another day closer to the next, inevitable, storm that could destroy his ships. His fateful decision to attack was thus based entirely on these ingredients of sea power. The difficulties crushed him. One sorry witness wrote:

> he is cruel to himself. We have seen him sick and attacked with scurvy, never desiring to make use of any remedies, working day and night, sleeping only an hour after dinner, his head resting upon his hands, sometimes lying down, but without undressing … There is not a man in his fleet who would believe that he has endured all the fatigue which he has undergone.[30]

The subsequent attack was disastrous. A handful of British sailors in well-made and well-positioned redoubts massacred a rampaging army of French and American sailors and soldiers who were not allowed to fire back – on pain of death – until they had taken the dominant British defensive position, the Spring Hill Redoubt. The carnage was almost inconceivable and the French searched for explanation: 'We know that the British filled their cannon with packets of scrap iron, the blades of knives and scissors, and even chains five and six feet long.'[31] The men who took down the French rush with this hail of iron death were British sailors. Arbuthnot subsequently praised them in a letter to the Admiralty.[32]

As usual there were attempts to find humour in the horror, and it was now so easy to poke fun at d'Estaing. A contemporary poem included these comic verses, which must rank as the finest produced in the war:

> Push round the brisk glass,
> He's surely an Ass,
> Who longer past losses does think on,
> Let us drink, laugh and sing,
> We've routed d'Estaing,
> And the Yankies fam'd General Lincoln.
>
> The French Grenadiers,
> With D'Estaing appears
> At the head of them boldly advancing,
> But approaching too nigh,
> A wounded arm and thigh
> Spoilt at once both his fencing and dancing.
>
> Of our powder the smell,
> They lik'd not so well,
> As they would that of garlick or onions,
> They roared out *'sacre dieu!'*
> Guns we thought they had few,
> But beggar they sprung up like *champignons*.
>
> My tale to cut short,
> They abandon'd the fort,
> Many hundreds behind them did stay,
> Tho to give them their due,
> I believe they had fled too,
> But the dead you know can't run away.[33]

Sadly beaten but permitted to return to their ships unchallenged, the French left Savannah in an operation blessed by fine weather. One British officer recorded the wonderful moment that 'the whole of the enemy's shipping that were at Tybee sailed over the bar, and left our port open' – an interesting inversion of the fear that had already been felt on numerous occasions in this war at the arrival of a fleet of warships.[34] This was the first time that Americans and Frenchmen had fought together against the British, and it had done nothing to heal the wounds of French and American antagonism suffered at Newport and Boston in 1778.* One Congressman said: 'Providence by another Striking Instance has ... tumbled our Towring Expectations to the ground.'[35] Always sensitive to such developments in the war, the Continental currency went into a tailspin.[36]

Weak and disoriented, d'Estaing's fleet split into several separate parts and eventually limped into Brest, Rochefort, L'Orient, Cádiz and Havana. It was frankly a miracle that the British captured none of their twenty-two ships of the line.[37] Lincoln wrote to the president of Congress blaming d'Estaing for abandoning him, just as Sullivan had done in 1778. He claimed, completely unreasonably, that, had the French fleet stayed, 'nothing could have prevented our success'.[38] These are the words of a farmer with no maritime experience who had been lucky enough not to visit any of the French ships. If d'Estaing had stayed any longer, it is far more likely that his ships would have been driven to their own destruction; by leaving when he did, at least he got them home.

Under the pressure of exercising sea power for so long, so far from significant dedicated naval repair and resupply facilities, and under the command of a soldier, French sea power in the Caribbean and in American waters had completely disintegrated. By the end of 1779 the French had managed to make a hash of their alliances with both the Americans and the Spanish, and the cherished expectations of sea power being a magic wand, shared by each of the allies, had been exposed as naïve.

It felt as if the tide was turning back in favour of the British. When news of d'Estaing's defeat reached England, the guns in the Tower of London were fired in victory, a

---

* Lincoln had been particularly angry that d'Estaing had summoned the British to surrender 'to the arms of the King of France', Mattern, *Benjamin Lincoln*, 82.

mark of just how desperate the British had been since 1778.[39] Could they now keep this momentum going and use the self-destruction of French sea power to drag themselves away from the precipice?

22

AMERICAN DESTRUCTION

With d'Estaing's departure from American shores the war at sea reverted to one fought between the British and the trident of American sea power: the Continental Navy, the various state navies and American privateers.

There were certainly some bright points for American forces at sea. A Scot with good maritime experience, who had settled in Virginia and had made sufficiently influential friends to secure a commission in the Continental Navy, wholeheartedly, if regretfully, took up the American cause. In his own words he had chosen to abandon the sea in the early 1770s in favour of 'calm contemplation and poetic ease', where he could appreciate 'the softer Affectations of the Heart and my prospects of Domestic Happiness', this being his 'favourite scheme for life'.[1] This all makes him sound like a monk and is more than a little disingenuous. When it came to war, this man was one of the most aggressive and single-minded officers in the Continental Navy, and his achievements would cause a sensation throughout Europe and America. His name was John Paul Jones.

In 1776 Jones had tasted success on Esek Hopkins's raid on the Bahamas, and he had subsequently been given his first command, the sloop *Providence*, in which he had made no fewer than sixteen captures in a cruise off the coast of Nova Scotia. He followed that up with even more success in the ship *Alfred*, which captured a British supply ship full of uniforms for Burgoyne's army. With a strange knack of being in the right place at the right time, Jones was operating off the coast of France when the Treaty of Alliance was formally declared in

1778, and his new ship, *Ranger*, was the first American warship to be saluted by a French warship – a hugely symbolic moment in the history of the revolution, as this was the occasion when the prickly French finally and openly accepted an American warship as representative of an independent nation. If behaving as if they were independent was one side of the coin of American independence, having that behaviour accepted was the other: it gave the American cause value, turning a counterfeit currency into the real thing.

Jones then headed for Whitehaven, a port on the Irish Sea that had grown wealthy through the export of coal. It may seem a strange choice, but Whitehaven lies on the Solway Firth directly opposite a little Scottish village called Kirkudbright – Jones's birthplace. Jones, therefore, was deliberately heading to waters he knew, where he could make his local knowledge count. He attacked Whitehaven, burned some shipping and then led a raid into Scotland, where he attempted, and failed, to kidnap a minor Scottish earl, the idea being that he could ransom the earl in exchange for American maritime prisoners held in British gaols. Although he never captured the earl, by raiding a British port he became the first enemy to set foot on English soil and cause significant damage for more than a century.*

Jones then had more success across the Irish Sea, near Carrickfergus, where he captured a British warship, HMS *Drake*.[2] Until now, the poster boys of American naval power in European waters had been Lambert Wickes, who had captured nine British ships in the Channel in January 1777 and then eighteen more in the Irish Sea in May, and Gustavus Conyngham, who had terrorized British merchant shipping in the Channel; but news of Jones's exploits, which reached America shortly after news of the alliance with France, transformed him into a personality whose adventures utterly dominated naval gossip, even though he had not yet fought the battle that would cement his name in naval legend.

---

* Since the Dutch raided the Medway and burned Sheerness in June 1667.

That battle took place off Flamborough Head on 24 September 1779.* Jones, leading a small squadron in the 40-gun *Bonhomme Richard*,† caught up with a British convoy on its way to the Baltic, which was escorted by a powerful 44-gun British ship, HMS *Serapis*. Captain Richard Pearson of the *Serapis* had been aware of Jones's presence for three full days and was fully prepared for him when they met.[3]

The two ships fell on each other, the Americans lashing theirs to the British in a display of seamanship and gallantry that was only possible once the fluke of the American anchor had become tangled up with the *Serapis*'s quarter. They were then so close that the muzzles of the American guns were touching the British hull.[4] The *Serapis*, with far superior guns and healthier, better-trained gunners, fired her guns constantly until, 'during the last hour of combat the shot passed through both sides of the *Bonhomme Richard*, meeting little or no resistance'.[5]

At the start of the action, the British ship had enjoyed a marginal advantage in firepower over the American, but shortly after firing began, one of Jones's 18-pounders exploded (and some accounts suggest two), causing massive damage to the lower deck and leading him to order the remaining 18-pounders not to be used.[6] The discrepancy in firepower thus became overwhelming. The American rudder was shattered, and only an odd timber here and there kept the poop from crashing down onto the gun-deck.[7]

The *Serapis*, however, was also in a terrible state, having suffered gravely at the hands of American sailors throwing grenades and other combustibles into the ship. The British had been on fire 'not less than ten or twelve times in different parts of the ship and it was with the greatest difficulty & exertion

---

* Interestingly, the vast majority of published accounts of the battle say it happened on 23 September, which is incorrect. Schaeper, *John Paul Jones*, 6–11.

† So named because she was the ex-French Indiaman *Duc de Duras*. It was the flagship of an entire squadron of seven 'American' warships financed by the French and was one of the two largest ships to serve under American colours, the other being the Dutch-built *South Carolina* (formerly called the *Indien*), armed with 40 guns.

imaginable at times that we were able to get it extinguished', and then, finally, they lost the fight and the flames took hold of a cartridge of gunpowder. A catastrophic explosion followed and 'blew up the whole of the people and officers that were quartered abaft the main mast, from which unfortunate circumstance all those guns were rendered useless for the remainder of the action'.[8] Ears ringing, skin scorched, with the mainmast on the verge of falling and with another ship in Jones's squadron, the frigate *Alliance*, still entirely undamaged, having skirted the action, Pearson surrendered his ship.[9]

There is no contemporary evidence at all that, moments before this, and with his own ship ruined, Jones rejected a British suggestion that he surrender by claiming 'I have not yet begun to fight.'[10] Nonetheless, Herman Melville and countless authors since have revelled in this clash, which, according to a rather overexcited Melville, was 'For obstinacy, mutual hatred, and courage ... without precedent or subsequent in the story of the ocean'.[11] More certain is that the battle ranks as one of the most hard-fought and bloody single-ship actions in British and American naval history, in which one witness recalled how they fought with 'the blood over one's shoes'.[12] Pearson was horrified by the state of the *Bonhomme Richard* when he went on board to hand over his sword: 'her quarter and counter on the lower deck entirely drove in, and the whole of her lower deck guns dismounted, she was also on fire in two places and six or seven foot of water in her hold.'[13] She sank two days later, which makes this one of those surprisingly rare occurrences when a sailing warship actually sank as the result of battle, and perhaps the only example when it was the victorious ship that actually sank.[14] George III knighted Pearson for his defence of the *Serapis* and, in his defence of that ship, the defence of the entire Baltic convoy which escaped unharmed.

* * *

Unfortunately for the American ships in North American waters, meanwhile, on 4 April 1779 Captain Sir George Collier had been placed in temporary command at New York after the detested and incompetent Gambier had been recalled. Energy came off Collier like sparks off a grindstone. He left behind an excellent diary that survives at the National Maritime Museum in Greenwich, England. If there is one word that leaps repeatedly off the pages in his lively prose, it is 'indignation'. The Americans really got under Collier's skin. While other British and Jäger servicemen wondered at the natural world of this remarkable continent, Collier's first recorded thought was, 'I see with indignation & concern the rebel colours insolently waving on the batterys of New York.'[15] He proved an unpleasant, barbed thorn in the American side. In July 1777 he had made the first capture at sea of an American frigate when he chased and took the *Hancock*.[16] In August he had ravaged the coast around Machias in Maine, where he had destroyed around thirty American vessels that had been gathered to invade British-held Nova Scotia.[17] He was insatiable.

Unusually for any British naval commander in New York, Collier got on very well with the usually intolerant Henry Clinton, who had taken over from William Howe after the latter's resignation had been accepted in May 1778. In the spring of 1779 Collier suggested a series of raids on rebel maritime strong points in the Chesapeake Bay, particularly around the area of Portsmouth and Hampton Roads. The Chesapeake was a focus of rebel shipbuilding, privateering and trade, all of which were instrumental in sustaining the rebel war effort. Clinton gave his consent.

For a fortnight in May 1779 Collier and his squadron rained shocking violence upon the rebels there, destroying or capturing no fewer than 137 vessels and stores worth at least £1 million. His troops were landed in beautifully conducted amphibious operations, in which flatboats were covered by galleys and gunboats, forming 'the most beautiful regatta in the world'.[18] The climax came on 24 May when Fort Nelson on the Elizabeth River was destroyed:

Night appeared grand beyond Description, tho' the light was a melancholy one: Five Thousand Loads of fine seasoned

Oak Knees for ship building, an infinite Quantity of Plank, Masts, Cordage, & numbers of beautiful Ships of War on the Stocks were all the Time in a blaze, & all totally consumed, not a vestage remaining, but the Iron Work, that such things *had* been.[19]

The most destructive British raid of the war, it fired both Collier and Clinton with energy for more. Within days of returning to New York they were off again, this time Collier's ships taking Clinton's soldiers far up the Hudson, where they seized crucial strong points which guarded north–south communication across the river. Collier then sailed downriver and into Long Island Sound, where his ships raided several Connecticut coastal towns, destroying shipping of any type wherever it was found. He was enraged at Norwalk, where, 'for the treacherous conduct of the rebels in murdering the troops from windows of houses after safeguards were granted them', he destroyed the entire town, 'together with five large vessels, two privateer brigs on the stocks and twenty whaleboats, as also two saw mills, a considerable salt work, [and] several warehouses of stores'. He rather nonchalantly added that the 'small town of Greenfield suffered the same Chastizement'.[20] Primarily thanks to Collier's ruthlessness, by July 1779 every ship in the Connecticut Navy had been captured or destroyed.

The most damning strike on American naval strength, however, fell far away from New York in the beautiful stillness, the colourful wilderness, the hitherto peacefulness of Maine. The reason that the war now descended on such an isolated spot was the result of a strategic jigsaw, every piece shaped by sea power.

In recent months Boston had become the leading centre of rebel maritime power. D'Estaing's arrival in American waters had forced the British to lift their blockade, and armed American ships now sailed in large numbers from Boston at will. Clinton complained of them growing 'insolent' and he 'trembled' for the fate of British supply convoys. British naval officers raged at their impotence.[21] In March seven British transports were captured, and in July eight rich prizes in a single cruise by the *Queen of France* and *Ranger*.[22] This new-found American strength, however, seemed threatened when the British decided to seize a dominant strategic location with an excellent anchorage to the north of Boston, in Maine.

The target was Bagaduce, modern-day Castine, a tiny headland near the mouth of the Penobscot River. The British would use it as a base from where they could police their maritime supply lines, which ran northward from New York, past rebel-held Boston, to the naval base at Halifax in Nova Scotia. Bagaduce was also a crucial source of shipbuilding timber, which was floated downstream from Maine's copious inland forests. It was hoped that a major military presence in the region would encourage loyalists displaced from Boston, Philadelphia and elsewhere to resettle. It was even hoped that this would be the start of a new colony called New Ireland. This British move, therefore, was far more than the small visible military operation that it seemed. Like an iceberg, that small military operation in forgotten Maine hid a far larger body of imperial weight.

A tiny British force, supported by just three naval sloops, seized Bagaduce on 12 June 1779. Rebel leaders in Massachusetts, chests puffed out in indignation at British temerity and faces flushed with pride in their new-found maritime power, decided to drive the British out. They drew on their own maritime history for inspiration. Bostonians had undertaken their own major maritime operations on several previous occasions: to capture Quebec in 1690, French Acadia (Nova Scotia) in 1704 and 1707, and Louisbourg in 1745. As a chance to demonstrate Massachusetts' ability to stand up for itself against its mighty imperial foe, and as a metaphor for the entire rebellion, this was too good an opportunity to miss. The British force in Bagaduce was nearby, it was small and it was utterly isolated. How difficult could it be?

*   *   *

The biggest naval force that had ever sailed under American colours gathered at Boston, their intention nothing less than to 'captivate, kill or destroy the whole force of the enemy'.[23] Manpower was a major problem. Abigail Adams noted how more than half of the men aged between sixteen and fifty had already been drafted into army service, and so the Penobscot expedition was forced to rely on whatever was left, a large portion of which was either small boys or old men. The need for men was so bad that Massachusetts was forced to issue a press to man their ships – something that was used regularly by the British but which, hitherto, had deliberately been avoided by the Americans, who were so keen to paint their cause as one of liberty fought by volunteers.

All three branches of American sea power – the Continental Navy, state navies and privateers – took part. The Massachusetts State Navy provided three armed ships, and the New Hampshire State Navy, in a rare example of interstate naval co-operation, its only warship, the *Hampden*. They were boosted by the presence of three warships from the Continental Navy, including the 32-gun frigate *Warren*, and sixteen Massachusetts privateers and twenty-two troop transports. The men involved did not suffer the language barriers experienced by the French and Spanish in their terrible attempt to work together in the English Channel, but they would soon discover that working such an alliance as a unified fleet raised more than enough problems of its own.

The American fleet consisted of ships of widely varying capabilities, captained by men with varying interests in the war. The majority of the captains were from Massachusetts, but their commander, Dudley Saltonstall, was an officer in the Continental Navy and was from Connecticut.[24] They did not have any shared culture or experience of working together. They would find it difficult to keep station in relation to each other in a flat calm, let alone in relation to an enemy who was firing back steadily, accurately, and with no intention of stopping. They had little experience of naval warfare at all. Most who had served on privateers knew next to nothing about battle because most merchantmen were either unarmed or poorly manned and their captains had no interest in risking their lives or the lives of their men for the sake of someone else's profit.

To wage naval warfare in the confines of an inland waterway was also to test the crews' seamanship in the most rigorous way. To avoid collision they would need to tack and wear with great accuracy and confidence, and in the noise of battle they would, ideally, execute those manoeuvres by hand signal alone. Their captains would have to cope with changes in their ships' capability as their men were wounded and the ships' rigging damaged. And they would have to do all of this in shallow water, near invisible mudbanks, in waters that raced this way and that with tidal flow and river currents.

Their enemy, on the other hand, had been able to nose their way into their anchorage at Bagaduce at their own pace, dropping a lead line here and there to sound the water. They would also, by now, be armed with detailed knowledge of winds, currents and tides in their new home. The ships would be anchored at bow and stern and probably attached to each other with giant hawsers, possibly even chains, to prevent their line from being broken. If attacked, therefore, none of the British sailors would be required to handle sail but could all focus on gunnery. Those men would have been trained to similar levels of competence according to similar rules by officers with similar professional expectations.

It is unclear how much of this the rebel leaders in Boston who had conceived the operation realized, but it is certain that the levels of American expectation associated with this expedition were unrealistic. Once again, sea power was seen as a type of cure-all: the Americans believed that they could just whisper its name to benefit from its strength, and they were now going to suffer for that misjudgement as both the French and the Spanish had already suffered.

When the Americans arrived, the British were unprepared to receive a major assault but immediately drew heart from the visibly woeful mismanagement of the American ships in the narrow tidewater.[25] This was a key characteristic of naval warfare in the age of sail: competence was *visible*, the motions

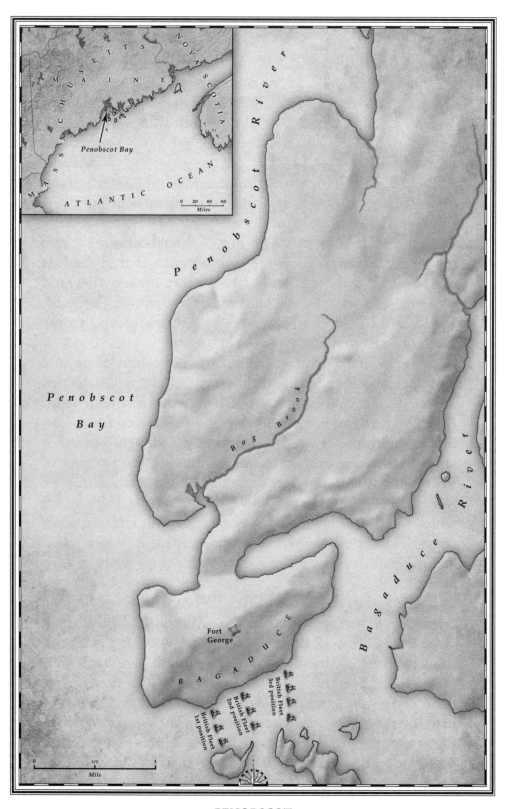

PENOBSCOT

of a ship a sensitive indicator of the ability and strength of her crew. The British, under command of Lieutenant Henry Mowat, quickly adopted a strong defensive position; the fleet of transports protected by the three British sloops carefully positioned and securely anchored near the newly constructed fort.

Faced with this, the man in command of the American land forces, Solomon Lovell, was unable to agree with the naval commander, Saltonstall, on the next step. Should Saltonstall's fleet take out the British sloops first or should the army secure the fort? At its most basic the conundrum was this: the first option would make it easier to take the fort; the second would make it easier to take the ships. The first option, however, would lead to the death of more sailors; the second to the death of more soldiers.

Saltonstall, at least, understood the difficulties of inshore naval operations and realized that to attack the well-defended Mowat was a dangerous proposal indeed. He stood up to Lovell and refused to take his ships into that 'dam hole',[26] an interesting choice of words that reveals the thought process of an experienced mariner. He was horrified at the prospect of sailing into a narrow waterway which, in his own words, he was 'totally not acquainted with'.[27] He knew that, if his attack failed, there would be no escape unless the wind miraculously changed direction at the exact moment that it was required and the British ships politely allowed his ships room to turn around.

It made far more sense for the American soldiers to launch a lightning raid on the unfinished British land defences, but Lovell, blinded by the presence of the British ships, refused to stand down. The distant, ignorant war-planners in Boston were also blinded by the presence of their own ships and rebuked Saltonstall from afar when news of the American inaction reached their ears. 'We have for some time been at a loss to know why the enemy's ships have not been attacked ... It is agreed on all hands that they are at all times in your power.'[28] Criticized from all sides,

Saltonstall prepared to launch a naval attack, but he never even got the opportunity.

On 12 August a British squadron under the fiery George Collier arrived at the mouth of the bay. Collier, based in New York, had rushed his ships to sea as soon as he heard of the American expedition, which was far too large to have escaped the network of loyalist spies that ran like an artery from Boston to New York.

At the sight of Collier's ships – at nothing more than the threat of British sea power – the Americans panicked. They could clearly see how the British manoeuvred their much larger ships with skill and efficiency, and they were all too aware that their own force was too inexperienced, too young, too old and too sick to prevail.

They fled upriver, in 'an unexpected and ignominious flight', wrote Collier, with the wind and the tide behind them, so tightly packed that only the rearmost few ships could fire safely at their pursuers without endangering the others. With the exception of two ships that were captured, the entire American force was destroyed on the riverbanks of the Penobscot. A chilling contemporary map of the action shows the American ships crammed into the river as the British chased, with the inscription 'Rebel Fleet on fire' [see fig. 11]. It was a stunning feat of seamanship by the British. Collier wrote how 'the King's ships continued their pursuit of the rebel fleet up the river Penobscot, & considerable hazard attended this part of the chace, from the extreme narrowness of the River, from the shoals & from the flaming ships on each side'.[29] In the words of Lovell, 'To attempt to give a description of this terrible Day is out of my Power ... Transports on fire. Men of war blowing up ... and as much confusion as can possibly be conceived.'[30] It ranks as one of the most one-sided and decisive battles in all naval history. 'We have lost a fine little navy', wrote Jabez Bowen, deputy governor of Rhode Island, a classic example of the Americans misunderstanding the nature of their sea power:[31] it was a terrible little navy and it was destroyed for its incompetence.

In time the British looted the American ships' guns and took them into their own service. The wrecks settled into the riverbanks. Some timbers remained exposed well into the twentieth century and served as climbing frames for children to play where once men and ships had burned. The thick, grey mud of the Penobscot, meanwhile, preserved immaculately the abandoned personal remains of hundreds of American sailors fleeing for their lives. One ship, the privateer *Defence*, was excavated between 1975 and 1981 by archaeologists who still purr over the quality of the artefacts left behind, undoubtedly the finest of any revolutionary-era shipwreck. We have tankards so perfect that they look like replicas used by modern-day re-enactors; we have initialled wooden name-tags for identifying lumps of meat boiled in a communal cauldron; we even have a potato skin. Most tellingly of all, however, we have immaculate leather shoes. Those shoes really are cause to pause and think. So easily celebrated simply as evidence of sailors' clothing from the era, that approach rather misses another crucial point: they are evidence that some poor sailors, assuming they survived the fleet's destruction, were forced to run for their lives through the Maine woods, possibly all the way to Boston, barefoot. Collier was convinced that the subsequent trial by wilderness those sailors now faced would kill many of them,[32] but in reality most made it home.[33] News of the destruction of the American fleet caused Arbuthnot in New York to jabber with excitement.[34]

*   *   *

The year 1779 was thus a disaster for the Americans, most of it at the hands of George Collier. The occasional bright point lit up the sky, including the American recapture of Stony Point and Paulus Hook on the Hudson in July and August,* and the capture of HMS *Serapis* by John Paul

---

* Stony Point was captured on 16 July in a daring night-time raid led by General Anthony Wayne and gave the Americans a huge morale boost at a dismal time. Paulus Hook was captured on 18 August by Major Henry Lee III, again in another night-time raid.

Jones off Flamborough Head in March, but the tide of allied American-French-Spanish failure seemed unstoppable. The state of the American army camp at Morristown, New Jersey, was also desperate. The horror of Valley Forge in the winter of 1777–8 survives in American folk memory as the nadir of Washington's army, but the winter of 1779–80 at Morristown was actually worse.

Washington now found himself immobilized by the ghost of French sea power. He needed to be ready to act in case d'Estaing appeared, but he had no idea where d'Estaing was or what he was planning to do. He ended up writing an extraordinarily servile letter that reveals the full extent to which the American army had been held hostage by d'Estaing's fleet. He begged d'Estaing 'to entreat that you will favour me as soon as possible with an account of your Excellency's intentions'.[35] Little did he know the shocking state of d'Estaing's fleet, which had been scattered to the far corners of the Atlantic, or that his faith in French sea power was entirely misplaced.

In blissful ignorance, Washington kept his soldiers blooded by allowing them to raid, with immense savagery, the Iroquois Indians of Pennsylvania and upstate New York who had sided with the loyalists. Led by Major-General Sullivan, the man who had failed to operate effectively with d'Estaing of Rhode Island in 1778, those raids are now famous for changing forever Indian and American history, but it is never acknowledged that Sullivan was unleashed for the simple reason that Washington was able to turn his mind and his forces to the interior because of the absence of d'Estaing's fleet: there is a direct link between d'Estaing's failure to maintain a naval presence in America in 1778 and the dramatic reshaping of American–Indian relations.

*   *   *

Winter then closed in. Temperatures plummeted and inflation rocketed. American credit was exhausted both at home and abroad. In the words of one young American, the Royal Navy's patrols had 'annihilated our commerce'.[36] The lush funding that had been available for the American navy at its inception vanished and all naval shipbuilding ceased. Captures at sea became the only means of increasing the numbers of American warships, though with so few ships now available and a far more wary and committed enemy, those prizes became harder to come by.[37]

The brief period of strength enjoyed by American armed ships sailing out of Boston in the spring and summer of 1779 was extinguished at Penobscot. Collier had done his bit in the south to shock American shipbuilding into submission, and isolated disasters befell the frigates that were actually at sea: the *Randolph* exploded in battle with HMS *Yarmouth* in February 1778; the *Alfred* was captured in the West Indies in March that year; the *Virginia* grounded in the Chesapeake and was easily captured the same month; the *Raleigh* was captured by two weaker ships off Maine in September. Though the Continental Navy had boosted its numbers with ships lent by France or purchased, of the original thirteen frigates Congress had set out to build in December 1775, by the end of 1779 only the *Boston*, *Trumbull* and *Providence* survived. In fact, five American ships – *Raleigh*, *Randolph*, *Alfred*, *Columbus* and *Independence* – had been lost or destroyed within just ninety days of each other.* While John Paul Jones often gets the headlines in the history of American naval power in 1779, this catastrophic loss is the story that matters far more. Jones's capture of a ship that was severely damaged in the fight – a fight in which his own ship was also ruined and therefore unable to continue his war against British merchantmen – was the only reason to 'celebrate' that year. In practice, those British observers with a keen understanding of naval warfare were more than happy that, for all the boost in morale Jones's action had caused in America, he had, effectively, put himself out of commission: he had shot himself in the foot, and it was actually Captain Pearson who could celebrate how he had

---

* Though the Continental Navy still had some eight frigates left, the numbers boosted by others purchased or borrowed.

'over set' the 'cruise and intentions' of Jones's troublesome squadron.[38]

The armed American ships now left at sea were small and outgunned by any British warship of comparative size. Few were coppered. Their masts and spars tended to be weak. They could barely afford to dress their sailors – something that the Navy Board described as a 'disgust to the service'.[39] 'In looking over the long list of vessels belonging to the United States taken and destroyed, and recollecting the whole history of the rise and progress of our navy, it is difficult to avoid tears', wrote Adams.[40] On the rare occasion that a capture was made, the British recaptured their prizes 35 per cent of the time.[41] On the occasions those American captures actually remained in American hands, the American legal and administrative naval infrastructure was so inadequate that it proved almost impossible to get the money from the prize's sale back to Philadelphia where Congress so desperately needed it.[42] In an attempt to tighten up the navy's administration, the Marine Committee's responsibilities were refined and centralized by the creation of a Board of Admiralty. It was intended that five officials, each from a different state, would constitute the board, but they struggled even to find three, the minimum required for a quorum. From the day of its creation onwards, the American Board of Admiralty gradually became less active.[43]

The state navies by now were also almost non-existent. Most of the ships in the Massachusetts and New Hampshire navies were destroyed at Penobscot, and Connecticut, Maryland, New Hampshire and Georgia had all abandoned their naval initiatives by the end of 1779.[44] The Pennsylvania Navy was shell-shocked from the Philadelphia campaign and its aftermath, and the Virginia Navy stunned by Collier's 1779 Chesapeake raid. Only South Carolina had a significant navy to speak of. It was clear to everyone that, at the level of both Continental and state navies, American sea power had been transformed from the effervescing draught that it had been in 1775–6 to a poisoned chalice.

'Our prospects are infinitely worse than they have been

at any period of the war',[45] wrote Washington. It was almost inconceivable that things could get any worse without the rebellion ending. But they did. Indeed, the greatest defeat inflicted on the Americans during the entire war had still not occurred.

1780

23

BRITISH DOMINANCE

In early 1780 two things happened that further shattered American dreams of a swift victory presented on a platter by Bourbon sea power. The first was that the British launched a long-planned amphibious attack on Charleston, South Carolina, inflicting the heaviest American army defeat of the war. The second was that the British managed to relieve Gibraltar, inflicting the heaviest Spanish naval defeat of the war.

*   *   *

By 1780 Clinton had been fuming over his failed 1776 attack on Charleston for three-and-a-half years. He had spent the past year doing what he could at New York with inadequate forces while working up a detailed plan to attack Charleston with yet another enormous British amphibious invasion force. More than 100 ships transported and escorted 8,708 men, an operation that would never have been possible were it not for the disintegration of d'Estaing's fleet. Just as the presence of French sea power had affected the shape of the war in 1778 and 1779, so did its absence now affect it in 1780.*

Clinton's attack on Charleston continued the British strategy, begun with the capture of Savannah in 1778, of conquering the southern states. Built on a spit of land at the confluence of the Ashley and Cooper rivers, the city was magnificent and unlike any other in America. There were no higgledy-piggledy

---

* Another example of the absence of French sea power affecting the war was Sullivan's 1779 raids on the Iroquois.

streets here as there were in Boston and New York; instead there were beautiful, broad boulevards lined with magnificent houses, built from the fat profits of the rice and indigo trades.* When war broke out, Charleston had swiftly become the main entry-point for much of the military supplies that had kept the American army in the field: arms, blankets, clothes.

If considered in isolation from the situation as it then stood, the attack on Charleston was a sensible strategy and a traditionally British strategy. Clinton would use the mobility provided by the navy to project British military strength to a distant location, where a victory would threaten his enemy's ability to wage war by targeting its maritime power and trading network. Whether or not it was the most appropriate strategy for that moment in the war, however, was another question entirely. The advantages of using British sea power were, of course, clear to see, but consider it this way: the plan to attack Charleston with a clothed, armed and well-supplied army was conceived in New York in the winter of 1779, almost within sight of Washington's shivering and starving army of stick-men. The British had been blinded by their sea power capability when they decided to attack Philadelphia in 1777, and the same thing now happened in 1780.

* * *

Vice-Admiral Marriot Arbuthnot, as insipid as a jellied eel, had finally arrived to take over from Collier, the tiger shark.[1] Clinton immediately loathed him, and theirs was a key relationship whose failure would have a big impact on the war.

The operation began in the winter of 1779 and immediately – and predictably – suffered from poor weather. Mini-icebergs invaded New York Harbour, forcing one British

---

* Indigo was the only way that any fabric could be dyed blue until the introduction of a synthetic substitute in the 1870s. In a curious way, therefore, the Royal Navy was about to attack a location that had played a crucial role in establishing its identity: blue sailors' jackets and officers' frock-coats were dyed with Charleston indigo.

transport ashore and damaging six others so badly that they were unable to make the voyage. The fleet left on Boxing Day and was immediately lashed by a week-long snowstorm, the first of three. A journey that was supposed to take ten days took over a month. One Hessian officer carefully calculated that fifteen of their fifty-six days at sea were spent in the grip of a storm.[2] Some of the ships were blown into the Gulf Stream, which took them northwards and eastwards, exactly the opposite direction to Charleston. One transport, with provisions for four weeks, drifted for eleven, and eventually ended up in St Ives in Cornwall.[3] The transport carrying Clinton's entire artillery train sank. Nearly all of the 396 British horses died and those that survived were in such a weakened state that they were all but useless when they arrived. The journey was horrific for the poor men on board. 'It may be safely said that the most strenuous campaign cannot be as trying as such a voyage', wrote one miserable Jäger, seasick to his boots. 'One takes every morsel with the greatest difficulty and discomfort.'[4]

When the weather finally cleared, the sea-birds returned. 'Today we saw wild ducks and sea gulls in great numbers, which looked as welcome to us in the air as when we saw them fried in a pan at other times', wrote one soldier.[5] A few days later he sighted land:

> I do not believe that the Ten Thousand Greeks, when they beheld the Black Sea after their difficult retreat through Asia, could have been more joyful over the sight of the sea than we were over the word 'Land'! Every face brightened.[6]

Clearly there would have been much less risk of such damage, death and misery if the operation had been undertaken in the summer of 1779 as originally planned, but d'Estaing's escape from the Caribbean had then forced Clinton to delay, and they sailed from New York almost as soon as they had received intelligence that d'Estaing had left America. French sea power was thus intricately linked to this failure, but Clinton chose to blame his new naval nemesis, Arbuthnot, for everything that went wrong.[7]

General Lincoln, meanwhile, was preparing for the British arrival in Charleston. The Americans planned to make a major stand. As a gesture of Congress's concern over the fate of Charleston, and as an important political move to both generate and secure loyalty to the rebellion in the south, Congress authorized Abraham Whipple to sail from Boston with three of the remaining Continental frigates.* They would be joined by three French frigates that had been left behind by d'Estaing after the Savannah campaign and also by the South Carolina State Navy. It would be a useful little squadron of six frigates, a sloop, two brigs, numerous armed boats and three galleys.[8]

As with the Penobscot expedition, expectations of the capability of American sea power were extremely high. Charleston, after all, was well protected by both natural and man-made obstacles. A long bar of shifting shell and sand lay offshore where the waters were so shallow that warships would have to take out most of their guns and stores before crossing. That crossing could then only be accomplished if the passage was buoyed and only then on a high, spring tide and with an easterly wind. The Americans, therefore, would know exactly when and where an attempt was to be made; there could be no surprise.

Once across the bar, the ships would have to wait in a very vulnerable state to reload their guns and stores. They would then, most likely, have to wait some more for a wind that would allow them to sail northwards, towards the next channel, between Sullivan's Island and the Middle Ground shoal. Guarded by Fort Moultrie, this is exactly where Clinton and Parker had come to grief in their 1776 attack. In this respect, at least, the Americans had history on their side; they

---

* *Boston, Providence* and *Queen of France*. The others were *Trumbull* (one of the original thirteen frigates ordered in 1776), *Alliance* (1777), *Deane* (purchased 1777) and *Confederacy* (1778). By then the Americans also had at their disposal the *Pallas*, lent by France in 1778.

drew strength from it and raised their expectations because of it.

The arrival of the Continental ships, visibly so large and powerful and flying the American flag, was a glorious occasion for the inhabitants and troops of Charleston, who could now celebrate Charleston's defiance. No one cradled these expectations more carefully than Lincoln, a man with absolutely no maritime experience,* who believed Whipple's ships would – of course – 'cover the harbor and preserve it from insult'. It was a 'general opinion' that armed ships lying off the bar would, by their presence alone, secure it.[9]

Everyone in Charleston, however, was blissfully ignorant of the true and shocking state of Whipple's ships. Caught in the same storm that had nearly destroyed the British invasion force, Whipple believed that his flagship the *Providence* was within just twelve hours of foundering and that the *Queen of France* was in such a poor state that she would be unable to go to sea again 'without more repair than she is worth'.[10] Lincoln, moreover, was also ignorant of the specific maritime challenges that went hand in hand with the defence of Charleston, but it was not long before he was disabused of his breezy ideas by Whipple, his captains, and no fewer than five Charleston pilots, all of whom signed a refreshingly honest report.

The first problem they identified was the defence of the bar. There was insufficient water to defend it without the constant risk of the American ships running aground. The British would also cross the bar on a flood tide with an easterly wind, ghastly conditions for a ship trying to maintain position on or near the bar. Lincoln's response is interesting. He was outraged that, until then, no one had given 'even one intimation that to occupy a station near the bar would be attended with hazard'.[11] He took to a boat and spent two full days examining

---

* Before the war Lincoln had been a farmer, deacon and town clerk in a small village in Massachusetts, though he had of course witnessed the horror of d'Estaing's fleet at Savannah.

the area for himself before admitting that there were unexpected 'difficulties' – essentially admitting that Whipple, his captains and the pilots were correct.[12]

The best defensive option was to build a strong line of ships between Fort Moultrie and the Middle Ground shoal, and Lincoln immediately began throwing orders around. The line was to be defended with chains and cables attached to anchors, with a line of ships sunk and a flotilla of fireships in the rear. As before, Lincoln had every expectation that this could be achieved. He was energized and enormously excited: 'there is so great a prospect of success nothing I think should divert us.'[13] But, as before, he was disappointed. Numerous attempts to block the channel were made, but it was soon discovered that the channel was too wide and too deep, and the current too strong for it to be blocked.

There was still hope, however. If the American fleet could work in close harness with Fort Moultrie, they might discourage or fight off the British. This plan, however, was based on the theory that the British would be unable to get their largest ships across the bar. And this time it was the American naval captains and pilots who had either miscalculated the depth of water in the harbour mouth or misjudged the ingenuity of their foe. If any had been in Charleston in 1776, they would surely have remembered the sight of Peter Parker taking the 50-gun *Bristol* over the bar,[14] but now they were convinced that only a frigate could make it over. The largest ship in Arbuthnot's fleet, the *Renown*, was of the exact same class as Parker's *Bristol*.

* * *

The British fleet arrived piecemeal off the mouth of Charleston Harbour, having escorted the army in its transports to a safe landing spot some thirty miles to the south, near the mouth of the North Edisto River. On the morning of 20 March they were finally ready to cross the bar, having scrapped with American galleys and small armed ships which attempted to prevent the British from buoying the channel.[15] This was an essential precursor to crossing the bar because the Americans had removed every possible navigation aid from the approaches to Charleston and had even painted black a church steeple that was used as an important transit marker. But with fire support from a land battery built near the lighthouse, the British drove away the American defenders, and soon after the Americans saw that symbol of British success and intent bobbing around with merry glee: a buoy dead in the centre of an awkward channel where no buoy should have been.

Stores and guns were then removed until the great British warships rode high out of the water, their masts swinging far more wildly in the swell than usual for want of ballast. They were now exceptionally vulnerable, not only for their want of guns but also for this alteration to their stability. A sudden storm would have destroyed them all. In this state, like medieval knights in their pyjamas, the British ships crossed the bar unmolested – first a shallow-drafted brigantine, then a galley, then the warships. Everyone held their breath. 'He whom luck forsakes loses everything in an instant', wrote one sailor.[16] Clinton, watching from his headquarters on James Island, knew the significance of the moment. 'Joy to you, Sir,' he wrote to Arbuthnot, 'to myself, and to us all upon your Passage of that infernal Bar.'[17] The British knew that simply by anchoring in their new position they had changed the war, because anchoring there 'ought to give new spirit to the army and discourage the enemy, for Charleston was now completely cut off by water'.[18]

The American squadron had done nothing to attack the vulnerable British as they crossed the bar, voting seven to one against the idea, and then, horrified at the size of the British fleet, chose not even to attempt to defend the channel at Fort Moultrie against the British squadron. They retreated back towards the city to block the entrance to the Cooper River on the city's northern boundary. This gave Lincoln a crucial advantage: he could get troops in and out of the city whenever he wanted. At least Whipple's hopelessly weak squadron and inexperienced men had brought Lincoln some hope.

CHARLESTON

Fort Moultrie

SULLIVAN'S ISLAND

Middle Ground Shoal

American Fleet

Charleston

Copper River

Ashley River

The Bar

ATLANTIC OCEAN

Landing site of British army under General Clinton

North Edisto River

Miles
0 1 2 3 4

Clinton had clearly learned from his experience of 1776: the British made no attempt to capture Fort Moultrie as they had with such incompetence in 1776 but now sailed magnificently past the fort, their passage serenaded by the roar of American cannon, which 'resembled a terrible thunderstorm'.[19] In a wonderful naval display they passed those American guns in perfect formation and 'with colors flying proudly, one ship behind the other, without firing a shot'.[20] Once past, each ship made a sudden turn, fired a broadside, and then sailed to its designated anchoring place. The last ship of the fleet, the 50-gun *Renown*, passed the fort and then 'lay to, took in her sails, and gave such an unrelenting, murderous fire that the whole ship seemed to flare up'.[21]

A display of such fine seamanship so close to a shore battery was immensely impressive stuff and the Americans knew it. One rebel, watching from the steeple of St Michael's Church, later noted:

> They really make a most noble appearance and I could not help admiring the regularity and intrepidity with which they approached, engaged and passed Fort Moultrie. It will reflect great honor upon the admiral and all his captains.[22]

One storeship grounded but the British had made enough of a demonstration of sea power to shatter the high expectations of the American squadron where confidence was replaced by despair. 'Horror, astonishment, fear, despondence, and shattered hopes seemed to befog their eyes, ears and hearts', claimed one Jäger captain.[23]

*   *   *

Clinton, meanwhile, had been marching up through the swamps and marshes of South Carolina and had taken up a strong position to the south. His progress had been helped from start to finish by a talented naval captain, George Elphinstone, who had been deliberately sent with the army because of his detailed knowledge of the area and who now commanded a large body of sailors embedded in the army.[24] Elphinstone had a high-enough rank to command large bodies of men with ease and confidence and he was respected for his abilities. He supervised the massive operation of crossing the Ashley River under the walls of the city. The Americans knew that the British would have to cross the river but Elphinstone out-thought them, crossing at an unexpected time and at an unexpected location. With muffled oars, no fewer than seventy-five flatboats crammed with troops swept passed the Americans at night and landed without the loss of a single man, an operation conducted 'with astonishing expedition'.[25] 'A million thanks', Clinton later wrote to Arbuthnot.[26]

We can see from the letters written in the aftermath of the event that Elphinstone had a network of talented captains with whom he worked, and that they in turn had a network of talented lieutenants and midshipmen on whom to rely. The reality, of course, was not perfect but, even allowing for the occasional boatload of rascals – 'such a set of scoundrels as I have about me would make a man go mad ... I may truly say to have no help at all, they are so fond of the damned grog'[27] – the British achieved their object with great energy and efficiency. Arbuthnot complimented them on the 'most perfect discipline'.[28]

Elphinstone and his men had, in effect, played the part that John Glover's Marblehead mariners had played with such success when attached to Washington's army in the New York and New Jersey campaigns of 1776. An important lesson of this war was that armies functioned in America with far greater success if they comprised a large group of professional sailors led by an experienced and high-ranking officer. In this, Elphinstone was a crucial unifier between army and navy – exactly what had been lacking in Burgoyne and Carleton's campaigns in Lake Champlain and the Hudson Highlands in 1776–7.[29]

The navy also contributed in another significant way. To make up for the loss of Clinton's siege-train on the voyage south, Arbuthnot lent, albeit grudgingly,[30] heavy guns from his ships to arm the British batteries ashore, a logistical feat that the British seem to have experienced no trouble with at all. Those guns had to be hauled out of the gun-decks, lowered into boats, rowed ashore and then dragged into position – a job that would normally have been done by horses. Because all the British horses had died on the voyage down, however, this job was done by sailors, 120 of them, harnessed to the guns by special rope harnesses made, of course, by the sailors.[31] When it came to the actual siege, the sailors again played a key part with 450 men, three captains and a lieutenant from each ship on duty on shore.[32] Comparison with the French siege at Savannah could not be starker. Their landings had been disastrous and their siege operations had been both delayed and then crippled by the French being forced to use naval guns in their land batteries and to man them with their zombie sailors.

With the army in position, the British were temporarily stalled by Whipple's clever defensive position. The American sailors had defended their ships well with a large and deep boom and their anchorage was covered by crossfire from shore positions.

There matters stood for several weeks until a reinforcement from New York allowed Clinton to send men around the north of the city to cut off the American escape by land. At the same time Elphinstone dragged a large boat on rollers overland from the Ashley to the Cooper River where he could police the rebel boat movements to and from the city.[33] The British envelopment of Charleston was thus complete, and it stands in such marked contrast to the New York campaign of 1776 that had been designed to drive the Americans from the city. Here, army and navy worked together brilliantly with the single, focused intention of trapping and capturing Lincoln's army. It worked like a dream and is a powerful reminder of what might have been had the Howes adopted a similar strategy at New York right at the very start of the war.

Lincoln had waited for too long. There had been ships and sailors aplenty to take his army and any civilians who wished to go with them to safety but, pressured by civilian officials and

Congress' blind desire not to abandon Charleston without a fight, he sacrificed his army.* He surrendered on 12 May 1780, the largest American defeat of the war. Some 2,571 Continental soldiers surrendered, but it was also a major naval defeat. Nearly 1,000 seamen surrendered, including Abraham Whipple, one of the Continental Navy's ablest commanders. Three of the largest remaining Continental warships – *Providence*, *Boston* and *Ranger* – were taken into British service, leaving only four of any significant size in the entire Continental Navy.[34] All but one of the ships of the South Carolina Navy were destroyed,[†] including the *Bricole*, a ship pierced for 60 guns and purchased from the French, the largest vessel to serve in any of the state navies during the war.[35] It was the worst defeat inflicted upon an American military force until 1862, when 10,700 Union troops surrendered to Stonewall Jackson at Harper's Ferry. Lincoln limped out at the head of the 'most ragged Rabble I ever beheld'.[36]

* * *

Although much focus tends to be thrown on the loss of Lincoln's army, the disaster at Charleston also needs to be considered in the context of the systematic British destruction of American shipping and shipbuilding that began in 1777 and peaked with Collier's raids and the victory at Penobscot in 1779. The loss of the American ships at Charleston had an impact that outweighed any of these previous losses: it is as if a threshold of disappointment had finally been reached. The American economy, sent into a tailspin by d'Estaing's defeat at Savannah, nosedived. John Adams, who was then in Holland desperately

---

* It is possible that his desire to resist was inspired by the huge fall-out which accompanied the loss of Ticonderoga without a fight in 1777.

† The Dutch-built frigate *South Carolina*, the most heavily armed warship that flew the American flag during the war, escaped destruction or capture because she was at sea at the time. She went on to make a few significant captures in 1781–2 and played a key role in the Spanish capture of the Bahamas in 1782. For histories of the ship, see J. A. Lewis, *Neptune's Militia*, 34–50, 65 ff.; Middlebrook, *South Carolina*, 31–8.

negotiating a loan with the Dutch, believed American affairs had been sent into a 'violent crisis' by the loss of Charleston,[37] and was now forced to argue that the defeat there should not be allowed to affect American credit. It is telling that Adams, a brilliant man, a wordsmith and a trained lawyer, sounded entirely unconvincing and desperate:

> But why were these four or five frigates of so much more importance than several times that number that we had lost before. We lost several frigates with Philadelphia and shipping to a much greater value than at Charlestown. We lost frigates with New York: but above all we lost at Penobscot armed vessels, to five times a greater amount than at Charlestown.[38]

Charleston was the final, catastrophic fault in the dam of artificial confidence that had been built by the American rebels since 1775. Lexington; Bunker Hill; a navy in the lakes; a Continental Navy; state navies; privateers; Trenton; the defence of the Delaware; Saratoga: all had played their part in demonstrating commitment, resolve and resourcefulness in the rebellion. Washington's army still survived, yet so much of the confidence that had been generated was weakened by the failure of d'Estaing at New York, Newport and Savannah, by the destruction of the state navies and the Continental Navy and, finally, by the capture of Charleston.

When news reached Paris, Fillipo Mazzei, an American agent, wrote to his friend Thomas Jefferson:

> Bad news have long legs ... I never was afflicted in Virginia by our bad events as I am now ... we are really dejected ... It is amazing the impression such an event makes in Europe. The greater the distance, the more it will be magnified in men's own imaginations.

Like Adams, he was forced to argue, entirely unconvincingly, that 'such a loss would not materially affect our operations, and that it is trifling in comparison to the unshaken constancy of the Americans'.[39]

The view from America really was far less rosy than that which both Adams and Mazzei were trying to paint. British concerns and fears had been soothed by the news just as those of the Americans had been piqued. The timing of Charleston's surrender simply could not have been any better: London was then in the grip of the Gordon Riots, the worst riots of the century;* the Opposition had finally begun to work together and had established some significant momentum, and North's government, though still with a good majority, was shaken. News of Charleston acted like an injection of political propane, allowing North to call and win a snap election.

The Americans knew that, without more significant foreign help, the war would soon be over, but their position was now far weaker than it had been in 1778 when they had first formally acquired such help. They now needed another, massive, commitment, from both France and Spain, if they were to stand any chance of victory, but this time both allies had even more reasons to leave the Americans to their own devices. D'Estaing had returned to France in tatters, having achieved nothing at all; the French had lost all their possessions in India; both navies had been ravaged by the horrific experience of the 1779 Channel operation; and the Spanish navy was about to suffer the misfortune of meeting a true British naval tornado, Admiral George Bridges Rodney, who would give them a proper beating.

* * *

In the winter of 1779 the fate of the Gibraltar garrison was on a bayonet's edge. A relief was planned but the operation was fraught with danger. Several large fleets lay between Britain and Gibraltar: there was an allied force in Brest and Spanish squadrons in Ferrol, Cádiz and Gibraltar itself. Whoever was chosen

---

* The riots began over religious issues but were quickly hijacked by others with a variety of grievances, many informed by the war.

to relieve Gibraltar would have to run the gauntlet of one, or perhaps all, of these fleets. The relief of Gibraltar was therefore a major naval commitment; so large, in fact, that it could only be provided by two British naval fleets combined. One fleet, ultimately bound for the Caribbean, would be diverted to sail the first leg of its journey via Gibraltar, and the other would consist of the most powerful ships in the Channel Fleet. The two would sail together as a massive naval escort but would then divide at Gibraltar, one sailing on to the Caribbean and the other sailing back to the Channel. Such an operation was only possible now because of the failure of the 1779 Bourbon Channel invasion campaign. In November 1779 the French invasion army on the north coast of Brittany had struck camp, allowing the British to look to their distant possessions once more.

The man chosen to spearhead this operation was Admiral George Rodney, whose appointment is further evidence of a new mindset in London. Rodney was experienced and he was aggressive. He was also, unfortunately, totally unpredictable, and had been deliberately bypassed for command until now. The primary concern was that he had a proven track record of being deeply and criminally irresponsible with public money. Investigations led by the Navy Board into his pre-war conduct as commander-in-chief at Jamaica led them to stop his pay, an exceptional act for an eighteenth-century administration. Rodney was also an eager – and bad – gambler and, since the start of the war, had actually been living in France to escape his creditors. One modern historian has described Rodney's behaviour in this troubled time as 'a staggering display of ill judgement' by a man who was 'over-bearing, avaricious and dysfunctional'.[40]

A true aristocrat, Rodney also had a rigid belief in the natural order of things that was visible in his command style. He had high expectations and no tolerance. His subordinates loathed him and the Admiralty knew that his subordinates loathed him. Rodney revelled in their fear. From the start of the American war, he had bombarded the Admiralty with letters begging for employment, and now he was about to get the answer he so craved. At a time when every officer in the Royal Navy was particularly touchy, Rodney's employment can be seen as something of a last, desperate, measure. Sandwich was only happy with the appointment once he had made certain that Rodney would be surrounded by carefully selected men with direct links to the Secretary of the Navy, who would control Rodney's budget.[41]

Nonetheless, Rodney was competent at certain things. He had an innovative mind that translated an obsession with naval victory and self-enrichment into a mad desire to increase the efficiency of the fleets under his command. Shortly after he had been given command, he began to fire out reams of new instructions and regulations for his fleet detailing expected duty. One of his most inspired decisions was to appoint a man named Gilbert Blane as physician of his fleet. Blane was a man of exceptional vision and skill who went on to become the greatest medical reformer in the history of the Royal Navy.

With safeguards in place, Sandwich was desperate to get Rodney to sea. It took only two months to equip and man Rodney's fleet, an amazing achievement and a very rare one in this war: the complexity of organizing long-distance resupply meant that most convoys were seriously delayed. When the weather changed on 8 December, Sandwich wrote: 'For God's sake go to sea without delay, you cannot conceive of what importance it is to yourself, to me, and to the public that you should not lose this fair wind.'[42] When he finally set sail, he led a fleet of around 100 ships, including an East India convoy that also required naval protection at least as far as Ferrol. This massive Armada in the eastern Atlantic matched Arbuthnot and Clinton's armada, bound for Charleston, which was then at sea in the western Atlantic: from Boxing Day 1779 for nearly a month, almost the entire might of British sea power was on the move.

Rodney's fleet was particularly well equipped. As a means of reducing the growth of weeds and the impact of the terrible shipworm which bored holes through ships' hulls, the British had been experimenting with nailing sheets of copper onto the hulls. By the autumn of 1779 its value was adequately proven, though its dangers inadequately understood,* and in a close meeting between Sandwich, the king and the new Comptroller of the Navy and administrative mastermind Charles Middleton, the monumental decision had been made to copper the entire British fleet. A huge financial gamble, it added a full 10 to 15 per cent to the cost of building a ship.[43]

Rodney was the first beneficiary of this order. He knew that his coppered ships would sail faster, closer to the wind, and manoeuvre with more precision than any un-coppered ship of a similar size, of any nation, and the French and Spanish, unable to match British industrial might, were miles behind in the race to copper their ships. Copper, therefore, would give him a massive tactical advantage in battle as it would confer on him the initiative. Immediately realizing its significance, Rodney issued new instructions to create a hunting pack of coppered ships that he could unleash with a specific signal.[44]

As always, such a big naval operation as the relief of Gibraltar was impossible to keep secret, though the British made special efforts to obfuscate its ultimate destination, and the ruse seems to have worked. The troops, supplies and pay for the Gibraltar garrison were embarked under orders from the American Department; no officers from the Gibraltar garrison's regiments were sent with the convoy; and even the coal for the garrison was procured from a source not usually associated with the supply of Gibraltar. Rodney's open orders were for the Leeward Islands and only sealed orders, to be opened miles offshore, mentioned Gibraltar.[45]

The French and Spanish thus heard only inexact rumours and they acted inexactly. The most prevalent belief was that any ships bound for Gibraltar would be lightly defended. As

---

* There was a chemical reaction in these early coppered ships between the iron nails that fastened the ships' hull timbers together and the copper. This 'galvanic action' slowly but surely destroyed the ships' structural integrity – a whisper of tragedy that would be heard as several thousand screams by the end of the war, not least in the wreck of the *Royal George*, which sank at her moorings at Spithead, with the loss of around 1,200 lives.

a result only a handful of allied ships actually made it to sea. Four hundred miles or so to the west of Rochefort, meanwhile, Rodney was making his way to Gibraltar at the head of a truly enormous battle fleet. On his way he stumbled into a convoy of fifteen Spanish supply ships destined for Spanish naval yards, escorted by several Spanish frigates and the *Guipuscoano*, a big and beautiful 64-gunner which belonged to the Company of Caracas.* In Rodney's rather nonchalant words, 'in a few hours the whole was taken',[46] and the *Guipuscoano* was renamed *Prince William* for the king's young son, Prince William Henry, the future William IV, who was sailing as a midshipman in Rodney's fleet aboard the *Prince George*.

Several days later Rodney came across his real prize, a Spanish squadron of eleven warships under the command of Don Juan de Lángara, which was heading for Cádiz, in the mistaken expectation of meeting up with the Cádiz fleet under Admiral Don Luis de Córdova to face a numerically inferior British fleet.[47] Like Lángara, Córdova knew of those plans but, unlike Lángara, he also knew that Rodney was out in force and was currently swooping down on the Spanish coast. Córdova stayed in Cádiz; no one warned Lángara.

Rodney, with a force more than twice the size of Lángara's, found the Spaniard's fleet fatally stretched out, 'at immense distances one from the other'.[48] It was midday when the fleets sighted each other and the sea was rising into a winter storm off Portugal: no place to be. Lángara ordered his ships to flee for Cádiz, believing that he could not 'expose others for his sake, as his vessel was not a good sailer'.[49]

The British pack lost no time in chasing and attacking. Fillipo Mazzei explains why:

It is undeniable that the extraordinary courage by which the English sailor have been hitherto animated, was chiefly owing to their persuasion of being invincible upon the water. Since

---

* The Company of Caracas was a Spanish trading company with a monopoly on the Venezuelan trade.

the beginning of this war they have experienced the contrary in almost every engagement of equal force with the French, but the Spaniards still continued to be in their opinion incapable of fighting.[50]

Rodney, struck down with gout, conducted the battle from his bunk through the capable hands of his flag captain, Walter Young. Rodney's coppered ships chased and came up with the Spaniards as the sun set, overwhelming the rearmost first before sweeping up the rest in a classic chase action. Rodney later explicitly attributed his fleet's greater speed to their new copper bottoms, the first operational confirmation of the value of coppering and another building block in a growing British psychological superiority at sea.

Engaging at night was fraught with difficulty and danger and was almost entirely unregulated by rules or instructions. Interestingly, however, and perhaps in anticipation of exactly this type of battle, Rodney had issued specific and detailed instructions for engaging at night shortly after his fleet had left Portsmouth.[51] The British would all have been equipped with specially designed night-time telescopes, but scientists had still not solved one crucial problem with their state-of-the-art night-vision technology: the image appeared upside down.[52]

The Spaniards undoubtedly fought well, their valour 'great beyond description',[53] particularly that shown by Lángara, who only gave up his ship at two in the morning when it was totally dismasted and he was seriously injured. British accounts describe him fighting until that moment against four British ships.[54] Several British ships were severely damaged, a full third of Rodney's fleet dismasted, and the British struggled in the darkness, high sea and strong wind to send prize crews across to the captured ships. The Spanish flagship was only boarded 'with infinite hazard' and a British longboat was lost in the process, overturned when a wave tossed it against the hull of the Spaniard. Miraculously, it seems that no British sailor lost his life in this accident.[55] Shockingly, one ship, the *Santo Domingo*, exploded, an event that appears in nearly every contemporary painting of the battle [*see fig. 13*]. 'Had this awful event taken place five minutes later, we most probably would have been partakers of her unhappy fate', wrote a shaken Captain John MacBride,[56] whose ship, the *Bienfaisant*, was closing in on her kill. The British ship's forecastle was scattered with debris from the explosion.

In amongst the carnage of the battle and its aftermath was an example of touching humanity. Captain MacBride, who secured the Spanish flagship *Fénix*, knew that he had an outbreak of smallpox on the *Bienfaisant*. He chose not to force any of the *Fénix*'s crew onto his ship as prisoners, the standard practice after a naval surrender. 'The feelings of a British officer cannot allow him to introduce an infection even amongst his enemies', he wrote.[57] This is just one example of several from this battle and its aftermath in which the British treated their Spanish prisoners with notable compassion – a particularly significant fact for the dark shadow it casts over the stunning harshness with which American maritime prisoners were treated by the British in this war.[58]

This, the 'Moonlight Battle' of 1780, has never received the attention from historians that it deserves. The first major British fleet victory of the war, it was won by a fleet tested by both enemy skill and hideous weather conditions, at night and in January. Six ships were eventually captured and the British were then forced to fight for their lives as the westerly wind and high swell remorselessly drove them towards the Portuguese coast. In a night of the highest drama two of the six prizes were lost on the rocks. Such a storm in the aftermath of battle has close parallels with the hurricane that struck the shattered fleets after the battle of Trafalgar in 1805. One can only imagine the pain in the sailors' fingers. Rodney was certain that the poor weather and the fact that the battle happened at night prevented them from capturing every ship in the squadron,[59] but the fact that they captured any at all, and that none of the damaged British ships were wrecked, is remarkable in itself. The reward that Rodney received was equally exceptional and was specifically tailored to his well-known debts. He received

£1,000 a year for life, to be continued after his death, with £500 going to Lady Rodney and £500 to their children.[60] The Royal Navy could be a good employer if it chose.

*   *   *

News of the battle, that 'Great Britain was Mistress of the Straits',[61] filtered through to the garrison at Gibraltar who had been teased by a rumour from the Spanish camp that they had actually won the battle.[62] Life in Gibraltar was transformed by the real news when it came. 'The Garrison are all on the wing', one witness wrote, 'the sound of the fleet is all that is to be heard and every rock and hill re-echoes the blissful tidings.'[63] Indeed, just the anticipation of the arrival of the British fleet was so influential that it drove down the exorbitant price of flour:

> This morning flour sold for six-pence per pound, which was some time past two shillings, and a great favour to obtain it at that price; the shops that were shut up, are now opened, and adorned with bread, biscuit, rusk &c. The garrison appears in an entire state of joyful commotion, and the people are so busy purchasing eatables, that it brings to my remembrance the festive fairs in Britain.[64]

Rodney's fleet was sighted in another dramatic night-time sea-scape, the ships' yards and masts only visible in the flashes of lightning that lit the sky.[65] They approached the Rock and then shot past it, caught by the westerly wind and current – exactly the same trap into which the blockading Spanish squadron had fallen the preceding summer.* It was nine full days before the British fleet was able to force its way back to the Rock and weigh anchor under a 21-gun salute. They appeared in such strength that Barceló's squadron, terrified of attack, darted behind the boom in Algeciras. Over the next few days the Spanish ships were dragged ashore and their guns mounted in land batteries to protect the ships.[66]

---

* See pp. 299–300.

On the other side of the bay, cranes were quickly built on the various moles and harbours, and goods piled high on the now bustling quays. The British took particular pleasure in unloading those supply ships that Rodney had captured from the Spanish before the main fleet battle: who could miss the irony that, thanks to British sea power, Gibraltar had been relieved by Spanish stores?[67] British gunners also had great fun testing the captured Spanish gunpowder, which proved greatly inferior to British and was surely a significant factor in the British victory at the Moonlight Battle.[68] A particular bonus for the garrison was that Rodney sent all his surgeons' mates ashore to help in the overflowing hospital.[69]

Lángara was carried ashore in a chair and the rumour went around, no doubt to the music of British sniggering, that he had been shot in the balls.[70] Through his haze of pain Lángara had been impressed with British seamanship and with their treatment of their prisoners, and also with the fact that one of the midshipmen in Rodney's fleet was none other than the king's son, Prince William Henry. Lángara is often quoted as having said, 'Well does Great Britain merit the empire of the sea, when the humblest stations in her Navy are supported by Princes of the Blood.'[71] Perhaps William was particularly polite to the captured admiral, but what Lángara had failed to notice was that everyone else thought that William was a royal pain in the arse. He went on to have a dangerously disruptive career in the Royal Navy that nearly ruined the careers of several talented seamen, including Nelson.

Rodney gloated over his victory as only he could gloat. He wrote to Sandwich a letter full of grovelling praise and flattery. It is so full of effluvia that Rodney can only have been drunk when he wrote it. 'I hope your enemies will now be confounded and that you may long continue at the head of that Board you so ably direct', he wrote. 'I am and ever will be grateful for the favors and friendship you honored me with in my youthful days, nor shall age or change of fortune ever make me deviate from my fixed resolution of ever proving myself a true and faithful friend to your Lordship.'[72] 'Spain in all her provinces severely feels the blow she has received', trumpeted Rodney. 'Despair, terror, fear and consternation prevails in every part.'[73] An impressive list of symptoms to have been caused by British sea power; a key one missing from the list is wrath. Lángara was apoplectic with the French. He believed, correctly, that the French had known that Rodney was at sea but had done nothing to warn him. He felt betrayed and deceived. Not only did he refuse to fight with the French again, but actually offered to fight with the British against them.[74] The allies were never going to help the Americans win the war if such distrust became endemic.

Another interesting result of the relief of Gibraltar was that the situation in the bay was suddenly turned on its head. Roads inland from Gibraltar were appalling and the Spanish relied as heavily upon maritime resupply as the British. Rodney's cruisers now patrolled the Gut providing protection for British merchant ships and trying to capture Spanish ones. It is no coincidence that, soon after the arrival of Rodney's fleet, a British Newfoundland ship, which was not part of the original resupply convoy, arrived with 500,000 pounds of salt cod.[75] Rodney's presence also allowed the sultan of Morocco to deliberately insult the Spanish at Ceuta.[76] The condition of the Spanish 'besiegers' quickly became miserable.

For some on the Rock itself, however, the arrival of the British fleet was a desperate affair because Rodney and Eliott used the opportunity presented by so many British ships to rid the Rock of what Eliott described as 'useless mouths'. They did this by initiating an enforced evacuation of women and children whose husbands or fathers were unable to demonstrate a sufficient quantity of stored food – an order that tore families apart.[77]

*　　*　　*

On 13 February 1780 Rodney was ready to set sail, no doubt with children and women weeping for their fathers and husbands who waved from ashore. High on his own success, and against all orders, Rodney left behind one of his ships of the line, an incongruous disregard for the value of a warship. Sandwich was incensed, not only because it was a stupid thing to have done, but also because – in anticipation of such behaviour – Rodney had received specific instructions not to do so.[78] The victory seems to have allowed a little of the real Rodney to bleed through his hitherto perfect, even fawning behaviour. It was not a good sign for the future.

His success, however, gave him some leeway, especially because it continued. He escaped European shores unmolested by Córdova, who lurked in Cádiz with fifty ships. Then, on his way to the Caribbean, Rodney detached a homeward-bound squadron which soon fell in with, and captured, a coppered French 64-gunner, stored for four years and with £60,000 in cash on board. Four merchant ships in her convoy were also taken.[79]

It was a fitting end to an operation of quite startling success. Finally the navy was doing what it was supposed to do. British expectations of sea power were, for the first time in this war, being met, though it only created a thirst for more. 'You cannot conceive the expectations we all have here from the great beginning you have made', purred Sandwich,[80] and the MP Lord Hobart declared, 'I beg you would go on beating the enemy ... as unanimity will be the consequence of it.'[81] 'The eyes of Europe are upon you', he continued, 'and I have no doubt that you will treat France there [the Caribbean] as you have done Spain in Europe and force them once more to ask [for] peace.'[82]

America, surely, was within Britain's grasp. However, the fact that Rodney sailed from Gibraltar directly to the Caribbean presented unwary, uninformed or over-eager observers with a trap, into which many historians have since fallen. Most of the coppered ships that Rodney had used to such great effect at the Moonlight Battle had been borrowed from the Channel Fleet whence they now returned,* and he took with him to the Caribbean a force designed to boost, rather than replace, the existing Caribbean squadron. The name of Rodney was

---

* Rodney took just four coppered ships with him to the Caribbean.

common to both theatres, therefore, but the overwhelming numerical superiority and quality of the ships that he had enjoyed in his Gibraltar campaign were not.

The British Leeward Islands fleet was now under the temporary command of Rear-Admiral Sir Hyde Parker.* It had been in a desperate state even before the battle of Grenada, but now it was only sixteen strong and really suffering.† Hyde Parker had been willing to take the war to the French but, with insufficient force, limited resources and hundreds of sick men, he had been foiled at every turn, though, given the resources, he avowed that he 'would have co-operated ... with any being but the Devil' to attack the French.[83] The Caribbean command was nothing but a curse, and it had already accounted, both professionally and physically, for the excellent Barrington and the resourceful Byron. Parker was now feeling that pressure. He had proved himself more than capable on numerous occasions in this war, but his eyesight was terrible, he was sick, and he feared for his own competence. His command weighed 'much too heavy for my shoulders'.[84]

Such self-doubt alone was a recipe for disaster because of Rodney's inherent suspicion of his subordinates, which had actually been aggravated, rather than soothed, as one might expect, by the conduct of his fleet at the Moonlight Battle. He railed and cursed at them.[85] 'If the fleet I am going to command', he wrote, 'should be as negligent and disobedient as part of that which sailed from England with me, you will hear of dismission, upon dismission, I must, I shall be obey'd.'[86] To make matters worse, Rodney now faced a completely different type of enemy from the one he had defeated at the Moonlight Battle. Then, Rodney had surprised a smaller number of slow ships crewed by sick men; now, his enemy was larger, skilled and prepared.

---

* Father to the Captain Hyde Parker who had so distinguished himself in that raid up the Hudson in 1776.

† There were three more ships under Peter Parker in Jamaica.

24

ALLIED RECOMMITMENT

The key lesson of 1780 is that the shocking failure of French and Spanish sea power in the first years of their alliance with America did not cause them to lose faith in sea power as a tool or weapon. In fact the opposite seems to have been the case: they still believed in it to the extent that they thought it would win them the war.

Every nation, it seemed, would forgive sea power anything. In 1778–9 the French had used a fleet to seize a handful of islands in the Caribbean but their balance was clearly in the red: d'Estaing's fleet had been proven impotent in America; the allied invasion attempt of Britain had failed catastrophically; thousands of French and Spanish sailors had died from epidemics; the Spanish had been unable to blockade Gibraltar and had been defeated by Rodney; millions upon millions of dollars had been spent by both France and Spain to little financial or territorial benefit. Indeed, the only tangible reward was that, thanks in part to the mere presence of French and Spanish warships, the American rebellion persisted, but as long as it persisted, the French and Spanish believed that, by using their sea power, there would be opportunities to further their own interests.

And so French and Spanish politicians and leaders lined more men up to die and heaped more coin to spend, as if they were deliberately testing the limits of their own system against the 'guarantee' of sea power. The year 1780 was a key moment. Near the end of the year the French naval minister Sartine fell from power and was replaced by an ally and protégé of Jacques Necker, the financial brain behind France's immense borrowing. It is very likely that a different political outcome in France at this time would have dramatically changed the direction of the war. Sartine's replacement, the marquis de Castries, now worked with Necker to sail France's crippled financial ship into even more distant waters, while logistical problems were solved on an ad hoc basis as they arose. The insatiable demand for labour in the dockyards, for example, was met with ever larger numbers of pressed men and convict labour: an unsustainable model for long-term dockyard efficiency and competence but one which injected enough muscle into the French navy to keep it going for another campaign.[1]

Earlier, important changes had also been made in terms of command. The previous French Caribbean campaign had failed to maximize its potential for numerous reasons, but chief among these was the maritime incompetence of its leader, the arrogant soldier d'Estaing. The man who would command this new fleet to be sent to America, however, the comte de Guichen, had spent almost his entire life at sea. Significantly, he had been entrusted with command of the fleet during the trials of the new French signalling system in 1775, and had then gone on to lead a division of d'Orvilliers's fleet at the battle of Ushant, where he had led with clarity, manoeuvred with precision and fought with bravery. Said to be the most accomplished admiral in the French navy, he also had a reputation as 'a very clever fellow'.[2] With this fleet came 16,000 soldiers hell-bent on retaking St Lucia and attacking Barbados. A dominant force on its own, this French fleet, however, was only one part of the opposition that Rodney now faced.

The second was a sizeable Spanish expedition that had amassed at Cádiz before setting out across the Atlantic. This fleet, consisting of 146 merchantmen, 11,000 troops and twelve ships of the line and commanded by Admiral Don Josef Solano, would either unite with the French in the Windward Islands or head to the Spanish city and naval base at Havana in the Leeward Islands. Solano, like de Guichen, was a life-long salt-blooded sailor. He had joined the Spanish navy as a teenager and had commanded his first 100-gun ship at the age of just thirty-six in 1762. The Spanish also made a massive new financial commitment in this period, and Charles III set out to borrow 60 million reals from the Five Greater Guilds of Madrid and a syndicate of other French, Spanish and Dutch financiers. Such borrowing was preferred over raising taxes or defaulting on the wages of public employees:[3] just like the French, the Spanish crown funded its support for a revolution in a way best calculated to avoid creating its own revolution at home. The Spanish had been sorely hurt by Lángara's defeat at the Moonlight Battle but remained committed to the war because there was sufficient evidence that Britain was cracking under pressure: their dreams of easy victories over imminent and lightly escorted British trade convoys seemed perfectly rational.[4]

This combined Bourbon campaign was designed to change the face of the war by threatening the British at their key power bases in the Caribbean. With the resources that Rodney had to hand, he would do well – very well indeed – if he could merely protect the status quo and see off the combined Bourbon threat that now hung over the British Caribbean like a tropical storm. If he could get to either fleet before they united, however, he would be given a real opportunity to knock either France or Spain out of the war. Both countries had bounced back once from significant disappointments, but now, for political, financial and logistical reasons, it was very unlikely indeed that they would be able to do so again. The British were thus under threat but simultaneously presented with a golden opportunity, and they fully anticipated that a 'lucky blow' now would win them the war. For once those expectations appear to have been entirely realistic.[5]

* * *

It did not begin well for the British because, on 22 March, de Guichen arrived in the Caribbean before Rodney, with seventeen ships of the line to add to the six already there, and headed straight for St Lucia. Parker, far outnumbered, took up a defensive position similar to Barrington's in 1778, strong enough to force de Guichen to return to Martinique and reassess: yet again, a well-positioned, well-prepared, anchored fleet had proved a formidable opponent and strategic game-changer.* During the operation and under constant threat from de Guichen, Parker slipped out of his anchorage, met a weak British convoy and escorted it to safety before resuming his defensive position: an operation that sings sweetly through the years of Parker's strategic grasp, command capability and maritime knowledge, and of his crews' fine seamanship.[6]

Rodney soon arrived and discovered that Parker's Caribbean fleet was too worn out and leaky to blockade the French by holding a position in the strong leeward currents off Martinique. He headed for St Lucia to seethe.

De Guichen's next move was against Barbados. Impressively, he escaped from Martinique at night, but the alarm was raised quickly enough for Rodney to find the French only eight leagues from the northernmost point of the island. Rodney was outnumbered but he planned to focus his attack on just a section of their line. His captains, however, misunderstood his signals. There is no evidence that he made any effort to explain his ideas to his captains before the battle.[7] Rodney's doctrine of fighting, when imposed on Parker's fleet, did not work. In the era before common command doctrine, this type of failure happened time and again as new admirals attempted to impose their own distinct operational vision onto an alien fleet. Almost always the result was confusion, impotence and failure. In this battle the British fleet, divided into three divisions, acted as three separate squadrons, rather than as a single body, and the tumbling circumstance of battle quickly ruined Rodney's plan. No ships were taken on either side, but the ships in the centre of both fleets, Rodney's flagship the *Sandwich* in particular, were badly damaged. A curious detail to survive is that a woman in the *Sandwich*'s crew worked a 24-pounder for the duration of the action and then sat up all night with the wounded.[8] Rodney blamed everyone but himself and painted

---

* Other examples are Howe at New York and Barrington at St Lucia, both in 1778.

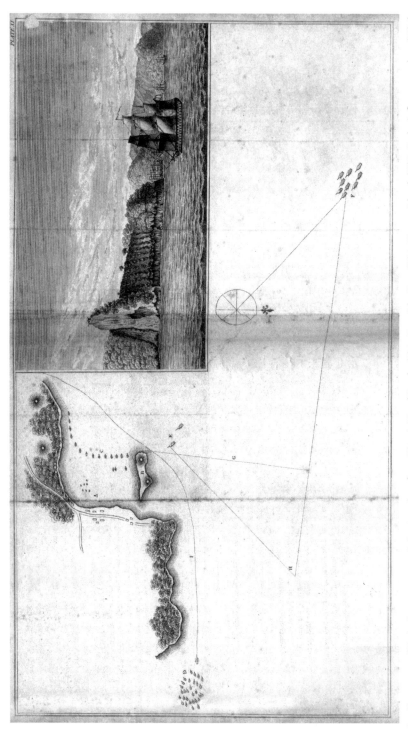

An illustration of Parker's operation at St Lucia, taken from Ekins' *Naval Battles*. 'A' is Gros Islet Bay; 'B' is Pigeon Island; 'C' is Parker's fleet at anchor; 'D' the English convoy of thirty troop transports; 'E' two French ships of the line chasing the convoy; 'F' the French fleet under Guichen with their anticipated course; 'G' is Parker's interception course; 'H' the position of the two French ships in chase, moments from reaching the convoy, but who bore up as soon as they saw Parker's fleet rounding Pigeon Island; 'I' is the safe course of the convoy to their planned anchorage at Carénage (modern Castries).

a completely unfair picture of a battle ruined by subordinate treachery:

> It is with concern inexpressible, mixed with indignation, that the duty I owe my sovereign and my country obliges me to acquaint your Lordships that during the action between the French fleet, on the 17th inst, and his Majesty's, the British flag was not properly supported.[9]

It was a shocking claim that was actually suppressed by British politicians.

Rodney also exploded at Parker in an outburst that could have come from the height of Elizabethan courtly intrigue: 'a dangerous man with a very bad temper,' he wrote, 'hostile in the highest degree to the Administration and capable of anything ... his cunning and art, however, has failed him ... his head will be at stake for palpable disobedience.'[10] Rodney sent him home with the next trade convoy. Parker was furious at such slander and prepared to defend himself in print but was urged to silence by Sandwich, who was desperate to avoid another damaging Keppel–Palliser affair.[11] Parker's subsequent silence should be read as commitment to the naval service by an impressive, skilled and loved commander. He was just extremely unfortunate to have crossed paths with Rodney.

Rodney also had special words for other subordinates. 'Had not Mr Rowley [Rear-Admiral Joshua Rowley] presumed to think, when his duty was only obedience,' wrote Rodney, unfairly, 'the whole French rear and the centre had certainly been taken.'[12] His gaze also came crashing down on Captain Nathaniel Bateman of the *Yarmouth*, who was later court-martialled and dismissed to his own astonishment, an event that was sorely felt throughout the fleet. Bateman was a captain who had risen from the lower decks and had no significant connections to protect him. Rodney, an aristocrat, crushed him. In the words of his peers, it was 'a harshness bordering on cruelty'.[13]

This fleet, which, a matter of days before Rodney's arrival, had demonstrated itself competent and united if physically weak when protecting St Lucia and saving a troop convoy, was thus torn apart and further weakened by Rodney's malign influence. It is a distinct shame that almost all the surviving correspondence from this theatre at this time is 'official', consisting of letters to and from the naval administration in London. Nothing has yet been uncovered that paints the picture from the perspective of Rodney's captains. One can only wonder at what they thought of their new commander.

After the battle the French were unable to get back to Martinique to repair because the British lay between them and the island, so they headed to Guadeloupe, where there were no repair facilities of any sort. The British returned to St Lucia, where there were no repair facilities of any sort either, but there were a handful of storeships and some supplies stowed ashore in tents.[14] Theoretically, therefore, the British held an advantage, but it was never realized because the Dutch came to the rescue of the French.

The Dutch island of St Eustatius was a key source of naval stores, imported in neutral Dutch ships from the Baltic. Exploiting a pre-existing Dutch–French relationship that Byron had sniffed out the previous year,[15] the Dutch now reached out to the French and sent to de Guichen's shattered fleet several ships packed to the gills with masts, rope, canvas and timber. At the same time they refused to do any business with Rodney. The French thus found themselves restored. News of the Dutch meddling reached Rodney's ears. It was not the kind of thing that he was likely to forget.

The French therefore achieved a significant operational advantage from the battle of Martinique by being able to repair their ships, which before the battle had already been in a better condition than Rodney's. In the coming weeks de Guichen and Rodney met on several occasions, but the British were unable to get their ships anywhere near the French. The disparity between these fleets is always forgotten by historians who too swiftly attribute a blanket superiority for British ships in this war to the magic of copper bottoms. De Guichen teased Rodney non-stop for a fortnight with his superior capability supported by excellent seamanship. Captain Boulton of the *Montagu* wrote:

> We were ten days together in sight of the enemy, the ships all cleared for action and men at their quarters in hourly expectation of an attack, as it was in their power at any time to come down upon us, [and] this constant attention night and day has worried the ship's crew sadly.[16]

This trial of endurance – a fascinating stand-off without parallel in the entire period – ended with both fleets cracking at exactly the same time, with French sailors on the point of starvation and British ships on the point of sinking.

In these first exchanges, therefore, both admirals had been stumped in their exercise of sea power: Rodney had failed to defeat de Guichen, who had, in turn, failed to attack St Lucia or Barbados. But how would the arrival of that large Spanish squadron from Cádiz affect this balance of power?

*   *   *

Solano's fleet was spotted off the Portuguese coast by a squadron of British frigates, which then raced across the Atlantic to various locations in the Caribbean to warn Rodney of his imminent arrival. He was then spotted again by a British frigate off Martinique, but altered course and then found de Guichen off Guadeloupe. Rodney's fleet was in a terrible state after his campaign against de Guichen, but even half of his ships would have been sufficient to capture Solano's convoy and in a stroke drive Spain out of the war. It was probably the closest that the British ever came to winning the war. Rodney then endured a horrible few weeks searching for this new enemy throughout the Caribbean, unaware that they had already arrived safely and his opportunity had passed. 'What to do I know not', he retched.[17]

Meanwhile his fleet and men rotted. The *Grafton*'s masts were 'totally unserviceable'; the *Fame* was condemned for her leaks; the *Centurion* was so leaky that there were claims that British sailors were dying at the pumps to keep her free; a very acute 'epidemical distemper' had struck the *Pearl*; and many men from the *Conqueror* had been forced ashore with 'old obstinate ulcers and other complaints and infirmities'.[18] Luckily for the British, Rodney's favourite surgeon, Gilbert Blane, was at the helm in this war against sickness, and he was full of ingenious ideas that transformed the health of British crews, one of which was to print medical instructions for officers based on the very latest medical research. His innovations, however, took time to have an impact. By 1782 he had transformed the health of British sailors in the Caribbean, but in the spring of 1780 he was still struggling to turn the situation around.

In the meantime men desperately ran from British warships in the Caribbean to avoid being killed by disease, and the crews of merchant ships armed themselves to avoid being pressed. The very nature of warfare in the Caribbean thus created great tension between the Royal Navy and the British merchant marine.[19] This had always been an issue, but by 1780 it had become a massive problem, simply because of the growing scale of the Royal Navy in Caribbean waters. The British fleet in the Caribbean was now larger than it ever had been during the war. By July 1780 32 per cent of the Royal Navy was in the Caribbean – in July 1778 it had been just 6 per cent. And by no means was disease the only health issue at stake. The rapid growth of the navy in the Caribbean also meant that victuallers were constantly delayed and obstructed by a lack of warehouse space and inadequate port facilities.[20]

While British sea power was trying not to self-destruct, the Spanish and French united near Dominica. Nothing had been done to prevent either fleet from leaving Europe and the British Caribbean forces had been too weak to prevent their arrival.

Rumour reached America that the allies had united and expectation rose, because, according to John Bondfield, 'So formidable a fleet never appeared in them seas.'[21] News also flashed back across the Atlantic and again expectations rose.

If that news was true, 'we may expect good News from that Quarter', wrote Edmund Jenings, an acquaintance of Adams living in Brussels.[22]

Now, however, the recent history of Franco-Spanish non-cooperation at sea came to bite them hard. The Spanish were so cross with the French for their conduct in the 1779 Channel campaign and in the events that led to the Moonlight Battle that – even with the British in a state of naval leprosy and with a huge numerical advantage, far larger than that which d'Estaing had enjoyed over Byron the year before* – they flatly refused even to consider the possibility of a combined operation with the French, who were doing their best to mollify them by lending them troops. Solano insisted on Havana as the centre of operations; de Guichen on Martinique.[23] Solano soon sailed north for Havana, but not before his crews, struck down with yet another epidemic, or possibly the same one that had ruined the 1779 Channel campaign, had infected the French fleet. The Bourbon allies were simply unable to maintain healthy crews. As time ran out before the onset of the hurricane season, de Guichen sailed for home, in escort of a huge French merchant convoy. Like d'Orvilliers in the Channel campaign, de Guichen had been broken by the loss of his son to fever.[24]

Unable to fight his unwilling enemies, Rodney spent the rest of his time in the Caribbean tackling the manning, supply and repair problems that had plagued the station since the start of the war. This lull in operations was a blessing in disguise. Rodney's innovations, bullying and disregard for rules and established practice, so disruptive in fleet battle, was stunningly successful when it came to this type of problem. In these crucial weeks, Rodney single-handedly dragged the navy out of the operational hole it had dug for itself in the Caribbean and made St Lucia a naval base worthy of the Royal Navy. He also focused on seamanship skill, watch-keeping discipline, fleet discipline and ship safety, with particular regard to gunnery

---

* By June the allies combined had thirty-five ships of the line; Rodney had eighteen. Jamieson, 'Leeward Islands', 219.

drill. Accidental collision and explosions, which had plagued the Caribbean squadron in battle hitherto, were eradicated. Powder horns were replaced with priming boxes and goose-quill tubes; linstocks were replaced with flintlocks. His doctor, Gilbert Blane, transformed the squadron's health, particularly by encouraging more responsibility among the officers for the health of their crews. Each ship's surgeon reported to Blane every month and Rodney did all he could to help, and even built a new hospital on breezy Pigeon Island. The scale of the British naval infrastructure on Pigeon Island is still visible today and is one of the most impressive surviving examples of British sea power in the Caribbean. Rodney was kind to those who laboured on its walls, making sure that they were not overworked and that they received a double allowance of grog.[25] Pigeon Island is as much a memorial to the strength, endurance and ingenuity of the sailors who built it as it is to Rodney's utter commitment to the success of the Royal Navy, achieved through care for, and training of, his men. If there is a single monument that encapsulates the dramatic change between the desperate Royal Navy in the Caribbean in the first years of the war and the bristling navy of the last, then this is it. Anyone with an interest in military history should visit it.

British politicians had wanted the Caribbean to be the key theatre in the naval war since 1779, and now, for the first time and thanks entirely to Rodney, the navy was going to be able to meet those expectations. It is a period of modernization and improvement that has few parallels in naval history. As the season came to an end, however, and now so distant from the Admiralty's gaze, Rodney allowed even more of his character to bleed out. Dr Jekyll was finished with his hospitals and health, his experiments and improvement; now it was time for Mr Hyde. Having heard a rumour that a French squadron was heading from the West Indies to America, and fearful of the imminent hurricane season, he left the Caribbean and sailed to New York, where he was not supposed to be. The Caribbean campaign of 1780, which at its inception had every appearance of a naval Armageddon, thus fizzled into nothing.

* * *

The spring of 1780 has a special place in French naval and maritime history. Consider this: in 1992 a fine French institution, the Centre International de la Mer, undertook a project to build a frigate from the age of sail, a multi-million-euro commitment. But what ship would they choose to build? One from the magnificent navy of Louis XIV, France's Sun King? Or perhaps one associated with the golden era of French privateering, when men like Jean Bart, René Douguay-Trouin and Robert Surcouf brought fear to British hearts? Or perhaps a frigate from the golden era of French exploration, the French equivalent of Captain Cook's *Endeavour* – Louis de Bougainville's *L'Aigle* or Lapérouse's *Astrolabe*? But no. They chose to rebuild the *Hermione*, the ship that sailed to America in March 1780 with news that the French would send another fleet, this time with an army, to America. They did this in spite of the numerous and significant operational disappointments suffered in 1778 and 1779; in spite of the growing and dark cloud of unsustainable debt hovering over the navy and the nation itself; in spite of the thousands of French sailors already dead from enemy action and disease; in spite of the inadequacy of the French manning system; in spite of the empty warehouses in French naval dockyards; and in spite of the ruinous tensions and incompetence of Spain.

The first plan, cooked up in Paris, so distant and disconnected from the provincial dockyards and from expert maritime knowledge, was hopelessly unrealistic: 8,000 troops were to be taken to America with 140 horses. By this stage in the war, however, there were too few sailors, too few soldiers, and too few ships available, and the idea of taking so many horses across the Atlantic, to expert eyes, was ludicrous. Each horse would take the space of ten men, and together the herd would require 45,000 gallons of fresh water and whole shiploads of forage just to survive the two months at sea. The plans were scrapped in favour of a scaled-down expedition whose preparation was overseen by the talented seaman, reliable officer and future explorer of great fame, the comte de Lapérouse. On 2 May, escorted by seven ships of the line and six frigates, 5,500 horseless French troops set sail aboard thirty-two transport ships crammed with artillery and military stores that would transform the condition of the American army.[26]

More lessons had been learned from d'Estaing's failures of 1778–9. The fleet was equipped with all the local navigational and hydrographical knowledge that d'Estaing had lacked upon his arrival on American shores in 1778,[27] and this time the roles of army and naval commander, disastrously united in 1778 under d'Estaing, were now divided and allocated to specialists. The fleet was commanded by the chevalier de Ternay, a thoroughbred sailor with forty years of naval service, and the entire expedition was commanded by the comte de Rochambeau, an equally experienced soldier. However, de Ternay was not well liked. A confidential memorandum on Ternay in 1779 described a character full of 'pride, hauteur and almost of severity'.[28] His quartermaster described him as a man who considered himself 'surrounded by rogues and idiots'. 'This character,' he continued, 'combined with manners far from courteous, makes him disagreeable to everybody.'[29] His appointment was no accident. Neither he nor Rochambeau was a born diplomat and both had been chosen to be strong and independent in their relationship with the Americans. Both had also compiled a superb record during the Seven Years' War (1754–63).[30]

Rumour of this French recommitment transformed the American economy, which had been suffering from extreme inflation since the autumn of 1779. Congress had become convinced that the war would not be won without further French intervention and then responded to news that the French would send both a powerful fleet and an expeditionary force to America by acting decisively with regard to the economy. The outstanding currency was redeemed at one fortieth of its nominal value. The new currency issued by Congress in the spring of 1780 was thus directly linked to the expected arrival – and expected subsequent success – of a French fleet.[31]

While the French made their preparations and the Americans rebuilt their finances, Lafayette, beaming with delight and cradling the secret confirmation of French help in the velvet pocket of his heart, dashed across the Atlantic in the newly built and sparkling *Hermione*. He arrived safely in Boston on 28 April simply bursting with naïve excitement. Washington had personally written to him explaining that he would now welcome a French army on American soil – a fundamental change in his stance towards the presence of French troops which had limited the 1778 French campaign to d'Estaing's limited perception of and clumsy use of sea power.[32]

The Bostonians loved the news and they loved this willowy French aristocrat who bore it. He disembarked 'in the midst of an immense crowd' and was welcomed 'with the roar of guns, the ringing of all the city's bells and the music of a band that marched ahead of us, and the huzzas of all the people that surrounded us'. That evening a crowd gathered outside his lodgings 'and built a great bonfire with much cheering, which lasted until after midnight'.[33] The scenes could not have been more different from the simmering tension that had last characterized the presence of French warships in Boston.

Lafayette dashed off a puppyish letter to Washington: 'Here I am, my dear General, and in the midst of the joy I feel in finding myself again one of your loving soldiers* ... I have affairs of the utmost importance which I should at first communicate to you alone.'[34] We know that Washington grew emotional as he read the message, and twelve days later they met at Washington's headquarters in Morristown. Lafayette's news and his beautiful new frigate promised great things. In spite of the many setbacks so far suffered by French and American sea power, Washington still firmly believed in its value; in fact he now believed that 'a constant naval superiority' was a prerequisite for the revolution's success.[35] John

---

* One of the first French officers to travel to America, Lafayette had already served in the American army from June 1777–January 1779 when he returned to Paris on leave.

Adams, then in Paris, who believed that the allies should have sent to America and the Caribbean fewer troops but more ships, shared his sentiment. To attack single locations with armies, Adams believed, 'is endeavouring to lop of[f] single Limbs', but to secure 'Dominion of the American Seas' was to lay 'the Ax to the root of the tree'.[36]

But would the French fleet that followed in the gleaming *Hermione*'s wake contradict the shiny impression she gave of French sea power? Would this new fleet be able to live up to the promises of the giddy Lafayette, the expectations of the distant French politicians, and the dreams of the desperate Washington?

* * *

Rochambeau's expedition provided thousands more young Frenchmen with the opportunity to experience the navy and to visit a strange land. The campaign is unusual for the quantity of diaries and sketchbooks that it generated; the French troops who travelled to America buzzed with excitement. It is likely that many had experienced the disappointment of the 1779 Channel campaign and that now, with the vast expanse of the eastern seaboard of America ahead of them, they knew that they had a far better chance of experiencing the war. First, however, they had to get there. Leaving posed an emotional challenge:

> The order for embarkation ... gave me the greatest pleasure, as a young soldier; but at the same time, the idea of such a long separation ... especially from a charming young fiancée endowed with wit and graces, naturally gave me many troubled moments, difficult to surmount without a certain fund of reason, which, unfortunately, was not one of my strong points.[37]

Many soldiers then experienced the sailors' gaze for the first time and saw their known world sink into the horizon. To view the land from this perspective and to be in the heart of such a fleet was transfixing. 'There is nothing more entertaining than to see the different ships get under way and proceed in succession to this narrow entrance to the harbour, which seems like a door of the sea', wrote Baron Ludwig von Closen, an observant aide-de-camp to General Rochambeau. Leaving the French part of Brest posed an emotional challenge:

> The port, which can be seen in the background toward the North; the city, whose higher fortifications appear much more clearly; the numerous villages on the shores of the harbour; the Landerneau River, flowing into it, whose winding course makes a very pretty view; a number of other ships in addition to those in our expedition: all these different objects together formed an extraordinarily beautiful picture at the moment of our departure.[38]

If one looks carefully, however, one can find smudges and cracks in the wonderful seascape painted in those diaries. The quality of French seamanship was poor. There were several collisions shortly after leaving Brest and then sheer surprise when they finally began to operate as a unit. On one such day, that same astonished soldier wrote, 'Never was a convoy better organized than was ours at that moment', but then added, rather tellingly, 'like a real fleet'.[39] One simply cannot shake the impression that the French were pretending.

The subsequent voyage followed the pattern of most voyages undertaken by armies in this war: it was an utter misery. To the inexperienced soldiers, even the noise of weighing anchor seemed 'unimaginable'.[40] The shipboard smell was horrific because of 'the exhalations and other bad odors produced by the passengers from men as much as from dogs'.[41] Seasickness and boredom clung to the troops like damp clothes. One officer, desperate for a fight, ran on deck armed to the teeth when a strange sail was sighted, only to be disappointed when the stranger proved friendly. 'I was left searing at the eternal peace that pursued me', he wrote.[42] One man was sent over the brink by the whole experience and attempted to set fire to his ship. He was keel-hauled.[43] On one French transport discipline was maintained by depriving men of wine rather than by the threat of physical punishment:[44] a wonderfully French solution to an eternal maritime problem.

Nonetheless, this new maritime environment filled them all with wonder. They caught sharks, peered at jellyfish, exclaimed at flying fish and laughed at dolphins. One French soldier was so starved of maritime experience that he compared diving dolphins to leaping sheep.[45] They were lucky enough to see the Aurora Borealis.[46] Those who had never crossed the Tropic of Cancer were baptized by Old Man Tropic in an extraordinarily colourful ceremony which involved men tarred and rolled in chicken feathers, ritual dunking, and young boys tied to cannon with their trousers around their ankles.[47] The sailors impressed the soldiers, particularly with their ability to withstand the unpleasantness of maritime travel, but also with their skill. 'The groaning masts and heaving ships made me reflect on the daring of men who risk themselves on an element that offers them a thousand dangers', wrote one army lieutenant.[48] Off Bermuda they witnessed a brief skirmish with a British convoy and were left to wonder at the strange experience of naval battle in which everything unfolded at a deathly slow pace, where nothing was easy to understand and still less easy to explain. The soldiers were, as one soldier put it, 'like blind men who like to talk about colours'.[49]

* * *

Rochambeau made the decision to head for Newport in Rhode Island at the last minute. It was a wise decision because it was an excellent destination. The harbour was now empty, having been abandoned by the British in October 1779 in a heavy-handed and panicky response to the threat posed by d'Estaing's reappearance in American waters. Thanks to survey work carried out by d'Estaing in 1778, de Ternay now had detailed charts of the harbour and was close enough to threaten New York. The only available shelter for a watching fleet was at Gardiners Bay on the very tip of Long Island, eighteen leagues to leeward.

Arbuthnot in New York had made no attempt to monitor Narragansett Bay and so the French fleet, weakened from its voyage and encumbered with its convoy of troop transports, sailed into Newport unchallenged; in fact they were not even *seen* by a British ship. The only moment of concern arose when the *Aimable Marie* lost contact in the seasonal fog that still haunts the Rhode Island coast in the summer months. And what was the source of the panic? Did she carry top-secret documents, new weaponry, or the army's pay? No. She was transporting Rochambeau's personal cooks and bakers.[50]

The Newport authorities, understandably hesitant in their response to an enormous invading army, soon became enthusiastic and ordered the town to be illuminated – a beautiful sight when viewed from the ships in the harbour. The French responded with a gunfire and rocket salute.[51]

Word flew to New York. Arbuthnot had recently received naval reinforcements that gave him a clear superiority over de Ternay. The French were suffering so badly from scurvy that no fewer than 1,500 had been immediately hospitalized upon their arrival and some had been so ill that they were 'unable to stand for an hour'.[52] Arbuthnot, in contrast, had fresh crews newly arrived from England, who were bursting with health having been fed 'essence of wort'* throughout their voyage.[53] And yet he made no move to force the French from Newport. He and Clinton had fallen out so badly during their success at Charleston that Captain Andrew Snape Hamond had been forced to step in to prevent a duel. Arbuthnot and Clinton, the head of the British army and the head of the British navy at New York, were now not even on speaking terms.[54] In such circumstances the organization of a complex combined operation was unlikely to succeed and was then entirely demolished when, reacting to a rumour that the French were about to sail, Arbuthnot abandoned a planned conference with Clinton without even leaving a message.[55]

The extent of this failure is revealed in two crucial facts: the first is that Rodney's recent arrival in New York had given the British total naval superiority in American waters; the second

---

* An oil derived from the herb of St John's wort, still used as a traditional remedy for a variety of illnesses.

that the British had first-hand intelligence of the state of the French fleet. Arbuthnot had sent a lieutenant, Josias Rogers, to Newport to discuss terms with Rochambeau for release of the French prisoners captured at Charleston. Rogers got aboard the French flagship without any alarm being raised anywhere; the French were neither rowing guard around the fleet nor keeping watch on the flagship itself. He eventually found de Ternay and discovered him to be very sick. The shipboard discipline that he witnessed was also appallingly slack. Arbuthnot's secretary, William Green, later claimed that he had 'no doubt, if we had gone in, the whole enemy's fleet must have surrendered or been destroyed'.[56] Certainly there was high risk in entering the well-defended harbour, but the British knew the waters well. It is certain that this was a clear-cut opportunity to heavily damage the French squadron that was never taken.

A balance was therefore struck. The French had secured Newport but the British now had naval superiority, exercised from New York. Thereafter the Royal Navy in North American waters was utterly dominant. Rochambeau refused to undertake any maritime-based operations of any type. Washington supported him. When the two met at the Hartford Conference on 20 September, the very first article that they agreed read:

> 1st. That there can be no decisive enterprise against the maritime establishment of the English in this country, without a constant naval superiority.[57]

Rochambeau's son was sent back to Paris to beg for more ships and more men, and a coded message was sent to de Guichen in the Caribbean. Unfortunately, however, Rochambeau's letter was encoded with the official French diplomatic code, and not the standard naval code: all de Guichen received was a page of meaningless numbers.[58] He was, in fact, lucky that the message even got through. De Ternay had written numerous letters to Paris begging for clothes and supplies, but his messages were intercepted four times by the blockading British force which kept the French fleet jammed into Newport as tight as a cork in a bottle. The British ships cruised so close to the beaches and headlands around the entrance to Narragansett Bay that French officers in shore batteries could make out the dress of the British sailors.[59]

The French settled in Newport. Although outnumbered and blockaded, their presence alone, in the words of Clinton, who could feel its effect in New York, gave 'additional animation to the spirit of the rebellion, whose almost expiring embers began to blaze up afresh upon its appearance'.[60]

French letter books and diaries from this period are filled with minute observations of American life. The Americans, it seemed, would 'sell their last shirt' for a cup of coffee and wiped their mouths on the table cloth. Most were noticeably tall; 'there are some, however, who are big and fat'. Newport's women were very fine, 'their complexion is white and clear; their hands and feet generally small; but their teeth are not very wonderful'.[61] The French also discovered that the British had been peddling untruths about them during their own long occupation of Newport. 'According to them [the British], we were the meanest and most abominable people on earth. They had carried their insolence to the point of saying that we were dwarfs, pale, ugly specimens who lived exclusively on frogs and snails'[62] – an interesting parallel to the insults hurled at the French in Boston. The barriers soon broke down, however, and in a short time the French were 'received as brothers rather than foreigners',[63] a marked contrast with the hostility that had characterized their relationship in Boston. The French moved their headquarters ashore into a house that still stands today on Washington Street [see fig. 15]. De Ternay and several French captains also moved ashore, staying in houses that also still stand.

The French used the time to educate and influence their soldiers with pro-war propaganda by producing their own newspaper, the *Gazette Française*, printed on an enormous press that had been carted across the Atlantic in space that could have been filled with tons of fresh fruit and vegetables to ease the suffering of their scurvy-ridden sailors. The press was set up on shore and given the grand title 'L'Imprimerie Royale de L'Escadre'. The link between the newspaper and the fleet – between French propaganda and the French navy, rather than the army – was therefore made explicit. This was probably the first service newspaper ever published by an expeditionary force.[64]

The French were also enlivened by a visit from local Native American tribes. The Indians danced and banged their drums while the French sailors fired their naval cannon from their towering ships.[65] The meeting seems to have gone well: 'these people have many good qualities and are basically much less barbarous than they appear', wrote one Frenchman.[66] One wonders what the Indians thought of the French: for some, and perhaps all, this would have been their first sight of a ship of the line.

The French presence in Newport provided a welcome shot in the arm for the New England regional economy, which rose magnificently to the challenge of supplying food and drink to the many men whose leaders could actually pay for what they needed. The very presence of French sea power thus allowed the Americans to abandon destructive policies such as embargoes, price-fixing and legal tender laws.[67]

* * *

Washington, meanwhile, despaired and raged as his bubbles of expectation burst. His resources were then so low that he was forced to send militiamen home, simply because he could not feed them. To make matters worse, Benedict Arnold, hero of the Quebec campaign, Valcour Island and Saratoga, defected to the British. His treachery was exposed by chance, and he escaped in a fascinating adventure. Major John André, the British army officer and spy whose capture exposed Arnold's complicity with the British, was caught travelling overland, and he was travelling overland because HMS *Vulture*, the British ship that was supposed to take him securely and swiftly downriver from West Point to New York in safe possession of

Arnold's plans of West Point, had been forced to move from its anchorage in the Hudson when it came under fire from gunnery from an American shore battery. Her log records that she received 'six shot in the hull, one between wind and water, three through the ship's boats on the booms; standing and running rigging shot away in many different places'.[68] This was more than enough to force her from her anchorage, leaving André utterly alone in hostile territory. Ironically, however, Arnold, warned of André's capture, did successfully escape to the *Vulture*. The captain's log records this, one of the most infamous moments of military treason in history, in a rather deadpan way: '24th Genl. Arnold in the American service delivered himself up with a boat's crew.'[69] Aboard the *Vulture*, in a dark cabin and with the desk gently rocking to the motion of the ship as she ran downstream for New York, Arnold wrote an extraordinary letter to Washington claiming that 'Love to my country actuates my present conduct', while acknowledging at the same time that everyone else in the world might not perhaps see it that way.

Washington was horrified and felt personally betrayed. The revolution survived, but American prospects were as bad as they had ever been, even with the arrival of Rochambeau. To make matters worse, if there was any hint at what the future might bring from what had already occurred, it was that, with the exception of overwhelming or uncontested amphibious operations, sea power as a weapon did not work as expected. It almost seemed like a confidence trick, with statesmen and politicians being the mark. Far from a means of expanding or defending the exercise of a nation's interest, sea power was nothing more than a guaranteed way of accruing debt, infecting sailors with deadly disease, and generating acrimony and disappointment.

Surprisingly, given their desperate performance so far in this war, the men who would show that this did not have to be the case were Spanish.

25

SPANISH SKILL

Control of the area around the Mississippi was a key Spanish war aim and it had been achieved by 1780. This territory, in the words of the Spanish Minister of the Indies, was to be 'the bulwark of the vast empire of New Spain'.[1] Bernardo de Gálvez, the governor of New Orleans who had already demonstrated considerable diplomatic skill in his handling of the Willing raid, had taken to military operations like a duck to water.

Gálvez had received news of the Spanish declaration of war long before any British forces in the area and had prepared a little fleet to raid up the Mississippi. His ships, apart from a single frigate, were then destroyed by a hurricane, but the determined and resourceful Gálvez went back to work and created another little fleet out of thin air by raising some wrecks from the seabed and sending troops far and wide to strip the Gulf Coast around New Orleans of every available craft. Once ready, his new fleet carried a jumble of men: Spanish veterans, Mexican recruits, Canary Islanders, carabiniers, militiamen, free blacks, mulattos and Indians.[2] The fleet was shadowed on the banks of the Mississippi by those soldiers who could not fit on the boats.

On 7 September this eclectic maritime force surprised the British at Manchac, thus securing the first Spanish victory of the war. The key strategic location of Baton Rouge fell soon after, and then Fort Panmure at Natchez. Also, and perhaps more importantly, they captured eight British vessels in the river and adjacent lakes, including one troop transport on its way to Manchac, which was taken by a Spanish crew that was five times smaller than that of its prize.[3] Not only had the Spanish taken control of the key British forts on the river, therefore, but they had also acquired a small fleet with which they could police the river and link their new possessions together. In total Gálvez and his men captured three forts, 550 soldiers, eight vessels and 430 leagues of the best land on the Mississippi. Quite a prize.

In the summer of 1780, therefore, the Hudson, the Mississippi and the mighty harbour of Newport were in American, Spanish and French hands: a three-way transnational allied claw on the American colonies that held them fast against British threats from north, south and east and provided a strong foundation from which to build. The French presence in Newport paralysed the Royal Navy at New York and Solano's massive fleet at Havana paralysed the British fleet at Jamaica. There were no significant British naval forces in the Floridas, Georgia or South Carolina at all, and Gálvez seized the opportunity.

He set about preparing for a strike against Mobile, the closest British base to New Orleans and a crucial harbour. Mobile Bay is like a tooth knocked out of the face of the Gulf of Mexico. Thirty miles long, six wide and protected by sandbanks, it was a fine anchorage. Some 1,200 men were readied in fourteen ships, but Gálvez's preparations were undone by another storm, this one so fierce that 400 Spanish sailors and soldiers drowned.[4] Yet again Gálvez was forced to resuscitate a fleet, and yet again he succeeded where many would have failed. For Gálvez the struggle for sea power was, more than anything else, a struggle against the elements.

When his fleet finally arrived at Mobile, things again went wrong. Six ships ran aground, one was wrecked, and the whole process of unloading troops and supplies, trying at the best of times, became almost farcical in the tempestuous weather. Gálvez lost so many supplies that he seriously considered retreating overland to New Orleans.[5] Ten days after his arrival, however, reinforcements arrived from Havana and the siege was on. The Spanish immediately began to make scaling ladders from their shattered ships.[6] The city was defenceless against such sea power and Fort Charlotte fell on 13 March. The Spanish thus took control of Mobile and with it secured access deep inland via the Alabama and Tombigbee rivers.

*   *   *

Gálvez's next goal was Pensacola, capital of British West Florida and only fifty miles or so further along the coast. Pensacola, however, was another type of target altogether, a fact which Gálvez knew well, having commissioned a detailed spying operation on the British defences there in the twilight years before official Spanish involvement in the war.[7] To take Pensacola would require a far more significant expedition than that which had taken Mobile, and it would rely entirely on Spanish ships: Pensacola was almost completely cut off from the interior by impassable swamps – it was, in effect, an island. Gálvez therefore travelled to Havana to urge Solano in person to let him borrow his fleet. Solano agreed.

In October nearly 4,000 troops boarded a fleet of seventy-two ships under Solano's command, left Havana for Pensacola, and immediately sailed into a horrific storm – the third time in three operations that natural forces destroyed Spanish fleets. 'The day began beautiful, with a clear horizon and a good wind', wrote one Spaniard, but things started to change, and fast. 'The wind rose at 9.30; at twelve it became violent; and at 4 there was a furious hurricane.' Three days later, their masts gave way, and 'water came in through the heads, the ports, and everywhere'. One ship, the *San Ramón*, was taking on fifty-eight inches of water every hour.[8]

Most surviving accounts of the storm are terse and echo shock and disappointment, rather than detailing the actual struggle with the elements, but one letter written by an educated Spaniard, perhaps an officer and certainly a seaman, offers a glimpse of the shocking destruction that visited the fleet. He reported that, of Gálvez's seven ships of the line, only one returned unscathed. One was never seen again and the rest were all left dismasted and adrift in the Gulf of Mexico. The fleet was scattered far and wide across the Gulf of Mexico: some survivors came ashore at their intended destination of Pensacola; others reached Mobile, New Orleans, even Campeche on the south-eastern tip of the Gulf of Mexico's crescent; others still, including Gálvez himself, were able to make it back to Havana. In many instances the sailors had thrown overboard everything that the ocean had not already claimed, simply to stay afloat. For warships the heaviest and most dangerous items in a storm were the cannon; for the horse transports it was the poor horses; for one of the hospital ships it was her entire supply of 'equipment and materials'. No detailed figures survive, but the British press boasted that over 2,000 Spaniards died.[9] The hurricane was so powerful that its existence can be physically demonstrated today in tree-ring isotopes in Georgia.[10]

*   *   *

This sequence of three storms endured by the Spanish in three separate operations raises the important question of weather forecasting in this period. In this campaign alone Gálvez had been frustrated at every turn, and in the war as a whole the weather repeatedly played a major role, not least in the storm that disrupted the battle between Howe and d'Estaing off Rhode Island in 1778, the storms that delayed and damaged Byron on his way to America and then the Caribbean in 1778, the storm that damaged d'Estaing's fleet at Savannah in 1779, the storm that nearly destroyed Arbuthnot and Clinton's expeditionary force to Charleston in 1780, and the major hurricane of October 1780 that would shortly tear apart the Royal Navy in the Caribbean.

It is important to realize that the men who navigated these ships, entirely dependent on the weather though charged with the fate of empires, actually knew very little about the science of the weather. Professional sailors had a general understanding that certain locations were dangerous at certain times of year, but apart from that their weather forecasting simply relied upon portents in the immediate environment: the behaviour of sea-birds; pods of dolphins moving in a certain direction; the appearance and behaviour of ocean swells. The science of meteorology was not unknown, but it was not yet a rigorous science, and instruments were very rare and neither standardized nor accurate. Certain crucial basics had not yet been discovered: atmospheric dynamics and the concepts of revolving storms and moving depressions were all unknown until the nineteenth century.[11]

It is all too easy to focus on a warship's guns and forget that these ships had no weapons at all with which to fight or outwit the weather. If caught out, all that the sailors could do was endure, though it is important to appreciate just how skilled they became at doing exactly that. A practised eighteenth-century crew could swiftly transform a ship set up to squeeze every last knot from a light breeze into one that could be punished by the elements for days at a time. Their repair skills were also exceptional. Wood or canvas could be taken from one part of a ship to be grafted onto another, like a bone transplant. Rudders could become jury-masts; capstan poles could become yards; sails could block breaches in the hull. We only have a dim sense now of just how they did what they did, however, and the question of seamanship during or after storms and battles remains one of the most interesting but least researched topics of naval history.[12] Indeed, one of the most fascinating hidden statistics of this period is not how many ships were wrecked by storms but how many were *saved* by exceptional seamanship and innovation – a type of knowledge that is now largely lost to history.

* * *

Gálvez's men endured this third storm and, eventually, returned with all but one of their ships to Havana, an impressive achievement indeed. Gálvez set about rebuilding the force. In Pensacola knowledge that this extraordinarily resilient man had his eyes set on them weighed heavily on the British, and they began to suffer from the same anxiety that had plagued the citizens and soldiers of New York in 1776, Philadelphia in 1777, and Charleston in 1780. Eyes nervously scanned the horizon for a force that they knew was coming but which they could do nothing to stop. Capture, rot and convoy duty had reduced the British 'squadron' at Pensacola to two armed schooners, and the same hurricane that shattered the Spanish fleet at Havana had nearly destroyed the British fleet at Jamaica. Parker was now unable to offer any help at all, even if he had been willing.[13]

The lack of British naval presence threw the Pensacolans into 'a state of disagreeable uncertainty'.[14] This was no Gibraltar; they had no expectations of succour at all. With the Spanish threat so clear and so close, the military and civilians of Pensacola fell to pecking at each other, the military claiming that the civilians were 'selfish and lazy' while at the same time coming up with plans to hand them all over to Gálvez as soon as he arrived so that they could be kept, for their own 'safety', in Spanish ships. Unsurprisingly, the idea appalled the civilians, who considered it 'unprecedented in any society'.[15]

*   *   *

The lesson of 1780 was that the worst British fears had come true: they had lost control of the sea. The combined American, French and Spanish threats meant that there were insufficient British warships to protect all their possessions. This had been a problem since the start of the war, but now, with competent men at the helm of the French and Spanish navies, it had become particularly acute. It is no surprise that the allies also began to make significant convoy captures in this period. On one occasion, on 9 August, a Franco-Spanish fleet of thirty-three ships sailed from Cádiz and captured a vast British convoy of over sixty ships, taking prisoner 1,350 seamen and 1,255 troops, and seizing £1.5 million in cargo and stores. It was the worst British convoy disaster in living memory,* and

---

* Since the Smyrna convoy disaster of 1693.

was felt so severely that it led to significant changes in British marine insurance.* Under pressure everywhere, the British had been unable to provide this convoy, which was travelling at a predictable time of year along a predictable course, with any more than a single line-of-battle ship and two frigates as escorts. The Channel Fleet was weak with sickness and the pressure of trying to control home waters with an inadequate force nearly killed Admiral Geary, then commander-in-chief of the home fleet. He appears to have had a complete break-down and remarkably the doctor's report still survives. 'The Admiral', wrote Dr James Lind, 'thro' a constant fatigue and hurry of business added to an over anxiety of mind, seems to have exhausted his strength, and spirits. He is feverish, his pulse weak, has for a violent headache, pain of his Breast, and profuse sweats.'[16] He simply had nothing left to give, broken by the challenge of exercising British sea power.

The British maritime empire was starting to fall apart because its maritime connections could not be guaranteed. This naval weakness, experienced empire-wide, was sensed intensely in Britain, particularly in London, where the pressure of exercis-ing inadequate sea power was crippling its already divided political hierarchy. The sudden outburst of riots in London, the worst riots of the century, is no coincidence. The very last thing that the British now needed was for Spain to open a new front in the Mediterranean; for France to reopen another front thousands of miles away in India; for several more countries, all equipped with their own navies, to flex their maritime muscles against Britain; and for the Spanish and French to ignore the festering wounds of their failed combined operations and to begin to co-operate once more.

But – quite extraordinarily – that is exactly what happened.

---

* It was a very rare example of British troop transports being taken in this war, the other occurring in June 1776, when four unescorted transports carrying 354 men of the 71st Regiment were captured by American ships off Boston. Syrett, *Shipping*, 182; Spilsbury, *Journal*, 21; Petrie, *Charles III*, 192; Woodman, *Britannia's Realm*, 23, 34–5.

26

RUSSIAN MEDDLING

The relationship between Britain, Holland and Russia during the American war was complex. The war had been received with mixed feelings in and around the Baltic and North Sea. American privateers had used Dutch ports as bases and they had been well received by the Dutch populace. On the diplomatic stage, however, their presence in the Baltic had actually acted against the Americans. The response in October 1779 to John Paul Jones's arrival in the Texel, the deep-water harbour that served Amsterdam, illustrates this well. Jones arrived in Holland with a small squadron including HMS *Serapis*, the ship he had recently captured from the British in that hard-fought action off Flamborough Head. Jones, however, was now burdened with the baggage of his own success. The *Serapis* wanted a mainmast, and his 600 prisoners, many injured or unwell, needed accommodation, medicine and victuals. Letters from the British captain reveal that the prisoners were, quite deliberately, treated appallingly by the Americans – an interesting observation that puts into context the better-known horrific treatment of American prisoners by the British in prison hulks off New York.

Jones's presence in the Texel was entirely involuntary; in such a weakened state he had wanted to find shelter in a French port, ideally Dunkirk, but had been ordered to Holland by the French, who wanted him to protect a Baltic supply fleet.[1] The Dutch public loved him. He was bold and daring, the embodiment of the rebellion. Here was flesh-and-blood proof that the most fascinating story of the age was true, that the American colonists had risen up against the might of the British and had, almost unbelievably, been so successful that they had brought their war across the Atlantic. Jones was quite the hero. 'Every day', wrote Jones, 'those blessed [Dutch] women come to the ships in great numbers – mothers, daughters, even little girls – bringing with them for our wounded all the numberless little comforts of Dutch homes, a tribute that came from the hearts of the people.'[2] One Dordrecht brewer was so impressed with Jones that he named a beer after him,[3] and children sang rhymes:

> Here comes John Paul Jones
> About him ev'ry Dutchman raves!
> His ship went down 'neath the waves,
> An English ship he boards and owns,
> If we had him here,
> If they had him there,
> There is still no end to all his pluck
> He's ready again to try his luck.[4]

By then his exploits had spread back across the Atlantic, and Abigail Adams wrote to her husband, begging for more information about this 'adventurous hero' who was so much 'the subject of conversation and admiration'.[5] Nor was he the only such subject of conversation and admiration. The Massachusetts-born privateer Daniel McNeil had made a similar splash with a number of stunning captures off the Russian port of Archangel in his ship *General Mifflin*. 'American Arms may truly be said to extend to the Poles', wrote John Bondfield.[6]

The Dutch politicians were far more circumspect than the public about Jones's presence in the Texel and, already divided over the war, fell to bickering.[7] This binary response to the American privateers is one of the clearest examples from the war that the news of naval success spoke to the masses in a far clearer way than they did to the politicians. One would suspect from Jones's own account that he was welcomed with open arms by everyone but that was far from the case. In fact the Dutch quickly mobilized a squadron under Vice-Admiral Rhynst – 'an Englishman at heart',[8] as Jones put it – to force him to leave, and he was forced to leave long before he was ready to go. He only had a single anchor, his rigging and sails were in very poor condition, and he had to abandon his prize and his prisoners. Jones described this as 'a sacrifice', with the implication of choice that term carries with it. In reality, however, he had no choice at all and was mercilessly forced to sea by the Dutch naval muscle of Rhynst and his massive squadron of thirteen two-decked warships.

Jones was thus left to fend for himself in the Channel, bristling with British cruisers and warships, in the autumn, known for its ferocious storms. It was not exactly a death sentence, nor was his capture guaranteed, but both were likely. 'As I put to sea the odds were a hundred to one* that we would soon have a serious affair with the enemy', wrote Jones.[9] With good luck, however, Jones avoided the British in a madcap dash down the Channel in which he logged some seventy miles in just seven hours, and made it safely to the Atlantic coast of France.[10] The diplomatic impact of his presence in Holland, meanwhile, waited to be felt.

Jones believed – and when he later wrote his memoirs, he certainly wanted others to believe – that the subsequent war between Britain and Holland was the result of his presence in the Texel alone.[11] His presence had certainly caused some political discomfort and, when war broke out, it was a specified reason for the declaration of hostilities, but it was only one of several given reasons, many of which were nothing more than flimsy excuses. Indeed, the relationship between Britain, Holland and America was far too complex and far too important for the mere presence of a single American rebel to shift off course. But if it was not Jones's presence that led Holland and Britain to war, then what did? The answer lies in Baltic, and particularly in Russian, sea power.

*   *   *

---

* His meaning was the reverse – 1:100 – in other words, virtually a certainty.

To understand the British declaration of war on the Dutch in December 1780, one must consider the Dutch as part of a broad collection of northern naval powers, which included the Swedes, the Danes and, above all, the Russians.

The Russians had no fewer than thirty ships of the line, they were the fourth-largest naval power in the world, and their navy had recently played a key role in winning a long-standing war against the Turks. The Dutch had an impressive force of twenty-six ships of the line and thirty-five frigates, and, if combined, the Danes and the Swedes could create a navy larger than the Dutch. The Danish and Swedish navies were designed for warfare in the shallow Baltic; only the Russians and the Dutch had significant numbers of warships capable of exercising sea power in the deep oceans.[12] Nonetheless, if considered together, these navies created a potent threat. The Thames estuary directly faces the estuaries of the Scheldt, Maas and Rhine across the narrow and shallow North Sea, and the ease with which one could sail to and from Britain across the North Sea was one of the main reasons for traditional British friendliness towards Holland and the Baltic countries. Indeed, the relationship with these northern navies, and particularly with the Dutch, was a crutch that supported the British empire: the British could only look to the west if their northern and eastern shores were secure.

The challenge that faced the North government in 1780 was how to manage the threat that this safety net might collapse. Their response was influenced by the way that the threat evolved. The driving force behind that threat was not created by the combined weight of Dutch politicians or by the lone energy of John Paul Jones, but by Catherine the Great, empress of Russia.

Catherine was concerned about the rights of neutral nations to trade with whom and in what they liked whenever they wanted. The American Revolution, don't forget, was both a 'Glorious Cause' and a glorious opportunity for entrepreneurs. The Dutch had already mobilized their maritime infrastructure and networks to make themselves rich by the war, by exporting weapons and military stores to America from Europe via their Caribbean colony, St Eustatius, and by trading in naval stores – Baltic flax, hemp, timber and copper – with French and Spanish dockyards. They had even been clever enough to facilitate the transfer of goods from British manufacturers to the rebellious colonies via Holland, and two frigates were secretly being built in Dutch shipyards for the Americans.[13]

The Russians had neither a significant deep-ocean merchant marine nor any colonies in the New World, but they did have a navy, they did have a good strategic location, and they did have an ambitious monarch who had seen the Dutch grow fat from the war. Hitherto Russian policy during the war had been focused on preserving the status quo between Britain and America and achieving a peaceful settlement. Now, however, with the British committed in the Caribbean, America, the Channel and Gibraltar, Catherine could see that the British could be pushed further than they had been pushed for nearly a century, and she wanted a piece of the action. She also wanted to raise the diplomatic profile of Russia to become a key player in European politics. She would do this by taking upon herself the role of champion of neutral nations' maritime rights, and one of the events that spurred her into action was Daniel McNeil's seizure of Russian trade goods off Archangel.[14] British, Spanish and French ships had all had their fun capturing Russian merchantmen, however, and Catherine's motivation was to protect her trade in general rather than to launch a calculated strike against America.

She had written to a friend to expect something 'du volcanique' and now she acted.[15] With no advice asked from her Council of State, she ordered the immediate armament of fifteen ships of the line and five frigates, an act that was foreshadowed by a dramatic growth in Russian merchant ships trading with other European cities. Catherine was making a mercantile statement backed up by naval power.

* * *

The British had always adapted their vision of neutral rights according to their own self-interest, and for nearly a century they had successfully imposed that vision with the weight of the Royal Navy behind their policy, occasionally with force, usually with threat. The key issue was this: during wartime they did not want neutral powers to trade in valuable naval stores with their naval enemies. So far in this war they had played this hand with great strength and ruthless inflexibility. Only twenty-five days after the declaration of war between England and France, the Royal Navy had been authorized to intercept and seize neutral vessels carrying 'Naval or Warlike stores' to French ports. This legal weight and naval muscle were assisted by an army of spies operating with great efficiency in ports all over north-eastern Europe – Helsingör, Göteborg, Gdansk, Riga, St Petersburg – providing the British squadron at the Downs with early intelligence of significant cargoes heading their way. The commander of that force, Francis Drake, constantly complained that his strength was insufficient but he still imposed an effective blockade.[16]

In March 1780 Catherine created a 'League of Armed Neutrality' to defend the rights of neutral nations. Initially it consisted of Russia, Sweden and Denmark.* The Americans were so keen on the idea that they made the inspired decision to attempt to join, rather overlooking the obvious fact that they were a belligerent.[17] The League was backed on paper by a total of eighty-four warships and was presented to the world in the same terms that the rebels had used to defend their revolution: this was a force gathered to protect itself against British tyranny. Seizures of Russian merchant ships were described in terms of 'cupidity', 'avidity' and 'arrogance', and it was claimed that the British had prosecuted them with 'uncontrolled violence'.[18] This was powerful stuff because, unlike much of the diatribe that had come out of the American colonies in the mid-1770s, much of what the Russians were now claiming was actually true. If the British had been tyrannical anywhere

---

* Prussia, Portugal and Austria joined in 1781, Naples in 1783.

and at any time, it was on the high seas, acting against neutral shipping, between 1778 and 1780. The shape of the war had therefore allowed the Russians to disguise their own imperial and mercantile ambitions with revolutionary rhetoric.

* * *

The British never saw it coming. Traditionally the Russians had been part of an important, though unofficial, anti-Bourbon balance of power. Catherine's league set off fireworks in London. Lord Stormont could make neither head nor tail of it, considering Russia's intentions 'so problematical that I know not what opinion to form',[19] and Sir James Harris, the British ambassador to St Petersburg, assumed wrongly that Catherine had been duped by her minister of foreign affairs, Nikita Panin, who he assumed, again wrongly, had been bribed by the French.[20] The Americans also misunderstood Catherine's intention, believing it to be consciously anti-British (and therefore pro-American), and a subsequent diplomatic mission to St Petersburg by Francis Dana was one of the most ill-judged diplomatic episodes of the war. Dana spent the best part of two years lurking in a St Petersburg lodging house, utterly ignored by the Russian court. Catherine, one of the chief bulwarks of the ancien régime, was never going to bend her own autocratic perceptions of the duties of subjects to divine-right monarchs.[21]

American interest in the League was based on the assumption that Baltic sea power would be able to stand up for its own rights.[22] But, yet again, this was an assumption about the effectiveness of sea power that was wholly wide of the mark. The British made no concessions to the League at all. Control over who traded with whom on the sea was as important a foundation to British imperial strength as the control of territory, and with so much British territory already so threatened in America, the Caribbean and India, control of the sea was the one thing that they would do everything they could to protect. If, as seemed likely, the worst came to the worst and territory was lost to the Americans or Bourbons, British control of the sea would provide them with a powerbase from which to rebuild.

There was also a key weakness with the first manifestation of Catherine's league: the Dutch were not members. The Dutch had been playing their cards carefully because they were profiting from the war and they wanted to continue to do so. Gradually, however, they slipped further and further towards Catherine's league when it became clear that her posturing was simply going to be ignored by the British. Without Dutch help the League was, in her words, nothing more than an 'armed nullity'.[23] Interestingly, it has been argued that the toothlessness of the Russian navy can be traced back to the presence of mercenary British naval officers at all levels of the Russian naval officer corps, who deliberately weakened the Russian naval stance towards Britain.[24]

The Dutch tried to insist that their convoys pass through the Channel safely and without inspection, and they tried to force their convoys through with the protection of Dutch naval vessels, but the British continued to make seizures even under the noses of Dutch warships.

The decision to declare war on the Dutch, thereby abandoning Britain's second-oldest alliance and the foundation of her foreign policy for more than a century, was taken at a cabinet meeting on 16 December 1780. In the traditional manner for foreign affairs the decision was taken towards the end of a long, heavy dinner, over the port and cheese. Rather wonderfully, we have an eyewitness account of that very moment written by Germain's undersecretary, William Knox. Even if one considers that Knox may have been keen to make Germain's cabinet rivals appear foolish, his account is stunning. Lord North, the prime minster, and Lord Bathhurst, the President of the Council, slept throughout the discussion. Lord Hillsborough, the Secretary of State for the Southern Department, 'nodded and dropped his hat', while Lord Sandwich, First Lord of the Admiralty, 'was overcome at first', but perked up after rubbing his eyes.[25]

This account has caused generations of historians some

mirth, but the actual reason for a lack of debate, which is surely the key question here, has never really been questioned. There was no debate because the answer was – then* – so obvious. Britain *had* to maintain her command of the sea, and war with the Dutch actually played to her interests. By making the Dutch belligerents the British denied to the French use of neutral Dutch ships and created the opportunity to reclaim some of the prestige and territory already lost in the war to the Americans, French and Spanish. British failure in the early years thus made war with the Dutch more, not less, likely. It was clearly argued by some at the time that Holland as a recognized enemy was less troublesome than Holland as a neutral. Sandwich firmly believed it and choreographed the dance to war.[26] The crucial consideration was to keep the Dutch isolated from the other neutral powers, particularly from Russia, and this, ultimately, was the primary motivation for war.† The British had heard that the Dutch were moving closer to Russia and were about to sign the League of Armed Neutrality. If they did join the League, then the Dutch could summon Russian, Swedish and Danish naval help if attacked, but if the British declared war first, then this could not, in theory, happen.

With commitments already made behind the scenes, all that was needed now was an event that would allow the British to declare war openly, rather like the *Belle Poule* action which the French had used to frame their entry into the war in 1778. It was provided by Henry Laurens, a leading figure in the rebellion and a recent president of the Continental Congress, who had been sent by Congress to Holland to

---

* It is not so clear now. It has been argued that the British overestimated the value of the Dutch maritime trade to the allied war effort. Dull, *Diplomatic History*, 125.

† Another, little-known reason for war was that the British had heard that the Dutch and French had nearly finished a scheme by which the Dutch would be able to continue to trade with France via a network of inland waterways which linked the Netherlands, Belgium and the French Channel ports with Nantes in the Bay of Biscay: an excellent route which would deny the Royal Navy its ability to control that trade via blockade. Syrett, *European Waters*, 125.

secure a massive loan. He sailed from Philadelphia in a newly built craft, the *Mercury*, 'as fast a sailer as any in America'.[27] She was supposed to be escorted by two American warships but only one, the *Saratoga*, was available, and she was so poorly ballasted that Laurens sent her back to Philadelphia. The *Mercury* continued alone. She was intercepted by a British frigate, the *Vestal*, off Newfoundland on 3 September 1780 and quickly surrendered. Laurens and his secretary set about throwing overboard all of their important mail, which they did with great success except for one bag, which was weighted down with shot but tied poorly at the throat, creating an air pocket. The bag floated, and the British spotted it and hauled it in with a boat hook.

Inside was a draft of a treaty between Holland and America that had been drawn up by no one in any position of authority, that had never been read by either government and that was intended to take force in the event of America achieving independence. It carried no authority, nor did it have any bearing on events in the winter of 1780.[28] Keppel, the first officer to see the papers, considered them irrelevant, but others with keener political minds saw their potential. It was, after all, a draft of a treaty between Holland and America – and *that* was an excuse for war.*

The British also swaggered to the tune of Lauren's capture, the first major American political figure that the British had seized. Instead of being treated as a soldier or sailor captured in battle and sent to rot in a prison hulk somewhere, Laurens was treated like a Tudor villain hell-bent on bringing down the monarchy: he was sent to the Tower 'upon suspicion of High Treason'.[29] He was the first and only American ever to have been imprisoned in the Tower of London. Smuggled in for fear of a rescue attempt, he was then denied pen and ink to prevent him from orchestrating any mischief. Laurens knew

---

* The fact that Laurens was carrying papers he did not need and that they were thrown into the water where they did not sink remains extremely suspicious. Nordholt, *Dutch Republic*, 148.

that this treatment was all for show: 'I looked upon all this parade to be calculated for intimidation, my Spirits were good & I smiled inwardly.'[30]

With Laurens in the Tower, the Americans had no ambassador working on their behalf in Holland, but in a curious twist of fate Laurens's capture did far more for the American cause than his presence in Holland could ever have achieved, for he had provided Britain with the excuse to go to war and the American chances of securing a loan from Holland had immeasurably increased. Laurens, sharp as a tack, instinctively and immediately knew this: 'I felt a satisfaction ... in being Captured by a British Ship of War, I shall now be sent to England where I shall be of more real service to my own Country that I could possibly be in any other part of Europe.'[31] What he did not know and could not possibly have foreseen, however, was the confoundingly convoluted path that would eventually link Dutch involvement in the war directly with American independence and which would also lead to a startling and permanent demise in Dutch mercantile, naval and imperial power.

*   *   *

Laurens's capture and Jones's former presence in the Texel were just two of several 'official' reasons given for the declaration of war, but for those in the know, none carried any weight. American politicians well versed in the real decision-making behind the scenes took great pleasure from the British doublespeak. John Adams described how the announcement provided a 'New Years Entertainment'.[32]

In the weeks after the declaration the British looked desperately to the east to see how the members of the League would react. It was, in the words of Lord Sandwich, a 'ticklish crisis' that 'might have the most decisive & fatal consequences'.[33] It was even proposed to the king that they should bribe Catherine with Minorca to keep her out of an alliance with the Dutch.[34] Such a distasteful proposal was never necessary, however, because the dice rolled in favour of the British.

The League's guard dogs never even barked and the Dutch were left on their own.

In terms of numbers the British were now massively out-gunned at sea. Combined, the French, Spanish and Dutch had 137 ships of the line to the British ninety-four, but naval warfare never worked in such a black and white way. There was no formal alliance between the Bourbons and the Dutch, and even if there had been, the war had demonstrated so clearly how difficult it would be to make such an alliance work. Adams, with his talent for seeing things as they really were, likened the Dutch predicament to that of a frog between the legs of two fighting bulls.[35] Their navy was relatively small, both in numbers and in the fact that it consisted of small ships designed for trade protection, and their empire was large and mostly undefended. The Dutch were in serious trouble.

PART 4

AMERICAN INDEPENDENCE
1781

27

DUTCH DISASTER

St Eustatius is a rocky volcanic outcrop at the northern tip of the Leeward Islands. Less than ten miles square and with only one reasonable harbour and one significant settlement, the value of St Eustatius lay not in acres of arable land but in the narrow strip of warehouses, a little over a mile long, which flanked its harbour. During the American war, these warehouses became some of the most valuable real estate in the world.[1] Using its status as a neutral power, the Dutch supplied the Americans with arms, powder and clothing, and they supplied the French with naval stores and food. The Dutch had helped the Americans from the start, but the real money began to be made when the French joined the war, because, with France a belligerent, French Caribbean islands suddenly became far more difficult to access for American merchants. The Dutch simply opened their arms even wider. In 1779 a Dutch rear-admiral noted how 3,182 vessels had sailed from St Eustatius in the thirteen months he had been there.[2] It is no exaggeration to claim that Dutch merchants operating from St Eustatius played a major role, perhaps *the* major role, in maintaining both the American army in the field and the French navy in the Caribbean Sea. The bellows of Dutch commerce fanned the American flame of liberty, and this was no secret: it is no coincidence that the password of General John Burgoyne's troops at the battle of Freeman's Farm was 'St Eustatius'.[3] War with Holland now gave the British the opportunity to do something about this irritating island.

* * *

In November 1780 Rodney returned to the Caribbean from a disastrous visit to New York, where he had assumed authority over the miserable and spineless Arbuthnot, thereby claiming, as the highest-ranking officer on station, the greatest portion of prize money seized during his stay. With the fresh taste of antagonism in his mouth, Rodney proceeded to annoy Peter Parker, the British commander of the Jamaica station. Parker, who had endured the most destructive and deadly Atlantic hurricane on record while Rodney had caroused in New York, was desperately trying to pick up the shattered pieces of his fleet and dockyard. Jamaica, 'the most Beautiful Island in the World', had the appearance of 'a Country laid waste by Fire and Sword'. Two ships of the line and five frigates had foundered, and seven ships of the line and three frigates had been dismasted. At the Jamaican port of Savanna la Mar, one of the ships in the harbour 'went over the fort, the parapet of which at other times is about fifteen feet above the level of the water'.[4]

Days earlier the storm had hit Barbados, killing 4,326 people, allowing slaves and prisoners to escape, and leading to, in the words of General Vaughan, 'a continuous scene of Rapine & Confusion' in the streets.[5] It then hit St Lucia 'with a degree of violence not to be described',[6] flattening Rodney's fledgling naval hospital and his temporary naval infrastructure ashore. The *Montague* was unfortunate enough to be at sea. 'Without a single blow of the ax', wrote her captain, 'all our masts were blown overboard.' She was soon rolling so deeply that her quarterdeck gun-ports, twenty-two feet above the surface of the water on a calm day, were repeatedly submerged, a motion that her captain could only describe as 'far beyond the conception of anyone but a seaman'.[7] The report from the captain of the *Amazon*, who was caught at sea by the storm, is truly terrifying.[8] Witnesses had no idea how to describe what they had seen and groped for words: 'irresistible fury ... incessant flood ... ruin, desolation, destruction ... incredible vehemence ... unusual and dreadful scene ... totally transformed.'[9] *Every single ship* that Rodney had left behind in the Leeward Islands had been sunk or damaged. Measured in these terms,

the 1780 hurricane season was far more destructive than any
fleet battle in the war, and by far the worst naval blow suffered
by the British. The French were also savaged by the hurricane,
with 4,000 fatalities on Martinique, which suffered from a
7.6-metre storm surge.*

Enter Rodney, whose own ships had been damaged on their
return to the Caribbean by the coat-tail storms of that hurricane. Parker now had to contend with Rodney, who wielded
his seniority like a boarding axe to demand priority in all
things. *His* ships were to be repaired first; *his* men were to be
given priority in getting food and medical supplies; *his* strategic demands were to be met and anyone who stood in his way
was a traitor to his country.

Having created his own hurricane of antipathy in Jamaica,
Rodney sailed to Barbados, where he received some wonderful
news among the carnage. The British, it seemed, had declared
war on the Dutch, and the politicians had suggested an early
strike against St Eustatius. Rodney now had an enormous
fleet under his command and 3,000 soldiers under General
Vaughan that he could summon to sing his song. In almost
delirious glee, Rodney fell on St Eustatius.

His motivation was a mixture of avarice and hatred. Rodney,
whose general intolerance was aggravated by raging gout and
prostatitis, hated a lot of people, but he reserved a special
loathing for the Dutch of St Eustatius. He hated them for
trading with the Americans, and he particularly hated them for
helping the French in the aftermath of the battle of Martinique
in 1780 while denying his own fleet critical supplies. The island
was, in his own colourful words, a 'receptacle for the outcast of
every nation' and was full of 'men who will make no scruple to
propagate every falsehood their debased minds can invent'.[10]
His attack on St Eustatius would be a punishment mission as
much as it would be a strategic move. *Everyone* in St Eustatius

* Only slightly smaller than the 8 metre storm surge created by Hurricane Katrina
in 2005 which devastated the Gulf Coast of America.

was in his sights, regardless of their nationality. Even British merchants were fair game. Such men, he argued,

> [have] meanly condescended to become Dutch burghers (and as such they shall be treated) ... Thank God that Providence has ordained General Vaughan and myself to be the instrument of a great, powerful, but injured nation to scourge them for their perfidy, and scourged they shall be.[11]

This conception of the attack as punishment was even immortalized in commemorative coins after the event. In the collections of the National Maritime Museum in Greenwich, one coin survives which applauds the 'Glorious Memory' of how Rodney 'Punished the Dutch at St Eustatia' [*see fig. 16*].[12]

This is what he did.

* * *

Rodney made his preparations exhaustively and in utter secrecy.[13] On 3 February 1781 Rodney arrived with fourteen ships of the line, 'as sudden as a clap of thunder'. The island was defenceless. In the words of one contemporary, 'Its inhabitants were a mixed body of all nations and climates; not reduced to any species of military duty or military discipline.' It had 'no fortifications for its defence; no garrison, no martial spirit, nor military regulations'.[14] To make matters worse, it had also been savaged by the hurricane, with 4,000 reported deaths. Rodney secured the island's surrender, all of the ships in her harbour, six warships and 150 merchantmen. A large convoy was then taken by surprise, and after a brief scuffle every ship was taken. The capture was so easy that the only evidence of conflict was 'part of a blue-sleeved arm with white trim ... seen floating in the sea',[15] and the captain of one of the British ships involved in the fight was left raging at the mortally wounded Dutch admiral for needlessly sacrificing his life and those of his men.[16] Back ashore, Rodney set about his work with conviction, all attempts to hide in sheep's clothing abandoned.

He and his men ignored centuries of convention regarding the sanctity of private property in wartime. Put simply, Rodney seized everything that was owned by anyone. He conducted 'a general confiscation of all the property found upon the island, public and private, Dutch and British; without discrimination, without regard to friend or foe ... the wealth of the opulent, the goods of the merchant, the utensils of the artisan, the necessaries of the poor'.[17] British merchants caught up in the plunder presented a petition to Rodney, who told them that he had a special place for their petition in his quarter-gallery – i.e. his loo.[18] We now understand quite how big a deal this was: modern archaeological excavation of St Eustatius in this period has revealed a wealth of British manufactured goods on the island.[19] Rodney even kept the Dutch flag flying over the town and fort to lure in ignorant merchants – a brazen deception which worked beautifully. In the subsequent days the British ensnared more than fifty American merchant ships and captured more than 2,000 American sailors. Thus, wrote one Dutchman, 'A sentence of general beggary [was] pronounced in one moment upon a whole people.'[20]

In an act of pointless malevolence the British also destroyed the Statian governmental archives: past and current lawsuits, notarial deeds, wills, probate inventories, manumission, prenuptial agreements, contracts, muster rolls, ships' manifests – everything. It was all simply wiped out. The aspect of Rodney's behaviour that has survived the centuries with most colour and controversy, however, is his treatment of the St Eustatius Jews. One hundred and one adult males were herded together and some were forcibly strip-searched in the belief that they were concealing money. Thirty were immediately set aside for deportation to St Christopher's, a nearby British island. Forced to leave behind their wives and children, they were marched to the shoreline and embarked on British boats under the guns of British sailors. They were taken aboard the British warship *Shrewsbury*, and their names still survive in her musterbook.[21] Those not selected for immediate deportation were imprisoned and their belongings auctioned. The question

'Great Britain lauds the enormities of Rodney and Vaughan in the most fulsome terms to
conceal their iniquity. I, for my part, filled with horror at their cruel behaviour, call Rodney
Nero and Vaughan Caligula.'

of anti-Semitism as motivation is unresolved, but there is no
evidence of anti-Semitism in Rodney's previous conduct and
there is some suggestion that this was all carried out without
his knowledge.[22]

Nonetheless, the entire operation was led by an admiral
and facilitated by the Royal Navy: the rape of St Eustatius
was a manifestation of British sea power. That fact is made
perfectly clear by a contemporary cartoon. Here, on a beach
lined by Dutch-style houses, are tons of trade goods, heaped
and stacked. Boats are crammed with people being taken
away, mournfully waving back to shore, where others reach
out to them in desperation. All this happens in the direct and
ominous shadow of a British warship.

Rodney acted throughout as supreme commander, admiral,

judge, jury, prize agent, accountant and auctioneer. As he filled his pockets, his critics filled envelopes with letters of condemnation. British Caribbean merchants, some of whom were currently under French control, were terrified that Rodney had set an appalling precedent. Rodney's most senior subordinate, Rear-Admiral Samuel Hood, who had not sailed with Rodney to St Eustatius, pondered his behaviour from afar and came to the conclusion that 'They will find it very difficult to convince the world that they have not proved themselves wickedly rapacious.'[23] Charles Goore, a prosperous Liverpudlian merchant, believed that the Dutch war 'has made some persons run mad'.[24] Most eloquent and far-sighted of all was the politician Edmund Burke, who instinctively knew that with great maritime power came great moral responsibility and a need to uphold universal values of jurisprudence, reason and justice.[25] This was one of the first times that a link between British maritime power and moral responsibility had been identified – a key feature by which the British empire would, in time, be judged.

* * *

Issues of anti-Semitism and morality aside, the British had struck a severe blow against the Dutch and through them against the Americans and French. 'There never was a more important stroke made against any state whatever', claimed an overexcited Rodney to his wife.[26] It was estimated, and by thoughtful and conservative men, that as much as £3 million had been seized, though no one really knew for sure. Samuel Hood simply said 'an amazing amount'.[27]

Back in England, Lady Rodney was soon to discover how sea power, exercised thousands of miles away, could transform the British social scene. 'Your express [letter]', she wrote to her husband,

... arrived on the morning of 13 March. My house has been like a fair from that time till this. Every friend, every acquaintance came. I went to the drawing-room on Thursday following. It was more crowded than on a birthday; and the spirits which every one was in was enlivening to a degree, and the attention and notice I received from their majesties were sufficient to turn my poor brain.[28]

The guns in the Tower of London were fired, no doubt deafening the captive Henry Laurens, and government stocks rose by one-and-a-half per cent.

John Adams was in Amsterdam when the news arrived. 'You have no idea, Sir,' he wrote to his friend Robert Livingstone, then American Secretary for Foreign Affairs, 'no man who was not upon the spot can have any idea, of the gloom and terror that was spread by this event.'[29]

Unfortunately for the Dutch, however, the loss of St Eustatius was only the start of their troubles. Back in European waters the British had raised more ships and more men to fight the Dutch, which weakened their ability to act in other theatres but allowed them to act decisively in the North Sea. They blockaded the Dutch coast, using their cruisers to prevent the Dutch from trading with the Spanish and French, and within only a few weeks they had captured 200 Dutch merchantmen with cargo estimated at 15 million guilders.[30] Meanwhile 300 more Dutch merchantmen were incarcerated in foreign ports by British warships. The most telling fact of all is that the number of Dutch ships passing into the Baltic via the Øresund at Copenhagen fell from 2,051 in 1780 to just nine in 1781.[31] That summer, intelligence reported that the harbour of Amsterdam, one of the pre-eminent hubs of global trade in this period, 'was like a desert'.[32]

*　*　*

The British rather easily absorbed this new war, therefore. The Dutch had no naval strength of any significance in foreign waters, and British strength in home waters had been maintained since the start of the war, for fear of invasion. The problem for the British remained their territories abroad: India, America, Canada, the Caribbean, Gibraltar and

Minorca. With limited resources some things would have to be prioritized. The obvious two contenders were the Caribbean, the economic engine of the British empire and war effort, and America, where the battle that could win this war might actually be fought. The answer settled upon by British politicians, however, was neither one nor the other.

28

BRITISH OBSESSION

There had been great celebrations in London when news of Rodney's 1779 relief of Gibraltar and victory over the Spanish at the Moonlight Battle reached British shores, but there had also been a national sigh of relief. At last – *at last* – the navy was doing what it was supposed to do. Rodney's isolated success in Spain was thus reason for renewed confidence and hope in the war in general. There was also, however, an important symbolic narrative in the relief of Gibraltar that appealed to the British because it seemed to reflect the war in microcosm and their favoured interpretation of it: threatened from all sides, Gibraltar, like Britain, was a lonely and isolated rock holding out against hordes of enemies. The Americans saw themselves as fighting for liberty against tyranny, but the British saw it as a defensive war, fought against the odds for the maintenance of the status quo. The British considered themselves under attack and could point to the French threats against Rhode Island, New York, St Lucia and Savannah, the French captures of Guadeloupe and Grenada, the Spanish threats against Jamaica and Pensacola, the Spanish captures on the Mississippi and at Mobile, and the combined Bourbon invasion threat which had so troubled British shores in both 1778 and 1779. Gibraltar, however, was different because Gibraltar had endured, because there the fear of invasion was sustained. The *story* of Gibraltar's resistance was therefore of immense political value.

Its strategic value, however, also rose in this specific period. The recent string of Spanish victories in the Floridas and Solano's threat hovering over Jamaica meant that, from mid-1780, Gibraltar rose in importance as a bargaining chip. If, as seemed likely, Jamaica, the cornerstone of the British empire, was to be lost to the Spanish, the British would stand a very good chance of getting it back at the negotiating table if they could bargain it for Gibraltar.

This, then, is the background to Gibraltar's surprisingly elevated position in British strategic thinking in the new year of 1781, and it led to a second major relief operation, led this time by Vice-Admiral George Darby. First, however, we must consider the situation as it then stood in Gibraltar, for the story of Gibraltar between the reliefs of Rodney and Darby is interesting, important and insufficiently known.

*   *   *

The practical value of Rodney's 1779 relief, as measured by its impact on the Gibraltar garrison rather than on the British newspaper-reading public, is easy to overstate. Rodney certainly brought ammunition, powder and salt provisions, but otherwise the relief was not what had been hoped for. Many of the supplies were inedible, the flour rotten, the peas maggoty, the meat stinking; many of the 'fresh' men were sick after the long voyage; and none of the colliers, so desperately needed, had been ready in time to make the journey.[1] This all meant that, in the words of one depressed soldier, 'The exigencies of the garrison since Admiral Rodney's departure had been as severe, if not more so, than before.'[2]

The situation in Gibraltar from 1780 therefore continued in much the same way as it had prior to Rodney's relief, which had been coloured by the inability of the Spanish squadron in Algeciras to impose an effective blockade of the Rock. Yet again it is striking how far distant were the realities of sea power and the expectations attached to it: in reality Barceló's squadron was a sorry jumble of ships, and yet rumours that the Spanish had actually taken Gibraltar reached America.[3]

Barceló had not come remotely close to taking the Rock, but his men had become increasingly ingenious. On one occasion, inspired by visible British naval weakness, they launched a fireboat attack. Shortly after two British warships had left their berths at the Mole, the location of the crucial powder store, the Spanish unleashed a tide of fireships. First one, then two and then nine shadowy masses appeared and then were ignited. The flames swiftly took and roared into life, illuminating the waters around them with bright orange tongues that caused shadows to dance all over the great Rock itself. They appeared like 'moving mountains of fire'[4] and threw out such heat that the pitch between the hull planks of the British warship *Panther*, lying at anchor nearby, melted.

Barceló's trap was well laid; he waited out in the bay with his warships to swoop on any British ship that might try to flee for safety.[5] His plan was foiled, however. British sailors swarmed to their boats and, 'notwithstanding the fierceness of the flames,'[6] threw grappling hooks and pulled the fireships off their path. It was a feat of exceptional courage. One witness wrote:

> The navy on this occasion can not be too highly recommended for their courage, conduct and alertness. Their intrepidity overcame every obstacle; and though three of the ships were linked with chains and strong cables, and every precaution was taken to render them successful, yet, with uncommon resolution and activity, the British seamen separated the vessels, and towed them ashore with no other injury to themselves than a few burns and bruises.[7]

The smouldering Spanish ships were then cut to pieces and used as fuel.[8]

The fireship attack really caused the British a fright. One witness noted how 'Everything here has been calculated upon a supposition we should always have a superiority at sea',[9] and they were forced to think anew. To protect the Mole they built a boom of masts joined by cables and held in position by anchors, and they moved the powder store to a safer location.[10]

The Spanish also built gunboats and bomb-vessels in this period that were used to bombard British positions and civilian houses. This brought a new kind of terror to the Rock: the fear of the unexpected cannon-strike. The boats would creep into range at night and then fire wildly, bringing down houses, killing and maiming. The Spanish also tightened the blockade. They did this in two different ways. First, they bought the friendship of the sultan of Morocco. An enormous bribe gave them access to his three major ports and the sultan expelled all British citizens.[11] A critical source of both supplies and intelligence was thus denied to the British. Second, they used a network of gunboats, oared vessels and warships to tighten up access to and from the bay:

> About ten of their armed cruizers are constantly under Cabritta, some at Tarifa, about eight near Tangier, three or four at Tetuan, some at Ceuta and several at the Gut's mouth … the gun-boats and gallies form a chain every night from Cabritta to Europa point, and in the morning return to their anchorage.[12]

This was quite a show of force compared with the Spanish 'blockade' at the start of the war, but these new ships were a shambles. 'From the patched and disorderly appearance of their sails and rigging, it was conjectured that they were fitted up in haste', wrote one unimpressed witness with a sailor's eye. Another noted how they were 'ill-finished'.[13]

Goods continued to leak into Gibraltar, therefore, just as they had prior to Rodney's relief. Merchantmen were still willing to run the blockade because they were lured by the attraction of the exceptionally high prices that Gibraltar offered. Bold merchants would nip silently past the Spanish xebecs and gunboats in the darkest of nights, hugging the great Rock – all well and good unless you were transporting a cargo of cockerels.[14] Morocco was neatly replaced as a source of supplies by Minorca. It took a while for the route to be set up and for merchants to be attracted to it, but once established it began to work very well indeed. By 9 February 1781 one diarist could write: 'Our supplies from the eastward were now pretty regular, and the boats and vessels in general very successful in their voyages.'[15]

Fishermen, sailors, soldiers, civilians and children continued to fish the bountiful bay from the Rock itself or from small boats that could dart to safety if threatened. Occasionally a skilled and bold naval crew would nip out and capture a lone merchantman, sometimes right under the noses of the Spanish. On one occasion two British warships did exactly that, working together, leaving Barceló 'baffled and disappointed'.[16] As before, the gulf in seamanship between the British and the Spanish was unmistakable.

The British in Gibraltar thus endured, but life was certainly miserable and the Gibraltarians began to suffer like sailors, as if they had been at sea for six months without fresh provisions. Scurvy became a major problem. Old fractures rebroke and old wounds reopened – classic symptoms of advanced scurvy. Smallpox ravaged the population, being particularly severe on children, who died in ghastly numbers. Nonetheless, the soldiers and sailors, as ever, had been prioritized over the civilians and the majority remained healthy.[17] They seem to have spent much of their time focused on gunnery innovation and research into ballistics. One soldier described with excitement how

> Experiments of every contrivance are now in agitation. Art and ingenuity which have been long employed for the preservation and destruction of mankind, are now studying their annihilation. Quadrants, Spirit-levels, and instruments of various forms and machinery, adorn the batteries for the more exact and certain method of killing. Everyone seems anxious to find out the safest, quickest, and surest method of despatch, in the elevation and depression of the ordnance.[18]

The Spanish were as far from taking Gibraltar as they had ever been. Nonetheless, the relief of Gibraltar dominated strategic thought back in London and, like an oarsman's blister, it began to have a disproportionate effect on the course of the war. Another fleet would be sent to the relief of Gibraltar, but that would only happen at the expense of something else – something that could be far, far more important to the future of the war. And that something was the containment of French sea power.

*   *   *

In the new year of 1781 the combined French naval force in European waters was imposing. No fewer than forty-seven ships of the line bobbed in Atlantic ports, the majority in Brest where, by their presence alone, they would, in the words of John Adams, 'keep the English in awe'.[19] With so much naval strength located in a single location so close to British shores, it seemed rash to send a relief to Gibraltar simply because of the threat that the French posed. From an aggressive standpoint it was also an excellent opportunity for the British to force a decisive encounter or to keep their enemy, hitherto maddeningly elusive, bottled up. A decisive encounter was certainly on the cards because the French were utterly committed to making some significant use of this fleet. They knew that their time was running out. In the words of the canny Vergennes, 'it is a war of hard cash, and if we drag it out the last shilling may not be ours'.[20] This growing sense of crisis was felt in America. Both Washington and Adams assumed that, unless the French made a decisive intervention in the coming season, the war would be decided in a conference in Europe.

But what would they do with their sea power? There were three major theatres in play. Rochambeau was well positioned in Newport, but his fleet and army were inadequate and needed reinforcement; the main Spanish fleet at Havana was pointed at Jamaica and would benefit from some help; and in spite of their losses at the start of the war, the Indian Ocean still presented some good opportunities for French imperial aggrandizement.

Alert to these possibilities, Vergennes embraced them all.

*   *   *

On 22 March an enormous French armada consisting of three separate fleets left Brest after several days of light easterly winds: one under the comte de Grasse bound for the Caribbean, another under the bailli de Suffren bound for India – both were skilled and lifelong sailors with aggressive reputations – and a third bound for Boston.[21] It was obvious weather for the French to leave harbour and perfect for maintaining a close blockade, but the British Channel Fleet was nowhere to be seen. The relief of Gibraltar had been prioritized over the containment of the French fleet, and Darby was then off the coast of Ireland, waiting to pick up a Gibraltar-bound convoy of victualling ships.

Finally, after weeks of delay caused by the enormous logistical difficulties of organizing such a maritime relief at the height of a war when shipping had to be drawn from one distant theatre to be used in another, Darby headed south to Gibraltar and met nothing more than three Spanish frigates on his journey. The Spanish fleet in Cádiz, which outnumbered Darby by five ships of the line, made no move to confront the British. This was a disappointment in London, where the king was hopping around in anticipation of a repeat of the Moonlight Battle: 'I know the justice of our cause; I know the excellence of our fleet; therefore have reason to expect success.'[22]

Now safely beyond Cádiz, Darby's entry into Gibraltar was guaranteed because Barceló's squadron was no match for such force. The fleet of Spanish gunboats, now some eighteen strong, rowed around firing frantically and the Spanish land batteries opened up on the British ships, but their sting was easily drawn, the British convoy 'being perfectly well covered by the ships and frigates'.[23] The Spanish vented their frustration by unleashing a staggering barrage onto the Rock, setting the town on fire with red-hot shot, 'a truly grand and awful spectacle of war'. At the height of this bombardment it was estimated that the Spanish were firing 3,000 shot per day, and those who witnessed it believed it to be the heaviest cannonade in history.[24] One witness offered a description:

The varied repercussion from the Rock, of exploding shells, and the reiterated sound of cannon and mortars, were such as stunned the air, whilst the eye traced with pain the ravaging effect, and gazed with anguish on the continual flash of ordnance, spreading desolation in every direction.[25]

Faced with such destruction, Darby's squadron kept moving at all times, tacking backwards and forwards incessantly. It must have been exhausting for the crews, but it was very effective and kept the British ships entirely unharmed.[26] Order within the town, meanwhile, disintegrated. 'Such a scene of drunkenness, debauchery and destruction was hardly ever seen before', wrote one witness.[27] 'Havock still continues!' wrote another. He went on:

Several of the inhabitants in endeavoring to save part of their property in town, have lost their lives. A corporal had his hand shot off as he was calling from a window to a man in the street. A soldier was found so miserably torn by a shell that he could not be known, only by part of his dress. A shot killed two soldiers this morning, one of whom was brushing his shoes for guard ... a Genoese youth, endowed with every amiable qualification, on the point of nuptial celebration, was unfortunately killed.[28]

Gibraltar was relieved again, therefore, though this time some of its inhabitants paid a terrible price for that relief. Many had failed to appreciate that the arrival of the British fleet would, by goading a Spanish response, bring their own destruction rather than their salvation.

* * *

Those who mourned the deaths of their husbands, wives, lovers and children in Gibraltar had no idea of the imperial cost that had yet to be paid for their relief. While they grieved, far out in the Atlantic the huge, combined, unopposed French fleet set off to change the war.

29

FRENCH ESCAPES

Once clear of Brest and deep in the Atlantic, the French armada split into its three distinct fleets: one of six ships of the line under Suffren bound for India via the Cape of Good Hope; another of twenty ships of the line under de Grasse bound for the Caribbean; and a third bound for Boston under escort of a 90-gun ship. If their unchecked escape from Brest was not bad enough, in two subsequent operational failures both de Grasse and Suffren were allowed to escape all over again.

*   *   *

The first French escape happened on the way to Good Hope. The British were all too aware of the importance of the Cape, which for several reasons was a cornerstone of British imperial security in the east. First, as a Dutch possession, it was the warehouse that kept the French Indian Ocean squadron operational, just as St Eustatius had been the warehouse that had kept the French Caribbean squadron operational. If the French were denied access to Good Hope, they would be unable to prosecute any campaign of any strength or duration from their island base at Île de France (Mauritius), a barren island barely able to sustain itself in peacetime, let alone in war with thousands of hungry and thirsty French soldiers and sailors bobbing around in French battle fleets. If the British could secure the Cape, therefore, they could secure India.

To secure Cape Town was also to secure the British island of St Helena. That hideous lump of Atlantic rock is famous as Napoleon's last prison, but its role in British naval and imperial strategy is not so well known. All of the high-value convoys coming from the east required protection for their return to home waters. They therefore needed a safe, remote location where they could meet their naval escort. They also needed a base where they could rest, repair, water and revictual after several gruelling months at sea. One thousand miles off what is now known as Namibia's Skeleton Coast, St Helena provided the perfect answer. It became, in the words of the chairman of the East India Company, 'the key to and from the East Indies',[1] and the only location from where it was possible to launch an attack on St Helena was Cape Town.

The attractiveness of Cape Town, moreover, was that it was clearly another soft target. The British and French were now, respectively, five and three years into the war and had armed forces at their fingertips in a way that the Dutch did not. Cape Town had more defences than the pathetic St Eustatius but none that could prevent a British or French army from landing. A British squadron of two ships of the line and three 50-gunners under Commodore George Johnstone was thus sent to Good Hope and became locked in a race with Suffren. The winner would be the man who could anchor his fleet in a strong defensive formation in Table Bay, secure the Dutch surrender and get any spare guns ashore to strengthen the weak Dutch defences.

Suffren, by any account, was unpleasant and difficult. Grossly fat and horribly sweaty, he was often badly dressed. One witness described him appearing in 'a coarse linen shirt entirely wet' worn over 'unbuttoned breeches, broken shoes, dirty stockings'. Renowned for being thoughtless and indiscreet, he was 'a man with whom one could not live, difficult to command, not prone to obedience, very prone to criticize', and he was a militant Provençal. He was, nonetheless, 'admired and appreciated by all' and had as much experience of warfare as any French naval officer.[2] He had witnessed the value of impetuous and relentlessly violent attacks at the British naval victories at Finisterre in 1747 and Lagos in 1759, and had also been present at the French tactical victory at Minorca in 1756, in which the French had outmanoeuvred the British to protect their army ashore. Suffren, therefore, knew the value of both dash and patience.

Command of the British squadron was given to Commodore George Johnstone, a man with barely any naval experience at all but with strong political connections. His appointment represents a significant shift of power in the British government away from Sandwich, who hitherto had done his best to match naval appointments with appropriate skill and experience, even if he had been given a very shallow pool from which to draw talent. Johnstone, however, was an accident waiting to happen.

The British won the first leg of the race, from European waters to the safety of the neutral Portuguese Cape Verde islands, where it was traditional for ships to water and victual on the way south. The claustrophobia of sea routine was broken at Porto Praya (now Praia on the island of Santiago), where the fleet anchored, and was replaced by the magical promise of a tropical island. The decks were encumbered with barrels and livestock and many of the men went ashore. The lure of revelry was further increased by the presence of several East Indiamen, all of which carried civilian – and female – passengers. Captain Thomas Pasley of the 50-gun *Jupiter*, one of the finest British naval diarists of the period, knew himself to have a weakness for the promise of female company: 'I delight to see a pretty face clothed in smiles', he wrote in anticipation of a dinner that night.[3] The war seemed thousands of miles away. Far enough south and close enough to Africa to appear entirely alien to any northern European, even today the Cape Verde islands seem utterly disconnected from the world around them. An experienced naval officer who had spent a life at sea in such places might not have been so easily distracted as the green Commodore Johnstone.

Shortly after his arrival at Porto Praya Johnstone heard interesting and troubling news. 'By the never-failing argument, Bribery', he had procured a number of letters that had recently been left at Porto Praya by none other than the *Serapis*, the British ship captured by John Paul Jones which had since become a French privateer. These letters told of 'Six Sail of French Ships of the Line close at our heel, to call at this very Bay for Water and Refreshments'.[4] It was said that this force consisted entirely of 74-gunners – far larger than the ships in Johnstone's squadron and even more reason to prepare for attack.

Scouts could have been sent out to survey the well-known approach route to the island; the officers and men could have been summoned back to their ships; the ships themselves could have been anchored in line, perhaps chained together, with anchors on their springs to allow for manoeuvrability. There was plenty of water in the bay for Johnstone to anchor his vulnerable ships inshore of, and thus protected by, his fleet.[5] But nothing – nothing at all – was done. In one of the most perplexing naval command decisions of the entire war, it is as if Johnstone had heard the news but dismissed it as untrustworthy or somehow irrelevant. There is some suggestion that he was seriously unwell.*

That night the British officers held a great party, in which 'high good humour reigned throughout'. They danced until after midnight and there was every expectation that the revelry would continue the next night. The following morning, 16 April, a ship on the edge of the British fleet made the signal for a sail, which would have made men stop their tasks and peer to the horizon. Then, with increasing dread, they would have seen the same ship make the same signal ten more times, for ten more ships. A pack of wolves had arrived at the edge of the forest. Johnstone, then in a rowing boat making his way through the anchored fleet, espied an East Indiaman that was slow on the uptake, her crew still cleaning the ship's sides

---

* Perhaps the fact that they were in a neutral port was sufficient reassurance, though it seems unlikely – the British themselves had merrily trodden all over Portuguese neutrality at the battle of Lagos in 1759, fought during the previous war, the Seven Years' War (1754–63); and then, as now, there was far too much at stake for such niceties to carry any weight. Unsurprisingly, there were no diplomatic repercussions for what Suffren was about to do. Dull, *French Navy*, 229n.21. Fabel, *Bombast and Broadsides*, 158.

with a water pump. According to one witness – one with a suspiciously good memory – he unleashed a brilliant tirade:

> Good God, Mr. Macpherson! Could I have expected this shameful conduct from you, whom I chose for my elephant in the hour of danger. And placed next myself in the line of battle, to be scratching your sides like a Highlander and pissing with this engine, when my signals for battle have been flying this half hour, and the enemy are actually caught off the point? Do you mean to engage them with this stream? A man ought to be crucified alive who can be guilty of this neglect.[6]

It was immediately clear that the French force was more powerful than the British and that it was advancing with 'Confident Impetuosity'.[7] One thousand five hundred British sailors were still ashore 'watering, fishing and embarking live cattle', while others were simply, in the words of Johnstone himself, 'taking the recreation of the shore'. At least one British officer, Colonel Fullarton, had to swim to his ship.[8]

The British had been caught with their trousers down. In his official report Johnstone admitted, through wonderfully gritted teeth, that the action 'bordered upon a surprise'.[9] The scene was set for a dramatic French victory, the likes of which had never been seen.

Luckily for the British, however, the French were equally unprepared for battle, and they were unprepared in two significant ways. Like the British, they were unprepared for immediate action then and there – we know that the decks of at least one of the ships, the *Annibal*, were encumbered with all sorts of boxes[10] – but they were also unprepared in terms of command and tactical expectation. Suffren was undoubtedly aggressive, but he was also divisive and an unwilling communicator. None of his fellow captains had any idea what their leader expected of them in such a situation. Suffren took his flagship boldly into the thick of the British fleet and attempted to anchor. A tricky manoeuvre even in one's home port, the attempt failed under the British guns and Suffren drifted close to the British flagship, where he was utterly mauled. Just one other ship mimicked his bold charge while the others ranged around the outskirts of the action and picked off easy targets.

At this stage the battle was a French victory but it was precarious. Four British ships, three of them almost defenceless, had been captured, but the French gunnery had been extraordinarily bad and the British as cool and competent as ever. In one delightful exchange Pasley's coxswain 'brought me one of the Enemy's Shot and requested my liberty to return it out of his Gun – so reasonable a request I could not refuse'.[11] The French casualty rate was far higher than the British and several of the French ships were now disabled. The French flagship itself was hampered with a warship in tow. Reduced in complement even before the action, Suffren had few men to spare for prize crews.

The nature of the French 'victory' was also coloured by the strategic situation. The British had lost four ships but had gained intelligence of far greater value. So much trouble had been caused in this war by ignorance of the location and condition of enemy squadrons, but Johnstone now knew exactly where his enemy was *and* its condition. A well-executed counter-strike could have eradicated the French threat to the Cape before they even reached it. But Johnstone did nothing. He held a council of war in which it was agreed that the damage sustained by the British fleet, the rising of the sea and the onset of night made any chase dangerous and worthless – a decision that was considered then, and has been ever since, as spineless.[12] The French escaped. 'What a Glorious opportunity was lost of destroying this Squadron and immortalizing ourselves', wrote a seething Pasley,[13] a loss felt so severely because, in his words, 'The French seem'd Damnably frightened'.[14]

It is often too easy to say that a naval battle was not what it could have been, but in this case the argument holds water. The British had been taken by surprise for sure, but they had savagely beaten the French warships that were bold enough to enter the harbour and they had received paltry damage in return.

All of the French prizes were almost immediately restored to British control. The crew of the fireship *Infernal* overcame their captors and the other prize crews abandoned their prizes. The intrigued and nosy British sailors returned full of juicy stories. Aboard the *Hinchinbrooke* Indiaman,

> The French Rascals had Plunder'd, Rob'd, and used them most inhumanly, more particularly the Ladies who they used with every indignity but the last, and by their conduct they wanted only time to accomplish even that.[15]

One French officer had lined the ladies up on the quarterdeck as an audience for his personal demonstration of a galloping hornpipe, 'which they confess he performed to a Miracle' before, in true pirate style, 'he pulled out a Pistol, presented it to Miss Johnstone's Breast with the most horrid Threats if they resisted, and Rob'd them of every thing they posessed'. This tale was too much for Pasley: 'I always detested a Frenchman, but now if possible more than ever. There were four ladies, one very Pritty.'[16]

One particularly interesting, though fleeting, observation of a marked difference between British and French sea power was made during this campaign – a difference that would actually go on to have a major impact on the outcome of the war.

In the aftermath of the battle a Swedish boy was captured who had recently spent 'five or six' weeks on board one of the French warships, the *Artésien*. Upon his arrival aboard Pasley's *Jupiter*, the boy was stunned by the cleanliness of the British ship. Pasley had his cleanliness regime expertly and rigorously maintained. His crew aired their bedding weekly and that of sick sailors daily. An 'air pump' operated constantly to ward off 'foul air' and windsails funnelled more fresh air down the hatches to boost circulation at night. Pasley toured the ship both above and below water every day, sometimes twice daily, to inspect for cleanliness.

The French, on the other hand, as reported by the Swedish boy, never once, in the six weeks he was with them, aired their hammocks, washed or cleaned the lower deck. 'Dirty Dogs', exclaimed Pasley, before wondering, 'How can they be healthy, when so crouded?'[17] The answer was that they couldn't. The French had been buckling under the pressure to man their ships ever since an epidemic had struck their Channel fleet in 1779. The men were few and inexperienced, and those who were not sick were weak. With inadequate infrastructure, it was impossible that the French navy could get any stronger without months, perhaps years, of recuperation.

Johnstone stayed in Porto Praya for two full weeks. His inactivity during those weeks was roundly condemned at the time and has been ever since. Pasley was not surprised, however. We know that he suspected the competence of his commander and his fellow captains. 'I have my doubts of some', he wrote, '– others I know to be *luke warm* and void of all enthusiasm in the service.'[18] Johnstone's ire, perhaps in a bid to deflect attention from himself, fell, entirely unreasonably, on Captain Sutton of the *Isis*.[19]

Suffren was also furious with his captains and believed he had missed a major opportunity in a battle that 'should have immortalized me',[20] but now he concentrated on the task in hand. He did all he could to race to the Cape with all his ships. He did not detach the damaged *Annibal* but drafted every carpenter in his command onto her, and in eight days she was 'as completely new masted and rigged as if in Brest'.[21] Other major repairs were conducted at sea in an impressive operation reminiscent of d'Estaing's repair at sea off Rhode Island in 1778.* Running low on water, which he had planned to replenish in Porto Praya, he chose not to replenish in Brazil, the obvious choice given the prevailing north-easterly winds, but rationed what was left and raced for the Cape.[22]

By demonstrating exactly the type of determination that Johnstone lacked, Suffren made it to the Cape first and secured

* See p. 246.

it for France, ending the 'Golden Dreams' of the British.[23] Johnstone abandoned any idea of challenging Suffren at the Cape, though he did capture four Dutch East Indiamen at anchor in Saldanha Bay, this is around 65 miles to the north, in an action that was characterized by exceptional bravery from Johnstone and his sailors, who boarded the Dutch Indiamen even though they had been set on fire. 'Some thing must be done, no matter what – a desperate game requires a desperate hazard', claimed Pasley.[24] There is little in the entire history of the Royal Navy that stands out like this action for blind courage. Receiving fire at point-blank range from an enemy warship was one thing, but boarding one that was on fire and full of gunpowder was quite another. His pyrrhic victory complete, Johnstone skulked back to St Helena,* away from 'this World [where] Poor Old England has not one friend. All hostile around us, no shore that will even yield us Water but at the point of our Guns.'[25]

The occupation of Good Hope was a great victory for the French. The British would now have to fight for their lives in India and feared greatly for their China trade. The poor Dutch, already immobilized in the north and destroyed in the Caribbean, were now gravely wounded in the east. The Cape of Good Hope, once the home of good, strict Dutch Protestants, became known as 'Little Paris' for its rapid conversion to French licentiousness. The statesman Jakob de Mist later complained that the French had

> entirely corrupted the standard of living at the Cape, and extravagance and indulgence in an unbroken round of amusements and diversions have come to be regarded as necessities … It will be the work of years to transform the citizens of Cape Town once again into Netherlanders.[26]

---

* Yet again, Johnstone could have acted differently here and headed to India, where Hughes was soon to need every ship that he could find to fight off Suffren.

Elsewhere the Dutch empire just fell away. All the West India Company's forts in West Africa were taken by the British, with the single exception of Elmina, and in India Sir Edward Hughes captured the strategically critical bases of Negapatam and Trincomalee, the only port in European possession to face the Bay of Bengal and offer safe year-round anchorage.

In August came another nail in the Dutch coffin. They finally snapped under the pressure of the British blockade and sent a huge merchant fleet to sea under the protection of a naval squadron. A British fleet, under the command of the excellent Hyde Parker, spotted the Dutch and attacked in one of the closest, fiercest and yet least-known engagements in naval history, the battle of the Dogger Bank. Parker's fleet was a mixture of relatively small ships described by one British sailor as 'totally unfit for the Line of Battle'; it had been together for only a limited time, 'and during that time but little attention was paid to make them expert in the forming of lines'.[27] The Dutch, by contrast, were fully prepared for battle and turned out very well. 'They appeared in great order; and their hammocks, quarter-cloths, &c., were spread in as nice order as if for show in harbour. Their marines also were well drawn up, and stood with their musquets shouldered, with the regularity and exactness of a review.'[28]

They met the British attack, resisting everything that was thrown at them. Casualties were high on both sides, though slightly higher on the Dutch. No ships were taken on either side but one Dutch ship sank. The difference, however, was that the Dutch fleet never left harbour again during the war because their naval infrastructure was unable to repair their broken ships and replace their dead men, and the Dutch politicians had no naval fight left. Nonetheless, the threat of their navy had severely affected the British war effort: with ships and men needed in the North Sea to confront the Dutch, too few had been available for North American waters.[29]

By the late summer of 1781, Dutch imperial and naval strength had entirely vanished.

* * *

The next French escape happened in the Caribbean. The scale of Rodney's success at St Eustatius created some real problems. He was so caught up in the moment, and his personal success was so tied to the operation's success, that he felt unable to pass its management on to a subordinate. So Rodney stayed in St Eustatius, and he stayed there for no less than three months, throughout the prime of the 1781 Caribbean campaigning season. He personally oversaw the cataloguing and sale of the loot and the gathering of a convoy that was, in his words, 'extremely valuable, more so, I believe, than ever sailed to Great Britain'.[30] Needless to say, the French did not stop to allow Rodney the leisure to complete his financial irregularities at his own pace.

Just like Johnstone in Porto Praya, Rodney knew that a French fleet was due to arrive. Unlike Johnstone, he did not know exactly where it would arrive, but it was a good bet that it would head for Martinique, the main French naval base in the Windward Islands. Rodney appointed his new second-in-command, Samuel Hood, to patrol to windward of Martinique to intercept them. His guess was correct – de Grasse was indeed headed for Martinique.

With no up-to-date intelligence of the French departure date from Brest, Hood lurked off Martinique for five entire weeks with no luck, long enough for his men to start to fall sick from scurvy. He spent much of his time grumbling about Rodney. It is ironic that Hood's letters are so full of bile because he had been chosen by Sandwich on the basis that he was one of the few men that might actually get on with Rodney.[31] But Sandwich seems to have failed to see the relationship from Hood's point of view. Hood was opinionated and, in his eyes, Rodney was incompetent.

That opinion was then confirmed when Rodney ordered Hood to abandon his station and take up a new one to leeward of Martinique. It is a curious move and has traditionally been interpreted to Rodney's detriment: that, with his treasure convoy now ready to sail, he was terrified it would be raided by French cruisers. He therefore wanted Hood at a station to leeward of Martinique, from where he could rush to Rodney's help at short notice. A major and often overlooked factor, however, is that Hood's fleet was desperate for provisions to the point that his men were dying, and one of his ships, the *Russell*, was in danger of sinking. A position to leeward of Martinique would, in theory, allow him to keep watch on the island and also to replenish his ships, one at a time, from St Lucia.[32]

This new position left the door open for de Grasse. Even if Hood was lucky enough to spot him, the prevailing current and wind would prevent him from attacking in a convincing manner. 'I do not feel myself at all pleasant in being to leeward', he wrote to Rodney, '... for would an enemy's fleet attempt to get into Martinique, and the commander of it inclines to avoid battle, nothing but a *skirmish* will probably happen, which in its *consequences* may operate as a defeat to the British squadron.'[33] He continued in a far more unguarded letter to the Deputy Secretary at the Admiralty, George Jackson: 'doubtless there never was a squadron so unmeaningly stationed as the one under my command.'[34] He was soon proven right.

De Grasse had finally taken his fleet to sea after months of frustration in the dockyards caused by poor administration and infrastructure. The men were unhappy, 'screaming like eagles' for pay, and he was forced to sail 'unsupplied with most of the articles absolutely necessary for a long voyage'.[35] Only half of his fleet was coppered, and the poor quality of his men immediately became apparent when several of his ships collided and two caught fire.[36] All this was further proof of the rotten state of French sea power. Nonetheless, on 29 April, at the head of a fleet twenty strong and escorting no fewer than 150 merchantmen, de Grasse rounded the windward point of Martinique. The Frenchman fired a handful of broadsides at Hood, who was both surprised at the size of de Grasse's fleet and immobilized to leeward by strong currents and light winds; his coppered ships were of no advantage against such natural forces. 'Never was more powder and shot thrown away in one day before', wrote Hood.[37]

However, the distant exchange of gunfire was enough to elevate this stand-off to the status of 'battle', and the fact that the French made it safely into Martinique transformed it into a 'victory'. On hearing the news, fellow American diplomat Charles Dumas wrote a wonderful letter to John Adams in which he freely stuck pins into Rodney:

> Je vous fais mon compliment, Monsieur, sur la victoire remportée par Mr. De Grasse près de la Martinique contre Hood. Voilà Rodney bien mortifié. Ce brigand le mérite.[38]
> ['My compliments, Sir, on Mr. Grasse's victory against Hood near Martinique. How Rodney is shamed. That brigand deserves it.']

* * *

This period was a total disaster for the British. In the Caribbean a newly arrived and powerful French fleet was now embedded in a well-protected French naval base. In South Africa, meanwhile, a French squadron had seized the Cape of Good Hope, from where it could threaten India and St Helena. It certainly had not helped that Johnstone had been incompetent at Porto Praya and Rodney preoccupied by treasure at St Eustatius, but all this could be traced back to the uncontested escape from Brest of the combined French fleet, caused by a British strategy that had prioritized the relief of Gibraltar over the containment of the French battle fleet in Brest. Thus the war turned, but there was still one more sting in the tail.

Darby had every available ship with him in Gibraltar, which meant that the Channel was undefended and British trade on the home stretch unprotected. On 25 April another French squadron, which had been operating unchallenged in the entrance of the Channel under the command of Rear-Admiral the comte de la Motte-Picquet, captured Rodney's entire treasure convoy on its return from St Eustatius.

News of the disaster caused a dramatic fall in the London stock market and gloating in America. Ben Franklin immediately wrote to John Adams with the news, reporting gleefully how the British had run away: 'The Men of War that were with them escaped; after making the Signal for every one to shift for himself.'[39] Adams, who had already pointed out the foolishness of attacking St Eustatius, trumpeted once again, this time with his lawyer's hat on:

> But what completes the Jest is, that De la Motte Piquet has carried safe into Brest two and twenty of the Vessels loaded with the spoils of St. Eustatia, which Rodney had sent under Convoy of Commodore Hotham and four Ships of the Line: so that Rodney after having lost his booty is like to have lawsuits to defend and very probably the whole to repay to the Owners. Thus the Cards are once more turned against the Gambler; and the Nation has gained nothing but an addition to their Reputation for Iniquity. This is good Justice.[40]

There was even more good news to come for America and her allies. In August the Spanish landed on Minorca and laid siege to the island, opening up yet another theatre to spread British commitments even further, and an enormously valuable treasure convoy, worth 25 million piastres, arrived safely in Spain from Havana.[41]

Adams subsequently mused on the remarkable fortunes of war. 'You know she is a great Changeling, and frowns upon one, sometimes in half an Hour after having lavished upon him her Smiles and Favours.'[42] The French were back in play in four key theatres: in the Channel with la Motte-Picquet, in India with Suffren, in America with Rochambeau and in the Caribbean with de Grasse. The Spanish were in play in four more: in Minorca with the duc de Crillon, in Gibraltar with Barceló, in Florida with Gálvez and in the Caribbean with Solano.

But could they make it work? Could Suffren work in tandem with Hyder Ali in India? Could Rochambeau work with Washington in America? Could de Grasse work with Gálvez or Solano in the Caribbean? History was against them all. The one thing that the French had demonstrated hitherto was a catastrophic inability to work in the field with anyone else. Timing was also against them. The French navy was falling apart, but so too was Washington's army. 'We have been half of our time without provisions, and are likely to continue so. We have no magazines, nor money to form them. We have lived upon expedients, until we can live no longer', wrote Washington.[43] The Continental Army mutinied in January. Hunger tore everything down.

The British, in contrast, were improving all the time. The new regime and infrastructure that Rodney had imposed on the Caribbean fleet in 1780 and the full mobilization of the Royal Navy that had begun in 1778 were now beginning to make their mark. Rodney had made strategic errors over both St Eustatius and the arrival of de Grasse, but his actual navy was rapidly improving. By the start of 1781 *all* the ships under his command were coppered – an outstanding logistical and industrial achievement.[44]

Back in England the dockyards were working at full tilt to finish the warships ordered in 1778. Thomas Byam Martin, a future admiral, visited Portsmouth at this time:

> Having for the first time planted my foot within a dock-yard, I found myself surrounded by the most busy, delight-ful scenes imaginable. Everything seemed to be in motion, and the clatter of the shipwright's hammers was a music quite in harmony with the notions I had picked up in my voyage across the harbour ... The busy, bustling scene often comes to my recollection like the renewal of a pleasant dream.[45]

Portsmouth, the largest of the Royal Dockyards and the most extensive industrial site in the world, now employed over 800 shipwrights and a workforce of 2,000. Scores of private yards assisted the Royal Dockyards with the massive building and repair programme: this was both a national and a private war effort, its success a tribute to British small business as much as it was to the scale of the national naval infrastructure.[46]

This was a defining moment in the war. Adams, always sniffing the wind, sensed it. 'There must be a Change soon for better or worse', he wrote.[47] He was right, but any gambling man who knew his history and had observed the war would have bet on worse.

30

ALLIED SUCCESS

The 1781 campaign in the Caribbean began with the French working in isolation from their Spanish and American allies. They captured Tobago, St Kitts, Nevis and Montserrat, and St Lucia was only saved by the lucky presence of three British frigates. Then something very interesting and important happened: almost out of the blue, the French began to work effectively with the Spanish. The French first offered, in January, four of their ships of the line to help protect the Spanish treasure convoy, and the ships went on to assist with the ongoing Spanish siege of Pensacola. The fate of the British garrison was sealed as soon as their access to the sea was successfully blocked, and on 9 May Campbell surrendered.[1] Here was an example of sea power well executed to exploit the weakness of an isolated British position in America. Had the French used their navy more effectively earlier in the war, this is exactly what could have happened at Philadelphia, New York and Newport in 1778, and at Savannah in 1779. Unfortunately for the British in 1781, there were still more examples of British forces in America in similar, vulnerable positions to Campbell's at Pensacola. The British were playing a dangerous game.

Benedict Arnold, the hero of Valcour and now turncoat, led one of those forces. In December 1780 he had launched a sizeable amphibious invasion of the Chesapeake Bay.* His arrival was unexpected. Neither Thomas Jefferson, the governor of

---

* Arnold had special boats made for this operation, drawing on his previous experiences of conducting amphibious operations for the Americans. Syrett, 'Methodology', 273.

Virginia, nor General von Steuben, a Prussian soldier in the service of the Continental Army and the ranking army officer, had made any plans to warn of an enemy approach by sea. The Virginia Navy, which by law was required to patrol the Chesapeake, was lying useless.[2]

The British arrival, with a fleet of almost fifty vessels, caused mass panic in and around the Chesapeake.[3] Arnold subsequently torched an important shipyard, several vessels and the state ropewalk at Warwick. Meanwhile, at Osborne's Wharf on the James River a 'very considerable force' of ships, perhaps twenty-one in total, was raised from slumber by the Virginia Navy, to face him down. Arnold offered terms, which were refused; the Americans were determined to defend their mini navy 'to the last extremity'.[4] The British mounted cannon on the riverbank opposite and unleashed an apocalyptic fire that routed the Americans. The British burned or captured all the American ships without the loss of a single British sailor or soldier.[5] In material terms the Virginia State Navy now no longer existed with the exception of a single vessel, the *Liberty*. Its sailors, however, had managed to scramble to safety, and they would go on to play a significant role in the coming campaign.

Since this dramatic victory, however, Arnold's advance had stalled. His presence had raised the blood of the Americans so severely that he had been forced to barricade himself into Portsmouth. Jefferson offered 5,000 guineas for Arnold taken alive.[6] With no significant naval protection he and his men were isolated, and the Americans and French knew it. A squadron was sent from Newport. The British in New York heard what was afoot and Arbuthnot chased. He caught up with the French off Cape Henry and brought them to battle. The fleets were evenly matched with eight of the line, but Arbuthnot had larger ships and more guns. He was, however, skilfully outmanoeuvred by the French commander, Captain Sochet des Touches. A British attack was then beset by confusion over signals, the signal for the line of battle apparently negating Arbuthnot's desire to engage. The solution to this apparent problem was a lesson that needed to be learned. 'I am tired of telling of our misfortunes', wrote one British officer. 'I wish I could obliterate such a day out of my memory.'[7]

Nonetheless, Arbuthnot's guns had a big impact on the packed French ships, not least the *Conquérant*:

> The greatest carnage was on the deck; the boatswains, the captain at arms and seven steersmen were among the dead, and its tiller and the wheel of the helm were carried away; notwithstanding which it held out.[8]

Had all of Arbuthnot's line actually engaged as he had intended, the result may have been different, but by no means is it certain. The French gunners were unquestionably skilled in this battle, and they were well led and controlled by the wily des Touches. French gunnery crippled the British ships so effectively that they were unable to pursue des Touches when he broke off the action.[9] A British officer much admired his foe: 'every captain of a gun in the French service is equal in ordnance abilities to the most experienced gunners in the navy', he wrote.[10] It was an important observation and it would have major consequences.

Nonetheless, the British had done enough to divert des Touches from Arnold, whose force survived.

* * *

Another example of a vulnerable British force in America was led by Cornwallis, who had burst out of Charleston to bring the war to South Carolina and Georgia and had since marched northwards into North Carolina, and then, having failed to control that state, into Virginia. In early August he occupied Yorktown, a small town on a peninsula in the Chesapeake Bay. He had not 'retreated' or 'holed up' but was there *because* of the navy. Germain was keen to secure a major post in Virginia, and Graves had supported the policy because it would give his ships an ice-free anchorage for the winter months – an excellent base from which to police the Chesapeake and the Atlantic coast of the southern colonies.[11]

Cornwallis thought it was a terrible idea but, following his orders, had occupied Yorktown at the narrow entrance of the deep York River. He was not sitting there waiting to be rescued but was waiting for the Royal Navy to come and occupy its new base. He had no immediate concerns about the enemy at all, at least in part thanks to a total breakdown in communication with Clinton. Greene, Lafayette and General Anthony Wayne had been trying, unsuccessfully, to pin Cornwallis down, but now the requirements of the Royal Navy had done it for them. Intelligent observers had had their eye on Cornwallis for some time. A full seven months earlier, John Adams had written with the prescient observation: 'Chesapeake Bay is a fine Trap. Our Allies will help Us catch a grand Flock of Vultures there by and by.'[12]

News of Cornwallis's position, meanwhile, had reached the ears of de Grasse in the Caribbean. From the allied perspective, the lure of catching Cornwallis, and the clear viability of the campaign, was stronger even than the attraction of the capture of Jamaica, the official target of the allies' 1781 campaign. But how to make it happen? Although de Grasse commanded the French fleet, overall command of the allied offensive for 1781 was actually in the hands of the Spanish. De Grasse would have to run any change of plan past them. Surely this was a recipe for disaster: the history of Franco-Spanish co-operation was atrocious and had already poisoned the war on numerous occasions. Here, however, and quite remarkably, things began to work in favour of the allies because the man in overall command of the allied campaign was the brilliant Bernardo de Gálvez, who had masterminded the Spanish conquests in the Mississippi basin and the Floridas. Gálvez, who could have insisted on an attack on Jamaica, instead became determined to move heaven and earth 'not [to] waste the most decisive opportunity in the whole war'.[13]

Gálvez released de Grasse from his West Indies campaign to travel north to America, which was, in turn, made possible by the Spanish agreeing to use their navy to protect French Caribbean possessions in his absence.[14] Not only was this a good idea but it was also well judged. The history of Spanish sea power in this war was one of disappointment, and yet this, with no major enemy battle fleet to face, was well within their capability. The French fleet, well led and well armed, would do the actual fighting. Crucially, the extent of Spanish aid offered also allowed de Grasse to take his *entire* fleet north – an unexpected move that subsequently gave him a critical numerical advantage.

One final hurdle was also overcome through allied co-operation. The operation had to be funded but the French had no money. Gálvez thus ordered his deputy, the excellent Francisco de Saavedra, to take some ships to Havana and secure the money from the expected treasure convoy. Unfortunately the treasure ships had not yet returned, but Saavedra managed to raise the necessary funds entirely through private donation, and he did so in little more than six hours.[15] Spanish warships then transferred those funds to de Grasse's fleet. Without that money the subsequent campaign would never have happened.

De Grasse now headed for the Chesapeake. In a distinct and highly significant change from previous French campaigns in this war, de Grasse took local pilots with him, men who had been rushed from America to the Caribbean by the French frigate *Concorde*.[16] Not only were the French co-operating with the Spanish, therefore, but they were also being far-sighted and professional. Washington, meanwhile, turned his back on the enemy army in New York and marched his soldiers to Virginia through Pennsylvania, a full 450 miles. His rear and flank were constantly exposed to attack. It was an immense gamble, all made on the promise of French sea power, which, on the basis of previous experience in the war, was almost certainly going to fail.

* * *

The British, in London, New York and the Caribbean, knew that something was brewing, though they did not know exactly what. One crucial assumption was made, however, that Rodney would contain any attack launched by de Grasse.[17]

There was every reason to be confident. Rodney was known to be aggressive; Rodney had already won a significant sea battle in the war; Rodney knew the Caribbean as well as anyone; and Rodney had sufficient ships to head off a French threat. But these arguments themselves rested on two further crucial assumptions: that Rodney would remain in command of his fleet and that his fleet would remain together.

Both of these assumptions were misplaced. Rodney threw the war off its axis by deciding to go home, probably to defend himself against the howling criticism over his conduct at St Eustatius. He was also ill. Not only did Rodney go home but he also took with him six precious ships. He sent Hood with the remains of the Caribbean fleet to New York, where overall command of the British fleet transferred to the useless Graves, who had now taken over from Arbuthnot but who outranked Hood. In one fell swoop, therefore, the situation was changed dramatically: the British had fewer ships than the French; their fleet was not a single entity but consisted of the North American fleet and the Caribbean fleet, each with its own distinct command doctrine; and overall command was in the hands of an inexperienced admiral who had never been destined for a significant sea-going command. Graves, in fact, was so suspect in his abilities that he had been sent to New York because it had become something of a naval backwater, and he was currently waiting to be replaced by Rear-Admiral Robert Digby, an officer junior to him in rank.

The British did nothing to improve their chances in America because they were paralysed by the threat posed by enemy fleets. Clinton was so terrified of leaving New York unprotected in case the French suddenly appeared off Long Island that he did nothing to stop Washington's bedraggled army from marching to Virginia. In Britain, meanwhile, the Channel Fleet was pinned down by two separate threats. The proximity of the Dutch navy meant that only three ships were sent to New York when far more were needed, and they also now faced a Bourbon naval threat in the Channel that was every bit as serious as that of 1778 and 1779.[18] The allies now had a fleet forty-nine strong near the Channel, more than double the strength of the British. When a French fleet took to sea from Brest in June, the quietly competent Vice-Admiral George Darby, now in command of the Channel fleet, had no choice but to barricade himself into Torbay. Luckily for him, the allied Channel campaign never came to much, and the fleet returned to Brest as sickly as it had been in 1779, but the operation had only ever been intended as a diversion and in that it was extremely effective: as long as there were large numbers of French ships in the Channel, no British ships would be sent from the Channel to the Caribbean or America. In creating that diversion, moreover, the allies had enjoyed total command of the western approaches to the British Isles for ten entire days and that had its own significant value.[19] Politicians, merchants and the public were utterly horrified. Pressure on the North government grew.

The result of all this was that the North American fleet, and Cornwallis, were left to fend for themselves, though there was still every chance that the French plans would fall apart through poor planning and execution, an entirely understandable inability to co-ordinate such an extraordinarily complex operation with the Americans during such a period of almost non-existent communication, or plain bad luck. There were three main players and the success of each was gravely threatened: Washington had to march to Virginia without his soldiers dying from starvation or exposure or deserting; de Grasse had to get his fleet in one piece from the Caribbean to the Chesapeake, avoiding the autumnal hurricanes which had already ruined so many naval operations during the war; and the French squadron under Rear-Admiral comte Barras de Saint-Laurent at Newport had to make its way to the Chesapeake with an all-important cargo of soldiers, provisions and Washington's entire siege train without being caught by the British fleet at New York. Finally, the allies had to hope that the British squadron under Hood would not head straight for the Chesapeake to secure Cornwallis before they arrived.

Surprisingly – amazingly – all of these things happened.

* * *

On 25 August Hood nosed into the Chesapeake, found it empty of French ships and continued north to New York. Five days later de Grasse arrived. On 31 August Cornwallis wrote a panicky letter to Clinton that reveals his complete surprise at the arrival of the French fleet.[20] He was not the only one to be surprised. Soon after the French arrived, a 'principal citizen of Virginia' rowed out to the French fleet, mistaking them for the British, to ask where Lord Rodney was. He was taken prisoner.[21] This surprise was partly the result of ignorance of what a French fleet looked like, but it was also the result of de Grasse's care – he had captured anything that came within a few miles of the French fleet on their voyage north.* He had then arrived safely and in good order and had made good use of the Chesapeake pilots he had brought with him. 'Now head banged against head in York and Gloucester', wrote one witness.[22]

News flew up the Chesapeake to Washington, marching south. He had been desperate to harness French sea power in an effective way from the very start of the war. During the preceding few weeks he had been twisted by fretfulness over de Grasse's intentions, location and fate. He begged for news, any news: 'If you get anything new from any quarter send it, I pray you, *on the spur of speed*, for I am almost all impatience and anxiety', he wrote to Lafayette.[23] The wonderful and unexpected news that de Grasse had actually arrived in the Chesapeake with twenty-eight ships of the line, four frigates and 3,500 troops sent him delirious and transformed that serious, dour man – albeit in a wonderfully eighteenth-century way: he 'waved his hat with demonstrations of joy'.[24] Claims that he actually hugged Rochambeau must be nonsense, but

---

* Including the packet *Queen Charlotte*, which was carrying home Colonel Lord Rawdon, one of the leading British commanders in the war who had repeatedly distinguished himself from Bunker Hill onwards. Grainger, *Battle of Yorktown*, 68; Shea, *French Fleet*, 152.

later descriptions of how he acted like a child whose every wish had been granted are far more convincing.

The trap now closed around Cornwallis. To save hundreds of miles of marching and an enormous amount of time, those American sailors from the Virginia Navy who had survived Arnold's onslaught at Osborne's Wharf helped French sailors to transport Rochambeau's and Washington's armies down the Chesapeake Bay in a massive convoy of ships and boats.[25] The Virginia State Navy not only provided sailors but also pilots, lookout boats and provisions. This voyage cut Washington's marching distance in half. It was a massive logistical challenge and large numbers of both French and American troops spent as many as fourteen days on the water, roughly the same amount of time that it took to sail from the Caribbean to the Chesapeake or from Plymouth to Cádiz. The soldiers either embarked at Head of Elk* in small boats, or marched a little further on to Annapolis, where larger ships could dock. They then made their way down the Chesapeake. One soldier was proud of this 'mosquito fleet' that made a 'grand appearance',[26] but the reality was far tougher than this suggests. The journey for most was horrific, for the Chesapeake is no calm inland lake but a wild stretch of water beset with unpredictable sand-banks and weather patterns, and it demands the highest levels of seamanship to navigate with confidence and safety. One soldier said 'the boats were vile' and noted how 'two or three of them foundered, and we have seven or eight men drowned'.[27] Another described the journey as an 'arduous and very hazardous undertaking' in which 'a number of boats were dismasted, sails torn to pieces and the whole in the utmost distress'.[28]

Once the Chesapeake had been negotiated, these men then had to get past the British at Yorktown. It is often assumed that Cornwallis was helpless, entirely reliant upon the navy for his rescue, but he was not: in fact he had at his disposal no

---

* Exactly where the British had disembarked for the Philadelphia campaign in 1777.

fewer than sixty-eight ships including the 44-gun *Charon*, the 32-gun *Guadeloupe*, the 24-gun *Fowey*, and seven sloops and brigs ranging from ten to sixteen guns. Added to these were thirty-two troop transports, victuallers, a shoal of small boats and about 1,000 sailors.[29] Not only might Cornwallis have whisked part, if not all, of his army to safety up the York River, which the British controlled as far as West Point some eighteen miles away, but he could also have posed a significant obstacle and threat to the exhausted crews on the overloaded boats that were ferrying American troops down the Chesapeake to Archer's Hope on the St James, a passage that took them very close to his position at Yorktown.[30] Cornwallis, however, had no eyes for his ships. He had landed all his ships' guns to arm his defences and had commandeered all their sails to make tents for the sick and wounded. Cornwallis did nothing to break his shackles other than to launch a fireship attack, which failed utterly, at least partly, and surprisingly, because of a lack of naval personnel used in the attack.[31] In a diluted sense, Cornwallis was suffering from the same problem experienced by Burgoyne in 1777. Then, Burgoyne's most senior naval officer had been a midshipman: now, Cornwallis had only a single lowly captain, Thomas Symonds of the *Charon*, upon whom to rely for naval advice. As was the case with Burgoyne, a naval officer equal or superior in rank to Cornwallis and embedded in his army would likely have changed the course of the war.

The result of all this was that the allied soldiers made it downriver quickly and relatively safely, which surprised them – they had fully expected Cornwallis to attack them on their way past the British position.[32] When they reached the mouth of the bay, they rejoiced at the sight of the French fleet. 'This is the most noble and majestic spectacle I ever witnessed, and we viewed it with inexpressible pleasure and the warmest gratitude … towards our great ally', wrote one.[33] Another was awestruck; to him, the French fleet resembled 'a swamp of dry pine trees'.[34] Meanwhile the boats that had brought the French and American troops down the Chesapeake were used to keep supply lines open back up the river.[35] They carried on this crucial business entirely unmolested by the British.

From this moment on, the only opportunity to upset the French plans fell on Graves, who was sailing as fast as he could from New York, but he had no idea of the exact situation. He did not realize that Cornwallis needed to be rescued and was merely hoping to meet, and fight, de Grasse.[36] His was a perception of sea power that was entirely divorced from the broader game that was being played. Barras was also sailing south, from Rhode Island, with extra ships and those crucial supplies for the French and American armies. Graves arrived before Barras, but even so he was massively outnumbered: de Grasse had five more ships of the line and 500 more guns.

An opportunity nonetheless presented itself. De Grasse left his anchorage in poor order with his van separated from his centre and rear. Graves, in 'best possible order, bowsprit to stern',[37] tried to pounce by bringing his entire force down onto the isolated French van, but he failed, and he failed because Hood, in command of the rear division, was confused by Graves's intentions and signals. He believed that Graves's signals to close the line and to engage the enemy more closely were contradictory and chose to do nothing – an odd decision from an otherwise impressive naval officer that confused contemporaries: 'To explain it [the battle] to one who was not there requires a considerable explanation', wrote one;[38] and it rightly still puzzles naval historians.[39]

Those British ships that were engaged were absolutely battered by the French; the boatswain's damage reports are staggering.[40] Five British ships were rendered useless, one of which, the *Terrible*, was abandoned and burned. In de Grasse's fleet only two ships were seriously injured. This point is often forgotten. As at the battle of Cape Henry, when Arbuthnot was hammered to a standstill, so here did the French perform very well indeed. Hood's later assertion that, had the signals not been so confusing, all would have been over in half an hour is nonsense.[41] There is no reason to believe that the French ships that had yet to engage would not have fought as their fellow sailors were already fighting, and the British, already outnumbered and with many ships in a poor state, were in no position to win easily if battle had become general. A contemporary journal from a British sailor leaves one in no doubt that the British were deeply impressed by the French seamanship in the aftermath of the battle: they were ready to go again.[42] De Grasse's men had fought well and his tactics had lured Graves away from the entrance to the Chesapeake to allow Barras to get in. Graves was out-thought and out-fought at the battle of the Chesapeake; he was soundly beaten. The only reason that the British could congratulate themselves was that a British frigate had sneaked behind the French fleet to their anchorage and had cut away all the buoys that marked the location of their anchors.[43]

As eighteenth-century naval battles go, it was hardly a heavyweight slug-fest, but therein lay the magic of sea power in this period. Even minor skirmishes could have the most profound consequences, and this is one of the finest examples of them all. The strategic consequences of the battle meant that this became the most significant battle in all of French, American and British naval history.

With Graves out of action, Barras made it safely to the Chesapeake, bringing the total of French ships of the line there to an insurmountable thirty-five. Graves returned to New York, where he spent a considerable time on necessary repairs to his shattered fleet while he planned another major relief. New York was then a particularly unpleasant place to be. With disaster so tangible, 'the spirit of party prevail[ed] in the highest degree, and our officers seem more anxious to ruin their private enemies than those of their country'.[44] Digby had arrived but refused to take over command.* This was Graves's mess.

Meanwhile the situation in Yorktown rapidly became alarming. The difference between this French force and that

---

* Digby brought with him Prince William Henry, the first ever royal visit to the colonies.

landed by d'Estaing at Savannah is quite remarkable. The French landed the siege train, which consisted of newly forged high-quality European cannon. Large numbers of the French sailors whose gunnery had been so impressive at the battles of Cape Henry and the Chesapeake were landed to operate them. Cornwallis was prepared for a siege, but he was not prepared for the savagery of the attack he was subjected to when the French batteries began their 'awful music'.[45] Red-hot shot rained onto the British fort and the trapped British ships until 'the whole peninsula tremble[d] under the incessant thunder of our infernal machines'.[46] The British marvelled at the allied artillerymen's prowess.[47]

The brand-new British frigate *Charon*, the most visible symbol of British military strength at Yorktown, was the first to be targeted and burned. The American doctor James Thacher reported:

> A red-hot shot from the French battery set fire to the *Charon*, a British 44-gun ship, and two or three smaller vessels at anchor in the river, which were consumed in the night. From the bank of the river, I had a fine view of this splendid conflagration. The ships were enwrapped in a torrent of fire, which spreading with vivid brightness among the combustible rigging, and running with amazing rapidity to the tops of the several masts, while all around was thunder and lightning from our numerous cannons and mortars, and in the darkness of night, presented one of the most sublime and magnificent spectacles which can be imagined. Some of our shells over-reaching the town, are seen to fall into the river, and, bursting, throw up columns of water like the spouting of monsters of the deep.[48]

Another was spurred to write:

> Never could a more horrible or beautiful spectacle be seen ... on a dark night, the ships with all their open portholes discharging sheafs of fire, the cannon shots that were going off, the appearance of the whole roadstead, the ships under

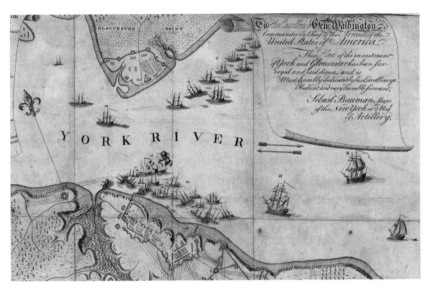

Sunken British ships are shown piled up off the coast of Yorktown. They are still down there in the gloom; the riverbed off Yorktown remains the largest known deposit of eighteenth-century shipwrecks in North America. One brig, *Betsy*, was excavated in the 1970s and produced some of the finest of all maritime artefacts from this war.

topsails flying from the burning vessels, all that formed a terrible and sublime spectacle.[49]

Charon's smouldering remains sank into the Yorktown mud alongside almost all of Cornwallis's ships, which had been either deliberately sunk by the British or destroyed by the French. With the water too shallow to cover the wrecks completely, the river off Yorktown looked like a shipwreck apocalypse.

The *Charon*'s crew was sent forward to an advance battery where their gunnery expertise would come in handy. It was a good idea but they faced an enemy of surprising power. After eight hours of continuous combat in this sailors' redoubt, only the lieutenant and midshipman survived: all thirty-six of their shipmates were dead. Cornwallis spent some time with them: he was not, as some American historians claim, hiding in a cave, but was where the battle would be hottest – with British sailors.

A brave sortie failed and Cornwallis set his mind to escape. At midnight sixteen boats were collected along the Yorktown wharves and were crammed with as many troops as they could fit. Priority was given to soldiers over sailors – an interesting decision. A deception was required if these soldiers were going to escape. The British guns would have to be fired consistently and accurately to convince the French and Americans that the British defences were well manned. The sailors, as expert gunners, were chosen for this task, though their selection had an unfortunate knock-on effect. A soldier takes up the story:

> At the critical moment, the weather from being moderate and calm, changed to a most violent storm of wind and rain, and drove all the boats, some of which had troops on board, down the river. It was soon evident that the intended passage was impracticable.[50]

Maybe this was so, but it is more than likely that, had Cornwallis let his sailors man the boats – just as Washington had let John Glover's Marblehead mariners man his boats at the similarly desperate evacuation of Brooklyn in 1776 – they would, at least, have stood a chance of escape.

Graves and Clinton made it back to the Chesapeake with their second relief but by then it was too late. They learned from three men escaping the trap in a small open boat that Cornwallis had surrendered on 17 October, the anniversary of Burgoyne's surrender at Saratoga – a point that was not lost on the Americans.[51]

So often the defeats of Cornwallis and Burgoyne go hand in hand in our perception of the revolution. Both armies were isolated from naval support and both paid the price. They are considered as parallel or twin defeats but there was one crucial difference. Burgoyne had no significant naval contingent but Cornwallis did. Yes, more than 7,000 soldiers surrendered, but so too did 840 sailors, and they left behind a ruined fleet of sixty-eight ships, their masts poking out of the sea. Perhaps, if used more wisely, these men could have saved themselves, Cornwallis, his soldiers – perhaps even America.

* * *

News of the defeat spread incredibly quickly by sea. An American schooner was sent directly from Yorktown to Newport, and it arrived with precise and accurate details on 24 October. It was in Boston only a day later. The news also flew to Brest in an unusually rapid crossing of just twenty-two days. From Brest it was taken to Paris, arriving in Versailles on 20 November, just as the king was celebrating the birth of the new Dauphin. From Paris it travelled to London. Even by that roundabout route the news reached London before Clinton's official dispatch, which was not sent by special courier but by the regular mail packet. Yet again the British lost the transatlantic maritime race for intelligence, just as they had ever since Lexington.[52]

The news was met with horror in London, where North took it, in the words of the MP Sir Nathanial Wraxall, 'As he would have taken a ball in his breast'.[53] It is claimed that he exclaimed, 'Oh God, it's all over', but things were not quite so simple. Certainly, foreign observers gloated. The Dutch radical François Van der Kamp wrote in full celebratory spate to John Adams and rather wonderfully described the victory as 'the Burgoynishing of that mighty Lord'. He went on: 'Now will the proud [sic] of the British nation be humiliated – now shall a venal and corrupt ministers learn – that the Servants of despotism must be vanquished by the Soldiers of Liberty.'[54] In Britain panic set in as fingers began to point. Rodney falsified his correspondence to show he had forewarned everyone, while Lord North blamed Rodney: 'For his part he solemnly believed that the capture of Lord Cornwallis was owing to the capture of St Eustatius.'[55] Graves and Hood, Cornwallis and Clinton – all hurled mud at each other. Clinton was the man most widely blamed by the press for letting it happen, Germain and Sandwich by the Opposition, and Sandwich by Germain.

In spite of their failure at the Chesapeake, however, the British had a strong and ever strengthening navy, and were still firmly ensconced in three of the most significant American ports: New York, Savannah and Charleston. Gibraltar was still secure, the British were in control of the North Sea, and the Indian and Caribbean theatres were still in the balance: by no means was the military situation ruined by Cornwallis's surrender. Technically the war continued until the Peace of Paris was signed in 1783, but the political situation had been utterly transformed by the battle of the Chesapeake. In reality, just as there were many beginnings to this war, so were there many endings, and Cornwallis's surrender was one.

EPILOGUE

There has been built in the port of Chatham a ship of war of 74 guns, called the *Atlas*. The figurehead represents that gigantic fabulous personage with an enormous globe on his shoulders. The head carver having tak[en] his measures badly, the globe was so high as to be in the way of the bowsprit, and it became necessary to take off part of the upper hemisphere. The part taken off was precisely North America.

Hague Gazette, 13 September 1782.[1]

The effects of Cornwallis's surrender took many months to directly change the war – which is why none of the diarists in the Yorktown campaign had any idea that they had just taken part in the most strategically decisive campaign of the century – but directly change the war they did. Cornwallis's surrender seemed to be the final proof that the British attempt to conquer the American colonies had failed. This was the shipwreck of British military expectations in America. Significantly, in a contemporary Dutch cartoon of the surrender laden with symbolism, a single wrecked ship, the *Eagle*, now represents the Royal Navy.* This was hardly news to the Opposition in Parliament, but what really mattered now was that supporters of the North government began to think this way also. Within weeks, general disgust was reflected in every opposition and neutral paper in Britain.[2] The political dice

* The choice of the *Eagle* is interesting. It was then in India, but had been Howe's flagship at the attack on New York in 1776 and it was the ship that had been targeted, without success, by David Bushnell's submarine.

America is shown as an Indian receiving British delegates on the beach; British commerce is an emaciated dairy cow being robbed by France, Spain, and Holland who stand at an altar representing American trade; the British lion is lame, having cut itself on a broken tea pot; next to the lion a frock-coated Englishman begs; the British ship, HMS *Eagle*, is aground; thistle and thorns in the foreground represent Scottish influence.

rolled, and the North government was fatally wounded and fell in March 1782. A new government, under the guidance of the Marquess of Rockingham, with the vehemently anti-French Charles James Fox as Foreign Secretary, committed itself to ending the war in America.

Meanwhile, the role of sea power in the war continued. It began immediately, at Yorktown, with yet another maritime evacuation exercised on British warships that further blended the Atlantic world into a new colour and texture. A huge fleet of runaway slaves, loyalists and paroled British officers sailed from Yorktown to New York, where, after a journey that was 'so extremely riotous' that one captain risked all in a storm just to get his passengers ashore,[3] the British ships spat out the chewed-up remains of the British American empire into the gutters of Manhattan.

Elsewhere the stakes had risen. The majority of the key politicians, if not all of the military commanders, had given

up hope of any further victory in America, but British possessions in the Caribbean, Mediterranean and India were still to
be saved. If possible, lost ground was also to be recovered to
set against the loss of America. The means by which this was
to be achieved created naval strategic problems of their own,[4]
and the various pathways that the subsequent naval war took
directly affected the shape of the peace.

* * *

The French envisaged a significant imperial presence in America
post-revolution but were unable to back up this policy with
military strength. The victory at the Chesapeake prevented the
allied campaign from collapsing in the autumn of 1781, but
the French navy could never win its fight against its mounting
burden of debt and long-term logistical inadequacies, and the
French had even discovered new ones to burden themselves
further. By 1782 the navy was in danger of defaulting on its
debts to war contractors, dockyard labour was provided principally by convicts, and the storehouses were empty. The royal
dockyards tried and failed to create and maintain the entire
French navy: there was little of the combined effort of royal
and private industry that so characterized the British success.
A notable new weakness, by the end of the war, was in the
quality the French officer corps. The French liked their officers
to be of noble birth, but they had been unwilling to expand
the pool from which they selected their officer corps as the
number of ships increased.[5]

Vergennes saw these problems clearly and now mourned
the condition of both French and Spanish sea power:

> Nos marines respectives qui auroient dû augmenter en
> nombre et en qualité pendant la guerre sont à ces deux Égards
> au dessous de ce qu'elles étoient [*sic*] à leur début.[6]
> ['Our respective navies, which should have increased in
> number and quality during the war, are in both respects less
> than they were at the start.']

The British, on the other hand, had grown ever stronger
from the moment that the decision was taken in 1778 to fully
mobilize. They had suffered, as all navies did, with the particular problems of waging war in the tropics – they were beset by
heat, sickness, a lack of stores, and hurricanes, and also had the
difficulty of maintaining a fleet of any size even in home waters
and close to major dockyards – but the unmistakable pattern
of British naval strength over time is one of improvement and
there was no sign of it stopping.

The key to this growth was a good supply of money, made
available by the relatively low interest on the British debt –
around 3 to 4 per cent. Crucially, this was at least half the
rate that the French paid.[7] The British had also discovered
that there was in fact a major advantage in fighting this war
alone, because the state's finances were unencumbered by
the large subsidies usually paid to foreign allies in return for
military aid. All spare cash, therefore, could be spent where
it was needed most – on the navy. That spending, moreover,
occurred with a good degree of control: British government
finances were strictly monitored, there was a system of annual
budgets, debt was funded, and all borrowing was subject to
public management. Nothing like this happened in France.
In fact no one actually had any idea what the French national
debt amounted to, and the naval minister Castries had been
receiving vast sums directly from the king with no strings
attached.[8]

The French were even unwilling to stop spending and continued the spiral into financial chaos that would spawn political and social chaos, and eventually revolution. The British,
on the other hand, by the end of the war had no fewer than
forty-two well-financed warships under construction in dockyards that were brimming with naval stores and teeming with
skilled workmen. By 1782 eighty-two capital ships, fourteen
ships of 50 guns, 115 frigates, and 102 sloops and cutters had
been coppered – an epoch-defining industrial achievement.[9]
Although the full implications of using iron nails to fasten the
copper were not yet fully understood and many ships were

weakened through electrolytic action, the introduction of copper meant that, even at this early stage, more of the British fleet could spend more time at sea. British sea power therefore went further in operational terms than French. By 1782 British ships, if measured rate for rate, were also more powerful than French ones because of the now widespread adoption of the carronade – a short-barrelled cannon that was devastating at close range.[10] In close action these guns were simply lethal and the French had nothing to compare.

All this added up to a significant advantage for the British that was given extra weight by new thinking on naval strategy conceived by Richard Kempenfelt and developed by Charles Middleton, which justified sending more squadrons to the Caribbean colonies rather than concentrating naval force in home waters.[11] It is fair to say that the French stood little chance when Rodney finally caught up with them in the Caribbean in April 1782 and thwarted an attempted Bourbon invasion of Jamaica by smashing a French fleet at the battle of the Saintes. One Frenchman described it as 'the hottest, longest and most terrible and I may say most dishonourable sea-fight since the invention of gunpowder'.[12] The British sailors unfortunate enough to board surrendered French ships found conditions not only of unimaginable carnage but also of unimaginable squalor, where the decks had been sealed by hatches rather than gratings and the scuppers had never been opened to let the filth run into the sea. Conditions were 'inconceivably putrid and offensive'.[13] When sailors of the *Ardent* opened the hold of one ship, every man that assisted was seized with fever within twenty-four hours. At that same battle, thanks to the work of Blane, Rodney's surgeon, every British ship except two had a perfect bill of health, and in that same month there was less sickness in the fleet than in any of the previous twenty-three months Blane had been in charge.[14]

At the Saintes the French lost five ships of the line captured or destroyed, 2,000 dead and some 5,000 captured. They were stunned by the difference between the two fleets. According to one British sailor, they were simply unable to comprehend 'how they came to lose so many men & we so few on that bloody day'.[15]

Even after this success, British naval problems continued and tension remained very high, creating its own political and operational headaches. The summer of 1782 was particularly awkward. In British waters, a third mighty combined fleet – though mainly consisting of Spanish ships – approached the Channel, leading to further political embarrassment. In American waters, British naval officers knew that there was a strong political resolution to end the war, but they had not actually received any orders to desist from attacking enemy shipping wherever possible. The tension was heightened by the arrival in Boston of the large portion of the French fleet that had not been destroyed or captured at the battle of the Saintes, under the command of Admiral le marquis de Vaudreuil. The tension and uncertainty were matched by a stunningly effective British naval blockade of the eastern seaboard, focused in particular on the Delaware.[16] So many of the problems experienced by the British early in the war had been caused by the Royal Navy being forced to support land operations and escort the many hundreds of supply ships that kept the army in America alive. Now, however, the British were actually prevented, by parliamentary order, from prosecuting any more land campaigns. This period of utter naval dominance clearly demonstrates that, if the navy had been left to its own devices and given sufficient resources, an effective blockade of the American coast would have been possible. It is perhaps the most tantalizing evidence that, had the British chosen a purely naval strategy in 1775 over one that favoured a land campaign, the revolution – or at least *this* revolution – would have been still-born.

In India the British fleet under Sir Edward Hughes tore apart Hyder Ali's fleet and captured the key Dutch base of Trincomalee before clashing repeatedly with Suffren in indecisive actions. Suffren was always bold and Hughes deserves far more credit than he has ever received for his repeated and skilful defensive actions in a very difficult naval theatre that favoured defence. Suffren's aggression remained hamstrung by the fact that the French had no repair facilities of any sort in India. Throughout his campaign he relied on Dutch materials to repair his ships, and the harbour in the Sultanate of Atjeh on Sumatra to shelter and carry out those repairs. He nevertheless enjoyed one significant success: the recapture of Trincomalee.[17]

The last shot of the war was actually fired during this campaign, at the battle of Cuddalore in the Bay of Bengal on 20 June 1783. The Boston Tea Party had demonstrated the clear and close links between the American colonies and the eastern empire at the birth of the war, and these naval struggles at its death were a sign of things to come. India would become ever more integrated into the British empire, though this was a process that had begun even before the revolution.[18]

The naval weakness of the French, so visible by 1782, dramatically undermined their position at the peace talks and directly led to the British recovering every one of the West Indies possessions that had been taken by France during the war, with the exception of the tiny island of Tobago. That naval weakness was also good news for the Americans who, during the course of the war, had come to realize that their pact with France might not turn out quite how they had hoped. Before the rottenness of the French navy was made manifest, France had real intentions of establishing a significant role for herself in America after the revolution, ostensibly by forcing the Americans to accept a tiny independent American state, restricted by the north–south line of the Appalachians in the west and the British in Canada.[19] Thus the possibility of a large America – one that might even incorporate a huge expanse of territory between the Appalachians and the Mississippi to provide the space that the colonies needed to grow – now actually increased as the value of French sea power fell: an irony of French naval assistance that is never acknowledged.

In the aftermath of Yorktown it was essential for the future of America and Britain that America become independent of

France as well as Britain and the visible collapse of French sea power at the Saintes made this possible. The British of course were happy to see this happen. They had no interest in either France or Spain growing strong in America and after this latest war were now less likely to co-operate with them than they ever had been. It was envisaged, therefore, that Britain and America would become friends by stripping the Americans of their French and Spanish alliances, though the Americans would still struggle by no longer benefiting from the traditional economic and mercantile advantages they had previously enjoyed as part of the British empire.[20] This, ultimately, was the price paid for their independence.

The British dominated the peace talks and ultimately granted America both territory and fishing rights beyond their wildest dreams. They received those areas of the thirteen colonies still under British occupation and immense territory between the Appalachians and the Mississippi, which now constitutes all or part of eleven states: Minnesota, Wisconsin, Michigan, Illinois, Indiana, Ohio, Kentucky, Tennessee, Mississippi, Alabama and Georgia. They also received access to the Mississippi and to the crucial Newfoundland fisheries. Nonetheless the European state that benefited most from the outcome of the war was, without doubt, Britain.[21]

The Spanish took Minorca in February 1782 but never came close to taking Gibraltar. In September, with French assistance, they launched a 'Grand Assault', which ended in an utter shambles, with hundreds of Spanish sailors actually having to be rescued by the men they were supposed to be attacking. The failure of this combined operation further damaged the diplomatic relationship between Spain and France.[22] Spanish impotence and incompetence at Gibraltar led to one of the best cartoons of the war, *The Bum-bardment of Gibralter*. Shortly after the Spanish bum-bardment, Howe led another successful relief. France was committed to continuing the war until Spain had obtained Gibraltar, but Vergennes managed to wriggle out of this in an impressive feat of diplomatic duplicity.[23] The Spanish had made gains during the war, notably

'Gainst Elliot the French & the Spaniards combin'd,
are throwing their Stink Pots you see from behind
That the Garrison's Safe you must own is no wonder
For all that they do is but F_t_g at Thunder.'

because of the skill of Gálvez, but their navy was now also in very poor shape.

At the peace talks the Spanish retained Minorca and both East and West Florida which, combined, created a territory that ran from the southern tip of the modern Florida peninsular all the way to the Mississippi. In these terms, the war for them had been a relative success, though their navy had suffered horribly ever since the epidemic that had ripped through the invasion fleet in 1779 and which had then infected the French navy. The Spanish navy had never lived up to its expectations. Barceló's inability to blockade Gibraltar and prevent its relief is a notable failure, as was their sustained inability to man their ships adequately. Spanish sea power was, and remained, all about show. Their ships looked wonderful and the numbers were impressive, but this was an illusion.

Their industrial infrastructure was also woefully inadequate. By the end of the war the British had coppered 313 ships; the

Spanish just one.[24] This naval weakness, ultimately, would be the undoing of their empire, which by 1830 had entirely disappeared. For the Spanish, therefore, the American war was something of a reprieve. Nonetheless, their strategy of threatening Britain in English waters, the Mediterranean and the Caribbean was crucial to the ultimate success of the war. An apocryphal story survives that construction work on the cathedral in Málaga had to be suspended to raise money for the American war, which primarily involved the expense of raising and manning their fleet. One can still clearly see how the tower and roof of the cathedral are incomplete, though one might not immediately think of the links between an unfinished roof, Spanish sea power and American independence.

The Dutch had been shattered by the war, a blow that was the first in a series of disasters to befall this once great empire. One Dutch spectator at the time commented how 'the evil of American Freedom' was the origin of 'all the subsequent disasters, sufferings and losses that befell the Republic'.[25] Their navy was rendered impotent by the battle of the Dogger Bank and some of their key colonies were left in the hands of their enemies or supposed allies: the English kept Negapatam and the French temporarily held the Cape and Trincomalee. Trading by the Dutch East India Company came to a standstill.[26] At the peace talks they reclaimed St Eustatius,* Good Hope and Ceylon, though they lost Negapatam in India and granted the British the right to free trade with their colonies in the east, opening highways for subsequent British aggrandizement in Malaysia. Though the politicians were severely disappointed and the public indignant at this result, they had at least benefited by building a new battle fleet that remained largely intact. By 1785 the Dutch had added no less than 90,000 tons of warships to their navy – an eye-opening figure considering that the Dutch had steadily maintained a battle fleet of roughly 60,000 tons in total for the preceding sixty years.[27]

---

* Which had been retaken from the British by the French in November on de Grasse's return to the Caribbean from Yorktown.

The Russian League of Armed Neutrality, with which the Dutch had flirted and which had played a significant role in bringing about war between Britain and the Netherlands, received no acknowledgement whatsoever in the peace treaty – a victory that would greatly benefit Britain in future wars. The Russian battle fleet, however, had massively expanded under Catherine's guidance. In terms of tons displacement, the Russian fleet of 1785 was more than twice the size it had been in 1770.[28] The navies of Denmark–Norway* and Sweden also increased and their combined navies significantly out-numbered the Russians. Within five years of the end of the American Revolution the Russians and Swedes were at each other's throats in a naval conflict, and the Baltic would remain a key theatre of naval war, both for the Baltic naval powers and for other European naval powers, who continued to source their naval stores from the Baltic for years to come.

The dust in America took generations to settle. The first great naval challenge posed by the treaty was the greatest of the entire war: the largest movement of ships and people in the history of the British empire in a maritime dance that would utterly transform the characteristics of the Atlantic world. Something like 9,000 slaves who had run away from their masters and 60,000 loyalists who chose to vote against independence by emigrating now left America in British ships, bound for Nova Scotia, East Florida and Quebec.[29]

The constant presence of the Royal Navy was a key charac-teristic of these evacuations and the decks of British warships provided some of the best seats from which to watch the play of independence unfold on the American stage. When the final evacuees left New York, the Americans held a fireworks display that was witnessed from a British deck by Ralph Henry, once enslaved to Patrick Henry, a key member of Congress, and by Daniel, once enslaved to Washington himself. The scene was described by one Hessian officer:

* Norway and Denmark were united for 436 years, from 1379 to 1814.

On all corners one saw the flag of thirteen stripes flying, cannon salutes were fired, and all the bells rang. The shores were crowded with people who threw their hats in the air, screaming and boisterous with joy, and wished us a pleasant voyage with white handkerchiefs. While on the ships, which lay at anchor with the troops, a deep stillness prevailed as if everyone were mourning the loss of thirteen beautiful provinces.[30]

Such evacuation was not an option for the Native Americans, many of whom had played key roles in assisting British fleets, particularly in the campaigns on Lake Champlain. They were not mentioned at all in the peace treaty and technically were still at war with the United States. For them the American Revolution was a significant episode in their extended decline. The promise of hope offered to the runaway slaves by evacuation in British ships also vanished into thin air, another collapse of expectation on an immense scale.[31]

While this was all happening in America, the American war at sea had carried on. British merchant ships continued to require an armed escort, and it was not until 24 March 1783 that Congress actually called home its remaining privateers and naval vessels.[32] The Admiralty had been entirely ineffective since the summer of 1781, when the Navy Boards had also been abolished, and in the intervening years, responsibility for the American navy had landed in the hands of a single man, Robert Morris, the Superintendent of Finance.[33] The last ship of the Continental Navy to be sold out of service was the *Alliance* on 3 June 1785.

This first phase of the life of American sea power was over, but it would come again and would surprise the world with its strength. In the interim America would have to learn to live with its independence, to pay its debts, and to trade with its allies and enemies.

Pre-existing trading patterns flourished. The largest and most obvious trading partner was, of course, Britain, and the Americans were utterly tied to the British economy. They may have been 'independent' but they certainly were not econom-ically independent.[34] The financially crippled French were unwilling to extend credit, and French goods did not suit the American market as English goods did. For the four years between 1786 and 1789 trade between Britain and America was worth £2,567,000, whereas trade between France and America was worth £56,000.[35]

The Spanish were simply unwilling to compromise their vision of colonial trading monopoly and refused to get involved with the Americans. The Dutch, however, were will-ing, and lent America 1.3 million dollars in the immediate aftermath of the peace.* Even so the Americans were never able to compete with the sheer size of the British economy, so strong that it absorbed the loss of the American economies with barely a shudder. Britain, therefore, was the key ally of the future. In the words of David Hartley, a British diplomat, Britain was 'the first of European nations in riches ... industry, commerce, manufactures ... together with civil liberty, which is the source of all, and naval power, which is the support of all'.[36] The British were happy to see the Americans eco-nomically dependent on their trade. Now reaching from the Atlantic to the Mississippi, America contained an inexhaust-ible source of riches. The building of American trade and the establishment of American–British co-operation were there-fore the most important first steps for America's new future as a major player in international relations.

Another major step towards that goal, but one for the future, was the creation of a new American navy, for a key lesson of this war was that, even if sea power was not the magic wand that so many thought it to be, it most certainly was a tool that would determine the rise and fall of empires. The creation of a new navy only became possible once the states had resisted fragmentation and combined under a new constitution, Congress had given itself the authority to tax the American

* Part of which, 70,000 in gold coin, was convoyed to America from Havana by an American frigate. Fowler, *American Crisis*, 130, 154.

people directly, and political will had once again looked to the sea.[37] Only then could the Americans even embark on the journey towards an effective, permanent navy. But, with these steps taken, and once they had experienced their own population explosion and industrial revolution, and had learned the principal lesson of this war that an effective navy could only be built and then maintained through 'unwearied attention' and even then with 'the utmost difficulty',[38] they would build a navy that would, eventually, change the world all over again.

In the meantime the Royal Navy existed in greater strength than ever before. Crucially, lessons had been learned during the war that now ensured that the fleet could be maintained in significant strength for a significant period of time – the exact challenge whose solution had so eluded them in the early 1770s. A sensible and well-funded cycle of construction and repair utilizing both private and royal yards was now in place. Britain now was both committed to, and capable of, maintaining a fleet of no fewer than 100 ships of the line, to be ready at all times,[39] and this was not just a question of infrastructure but of personnel: it is no coincidence that one of the subsequent generation's most influential and talented naval administrators – Andrew Snape Hamond – was one of this war's most talented serving naval officers.

The war taught the British significant lessons about the deployment of fleets, if not quite 'strategy' as we know it. The most important was that large naval fleets were far easier to maintain and control in home waters, near major permanent dockyards, than in foreign waters, supported by ad hoc or small local infrastructure; and so too was it far easier to keep the enemy trapped at home than to chase him all around the world. By no means is it a coincidence that the battle of the Saintes in 1782 was the first and last major action fought outside British waters by the principal British fleet; indeed it did not leave European waters again until 1944.[40] The key to the British future would be small, relatively inexpensive locations that could be used as naval bases from which to police the global British maritime trade network. This global web of naval protection, occasionally boosted by large squadrons, would be augmented by immense naval strength permanently maintained in European waters, where the British could protect its own shores and homeward- and outward-bound trade convoys, and bottle up enemy warships.

The Royal Navy was thus finally primed as the weapon it was always supposed to be – a weapon that could realize the dreams of the politicians and the public who so worshipped the god of sea power. More than anything else, this naval progress in the process of imperial loss is why, ironically, the independence of America heralded the period of Britain's greatest imperial strength.

A still broader lesson concerns our ability and desire to analyse and question our own behaviour. We are always happy to mishear, mis-see and misunderstand something so that the stories we weave add up. To protect us from this tendency, historians need to tell the story of what, actually, *was* there, and without any doubt the strongest theme of this particular history is one of collapsed expectation, of the appearance or belief in sea power not being realized in its application. Admiral Pasley summed up this problem in microcosm when his crew, having returned to Plymouth from a lengthy cruise in August 1780, were so shattered by scurvy that most were 'incapable of moving'. And yet he knew that, from a distance, his was a ship of immense power and influence – in his words, 'a ship of apparent force without abilities'.[41] The Americans, French and Spanish were exceptionally lucky that their continued misreading, misunderstanding and mishandling of sea power did not lead to failure during the war, and the British were exceptionally lucky that *their* misreading, misunderstanding and mishandling of sea power did not lead to even greater losses than America – as we have seen, the entire British empire was left hanging by a thread on several occasions. By placing blind faith in a poorly understood system, all parties in this war repeatedly exposed themselves to disaster.

There is a lesson for us all here, but at the same time, for all these difficulties faced, a little blind faith (and sometimes a lot) meant that this was a period of the most extraordinary endeavour, of the greatest military and administrative achievements of the eighteenth century, a period unique in the history of the world, and those who had been part of it knew that they had been part of something special. Thomas Paine declared, 'Could we clear away the mist of antiquity, it is more than probable the ancients would admire us, rather than we them.'[42] At the end of the war, Ezra Stiles, President of Yale, proclaimed: 'We have lived an age in just a few years; we have seen more wonders accomplished than are unfolded in a century.'[43] For, sometimes, it takes such blind faith, such willingness not to give up against all known odds, to shape the history of the world in a new way.

GLOSSARY OF NAUTICAL TERMS

Bateau: A shallow-draft flat-bottomed boat used extensively across North America in the colonial period around 30ft long and 6ft wide. The largest were capable of mounting small cannon and swivel guns.

Bilge: The lowest compartment on a ship, where the sides meet the keel.

Bow: The foremost part of a ship's hull.

Bowsprit: A spar extending forwards over the bow.

Brig: A vessel square-rigged on two masts.

Brigantine: A two-masted vessel with square-rigged foremast and a mainmast rigged fore and aft.

Broadside: The side of the ship; the number of guns mounted on one side; the simultaneous fire of these guns.

Bulwark: A barrier around the side of the deck.

Companionway: A hatchway in a ship's deck leading below.

Corvette: A small warship with only one deck. Smaller than a frigate, larger than a sloop.

Cot: A canvas hammock sewn into a wooden bed frame and suspended from the deck-head. An officer's bed.

Cutter: A small vessel fore-and-aft rigged on a single mast.

Cutwater: Part of the hull, the foremost part of the prow.

Double: To attack a ship or squadron from both sides.

Draught: The depth of water required to float a ship.

Fish: To strengthen a damaged spar or mast by lashing spars to it in the manner of splints.

Frigate: A small sailing warship of fine form and high speed. Carries her armament on a single deck, her main deck, while her lower deck is unarmed.

Galley: A type of small boat; a small sailing warship or merchantman fitted to row with sweeps; a type of inshore warship propelled primarily by oars; the kitchen of a ship.

Gallivat: A small armed vessel, with sails and oars; used on the Malabar coast.

Grave: To ground a ship in order to work on her hull when it is exposed at low water.

Gun-port: A port cut in the hull to allow guns mounted below deck to fire out.

Gunwale: A heavy timber forming the top of the ship's side.

Hatch coaming: The raised section of timber around the entrance to a hatchway to deflect or prevent entry of water.

Heave to: To stop or lie to by backing some of the sails.

Jury-mast: A makeshift and temporary mast, improvised because of loss or damage to the original mast.

Kedge: To move a ship, typically against wind or tide, by hauling on a line attached to a kedge anchor.

Ketch: A small vessel square or fore-and-aft rigged on a main mast with a distinctive small mizzen mast aft.

Lateen sail: A large triangular sail rigged fore and aft on a long yard running diagonally to the bow.

League: A measure of distance, three miles.

Leeward: Relating to the direction towards which the wind is blowing.

Lugger: A small sailing vessel rigged fore and aft with quadrangular sails.

Magazine: A storehouse for explosives; a compartment in the ship for storing powder.

Mast cap: A strong block of wood used to bind two masts together.

Packet-boat: A vessel employed under Post Office contract to carry mail.

Pinnace: A small boat, propelled by sail or oars, carried on a large ship to act as a tender.

Portage: To carry water craft or cargo overland.

Quarter: The sides of a ship's stern.

Quarter-gallery: A walkway or balcony projecting from the stern or quarters of a ship.

Radeau: A type of ship used as a naval gun platform. Very basic in construction and difficult to manoeuvre. The term is derived from the French meaning 'raft'.

Rating: A man's rate; a man so rated, one of the 'common men' of a ship's company, having no rank.

Rowlock: A brace that attaches an oar to a boat's gunwales and provides a fulcrum for rowing.

Schooner: A small sailing vessel fore-and-aft rigged on two masts.

Scow: A flat-bottomed boat with a blunt bow, often used to transport freight.

Scupper: A port or channel to carry water off a deck and over the ship's side.

Shallop: A small cruising warship.

Shroud: A stay supporting a mast from the side.

Sloop: A small cruising warship with only one internal deck and mounting her main battery on the upper deck.

Spar: A mast, pole or boom.

Spring: A hawser led from the capstan, out of the ship aft and made fast some way along the anchor cable, hauling on which will cant an anchored ship to bring her broadside to bear as desired.

Stern: The after end of a ship.

Strike: To lower a mast, spar or sail; to surrender; to run aground.

Stunsail or **studding sail**: A light sail temporarily spread outboard of a square sail in light airs.

Tender: A vessel employed to assist another: an auxiliary vessel.

Thole-pin: Pegs mounted vertically in the gunwale of a rowing boat, against which the oars are pulled. An alternative to a rowlock.

Topgallant: A square sail set on the topgallant mast, above the topsail.

Warp: To manoeuvre a ship using hawsers made fast to the shore or buoys.

Wear (ship): To alter course from one tack to the other by turning before the wind.

Weather deck: A deck exposed to the sky.

Weather gage: The windward position in relation to another ship or fleet.

Windsail: A sail rigged as an air scoop over a hatch or companionway to catch breezes and divert them below.

Windward: Relating to the direction from which the wind is blowing.

Xebec: A small three-masted Mediterranean vessel with both square and lateen sails.

Yard: A spar hung horizontally from a mast to spread the head or foot of a square sail.

NOTES

Introduction

1 GWP: G. Washington to J. Hancock, 10 July 1777; NYPL: Mazzei Papers, 8 February 1780.
2 See, for example, Mahan, *Major Operations*, 163; Clowes, *Royal Navy*, III, 543.
3 Quoted in Mackesy, *War for America*, 183.
4 Explained in Syrett, *European Waters*, 125–6.
5 Many thanks to Dr Michael Crawford for bringing this to my attention.
6 Baxter, *British Invasion*, 92.
7 Billias, *Washington's Generals and Opponents*, vii.

1 British Pyre

1 Oertling, *Bilge Pumps*, 1–9.
2 Oertling, *Bilge Pumps*, 59.
3 Lavery, *Shipboard Life*, 42, 53, 100, 196.
4 Park, 'HMS *Gaspee*', 31.
5 Patton, *Patriot Pirates*, xxii.
6 Park, 'HMS *Gaspee*', 34.
7 Park, 'HMS *Gaspee*', 36n.106.
8 Park, 'HMS *Gaspee*', 33–4.
9 Bartlett, *History*, 19.
10 Bartlett, *History*, 34.
11 Falconer, *Dictionary*, 128; Caruana, *English Sea Ordnance*, II, 449–52.

2 American Origins

1 T. C. Barrow, *Trade and Empire*, 244; Lemisch, 'Jack Tar', 398–9; Park, 'HMS *Gaspee*', 52, 80–3.
2 Magra, *Fisherman's Cause*, 8–9, 12, 142 ff.; Brunsman, *Evil Necessity*, 222 ff., 242.
3 T. C. Barrow, *Trade and Empire*, 177.

4 Park, 'HMS *Gaspee*', 10.

5 Park, 'HMS *Gaspee*', 10–14.

6 From Dudingston's immediate generation we know that James Hawker, Jeremiah Morgan and Robert Keeler were British naval officers with a similar reputation. Stout, *Navy in America*, 168; Bunker, *Empire on the Edge*, 51–3.

7 Quoted in Stout, *Navy in America*, v.

8 Stout, *Navy in America*, 141.

9 Maier, *Resistance to Revolution*, 8–11; Leslie, 'Gaspee Affair', 234; Maier, 'Popular Uprisings', 15. The Rhode Islanders were also irate that Dudingston had taken some smugglers to Boston, which was in a different state, for trial. He was perfectly entitled to do so, but it irritated the Rhode Islanders that their own judicial system was not responsible for trying their own criminals. Stout, *Navy in America*, 141. For more on the role of the Vice-Admiralty Courts as a cause of revolution, see Ubbelohde, *Vice-Admiralty Courts*, 203 ff.

10 Maier, *Resistance to Revolution*, 8, 15; Stout, *Navy in America*, 168; Bunker, *Empire on the Edge*, 68–9.

11 Park, 'HMS *Gaspee*', 27–8; Stout, *Navy in America*, 141.

12 Butler, *Becoming America*, 233; Park, 'HMS *Gaspee*', 36, 164.

13 Bunker, *Empire on the Edge*, 229–30; Fischer, *Revere's Ride*, 26.

14 Brogan, *History*, 164.

15 Barnes and Owen, *Sandwich Papers*, I, 49–54; Stout, *Navy in America*, 161; Park, 'HMS *Gaspee*', 29–31; Bunker, *Empire on the Edge*, 55.

16 For details of the political process behind the Commission, see Wickwire, 'John Pownall', 549.

17 Leslie, 'Gaspee Affair', 241.

18 Park, 'HMS *Gaspee*', 2.

19 Maier, *Resistance to Revolution*, 215, 231; Bumsted and Clark, 'Tom Paine', 566; Stout, *Navy in America*, v; Bunker, *Empire on the Edge*, 113.

20 Stout, *Navy in America*, 158.

21 Schlesinger, 'Political Mobs', 248.

22 Leslie, 'Gaspee Affair', 243–4.

23 Park, 'HMS *Gaspee*', 2, 133.

24 Park, 'HMS *Gaspee*', 10.

25 Weintraub, *Iron Tears*, 5.

26 Bowen, *John Adams*, 439.

27 Bowen, *John Adams*, 439; Bunker, *Empire on the Edge*, 373 ff.

28 Anson, *Grafton Correspondence*, 266 ff.; Donoughue, *British Politics*, 284–5; Bunker, *Empire on the Edge*, 369.

29 Baugh, 'Why did Britain?', 155.

30 Tilley, *British Navy*, 9.

31 Tilley, *British Navy*, 9.

32 Alcedo, *Geographical and Historical Dictionary*, 178.

33 NDAR I: 24, 58, 59, 177; Stout, 'Manning', 185; Mercer, 'Northern Exposure', 207–11; Barnes and Owen, *Sandwich Papers*, I, 41.
34 NDAR I: 61; N. Miller, *Sea of Glory*, 17.
35 Stout, *Navy in America*, 161.
36 Tilley, *British Navy*, 11–13.
37 Tilley, *British Navy*, 11; T. C. Barrow, *Trade and Empire*, 249–50.
38 Barnes and Owen, *Sandwich Papers*, I, 42.
39 Tilley, *British Navy*, 3; Rodger, *Insatiable Earl*, 225–7; Yerxa, 'Samuel Graves', 372; ODNB: 'Graves, Samuel (1713–1787)'.
40 Higginbotham, 'State Formation', 58–9.
41 Magra, *Fisherman's Cause*, 98; Marshall, *Making and Unmaking*, 13; Buel, *In Irons*, 1, 31.
42 Ramsay, *History*, 74–5. Many thanks to Dr Mike Duffy for this reference.

3 European Gunpowder

1 G. Cole, 'Ordnance Office', 166.
2 G. Cole, 'Ordnance Office', 143; West, *Gunpowder*, 171.
3 West, *Gunpowder*, 172; Stephenson, 'Supply', 274–5; Salav, 'Production', 425.
4 Magra, *Fisherman's Cause*, 162.
5 Glete, *Navies and Nations*, I, 271.
6 Syrett, *European Waters*, 4.
7 R. P. Richmond, *Powder Alarm*, 96.
8 Caughey, *Gálvez*, 87.
9 Syrett, *American Waters*, 22, 30; Magra, *Fisherman's Cause*, 166.
10 An extraordinary story in itself. See Morton and Spinelli, *Beaumarchais*; R. R. Butler, *Figaro's Fleet*; Dull, *Diplomatic History*, 60–1.
11 O'Shaughnessy, *Men Who Lost America*, 14.
12 NDAR I: 388; Jamieson, 'Leeward Islands', 111.
13 Tuchman, *First Salute*, 9.
14 O'Shaughnessy, *Men Who Lost America*, 331.
15 NDAR I: 23–4; MHS: *Graves Conduct*, 418; Yerxa, 'Samuel Graves', 373.
16 NDAR I: 178.
17 Stout, *Navy in America*, 162–3; NDAR I: 124.
18 Moomaw, 'Captain Hamond', 247.
19 Magra, *Fisherman's Cause*, 172.
20 Bunker, *Empire on the Edge*, 306–7; Fischer, *Revere's Ride*, 48.
21 Stout, *Navy in America*, 163; Ward, *War for Independence*, 13; Tilley, *British Navy*, 15–16; NDAR I: 38.
22 Fischer, *Revere's Ride*, 57; NDAR I: 15, 40.
23 Stephenson, 'Supply', 273.

24 C. E. Carter, *Gage Correspondence*, I, 377; II, 654.

25 Bunker, *Empire on the Edge*, 330.

26 McCurry, 'North Government', 143.

27 R. P. Richmond, *Powder Alarm*, 105.

28 McCurry, 'North Government', 145; Bunker, *Empire on the Edge*, 343–63.

29 NDAR I: 179.

30 Tilley, *British Navy*, 23.

31 Knight, 'Recovery', 12.

32 NDAR I: 192; Mackenzie, *Diary*, I, 18.

33 Olson and Doescher, 'Astronomical', 439–40.

34 Fischer, *Revere's Ride*, 262.

35 NDAR I: 372.

36 NDAR I: 206.

37 Fischer, *Revere's Ride*, 284; NDAR I: 202.

38 NDAR I: 249.

39 NDAR I: 226.

40 NDAR I: 224–6, 229, 476–7, 480–1, 967–8, 991, 1306.

41 Rantoul, 'Quero', 13.

42 Tilley, *British Navy*, 46; Rantoul, 'Quero', 11.

43 Rantoul, 'Quero', 10.

44 Rantoul, 'Quero', 6.

45 NDAR I: 325, 484.

46 Rantoul, 'Quero', 14.

47 Fischer, *Revere's Ride*, 416 n.50.

48 Fischer, *Revere's Ride*, 275.

49 Fischer, *Revere's Ride*, 290.

50 Stout, *Navy in America*, 135; Tilley, *British Navy*, 32.

51 Bunker, *Empire on the Edge*, 349.

4 Canadian Invasion

1 For a brief discussion of this point with particular relevance to the prehistory of the Royal Navy, see Rodger, *Safeguard*, xxiv–xxv. See also Hattendorf, *Talking about Naval History*, 185; and for the prehistory of the American navy, see Dull, *American Naval History*, 1–16.

2 Randall, *Benedict Arnold*, 94.

3 E. Allen, *Narrative*, 6.

4 Nelson, *Arnold's Navy*, 24–9.

5 Bellesiles, *Outlaws*, 118.

6 NDAR I: 367, 503–4.

7 Randall, *Benedict Arnold*, 109.

8 NDAR I: 671–3.

9 NDAR I: 340.

10 NDAR I: 763; Higginbotham, 'State Formation', 59.

11 NDAR I: 1217.

12 NDAR II: 145, 162–3, 217–18, 867.

13 NDAR II: 531–5.

14 NDAR II: 1078.

15 NDAR II: 1221.

16 NDAR II: 1104.

17 Desjardin, *Howling Wilderness*, 20.

18 NDAR II: 38; Smith and Knight, *Troubled Waters*, 32.

19 Desjardin, *Howling Wilderness*, 21.

20 There are several important sources for the cost of pre-revolutionary bateaux, one of the most interesting being the daybook from a general store in Schenectady, New York, 1772–4; NYSA: BD 20583. Another excellent source is the Account Books of Daniel Campbell, a wealthy Schenectady merchant. These are also in the New York State Archives, SC 11062. Many thanks to the deeply knowledgeable David Manthey for sources and advice on all things bateau-related that appear in this book.

21 Desjardin, *Howling Wilderness*, 61.

22 Middlekauff, *Glorious Cause*, 310.

23 NDAR II: 431.

24 NDAR II: 433.

25 Desjardin, *Howling Wilderness*, 60–1.

26 Desjardin, *Howling Wilderness*, 61.

27 NDAR II: 1006.

28 NDAR II: 1016.

29 Nelson, *Arnold's Navy*, 125.

30 J. H. Smith, *Our Struggle*, 24.

31 NDAR II: 1016.

32 NDAR II: 1027.

33 Desjardin, *Howling Wilderness*, 119, 189.

34 NDAR II: 1171, 1173; Wrong, *Canada*, 93; Desjardin, *Howling Wilderness*, 122.

35 NMM: BGR/9.

36 Wrong, *Canada*, 101.

37 Mackesy, *War for America*, 50; Higginbotham, *War of American Independence*, 143.

38 ODNB: 'Palliser, Sir Hugh'.

39 NDAR I: 127; NMM: SAN/F/7; TNA: ADM 2/372; ODNB: 'Palliser, Sir Hugh'; Barnes and Owen, *Sandwich Papers*, I, 85.

40 NDAR III: 541; Rodger, *Insatiable Earl*, 227.

41 Douglas, 'Account', 41.

42 ODNB: 'Douglas, Sir Charles'.

43 There are several important studies of ice and ice seamanship, but nothing can take the place of actually experiencing it. For historians a particularly

interesting starting point is the US Navy Hydrographic Office's *Manual of Ice Seamanship* (Washington, 1950).

44 TNA: ADM 1/1706, 8 May 1776.
45 TNA: ADM 51/484, ff. 27–8.
46 NDAR V: 225–7.
47 Higginbotham, *War of American Independence*, 115.

5 Colonial Sea Power

1 NDAR I: 202, 221–2, 297, 302–3, 325, 339.
2 NDAR I: 221, 252, 263.
3 Syrett, *American Waters*, 5.
4 For more examples of whaleboat attacks, see NDAR I: 602, 672, 786, 835, 858; MHS: *Graves Conduct*, 468.
5 Hattendorf, *Talking about Naval History*, 188.
6 Quoted in Daughan, *If By Sea*, 40.
7 NDAR I: 721–2.
8 NDAR I: 622.
9 Willis, 'Archaeology', 7–26.
10 Freeman, *Washington*, I, 151.
11 Middlekauff, *Glorious Cause*, 299.
12 Nelson, *Secret Navy*, 54.
13 Bowen, *John Adams*, 547; Hattendorf, *Talking about Naval History*, 190.
14 Fowler, 'Esek Hopkins', 6.
15 Buel, *In Irons*, 80.
16 Daughan, *If By Sea*, 49.
17 Tilley, 'Naval Policy Development', Part II, 119.
18 Bowen, *John Adams*, 523; Middlekauff, *Glorious Cause*, 317; Tilley, 'Naval Policy Development', Part I, 69–78.
19 O'Shaughnessy, *Men Who Lost America*, 332. Fowler, *Rebels*, 4; Buel, *In Irons*, 30n.6.
20 Neeser, *Shuldham Despatches*, xxiii.
21 NDAR I: 287–9.
22 NDAR II: 36.
23 *Chaleur* (1764) NMM: ZAZ6084; *Halifax* (1768) ZAZ6199; *Sultana* (1768) ZAZ6088; *Sir Edward Hawke* (1768) ZAZ6085. The two from the war years are the *Coureur* (captured 1780) ZAZ6170 and *Berbice* (purchased 1780) ZAZ6119.
24 Smith and Knight, *Troubled Waters*, Plate 3. From the Peabody Museum in Salem.
25 Smith and Knight, *Troubled Waters*, 24.
26 Hattendorf, *Talking about Naval History*, 188.
27 Several ships in the US Navy have been named *Jeremiah O'Brien* and even a Second World War merchant ship, which survives as a museum

ship in San Francisco. For more on the affair, see NDAR I: 655–6, 676–7; Churchill, 'Margaretta Affair', 60–74.

28 Paullin, *Navy*, 322; Hattendorf, *Talking about Naval History*, 189.

29 Jackson, *Pennsylvania Navy*, 11 ff.

30 Stewart, *Virginia's Navy*, 3–15; Paullin, *Navy*, 398–401; Selby, *Virginia*, 76.

31 Paullin, *Navy*, 455–7.

32 Paullin, *Navy*, 356.

33 NDAR I: 764.

34 NDAR I: 764–5; Paullin, *Navy*, 418–20, 459–60.

35 Ansoff, 'First Navy Jack', 33–41; Jackson, *Pennsylvania Navy*, 17; Paullin, *Navy*, 327.

36 Gordon, *Maritime Medicine*, 112.

37 For more on the manning of the state navies and the interesting topic of motivation for service, see Gilje, 'Loyalty and Liberty'.

38 Tilley, 'American Revolutionary Naval Policy', Part I, 70; Tilley, 'Naval Policy Development', Part II, 119; Tilley, 'Naval Policy Development', Part III, 194.

39 NDAR II: 442.

40 Hattendorf, *Talking about Naval History*, 193. For detailed study of the first frigates, see Brewington, 'Designs'.

41 Hattendorf, *Talking about Naval History*, 194.

42 Hattendorf, *Talking about Naval History*, 192; Magra, *Fisherman's Cause*, 179.

43 Hattendorf, *Talking about Naval History*, 191.

44 The first draft still survives in the archives of the Connecticut Historical Society. NDAR II, 649–53; Hattendorf, *Talking about Naval History*, 193.

45 APDE: 28 November 1775.

46 APDE: to James Warren, 13 October 1775.

47 Dull, *American Naval History*, 31; Hattendorf, *Talking about Naval History*, 195.

48 Buel, *In Irons*, 94; Silverstone, *Sailing Navy*, xvii.

49 Rankin, 'Naval Flag', 341; Tuchman, *First Salute*, 48. The Grand Union flag existed until the Stars and Stripes was introduced in June 1777.

50 There is some debate over this. See NDAR II: 1307.

51 NDAR VII: 190, 313, 1018–19; Tuchman, *First Salute*, 5–8.

52 Armitage, *Declaration*, 36.

53 Tilley, 'American Naval Policy Development', Part III, 196.

54 Paullin, *Navy*, 321; Tilley, 'Naval Policy Development', Part II, 121, 126.

55 Buel, *In Irons*, 37; Tilley, 'American Naval Policy Development', Part III, 194–9.

56 Tilley, 'American Naval Policy Development', Part III, 198.

57 Foy, 'Ports of Slavery', 275, 280.

58 Alberts, *Golden Voyage*, 36.

59 Patton, *Patriot Pirates*, 79–80.

60 APDE: J. Adams to A. Adams, 22 May 1777; GWP VI: 396; Patton, *Patriot Pirates*, 34.

61 Syrett, 'Germain', 395–405.

62 MHS: *Graves Conduct*, 4 December 1775.

63 Patton, *Patriot Pirates*, 31.

64 NDAR III: 69–72; MHS *Graves Conduct*, 4 December 1775.

65 GWP IV: 130.

66 Daughan, *If By Sea*, 43.

67 Syrett, *American Waters*, 23.

68 Bowler, *Logistics*, 96.

69 NDAR IV: 697, 708–9, 746–7; Tuchman, *First Salute*, 49; Morison, *John Paul Jones*, 43–8.

70 The names chosen for the early Continental vessels are interesting. See NDAR III: 173.

71 Most of the powder was secured, however, because the Americans delayed their attack until daylight. NDAR IV: 133; McCusker, 'Invasion of Nassau', 189–217; Morison, *John Paul Jones*, 43–8; Callo, *John Paul Jones*, 25–8.

72 NDAR VI: 619; Syrett, *European Waters*, 6.

73 O'Shaughnessy, *Empire Divided*, 155.

74 Alberts, *Golden Voyage*, 25–35; Patton, *Patriot Pirates*, 71–2; Jamieson, 'Leeward Islands', 119.

75 TNA: ADM 1/487. Other copies in the National Archives are TNA: Co5/177 and Co5/40.

76 Berger, *Broadsides*, 198.

77 Armitage, *Declaration*, 70.

78 NDAR III: 96, 122.

79 NDAR III: 9–10.

80 Patton, *Patriot Pirates*, 34.

81 Syrett, 'Organisation', 169–81.

82 O'Shaughnessy, *Men Who Lost America*, 328.

83 Ramsay, *History*, 224.

84 NDAR III: 112n.

85 MHS: *Graves Conduct*, 13 May 1775; Neeser, *Shuldham Despatches*, 49.

86 MHS: *Graves Conduct*, 392.

6 British Evacuation

1 Horowicz and Robson, *Colonial Posts*, 6; T. B. Allen, *Tories*, 160.

2 Moomaw, 'Captain Hamond', 66.

3 NDAR III: 135–6, 227; Quarles, *Negro*, 27; Berger, *Broadsides*, 87–92; T. B. Allen, *Tories*, 154–6; Selby, *Virginia*, 66.

4 Pybus, *Epic Journeys*, 8.
5 Selby, *Virginia*, 67–8; Pybus, *Epic Journeys*, 8.
6 Foy, 'Ports of Slavery', 274; Quarles, *Negro*, 31; Berger, *Broadsides*, 96.
7 Foy, 'Ports of Slavery', 5–11, 256–60; Quarles, *Negro*, 29; Pybus, *Epic Journeys*, 8.
8 Chernow, *Washington*, 195. For shock at the losses sustained on Bunker Hill, see TNA: ADM 1/486, 10–12.
9 NDAR III: 433, 443, 468, 1312–14; Hattendorf, *Talking about Naval History*, 186; Tilley, *British Navy*, 58–61.
10 Chernow, *Washington*, 227.
11 Weintraub, *Iron Tears*, 57.
12 Weintraub, *Iron Tears*, 55.
13 Neeser, *Shuldham Despatches*, 137.
14 McCullough, *John Adams*, 98.
15 Jasanoff, *Liberty's Exiles*, 29.
16 McCullough, *John Adams*, 98.
17 Lydenberg, *Robertson Diaries*, 79.
18 T. B. Allen, *Tories*, 114.
19 TNA: ADM 1/21680, f. 102; T. B. Allen, *Tories*, 113, 121.
20 NDAR IV: 376, 379, 405–7; Gordon, *Maritime Medicine*, 116.
21 McCullough, *1776*, 103.
22 McCullough, *1776*, 107.
23 GWP IV: 449.
24 There are various estimates of the strength of the British forces in Boston. William Howe reported 8,906 but other figures of 7,579 and 9,192 have survived. See French, *First Year*, 672 and appendices. Also, NDAR IV: 360; Syrett, *Shipping*, 207.
25 Jasanoff, *Liberty's Exiles*, 158; Neeser, *Shuldham Despatches*, xxxii, 187.
26 Chernow, *Washington*, 227.
27 NDAR IV: 496–7; McCullough, *1776*, 105.
28 Klooster, *Revolutions*, 42; Pybus, *Epic Journeys*, 17; NDAR IV: 244; NDAR V: 321–2.
29 Pybus, *Epic Journeys*, 18.
30 Moomaw, 'Colonial Virginia', 147.
31 Moomaw, 'Captain Hamond', 68.
32 NDAR V: 420–1, 781–2, 802–4, 860; Thacher, *Journal*, 58; Servies, *Log*, 8.
33 Moore, *Songs and Ballads*, 137; Weintraub, *Iron Tears*, 62.
34 Wilson, *Southern Strategy*, 54.
35 Mahan, *Major Operations*, 34.
36 Jasanoff, *Liberty's Exiles*, 49; Sweet and Nash, *Struggle*, 74; Pybus, *Epic Journeys*, 23.
37 Fischer, *Washington's Crossing*, 10.

7 British Attack

1 Knight, 'Recovery', 17.
2 Gruber, *Howe Brothers*, 51–2.
3 Knight, 'Recovery', 19; T. S. Anderson, *Howe Brothers*, 58; Gruber, *Howe Brothers*, 12–14, 32–8.
4 Baugh, 'Politics', 222–3; Conway, 'Politics', 1185.
5 Conway, 'Fellow Nationals', 86; T. S. Anderson, *Howe Brothers*, 84–5.
6 O'Shaughnessy, *Men Who Lost America*, 92.
7 Quoted in Baugh, 'Why did Britain?', 159.
8 Mackesy, *War for America*, 62. The original plan had been to use Russian troops to augment the few British soldiers available. This had been stopped by Catherine the Great. Dull, *Diplomatic History*, 47.
9 Stone, *Letters and Journals*, 3.
10 Tustin, *Diary*, 6.
11 Acomb, *Revolutionary Journal*, 29.
12 Quoted in Syrett, *Shipping*, 183. See also Pfister, *Voyage*, 10–30.
13 Tustin, *Diary*, 7.
14 Stirling, *The Hothams,* II, 303. The letter reporting Hotham's arrival in Halifax is in NDAR V: 942.
15 McCullough, *1776*, 131.
16 NDAR V: 815–17, 836–8, 874–5, 893–7; 917–18; Chernow, *Washington*, 235.
17 NDAR VI: 156.
18 NDAR V: 1038, 1–40, 1042–5; Laughton, 'Duncan Journals', 118.
19 NDAR V: 836, 935; Golway, *Washington's General*, 80.
20 Fischer, *Washington's Crossing*, 106.
21 NDAR V: 918, 1088, 1350; Ketchum, *Saratoga*, 7.
22 Callahan, 'Henry Knox', 243; O'Shaughnessy, *Men Who Lost America*, 92.
23 NDAR V: 662, 838; Thacher, *Journal*, 64; Chernow, *Washington*, 232; McCullough, *1776*, 133.
24 Chernow, *Washington*, 233.
25 GWP V: 180.
26 BL: Add 21680, f. 127; NDAR V: 1038, 1040–1; NDAR VI: 20, 37, 50, 1178–83; Walker, *Engineers*, 121–2; Diamant, *Chaining the Hudson*, 42–3.
27 GWP VI: 54.
28 Chernow, *Washington*, 238.
29 Lefkowitz, *Long Retreat*, 19n.1.
30 Laughton, *James Journal*, 28.
31 Tilley, *British Navy*, 87; Moomaw, 'Captain Hamond', 268–72.
32 NDAR V: 1309; Syrett, *Shipping*, 191; Moomaw, 'Captain Hamond', 248, 256.

33 A wonderful account of the negotiations can be read in NYPL 847: 11 September 1776, 'Memorandum of an interview between Lord Howe and Delegates from Congress'. See also Gruber, *Howe Brothers*, 117–20.

34 Crawford, 'Naval Support', 3. For more on the background see Harding, *Amphibious Warfare*; Syrett, 'British Amphibious Operations' and Syrett, 'Methodology'; Hore, *Seapower Ashore*; J. M. Johnson, 'Best Use'.

35 The many difficulties of getting horses from a ship to shore are described in Boniface, *Cavalry*, 290–1.

36 For details of the signalling system used, see a naval signal book *c.*1775–83 in MHS: SBd–186.

37 There is an interesting description in BL: Add 21680, f. 136.

38 Syrett, 'Methodology', 270–5.

39 GWP III: 461–5.

40 T. B. Allen, *Tories*, 169.

41 Chernow, *Washington*, 238.

42 NDAR VI: 267–70, 838–49, 861–2, 884–8; Laughton, 'Duncan Journals', 123.

43 Scull, *Evelyn Memoir*, 83.

44 Chernow, *Washington*, 248; BL: Add 21680, f. 149.

45 Laughton, 'Duncan Journals', 125.

46 Billias, *Glover*, 101.

47 Billias, *Glover*, 6, 99; Fischer, *Washington's Crossing*, 101; Magra, 'Soldiers', 535–8.

48 NDAR VI: 351, 354, 364; Chernow, *Washington*, 251.

49 NDAR VI: 336, 354, 364.

50 NDAR VI: 350–1. British ships made it to the East River on 2 September; NDAR VI: 655.

51 The drawing is by Lieutenant Francis M. Barber, prepared for a lecture in 1875 on 'submarine boats'. The *Gentleman's Magazine* of 1747 has an earlier and far less elaborate image, in an article on submarines that Bushnell is believed to have read. Lefkowitz, *Turtle*, 25.

52 Lefkowitz, *Turtle*, 97.

53 NDAR VI: 1499 ff.; Walker, *Engineers*, 139.

54 Lefkowitz, *Turtle*, 91, 103.

55 Hagist, 'New Interpretation', 328.

56 Fischer, *Washington's Crossing*, 103.

57 Scull, *Evelyn Memoir*, 85; Lydenberg, *Robertson Diaries*, 97.

58 Hagist, 'New Interpretation', 330.

59 Moomaw, 'Captain Hamond', 263.

60 Syrett, 'Methodology', 280n.43; Scull, *Evelyn Memoir*, 84; Mackenzie, *Diary*, I, 47.

61 NDAR VI: 928–33; W. Carter, *Genuine Detail*, 41; Laughton, 'Duncan Journals', 130; Mackenzie, *Diary*, I, 59; Schecter, *Battle for New York*, 202.

62 NDAR VI: 928–33, 974; Lydenberg, *Robertson Diaries*, 99; Mackenzie, *Diary*, I, 59; Fischer, *Washington's Crossing*, 107; Scull, *Evelyn Memoir*, 86–7.

63 Lefkowitz, *Turtle*, 17.

64 There is some suggestion that it was recovered by Bushnell. Lefkowitz, *Turtle*, 102.

65 NDAR VI: 1182–5; VII: 88–9; Patton, *Patriot Pirates*, 102; Lefkowitz, *Long Retreat*, 25–34.

66 Mackenzie, *Diary*, I, 109. See also NDAR VII: 259.

67 TNA: ADM 1/487, 149–50, 155–6; NDAR VII: 259–62, 386–7, 399–401.

68 Tilley, *British Navy*, 94.

69 NDAR VII: 1167–8, 1234–5, 1275–7.

70 Lefkowitz, *Long Retreat*, 43–9 and Figs 6–8. See also pages 181, 352.

71 Lefkowitz, *Long Retreat*, 103.

72 NDAR VII: 437; Lefkowitz, *Long Retreat*, 93, 106n.2. Many thanks to Arthur Lefkowitz for drawing my attention to this.

73 NDAR III: 1235, 1322, 1304; Jackson, *Pennsylvania Navy*, 17–19.

74 NDAR VII: 352, 414; Jackson, *Pennsylvania Navy*, 269; Lefkowitz, *Long Retreat*, 106.

75 Fischer, *Washington's Crossing*, 134.

76 McCullough, *1776*, 262.

77 Chernow, *Washington*, 268.

78 Tustin, *Diary*, 27; Lefkowitz, *Long Retreat*, 106.

79 Jackson, *Pennsylvania Navy*, 76, 79, 82.

80 Fischer, *Washington's Crossing*, 135; Lefkowitz, *Long Retreat*, 124.

81 The strategic concept of the 'fleet in being' is most recently discussed in Hattendorf, 'Fleet in Being'.

8 Freshwater Fleets

1 Graham, *Royal Navy*, 7; Baxter, *British Invasion*, 115.

2 Nelson, *Arnold's Navy*, 218.

3 Baxter, *British Invasion*, 117.

4 Baxter, *British Invasion*, 88–92.

5 Hadden, *Journal*, 10.

6 Baxter, *British Invasion*, 113, 120.

7 Fowler, *Rebels*, 196.

8 NDAR III 490; NDAR IV 890–1; NMM: BGR/9; Hadden, *Journal*, 540.

9 Nelson, *Arnold's Navy*, 273.

10 Baxter, *British Invasion*, 119.

11 Hadden, *Journal*, 541.

12 TNA: ADM 1/487, f. 93; Baxter, *British Invasion*, 119.

13 Anon, 'America: Affairs in Canada', 427. See also NMM: BGR/9.

14 NDAR VI: 45–7, 55, 55n.; Fowler, *Rebels*, 200.

15 Bratten, *Gondola Philadelphia*, 40.
16 NDAR VI: 45–7, 136, 1081; Bratten, *Gondola Philadelphia*, 41.
17 NDAR VI: 1437 (ship plan).
18 Bratten, *Gondola Philadelphia*, 41.
19 Baxter, *British Invasion*, 154–6.
20 Baxter, *British Invasion*, 143.
21 Bratten, *Gondola Philadelphia*, 38.
22 Hadden, *Journal*, 540.
23 NDAR VI: 1343–4; Bratten, *Gondola Philadelphia*, 42.
24 Nelson, *Arnold's Navy*, 288.
25 Baxter, *British Invasion*, 153.
26 BL: Add 38260, f. 9.
27 Northcote Parkinson, *Pellew*, 29; Baxter, *British Invasion*, 115.
28 *British Invasion*, 153; Bratten, *Gondola Philadelphia*, 42.
29 Nelson, *Arnold's Navy*, 237.
30 Fowler, *Rebels*, 187.
31 Much of the shipbuilding effort can be followed in NDAR VI.
32 Pell, 'Schuyler', 61.
33 Pell, 'Schuyler', 61.
34 Pell, 'Schuyler', 63.
35 Nelson, *Arnold's Navy*, 243.
36 Bratten, *Gondola Philadelphia*, 25.
37 See Varick Papers in NYHS: MS655 and Schuyler Papers in NYPL: Mss Col 2701.
38 Nelson, *Arnold's Navy*, 241; Fowler, *Rebels*, 190.
39 Fowler, *Rebels*, 190.
40 N. Miller, *Sea of Glory*, 170.
41 Bird, *Navies in the Mountains*, 175; Nelson, *Arnold's Navy*, 276.
42 Nelson, *Arnold's Navy*, 257.
43 BL: Add 38260, f. 9.
44 American accounts can be followed in NDAR VI: 1234–7, 1289–90, 1350–1; British accounts, 1198, 1228–30, 1244–5, 1257–61, 1272–7, 1341.
45 Osler, *Exmouth*, 20; Taylor, *Commander*, 38.
46 Nelson, *Arnold's Navy*, 326.
47 BL: Add 35371, f. 179.

9 American Riposte

1 GW-LOC: Washington to J. A. Washington, 18 December 1776.
2 Chernow, *Washington*, 269.
3 Syrett, *Shipping*, 124.
4 For more on this, see Willis, *Fighting Temeraire*.
5 Fischer, *Washington's Crossing*, 203.
6 Billias, *Glover*, 7.

7 Haven, *Thirty Days*, 44.
8 Haven, *Thirty Days*, 14.
9 Magra, 'Soldiers', 559.
10 Fischer, *Washington's Crossing*, 212.
11 For a list of the ferries see Fischer, *Washington's Crossing*, 397.
12 Jackson, *Pennsylvania Navy*, 17.
13 Haven, *Thirty Days*, 218–19.
14 Chernow, *Washington*, 273.
15 Hutton, *Portrait*, 100.
16 Fischer, *Washington's Crossing*, 257–9; Rodney, *Diary*, 13.
17 Billias, *Glover*, 8.
18 Fischer, *Washington's Crossing*, 208.
19 Chernow, *Washington*, 282–3.
20 Fischer, *Washington's Crossing*, 343.
21 Syrett, *Shipping*, 128.
22 Olton, *Artisans*, 1.
23 O'Shaughnessy, *Men Who Lost America*, 18.
24 Quoted in Ketchum, *Saratoga*, 104.
25 O'Shaughnessy, *Men Who Lost America*, 112–14; Billias, 'Burgoyne', 172;
    Willcox, 'Too Many Cooks', 57. It was only after Burgoyne's surrender
    that he complained of a lack of co-operation.
26 Ketchum, *Saratoga*, 61.
27 Syrett, *Shipping*, 239.
28 Chernow, *Washington*, 300.
29 NDAR IX: 336–7, 721, 723.
30 Syrett, *Shipping*, 230.
31 NDAR IX: 723.
32 O'Shaughnessy, *Men Who Lost America*, 107.
33 BL: Add 8010/2; Syrett, *Shipping*, 191.
34 BL: Add 8010/2; NDAR IX: 363; Tilley, *British Navy*, 106; Moomaw,
    'Captain Hamond', 319–27.
35 Moomaw, 'Captain Hamond', 326.
36 NDAR IX: 327, 354, 363; Tilley, *British Navy*, 106.
37 Chernow, *Washington*, 301.
38 O'Shaughnessy, *Men Who Lost America*, 107.
39 BL: Add 8010/2; NDAR IX: 795.
40 See WCL: Simcoe Papers, 'General disposition preparative to the landing
    of the army 24 August 1777'; NDAR IX: 785–8, 793–9.
41 BL: Add 8010/2.
42 NDAR IX: 835, 856–7.
43 Tilley, *British Navy*, 107.
44 Syrett, *American Waters*, 80.
45 Jackson, *British Army*, 12.
46 NDAR IX: 793, 808–9; Chernow, *Washington*, 301.

47 Quoted in Jackson, *British Army*, 13.
48 NDAR IX: 793, 960–1.
49 Foy, 'Ports of Slavery', 267.
50 Jackson, *British Army*, 17; T. B. Allen, *Tories*, 241–3.
51 BL: Add 8010/2.
52 NDAR IX: 972–7. Follow the campaign in Taaffe, *Philadelphia Campaign*.
53 NDAR IX: 972–7, 984; Dorwart, *Fort Mifflin*, 31.
54 Walker, *Engineers*, 150–2, 57–9; Dorwart, *Fort Mifflin*, 44–9.
55 Moomaw, 'Captain Hamond', 117; Jackson, *Pennsylvania Navy*, 353 ff.
56 Harte, 'River Obstructions', 139.
57 Jackson, *Pennsylvania Navy*, 359.
58 NDAR IX: 91, 107, 110, 294.
59 Fitzpatrick, *Washington Writings*, IX, 255–6, 259.
60 Syrett, *American Waters*, 81.
61 Dorwart, *Fort Mifflin*, 36.
62 Syrett, *American Waters*, 81.
63 NDAR X: 248; Leach, 'Hazlewood', 3–5; Walker, *Engineers*, 166.
64 NDAR X: 246–50, 260–4; Tilley, *British Navy*, 114; Moomaw, 'Captain Hamond', 363.
65 Dorwart, *Fort Mifflin*, 41.
66 Syrett, *American Waters*, 84; Jackson, *British Army*, 71, 200; Dann, *Nagle Journal*, 11–12.
67 Dorwart, *Fort Mifflin*, 41; Jackson, *Pennsylvania Navy*, 205.
68 NDAR X: 396–7.
69 Bass, *Ships and Shipwrecks*, 150.
70 NDAR X: 246–54, 260–4.
71 Jackson, *Pennsylvania Navy*, 204.
72 NDAR X: 265, 286–7, 305–8; Jackson, *Pennsylvania Navy*, 202.

10 British Surrender

1 Baxter, *British Invasion*, 178.
2 Nelson, *Arnold's Navy*, 341.
3 J. Baldwin, *Journal*, 94; Walker, *Engineers*, 102.
4 J. Baldwin, *Journal*, 94.
5 Thacher, *Journal*, 96.
6 Thacher, *Journal*, 96; Osler, *Exmouth*, 25.
7 Walker, *Engineers*, 104–5.
8 MHS: 'The Diary of Moses Greenleaf', 27 April 1777.
9 Mackesy, *War for America*, 107.
10 Mintz, *Generals of Saratoga*, 112–13.
11 BL: Add 32413; Mackesy, *War for America*, 108.
12 NDAR X: 587; Hadden, *Journal*, 53.
13 Hadden, *Journal*, 56.

14 Hadden, *Journal*, 52.
15 NDAR IX: 187; Anburey, 'Ticonderoga', 15.
16 O'Shaughnessy, *Men Who Lost America*, 146.
17 Anburey, 'Ticonderoga', 15–17.
18 M. L. Brown, *Baroness von Riedesel*, 26–7, 31–2; Furneaux, *Saratoga*, 139.
19 Thorp, *Acland Journal*, xxviii–xxix, 8, 12, 14, 18.
20 NDAR IX: 174–5; Anburey, 'Ticonderoga', 15.
21 Hadden, *Journal*, 84.
22 Nelson, *Arnold's Navy*, 342.
23 Walker, *Engineers*, 106.
24 BL: Add 32413, f. 48; Thacher, *Journal*, 102; Preston, Lyon and Batchelor, *Navies*, 26; Mintz, *Generals of Saratoga*, 144–6.
25 J. Baldwin, *Journal*, 109.
26 NDAR IX: 212–13, 284, 349, 594; Hadden, *Journal*, 80 ff.; Northcote Parkinson, *Pellew*, 43; Lynn, *Specht Journal*, 53; Bird, *Navies in the Mountains*, 239.
27 Hadden, *Journal*, 89; Lynn, *Specht Journal*, 54.
28 J. Baldwin, *Journal*, 110–11.
29 Thacher, *Journal*, 100; Lynn, *Specht Journal*, 54; Bird, *Navies in the Mountains*, 239.
30 NDAR IX: 225.
31 Thacher, *Journal*, 102.
32 Walker, *Engineers*, 106.
33 Chernow, *Washington*, 301.
34 The many balancing factors in Schuyler's failure can best be followed in Mintz, *Generals of Saratoga*, 142–4.
35 Hadden, *Journal*, 96.
36 Hadden, *Journal*, 94.
37 Billias, 'Burgoyne', 177.
38 Hadden, *Journal*, 106.
39 Pell, 'Schuyler', 67.
40 Furneaux, *Saratoga*, 134.
41 Beatson, *Memoirs*, IV, 233.
42 NDAR X: 70, 90, 94, 96–9.
43 Harte, 'River Obstructions', 176.
44 There has been some very promising underwater survey work undertaken to identify possible wrecks in these locations. Napolitano, 'Multibeam Acoustics', 23–4; NDAR X: 47, 57–8, 73.
45 NDAR X: 109, 118.
46 Ketchum, *Saratoga*, 378; Mintz, *Generals of Saratoga*, 200.
47 Stone, *Visits*, 298.
48 NMM: PEL Misc 92/027 f.139.
49 Stone, *Visits*, 241; Billias, *Glover*, 132–49; Mintz, *Generals of Saratoga*, 183, 189, 196–7.

50 Osler, *Exmouth*, 39.

51 O'Shaughnessy, *Men Who Lost America*, 219.

52 Many thanks to Mr Robert Bellamy for this observation. NDAR X: 665; NDAR XI: 407–8, 709 and n.

53 NDAR X: 392. This would not have been that much of a surprise. The *Thunderer* was a very bad sea boat and nearly sank after the battle of Valcour, when her lee boards gave way and she heeled alarmingly. Cometti, *Enys Journals*, 20; Malcomson, *Warships of the Great Lakes*, 29.

11 American Sea Power

1 NDAR X: 456–68, 512–14, 549–50; Moomaw, 'Captain Hamond', 349 ff.

2 Walker, *Engineers*, 173–4.

3 NDAR X: 557–9, 653–4: Moomaw, 'Captain Hamond', 364; Crawford, 'Naval Support', 6.

4 NDAR X: 25, 28 and n., 288, 321; Moomaw, 'Captain Hamond', 373.

5 Jackson, *British Army*, 89.

6 Cobbett, *Parliamentary History*, XVIII, 1427.

7 Knight, 'Recovery', 13.

8 NDAR VIII: 1028; Collins, 'Whaleboat Warfare', 197–9.

9 G. W. Allen, *Naval History*, 231–2.

10 G. W. Allen, *Naval History*, 239.

11 Alberts, *Golden Voyage*, 49; Jamieson, 'Leeward Islands', 122.

12 Jamieson, 'American Privateers', 20.

13 Knight, *Pursuit*, 44.

14 O'Shaughnessy, *Men Who Lost America*, 118; Gruber, 'Lord Howe', 244; N. Miller, *Sea of Glory*, 293.

15 For a detailed example, see Crawford, 'Hawke and the Dove', 49–66. The Portuguese, Danes and Prussians (until 1779) took a pro-British stance. NDAR VI: 467–8.

16 NDAR VIII: 514, 529, 603, 614–15; Bemis, *Diplomacy*, 54; Johnston, 'American Privateers', 359–61; Dull, *Diplomatic History*, 80–1; Crawford, 'Hawke and the Dove', 64.

17 NDAR IX: 600, 606, 615–16, 634–5; N. Miller, *Sea of Glory*, 298–9.

18 Syrett, 'Germain', 395–405; N. Miller, *Sea of Glory*, 298–9.

19 Though calculating the figures is fraught with difficulty. Syrett, *American Waters*, 88; O'Shaughnessy, *Men Who Lost America*, 332.

20 British exports averaged about 15 per cent less between 1776 and 1782 than between 1772 and 1775, though it is unclear precisely how this is related to the war. Dull, *Diplomatic History*, 68.

21 NDAR VIII: 282; Hattendorf, *Talking about Naval History*, 194–5; Fowler, *Rebels*, 74–7.

22 APDE: Warren to Adams, 7 September 1777.

23 Hattendorf, *Talking about Naval History*, 196.

24 NDAR VIII: 89 and n., 224; N. Miller, *Sea of Glory*, 225.

25 MML: 'Letterbook of Esek Hopkins', 33–4.

26 NDAR V: 265.

27 NDAR V: 280.

28 NDAR IX: 627, 877–8, 881–2.

29 Syrett, *American Waters*, 85.

30 Laughton, *James Journal*, 41.

31 APDE: Warren to Adams, 22 June 1777.

32 APDE: Warren to Adams, 23 March 1777. Manley outranked McNeill, who was abrasive and doubted Manley's competence.

33 NDAR IX: 47, 51, 85–7, 282–4, 305–6; G. W. Allen, *Naval History*, 205.

34 P. C. F. Smith, *Manley Zeal*; held in the collections of the Peabody Essex Museum in Salem, MA.

35 P. C. F. Smith, *Manley Zeal*, 59.

36 NDAR IX: 226–30, 279–80.

37 APDE: Warren to Adams, 7 September 1777; NDAR IX: 299–300, 307–9, 875.

38 APDE: Gordon to Adams, 5 June 1777.

39 Buel, *In Irons*, 47.

40 Braake, *Posted Letter*, F-42.

41 NDAR VII: 677, 777, 780–1, 790–1.

42 Rodger, *Insatiable Earl*, 235.

43 Bonnichon, 'Objectifs Français', 52.

44 Dull, *Ship of the Line*, 94–5; Dull, 'Mahan', 61; Dull, 'Tragedy', 81; Baugh, 'Why did Britain?', 158, 162. A belief that was not, in fact, widely shared in the British treasury; Mackesy, *War for America*, 37.

45 Dull, 'Tragedy', 94.

46 Knight, 'Recovery', 12–14; Dull, *Ship of the Line*, 101; G. S. Brown, 'Anglo-French Naval Crisis', 8; Rodger, *Insatiable Earl*, 238; Tilley, *British Navy*, 121.

47 Bemis, *Diplomacy*, 60–6.

48 Dull, *Ship of the Line*, 97–8.

49 NDAR IX: 1139; Dull, *Ship of the Line*, 98; Dull, *French Navy*, 90; Dull, 'Tragedy', 91; Dull, *Diplomatic History*, 89–92; Dull, *Franklin the Diplomat*, 23.

50 NDAR X: 667–8, 764n.; NDAR XII: 310; Morton and Spinelli, *Beaumarchais*, 128, 138.

51 Dull, *Benjamin Franklin*, 72–6; Mintz, *Generals of Saratoga*, 234.

12 Bourbon Alliance

1 Ribiero, *Dress*, 142.

2 Bishop, 'Rochambeau', 786–7.

3 Herring, *Colony*, 22.

4 Conway, 'Fellow Nationals', 96.

5 Bishop, 'Rochambeau', 786–7.

6 WCL: Abraham Whipple Papers, M-115, 5 July 1778.

7 Morton and Spinelli, *Beaumarchais*, 167–71, 180, 197.

8 Dexter, *Stiles Diary*, II, 458.

9 Conway, 'Fellow Nationals', 96.

10 TNA: ADM 1/5117/12; Syrett, *European Waters*, 13; Willcox, 'Admiral Rodney', 193–8; Bemis, 'Secret Service', 474–95.

11 Rodger, *Insatiable Earl*, 235; Boudriot, 'French Fleet', 79–86.

12 Brunsman, *Evil Necessity*, 245.

13 Dull, *French Navy*, 15.

14 For the background context, see Black, *European Powers* and Black, *Necessary Enemies*.

15 H. W. Richmond, *Statesmen and Seapower*, 144; Bonnichon, 'Objectifs Français', 49–50.

16 Gillispie, *Science and Polity*, 51. Lavoisier was guillotined during the Reign of Terror in the summer of 1794. Kelly, *Gunpowder*, 166, 177.

17 C. L. Lewis, *de Grasse*, 46.

18 Boudriot, *Seventy-Four Gun Ship*, IV, 9.

19 Jenkins, *French Navy*, 149–50.

20 The first book on naval tactics ever published in the English language had only appeared twelve years before war broke out with America. Depeyre, *Tactiques et Stratégies*, 99–148; O'Bryen, *Naval Evolutions*.

21 Chernow, *Washington*, 336.

22 TNA: ADM 1/94, f. 337.

23 TNA: ADM 51/59, 18 June 1778.

24 TNA: ADM 1/94, ff. 375–7.

25 Anon, *Maritime Campaign*, 6.

26 Syrett, *European Waters*, 38.

27 Conway, 'Fellow Nationals', 97.

28 Conway, 'Fellow Nationals', 98.

29 Conway, 'Fellow Nationals', 67–8, 94–6; Conway, 'Politics', 1200.

13 French Firepower

1 For a charming personal letter revealing this fear, see Macleod, 'Thinking Minds', 250; see also Patterson, *Other Armada*, 39.

2 Dull, *French Navy*, 108n.5.

3 Goodwin, *Nelson's Ships*, 234–5.

4 Goodwin, *Nelson's Ships*, 236.

5 Bonner-Smith, *Barrington Papers*, II, 4.

6 O'Shaughnessy, *Men Who Lost America*, 48.

7 Knight, 'Recovery', 13–14.

8 O'Shaughnessy, *Men Who Lost America*, 31.

9   Chaline, 'Escadres d'Évolution', 365–81.
10 Clowes, *Royal Navy*, III, 413; Tilley, *British Navy*, 130.
11 Villiers, 'La Stratégie', 211–47.
12 Mackesy, *War for America*, 210.
13 *Keppel Trial*, 119; de Goussencourt, 'Journal', 91.
14 Willis, *Fighting at Sea*, 129–51; Syrett, *European Waters*, 71.
15 Dull, *French Navy*, 121, 359–60.
16 Jenkins, *French Navy*, 151.
17 Rodger, *Insatiable Earl*, 245.
18 TNA: ADM 51/1036/1.
19 NMM: MKH/508; Goodwin, *Nelson's Ships*, 238; Forrer and Roussel, *La Bretagne*, 57–60.
20 Anon, *Letter from a Sea-Officer*, 13.
21 Rodger, *Insatiable Earl*, 244.
22 Rodger, *Command of the Ocean*, 2, 337.
23 Hodges, *Naval Documents*, 163.
24 TNA: ADM 51/1036/1; NMM: SAN/F/17; Cobbett, *Parliamentary History*, XX, 448.
25 Tunstall, *Naval Warfare*, 119, 127, 135, 146; Willis, *Fighting at Sea*, 69–71.
26 Tracy, 'British Assessments', 83.
27 Conway, 'Fellow Nationals', 68; Conway, 'Politics', 1200.
28 Knight, 'Recovery', 17.
29 O'Shaughnessy, *Men Who Lost America*, 70.
30 Hunt, *Life of Palliser*, 300.
31 Wright, *Cowper Poems*, 33–4.
32 Mahan, *Major Operations*, 69.
33 Anon, *Nereus's Prophecy*, B.
34 Mackesy, *War for America*, 243.
35 Cohen, *Yankee Sailors*, 95.
36 Rankin, 'Lord Cornwallis', 199.

14 British Survival

1   NDAR XII: 266, 282, 319; F.-H. Smith, 'French at Boston', 13.
2   F.-H. Smith, 'French at Boston', 14.
3   NDAR XII: 517–19, 611–12; Mahan, *Major Operations*, 47.
4   Hattendorf, *Newport*, 4. A 1746 operation with some parallels can be followed in Pritchard, *Anatomy of a Naval Disaster*.
5   NDAR XII: 583, 718–19; Hattendorf, *Newport*, 38.
6   Wilson, *Southern Strategy*, 134.
7   Chaline, 'Admiral d'Orvilliers', 6.
8   Hattendorf, *Newport*, 4.
9   NYPL: Mss Col 1216, Captain Henry Duncan to a friend, 14 September 1778.

10 Mackesy, *War for America*, 154–9; Gruber, *Howe Brothers*, 280–1.

11 Syrett, *American Waters*, 95; Jackson, *British Army*, 261.

12 Tilley, *British Navy*, 139.

13 Chernow, *Washington*, 338.

14 T. B. Allen, *Tories*, 247; Jackson, *British Army*, 259–62; W. Brown, *Good Americans*, 61.

15 Moomaw, 'Captain Hamond', 399.

16 Foy, 'Ports of Slavery', 269.

17 NYPL: Mss Col 1216, Captain Henry Duncan to a friend, 14 September 1778; Syrett, *American Waters*, 99; Syrett, *Howe*, 79; Hattendorf, *Newport*, 9.

18 O'Beirne, *Narrative*, 15.

19 Mahan, *Major Operations*, 50.

20 Tustin, *Diary*, 140.

21 APDE: J. Bondfield to the Commissioners, 8 and 15 September 1778. For an interesting American perspective see BPL: A. Adams to J. Thaxter, 21 May 1778, MS. AM.229 (3).

22 O'Beirne, *Narrative*, 16.

23 Moomaw, 'Captain Hamond', 405.

24 Kerallain, *Bougainville*, 164; Syrett, *American Waters*, 99; Tilley, *British Navy*, 145.

25 Moomaw, 'Captain Hamond', 403.

26 Tilley, *British Navy*, 142.

27 Hattendorf, *Newport*, 8.

28 Mahan, *Major Operations*, 49.

29 The question of British masts in this war is an interesting one. See Knight, 'New England Forests'; Albion, *Forests*; Carlton, 'New England Masts', 13.

30 TNA: ADM 1/486, ff. 115–19; Barrington, 'Some Letters', 387; Syrett, *Howe*, 81; Jamieson, 'Leeward Islands', 79.

31 Whittemore, 'John Sullivan', 153.

32 Hattendorf, *Newport*, 13.

33 Crawford, 'Joint Allied Operation', 233.

34 Crawford, 'Joint Allied Operation', 236.

35 Clowes, *Royal Navy*, III, 169.

36 Hattendorf, *Newport*, 16.

37 NYPL: Mss Col 1216, Captain Henry Duncan to a friend, 14 September 1778.

38 NYPL: Mss Col 1216, Captain Henry Duncan to a friend, 14 September 1778; F.-H. Smith, 'French at Boston', 16.

39 O'Beirne, *Narrative*, 35.

40 TNA: ADM 1/488, ff. 314–16; Moomaw, 'Captain Hamond', 403–7.

41 N. Miller, *Sea of Glory*, 349.

42 McBurney, *Rhode Island*, 151–2.

43 N. Miller, *Sea of Glory*, 349; McBurney, *Rhode Island*, 150.

44 NYPL: Mss Col 1216, Captain Henry Duncan to a friend, 14 September 1778; Moomaw, 'Captain Hamond', 413; O'Beirne, *Narrative*, 40.

45 Chernow, *Washington*, 348.

46 Chernow, *Washington*, 348; McBurney, *Rhode Island*, 152. N. Miller, *Sea of Glory*, 346.

47 BPL: A. Adams to J. Thaxter, 26 August 1778, MS. Am. 229 (6).

48 BPL: A. Adams to J. Thaxter, 26 August 1778 , MS. Am. 229 (6).

49 McBurney, *Rhode Island*, 153.

50 Chernow, *Washington*, 349.

51 Moore, *Songs and Ballads*, 233.

52 N. Miller, *Sea of Glory*, 353.

53 NYPL: Navy Board of the Eastern Division Letter Book, 31 October 1778.

54 Buel, *In Irons*, 27.

55 F.-H. Smith, *Memorial*, 6–8.

56 APDE: *Adams Family Papers*, III, 'Descriptive List of Illustrations'.

57 APDE: A. Adams to J. Adams, 21 and 25 October 1778.

58 APDE: J. Adams to A. Adams, 18 December 1778.

59 Barnes and Owen, *Sandwich Papers*, II, 308.

60 Hattendorf, *Talking about Naval History*, 197; Mahan, *Major Operations*, 72; Dull, *Diplomatic History*, 107.

61 Barnes and Owen, *Sandwich Papers*, II, 355.

15 Caribbean Sea

1 Marshall, *Making and Unmaking*, 363.

2 O'Shaughnessy, *Empire Divided*, 210; Mackesy, *War for America*, 524–5.

3 Bonner-Smith, *Barrington Papers*, II, xvii.

4 Jamieson, 'Leeward Islands', 53.

5 Crewe, *Yellow Jack*, 7–9, 213, 298.

6 Jamieson, 'Leeward Islands', 55–8.

7 O'Shaughnessy, *Empire Divided*, 9.

8 Barnes and Owen, *Sandwich Papers*, II, 337. For deaths at the siege, see F. Anderson, *Crucible of War*, 501.

9 Jamieson, 'Leeward Islands', 76.

10 Laughton, *James Journal*, 53.

11 Jamieson, 'Leeward Islands', 135.

12 Bonner-Smith, *Barrington Papers*, II, 288.

13 O'Shaughnessy, *Men Who Lost America*, 104.

14 O'Shaughnessy, *Empire Divided*, 152–3.

15 O'Shaughnessy, *Empire Divided*, 163; Carrington, *Sugar Industry*, 47.

16 O'Shaughnessy, *Empire Divided*, 162.

17 Higginbotham, *War of American Independence*, 106. Though a minority

of whites did support the revolution. O'Shaughnessy, *Empire Divided*, 182; Carrington, *British West Indies*, 127.

18 NDAR X: 151, 660, 667, 737; O'Shaughnessy, *Empire Divided*, 169; Barnes and Owen, *Sandwich Papers*, I, 369.

19 Jamieson, 'Leeward Islands'.

20 Barrington, 'Some Letters', 288–90.

21 Bonner-Smith, *Barrington Papers*, II, 39; Barnes and Owen, *Sandwich Papers*, I, 414–15; Clowes, *Royal Navy*, IV, 19; Boromé, 'Dominica', 36.

22 Jamieson, 'Leeward Islands', 56.

23 Boromé, 'Dominica', 38–40.

24 Barnes and Owen, *Sandwich Papers*, II, 345.

25 During the Philadelphia campaign of 1777 Hotham remained behind in New York as the senior naval officer. Gill Jr and Curtis III, *Man Apart*, 200n.47.

26 Bonner-Smith, *Barrington Papers*, II, 168–9.

27 Anon, *Observations on the Diseases*, 1.

28 Bonner-Smith, *Barrington Papers*, II, 119.

29 Bonner-Smith, *Barrington Papers*, II, 116.

30 Barrington, 'Some Letters', 386–9.

31 Barnes and Owen, *Sandwich Papers*, II, 345.

32 Barnes and Owen, *Sandwich Papers*, II, 345.

33 Barrington, 'Some Letters', 387.

34 Barnes and Owen, *Sandwich Papers*, II, 346, 357; Bonner-Smith, *Barrington Papers*, II, 151.

35 Bonner-Smith, *Barrington Papers*, II, 120.

36 Whinynates, *Francis Downman*, 94.

37 Bonner-Smith, *Barrington Papers*, II, 167; Barrington, 'Some Letters', 389.

38 Bonner-Smith, *Barrington Papers*, II, 120–5; Jamieson, 'Leeward Islands', 156.

39 Barnes and Owen, *Sandwich Papers*, II, 347; Whinynates, *Francis Downman*, 95.

40 James, *British Navy*, 119.

41 Barnes and Owen, *Sandwich Papers*, II, 354.

42 Bonner-Smith, *Barrington Papers*, II, 131.

43 Barrington, 'Some Letters', 382.

44 Bonner-Smith, *Barrington Papers*, II, 141; Barnes and Owen, *Sandwich Papers*, II, 350.

45 Barnes and Owen, *Sandwich Papers*, II, 354.

46 Bonner-Smith, *Barrington Papers*, II, 157.

47 Carrington, *Sugar Industry*, 50.

48 TNA: ADM 1/486, ff. 118, 128–9; Jamieson, 'Leeward Islands', 77; James, *British Navy*, 114.

49 Jamieson, 'Leeward Islands', 57.

50 Barrington, 'Some Letters', 391.
51 Syrett, 'D'Estaing's Decision', 162n.21; Barnes and Owen, *Sandwich Papers*, II, 357.

16 Indian Empire

1 Marshall, *Making and Unmaking*, 221, 252–3, 264.
2 Parsons, *Travels*, 214–15; Falconer, *Dictionary*, 400. Nelson, who visited Bombay around this period, twice in 1775 and once in 1776, greatly admired the infrastructure. Sugden, *Dream of Glory*, 96.
3 H. W. Richmond, *Navy in India*, 76, 81.
4 There is lots of unexplored material from the India Office in the British Library concerning the opening of the Suez route in 1777. See, for example, BL: IOR/G/17/5. A chart survives of a voyage undertaken by HMS *Swallow* in 1777. BL: IOR/X/14692/97 and IOR/X/14692/100. Also see NMM: GRENiD/3 and JRL: GB 133 Eng MS 469.
5 G. Baldwin, *Political Recollections*, 7; Hoskins, *British Routes*, 18n.63.
6 H. W. Richmond, *Navy in India*, 81.
7 TNA: ADM 1/165, 16 August 1778.
8 BL: IOR/H/166, page 217.
9 Gleig, *Hastings Memoirs*, 205.
10 MacDougall, 'British Seapower', 303.
11 Roy, *War*, 21.
12 Anon, 'Biographical Memoir', 4.
13 Baugh, 'Why did Britain?', 163.
14 Dull, *French Navy*, 364.

17 Spanish Patience

1 For the background see R. White, *Middle Ground*. For specifics on a raid led by Christopher Carleton in 1778 with Indian help, see Washington and Washington, *Carleton's Raid*. A nephew of Guy Carleton, Christopher had spent some time actually living among the Mohawk Indians before the war. Heavily tattooed, he wore a ring in his nose.
2 Knight, *Pursuit*, 49.
3 Chavez, *Spain*, 108; Caughey, *Gálvez*, 87,101; McCarthy, 'Attitude of Spain', 50.
4 Chavez, *Spain*, 104; Haarmann, 'Spanish Conquest', 109; Paullin, *Navy*, 308; Shaw, *British Administration*, 276.
5 Alden, *The South*, 275; Shaw, *British Administration*.
6 NDAR XI: 682.
7 NDAR XI: 492, 775–6, 792; Haynes, 'James Willing', 12; Caughey, *Gálvez*, 113; Abbey, 'Peter Chester', 20; Abbey, 'Intrigue', 398; Crawford, 'Naval Conquest', 9–10.

8   Haynes, 'James Willing', 13.
9   NDAR XI: 606–7, 643, 649, 704, 706; NDAR XII: 436–7; Chavez, *Spain*, 106; Haynes, 'James Willing', 16–17, 38. Willing was subsequently captured by the British at sea and, considered a 'person of consequence', spent the rest of the war in a British prison.
10 Haynes, 'James Willing', 27; Chavez, *Spain*, 105.
11 Chavez, *Spain*.
12 Bemis, *Diplomacy*, 110.
13 Dull, *Diplomatic History*, 107–9; Chavez, *Spain*, 133.
14 Syrett, *European Waters*, 69.
15 Dull, *Ship of the Line*, 103; Patterson, *Other Armada*, 6; Mackesy, *War for America*, 279.
16 Dull, *Diplomatic History*, 107.
17 Syrett, *European Waters*, 69.
18 Chernow, *Washington*, 362.
19 C. C. Jones, *Siege of Savannah*, 10–11.
20 O'Shaughnessy, *Men Who Lost America*, 47.
21 O'Shaughnessy, *Men Who Lost America*, 66.

18 Bourbon Invasion

1   Patterson, *Other Armada*, 166.
2   Patterson, *Other Armada*, 41.
3   Patterson, *Other Armada*, 42.
4   Patterson, *Other Armada*, 60. Dull, *French Navy*, 134; Forrer and Roussel, *La Bretagne*, 70–1.
5   Patterson, *Other Armada*, 160.
6   Patterson, *Other Armada*, 46.
7   Parès, *Imprimeries d'Escadre*, 5–7.
8   Tunstall, *Naval Warfare*, 143.
9   Patterson, *Other Armada*, 181.
10 TNA: ADM 1/1806, ff. 243, 245, 253, 257.
11 Patterson, *Other Armada*, 207.
12 TNA: ADM 1/806, f. 248.
13 Chavez, *Spain*, 139; Forrer and Roussel, *La Bretagne*, 73, 77.
14 Patterson, *Other Armada*, 209.
15 Dull, *French Navy*, 157.
16 Butterfield, *George III*, 66n.
17 Patterson, *Other Armada*, 214; Mackesy, *War for America*, 295.
18 *Annual Register*, 1780, page 15.
19 Knight, 'Recovery', 10.
20 Mackesy, *War for America*, 263.
21 WCO: J. Wesley to S. Bradburn, 10 July 1779.
22 Conway, 'Fellow Nationals', 95.

23 Tunstall, *Naval Warfare*, 146.
24 Dull, 'Tragedy', 99; Dull, *French Navy*, 163–7, 202.

19 British Resourcefulness

1   Chavez, *Spain*, 132.
2   Ancell, *Journal*, 6.
3   Ancell, *Journal*, 10; J. Russell, *Gibraltar*, 44; McGuffie, *Siege*, 49.
4   McGuffie, *Siege*, 44.
5   NMM: DUF/2; ADM L/P 142.
6   Petrie, *Charles III*, 187; Drinkwater, *History*, 62.
7   Barnes and Owen, *Sandwich Papers*, III, 171.
8   J. Russell, *Gibraltar*, 51; Ancell, *Journal*, 9; Spilsbury, *Journal*, 5, 8.
9   See for example Spilsbury, *Journal*, 9; Ancell, *Journal*, 12.
10 Harding, 'Two Sieges', 37; McGuffie, *Siege*, 48.
11 For more on this see Dull, *Miracle*.
12 J. Russell, *Gibraltar*, 42.
13 J. Russell, *Gibraltar*, 62.
14 NMM: Ell/501 f.50.
15 Drinkwater, *History*, 86.

20 Caribbean Crisis

1   Bonner-Smith, *Barrington Papers*, II, xxv. There is some suggestion that Byron acted in this way to lure the French out of Martinique. Jamieson, 'Battle of Grenada', 58–9.
2   Jamieson, 'Battle of Grenada', 55–8.
3   Barrow, *Life of Macartney*, I, 56.
4   Wilson, *Southern Strategy*, 135.
5   Mahan, *Major Operations*, 76.
6   Jamieson, 'Leeward Islands', 187; Log of the *Fortunée*, 6 July 1779, BPL: MSf Eng 514.
7   Bonner-Smith, *Barrington Papers*, II, xxii, 288.
8   Bonner-Smith, *Barrington Papers*, II, 287, 326; Jamieson, 'Leeward Islands', 40.
9   Bonner-Smith, *Barrington Papers*, II, 331.
10 Log of the *Fortunée*, 6 July 1779, BPL: MSf Eng 514; Dunmore, *Pacific Explorer*, 135.
11 Ekins, *Naval Battles*, 78; Mahan, *Major Operations*, 78. It is unclear why it was described as black. British ships in this period were usually painted yellow.
12 Bonner-Smith, *Barrington Papers*, II, 319; Ekins, *Naval Battles*, 78.
13 Jamieson, 'Leeward Islands', 190; Cavaliero, *Admiral Satan*, 39–41.

14 C. C. Jones, *Siege of Savannah*, 10; McLarty, 'Jamaica', 63; Jamieson, 'Battle of Grenada', 61.

15 Jamieson, 'Battle of Grenada', 62.

16 Jamieson, 'Battle of Grenada', 55.

17 Pocock, *Young Nelson*, 43. The British preparations are detailed in TNA: ADM 1/241, ff. 303–4, 311.

18 Jamieson, 'Leeward Islands', 164.

21 French Incompetence

1 The Admiralty decided to replace Gambier with Arbuthnot on 23 January 1779. TNA: ADM 3/86.

2 TNA: ADM 1/486, ff. 250–1.

3 Clinton's decision-making process can be followed in Barnes and Owen, *Sandwich Papers*, III, 136–41, 237 ff.

4 Paullin, *Navy*, 459–60.

5 Wilson, *Southern Strategy*, 77.

6 Dull, *French Navy*, 161.

7 TNA: ADM 1/486, f. 306; Wilson, *Southern Strategy*, 138.

8 C. C. Jones, *Siege of Savannah*, 16, 59.

9 Hough, *Siege of Savannah*, 54, 146; C. C. Jones, *Siege of Savannah*, 57, 61.

10 For d'Estaing's motivations, see Anon, 'Siege of Savannah', 130; Chernow, *Washington*, 365; Mattern, *Benjamin Lincoln*, 80; Dull, *French Navy*, 161–2n.15.

11 Hough, *Siege of Savannah*, 106–9.

12 Lawrence, *Storm*, 20–1.

13 Anon, 'Siege of Savannah', 130; Wilson, *Southern Strategy*, 175; C. C. Jones, *Siege of Savannah*, 19.

14 C. C. Jones, *Siege of Savannah*, 13.

15 C. C. Jones, *Siege of Savannah*, 59; Wilson, *Southern Strategy*, 139.

16 Hough, *Siege of Savannah*, 51n.1.

17 Lawrence, *Storm*, 31.

18 C. L. Lewis, *de Grasse*, 80.

19 TNA: ADM 1/486, f. 305; Wilson, *Southern Strategy*, 144; Lawrence, *Storm*, 49–51.

20 Wilson, *Southern Strategy*, 145; Mattern, *Benjamin Lincoln*, 82.

21 Crawford, 'Naval Support', 5.

22 C. C. Jones, *Siege of Savannah*, 61–62; Lawrence, *Storm*, 86–7, 89–90.

23 Hough, *Siege of Savannah*, 54.

24 C. C. Jones, *Siege of Savannah*, 62.

25 Mattern, *Benjamin Lincoln*, 83.

26 Wilson, *Southern Strategy*, 151; C. C. Jones, *Siege of Savannah*, 25.

27 Hough, *Siege of Savannah*, 62.

28 Wilson, *Southern Strategy*, 153.

29 Five of the seventy-six guns were field pieces. C. C. Jones, *Siege of Savannah*, 27. HMS *Rose* and *Fowey* had been stripped of their armaments.
30 Wilson, *Southern Strategy*, 135.
31 Wilson, *Southern Strategy*, 173.
32 TNA: ADM 1/486, f. 328; Lawrence, *Storm*, 104 ff.
33 Anon, 'D'Estaing Eclipsed', [no date].
34 Anon, 'Siege of Savannah', 139.
35 D. L. Russell, *Southern Colonies*, 146.
36 Buel, *In Irons*, 144.
37 Though three frigates were taken: C. L. Lewis, *de Grasse*, 81; C. C. Jones, *Siege of Savannah*, 69. And Thomas Pasley came close: TNA: ADM 1/2306, 15 December 1779.
38 Mattern, *Benjamin Lincoln*, 86.
39 R. C. Cole, 'Savannah and the British Press', 190.

22 American Destruction

1 NDAR XII: 676.
2 NDAR XII: 589–90, 595–606, 675–6; Callo, *John Paul Jones*, 48–51.
3 TNA: ADM 1/2305.
4 TNA: ADM 1/2305.
5 Gawalt, *Jones' Memoir*, 37.
6 Schaeper, *John Paul Jones*, 72; Boudriot, *John Paul Jones*, 53 ff.
7 Gawalt, *Jones' Memoir*, 37.
8 TNA: ADM 1/2305.
9 The reasons for which are discussed in Schaeper, *John Paul Jones*, 41–4.
10 C. L. Lewis, 'Yet Begun to Fight', 229–37. The suggestion that he surrender was certainly made, however. TNA: ADM 1/2305.
11 Melville, *Israel Potter*, 120.
12 J. S. Barnes, *Fanning's Narrative*, 53; Schaeper, *John Paul Jones*.
13 TNA: ADM 1/2305.
14 For more on the difficulty of sinking wooden sailing ships, see Introduction, pages xxx–x and Willis, *Fighting at Sea*, 152 ff.
15 NMM: JOD/9.
16 Sketches of the action made by the *Hancock*'s captain, Hector McNeill, held in the MHS, are published in NDAR IX: 989–1000. Collier's account is in the same volume, pages 269–73.
17 NDAR IX: 683, 750–3, 845.
18 Fallaw and Stoer, 'Old Dominion', 445.
19 TNA: ADM 1/1612, ff. 30–1; Syrett, *American Waters*, 123; Stewart, *Virginia's Navy*, 73–7; Selby, *Virginia*, 205.
20 TNA: ADM 1/1612, ff. 40–2.
21 WCL: H. Mowat to P. Cosby, 23 May 1780, Christopher Mason Letterbook, M-132; Bowler, *Logistics*, 262.

22 Hattendorf, *Talking about Naval History*, 197; Buel, *In Irons*, 88.
23 Norton, *Captains Contentious*, 73.
24 For more on his background see Buker, *Penobscot Expedition*, 19–22.
25 Fowler, *Rebels*, 115.
26 N. Miller, *Sea of Glory*, 415.
27 Norton, *Captains Contentious*, 81; Buker, *Penobscot Expedition*, 61–3.
28 N. Miller, *Sea of Glory*, 415.
29 TNA: ADM 1/1612, ff. 47–9.
30 Norton, *Captains Contentious*, 82.
31 WCL: J. Bowen to N. Greene, 6 September 1779, Hubert Smith Collection, II.
32 TNA: ADM 1/1612, ff. 48.
33 Buker, *Penobscot Expedition*, 97.
34 TNA: ADM 1/486, ff. 219.
35 Chernow, *Washington*, 265.
36 Rankin, *Narratives*, 39.
37 Hattendorf, *Talking about Naval History*, 198; Buel, *In Irons*, 93.
38 TNA: ADM 1/2305.
39 NYPL: Navy Board of the Eastern Division [Boston] Letter Book; Buel, *In Irons*, 94.
40 Toll, *Six Frigates*, 18.
41 Buel, *In Irons*, 96.
42 Buel, *In Irons*, 93.
43 Hattendorf, *Talking about Naval History*, 196–8.
44 Buel, *In Irons*, 90.
45 N. Miller, *Sea of Glory*, 419.

23 British Dominance

1 For some important background to Arbuthnot's appointment see Rodger, *Insatiable Earl*, 284–7.
2 Borick, *Gallant Defense*, 24–5.
3 Mackesy, *War for America*, 340.
4 Uhlendorf, *Siege of Charleston*, 119.
5 Tustin, *Diary*, 194.
6 Tustin, *Diary*, 194.
7 Tilley, *British Navy*, 174; Syrett, *American Waters*, 134.
8 Borick, *Gallant Defense*, 73.
9 Wilson, *Southern Strategy*, 209; Mattern, *Benjamin Lincoln*, 94–5.
10 N. Miller, *Sea of Glory*, 421.
11 Wilson, *Southern Strategy*, 209.
12 Borick, *Gallant Defense*, 74.
13 Borick, *Gallant Defense*, 80.

14 Many thanks to Carl Borick for this observation. For the problems encountered in the first attack, see TNA: ADM 1/486, ff. 64–9.

15 TNA: ADM 1/486, f. 355.

16 Tustin, *Diary*, 210.

17 Tilley, *British Navy*, 179.

18 Tustin, *Diary*, 210.

19 Wilson, *Southern Strategy*, 211.

20 Wilson, *Southern Strategy*, 211.

21 Wilson, *Southern Strategy*, 212.

22 Lloyd, *Keith Papers*, I, 143.

23 Wilson, *Southern Strategy*, 213.

24 TNA: ADM 1/486, f. 355; Lloyd, *Keith Papers*, 145.

25 Lloyd, *Keith Papers*, 140.

26 Willcox, *American Rebellion*, 161, 163.

27 Lloyd, *Keith Papers*, 167.

28 Lloyd, *Keith Papers*, 142.

29 Campbell, 'Jointness', 66.

30 Wilson, *Southern Strategy*, 210.

31 Tilley, *British Navy*, 179.

32 Lloyd, *Keith Papers*, 173; Mattern, *Benjamin Lincoln*, 98.

33 Tustin, *Diary*, 225.

34 *Alliance, Confederacy, Deane* and *Trumbull*. The sloop *Saratoga* was launched in April 1780. For a list of the American ships captured, see TNA: ADM 1/486, ff. 369–70.

35 Paullin, *Navy*, 433.

36 Shipton, 'Benjamin Lincoln', 203.

37 APDE: J. D. van der Capellen, 28 November 1780.

38 APDE: J. Adams to J. D. van der Capellen, 21 January 1781.

39 NYPL: Mazzei Papers, F. Mazzei to T. Jefferson, 22 June 1780.

40 Syrett, *Rodney Papers*, II, 3.

41 Syrett, *European Waters*, 83.

42 Syrett, *Rodney Papers*, II, 270.

43 Knight, 'Recovery', 23.

44 Corbett, *Signals and Instructions*, 211.

45 Mackesy, *War for America*, 312; Drinkwater, *Narrative*, 91.

46 Syrett, *Rodney Papers,* II, 304.

47 J. Russell, *Gibraltar*, 58.

48 Mahan, *Major Operations*, 89.

49 NYPL: Mazzei Papers, 8 February 1780.

50 NYPL: Mazzei Papers, 8 February 1780.

51 Corbett, *Signals and Instructions*, 233.

52 Warner, 'Telescopes for Land and Sea', 45.

53 NYPL: Mazzei Papers, 8 February 1780.

54 Chavez, *Spain*, 141.

55 Syrett, *Rodney Papers*, II, 313.
56 Syrett, *Rodney Papers*, II, 313.
57 Barnes and Owen, *Sandwich Papers*, III, 198.
58 For more British humanity, see Syrett, *Rodney Papers*, II, 342.
59 Syrett, *Rodney Papers*, II, 321.
60 Syrett, *Rodney Papers*, II, 408.
61 Syrett, *European Waters*, 89.
62 Ancell, *Journal*, 22.
63 Ancell, *Journal*, 25.
64 Ancell, *Journal*, 25.
65 Drinkwater, *Narrative*, 91.
66 Barnes and Owen, *Sandwich Papers*, III, 194; J. Russell, *Gibraltar*, 53.
67 Barnes and Owen, *Sandwich Papers*, III, 194.
68 McGuffie, *Siege*, 60.
69 Syrett, *Rodney Papers*, II, 328.
70 Ancell, *Journal*, 26.
71 J. Russell, *Gibraltar*, 60.
72 Barnes and Owen, *Sandwich Papers*, III, 193.
73 Syrett, *Rodney Papers*, II, 347.
74 Barnes and Owen, *Sandwich Papers*, III, 195; Syrett, *Rodney Papers*, II, 348; J. Russell, *Gibraltar*, 61.
75 J. Russell, *Gibraltar*, 60.
76 Barnes and Owen, *Sandwich Papers*, III, 194.
77 Hills, *Rock of Contention*, 318.
78 Mahan, *Major Operations*, 91.
79 Barnes and Owen, *Sandwich Papers*, III, 203–4; Syrett, *Rodney Papers*, II, 381.
80 Syrett, *Rodney Papers*, II, 376.
81 Syrett, *Rodney Papers*, II, 370.
82 Syrett, *Rodney Papers*, II, 369.
83 Owen, 'Rodney and de Guichen', 195; Jamieson, 'Leeward Islands', 198.
84 Syrett, *Rodney Papers*, II, 419.
85 Barnes and Owen, *Sandwich Papers*, III, 201; Syrett, *European Waters*, 90.
86 Syrett, *European Waters*, 90.

24 Allied Recommitment

1 MHS: Journal of Josiah Bartlett, 136; Dull, *Ship of the Line*, 107; Price, *Preserving the Monarchy*, 52; Dull, *French Navy*, 198–9, 227; Knight, 'Recovery'.
2 NYPL: Mazzei Papers, 8 February 1780; Owen, 'Rodney and de Guichen', 198; Jamieson, 'Leeward Islands', 207.
3 Hamilton, 'War and Inflation', 36–41; Harris, 'Comte Rendue', 161.

4 Petrie, *Charles III*, 191; Chavez, *Spain*, 143; Dull, *French Navy*, 179–80.

5 Dull, *French Navy*, 189; Mackesy, *War for America*, 384.

6 Ekins, *Naval Battles*, 111–12.

7 Jamieson, 'Leeward Islands', 214.

8 Ekins, *Naval Battles*, 114. It was not uncommon for women to serve aboard warships, though it does seem to have been uncommon for them to work the guns in battle. A good general survey is Cordingly, *Heroines and Harlots*. See also Rodger, *Wooden World*, 55, 67, 76–8. For a baby born in battle see Rodger, *Command of the Ocean*, 2, 506.

9 Syrett, *Rodney Papers*, II, 471.

10 Tunstall, *Naval Warfare*, 167.

11 Mackesy, *War for America*, 331.

12 Tunstall, *Naval Warfare*, 167.

13 Syrett, *Rodney Papers*, II, 390.

14 Syrett, *Rodney Papers*, II, 456, 486.

15 Barnes and Owen, *Sandwich Papers*, III, 167.

16 Jamieson, 'Leeward Islands', 216.

17 Syrett, *Rodney Papers*, II, 394.

18 Syrett, *Rodney Papers*, II, 486; Owen, 'Rodney and de Guichen', 433.

19 Servies, *Log*, 10.

20 For figures, see Dull, *French Navy*, 315–16; Syrett, *Shipping*, 167.

21 APDE: J. Bondfield to J. Adams, 28 May 1780.

22 APDE: E. Jennings to J. Adams, 15 July 1780.

23 Hargreaves-Mawdsley, *Eighteenth-Century Spain*, 133.

24 Owen, 'Rodney and de Guichen', 438; Syrett, *Rodney Papers*, II, 395; Jamieson, 'Leeward Islands', 220–2.

25 Syrett, *Rodney Papers*, II, 452; Barck, *Rodney Letter-books*, I, 187.

26 Kennett, *French Forces*, 14–15; Anon, *Gazette Françoise*, 5; Hattendorf, *Newport*, 55–7; Dunmore, *Pacific Explorer*, 142.

27 Kennett, *French Forces*, 28.

28 Kennett, *French Forces*, 12.

29 Chernow, *Washington*, 377.

30 Dull, *French Navy and the Seven Years' War*, 172, 180–1.

31 Buel, *In Irons*, 146–8.

32 Dull, *Benjamin Franklin*, 78–9.

33 Idzerda et al., *Lafayette*, 89; Hattendorf, *Talking about Naval History*, 206.

34 Chernow, *Washington*, 372.

35 Hattendorf, *Newport*, 69; Knox, *Naval Genius*, 70.

36 APDE: J. A. to W. Carmichael, 12 May 1780.

37 Acomb, *Revolutionary Journal*, 3.

38 Acomb, *Revolutionary Journal*, 7.

39 Acomb, *Revolutionary Journal*, 21.

40 Acomb, *Revolutionary Journal*, 7.

41 Acomb, *Revolutionary Journal*, 10.
42 Rice and Brown, *American Campaigns*, I, 224.
43 Hattendorf, *Newport*, 53.
44 Acomb, *Revolutionary Journal*, 12.
45 Acomb, *Revolutionary Journal*, 18.
46 Rice and Brown, *American Campaigns*, I, 120.
47 Rice and Brown, *American Campaigns*, I, 226; Lydenberg, *Crossing the Line*, LIX–LXI.
48 Kennett, *French Forces*, 31.
49 Acomb, *Revolutionary Journal*, 21; Rice and Brown, *American Campaigns*, I, 16.
50 Hattendorf, *Newport*, 59.
51 Hattendorf, *Newport*, 61. The reference to rockets is interesting; we know that the French were developing phosphorous shells in the 1780s. Knight, *Pursuit*, 296.
52 Rice and Brown, *American Campaigns*, I, 120; Kennett, *French Forces*, 46; Acomb, *Revolutionary Journal*, 28.
53 Tilley, *British Navy*, 193.
54 Moomaw, 'Captain Hamond', 447; Willcox, 'Old Women', 268.
55 Mackesy, *War for America*, 348–9.
56 Tilley, *British Navy*, 195.
57 Knox, *Naval Genius*, 70.
58 Kennett, *French Forces*, 62.
59 Hattendorf, *Talking about Naval History*, 209–11.
60 Rice and Brown, *American Campaigns*, I, vi.
61 Acomb, *Revolutionary Journal*, 50–1; Rice and Brown, *American Campaigns*, I, 20–1.
62 Rice and Brown, *American Campaigns*, I, 21.
63 Rice and Brown, *American Campaigns*, I, 21.
64 Anon, *Gazette Françoise*, 5–7.
65 Rice and Brown, *American Campaigns*, I, 123.
66 Rice and Brown, *American Campaigns*, I, 20.
67 Buel, *In Irons*, 157.
68 TNA: ADM 51/1044.
69 TNA: ADM 51/1044.

25 Spanish Skill

1 Haarmann, 'Spanish Conquest', 108.
2 Haarmann, 'Spanish Conquest', 110; Caughey, *Gálvez*, 152; Thonoff, 'Texas and the American Revolution', 516.
3 McCarthy, 'Attitude of Spain', 61; Haarmann, 'Spanish Conquest', 113; Chavez, *Spain*, 171; Abbey, 'Peter Chester', 30; Caughey, *Gálvez*, 161.
4 Chavez, *Spain*, 175.

5   Haarmann, 'Spanish Conquest', 116.
6   Chavez, *Spain*, 175.
7   Gold, 'Bernardo de Galvez', 92–3; Crawford, 'Naval Conquest', 2.
8   Wilkie, 'New Light', 198.
9   Chavez, *Spain*, 182; Caughey, *Gálvez*, 193; Wilkie, 'New Light', 198.
10 D. L. Miller et al., 'Tree Ring Isotope', 14294.
11 Many thanks indeed to Dr Clive Wilkinson for help on this topic. Frangsmyr, Leibron and Rider, *Quantifying Spirit*, 149, 153n.37.
12 For more, see Willis, *Fighting at Sea*.
13 Crawford, 'Naval Conquest', 14–15.
14 Fabel, 'Ordeal by Siege', 294.
15 Fabel, 'Ordeal by Siege', 286.
16 TNA: ADM 1/96, f. 131.

26 Russian Meddling

1   D. A. Miller, *Joseph Yorke*, 78; Morison, *John Paul Jones*, 251–2.
2   Haley, *British and the Dutch*, 216.
3   Bruijn, 'Long Life', 52.
4   Nordholt, *Dutch Republic*, 76.
5   APDE: A. Adams to J. Adams, 18 January 1780.
6   APDE: J. Bondfield to the Commissioners, 26 August 1778; Bemis, *Diplomacy*, 151.
7   Bradford, 'John Paul Jones', 31; Morison, *John Paul Jones*, 253.
8   J. P. Jones, *John Paul Jones*, 43.
9   J. P. Jones, *John Paul Jones*, 44.
10 Morison, *John Paul Jones*, 265; Callo, *John Paul Jones*, 109–11.
11 J. P. Jones, *John Paul Jones*, 42.
12 Glete, 'Navies and Power Struggle', 67, 83.
13 Middlebrook, *South Carolina*, 1–3; J. A. Lewis, *Neptune's Militia*, 7–9; Glete, *Navies and Nations*, I, 284; Fowler, *Rebels*, 213, 216; Haley, *British and the Dutch*, 215.
14 Griffiths, 'Nikita Panin', 7.
15 de Madariaga, *Armed Neutrality*, 157.
16 Syrett, *European Waters*, 96, 99, 109.
17 Dull, *Diplomatic History*, 129.
18 de Madariaga, *Armed Neutrality*, 78; Mackesy, *War for America*, 377.
19 Syrett, *European Waters*, 122.
20 Griffiths, 'Nikita Panin', 9.
21 Griffiths, 'Nikita Panin', 1, 9, 21; Bemis, *Diplomacy*, 164–5; Griffiths, 'Catherine the Great', 86; Dull, *Diplomatic History*, 130–1.
22 Van Alstyne, *Empire and Independence*, 213.
23 H. W. Richmond, *Statesmen and Seapower*, 154.
24 Tredrea and Sozaev, *Russian Warships*, 60.

25 Rodger, 'British View', 26; Rodger, *Insatiable Earl*, 293.

26 Rodger, *Insatiable Earl*, 292.

27 Chesnutt and Taylor, *Laurens Papers*, XV, 332.

28 Chesnutt and Taylor, *Laurens Papers*, XV, 332.

29 Chesnutt and Taylor, *Laurens Papers*, XV, 340; Conway, 'Fellow Nationals', 68–9.

30 Chesnutt and Taylor, *Laurens Papers*, XV, 340.

31 Chesnutt and Taylor, *Laurens Papers*, XV, 335.

32 APDE: J. Adams to the President of Congress, 1 January 1781.

33 Syrett, *European Waters*, 129.

34 Mackesy, *War for America*, 382.

35 Kubben, *Regeneration*, 152.

27 Dutch Disaster

1 Jameson, 'St. Eustatius', 699.

2 Jameson, 'St. Eustatius', 686.

3 O'Shaughnessy, *Men Who Lost America*, 291.

4 Mulcahy, *Hurricanes and Society*, 25.

5 Mulcahy, *Hurricanes and Society*, 98.

6 TNA: ADM 1/310, f. 52.

7 Jamieson, 'Leeward Islands', 227.

8 TNA: ADM 1/310, ff. 55–6.

9 TNA: ADM 1/310, f. 52.

10 Jameson, 'St. Eustatius', 702.

11 Tilley, *British Navy*, 238.

12 NMM: MEC1446.

13 Barck, *Rodney Letter-books*, 1, 181–3, 185–6, 188–9.

14 Jameson, 'St. Eustatius', 684.

15 Hurst, *Golden Rock*, 125.

16 NMM: JHS/1.

17 Jameson, 'St. Eustatius', 703.

18 O'Shaughnessy, *Men Who Lost America*, 300.

19 O'Shaughnessy, *Empire Divided*, 227.

20 Jameson, 'St. Eustatius', 703.

21 TNA: ADM 36/10243.

22 de Madariaga, *Armed Neutrality*, 363; Hurst, *Golden Rock*, 143.

23 Lloyd, 'Sir George Rodney', 343.

24 WCL: C. Goore Letterbook, 2 February 1781.

25 Abbatista, 'Edmund Burke', 3–4.

26 Jameson, 'St. Eustatius', 701.

27 NMM: JHS/1.

28 Jameson, 'St. Eustatius', 701.

29 APDE: J. Adams to R. Livingstone, 21 February 1782.

30 An interesting journal from this period and location is NMM: HSR/B/18.
31 de Madariaga, *Armed Neutrality*, 363.
32 Syrett, *European Waters*, 130. Some trade with America continued, however, under Russian and Prussian flags, some of it in Dutch boats. Dull, *Diplomatic History*, 26.

28 British Obsession

1 Drinkwater, *History*, 112, 122; McGuffie, *Siege*, 65; J. Russell, *Gibraltar*, 63.
2 Drinkwater, *History*, 144.
3 APDE: T. Digges to J. Adams, 5 January 1780.
4 McGuffie, *Siege*, 71.
5 Ancell, *Journal*, 41; McGuffie, *Siege*, 72.
6 Drinkwater, *History*, 111.
7 Drinkwater, *History*, 112.
8 Drinkwater, *History*, 112; Spilsbury, *Journal*, 19.
9 Harding, 'Two Sieges', 39.
10 Drinkwater, *History*, 122; McGuffie, *Siege*, 85.
11 Drinkwater, *History*, 132–3; Chavez, *Spain*, 145; Spilsbury, *Journal*, 25.
12 Ancell, *Journal*, 51.
13 Drinkwater, *History*, 113.
14 Ancell, *Journal*, 36.
15 TNA: ADM 1/1613, Curtis letters; Spilsbury, *Journal*, 22–9; Drinkwater, *History*, 114–15, 123, 133, 142; McGuffie, *Siege*, 83.
16 Ancell, *Journal*, 36.
17 McGuffie, *Siege*, 91.
18 Hills, *Rock of Contention*, 325.
19 APDE: J. Adams to J. D. van der Capellan, 21 January 1781.
20 Mackesy, *War for America*, 386.
21 H. W. Richmond, *Navy in India*, 136.
22 Barnes and Owen, *Sandwich Papers*, IV, 34.
23 Barnes and Owen, *Sandwich Papers*, IV, 35.
24 Ancell, *Journal*, 92.
25 Ancell, *Journal*, 90.
26 Ancell, *Journal*, 100.
27 Spilsbury, *Journal*, 30.
28 Ancell, *Journal*, 95.

29 French Escapes

1 Frost, *Convicts and Empire*, 52.
2 Cavaliero, *Admiral Satan*, 6, 20, 24–6; H. W. Richmond, *Navy in India*, 141.

3 Pasley, *Sea Journals*, 143.
4 Pasley, *Sea Journals*, 136.
5 Blake, *Blake's Remarks*, 15.
6 Fabel, *Bombast and Broadsides*, 154.
7 Pasley, *Sea Journals*, 137.
8 Mackesy, *War for America*, 390; Blake, *Blake's Remarks*, 16, 28.
9 Blake, *Blake's Remarks*, 31.
10 Fabel, *Bombast and Broadsides*, 155; Cavaliero, *Admiral Satan*, 65.
11 Pasley, *Sea Journals*, 138.
12 Johnstone's official reasoning can be followed in Blake, *Blake's Remarks*, 34.
13 Pasley, *Sea Journals*, 140.
14 Pasley, *Sea Journals*, 140.
15 Pasley, *Sea Journals*, 141.
16 Pasley, *Sea Journals*, 142.
17 Pasley, *Sea Journals*, 150.
18 Pasley, *Sea Journals*, 136.
19 TNA: ADM 1/2485, 13 June 1781.
20 Castex, *Manœuvre*, 264; Sen, *French in India*, 233.
21 Fabel, *Bombast and Broadsides*, 158; Sen, *French in India*, 235.
22 Cavaliero, *Admiral Satan*, 72 ff.
23 Pasley, *Sea Journals*, 142, 167.
24 Pasley, *Sea Journals*, 168–70.
25 Pasley, *Sea Journals*, 162.
26 A. B. Smith, 'French Period'.
27 Ekins, *Naval Battles*, 115.
28 Ekins, *Naval Battles*, 117.
29 Dull, *French Navy*, 246.
30 Abbatista, 'Edmund Burke', 10–11.
31 Tilley, *British Navy*, 239.
32 Baugh, 'Superior Subordinate', 303–4; Jamieson, 'Leeward Islands', 243.
33 Tilley, *British Navy*, 240.
34 Tilley, *British Navy*, 240.
35 Shea, *French Fleet*, 31.
36 Shea, *French Fleet*, 30–5, 148.
37 Ekins, *Naval Battles*, 111.
38 APDE: C. Dumas to J. Adams, 3 July 1781.
39 APDE: B. Franklin to J. Adams, 11 May 1781.
40 APDE: J. Adams to the President of Congress, 29 May 1781.
41 Dull, *French Navy*, 254.
42 APDE: J. Adams to J. Warren, 18 March 1781.
43 Ramsay, *Life*, 103.
44 Jamieson, 'Leeward Islands', 48.
45 Knight, *Portsmouth Dockyard Papers*, xvii.

46 Knight, *Portsmouth Dockyard Papers*, liv–lv.
47 APDE: J. Adams to the President of Congress, 29 May 1781.

30 Allied Success

1   The maritime aspects of the siege are interesting and can be followed in Crawford, 'Naval Conquest', 6–8, 16; Caughey, *Gálvez*, 201–4; Servies, *Log*, 21, 163, 169. For the French loan of ships, see Dull, *French Navy*, 234.
2   Lassiter, 'Arnold's Invasion of Virginia', 82.
3   Anon, 'Arnold's Invasion', 131; Selby, *Virginia*, 224.
4   Paullin, *Navy*, 414.
5   Linder, *Tidewater's Navy*, 18; Fallaw and Stoer, 'Old Dominion', 468; Goldenberg and Stoer, 'Virginia State Navy', 194–5.
6   Fallaw and Stoer, 'Old Dominion', 464.
7   Ekins, *Naval Battles*, 105.
8   Tilley, *British Navy*, 226.
9   Tilley, *British Navy*, 226; TNA: ADM 1/486, ff. 575–80.
10 Ekins, *Naval Battles*, 105.
11 Willcox, 'Sir Henry Clinton', 92; Rankin, 'Lord Cornwallis', 216; Sands, 'Seapower at Yorktown', 53–8.
12 APDE: J. Adams to J. Searle, 8 February 1781.
13 Chavez, *Spain*, 201.
14 Shea, *French Fleet*, 150; Chavez, *Spain*, 201–2.
15 Padrón, *Saavedra Journal*, 208–12; Chavez, *Spain*, 202; Dull, *French Navy*, 245.
16 Dull, *French Navy*, 242, 247.
17 Syrett, *American Waters*, 180–1.
18 Dull, *French Navy*, 246.
19 A chart of the French operation in the Channel is in Forrer and Roussel, *La Bretagne*, 94–5.
20 Grainger, *Battle of Yorktown*, 68; Willcox, *American Rebellion*, 563.
21 Shea, *French Fleet*, 63.
22 Tustin, *Diary*, 325.
23 Chernow, *Washington*, 408.
24 Grainger, *Battle of Yorktown*, 77.
25 Linder, *Tidewater's Navy*, 15; Eller, 'Washington's Maritime Strategy', 509; Selby, *Virginia*, 301; Stewart, *Virginia's Navy*, 102.
26 Grainger, *Battle of Yorktown*, 85; Shea, *French Fleet*, 154.
27 Grainger, *Battle of Yorktown*, 84.
28 Grainger, *Battle of Yorktown*, 86.
29 Sands, 'Seapower at Yorktown', 211 ff.; Tustin, *Diary*, 325.
30 Sands, 'Seapower at Yorktown', 68.
31 TNA: ADM 1/489, f. 413; C. L. Lewis, *de Grasse*, 176; Grainger, *Battle of Yorktown*, 87; Sands, 'Seapower at Yorktown', 76–87; Tustin, *Diary*, 328.

32 Shea, *French Fleet*, 66; Eller, 'Washington's Maritime Strategy', 504.

33 Linder, *Tidewater's Navy*, 18.

34 Grainger, *Battle of Yorktown*, 85.

35 Grainger, *Battle of Yorktown*, 118.

36 O'Shaughnessy, *Men Who Lost America*, 312; Tilley, *British Navy*, 248; Chadwick, *Graves Papers*, 25.

37 Shea, *French Fleet*, 69.

38 Rankin, 'Lord Cornwallis', 218.

39 Breen, 'Graves and Hood', 53–65; Sullivan, 'Graves and Hood', 175–94; Pengelly, *Samuel Hood*, 124–50.

40 TNA: ADM 1/489, f. 425; Chadwick, *Graves Papers*, 66–75; Grainger, *Battle of Yorktown*, 92; C. L. Lewis, *de Grasse*, 159; Shea, *French Fleet*, 156.

41 Grainger, *Battle of Yorktown*, 73.

42 NMM: GRE/6.

43 Chadwick, *Graves Papers*, 82.

44 Grainger, *Battle of Yorktown*, 135.

45 Rankin, 'Lord Cornwallis'.

46 Callahan, 'Henry Knox', 254.

47 Callahan, 'Henry Knox', 255.

48 Bass, *Ships and Shipwrecks*, 163.

49 C. L. Lewis, *de Grasse*, 183.

50 Grainger, *Battle of Yorktown*, 143. See also Sands, 'Seapower at Yorktown', 89.

51 Chadwick, *Graves Papers*, 141–3; Grainger, *Battle of Yorktown*.

52 Fowler, *American Crisis*, 35.

53 Whitely, *Lord North*, 195.

54 APDE: F. A. Van der Kamp to J. Adams, 26 November 1781.

55 O'Shaughnessy, *Men Who Lost America*, 292, 347; Rodger, *Command of the Ocean*, 2, 352.

Epilogue

1 Quoted in Weintraub, *Iron Tears*, xvii.

2 Lutnick, *British Press*, 187.

3 D. L. Russell, *Southern Colonies*, 304; Sands, *Yorktown's Captive Fleet*, 101.

4 Explored in Hattendorf, 'Fleet in Being', 53–6.

5 Dull, *Ship of the Line*, 114; Stockley, *Britain and France*, 88; Dull, *French Navy*, 279–80; Glete, *Navies and Nations*, I, 275.

6 Stockley, *Britain and France*, 87–8.

7 Dull, *Ship of the Line*, 119.

8 Stockley, *Britain and France*, 89.

9 Knight, 'Introduction of Copper', 303; Lavery, *Ship of the Line*, I, 116.

10 Hattendorf, 'Fleet in Being', 56; Lavery, *Arming and Fitting*, 106; Knight, *Britain Against Napoleon*, 354.

11 Hattendorf, 'Fleet in Being', 53–6.

12 Shea, *French Fleet*, 119.

13 Jamieson, 'Leeward Islands', 90.

14 Jamieson, 'Leeward Islands', 74, 87.

15 BL: Add 35525, f. 94.

16 Buel, *In Irons*, 217, 240-2.

17 The campaign can be followed in Cavaliero, *Admiral Satan*, 81 ff.; H. W. Richmond, *Navy in India*; Sen, *French in India*.

18 Longer-term processes are identified in Marshall, *Making and Unmaking*.

19 The Americans also believed that the Spanish planned to 'coop us up within the Allegheny Mountains'. Morris, *Peacemakers*, 308–9; Van Alstyne, *Empire and Independence*, 217; Fleming, *Perils of Peace*, 219–21. The French position at the peace talks was also undermined by their fear that the Russians were about to annex the Crimea. Dull, 'Vergennes', 111.

20 Hattendorf, 'US Navy', 156; Rodger, 'Cause and Effect', 107.

21 Dull, *Diplomatic History*, 146, 161; Bemis, *Diplomacy*, 230; Van Alstyne, *Empire and Independence*, 220–2; Magra, *Fisherman's Cause*, 233; Fleming, *Perils of Peace*, 237–9.

22 Fleming, *Perils of Peace*, 227–8.

23 Conn, *Gibraltar*, 189 ff.; Harlow, *Second British Empire*, I, 344 ff.; Fowler, *American Crisis*, 127.

24 Knight, 'Recovery', 22.

25 Nordholt, *Dutch Republic*, 17.

26 Bruijn, 'New World', 115.

27 Glete, *Navies and Nations*, I, 274.

28 Glete, *Navies and Nations*, I, 297.

29 Pybus, *Black Founders*, 38; Fowler, *American Crisis*, 114; Jasanoff, *Liberty's Exiles*, 70–7.

30 Klooster, *Revolutions*, 36.

31 Klooster, *Revolutions*, 42–4; Ward, *War for Independence*, 208; Foy, 'Ports of Slavery', 282.

32 Hattendorf, *Talking about Naval History*, 198.

33 His role in American sea power post-Yorktown is fascinating and little studied. See Nuxoll, 'Naval Movement', 3–34. See also the excellent Powers, 'Decline and Extinction'.

34 Harlow, *Second British Empire*, I, 230; Dull, *Diplomatic History*, 162–3; Woodman, *Britannia's Realm*, 60.

35 Knight, *Britain Against Napoleon*, 23.

36 Van Alstyne, *Empire and Independence*, 230.

37 Examined in Hattendorf, 'US Navy', 151–76; Hattendorf, *Talking about Naval History*, 199; Klooster, *Revolutions*, 39; Buel, *In Irons*, 253; Nuxoll, 'Naval Movement', 3–13; Marshall, *Remaking*, 1.

38 Sir John Sinclair, *Thoughts on the Naval Strength of the British Empire* (1782), quoted in Knight, *Britain Against Napoleon*, 21.

39 Knight, 'Recovery', 14; Knight, *Britain Against Napoleon*, 5–6.

40 Rodger, 'Cause and Effect', 106–9.

41 TNA: ADM 1/2306, 22 August 1780.

42 Diamant, *Chaining the Hudson*, xi.

43 Diamant, *Chaining the Hudson*, xi.

BIBLIOGRAPHY

Abbreviations

APDE   Adams Papers Digital Editions; www.masshist.org/publications/apde2
BL   British Library, London
BPL   Boston Public Library
GWP   George Washington Papers (Revolutionary War Series, 22 vols)
JCBL   John Carter Brown Library, Providence, Rhode Island
JRL   John Rylands Library, University of Manchester
LOC   Library of Congress, Washington DC
MHS   Massachusetts Historical Society
MML   Mariner's Museum Library, Newport News, Virginia
NDAR   Naval Documents of the American Revolution (12 vols)
NYHS   New York Historical Society
NMM   The Caird Library, National Maritime Museum, Greenwich, London
NYPL   New York Public Library
NYSA   New York State Archives
ODNB   Oxford Dictionary of National Biography
PEM   Peabody Essex Museum, Salem, Massachusetts
PML   Pierpoint Morgan Library, New York
TNA   The National Archives, Kew, London
WCL   William Clements Library, Ann Arbor, Michigan
WCO   Wesley Centre Online; http://wesley.nnu.edu/john-wesley

Abass, D. K., 'Endeavour and Resolution Revisited: Newport and Captain James Cook's Vessels', *Newport History*, 70, no. 1 (1999), 15
—— 'Newport and Captain Cook's Ships', *The Great Circle*, 23, no. 1 (2001), 3–20
Abbatista, G., 'Edmund Burke, the Atlantic American War and the "Poor Jews at St. Eustatius": Empire and the Law of Nations', *Cromohs*, 13 (2008), 1–39
Abbey, K. T., 'The Intrigue of a British Refugee Against the Willing Raid, 1778', *William and Mary Quarterly*, 1, no. 4 (1944), 397–404

———— 'Peter Chester's Defense of the Mississippi After the Willing Raid', *Mississippi Valley Historical Review*, 22, no. 1 (1935), 17–32

Abbot, W. W. et al. (eds), *The Papers of George Washington: Revolutionary War Series* (22 vols, Charlottesville, VA, 1985–2014)

Acomb, E. A., *The Revolutionary Journal of Baron Ludwig von Closen, 1780–3* (Williamsburg, VA, 1958)

Alberts, R. C., *The Golden Voyage: The Life and Times of William Bingham, 1752–1804* (Boston, MA, 1969)

Albion, R. G., *Forests and Seapower: The Timber Problem of the Royal Navy, 1652–1862* (Annapolis, MD, 2000)

Alcedo, A., *The Geographical and Historical Dictionary of America and the West Indies . . .* (London, 1812–5)

Alden, J. R., *The South in the Revolution* (Louisiana, 1957)

Allen, E., *A Narrative of Colonel Ethan Allen's Captivity . . .* (New York, 1930)

Allen, G. W., *Naval History of the American Revolution* (Boston, 1913)

Allen, T. B., *Tories Fighting for the King in America's First Civil War* (New York, 2010)

Anburey, T., 'The Taking of Ticonderoga, 1777', *Bulletin of the Fort Ticonderoga Museum*, 2, no. 1 (1930), 15–22

Ancell, S., *A Journal of the Blockade and Siege of Gibraltar* (Cork, 1793)

Anderson, F., *Crucible of War: The Seven Years' War and the Fate of Empire in British North America, 1754–1766* (New York, 2000)

Anderson, T. S., *The Command of the Howe Brothers During the American Revolution* (Cranbury, NJ, 1936)

Anon, 'Account of the Siege of Savannah', *Collections of the Georgia Historical Society*, 5, 129–39

———— 'America: Affairs in Canada', *Scots Magazine*, 38 (1776), 427

———— 'Arnold's Invasion', *William and Mary Quarterly*, 6, no. 2 (1926), 131–2

———— *An Authentic and Impartial Copy of the Trial of the Hon. Augustus Keppel, Admiral of the Blue* (Portsmouth, 1779)

———— 'Biographical Memoir of Captain Joseph Ellis', *Naval Chronicle*, XIX (1808), 1–29

———— *Gazette Françoise: An Account of the French Newspaper Printed on the Press of the French Fleet at Newport, Rhode Island, 1780 and 1781* (Providence, RI, 1926)

———— *A Letter from a Sea-Officer of France to the Honourable Admiral Keppel* (London, 1778)

———— *The Maritime Campaign of 1778* (London, 1779)

———— *Nereus's Prophecy: A sea-piece, sketched off Ushant on the memorable morning of the 28th of July, 1778* (London, 1779)

———— *Observations on the Diseases which Appeared in the Army on St Lucia . . .* (Barbados, 1780)

Ansoff, P., 'The First Navy Jack', *Raven: A Journal of Vexillology*, no. 11 (2004)

Anson, W. R. (ed.), *Autobiography and Political Correspondence of Augustus Henry, Third Duke of Grafton* (London, 1898)

Armitage, D., *The Declaration of Independence: A Global History* (London, 2007)

Baldwin, G., *Political Recollections Relative to Egypt* ... (London, 1802)

Baldwin, J., *The Revolutionary Journal of Col. Jeduthan Baldwin* (New York, 1971)

Barck, D. C. (ed.), *Letter-books and order-book of George, Lord Rodney, Admiral of the White Squadron, 1780–1782*, I (New York, 1932–3)

Barnes, G. R. and J. H. Owen (eds), *The Private Papers of John, Earl of Sandwich, First Lord of the Admiralty, 1771–1782*, 4 vols (London, 1932–8)

Barnes, J. S. (ed.), *Fanning's Narrative: Being the Memoirs of Nathaniel Fanning, an Officer of the Revolutionary Navy, 1778–1783* (New York, 1912)

Barrington, S., 'Some Letters of Admiral the Hon. Samuel Barrington', *Mariner's Mirror*, 19 (1933), 279–91, 381–403

Barrow, J., *Some Account of the Public Life and a Selection from the Unpublished Writings of the Earl of Macartney*, 2 vols, Vol. I (London, 1807)

Barrow, T. C., *Trade and Empire: The British Customs Service in Colonial America, 1660–1775* (Cambridge, MA, 1967)

Bartlett, J., *A History of the Destruction of His Britannic Majesty's Schooner Gaspee* ... (Bedford, MA, 1861)

Bass, G. F. (ed.), *Ships and Shipwrecks of the Americas* (London, 1996)

Baugh, D. A., 'The Politics of British Naval Failure, 1775–7', *American Neptune*, 52, no. 4 (1992), 221–46

—— 'Sir Samuel Hood: Superior Subordinate', in G. A. Billias (ed.), *George Washington's Generals and Opponents* (New York, 1994), 291–326

—— 'Why did Britain Lose Command of the Sea during the War for America?', in J. Black and P. Woodfine (eds), *The British Navy and the Use of Naval Power in the Eighteenth Century* (Atlantic Highlands, NJ, 1988), 149–70

Baxter, J. P., *The British Invasion from the North: The Campaigns of Generals Carleton and Burgoyne from Canada 1776–7 with the Journal of Lieutenant William Digby* (Albany, 1887)

Beatson, R., *Naval and Military Memoirs of Great Britain from 1727 to 1783*, Vol. IV (London, 1804)

Bellesiles, M. A., *Revolutionary Outlaws: Ethan Allen and the Struggle for Independence on the Early American Frontier* (London, 1995)

Bellico, R. P., *Sail and Steam in the Mountains: A Maritime and Military History of Lake George and Lake Champlain* (Fleischmanns, NY, 1991)

Bemis, S. F., 'British Secret Service and the French-American Alliance', *American Historical Review*, 29 (1923), 474–95

—— *The Diplomacy of the American Revolution* (Bloomington, IN, 1957)

Berger, C., *Broadsides and Bayonets* (San Rafael, CA, 1976)

Billias, G. A., *General John Glover and his Marblehead Mariners* (New York, 1960)

———— (ed.), *George Washington's Generals and Opponents* (New York, 1994)

———— 'John Burgoyne: Ambitious General', in G. A. Billias (ed.), *George Washington's Generals and Opponents* (New York, 1994), 142–92

Bird, H., *Navies in the Mountains: The Battles on the Waters of Lake Champlain and Lake George, 1609–1814* (New York, 1962)

Bishop, G. P., 'Rochambeau: An Appreciation', *North American Review*, 205, no. 738 (1917), 786–7

Black, J., *Natural and Necessary Enemies: Anglo-French Relations in the Eighteenth Century* (London, 1986)

———— *The Rise of the European Powers* (London, 1990)

Black, J. and P. Woodfine (eds), *The British Navy and the Use of Naval Power in the Eighteenth Century* (Leicester, 1988)

Blake, *Blake's Remarks on Com. Johnstone's Account of His Engagement With a French Squadron . . .* (London, 1782)

Boniface, J. J., *The Cavalry Horse and His Pack* (Kansas City, 1903)

Bonner-Smith, D. (ed.), *The Barrington Papers, selected from the letters and papers of Admiral the Hon. S. Barrington*, 2 vols, Vol. II (London, 1937–41)

Bonnichon, P., 'Les Objectifs Français de la Guerre d'Amérique', in O. Chaline (ed.), *La France et l'Indépendance Américaine* (Paris, 2008), 49–62

Borick, C. P., *A Gallant Defense: The Siege of Charleston, 1780* (Colombia, SC, 2003)

Boromé, Joseph A., 'Dominica during French Occupation, 1778–1784', *English Historical Review*, 84, no. 330 (1969), 36–58

Boudriot, J., 'The French Fleet During the American War of Independence', *Nautical Research Journal*, 25, no. 2 (1979), 79–86

———— *John Paul Jones and the Bonhomme Richard: A Reconstruction of the Ship and an Account of the Battle* (Paris, 1987)

Boudriot, J., *The Seventy-Four Gun Ship: A Practical Treatise on the Art of Naval Architecture*, 4 vols (Paris, 1988)

Bowen, C. D., *John Adams and the American Revolution* (New York, 1950)

Bowler, R. A., *Logistics and the Failure of the British Army in America* (Princeton, NJ, 1975)

Braake, A. L. ter, *The Posted Letter in Colonial and Revolutionary America, 1628–1790* (State College, PA, 1975)

Bradford, J. C., 'John Paul Jones: Honor and Professionalism', in J. C. Bradford (ed.), *Command Under Sail: Makers of the American Naval Tradition* (Annapolis, MD, 1985), 18–45

Bratten, J. R., *The Gondola Philadelphia and the Battle of Lake Champlain* (Texas, 2002)

Breen, K., 'Graves and Hood at the Chesapeake', *Mariner's Mirror*, LXVI, no. 1 (1980), 53–65

Brewington, M. V. , 'The Designs of Our First Frigates', *American Neptune*, 8, no. 1 (1948), 11–25

Brogan, H., *The Pelican History of the United States of America* (London, 1985)

Brown, G. S., 'The Anglo-French Naval Crisis, 1778: A Study of Conflict in the North Cabinet', *William and Mary Quarterly*, 13, no. 1 (1956), 3–26

Brown, M. L. (ed.), *Baroness von Riedesel and the American Revolution* (Williamsburg, VA, 1965)

Brown, W., *The Good Americans: The Loyalists in the American Revolution* (New York, 1969)

Bruijn, J. R., 'Facing a New World: The Dutch Navy Goes Overseas (c.1750–1850)', in B. Moore (ed.), *Colonial Empires Compared: Britain and the Netherlands, 1750–1850* (Aldershot, 2003), 113–28

——— 'The Long Life of Treaties: The Dutch Republic and Great Britain in the Eighteenth Century', in R. Hobson and T. Kristiansen (eds), *Navies in Northern Waters, 1721–2000* (London, 2004), 41–58

Brunsman, D., *The Evil Necessity: British Naval Impressment in the Eighteenth-Century Atlantic World* (Charlottesville and London, 2013)

Buel, R., *In Irons: British Naval Supremacy and the American Revolutionary Economy* (London, 1998)

Buker, G. E., *The Penobscot Expedition: Commodore Saltonstall and the Massachusetts Conspiracy of 1779* (Annapolis, MD, 2002)

Bumsted, J. M. and C. E. Clark, 'New England's Tom Paine: John Allen and the Spirit of Liberty', *William and Mary Quarterly*, 21, no. 4 (1964), 561–70

Bunker, N., *An Empire on the Edge: How Britain Came to Fight America* (New York, 2014)

Butler, J., *Becoming America: The Revolution Before 1776* (Cambridge, MA, 2000)

Butler, R. R., *Figaro's Fleet* (Stroud, 2008)

Butterfield, H., *George III, Lord North and the People, 1779–80* (London, 1949)

Callahan, N., 'Henry Knox: American Artillerist', in G. A. Billias (ed.), *George Washington's Generals and Opponents* (New York, 1994), 239–59

Callo, J., *John Paul Jones: America's First Sea Warrior* (Annapolis, MD, 2006)

Campbell, J., 'Jointness in 1780 Charleston and 1861–5 Charleston' (MA Thesis: US Army Command and General Staff College, 2004)

Carlton, W. R., 'New England Masts and the King's Navy', *New England Quarterly*, 12, no. 1 (1939), 4–18

Carrington, S. H. H., *The British West Indies During the American Revolution* (Dordrecht, NL, 1988)

———— *The Sugar Industry and the Abolition of the Slave Trade, 1775–1810* (2002)

Carter, C. E. (ed.), *The Correspondence of General Thomas Gage with the Secretaries of State, 1763–1775*, 8 vols, Vols I and II (New Haven, CT, 1931)

Carter, W., *A genuine detail of the several engagements: positions, and movements of the royal and American armies; with an accurate account of the blockade of Boston, and a plan of the works on Bunker's Hill, at the time it was abandoned by His Majesty's forces, on the seventeenth of March, 1776: In a series of letters to a friend* (London, 1784)

Caruana, A. B., *The History of English Sea Ordnance, 1523–1875*, Vol. II (Rotherfield, 1997)

Castex, R. V. P., *La Manœuvre de La Praya 16 avril 1781. Étude politique, stratégique et tactique, d'après des nombreux documents inédits* (Paris, 1912)

Caughey, J. W., *Bernardo de Gálvez in Louisiana, 1776–1783* (Berkeley, CA, 1934)

Cavaliero, R., *Admiral Satan: The Life and Campaigns of Suffren* (London and New York, 1994)

Chadwick, F. A. (ed.), *The Graves Papers* (New York, 1916)

Chaline, O., 'The Admiral d'Orvilliers: A style of command in the age of the American War', *Naval Leadership in the Age of Sail (1750–1840)*, Conference, NMRN Portsmouth (2011)

———— 'Les Escadres d'Évolution à la Veille de la Guerre d'Indépendance Américaine', in O. Chaline et al. (eds), *Les Marines de la Guerre d'Indépendance Américaine, 1763–1783* (Paris, 2012), 365–80

Chavez, T. E., *Spain and the Independence of the United States* (Albuquerque, NM, 2002)

Chernow, R., *Washington: A Life* (London, 2010)

Chesnutt, D. C. and C. J. Taylor (eds), *The Papers of Henry Laurens*, XV (Colombia, SC, 2000)

Churchill, E. A., 'The Historiography of the Margaretta Affair, or How Not to Let the Facts Interfere with a Good Story', *Maine Historical Society Quarterly*, 15, no. 2 (1975), 60–74

Clowes, W. L., *The Royal Navy: A History from the Earliest Times to 1900*, 7 vols (London, 1897–1903)

Cobbett, W. (ed.), *The Parliamentary History of England*, 36 vols, Vols XVIII and XX (London, 1806–20)

Cohen, S. S., *Yankee Sailors in British Gaols: Prisoners of War at Forton and Mill, 1777–1783* (London, 1995)

Cole, G., 'The Office of Ordnance and the Arming of the Fleet in the French Revolutionary Wars, 1793–1815' (PhD: University of Exeter, 2008)

Cole, R. C., 'The Siege of Savannah and the British Press, 1779–1780', *Georgia Historical Quarterly*, 65, no. 3 (1981), 189–202

Collins, J. F., 'Whaleboat Warfare on Long Island Sound', *New York History*, 25, no. 2 (1944), 195–201

Cometti, E. (ed.), *The American Journals of Lt John Enys* (Syracuse, NY, 1976)

Conn, S., *Gibraltar in British Diplomacy in the Eighteenth Century* (New Haven, 1942)

Conway, S., 'From Fellow Nationals to Foreigners: British Perceptions of the Americans, circa 1739–1783', *William and Mary Quarterly*, 59, no. 1 (2002), 65–100

———— 'The Politics of British Military and Naval Mobilization, 1775–83', *English Historical Review*, 112, no. 449 (1997), 1179–201

Corbett, J. S., *Signals and Instructions, 1776–1794* (London, 1971)

Cordingly, D., *Heroines and Harlots: Women at Sea in the Great Age of Sail* (London, 2001)

Crawford, M. J., 'The Hawke and the Dove. A Cautionary Tale: Neutral Ports and Prizes of War during the American Revolution', *Northern Mariner/Le Marin du Nord*, 18, no. 3 (2008), 49–66

———— 'The Joint Allied Operation at Rhode Island, 1778', in W. R. Roberts (ed.), *Naval History: Selected Papers form the Ninth Naval History Symposium* (Annapolis, MD, 1991), 227–42

———— 'The Naval Conquest for the Gulf Coast in the American Revolution', *North American Society for Oceanic History Conference* (Galveston, TX, 2012)

———— 'Naval Support of Land Operations During the American War of Independence', *Les Marines de la Guerre d'Indépendance Américaine, 1763–1783: Leur mise en œuvre Opérationnelle*, Paris Conference (2013)

Crewe, D. G., *Yellow Jack and the Worm: British Naval Administration in the West Indies, 1739–48* (Liverpool, 1993)

Dann, C. (ed.), *The Nagle Journal: A Diary of the Life of Jacob Nagle, Sailor, From the Year 1775 to 1841* (New York, 1988)

Daughan, G. C., *If By Sea: The Forging of the American Navy from the American Revolution to the War of 1812* (New York, 2008)

De Goussencourt, Chevalier, 'A journal of the Cruise of the fleet of his most Christian Majesty, under the command of the Count de Grasse-Tilly in 1781 and 1782', in *The Operations of the French Fleet under the Comte de Grasse in 1781–2: As Described in Two Contemporary Journals*, edited by Anon. (New York, 1971), 26–134

De Madariaga, I., *Britain, Russia, and the Armed Neutrality of 1780: Sir James Harris's Mission to St Petersburg during the American Revolution* (London, 1962)

Depeyre, M., *Tactiques et Stratégies Navales de la France et du Royaume-Uni de 1690 à 1815* (Paris, 1998)

Desjardin, T. A., *Through a Howling Wilderness* (New York, 2006)

Dexter, F. B. (ed.), *The Literary Diary of Ezra Stiles*, 3 vols, Vol. II (New York, 1901)

Diamant, L., *Chaining the Hudson: The Fight for the River in the American Revolution* (New York, 1989)

Donoughue, B., *British Politics and the American Revolution: The Path to War, 1773–75* (London, 1964)

Dorwart, J. M., *Fort Mifflin of Philadelphia: An Illustrated History* (Philadelphia, 1998)

Douglas, C., 'An Account of the Result of Some Attempts Made to Ascertain the Temperature of the Sea in Great Depths, Near the Coasts of Lapland and Norway; as Also Some Anecdotes, Collected in the Former', *Philosophical Transactions (1683–1775)*, 60 (1770), 39–45

Drinkwater, J., *A History of the Siege of Gibraltar, 1779–1783* (London, 1905)

—— *Narrative of Proceedings of the British Fleet Commanded by Admiral Sir J. Jervis, 1797*, 2nd edn (London, 1840)

Dull, J. R., *The Age of the Ship of the Line: The British and French Navies, 1650–1815* (Lincoln, NE, 2009)

—— *American Naval History, 1607–1865: Overcoming the Colonial Legacy* (Lincoln and London, 2012)

—— *Benjamin Franklin and the American Revolution* (Lincoln, NE, 2010)

—— *A Diplomatic History of the American Revolution* (New Haven, 1985)

—— 'France and the American Revolution Seen as Tragedy', in R. Hoffman and P. J. Albert (eds), *Diplomacy and Revolution: The Franco-American Alliance of 1778* (Charlottesville, VA, 1981), 73–106

—— *Franklin the Diplomat: The French Mission* (Philadelphia, 1982)

—— *The French Navy and American Independence: A Study of Arms and Diplomacy, 1774–1787* (Princeton, 1975)

—— *The French Navy and the Seven Years' War* (London, 2005)

—— 'Mahan, Sea Power, and the War for American Independence', *International History Review*, 10, no. 1 (1988), 59–67

—— *The Miracle of Independence: Twenty Ways Things Could Have Turned Out Differently* (forthcoming)

—— 'Vergennes, Rayneval and the Diplomacy of Trust', in R. Hoffman and P. J. Albert (eds), *Peace and the Peacemakers: The Treaty of 1783* (Charlottesville, VA, 1986), 101–31

Dunmore, J., *Pacific Explorer: The Life of Jean-François de La Perouse, 1741–1788* (Palmerston, NZ, 1985)

Ekins, C., *Naval Battles from 1744 to the Peace of 1814, Critically Reviewed and Illustrated* (London, 1824)

Eller, E. M., 'Washington's Maritime Strategy and the Campaign that Assured Independence', in E. M. Eller (ed.), *Chesapeake Bay in the American Revolution* (Centreville, MD, 1981), 475–524

Fabel, R. F. A., *Bombast and Broadsides: The Lives of George Johnstone* (London, 1987)

—— 'Ordeal by Siege: James Bruce in Pensacola, 1780–1', *Florida Historical Quarterly*, 66, no. 3 (1988), 280–97

Falconer, W. (ed.), *Universal Dictionary of the Marine* (London, 1780)

Fallaw, R. and M. W. Stoer, 'The Old Dominion Under Fire: The Chesapeake Invasions, 1779–1781', in E. M. Eller (ed.), *Chesapeake Bay in the American Revolution* (Centreville, MD, 1981), 432–74

Ferling, J., *Almost a Miracle: The American Victory in the War of Independence* (New York, 2009)

Fischer, D. H., *Paul Revere's Ride* (New York, 1994)

———— *Washington's Crossing* (Oxford, 2004)

Fitzpatrick, J. C. (ed.), *The Writings of George Washington*, 39 vols (Washington, DC, 1931–44)

Fleming, T., *The Perils of Peace: America's Struggle for Survival after Yorktown* (New York, 2007)

Forrer, C. and C.-A. Roussel, *La Bretagne: Un Vaisseau de 100 Cannons Pour le Roi et la République* (Gourin, FR, 2005)

Fowler, W. M., *American Crisis: George Washington and the Dangerous Two Years after Yorktown, 1781–3* (New York, 2011)

———— 'Esek Hopkins: Commander-in-Chief of the Continental Navy', in J. C. Bradford (ed.), *Command under Sail: Makers of the American Naval Tradition* (Annapolis, MD, 1985), 3–17

———— *Rebels under Sail: The American Navy During the Revolution* (New York, 1976)

Foy, C. R., 'Ports of Slavery, Ports of Freedom: How Slaves used Northern Seaports' maritime Industry to Escape and Create Trans-Atlantic Identities, 1713–1783' (PhD: University of New Jersey, 2008)

Frangsmyr, T., J. L. Leibron and R. E. Rider (eds), *The Quantifying Spirit in the 18th Century* (Los Angeles, 1990)

Freeman, D. S., *George Washington*, Vol. I (London, 1948)

French, A., *The First Year of the American Revolution* (Boston, 1934)

Frost, A., *Convicts and Empire: A Naval Question, 1776–1811* (Oxford, 1980)

Furneaux, R., *Saratoga: The Decisive Battle* (London, 1971)

Gawalt, G. W. (ed.), *John Paul Jones' Memoir of the American Revolution: Presented to King Louis XVI of France* (Washington, DC, 1979)

Gilje, P. A., 'Loyalty and Liberty: The Ambiguous Patriotism of Jack Tar in the American Revolution', *Pennsylvania History*, 67, no. 2 (2000), 165–93

Gill Jr., H. B. and G. M. Curtis III (eds), *A Man Apart: The Journal of Nicholas Cresswell, 1774–1781* (Lanham, MD, 2009)

Gillispie, C. C., *Science and Polity in France at the End of the Old Regime* (Princeton, 1980)

Gleig, G. R., *Memoirs of the Life of Warren Hastings* (Rich. Bentley, 1841)

Glete, J., *Navies and Nations: Warships, Navies and State Building in Europe and America, 1500–1860*, 2 vols (Stockholm, 1993)

———— 'Navies and Power Struggle in Northern and Eastern Europe,

1721–1814', in R. Hobson and T. Kristiansen (eds), *Navies in Northern Waters, 1721–2000* (London, 2004), 66–93

Gold, R. L., 'Governor Bernardo de Gálvez and Spanish Espionage in Pensacola, 1777', in J. F. McDermott (ed.), *The Spanish in the Mississippi Valley, 1762–1804* (Chicago, 1974), 87–99

Goldenberg, J. A. and M. W. Stoer, 'The Virginia State Navy', in E. M. Eller (ed.), *Chesapeake Bay in the American Revolution* (Centreville, MD, 1981), 170–203

Golway, T., *Washington's General: Nathanael Greene and the Triumph of the American Revolution* (New York, 2007)

Goodwin, P., *Nelson's Ships: A History of the Vessels In Which He Served, 1771–1805* (London, Conway, 2002)

Gordon, M. B., *Naval and Maritime Medicine During the American Revolution* (Ventnor, NJ, 1978)

Graham, G., *The Royal Navy in the War of American Independence* (London, 1976)

Grainger, J. D., *The Battle of Yorktown, 1781: A Reassessment* (Woodbridge, 2005)

Griffiths, D. M., 'Catherine the Great, the British Opposition and the American Revolution', in L. A. Kaplan (ed.), *The American Revolution and 'A Candid World'* (Kent State, 1977), 85–110

——— 'Nikita Panin, Russian Diplomacy, and the American Revolution', *Slavic Review*, 28, no. 1 (1969), 1–24

Gruber, I. D., *The Howe Brothers and the American Revolution* (New York, 1972)

——— 'Richard Lord Howe: Admiral As Peacemaker', in G. A. Billias (ed.), *George Washington's Generals and Opponents* (New York, 1994), 233–59

Haarmann, A. W., 'The Spanish Conquest of British West Florida', *Florida Historical Quarterly*, 39, no. 2 (1960), 107–34

Hadden, J. M., *Hadden's Journal and Orderly Books* (Albany, NY, 2009)

Hagist, D. H., 'A New Interpretation of a Robert Clevely Watercolour', *Mariner's Mirror*, 94, no. 3 (2008), 326–30

Haley, K. H. D., *The British and the Dutch: Political and Cultural Relations Through the Ages* (London, 1988)

Hamilton, E. J., 'War and Inflation in Spain, 1780–1800', *Quarterly Journal of Economics*, 59, no. 36–77 (1944)

Harding, R., 'A Tale of Two Sieges, Gibraltar 1726–7 and 1779–83', *Transactions of the Naval Dockyards Society*, 2 (2006), 31–46

——— *Amphibious Warfare in the Eighteenth Century: The British Expedition to the West Indies, 1740–2* (Woodbridge, 1991)

Hargreaves-Mawdsley, W. N., *Eighteenth-Century Spain, 1700–1788* (London, 1979)

Harlow, V. T., *The Founding of the Second British Empire, 1763–1793*, Vol. I (London, 1952)

Harris, R. D., 'Necker's Compte Rendu of 1781: A Reconsideration', *Journal of Modern History*, 42, no. 2 (1970), 161–83

Harte, C. R., 'The River Obstructions of the Revolutionary War', *Annual Report of the Connecticut Society of Civil Engineers*, 62 (1946), 135–86a

Hattendorf, J. B., 'The Idea of "A Fleet in Being" in Historical Perspective', *Naval War College Review*, 67, no. 1 (2014), 43–60

—— *Newport, the French Navy, and American Independence* (Newport, 2005)

—— *Talking about Naval History: A Collection of Essays* (Newport, 2011)

—— 'The US Navy and the "Freedom of the Seas", 1775–1917', in R. Hobson and T. Kristiansen (eds), *Navies in Northern Waters, 1721–2000* (London, 2004), 151–76

Haven, C. C., *Thirty Days in New Jersey Ninety Years Ago* (Trenton, 1867)

Haynes, R. V., 'James Willing and the Planters of Natchez: The American Revolution Comes to the Southwest', *Journal of Mississippi History*, XXXVII (1975), 1–42

Heath, W., *Memoirs of Major General William Heath* (New York, 1901)

Herring, G. C., *From Colony to Superpower: U.S. Foreign Relations since 1776* (Oxford, 2008)

Higginbotham, D., 'War and State Formation in Revolutionary America', in E. H. Gould and P. S. Onuf (eds), *Empire and Nation: The American Revolution in the Atlantic World* (Baltimore, 2005), 54–71

—— *The War of American Independence: Military Attitudes, Policies, and Practice, 1763–1789* (London, 1977)

Hills, G., *Rock of Contention* (London, 1974)

Hinkhouse, F. J., *The Preliminaries of the American Revolution as Seen in the English Press* (London, 1969)

Hodges, H. W. (ed.), *Select Naval Documents* (Cambridge, 1922)

Hore, P. (ed.), *Seapower Ashore: 200 Years of Royal Navy Operations on Land* (London, 2001)

Horowicz, K. and L. Robson, *The Colonial Posts in the United States of America, 1606–1783* (London, 1967)

Hoskins, H. L., *British Routes to India* (London, 1966)

Hough, F. B., *The Siege of Savannah by the Combined American and French Forces . . .* (Spartanburg, SC, 1866)

Hunt, R. M., *The Life of Sir Hugh Palliser, Bart.* (London, 1844)

Hurst, R., *The Golden Rock: An Episode of the American War of Independence* (London, 1996)

Hutton, A. H., *Portrait of Patriotism: 'Washington Crossing the Delaware'* (Philadelphia, 1959)

Idzerda, S. J. et al. (eds), *Lafayette in the Age of the American Revolution*, 5 vols (Ithaca, NY and London, 1980–3)

Jackson, J. W., *The Pennsylvania Navy, 1775–1781* (New Brunswick, 1974)

—— *With the British Army in Philadelphia, 1777–8* (San Rafael, CA, 1979)

James, W. M., *The British Navy in Adversity: A Study of the War of American Independence* (London, 1926)

Jameson, J. F., 'St. Eustatius in the American Revolution', *American Historical Review*, 8, no. 4 (1903), 683–708

Jamieson, A. G., 'American Privateers in the Leeward Islands', *American Neptune*, 43 (1983), 20–30

———— 'The Battle of Grenada and Caribbean Strategy, 1779', in W. B. Cogar (ed.), *Naval History: The Seventh Symposium of the U.S. Naval Academy* (Annapolis, MD, 1988), 55–62

———— 'War in the Leeward Islands, 1775–83' (PhD: Oxford, 1981)

Jasanoff, M., *Liberty's Exiles: The Loss of America and the Remaking of the British Empire* (London, 2011)

Jenkins, E. H., *A History of the French Navy* (London, 1973)

Johnson, J. M., 'Making the Best Use of Your Joint Forces: Joint and Combined Operations on the Hudson River, 1777 and 1781' (MA: Naval War College, 1995)

Johnston, R. Y., 'American Privateers in French Ports, 1776–8', *Pennsylvania Magazine of History and Biography*, 53 (1929), 352–74

Jones, C. C., *The Siege of Savannah of 1779 As Described in Two Contemporaneous Journals of French Officers* (Albany, NY, 1874)

Jones, J. P., *John Paul Jones' Memoir of the American Revolution Presented to King Louis XVI of France* (Honolulu, 2001)

Kelly, J., *Gunpowder: A History of the Explosive That Changed the World* (2004)

Kennett, L., *The French Forces in America, 1780–3* (Westport, CT, 1977)

Kerallain, R. de, *Bougainville à L'Escadre du Comte d'Estaing, Guerre d'Amerique, 1778–1779* (Paris, 1927)

Ketchum, R. M., *Saratoga: Turning Point in America's Revolutionary War* (London, 1999)

Klooster, W., *Revolutions in the Atlantic World: A Comparative History* (New York, 2009)

Knight, R. J. B., *Britain Against Napoleon: The Organization of Victory, 1793–1815* (London, 2013)

———— 'The Introduction of Copper Sheathing into the Royal Navy, 1779–86', *Mariner's Mirror*, LIX (1973), 299–309

———— 'New England Forests and British Seapower: Albion Revised', *American Neptune*, XLVI (1986), 221–9

———— *Portsmouth Dockyard Papers, 1774–1783: The American War* (Portsmouth, 1987)

———— *The Pursuit of Victory: The Life and Achievement of Horatio Nelson* (London, 2005)

———— 'The Royal Navy's Recovery after the Early Phase of the American Revolutionary War', in G. J. Andreopoulos and H. E. Selesky (eds), *The Aftermath of Defeat: Societies, Armed Forces and the Challenge of Recovery* (New Haven, CT, 1994), 10–25, 160–2

Knox, D. W., *The Naval Genius of George Washington* (Boston, 1932)

Kubben, R., *Regeneration and Hegemony: Franco-Batavian Relations in the Revolutionary Era, 1795–1803* (Leiden, 2011)

Lassiter, F. R., 'Arnold's Invasion of Virginia', *Sewanee Review*, 9, no. 1 (1901), 78–93

Laughton, J. K. (ed.), *Journal of Rear-Admiral Bartholomew James* (London, 1896)

———— 'The Journals of Henry Duncan', in J. K. Laughton (ed.), *The Naval Miscellany I* (London, 1902), 105–211

Lavery, B., *The Arming and Fitting of English Ships of War, 1600–1815* (London, 1987)

———— *The Ship of the Line*, Vol. I (London, 1983)

———— (ed.), *Shipboard Life and Organisation, 1731–1815* (Aldershot, 1998)

Lawrence, A. A., *Storm Over Savannah: The Story of Count d'Estaing and the Siege of the Town in 1779* (1951)

Leach, J. G., 'Commodore John Hazlewood, Commander of the Pennsylvania Navy in the Revolution', *Pennsylvania Magazine of History and Biography*, 26, no. 1 (1902), 1–6

Lefkowitz, A., *The American Turtle Submarine: The Best-Kept Secret of the American Revolution* (Gretna, LA, 2012)

———— *The Long Retreat: The Calamitous American Defense of New Jersey, 1776* (Metuchen, NJ, 1998)

Lemisch, J., 'Jack Tar in the Streets: Merchant Seamen in the Politics of Revolutionary America', *William and Mary Quarterly*, 25, no. 3 (1968), 371–407

Leslie, W. R., 'The Gaspee Affair: A Study of its Constitutional Significance', *Mississippi Valley Historical Review*, 39, no. 2 (1952), 233–56

Lewis, C. L., *Admiral de Grasse and American Independence* (New York, 1980)

———— 'I Have Not Yet Begun to Fight', *Mississippi Valley Historical Review*, 29 (1943), 229–37

Lewis, J. A., *Neptune's Militia: The Frigate South Carolina during the American Revolution* (Kent, OH, 1999)

Linder, B., *Tidewater's Navy: An Illustrated History* (Annapolis, MD, 2005)

Lloyd, C. (ed.), *The Keith Papers: Selected from the Letters and Papers of Admiral Viscount Keith*, 3 vols (London, 1927–55)

———— 'Sir George Rodney: Lucky Admiral', in G. A. Billias (ed.), *George Washington's Generals and Opponents* (New York, 1994), 327–54

Low, C. R., *History of the Indian Navy*, 2 vols (London, 1887)

Lutnick, S. (ed.), *The American Revolution and the British Press* (Columbia, MO, 1967)

Lydenberg, H. M. (ed.), *Archibald Robertson: His Diaries and Sketches in America, 1762–1780* (New York, 1930)

———— *Crossing the Line: Tales of the Ceremony During Four Centuries*, Vols LIX–LXI, New York Public Library Bulletin (1955–7)

Lynn, M. C. (ed.), *The Specht Journal: A Military Journal of the Burgoyne Campaign* (Westport, CT, 1995)

MacDougall, P., 'British Seapower and the Mysore Wars of the Eighteenth Century', *Mariner's Mirror*, 97, no. 4 (2011), 299–314

Mackenzie, F., *Diary of Frederick Mackenzie*, Vol. I (Cambridge, MA, 1930)

Mackesy, P., *The War for America, 1775–1783* (London, 1964)

Macleod, E. V., 'Thinking Minds of Both Sexes: Patriotism, British Bluestockings and the Wars against Revolutionary America and France', in K. Hagemann, G. Mettele and J. Rendall (eds), *Gender, War and Politics: Transatlantic Perspectives, 1775–1830* (Basingstoke, 2010), 247–64

Magra, C. P., *The Fisherman's Cause: Atlantic Commerce and Maritime Dimensions of the American Revolution* (Cambridge, 2009)

—— '"Soldiers . . . Bred to the Sea": Maritime Marblehead, Massachusetts, and the Progress of the American Revolution', *New England Quarterly*, 77, no. 4 (2004), 531–62

Mahan, A. T., *The Major Operations of the Navies in the War of American Independence* (London, 1913; reprint Stroud, 2006)

Maier, P., *From Resistance to Revolution: Colonial Radicals and the Development of American Opposition to Britain, 1765–1776* (New York, 1974)

—— 'Popular Uprisings and Civil Authority in Eighteenth-Century America', *William and Mary Quarterly*, 27, no. 1 (1970), 3–35

Malcomson, R., *Warships of the Great Lakes* (London, 2001)

Marshall, P. J., *The Making and Unmaking of Empires: Britain, India, and America, c.1750–1783* (Oxford, 2005)

—— *Remaking the British Atlantic: The United States and the British Empire after American Independence* (Oxford, 2012)

Mattern, D. B., *Benjamin Lincoln and the American Revolution* (Colombia, SC, 1995 and 1998)

McBurney, C. M., *The Rhode Island Campaign: The First French and American Operation in the Revolutionary War* (Yardley, PA, 2011)

McCarthy, C. H., 'The Attitude of Spain during the American Revolution', *Catholic Historical Review*, 2, no. 1 (1916), 47–65

McCullough, D., *1776: America and Britain at War* (London, 2005)

—— *John Adams* (New York, 2001)

McCurry, A. T., 'The North Government and the Outbreak of the American Revolution', *Huntingdon Library Quarterly*, 34, no. 2 (1971), 141–57

McCusker, J. J., 'The American Invasion of Nassau in the Bahamas', *American Neptune*, 25, no. 3 (1965), 189–217

McGrath, T., *John Barry: An American Hero in the Age of Sail* (Yardley, PA, 2010)

—— *Give Me a Fast Ship: The Continental Navy and America's Revolution at Sea* (New York, 2014)

McGuffie, T. H., *The Siege of Gibraltar, 1779–1783* (London, 1965)

McLarty, R. N., 'Jamaica Prepares for Invasion, 1779', *Caribbean Quarterly*, 4, no. 1 (1955), 62–7

Melville, H., *Israel Potter* (Evanston and Chicago, 1982 [first published 1854])

Mercer, K., 'Northern Exposure: Resistance to Naval Impressment in British North America, 1775–1815', *Canadian Historical Review*, 91, no. 2 (2010), 199–232

Middlebrook, L. F., *The Frigate 'South Carolina': A Famous Revolutionary War Ship* (Salem, MA, 1929)

Middlekauff, R., *The Glorious Cause: The American Revolution, 1763–1789* (New York, 2005)

Miller, D. A., *Sir Joseph Yorke and Anglo-Dutch Relations, 1774–1780* (The Hague, 1970)

Miller, D. L. et al., 'Tree-Ring Isotope Records of Tropical Cyclone Activity', *Proceedings of the National Academy of Science of the United States of America*, 103, no. 39 (2006), 14294–97

Miller, N., *Sea of Glory: A Naval History of the American Revolution* (Charleston, SC, 1974)

Mintz, M. M., *The Generals of Saratoga: John Burgoyne and Horatio Gates* (New Haven and London, 1990)

Moomaw, H. W., 'The Naval Career of Captain Hamond, 1775–79' (PhD: University of Virginia, 1955)

———— 'The British Leave Colonial Virginia', *The Virginia Magazine of History and Biography*, vol. 66, no. 2 (April 1958), 147–160.

Moore, F. (ed.), *Songs and Ballads of the American Revolution* (New York, 1855)

Morison, S. E., *John Paul Jones: A Sailor's Biography* (Boston, 1959)

Morris, R. B., *The Peacemakers: The Great Powers and American Independence* (New York, 1965)

Morton, B. N. and D. C. Spinelli, *Beaumarchais and the American Revolution* (Latham, MD and Oxford, 2003)

Mulcahy, M., *Hurricanes and Society in the British Greater Caribbean, 1624–1783* (Baltimore, 2006)

Napolitano, M. F., 'A Baseline inventory of multibeam acoustic targets from the Hudson River between New York Harbor and Wappingers Falls', in W. C. Nieder and J. R. Waldman (eds), *Final Reports of the Tibor T. Polgar Fellowship Program, 2003* (New York, 2004), Section VIII, 1–29

Neeser, R. W. (ed.), *The Despatches of Molyneux Shuldham: Vice-Admiral of the Blue and Commander-in-Chief of His Britannic Majesty's ships in North America, January–July, 1776* (New York, 1913)

Nelson, J. L., *Benedict Arnold's Navy* (Camden, ME, 2006)

———— *George Washington's Secret Navy* (New York, 2008)

Nordholt, J. W. S., *The Dutch Republic and American Independence* (London, 1982)

Northcote Parkinson, C., *Edward Pellew, Viscount Exmouth* (London, 1934)

Norton, L. A., *Captains Contentious: The Dysfunctional Sons of the Brine* (Columbia, SC, 2009)

Nuxoll, E. M., 'The Naval Movement of the Confederation Era', in M. J. Crawford and W. S. Dudley (eds), *The Early Republic and the Sea: Essays on the Naval and Maritime History of the Early United States* (Washington, DC, 2001), 3–34

O'Beirne, T. L., *A Candid and Impartial Narrative of the Transactions of the Fleet under the Command of Lord Howe, From the Arrival of the Toulon Squadron, On the Coast of America, to the Time of His Lordship's Departure for England, With Observations* (London, 1799)

O'Bryen, C., *Naval Evolutions: or a System of Sea Discipline* (London, 1762)

O'Shaughnessy, A. J., *An Empire Divided: The American Revolution and the British Caribbean* (Philadelphia, 2000)

——— *The Men Who Lost America: British Command During the Revolutionary War and the Preservation of the Empire* (London, 2013)

Oertling, T., *Ships' Bilge Pumps* (Texas, 1996)

Olson, D. W. and R. L. Doescher, 'Astronomical Computing: Paul Revere's Midnight Ride', *Sky and Telescope*, 83 (1992), 437–40

Olton, C., *Artisans for Independence: Philadelphia Mechanics and the American Revolution* (Syracuse, 1975)

Osler, E., *The Life of Admiral Viscount Exmouth* (London, 1835)

Owen, J. H., 'Rodney and de Guichen', *Naval Review*, 13 (1925), 195–212, 433–46

Padrón, F. M. (ed.), *Journal of Don Francisco Saavedra de Sangronis during the commission which he had in his charge from 25 June 1780 until the 20th of the same month of 1783* (Gainesville, FL, 1989)

Parès, J., *Imprimeries d'Escadre* (Paris, 1928)

Park, S. H., 'The Burning of HMS Gaspee and the Limits of Eighteenth-Century British Imperial Power' (PhD: University of Connecticut, 2005)

Parsons, A., *Travels in Asia and Africa* (London, 1808)

Pasley, T., *Private Sea Journals, 1778–1782* (London, 1931)

Patterson, A. T., *The Other Armada: The Franco-Spanish Attempt to Invade Britain in 1779* (Manchester, 1960)

Patton, R. H., *Patriot Pirates: The Privateer War for Freedom and Fortune in the American Revolution* (New York, 2008)

Paullin, C. O., *The Navy of the American Revolution: Its Administration, Its Policy and Its Achievements* (Chicago, 1906)

Pell, J. H. G., 'Philip Schuyler: The General as Aristocrat', in G. A. Billias (ed.), *George Washington's Generals and Opponents* (New York, 1994), 54–78

Pengelly, C., *Sir Samuel Hood and the Battle of the Chesapeake* (Gainesville, FL, 2009)

Petrie, C., *King Charles III of Spain: An Enlightened Despot* (London, 1971)

Pfister, A., *The Voyage of the First Hessian Army from Portsmouth to New York, 1776* (unknown, 1915)

Pocock, T., *The Young Nelson in the Americas* (London, 1980)

Powers, S. T., 'The Decline and Extinction of American Naval Power, 1781–1787' (PhD: Notre Dame, 1965)

Preston, A., D. Lyon and J. H. Batchelor, *Navies of the American Revolution* (London, 1975)

Price, M., *Preserving the Monarchy: The Comte de Vergennes, 1774–1787* (Cambridge, 1995)

Pritchard, J., *Anatomy of a Naval Disaster: The 1746 French Expedition to North America* (Montreal, 1995)

Pybus, C., *Black Founders: The Unknown Story of Australia's First Black Settlers* (Sydney, 2006)

————— *Epic Journeys of Freedom: Runaway Slaves of the American Revolution and Their Global Quest for Liberty* (Boston, 2006)

Quarles, B., *The Negro in the American Revolution* (Chapel Hill, NC, 1961)

Ramsay, D., *A History of the American Revolution* (Philadelphia, 1789)

————— *The Life of George Washington* (Baltimore, 1832)

Randall, W. S., *Benedict Arnold: Patriot and Traitor* (New York, 1990)

Rankin, H. F., 'Charles Lord Cornwallis: Study in Frustration', in G. A. Billias (ed.), *George Washington's Generals and Opponents* (New York, 1994), 193–232

————— (ed.), *Narratives of the American Revolution as told by a young sailor, a home-sick surgeon, a French volunteer, and a German general's wife* (Chicago, 1976)

————— 'The Naval Flag of the American Revolution', *William and Mary Quarterly*, II, no. 3 (1954), 339–53

Rantoul, R. S., 'The Cruise of the Quero: How We Carried the News to the King', *Essex Institute Historical Collections*, 36 (1900), 1–30

Ribiero, A., *Dress in Eighteenth-Century Europe, 1715–1789* (London, 1984)

Rice, H. C. and A. S. K. Brown (eds), *The American Campaigns of Rochambeau's Army, 1780–3*, 2 vols (Princeton, NJ, 1972)

Richmond, H. W., *The Navy in India, 1763–83* (London, 1931)

————— *Statesmen and Seapower* (Oxford, 1946)

Richmond, R. P., *Powder Alarm, 1774* (Princeton, NJ, 1971)

Rodger, N. A. M., 'The British View of the Functioning of the Anglo-Dutch Alliance, 1688–1795', in G. J. A. Raven and N. A. M Rodger (eds), *Navies and Armies: The Anglo-Dutch Relationship in War and Peace, 1688–1988* (Edinburgh, 1990), 12–32

————— *The Command of the Ocean: A Naval History of Britain, 1649–1815*, Vol. II (London, 2004)

————— *The Insatiable Earl: A Life of John Montagu, 4th Earl of Sandwich, 1718–92* (London, 1993)

————— *The Safeguard of the Sea: A Naval History of Britain, 660–1649* (London, 1997)

―――― 'Seapower and Empire: Cause and Effect?', in B. Moore (ed.), *Colonial Empires Compared: Britain and the Netherlands, 1750–1850* (Aldershot, 2003), 97–112

―――― *The Wooden World: An Anatomy of the Georgian Navy* (London, 1986)

Rodney, C. A. (ed.), *The Diary of Captain Thomas Rodney, 1776–1777* (Wilmington, PA, 1879)

Roy, K., *War, Culture and Society in Early Modern South Asia, 1740–1849* (Abingdon, 2011)

Russell, D. L., *The American Revolution in the Southern Colonies* (Jefferson, NC, 2000)

Russell, J., *Gibraltar Besieged, 1779–1783* (London, 1965)

Salav, D. L., 'The Production of Gunpowder in Pennsylvania during the American Revolution', *Pennsylvania Magazine of History and Biography*, 99, no. 4 (1975), 422–42

Sands, J. O., 'Sea Power at Yorktown: The Archaeology of the Captive Fleet' (PhD: George Washington University, 1980)

―――― *Yorktown's Captive Fleet* (Newport News, VA, 1983)

Schaeper, T. J., *John Paul Jones and the Battle off Flamborough Head: A Reconsideration* (New York, 1989)

Schecter, B., *The Battle for New York* (New York, 2002)

Scheina, R. L., 'A Matter of Definition: A New Jersey Navy, 1777–1783', *American Neptune*, 39, no. 3 (1979), 209–17

Schlesinger, A. M., 'Political Mobs and the American Revolution', *Proceedings of the American Philosophical Society*, 99, no. 4 (1955), 244–50

Scull, G. D. (ed.), *Memoir and Letters of Captain W. Glanville Evelyn, of the 4th Regiment ('King's Own')* (Oxford, 1879)

Selby, J. E., *The Revolution in Virginia, 1775–1783* (Williamsburg, VA, 1988)

Sen, S. P., *The French in India, 1763–1816* (Calcutta, 1958)

Servies, J. A. (ed.), *The Log of HMS Mentor, 1780–1* (Pensacola, FL, 1982)

Shaw, L., *British Administration of the Southern Indians, 1756–63* (Lancaster, 1931)

Shea, J. G. (ed.), *Operations of the French Fleet under the Comte de Grasse, 1781–2: As Described in Two Contemporaneous Journals* (New York, 1864)

Shipton, C. K., 'Benjamin Lincoln: Old Reliable', in G. A. Billias (ed.), *George Washington's Generals and Opponents* (New York, 1994), 193–211

Silverstone, P. H., *The Sailing Navy, 1775–1854* (New York, 2006)

Smith, A. B., 'The French Period at the Cape, 1781–1783: a report on excavations at Conway Redoubt, Constantia Nek', *South African Military History Society*, 5, no. 3 (1981)

Smith, F.-H., 'The French at Boston During the Revolution', *Bostonian Society Publications*, 10 (1913), 9–78

―――― *The Memorial to the Chevalier de Saint-Sauveur* (Boston, 1918)

Smith, J. H., *Our Struggle for the Fourteenth Colony, Canada and the American Revolution* (New York, 1907)

Smith, P. C. F., *Fired by Manley Zeal: A Naval Fiasco of the American Revolution* (Salem, MA, 1977)

Smith, P. C. F. and R. W. Knight, *In Troubled Waters: The Elusive Schooner Hannah* (Salem, MA, 1970)

Spilsbury, J., *A Journal of the Siege of Gibraltar, 1779–1783* (Gibraltar, 1908)

Stephenson, O. S., 'The Supply of Gunpowder in 1776', *American Historical Review*, 30, no. 2 (1925), 271–81

Stewart, R. A., *The History of Virginia's Navy of the Revolution* (Richmond, VA, 1933)

Stirling, A. M., *The Hothams*, Vol. II (London, 1918)

Stockley, A., *Britain and France at the Birth of America: The European Powers and the Peace Negotiations of 1782–3* (Exeter, 2001)

Stone, W. L. (ed.), *Letters and Journals Relating to the American Revolution and the Capture of the German Troops at Saratoga by Mrs General Riedesel* (Albany, NY, 1867)

——— *Visits to the Saratoga Battle-Grounds, 1780–1880* (Port Washington, 1895)

Stout, N. R., *The Royal Navy in America, 1760–1775: A Study of Enforcement of British Colonial Policy in the Era of the American Revolution* (Annapolis, MD, 1973)

——— 'Manning the Royal Navy in North America, 1763–1775', *American Neptune*, 23 (1963), 174–85

Sugden, J., *Nelson: A Dream of Glory* (London, 2005)

Sullivan, J. A., 'Graves and Hood', *Mariner's Mirror*, LXIX (1983), 175–94

Sweet, D. G. and G. B. Nash (eds), *Struggle and Survival in Colonial America* (Berkeley, CA, 1982)

Syrett, D., *Admiral Lord Howe* (Stroud, 2006)

——— 'British Amphibious Operations during the Seven Years and American Wars', in M. L. Bartlet (ed.), *Assault from the Sea: Essays on the History of Amphibious Warfare* (Annapolis, MD, 1983), 51–9

——— 'D'Estaing's Decision to Steer for Antigua, 28 November 1778', *Mariner's Mirror*, 61, no. 1 (1975), 155–62

——— 'Lord George Germain and the Protection of Military Storeships, 1775–1778', *Mariner's Mirror*, 60 (1974), 395–405

——— 'The Methodology of British Amphibious Operations during the Seven Years and American Wars', *Mariner's Mirror*, 58, no. 3 (1972), 269–80

——— 'The Organisation of British Trade Convoys, 1775–1783', *Mariner's Mirror*, 62 (1976), 169–81

——— *The Rodney Papers*, Vol. II (Aldershot, 2007)

——— *The Royal Navy in American Waters, 1775–1783* (Aldershot, 1989)

——— *The Royal Navy in European Waters during the American Revolutionary War* (Columbia, SC, 1998)

———— *Shipping and the American War, 1775–1783: A Study of British Transport Organisation* (London, 1970)

Talbot, J. E., *The Pen and Ink Sailor: Charles Middleton and the King's Navy, 1778–1813* (London, 1998)

Taaffe, S. R., *The Philadelphia Campaign, 1777–1778* (Lawrence, KS, 2003)

Taylor, S., *Commander: The Life and Exploits of Britain's Greatest Frigate Captain* (London, 2012)

Thacher, J., *A Military Journal During the American Revolutionary War from 1775 to 1783 …* (Boston, 1823)

Thonoff, R. H., 'Texas and the American Revolution', *Southwestern Historical Quarterly*, 98, no. 4 (1995), 511–17

Thorp, J. D., *The Acland Journal: Lady Harriet Acland and the American War* (Winchester, 1993)

Tilley, J. A., *The British Navy and the American Revolution* (Columbia, SC, 1987)

———— 'The Development of American Revolutionary Naval Policy, April 1775–July 1776', Part I, *Nautical Research Journal*, 25, no. 2 (1979), 69–72

———— 'The Development of American Revolutionary Naval Policy, April 1775–July 1776', Part II, *Nautical Research Journal*, 25, no. 3 (1979), 119–26

———— 'The Development of American Revolutionary Naval Policy, April 1775–July 1776', Part III, *Nautical Research Journal*, 25, no. 4 (1979), 194–9

Toll, I. W., *Six Frigates: How Piracy, War and British Supremacy at Sea Gave Birth to the World's Most Powerful Navy* (London, 2006)

Tracy, N., 'British Assessments of French and Spanish Naval Reconstruction', *Mariner's Mirror*, 61, no. 1 (1975), 73–85

———— *Navies, Deterrence, and American Independence* (Vancouver, 1988)

Tredrea, J. and E. Sozaev, *Russian Warships in the Age of Sail, 1696–1860* (Barnsley, 2010)

Tuchman, B. W., *The First Salute* (London, 1988)

Tunstall, W. C. B., *Naval Warfare in the Age of Sail* (London, 1990)

Tustin, J. P. (ed.), *Diary of the American War: A Hessian Journal* (New Haven and London, 1979)

Ubbelohde, C., *The Vice-Admiralty Courts and the American Revolution* (Williamsburg, 1960)

Uhlendorf, B. A. (ed.), *The Siege of Charleston with an Account of the Province of South Carolina: Diaries and Letters of Hessian Officers from the von Jungken Papers in the William L. Clements Library* (Ann Arbor, 1938)

Van Alstyne, R., *Empire and Independence: The International History of the American Revolution* (New York, 1965)

Villiers, P., 'La Stratégie de la Marine Française de l'Arrivée de Sartine à la Victoire de la Chesapeake', in M. Acerra, J. Merino and J. Meyer (eds),

Les Marines de guerre européennes XVIIe–XVIIIe siècles (Paris, 1998), 211–47

Walker, P. K., *Engineers of Independence: A Documentary History of the Army Engineers in the American Revolution, 1775–1783* (Washington, DC, 1981)

Ward, H., *The War for Independence and the Transformation of American Society* (London, 1999)

Warner, D. J., 'Telescopes for Land and Sea', *Rittenhouse*, XII, no. 2 (1998), 33–54

Washington, I. and P. Washington, *Carleton's Raid* (Canaan, 1977)

Weintraub, S., *Iron Tears: Rebellion in America, 1775–1783* (London, 2005)

West, J., *Gunpowder, Government, and War in the Mid-Eighteenth Century* (Woodbridge, 1991)

Whinynates, F. A. (ed.), *The Services of Francis Downman in France, North America, and the West Indies* (London, 1898)

White, R., *The Middle Ground: Indians, Empires, and Republics in the Great Lakes Region* (Cambridge, 2011)

White, T., *Naval Researches; or, a candid inquiry into the conduct of Admirals Byron, Graves, Hood, and Rodney, in the actions off Grenada, Chesapeake, St. Christopher's, and of the ninth and twelfth of April, 1782: being a refutation of the plans and statements of Mr. Clerk, Rear Admiral Ekins and others* (London, 1830)

Whitely, P., *Lord North: The Prime Minister Who Lost America* (London, 1996)

Whittemore, C. P., 'John Sullivan: Luckless Irishman', in G. A. Billias (ed.), *George Washington's Generals and Opponents* (New York, 1994), 137–62

Wickwire, F. B., 'John Pownall and British Colonial Policy', *William and Mary Quarterly*, 20, no. 4 (1963), 543–54

Wilkie, E. C., 'New Light on Gálvez's First Attempt to Attack Pensacola', *Florida Historical Quarterly*, 62, no. 2 (1983)

Wilkinson, C., *The British Navy and the State in the Eighteenth Century* (Woodbridge, 2004)

Willcox, W. B., 'Admiral Rodney Warns of Invasion, 1776–1777', *American Neptune*, IV, no. 3 (1944), 193–8

—— (ed.), *The American Rebellion: Sir Henry Clinton's Narrative of His Campaigns, 1775–1782* (New Haven, 1954)

—— 'Arbuthnot, Gambier, and Graves; "Old Women of the Navy"', in G. A. Billias (ed.), *George Washington's Generals and Opponents* (New York, 1994), 260–90

—— *Portrait of a General: Sir Henry Clinton in the War of Independence* (New York, 1964)

—— 'Sir Henry Clinton: Paralysis of Command', in G. A. Billias (ed.), *George Washington's Generals and Opponents* (New York, 1994), 73–102

—— 'Too Many Cooks: British Planning before Saratoga', *Journal of British Studies*, 2, no. 1 (1962), 56–90

Willis, S. B. A., 'An Archaeology of Smuggling: The Falmouth King's Pipe in Context' (MA: University of Bristol, 2006)

—————— Fighting at Sea in the Eighteenth Century: The Art of Sailing Warfare (Woodbridge, 2008)

—————— The Fighting Temeraire (London, 2009)

Wilson, D. K., The Southern Strategy: Britain's Conquest of South Carolina and Georgia, 1775–1780 (Columbia, SC, 2005)

Woodman, R., Britannia's Realm: In Support of the State, 1763–1815 (Stroud, 2009)

Wright, T. (ed.), The Unpublished and Collected Poems of William Cowper (London, 1890)

Wrong, G. M., Canada and the American Revolution: The Disruption of the First British Empire (New York, 1935)

Yerxa, D. A., 'Vice-Admiral Samuel Graves and the North American Squadron, 1774–76', Mariner's Mirror, 62, no. 3 (1976), 371–86

INDEX

Page numbers in **bold** refer to figures.

100 200 300 400 500 600 700 800 900 1000 Yards.

Isthmus Fortified

Abbatis &

Fleche Occupied by 150 Men from the Fort and to prevent the Rebels from landing which they were afterwards Obliged to abandon

1 Mortar

2 9-18 Pounders

Rocket Batterie

Rebels

Battery ... of the ...

Defence Rebel Brig of 16 Guns blown up

in the morning of the 03 of July the Rebels effected a landing under cover of a heavy fire from their Ship and erected a Battery to cannonade the Fort

Hunter of 18 Guns taken by Lieut Mulroy of the Raisonable both their Ships were endeavouring to make their escape up Penobscot of Long Island the 14 August

The Camilla Cap.t Collins of 20 Guns in pursuit of the Defence and Hunter Rebel Ships

LONG ISLAND

Commodore Sir George Collier's Squadron of August obliges the Rebels to quit their position and retire with precipitation ... River

Greyhound 20 Guns

Raisonable 64 Guns